Praise for *Fighting the Odds*

Fighting the Odds is first-class political biography, solidly researched, crisply written, both objective and perceptive in its portrayal of a valiant and significant senator.

Arthur Schlesinger, Jr.
Pulitzer Prize Winner

One frequently encounters good people in politics but seldom great people. Frank Church was a great and good man. This superb biography captures both his greatness and essential goodness—as well as the human qualities. As a long-time admiring friend and colleague, I am delighted to see this important life captured so brilliantly in this important biography.

George McGovern
U. S. Senator

This fine, lively, comprehensive biography couldn't be more welcome. Frank Church was brave, bright, articulate nearly to a fault, and a good and principled man besides. *Fighting the Odds* is the kind of biography so greatly needed for the powerful, influential men and women of Congress who have put their marks on our history. In choosing Senator Church, authors Ashby and Gramer have brought to life one of the most important and appealing figures of them all.

David McCullough
Pulitzer Prize Winner

LeRoy Ashby and Rod Gramer have done Frank Church justice in a biography that is very like him: conscientious, thorough, and politically meticulous. They have given us a speaking likeness of this man in the context of his tumultuous times.

Mary McGrory
The Washington Post

Fighting the Odds combines comprehensive and impeccable scholarship with a fast pace and a sense of appropriate detail that make it a pleasure to read. It is the definitive biography for scholars and the enjoyable one for the thousands of people around the world who knew and admired Frank Church.

Cecil D. Andrus
Governor of Idaho

… a meticulously researched, comprehensive, eminently fair biography of the late Frank Church. Church led in the fights for peace and for saving the environment. He battled against the imperial presidency. This definitive biography reminds us of what public life lost when Church failed to gain a fifth Senate term in 1980. Brave and gallant to the end, and true to his life-long beliefs, Church deserves to be remembered. Gramer and Ashby have contributed much to that end with this important book.

William L. O'Neill
Rutgers University

LeRoy Ashby and Rod Gramer have authored a well-researched and engaging portrayal of one of the Senate's best-remembered figures. The book offers a comprehensive examination of the life and career of Frank Church, from his political victories to his ultimate defeat in his battle against cancer. Students of American political history will enjoy this superb book.

Mark O. Hatfield
U. S. Senator

The story of Senator Frank Church is a modern-day "Pilgrim's Progress" that reflects the American political system at its best. For twenty-four brilliant years, he was a profile in courage in Congress, tackling the toughest issues, inspiring others to try harder. This excellent biography tells his story in vivid detail—it should be required reading for all who want to know more about Congress and this extraordinary period in America's recent history.

Edward M. Kennedy
U. S. Senator

My first memories of Senator Frank Church are from the days when my father took me as a young child to the Senate Chamber. Senator Church was easily the nicest and kindest person I met. He claimed we should be pals because he was the youngest senator. He made me smile. I watched him and my father as they led many important debates of the post-World War II era. Since that time, Senator Church and his family have been an important part of my life and have helped shape my views of public service.

Frank Church was a visionary leader of conviction and principles. He was a strong proponent of civil rights, environmental legislation, and the Panama Canal treaties of 1978. He foresaw the end of Communism. But Senator Church's greatest gift to his country was his willingness to always—always—fight for the causes in which he believed, even if his views went against public opinion. He kept his expectations high and he showed the American people by example how to move our country forward.

Senator Church was devoted to his country, his home state of Idaho, and to his family. His legacy will remain in our memories, and his memory in my heart.

Al Gore
Vice President of the United States

Fighting the Odds

Fighting the Odds

THE LIFE OF SENATOR

FRANK CHURCH

LeRoy Ashby & Rod Gramer

WSU PRESS

Washington State University Press
Pullman, Washington

Washington State University Press, Pullman, Washington 99164-5910

First printing 1994
Printed and bound in the United States of America on pH neutral, acid-free paper.

Library of Congress Cataloging-in-Publication Data

Ashby, LeRoy.
Fighting the odds : the life of Senator Frank Church / LeRoy Ashby, Rod Gramer.
p. cm.
Includes bibliographical references (p.) and index.
ISBN 0-87422-103-X (acid-free paper)
1. Church, Frank. 2. Legislators—United States—Biography. 3. United States. Congress. Senate—Biography. I. Gramer, Rod, 1953- . II. Title.
E840.8.C49A84 1994
328.73'092—dc20
[B] 93-43250
CIP

Part of Chapter 3 of the present work appeared in a different form in LeRoy Ashby, "Frank Church Goes to the Senate: The Idaho Election of 1956," *Pacific Northwest Quarterly,* Vol. 78 (1987), 17-31.

To Mary, again and always, and to Steve and Kris—with pride, thanks, and much love.

L. A.

To my wife, Julie, with great love and appreciation; to my children, Jennifer and Robert, with pride; and to my mother, Virginia Gramer Bremner, with love and thanks.

R. G.

It's never too late—nor are the odds ever too great—to try. In that spirit the West was won, and in that spirit I now declare my candidacy for President of the United States.

Frank Church
March 18, 1976

Contents

Senator Frank Church. *Courtesy Boise State University.*

Prologue

IN EARLY 1984, former Idaho senator Frank Church lay dying of pancreatic cancer. Despite his rapidly deteriorating condition, he resolved to complete a final, desperate appeal for responsible government and against American interventionism, causes for which he had fought for years in the Senate. The Reagan administration's efforts to overthrow the Nicaraguan government dismayed him, driving him on. Propped up in bed, in growing pain, he scribbled on yellow legal pads an impassioned plea to end U. S. gunboat diplomacy and " 'cloak and dagger' " covert activities. When he sometimes sagged back in his pillows, too tired to write, his friend Jerry Levinson tried to take down his comments verbatim. Church, always the perfectionist, edited his essay endlessly. Seeming to draw upon sheer will power, he concentrated his fading energy on making a point that he had articulated for some twenty years: America's obsession with " 'monolithic' communism" had led the U. S. into a swampland of bloody foreign policy mistakes from Latin America to Vietnam. Communism was in fact "a waning force," he wrote, and he emphasized yet again that the United States simply had to learn to live in a world of revolutionary change.[1]

For much of his life Church had battled political and physical odds. "My wife says I have a St. George complex," he laughed. His opposition in the 1980s to U. S. interventionism was not new; neither was his fight against cancer. In 1949 doctors discovered that he had testicular cancer and predicted he would be dead within six months. He had been twenty-four then, a young veteran of World War II, just starting a family. With the help of radiation treatments and his wife Bethine, he survived. Following his terrifying brush with death he concluded that "the only way to live. . .is by taking great chances."[2]

Living on what he viewed as borrowed time, Church had indeed taken chances.[3] In 1956 he ran for the Senate as a Democrat in largely Republican Idaho. He was only thirty-two and had never held political office; yet he won. No Idaho Democrat had ever been reelected to the Senate; yet Church won reelection three times, and missed a fifth term in 1980 by less than 1 percent of the vote. A self-styled liberal, he represented a state that conservative Republicans increasingly controlled. Numerous times he resisted the prevailing opinion among his constituents—on civil rights, social welfare programs, foreign policy, defense buildups, and the Panama Canal treaties of 1978. Despite the power of lumber, mining, and ranching interests in Idaho, he built a distinguished environmental record and led the way in passing wilderness legislation.

He braved the odds not only within his state, but nationally. From the start of his career, he placed himself at the center of the dominant legislative struggles of the post-World War II era. He had no elective experience before entering the Senate; but within months after taking office he played a significant role in the passage of the 1957 Civil Rights Act. He was a product of the Cold War; yet in the early Sixties he began to question the wisdom of Cold War foreign policy. By the decade's end he was a foremost Senate critic of the orthodox assumption that Soviet-inspired communism was the main source of world upheaval and turbulence. Barely forty and still a junior senator, he defied Lyndon Johnson, a strong president from his own party, on the issue of the Vietnam war. As a leading Senate "dove" during that long, ugly conflict, he stood up against the Johnson and Richard Nixon administrations, popular opinion, and the sentiments of most of his colleagues. In the early Seventies, the landmark Cooper-Church amendment marked a shift in public opinion against the war.

At considerable political risk during his last two terms, Church challenged the bastions of the national security state: the "imperial Presidency," giant multinational corporations, and the Central Intelligence Agency. In 1978 he resisted a huge groundswell of opposition against the Panama Canal treaties and steered them through the Senate. By 1979, when the public hungered for good news and reassurances, he warned instead of America's declining competitiveness in the global economy.

Considerable irony marked his life. He rightly saw himself as a quixotic fighter for great causes and as a political revivalist who roused the people to defend their country's ideals; yet he was a shrewd politician who prided himself on building coalitions and knowing how to obtain votes. Some critics claimed that he compromised too easily; others viewed him as a crusading moralist. He was basically shy, yet became a skilled and eloquent speaker—one of the twentieth century's "great debaters," according to Massachusetts senator Ted Kennedy. Some people believed that he was primarily a speech-maker, the "boy orator of the Snake River"; yet his name was attached to such legislative milestones as the Cooper-Church and Case-Church amendments, and he presided over several of the most important Senate investigations in modern American history. He often exemplified Western independence, yet reminded many observers of a well-bred Easterner.[4]

Church was a resolute patriot, even though the conservative *National Review* castigated him as "a major figure in America's attempted suicide during the Sixties and Seventies." His dissent against the Vietnam war, his investigations of the CIA and America's multinational corporations, and his fight for the Panama Canal treaties attested both to his courage and to his affection for his country's historic ideals. "No one sang 'God Bless America' with more ardor," columnist Mary McGrory recalled. Precisely because he believed so deeply in America's ideals and constitutional principles he found the 1960s and 1970s a particularly wrenching era. Again and again, he applied high standards of morality to America's actions at home and abroad.[5]

Far more than most politicians, Church was his own person. "Sometimes it is necessary to take the unpopular positions," he said. "I have to live with my conscience a lot longer than I have to live with my job."[6]

Paradoxically, his willingness to stand by his principles may have extended his political life in Idaho, despite the state's growing conservatism. He guessed that "Idaho is still close enough to 'High Noon' " that people appreciated his independence. In 1968, for example, substantial numbers voted for him despite their own hawkish reputation and his "dovish" stand on Vietnam. Among them was Jack Hawley. The conservative Republican had run against Church in 1962; Hawley thereafter voted for him because of his "real gutty stand against the war." In 1980, when Church discussed his support for the Panama Canal treaties in one Idaho town, the audience seethed with hostility. But when he finished his thirty-minute explanation, he received a standing ovation. As the people left, a number of them indicated that they still might not vote for him, but they respected him.[7]

Although some Idahoans loathed him, he provided others with a sense of pride. Long-time resident Alice Dieter liked to believe that he countered the state's image as "a provincial backwater." Another Idahoan, when visiting Boston in the mid-Seventies, regretted that most people seemed not to know where Idaho was. But at least "they knew we grow potatoes and they knew Frank Church was our senator."[8]

In early 1984, many of them also knew that Church was dying. The announcement that he had inoperable malignancies received considerable media attention. His second, deadly battle with cancer allowed no hope for recovery. The odds had finally caught up with him, but not before he published his final essay criticizing the Reagan administration for arming "an exile army" to topple the Nicaraguan government. "Why," he asked in his last public statement, "does America, the first nation born of revolution in the modern age, find it so difficult to come to terms with revolutionary change. . . ?" Church had no more time to borrow. He could only hope that his country did.[9]

"No one is more quickly forgotten in Washington than a defeated politician," he once told his son. Although generally true, his comment did his own career a disservice. There were many reasons to remember Frank Church.[10]

High school sweethearts Frank Church and Bethine Clark in her convertible. *Courtesy Bethine Church.*

Chapter One
Beginnings: 1924-1942

ONCE AGAIN THE COUGH was coming, welling up from deep within the boy's chest, giving him the sensation of drowning, forcing him to fight for oxygen. His anxious parents sat with him through the night, holding him, rocking him, sometimes hitting him on the back in frantic efforts to clear his blocked air passages. Years later, his mother still shuddered at memories of his acute bronchial infections and dreaded coughing spells. More than once, she had feared that he would not survive until morning.[1]

For the boy, Frank Forrester Church III, the bronchitis attacks were indeed frightening, but they were random counterpoints to a childhood otherwise remarkably secure and happy. Although he was frail and sickly, his sense of self was strong, even protected. From childhood onward, he would feel comfortable with who he was, where he was from, and what he could do. Fixed reference points—geographical, familial, economic, and cultural—bounded his early years, providing him with a feeling of place, respectability, and identity that he never lost.

I

Frank Church III, or "Frosty" as his family nicknamed him, was born in Boise, Idaho, on July 25, 1924. In retrospect he joked that he had been "going down hill" physically since his birth. Serious complications forced his delivery by cesarian section, and hospitalized him for two weeks. Shortly thereafter, the bronchial infections started. Time and again over the next few years, doctors inserted large needles into his nose to drain his sinus passages.[2]

His health was frail, but his family offered him bedrock security. It was a family proud of its pioneer Idaho stock, but able to trace its American ancestry back to 1630 when Englishman Richard Church debarked in Boston. Richard subsequently married Elizabeth Warren, whose father had sailed to America on the *Mayflower.* Frank Forrester Church I was the first family member to leave New England, moving in 1872 from Maine to Idaho City, a mining town some twenty miles from Boise. There he met and married Mary Elizabeth Barry, the daughter of Irish immigrants who had followed the early 1860s gold rush into the Boise Basin.[3]

In 1893, when President Grover Cleveland placed him in charge of the United States Assay office in Boise, the first Frank Church moved to Idaho's capital city. His son, Frank II, was born in 1890, and in 1913 married Laura Bilderback, a second-generation Idahoan whose pioneer credentials in the state matched those of her husband. She and Frank II, who operated a small sporting-goods store in Boise, were solidly middle-class, Idahoan, and Republican. They had two sons, Richard in 1916, and, eight years later, Frank Forrester III.[4]

The Church family was economically modest but stable, supportive, and religious. Tranquility governed it, sparing the two brothers from the domestic feuds that often racked other households. Laura Church was a loving, good-natured, caring mother. Her sons and their friends remembered her striking brown eyes, slender frame, and long, black hair. She had an outgoing disposition and a relaxed, unruffled manner.[5]

Her younger son's health nevertheless worried her, making her sometimes overly protective. Only when he was twelve did she reluctantly consent to his visiting relatives at Warm Lake in central Idaho. Afraid even then that the mountain air might affect him adversely, she admonished his hosts to watch him carefully.[6]

Frank Sr., equally concerned about young Frank, was a more remote figure. Hardworking and frugal, he was as protective of his emotions as he was of his possessions. A furniture store clerk before he entered the sporting goods business, he personified the stereotypical small shopkeeper—morally upright, cautious, nervous about the future, and defensive of his hard-won gains. Balding and chunky, he kept his feelings hidden behind a typically expressionless, round face. Richard could not recall hearing his father ever say that he loved anyone. The elder Church's rather uncommunicative, even brooding, demeanor gave some people the impression that he was unfriendly, even cold. His grandson, Forrest, could not remember any pictures of him smiling. But Frank Sr. cared a great deal for his family and took considerable pride in it. Although strict, he was not unkind and his concern for his family's welfare was never in doubt.[7]

Despite his emotional distance, he spent considerable time with his family, occasionally taking his sons on fishing expeditions and duck hunting trips. During the summers, the family sometimes camped in the mountains, particularly in the Warm Lake area. When Frosty was too small to fish, he played for hours outside the tent or had someone take him to the water's edge so that he could dig in the sand. Each year the family gathered huckleberries for pies and jam. Back home in Boise, Laura Church loved to play the piano; her husband, eyes closed, would sit listening while her sons read quietly on the couch. On occasion the family ventured out to a movie.[8]

A reassuring network of outside friendships surrounded the Churches. Grandmother Bilderback lived with them for a while, doting on her grandsons. The boys' other grandmother, an aunt, and an uncle lived nearby and frequently visited. Frank Sr. much enjoyed socializing with a small group of friends, typically at each other's homes. Laura, more outgoing than her husband, had a larger circle of acquaintances that gathered often at the Church residence for bridge games. When Frosty was only a few years old, his father converted the upstairs into four, one-bedroom apartments. The Churches enjoyed open, friendly relationships with their tenants, often sitting with them on the front steps during the summertime.[9]

Discipline in the Church home came almost entirely through the force of example, well-defined rules, and encouragement for jobs well done, especially schoolwork. The parents believed and practiced the virtues of perseverance, frugality, and honesty. For their sons, those virtues were indisputable. Lying was the one infraction that elicited "very harsh punishment," as Richard recalled. The brothers knew that they could best please their father by doing well with their classes. That their schoolwork would prepare them for college was a given. Frank Sr. valued higher education, something he had sought briefly at a Catholic college in nearby Washington, until a near-fatal diphtheria attack had forced him out. Although the elder Church could be stern, he was not very imposing physically and not inclined to play the tyrant's role. Laura recalled reprimanding Richard only once, and never physically punishing either son.[10]

The parents tended to be especially permissive with Frank when he was small because they wanted to avoid anything that might provoke his choking spells. The youngster, quick to take advantage of the situation, occasionally staged temper tantrums, falling to the floor, screaming and kicking when he did not get his way. His parents generally indulged such behavior until, eventually, he outgrew it. Even when he once opened his father's store and sold Fourth of July fireworks at well below cost to grateful customers, his mother and father kept up a cheerful front. Frank Sr. rationalized the situation by noting that at least he did not have to carry surplus fireworks over for a year.[11]

To the envy of his friends, Frank Jr. always enjoyed considerable personal freedom. For the most part he used that freedom with responsibility, seldom giving his parents reason to question his conduct.[12]

His parents rewarded him with a remarkably open environment, even when it came at the expense of Frank Sr.'s devout Catholicism. Determined to rear his sons in the Catholic faith, the elder Church insisted initially that they accompany him every Sunday to mass and attend parochial school. Eventually, despite his deeply felt convictions, he allowed his younger son to switch to the public schools. Laura may have accounted in part for his acquiescence on this point; although nominally Episcopalian, she was not particularly religious and rarely attended services. But Frank Sr.'s own desire to accommodate his children may have made the difference.[13]

From an early age, Frosty showed little enthusiasm for his father's religion. Between weekly catechism classes he left his catechism book at a friend's house, ignoring his lessons. In the second grade he said he wanted to transfer from St. Joseph's to the public school. His father ultimately relented, conceding that his younger son was struggling in the parochial school and needed a different environment. For one thing, the youngster's frail physique offered a prime target for several bullies who hassled and sometimes beat up on him. "Those Catholic boys were meaner than mean," recalled neighborhood friend, Jim Baxter. "They used to love to have fights with us. They were tough." Richard, who graduated from St. Joseph's, once intervened to save his frightened little brother, who was fleeing through a backyard from four adversaries. Convinced that Frosty would be safer and happier in the public school, Richard argued at length with his father, helping to persuade him that the transfer would offer a greater range of opportunities.[14]

After switching to the public schools, young Frank flourished socially and academically. He was quick, well-behaved, and intellectually curious. "He used to dazzle us with the fact that he read the newspaper," recalled one friend. His cousin Harmon remembered, "My mother always used to say that the problem was I was reading comic books and Frank was reading *The Atlantic Monthly*."[15]

Some classmates at first viewed him as a "teacher's pet." One of them recalled that, in the fourth grade, "we kids in the back would sit back and say, 'Oh, there he goes again,' " when he seemed to be showing off his abilities. "He would start in, and we'd all just sit there dying. The teachers loved it; they adored him." Indeed, they sometimes refused to believe that he could do anything wrong, even when he did. He once jabbed his Parker pen through the cracks in the seat in front of him, stabbing a girl in the rear end. Startled, she rose out of her seat angrily and hit him. Despite her protests that she had not initiated the episode, it was she whom the teacher suspended from school.[16]

While Church continued to impress his teachers, he for the most part overcame the stigma of teacher's pet through sheer personality. He developed a reputation among his peers for being witty and good-natured. Although talented and confident, he had a self-deprecating sense of humor and avoided displays of arrogance. Indeed, by all accounts his demeanor was infectious. "You always felt better being around him," recalled one classmate. By junior high, he was the magnet for a large and lively circle of friends, among them Bob Wardwell, a neighbor he had known since childhood. The two boys had become inseparable, mowing lawns together, investing jointly in a pair of toy binoculars, sketching out plans for a rocket ship to take them to the moon. They had also formed a club in which Frank was president and Wardwell the sergeant in arms, even though they sometimes had to stuff the ballot box to maintain power. In retrospect, Church recalled his childhood relationship with Wardwell as providing some of the happiest days of his life.[17]

In the seventh grade Church met Stan Burns and Carl Burke, who also became his close friends. For these youngsters, and a half dozen others, the Church home became a gathering place to study, play poker or ping pong, talk, telephone girls, and raid the refrigerator. Laura Church, ever congenial, seemed to let nothing bother her, even a mess of feathers in the house following a pillow fight. In turn, Frosty and his friends gave her little to complain about.[18]

"We certainly weren't a wild bunch," Frank Church recalled, "but probably the goody-goodys." They were neither rowdy nor destructive. Their idea of fun was a visit to the soda fountain at Murray's drug store, or purchasing ice cream cones at Joe Albertson's new supermarket.[19]

Although Church's "goody-goody" reputation hardly charmed all of his peers, he was extremely popular. "His classmates had an 'isn't-he-something' way of showing him off," recalled one observer, yet "he knew how to transform that 'isn't-he-something' aura into an aren't-we-wonderful group feeling." He reportedly did not "exploit his Hollywood looks with the girls, seemed in no sense to be an advantage taker," and had a capacity to disarm critics and possible foes. In junior high even a large, somewhat older youth with a bully's reputation became devoted to Church, promising to protect him against all comers. In Stan Burns's words, Church "was very capable in human engineering," not in a cynical sense of using people, but in his adeptness in getting along with virtually everyone. "He was an artist" at diplomacy, according to another friend, Tom Spofford, who marveled at his ability to avoid conflict and trouble.[20]

II

To Church and his friends, Boise seemed a perfect place in which to grow up. With a population of around 22,000 in 1930, and 26,000 a decade later, it combined a small city's diversity and opportunity with village neighborliness and familiarity. Nestled in a valley in southwestern Idaho, it featured mountains and plains, swift-running streams and wide meadows. Geographically remote from major urban areas, or even other communities of comparable size, it was the state's political, cultural, and economic center. The Boise River, lined with cottonwoods, cut through the valley. To the south sprawled a high plateau and the Owyhee Mountains. To the east for several hundred miles stretched a high, arid desert. Early pioneers had regarded that endless, dry expanse as inhospitable for settlement, but by the early twentieth century irrigation had turned the area into farm country. Along the slightly elevated "bench" outside of Boise, hundreds of small farms emerged, attesting to the virtues of sturdy work and the importance of water, a crucial state resource and political issue. Frank Church's family, like many others in the Boise area, typically took pleasant evening drives, or went swimming below the diversion dam which channeled water from the river into the irrigation canals.[21]

North of Boise, foothills rose sharply to a forested ridge bordering a beautiful mountain area that extended into Canada. The sparsely covered hills leading to the ridge provided a superb hiking and playing area for Church and his friends, a marvelous place to roast hot dogs, hunt Indian arrowheads, and reenact the dramas of Hollywood westerns. Church and Wardwell once discovered a cave, dubbed it their "hideout," and carefully covered their tracks so that no one else would discover it. From here they plotted "attacks" on Boise, which in the summertime beckoned below like a green oasis in the midst of interminable flatlands. During winters, the foothills provided ideal sledding.[22]

"Sometimes," wrote Carl Burke, "I think Boise is a changeless place."[23] In some respects Burke could have described all of Idaho. A massive state that reminded one observer of "a pregnant capital *L*,"[24] it has several distinct regions. Boundless acres of spectacular and often-remote mountain wilderness stretch from the long northern panhandle through the middle part of the state. The immense bottom part of Idaho's "L" configuration, semi-arid and flat, extends more than three hundred miles along the meandering Snake River, which annually carries more water than either the Colorado or Rio Grande. In important respects, the two sprawling geographical sections developed quite differently. In the late 1800s, for example, when the mining and lumbering areas of the northern mountain sections exploded with labor violence, the eastern part of the state remained quiet, attracting mainly Mormon farmers from Utah. Although strikingly different topography, economies, and religious temperaments distinguished the two regions, they were nevertheless alike in their lack of significant population centers or major industrial giants. By 1930 fewer than eight million of the state's fifty-four million acres were under cultivation. Idaho's dominant physical terrain, its small-business economy, its scattered population, its celebration of individualistic frontier values, and its comparative isolation within the United States seemed as "changeless" as its capital.

Certainly Boise grew very little during Frank Church's childhood. A visitor in 1929 described it as "one of the most beautiful cities of the West," with wide streets and "stately" buildings. The Church family's large, two-story brick dwelling near the corner of Ninth and Franklin streets was only a few blocks from the downtown business section and the state capitol building. For Frank and Richard, it was easy to believe that their home rested at a kind of religious and educational crossroads. Across the alley was the Mormon Church. To one side, and so close that the brothers could touch it out their dining room window, was the Christian Church. St. John's Catholic Church and St. Joseph's parochial school were a little over a block away. Nearby was Boise High School with an enrollment of around two thousand. During weekdays, students constantly walked and drove by; and on Sundays the sounds of various religious congregations competed for attention. It was easy for young Frank Church to believe he lived at the center of the universe.[25]

Looking back, Church's good friend Stan Burns laughingly described the self-satisfaction with which Boise youths in the Thirties perceived people who lived outside of Idaho's capital city: "They were out in cow country, and milked animals and did all that sort of rural thing. They were hicks. . . . We were very sophisticated people" with seven movie theaters and "restaurants that stayed open day and night." To young people such as Burns, Carl Burke, and Frank Church, Boise was not simply home; it was a cosmopolitan mecca, the centerpiece of a spacious state for which they felt great pride.[26]

In a number of ways, Frank Church's early years were thus full of advantages and opportunities. Even the Great Depression spared him personal discomfort or worry. His father's sport shop on Eighth street continued to do moderately well, benefiting from dedicated effort, penny-pinching, and supplementary income in the summer from a soft-drink stand. Frank at one point was fortunate enough to own a new ivory-colored Schwinn bicycle, which he allowed his envious friends to ride.[27]

Academically, Church also continued to prosper. He was imaginative, creative, and confident. "I don't think Frank ever doubted that he had unusual ability," Stan Burns later said. "This was a fellow with a great deal of inner resource. . . . When he decided to do something, or go in a certain direction, he brought about as much personal horsepower to the mission as anybody you would run into." In this respect, he dazzled friends and teachers alike. At age fourteen, he wrote a letter to a local newspaper urging the United States to stay out of the growing war in Europe. The editor, skeptical that someone so young could have written such a thoughtful letter, checked its authenticity with Church's teachers. He decided to print it on the front page, but several readers remained skeptical that it had come from the pen of an eighth grader.[28]

By then, however, Church was fascinated with words—how they looked, how they sounded, what nuances they conveyed. He never lost that fascination. His eleventh grade English teacher, Esther Huse, after teaching some two hundred students annually over twenty-five years, remembered him as her best pupil. Every Friday she had someone bring a word for the class to define and analyze. Once, Church wrote "antidisestablishmentarianism" on the chalkboard. The students looked at it blankly until he began to coax them: "You can get it. You find a word that you recognize right in the middle of that long word." When they identified "establish," he got them to look for prefixes and suffixes. At the end of the class, one student asked Huse, "How does he always wow us like that?" As Huse later reflected, "Even the kids thought he was something special."[29]

Church's affection for language was most evident when he was speaking. Visiting his cousin at Warm Lake, he would climb on a log and lecture to the expansive alpine meadow. At home, he practiced oratory in front of a mirror, or stood on the steps and held forth to the neighborhood children. His high school speech teacher dubbed him "a natural," and gave him special instruction. As a member of the debate team, he was a fearsome opponent, leading Boise High School to the state championship his junior year. Some fourteen years after one debate, a former rival from Blackfoot High School recalled Church's "just beating hell out of us" with "an unforgettable performance."[30]

In 1941, as a junior, he emerged from a field of 108,000 contestants to win the fourth annual American Legion National High School Oratorical Contest. "Champion orator of United States!" the Boise high school newspaper proudly announced. The finals that year were held on The Citadel campus in Charleston, South Carolina. For the sixteen-year-old Church, the contest was a heady experience. At the regional competition in Pocatello he had been "simply awesome," according to one observer. "No one else there was in his league." After dominating the elimination rounds, he went by train to Charleston to compete against eight other regional champions.[31]

Each contestant initially had to deliver a ten-to-twelve-minute prepared address on some aspect of Americanism and then, after drawing a topic concerning the Constitution, to speak extemporaneously for around five minutes. Church did not bring a commanding physical presence to the platform. Thin to the point of emaciation, with long, skinny arms that dangled awkwardly, he relied upon an expressive face, a vigorous speaking style, careful articulation, and control of "stage fright." In his prepared speech, "Our American Way of Life," he asserted patriotically that "a free and equal society was inevitable in America," and that "efficiency-making competition of free, rival enterprise has built our dynamic economy." Then he ventured onto more controversial ground. Drawing upon a theme that had long resonated in Idaho politics, he warned of the dangers of economic monopoly and its inevitable abuse of power. He urged greater federal authority to harness monopolies and save common citizens. He also pleaded with his listeners not to destroy American freedoms at home in the name of protecting them. His conclusion was appropriately upbeat. If Americans respected and defended their freedoms, "no matter how dark the future may be, a united America will move forward with unshakable courage and irresistible power toward unlimited democracy and happier times."[32]

His prepared comments impressed the judges, but he reportedly "scored heavily" with his extemporaneous presentation on the Fifth Amendment. He had only five minutes to organize his thoughts. Then, "like a master," according to one contest official, he skillfully dissected the topic, winning first place and a $4000 scholarship. Although his chances of attending college had never been in doubt, the scholarship offered academic opportunities far beyond what his family could otherwise have afforded. He was not yet sure which school he wanted to attend, but, as a junior, he had time to consider his options.[33]

Much was going right for young Church. Shortly after returning from South Carolina, he was elected student body president. On paper, at least, the election was a classic confrontation. The "skinny little runt" from the debate team ran against the star quarterback. Church was no athlete. Indeed, according to Carl Burke, he had little interest in sports and was simply "awful" on the playing field. Looking back, Church attributed his election as student body president to "a kind of a political uprising of the non-athletic types." Although the proverbial "jock versus egghead" division may not have been decisive, Burke, who served as his campaign manager, guessed that Church had drawn his greatest support from "at least half the students [who] never attended football games." Although Burke conceded that his friend had pulled off "a bit of an upset," he believed the election result was not altogether surprising: Church was widely popular and campaigned much harder than his opponent.[34]

By his senior year, however, he had more than school politics on his mind. The gathering war clouds around the world grew increasingly ominous. Closer to home, Frank focused his attention on Bethine Clark, the governor's daughter. He had met her earlier at a state gathering of student government representatives in Boise, when she still lived in Idaho Falls. A year older than he, she had moved to Boise midway through her senior year in early 1941, after her father's election as governor.

The Clarks constituted one of Idaho's leading Democratic families. Chase, Bethine's father, was a state senator, mayor of Idaho Falls, and one-term governor. Subsequently, Franklin D. Roosevelt appointed him to the federal district court in Boise. Barzilla Clark, Bethine's uncle, had been a very popular mayor of Idaho Falls and then governor in the Thirties. And Bethine's cousin D. Worth Clark became a congressman and a U. S. senator. Bethine took avidly to her political environment. By age seven or eight she was asking strangers if they were going to vote for her father.[35]

Slender, medium in height, attractive, and smart, Bethine Clark spurned the role of a flirt. Although Church, Wardwell, and others asked her out, she had little interest in the rituals of high school dating or in playing the coquette. As Stan Burns recalled, "She was one of the guys." With an outgoing personality, an irresistible enthusiasm, and an informed awareness of the world around her, she was simply fun to be with, a person whose considerable appeal was both personal and cerebral. She moved quickly into Frank Church's circle of friends. Her parents' house—the governor's mansion—became a popular hangout, a place for snacking and endless hours of debate. At one point her mother asked why she did not sometimes invite some girls over. "We're talking politics and they're not interested," Bethine replied.[36]

III

There was no doubt that Frank Church was interested in talking politics. He had been since at least the fifth grade. By the time he entered junior high school, he had already decided to follow the footsteps of his hero, William E. Borah, the celebrated "Lion of Idaho." A U. S. senator from 1907 until his death in 1940, Borah was one of the nation's political giants. In Idaho no one cast a larger shadow. Church later liked to recall the story of a little boy who spotted Borah shaking hands in a Boise hotel and ran home to inform his father. "Don't be ridiculous," the father supposedly answered. "What would a big man like Borah be doing way out here in Boise, Idaho?" When Borah died in January, 1940, fifteen-year-old Frank Church watched in awe as huge throngs of famous people descended on Boise to honor the senator. The popping flashbulbs, newsreel cameras, and massive crowds had evoked "the unaccustomed feeling of being a part of a larger drama than our little city could wholly comprehend." Church remembered walking by the opened coffin in the rotunda of the state capitol, catching his only glimpse of Borah in person. "Because he was a Senator," Church later said, "I wanted to become one."[37]

Young Frank's idolization of Borah certainly pleased his parents, as well as his aunt Eva. In 1931, after working in the offices of Republican governors for over twenty years, Eva had politely refused to continue the job under Democrat C. Ben Ross. It was nothing personal; she simply would not work for anyone but a Republican. Church's father wavered only once in his allegiance to the G. O. P. At the depths of the Great Depression in 1932, he voted for Franklin Roosevelt, a decision he quickly regretted. "He had much of the Main Street outlook of a small businessman in a highly Republican community," recalled his younger son. Roosevelt's spending policies infuriated him, and he feared that the president was bankrupting the nation. He once became so agitated at Roosevelt's image on a ten-cent coin that he threw the dime away.[38]

Young Frank, ever the debater, liked to go to the library to look up favorable things about Democrats so that he could engage his father in spirited exchanges over dinner. This was just fine with the elder Church who, his son recalled, loved to argue about politics. Frank Jr.'s reading of history persuaded him that the Democratic Party from its origins had been more sympathetic to the common people than had Republicans. "I learned all about the Democrats so I could argue with Dad," he said later. "I ended up by converting myself." The father apparently enjoyed the friendly give-and-take and was proud of his son's intellect. Young Frank's enthusiasm for Democrats undoubtedly puzzled him, but he accepted his son's political apostasy with grace.[39]

In the end, the son resembled his father almost not at all. He felt affection for him but in most respects did not want to be like him. By the time he entered high school, his break with his father's religion was as clear as their political separation. Richard Church guessed subsequently that his brother found the Catholic church too rigid and hierarchical—"too much of a religious dictatorship." To young Frank, who in Richard's words "questioned everything," Catholicism seemed neither practical nor logical. The occasional kidding from Protestant friends about such subjects as the Spanish Inquisition hardly challenged that judgment. He had, according to Richard, concluded at a fairly young age that the Catholic church was run by "too many self-righteous people" who "were wrong about an awful lot of things."[40]

It had not taken Frank Church III long to reject his father's Republican politics, his shopkeeper's world, and his religion. Later on, he talked little to his own children about Frank Sr. "He said his father was a very dear and sweet man, a very kind man," his son Forrest recalled. But he believed that the elder Church had worried too much to enjoy life, and had been excessively prudent. He "didn't want to be that way at all," Forrest surmised. He was uncomfortable with his father's "cautious approach—conservative, solid," averse to risk.[41]

Frank Sr., to his credit, did nothing to thwart his son's independent streak; in fact, through such things as the free-wheeling, political debates at the dinner table, he in many ways encouraged autonomy, however unintentionally. "I don't understand him," he once conceded to a neighbor.[42] But he nevertheless allowed him to go his own way, even on such heart-felt issues as politics and religion.

Franklin Roosevelt's visit to Boise in 1938 hastened the younger Church's shift to the Democratic Party. Church was then attending eighth grade in Boise's new junior high school, built by Roosevelt's Works Progress Administration. He watched the president's caravan drive by, initially intending neither to cheer nor applaud a man so offensive to his parents. But, as Church remembered, Roosevelt's "smile was so infectious, and his wave so friendly—his whole appearance so magnetic—that I found myself waving and cheering with the others."[43]

He cheered for the New Deal as well. Although his own family was never severely pinched, he was keenly aware of the social and political ferment of the era. It was difficult not to develop a social consciousness. There were too many reminders, even for a relatively protected teenager, of economic dislocation and misery. Boise bore witness to its own examples of suffering, especially among people who lived hand-to-mouth in cardboard shacks along the river and who waited in breadlines and knocked on doors in Church's neighborhood asking for food. The New Deal was controversial, but to Church and his friends its work relief programs offered examples of government responsiveness to problems. "We were very conscious of the haves and have nots," Stan Burns recalled. "We read these books about the Robber Barons and how they raped the West and how they stripped the resources of this country."[44]

According to Church's brother, Frank had developed by his early teens a strong suspicion of concentrated wealth. On a family trip to Annapolis in 1938, when Richard graduated from the Naval Academy, Frank's reaction to a neighborhood of wealthy homes had been one of outrage: "Look at that, look at that," the thirteen-year-old kept saying angrily.[45]

For Church, there was also the wisdom of Senator Borah, a maverick Republican who criticized the influence of organized wealth upon his own party. Church later liked to quote what Borah had reportedly said of the G. O. P. in the 1920s: "I do not know for sure what would happen, but I think the present administration would most assuredly flounder, if somebody were to cut the telephone lines between Wall Street and Washington."[46]

Borah had another message that appealed to Church, one that seemed particularly relevant amid the deteriorating international conditions of the late 1930s and early 1940s. The ever-vigilant senator issued a series of renewed warnings against America's possible involvement in the spreading European and Asian wars. For Borah, the avoidance of entangling foreign alliances was a touchstone for American foreign policy.

It was in fact this issue that had elicited Church's eighth-grade letter to the *Boise Capital News*. The youngster had written to defend a recently published article in which Borah had begged Americans to "beware of war mongers" who would ensnare America abroad. Describing himself as an isolationist, Church had reminded Americans of the blundering and ineffectual efforts to make the world safe for democracy during the Great War. "Only a widespread call from an outraged public," he had argued, could save the United States from recycled English-French propaganda and misguided internationalists, who, for the sake of world trade, would destroy their own country. If the United States again played the role of " 'International Sucker,' " it would probably mean the end of democracy along with the deaths of millions of Americans. The editor had printed Church's letter beneath the headline, "A Junior High Student Says America 'Sucker.' "[47]

IV

Japan's December 7, 1941 attack on Pearl Harbor destroyed Church's faith in American isolationism, just as it did that of many Americans.

On that fateful Sunday he had driven his father's car to Joe Albertson's store on State street to buy ice cream cones with Carl Burke. On their way back home, they had turned on the car radio to hear the stunning news from Hawaii. Both recognized immediately that the United States was now at war and that they themselves would probably soon be in uniform.[48]

A few days later, Church as student body president summoned his classmates to duty: "We seniors have this high school year to finish—then we can *all* enlist." To help galvanize patriotic feelings, Church once dressed up to resemble Adolph Hitler and subjected himself to a mock hanging.[49]

The war added a frantic dimension to Church's last high school semester. Patriotic rallies and flag-waving efforts competed with the usual extracurricular activities such as debating, acting in the senior class play, and even filling the auditorium with a magic show in which Church supposedly hypnotized a student named Orville Porritt. Indeed, the hypnotism act proved so successful that Church later carried it a step further: he allegedly put a spell upon Porritt, who by prearrangement suddenly stood up in biology class in a trance, announced that "Frank Church wants me," and walked out. Complicating the situation was the fact that some people seemed to believe that Church had actually cast a spell over Porritt. One teacher warned Carl Burke in all seriousness, "We must stop this evil before it goes further. Church has power over Orville that is witch-like." Church, Burke, Porritt, and several others ended up in the principal's office, trying to explain that they really had been playing a prank, and that nothing more sinister was involved.[50]

A more serious run-in with authorities in early 1942 resulted in Church's spending a few hours in jail. Following a basketball game in nearby Nampa a fight broke out, ending in the arrest of a Boise student. Church hurried to the jail, convinced that the Nampa police had violated the youth's civil liberties. He did so with a sense of the rightness of his cause and the power of his persuasive abilities. His months of preparing for the American Legion's national debate the previous year had made him familiar indeed with the Bill of Rights, which had been the selected topic for the extemporaneous part of the competition. Surely he could convince the sheriff as effectively as he had the debate judges. By the time he reached the jail, a small mob of Boise students was behind him. Before he could argue his case, however, the police chief who met him at the door grabbed him by the collar and threw him in a cell. Protesting vigorously that the police were now violating his rights, as well as those of the other student, Church quoted loudly from the Constitution and the Declaration of Independence. It was a sobering and humiliating moment. "Frank had won this national oratorical contest which gave him lots of confidence about his ability to speak to the issues," Stan Burns reflected later. But this time "reason" did not prevail. "This big, old, red-neck cop just put him in the slammer with the rest of them." A few hours later the police released the students without booking them, but Church was justifiably worried about the bad publicity that could come from the incident. When he informed Bethine what had happened, she was horrified. "I just thought it was the end of the world," she recalled. Her father's response was apparently more typical of the community's reaction to the matter. The governor shrugged off her young friend's scrape with the law as harmless, no worse than the time he himself as a youngster had put a cow in the belfry of a church.[51]

Following high school graduation, Church spent the summer of 1942 working for the highway district office with Burke, Burns, and another friend, Wade Fleetwood. They spent days combing gravel roads in the desert, tossing the larger rocks off to the side, struggling along in searing temperatures that soared to over 100 degrees in the shade. But offsetting the physical discomfort was a sense of camaraderie and good times. Those days were, in a sense, high school's epilogue.[52]

By fall, the old gang was scattering. Bethine left for the University of Michigan. Wardwell headed north to the University of Idaho. Burns enrolled in Boise Junior College. Church had decided to use his American Legion Scholarship at Stanford, Burke's choice as well. But they were all aware that the war would shortly impose its own imperatives upon them.[53]

Before entering the army in early 1943, Church attended Stanford for two quarters, time enough to involve him in controversy and jeopardize his friendship with Burke. Anxious to prove himself, and perhaps even somewhat cocky, Church refused to play the expected role of humble freshman. He challenged and defeated the upper-class members of the debate team, clearing the way for a dramatic confrontation with the university's top senior debater, Jim Kessler, who also happened to be coach of the freshman team. Incredibly, he then defeated Kessler, establishing himself as Stanford's top debater within his first several months on campus. He also challenged a respected Stanford political tradition, angering at least one of the deans in the process. The incident flowed from Church's discovery that freshmen could not serve on the Student Executive Committee. Perhaps with an eye on democratic principles, perhaps fired by his own ambitions, he launched a campaign for freshmen representation on the committee and, thus, in student government. His unsuccessful efforts upset not only some university administrators, but even Burke, who believed that Church had conducted himself poorly. The two old friends began to pull apart, even before military service sent them in separate directions.[54]

When Church departed Stanford for the army, he may have suspected that he was leaving behind far more than his initials carved on a tabletop at a popular bar near the university. He was also separating himself from the familiar world of his youth, a world that for him had been fairly charmed, free of tragedy, full of success. His family had provided him with a protective and nurturing environment. His public school years had been happy, productive, and fun. His considerable talents and popularity had helped him win the student body presidency, a national debate championship, and a university scholarship. His health had improved, although he was still skinny and subject to colds. His first seventeen years had indeed been full of promise. Perhaps for the first time, he peered into a future in which his previous triumphs might count for nothing.[55]

Church in Kweiyang, China, August 1945. *Courtesy Bethine Church*.

Chapter Two

A Wartime and Postwar Education: 1943-1955

"I LEFT A BOY and I think I came back a man," Frank Church said, as he reminisced about his World War II Army experience.[1] The war undoubtedly changed him. It introduced him to new worlds and expanded his political consciousness. He returned from military service in Asia convinced, for example, that colonialism was a modern tragedy, a tragedy that could only worsen if imperial powers tried to hold back the forces of nationalism. The postwar decade provided a different kind of education. He completed his undergraduate and law degrees, but he also learned how to build a strong marriage and face life anew, after a terrifying bout with cancer.

I

From late 1942 until mid-1946, Church zig-zagged through the military. On December 7, 1942, after a brief stint in the Reserve Officers Training Corps at Stanford, he enlisted in the Army. He took his basic training in the Army Air Corps and then transferred to a specialized Army program in foreign languages and an apparent assignment in Europe. But, after switching into Army Intelligence and Officer's Candidate School (OCS), he ended up in the Asian theater of combat, especially China.[2]

His military journey provided additional proof of his intellectual abilities. He was one of seven out of a class of four hundred who gained admission to OCS at Fort Benning, Georgia. Moreover, the colonel who headed the selection committee warned him that only one other nineteen year old had gone to Benning and successfully completed OCS training. Yet Church, on his twentieth birthday, received his commission as a second lieutenant in the infantry.[3]

Despite his achievement he was well aware of his awkward adjustment to the military. A particularly humiliating reminder came during his final field exam at Fort Benning. Weakness and a high fever, resulting from yet another bronchial cold, threatened to keep him from the last simulated battle-range maneuvers and the completion of his commission. Determined to finish the final drill, he donned two pairs of long underwear to protect him from the weather. But as he crawled over the dirt with bullets flying overhead, he realized that the buttons on his "long-johns" were popping off as they dragged across the ground. To his horror, his underwear began to slip down his legs, "hobbling him," as he later remembered, "like a western range horse meant not to roam." He struggled to his feet for the concluding charge with fixed bayonet. The best he could do was jerk along clumsily with tiny steps, while successive waves of soldiers passed by him. His future as an officer wavered before his eyes. Fortunately, as he later put it, "Fate, which takes care of an occasional botch, looked the other way," and he received his second lieutenant's bar.[4]

In mid-February 1945, Church shipped out for Asia. He learned in India that Franklin Roosevelt had died on April 12. For Church the news was dispiriting because the Democratic president had, more than anyone, determined his political allegiance. He may have recalled an evening in 1943 when he had been on a Labor Day weekend pass and had stood outside the White House in a gloomy drizzle. That night in the rain he had felt a powerful sense of tragedy as he pondered the huge responsibilities pressing upon Roosevelt. He remembered that a powerful rightward political tide had engulfed Woodrow Wilson during World War I, and he feared that events would be no kinder to Roosevelt. The nation seemed "already stumbling and hesitant," Church had written after his White House vigil, "already divided in ill-confidence and petty politics." Although he believed that Roosevelt had "become the dominant figure of the world," he had concluded as early as mid-1943 that "the baffling, almost hopeless problems of the coming peace" would overwhelm Roosevelt as surely as they had Wilson.[5]

The 1944 election had not persuaded him otherwise. Even Roosevelt's campaign speeches had disappointed him. They had seemed timid and shallow, surpassed only by the clichés of the Republican candidate, Thomas E. Dewey. After listening to a radio broadcast of Dewey addressing "a nondescript crowd of clowns and bell ringers," Church had concluded that Dewey's "least objectionable" words were his "Fellow Americans" salutation. The level of the campaign had disheartened him, even though he assuredly wanted Roosevelt to win. "If both candidates are going to subject the American people to vacuum addresses," he had said, "I prefer [Roosevelt's dog] 'Fala' stories to simple trite." By early 1945 Church was convinced that "we need Liberal leadership desperately."[6]

Roosevelt's death deepened his despair in that regard. "News of the President's death struck the Orient with ominous suddenness," Church observed as he dejectedly viewed the flags at half-mast in New Delhi. He guessed "that Franklin Roosevelt was held in greater esteem by more ordinary people all over the world than any living figure. His successor, God pity him, may well turn tragedy to calamity."[7]

With those troubling thoughts, Church in late April headed up the Burma Road into China with his Intelligence unit, winding along the lower Himalayas and through a vast countryside more spectacular than any he had seen before. For the remaining months of the war he worked with the G-2 Section located at Kunming, in southern China's Yunnan Province.

His "absorbing" Intelligence work allowed him to feel at last that he was making a worthwhile contribution to the war effort, even though he was not near the fighting. He sorted through intelligence reports, analyzing them, charting the movement and strength of Japanese troops. When he substituted in mid-July for his immediate senior officer at a daily staff briefing, he so impressed the commanding general, Robert B. McClure, that he ended up officiating at the subsequent briefings. McClure believed that Church's reports on Japanese troop movements were so good that he recommended the young lieutenant for a Bronze Star. The commendation praised Church's files on enemy units as "so well prepared that intelligence agencies made requests for additional copies and language personnel in the field used the special studies as chief guides in interrogations." Moreover, according to the citation, Church's "daily presentations to the Combined Staff sections. . .were so unanimously acclaimed that the Commanding General personally commended him." Privately, McClure contended that Church spoke with "the finest diction in the army."[8]

II

Although Church performed at a high level in the Army, he did not like military life. Indeed, on at least one occasion, he said he loathed it. His brother suspected that he found it too much like the Catholic religion, too hierarchical and rigid. Richard, who remained a Catholic and followed a military career after graduating from the Naval Academy, could not account for his brother's predisposition. The one time that he saw him during the war was just before Frank left for Asia. Richard, back in the United States after suffering serious battle wounds, sensed that Frank was proud to be in uniform and doing his part in the war, but "wasn't really oriented toward military life."[9]

Certainly the military's emphasis on rank annoyed Frank Church, reaffirming that he was "a civilian at heart." In this regard, he laughed at the displeasure of some senior officers when General McClure brought him along to various social functions in China. Once, after he had "taken about all of the rank snobbishness" that he could tolerate, he was delighted to note "the obvious bewilderment. . .of one or another haughty Colonel who simply can't understand why a lieutenant should be present at all. What a gratifying spectacle it is!"[10]

On another level, when Church said that "the devil wears a military uniform," he addressed a problem common to many people during the war: a pronounced sense that outside events were in control, running roughshod over personal dreams and plans. "This awful war and everything that goes with it is bearing down on me with mounting weight," he complained at one point. "I'm sick of it." Because no one could predict how long the fighting would last or what its consequences would be, "you just plod along cursing your own fate, brooding over your own feeble ability even to protest." That sense of helplessness, of being a pawn in some larger struggle, had gripped him with particular force on board the ship to Asia. "The whole of the universe—with all its magnificence, cold and barren—seems to look down and mock our puny impudence," he wrote.[11]

III

Caught up in a drama quite apart from his own choosing, Church nevertheless remained alert to whatever lessons he might learn from it. For the first time, he confronted something other than "Mainstreet USA." Asia's incredible poverty and human suffering left him unsettled and regretful. In Shanghai, for example, he saw a city with staggering inflation but no coal or heat or sufficient food. "Many Chinese will die before Spring," he observed sadly. "These are things that few Americans think about. . . . We will eat well and live well," while remaining "largely oblivious to the tragic spectacle about us." In India, he felt pangs of guilt when he contrasted his own spacious living quarters with the abominable conditions of the native population. He even had a "bearer" who waited on him. "I find myself the champion (so I like to think!) of the down-trodden, with a personal servant," he noted uncomfortably.[12]

While the war made him more aware of human deprivation, it also expanded his appreciation of cultural differences. "I hate to see the gradual deterioration of national cultures," he said after seeing the parts of Nanking that had become "fully Westernized."[13]

His own perspectives were those of a Westerner, however. Thus the "often unbearable" stench in India bothered him and he lamented that "nothing in China ever works very well." Although he liked the Chinese as a people and believed they were "more industrious" than those in India, he concluded that theirs was "a 17th Century civilization." Exasperated with an environment in which nothing seemed to work, he commented that " 'Made in China' is the trade-mark of inferiority." Windows and doors refused either to open or to close. Hinges and doorknobs fell off. The coming of the rainy season made the situation worse. "No roof in all of China will satisfactorily contain water," he protested. Gray, humid days and torrential downpours meant leaking roofs, mud, and an "omnipresent dreariness" that he found oppressive. Not surprisingly, he longed for "the hills of Idaho." Nostalgic almost to tears, he wrote that people who really knew Idaho could never break from it. "Wherever else we may live, however fond we may become of another place, or of many others, there lingers an appetite only Idaho can appease."[14]

However much he remained a prisoner of his own culture, he was nonetheless a remarkably perceptive observer. He quickly recognized that Asia was on the brink of immense upheaval. China, for example, suffered from wild inflation, scarce commodities, a flourishing black market, and savage conflict. Even as he relished the news of Germany's May 7, 1945 surrender and the end of the war in Europe, he suspected that China symbolized "the chaos and confusion of our time." He predicted that, at the least, China would "become the focal point for the momentous events that will shape the destiny of Asia for a century to come."[15]

The popularity of the Chinese communists did not surprise him. They had fought the Japanese "brilliantly," and had done so with ingenuity and discipline. Moreover, they seemed far more responsive than the Nationalist government to China's huge domestic problems. "In the organization of their society, and in the extent of their sweeping reforms," Church observed, "they appear to have equalled their astonishing military success." The government of Chiang Kai-shek, in contrast, was hopelessly corrupt, apparently "capable of nothing other than throwing its weight around." In Church's estimation, Chiang was "fast losing prestige among the people," and would probably soon fall from power.[16]

Church also concluded that European imperialism was justifiably doomed. His disdain for colonialism had previously been remote and abstract, but in Asia he met subject peoples whose hatred of it was immediate and personal. He quickly sensed "the stoic hostility of the Indian." During his brief stay in New Delhi he talked with young Indians in British uniforms "who really were young revolutionaries. . .waiting and planning for the day after the war when they would assert India's right to independence." Church never forgot his first encounter with one of them. He discovered to his surprise that the man was "motivated by the same things that motivated George Washington and the American rebels" when they challenged George III. Much humbled, Church on another occasion listened in amazement while a young Indian sergeant quoted extensively from American revolutionaries and the Federalist Papers. The surging power of anti-colonialism had never been clearer to Church. "I suddenly found that I was living in a world full of ferment," he recalled.[17]

His education in nationalism continued when he moved to China. During his first discussion with a class of Chinese interpreters, for example, he was taken aback when one of them asked why the British should be allowed to retain Hong Kong. "Now there," Church wrote, "is a good question." In that context, he was delighted to learn in August 1945 that Winston Churchill had lost the recent British election. He hoped that Churchill's defeat signalled a weakening of the British "will for imperialism."[18]

When Church reflected later on his military service in China and India he had no doubt about what he had learned: nationalism, not communism, was "the great force of our times." He was not surprised when revolutionary turbulence shook much of the postwar world, from Asia through the Mideast and into Africa and Latin America. In his opinion, the breaking up of "the old colonial empires" was as predictable as what happens to "icebergs in the spring."[19]

IV

While in Asia he began to worry that his own country would resist the anti-colonial trend. By mid-1945 the prospect of U. S.-style expansionism agitated him considerably. Apologizing for his tendency to lecture and sound pompous—"a pitfall of mine," he admitted[20]—he sketched out his concerns in several letters to Bethine Clark.

He saw disconcerting signs "that the United States is about to launch itself into a program of unprecedented imperialism." The American economy was largely to blame. That economy, he insisted, had little to do with free enterprise, being instead the product of "a highly industrialized, complex system of capitalism, limited only by certain, inadequate public control." The search for profits and the need to find outlets for surplus goods had forced the U. S. to seek new markets. Annexation of the Philippines and intrusions into Latin America at the turn of the century were early examples. Until recently, Church reasoned, this search for markets had been less urgent in the United States than in Britain and France. But now, because of rising U. S. productivity and the need to maintain wartime employment levels, American businesses would be more anxious than ever about foreign investments and sales. Church speculated bleakly that the U. S. would increasingly intervene in other countries, relying on "actual or threatened military protection." The result would be "imperialism, in its. . . most dangerous form!" If the U. S. remained on this path, nothing but "very real trouble" lay ahead.[21]

This outburst was certainly not the first indication of Church's displeasure with big business. He had, for instance, already indicated to his family and friends how much he disliked the National Association of Manufacturers (NAM). In 1943 the NAM had invited him, as a former winner of the American Legion oratorical contest, to speak at its December 8 convention in New York City's Waldorf-Astoria hotel. He had received the Army's permission to deliver the address, but as the date drew closer his enthusiasm waned. Two days before he was to speak, the NAM sent him some suggestions about what he might say. He was not fooled a bit. These supposedly helpful recommendations were intended to keep him within the organization's desired agenda. Church irritably informed his family that the NAM wanted "the same old patter and bunk that we have been fed for years in the best Hollywood traditions." Finally, after talking to the NAM's publicity chairman, he agreed to use only some of the organization's suggestions and otherwise to abide by his own script. "I adopted what I could without compromising myself, and without doing an injustice" to major principles, he reported home. He headed off to New York City, "fortified in the conviction that I shall speak honestly. . . , or I shall not speak at all!"[22]

He had approached the NAM convention with a remarkable lack of awe. Laughingly, he liked to think that he had fared better than had all "the notoriety" on stage with him, including the head of the DuPont corporation. After the speech, he took lightly the offer from an NAM leader for a position in the organization following the war. There was, he told a friend, no way that he would ever join up with the NAM: "They represent an extremely reactionary viewpoint" and were determined "to maintain their own power without acknowledgement of the crying social injustices that must be met and solved." Indeed, he insisted that the convention had fortified his "Liberal conviction."[23]

His liberal predilections were clear in his mid-1945 correspondence with Bethine Clark. At one point he set down some ideas about how the United States might harness the power of big business and avoid a tragic plunge into imperialism. His proposals were hardly original, but they clearly showed his affinity for modern American reform movements ranging from populism to the New Deal.

He shared the basic assumptions of New Deal liberalism. Thus he believed that the U. S. needed to rely upon domestic planning rather than foreign markets. To provide the framework for this planning, Church favored three policies: using governmental tax powers to bring predictability into the economy, abolishing industrial monopolies, and achieving more "economic democracy." Without specifically naming English economist John Maynard Keynes, he supported the kind of Keynesian program that New Dealers had implicitly followed, however erratically. This required, as Church summarized it, higher taxes in prosperous times and relaxed rates during economic slumps. If the economy turned downward, the government would provide temporary relief through federal spending, just as it had done during the New Deal.[24]

His animus against monopolies was not only personal, but also tapped a rich political vein in America and certainly in Idaho, where resentment against outside profiteers ran deep into the populist era. To combat monopolies, Church recommended an old idea: licensing industry. Like three-time Democratic presidential candidate William Jennings Bryan forty years earlier, he viewed the licensing of big business as a way to revive economic competition, keep prices down, and open opportunities.[25]

For the U. S. to enjoy more economic democracy, another familiar goal among American liberals, Church advocated "public support and protection of independent labor unions." Indeed, the key to the purchasing power of wage earners rested with "healthy, responsible unions." Economic democracy also demanded government aid to small businesses and cooperatives.[26]

As Church considered his ideas, he admitted that they were anything but daring or radical. He nevertheless liked them because they avoided extreme ideologies on both the right and the left. As "a compromise program" they might well win passage, he told Bethine, "if the Liberals can ever get together."[27]

Church's wartime experiences had unquestionably solidified his political convictions. He instinctively favored the middle ground, the preferred turf of Borah and Franklin Roosevelt, his political models. Suspicious of economic bigness, he believed in the role of an active government to protect the public and sympathized with the needs of workers and small business people. And he opposed foreign policies that smacked of colonialism.

America's use of nuclear weapons against Japan in early August added another element to his political creed. More than ever, he recognized the folly of seeking national security through arms races or unilateral action. The best hope for peace, he concluded, rested with a world organization of nations.[28]

Significantly, his response to the dropping of atomic bombs on Hiroshima and Nagasaki was darkly philosophical. Rather than celebrate the war's conclusion, and the prospects of returning home earlier than might otherwise have been possible, he shuddered at the arrival of a nuclear age. "The atomic bomb is not the 'marvel of the Age' but the monster of all time," he argued shortly after the war ended. Humanity's lamentable effort "to advance the cause of death" via new military technology had finally produced the ultimate "weapon of self-destruction." Church was astonished that most people whom he knew were enthusiastic about the atomic bomb: "We even applaud reaching our doom!" How ironic, he believed, that a triumph of the human intellect would come at the expense of the human soul. He conceded that, in the hands of the United States, England, and Canada, the atomic bomb would temporarily help to keep the peace. Other nations would soon develop their own nuclear arsenals, however. Once that happened, "the criterion by which we have heretofore measured the relative power of nations, great and small, will no longer hold." The bomb had forever changed the modern world, just as "gunpower leveled Feudalism." Anticipating a futile arms race, Church warned that no nation could find security by constructing huge military arsenals. "It will no longer make any difference whether the United States can build a hundred thousand planes or a million atomic bombs."[29]

On occasion, in the weeks after the war ended, Church tried to find some way to interpret the development of atomic weapons as a story of progress. Perhaps, for example, the atomic bomb would at last reveal the necessity of "a genuine federation of nations." Governments had previously sought security through their own defenses. Leaders might now finally recognize that international laws and institutions held the key to genuine national security.[30]

Sometimes, however, cynicism got the best of Church. He had witnessed "so much filth, misery, and hopeless poverty," so much exploitation, "starvation, mass-murder, and unbelievable barbarity," that he wondered if the earth would be better off without humans. "Leave it to the rats and dandelions," he said dejectedly.[31]

The atomic threat aside, he was not optimistic about future peace. The dreary truth, he maintained, was that "our system of living made war profitable for the few most influential" people and groups. For them, war was a necessary means to gain or keep their property and power.[32]

Not all was bleak for Church. On September 9, he was one of only several Americans who witnessed the official Japanese surrender to the Chinese at Nanking. General McClure took him to Nanking as the acting intelligence officer. Church believed he had the best seat available, a front row balcony spot directly overlooking the signatories' tables. "Today will be one of the most celebrated in Chinese history," he wrote excitedly, "and if I make no mark elsewhere, at least some Chinese scholar many years hence will find my signature buried among those of the guests who were invited to attend."[33]

A few days later he flew with McClure in Generalissimo Chiang Kai-shek's personal plane to another momentous event: the victorious entry of Chinese troops into the city of Hangchow. For almost an hour, he, McClure, and the general's aide constituted the three-person American party that participated in the massive parade. "The streets were jammed with shouting people," Church reported. "Exploding firecrackers and aerial bombs sounded loudly everywhere." That evening the Americans were guests at the provincial governor's mansion, where they literally feasted on a meal of some twenty courses, drank innumerable toasts, danced, and rowed in gondolas across a lake that shimmered in the harvest moonlight. Before leaving Hangchow, Church ended up singing old American songs such as "The Strawberry Blonde" with the mayor, who had graduated years earlier from the Massachusetts Institute of Technology. "It was like a tale from the Arabian Nights," in Church's estimation.[34]

Barely twenty-one and newly promoted to first lieutenant, Church had experienced some heady moments indeed. "Things have always happened to me in a big way," he told his parents. "It has so far been my good fortune that the 'ups' should greatly out-number the 'downs.' If the laws of averages ever begin to take effect, I'm in store for a wretched future."[35]

V

Some of the "downs" made a quick appearance. Church soon realized he would not get out of the Army for months, probably not until Easter. His spirits plummeted. "It is going on three years now that I've floundered in the army," he protested in late September, 1945. "The war is over. It took me out of my freshman year in college, and a man has a right to get back to his pursuits. I want to begin to live!"[36]

"It looks like I'll lock the place up when the last man has left Shanghai," he wrote his parents more than four months later. By then he had lost his interest in intelligence work and was anxious to put it behind him forever.[37]

He talked about returning to college, although he suspected he would not get out of the Army in time for fall enrollment. He felt "no particular attachment to Stanford" and speculated that he might transfer to an eastern school. The real problem, he conceded cheerlessly, was that he could not get excited about attending college anywhere. He dreaded "listening to mindless lectures largely for the purpose of condensing them" for exams; hearing "the vacuous grade-getters" prate about their high marks; wearing a freshman beany cap; participating in "the sordid rituals" of campus life. He cared not who won athletic events and he despised the rah-rah atmosphere. "No, I am obligated by social pressure to return to college, and to obtain a degree." This obligation, he wrote gloomily, reenforced what he had come to resent over the past several years: "outside pressures of different kinds, and not my own free choice, have acted to mold my life against my will."[38]

VI

Yet Church seemed uncertain about how he wanted to mold his own life—at least as it involved Bethine Clark. By the spring of 1946 his unraveling romantic relationship with her undoubtedly contributed substantially to his despondency. And he, more than anyone, was to blame.

He was undoubtedly very fond of her. While he was in the service, her frequent letters boosted his morale. In the spring of 1944 he had even speculated that, without the war, he "might have had a ring on her finger by now."[39]

But he could not decide how she fit his future plans. In late July 1944, when he was on a brief furlough, they had picnicked alongside a mountain stream north of Boise. Although she had felt very close to him, he had refused to make any long-term commitments to her.[40]

Wartime uncertainties influenced his indecision, but so did ambition. As he informed one friend, "My first love is still politics." This was basically what he had told Bethine during their picnic. He hoped to complete his law degree after the war and eventually to run for political office. But that dream, he feared, might fall victim to an early marriage and the pressures of building a family. He wanted to close off neither his options nor hers, he said. Thus he urged that they postpone any firm promises to each other. He still viewed her as his "sweetheart," but for the present he could guarantee her no lasting relationship. "Frank was always afraid he was going to do the things everybody else did," she said later of that day which was, for her, so disappointing. "And he didn't want to. Marriage, or anything else. He just wanted a different kind of life."[41]

Unwilling to make any commitment to her, he nevertheless seemed unable to do without her. He informed his parents that she was as "wonderful" as ever. "You are always in my thoughts," he told her. He apologized for treating her in a "a callous and rotten" way, for being inconsiderate, and for hurting her. In his relationship with her, he confessed, "I qualify for a dunce's booby prize." He admitted that he was "green with envy" and felt "blue" whenever he thought about her dating someone else. Candidly, he wished bad luck on anyone who might be courting her.[42]

Not surprisingly, she had difficulty interpreting all of this. She found his reference to feeling "green" and "blue" about her dating other men downright perplexing. After all, just a few months earlier he had encouraged her to do just that. "I've been under the impression that I was working under *your instructions* and it was the least of your worries," she wrote. How, she wondered, should she read his mixed signals? He signed his letters with "love"; yet, she noted, "you've said nothing of loving me."[43]

He remained ambivalent, unable to assess his own feelings. "You are the only girl I have ever wanted to love," he assured her. But he was still struggling within, "half-trying to say that I do love you, half-trying to let you know that I've no right to say that I do love you." Probably, he conceded, none of this made any sense. "When it comes to you, I always bungle things. . . ."[44]

This time the damage seemed permanent. In early 1946 Bethine Clark became engaged to a West Point cadet she had been dating at the University of Michigan. Frank Church's wartime education had left him wiser about the world, but not necessarily about himself and his future.

VII

Church undoubtedly had mixed feelings when he finally returned to Idaho following his June 11 discharge from the Army. It was good to be back home, but much had changed. Even when he had last visited Boise, during Christmas of 1944, he had felt as if he were "in the midst of strangers," or "like a transient in his own home town." Because of the war, the city's economy was now slightly more diversified and industrialized. Old friends were often different or gone. Bob Wardwell, for instance, had died in a plane crash in Japan several weeks after the war ended, leaving Church painfully aware of "a vacuum that won't be filled."[45]

Bethine Clark's decision to marry the West Pointer had created another vacuum in his life, one that he apparently now regretted considerably. But it was too late to repair that situation. Her engagement had ended any romance between them. Or at least he thought so, until he talked with his old friend Stan Burns. Burns had returned from the Pacific several weeks earlier to learn, much to his surprise, that Bethine was engaged to someone other than Frank. She explained to him that Church had hurt her deeply by showing no interest in marrying her. When Burns guessed that she was still fond of Church, she fought back tears and replied, no matter, he had rejected her. She had no intention even of seeing him when he got back to Boise, a point she finally relented on after talking at length with Burns. Shortly after

Church arrived in town, Burns surprised him with information that Bethine seemed still to care for him. Church immediately dropped by her home and asked her to go for a drive.[46]

It took Church only about twenty minutes that evening to ask Bethine Clark to marry him. She accepted conditionally. Her previous engagement was not the problem; she had already decided it was a mismatch and that she would break it off. The problem was timing. She wanted Church to make sure that he was certain about his sudden proposal. She recommended that he see if he still felt the same way after he had been enrolled for a few months that fall at Stanford. In the meantime, she would end her engagement. This was fine with Church.[47]

It was not fine with her parents. The morning after Church's proposal to Bethine, he placed an anxious phone call to Burns. Much distressed, Church claimed that he had ruined everything. Bethine's father had virtually thrown him out of the house when he had learned about the new marriage plans. Although Chase and Jean Clark liked Church personally, they resented his sudden reentry into their daughter's life and what they perceived as a terrible breach of etiquette. After all, Bethine was still engaged to another man. Chase Clark worried, moreover, that Frank and Bethine would not be able to build a marriage. He was convinced that Bethine, high strung and volatile, needed a steadier influence than Church, who was bursting with energy and ambition. Their competitive natures would hardly be conducive to marital harmony. Bethine, using her influence as an only daughter, eventually prevailed, persuading her parents that she and Frank Church were suited for each other. In December, their engagement became official.[48]

VIII

With Bethine Clark and recent wartime memories much on his mind, Church had difficulty readjusting to undergraduate life at Stanford. The conspicuous wealth of many students made him uneasy. Although he lived in a fraternity, he objected to its "unbelievable" rituals and worked out an arrangement by which others in the house left him alone. Politically, he felt like an alien. When the Republicans captured both houses of Congress in the 1946 elections, he wrote disgustedly that "Stanford wildly applauds. I wonder how I ever chose for my university such a pesthole of reaction."[49]

Eager to stir the complacent political waters on campus, he seized an opportunity in late October to address a School of Education assembly about China. Admittedly "anxious for the chance to strike out against Chiang's China," he joked beforehand that his speech might result in his being run out of Stanford. By his own account, his "no-holds-barred" attack on the Chiang government "created quite a sensation." The one-hour lecture stirred up "something of a teapot tempest," and elicited other speaking invitations. He speculated that people back in Boise would have found his address very upsetting. They probably would have concluded that "the Legion protege" had been transformed into the " 'menace on Franklin Street.' "[50]

But he did not accuse only Boise of political timidity. "Even our most liberal and advanced colleges quake at having the fragile myths attacked," he complained. He objected to a tendency across the country either to avoid controversial subjects or to relegate them to private discussions behind closed doors.[51]

In January 1947 he "weathered a minor crisis in the Speech and Drama Department" when he refused to lecture on China at the Toastmaster's Club in Redwood City, California. The group, he discovered, wanted him to deliver an innocuous travelogue on China. Only after the Toastmasters agreed that he could talk on his own terms did he speak to them. Telling the group at the outset that he could not discuss China in a non-controversial manner, he lambasted the Chiang regime as "Fascistic"—a "single-party state" in which a few wealthy families enjoyed "power, plunder, and profit." He accused Chiang of having held back his own military forces during the war on the assumptions that the United States would defeat the Japanese and that the Nationalists would need troops to continue the civil war against the communists. Emphasizing that corruption pervaded the Nationalist government, Church argued that Chiang tried to deflect public anger onto scapegoats, including the communists. Insofar as Americans attempted to save the Chiang regime, Church warned, "we make ourselves party to China's sorrow."[52]

Church took his "China talk" to a variety of other groups. He delighted in shocking the "well-fed matrons of San Jose" and accepted a $25 honorarium for speaking to a group of Rotarians. "Taking money from the Rotarians is practically as worthy a cause as damning the regime of Chiang Kai Chek [sic]," he told Bethine. "If I can manage to get things well enough organized, perhaps I'll be able to buy a dress suit for our wedding."[53]

While speaking out publicly against the Chiang regime, Church continued his college debating career as spectacularly as he had started it in 1942. In Hawaii he competed before a standing-room only crowd of more than a thousand. Back in California he recovered from a bad chest cold to win the fifty-third annual debate between Stanford and the University of California, thereby earning the coveted Medaille Joffre award. The Associated Students of Stanford recognized him as the school's top debater.[54]

"I've had a hell of a time settling down to study," Church had written when he first returned to college. "The thought of it is deadening." But study he had, carrying double the normal course load. That heavy load, combined with the credit hours he had already accumulated, allowed him to complete his whirlwind undergraduate education in the summer of 1947. He graduated "with great distinction" as a Political Science major in the top 5 percent of his class.[55]

IX

On June 21, 1947, Frank and Bethine took their wedding vows on the porch of the Clark family's Robinson Bar Ranch in the Salmon River mountains. The seventy-acre ranch, with a natural hot spring, lay nestled in a little valley near Challis, Idaho. The setting was magnificent.

After driving around Mexico for several weeks on their honeymoon, the Churches moved to Boston where he enrolled in Harvard Law School. The move provided what Bethine, in retrospect, described as "a terrible and wonderful time." Living in Boston had its "magical" moments, including even their struggle to make a home out of a small, fourth-floor apartment with a kitchen more like a phone booth. Because she worked at the Radcliffe library, they commuted together to Cambridge in their DeSoto convertible—usually very fast, invariably behind schedule, and with the Boston Pops Orchestra turned up loudly on the radio. Church also enjoyed the opportunity to see his brother on a regular basis. In 1947 Richard was still in the Navy but attending Harvard Business School. Each Friday afternoon, the brothers ate lunch together.[56]

There were nevertheless difficulties for the newlyweds, including the challenge of learning to live together. He was exceedingly well-organized, disciplined, and orderly. She was less so and, by her own admission, had "an incendiary temper." Inevitably, collisions occurred.

Once, she spent considerable time cleaning the apartment only to have him comment that the place looked awful. She burst into tears and thought about leaving. He apologized, explaining that the place was "chaotic," not dirty. Clutter of any kind bothered him. Just as he always tried to keep his thoughts in logical order and his emotions controlled, so he favored tidy surroundings.[57]

As the young couple sought a formula for domestic harmony, they wrestled with limited finances and other problems. He studied most of the time, and neither of them particularly liked the Northeast. Law school turned out to be "a veritable purgatory for work," as Church described it. He excelled nonetheless, winning an early appointment to the *Harvard Law Review.* All too symbolic for him, however, were the "austere, forbidding portraits of the great jurists" that hung in the classrooms. Their cold, stern faces typified the dour mood inside and the punishing weather outside, courtesy of one of Boston's worst winters in years. During his first final exam, moreover, someone stole his car.[58]

By then Church was also suffering from a severe backache and doubts about his chosen law school. He told his brother that a Harvard degree would assuredly open up many opportunities, but not necessarily the ones he sought. Richard sensed that Frank was afraid "Harvard law was going to lead him down a path he didn't want to go"–one leading to a career in a large, eastern law firm. Frank Church himself later conceded that, from the outset, he had viewed the law as a doorway into politics. It thus seemed essential, he recalled, that he return "to Idaho to establish my home, my practice, and to find a political base." Stanford Law School, from this perspective, seemed to offer more advantages than Harvard.[59]

In Boston, meanwhile, bad news continued to mix with the good. The Churches were thrilled to learn that Bethine was expecting a baby by early fall, but she found it increasingly taxing to negotiate the four flights of steps to their apartment. Frank flourished academically at Harvard, but his back pains worsened, sometimes doubling him over in agony. The doctor's nonchalant dismissal of his discomfort as "student's backache" provided no relief.[60]

Circumstances seemed to dictate a change of location. Frank had decided to transfer to Stanford, where he hoped, among other things, the warmer weather would help his back. And Bethine was not anxious to spend another year in Boston. Thus in the summer of 1948, the Churches moved back West.

On September 23, shortly after Frank Church entered Stanford's law school as a second-year student, Bethine gave birth to Frank Forrester IV, nicknamed "Twig." With a new baby and a new residence, the Churches looked optimistically ahead. Palo Alto promised an easier winter than what they had just experienced. They were delighted to replace the fourth-floor walkup in South Boston with a small rented house complete with a yard, and even a sandbox for Twig. It was good, additionally, to be close again to Church's old friend, Carl Burke, also a law student at Stanford.

X

Then, in February, 1949, came shocking news. Church, still experiencing serious back pains, had suddenly developed a swelling in his groin area–"Mr. Trouble" as the doctor described it. Church faced greater danger than he realized. He entered the hospital for a routine one-hour operation for a hernia. In the waiting room, Bethine watched the clock with growing alarm. Six hours after her husband entered surgery, she received a distressing report. The doctors had discovered testicular cancer, and the situation was bad, very bad. Despite the removal of a tumor, as well as lymph nodes and glands on Church's left side all the way up to his kidney, there was little hope. He had *choriocarcinoma*, an incurable condition. In three to six months he would probably be dead. Shortly after receiving this devastating news, Frank and Bethine discussed ending their lives together. Profoundly depressed, they sat in a San Francisco restaurant, talking about how they would leave the baby with his four grandparents in Boise, take one last trip together to Italy and drive off a cliff.[61]

A week after the initial diagnosis of cancer, however, fright and despair suddenly gave way to a flicker of hope. A routine check at Stanford Medical School produced another diagnosis. Dr. David A. Wood, head of the pathology department, concluded that Church suffered from *seminoma*, a somewhat less lethal strain of cancer which might respond to Stanford's experimental program in X-ray treatment.[62]

The following seven weeks were dreadful. Daily X-ray therapy exacted a terrible physical toll. Megadoses of radium burned Church's flesh, turning it purple, and wracked him with nausea. A loss in appetite and violent fits of vomiting sent his weight plunging to ninety pounds. After the third week, doctors temporarily stopped the treatments and ordered him back to the hospital for intravenous feeding. Bethine, however, was determined, if at all possible, to keep him at home. "While you are curing his cancer," she told the doctors, "you are killing his body." At home she had been able to distract him somewhat from his nausea by reading aloud from books such as *Mr. Roberts*, which made him laugh. The doctors agreed that he could remain with her, but only if she could get some food and a daily minimum of four quarts of liquid into him. When it turned out that root beer settled satisfactorily in his stomach, she constantly kept a cold glass beside him. The root beer, along with some kinds of food such as lamb chops and baked potatoes, worked well enough for Church to remain at home during his remaining treatments. Even then, there were scary moments. The discovery of spots on his lungs suggested that the cancer had spread. The spots, however, turned out to be old scars from earlier childhood illnesses. When his jaw suddenly went numb, he was convinced that the cancer had reached his brain. "It was," he recalled, "the lowest I'd ever been in my life." But the cancer, it turned out, was not spreading.[63]

In the spring of 1949, following the last X-ray treatment, the Churches loaded up their car and left for Boise. The final verdict on Frank's cancer was not yet in, of course. According to the doctors he needed to go another five years without recurring problems to ensure that he had beaten the disease. Even then, they estimated that the ordeal had probably lopped ten to fifteen years off his life.[64]

As the Churches drove toward Idaho they chose to interpret an initially disturbing event as a favorable sign. To facilitate her driving, Bethine had removed her diamond ring, a favored family heirloom. Frank, sitting next to her, had placed it on one of his long, bony fingers. When they passed over a small river in Nevada, he tossed an empty root beer bottle out the window and into the water. As he did, Bethine's ring slipped off, flying out the window. Still weak from his X-ray treatments, but determined to find her ring, he insisted on searching for it in the shallow stream. Increasingly frantic and having no success, he suddenly had an idea—perhaps the ring had not traveled as far as the bottle. Sure enough, he found it on the edge of the bridge. Although a car had run over it, fracturing the diamond, it could be fixed. "Finding that ring," Church remembered, "seemed to be a symbol that our luck would change."[65]

Church not only survived his battle with cancer, he came away from it with a firmer sense of life's possibilities and challenges. As he later put it, "I'd had a sentence of death passed upon me—a sentence that had been lifted. I was determined to make my life the better for it—personally, with my wife and children, and professionally in my career." He was now, he said, more willing to take chances, even when the odds seemed outlandishly high.[66]

Additionally, his relationship with Bethine deepened. They had shared a harrowing time. She had been instrumental in his recovery, nursing him, encouraging him, being constantly with him. Their marriage ties were knotted more tightly. She was ever after more protective of him, and he was more appreciative of her.

XI

After a summer's convalescence in Boise, Church resumed his studies at Stanford, where he helped edit the law review. Within a year, in 1950, he received his degree. He returned immediately to Idaho and passed the bar exam without studying for it nor waiting the customary months after graduation to take it.[67]

Financial considerations dictated his choice of a first job, as legal counsel for the Idaho Office of Price Stabilization. As a beginning attorney eager to generate some income, and still weak from his last cancer treatment, he viewed the position as a way to gain time until he could start his own practice. Sentiment also influenced his decision. During World War II his father had come out of retirement to serve on the county ration board of the Office of Price Administration (OPA), predecessor of the Office of Price Stabilization (OPS).[68]

The OPS was part of the Truman administration's cautious effort to curb inflation after the outbreak of the Korean war in June, 1950. Wage-price controls pleased few Americans, however. Roosevelt's OPA had always been unpopular, until it ceased operating in 1946. The OPS fared no better. Despite indications by late 1950 that the public would accept some controls, the task of administering economic restraints was staggering. Anti-control sentiment surfaced quickly among numerous groups, ranging from organized labor to the farm bloc, the National Association of Manufacturers, and chambers of commerce. "This is just the same old fight," Truman told the press wearily in the spring of 1951. "Whenever you tread on the toes of anybody, he has to scream."[69]

As legal counsel for the Idaho OPS, Frank Church soon heard plenty of screams, just as his father had earlier with the OPA. The elder Church had administered local rationing out of a sense of good citizenship; the job, however, had been an emotional strain, opening him up to considerable abuse and pleas for special treatment. Indeed, Frank Church suspected that the stressful OPA experience had shortened his father's life. Frank Sr. died of a heart attack in January 1950, a few months before his son signed on with the OPS.[70]

Frank Jr. quickly learned how "tough and thankless" controlling prices could be. Like some of Truman's liberal advisors, Church nonetheless believed that the Korean war dictated controls. Without them, runaway inflation could create a host of other evils. In the mid-1940s he had personally watched the "beast" of inflation tear apart the Chinese. He knew that, unchecked, inflation could destroy a nation, savaging family incomes, and encouraging deadly political scapegoating. In Church's opinion, inflation demanded an energetic governmental response. But after a year's work with the OPS, he concluded that Congress had given the unpopular agency "a wooden sword and no shield to wage the battle." In the fight against the "Goliath" of soaring prices, success unfortunately seemed to depend upon "the luck of David."[71]

In 1951 Church happily departed the OPS in favor of his own Boise law practice. He also taught night classes in public speaking at Boise Junior College. He required no textbook in his courses, emphasizing instead that people learned to speak publicly just as they learned to swim: "by actually doing it." A good speech, he insisted, was well-prepared, logical, persuasive, and avoided either "name-calling or flag-waving."[72]

Meanwhile, the paths of Church and Carl Burke continued to cross. The rift that had separated them briefly during the early 1940s faded. Each had served as best man at the other's wedding. Burke had also returned to Boise with a Stanford law degree and worked briefly as a counsel for the OPS. In the early 1950s, the Churches and Burkes even became neighbors, living next to each other in small houses on Logan Street. Of the things the two men shared—schooling, ideals, and careers—their interest in politics kept them closest.

In 1948, while they were in law school, they had gone together to vote in their first presidential election. After casting ballots for Harry Truman, they had driven into San Francisco to await the returns. At several Democratic rallies they had joined in the excitement as the underdog Truman prevailed over the heavily favored challenger, Tom Dewey. For the fun of it, they had also visited what was supposed to have been a huge Republican celebration in one of the city's grandest hotels. To their delight, they had found magnificent offerings of food and drink, but virtually no Republicans on hand.[73]

In the Boise area by the early 1950s, however, Democrats were the ones largely missing; indeed, Church joked that few things sounded more ghostly than the voice of an Ada County Democrat. For the politically ambitious Church and Burke, the local scene was anything but encouraging. The Democratic headquarters on Jefferson street in Boise resembled a hovel compared with its Republican counterpart in the stately Owyhee Hotel. For years no Democrat had won office in Ada county, and in 1952 only three candidates initially filed for positions on the party ticket.[74]

Church and Burke concentrated on revitalizing the sleepy local organization. They had little sympathy for the old leadership which, all the way down to precinct levels, consisted primarily of hangers-on, intent on protecting their own positions. The Church-Burke faction, "Young Turks," as someone dubbed its members, gathered at Church's home evening after evening to pore over precinct maps and recruit people to challenge the party's Old Guard. Over a number of months, the "Young Turks" gained control of the county Democrats. "It was not so much that the people we ousted were all that bad," Burke said in retrospect, "but we thought they were at that time. Anyway, from that point on, the Ada County organization strongly backed Frank Church."[75]

XII

In 1952, buoyed up by their success within the local Democratic party, Church and Burke announced their candidacies for the state legislature. Their chances for success hardly rested upon bulging campaign chests—each spent only about $100. Instead, they hoped to persuade the county's residents of the need to build a healthy two-party system. This, Church told prospective voters, would end "the complete monopoly control of one party over all our local offices." Intending primarily to publicize themselves and energize the Democratic organization, neither expected to win.[76]

Probably neither expected to lose quite so badly, however. Church finished fifth in a field of eight, only slightly ahead of Burke. Each of the four Republican front-runners almost doubled the number of votes that either Church or Burke received.[77]

Within the friendlier confines of the state Democratic party, Church fared far better. In 1952 he was elected head of the Idaho Young Democrats, and he delivered the keynote address at the party's state platform convention. Although his speech contained the kinds of name-calling and flag-waving that he banned from his own public speaking course, it undoubtedly impressed state Democrats, anxious to thump the opposition and celebrate their party's accomplishments.[78] In Church they could see a "comer," a young, good-looking, dynamic individual, with solid Idaho credentials and a promising future—the very kind of person the party desperately needed.

At this point, however, Church offered more style and youthful exuberance than new ideas, especially when he discussed foreign policy issues. A few years earlier, in his letters from Asia as a young soldier, he had worried that America's search for markets would encourage aggressive, expansionist policies detrimental to peace. Immediately after the war, he had taken issue with the increasingly popular Cold War rendition of China's fate—a rendition that pitted the evil communists against the democratic forces of Chiang Kai-shek. But, by 1952, he was content to echo the prevailing Cold War views about America's need to stand firm against communist belligerence. In his keynote address at the state party convention he thus praised Truman's "aggressive foreign policy" and urged Democrats not to sit quietly while Republicans accused them of being insufficiently tough with the Soviets.[79]

XIII

His stridency was probably for political effect, but it also reflected the grip of conventional Cold War thinking upon him. By the late Forties and early Fifties, Cold War anti-communism pervaded American society and politics, its hold on liberals particularly evident in the Americans for Democratic Action. The ADA had emerged in 1947 as both a champion of civil rights and New Deal-style reforms and an advocate of vigorous resistance to Soviet expansionism abroad, mainly through economic aid programs and military preparedness. Although the ADA, which drew its membership primarily from several northeastern states, was scarcely a political factor in Idaho, it was one of the most significant barometers of liberal opinion in the United States. Some American liberals, including a few within the ADA, warned against excessive fears of the Soviet Union; but most agreed with ADA member Gus

Tyler that the Soviets were following a "continuous zig-zag policy to win the entire world for Communism." Frank Church's views in the early 1950s corresponded with Tyler's.[80]

Church's willingness to blame the Cold War on Soviet aggression attested to the prevalence of that orthodox interpretation, but his foreign policy views were perhaps less considered and reflective than they might have been. For some time, personal matters had preoccupied him. Following his last X-ray treatment in 1949, the outcome of his battle with cancer would remain in doubt for at least five years. Additionally, the demands of beginning a family, wrestling with his OPS job, building a law practice, teaching a college course, and trying to launch a political career absorbed much of his attention.

His uncritical acceptance of prevailing Cold War attitudes was especially evident in 1954 and 1955 when he chaired Idaho's Crusade for Freedom organization, a reputedly private effort to raise money on behalf of Radio Free Europe. Years later, he found his mid-Fifties' zeal for the Crusade an embarrassment, indicative of his naiveté as well as of the mood of the times. The Crusade "had a great appeal to me," he remembered. "I believed wholeheartedly in it." He had been much flattered at the opportunity to raise funds for broadcasting across the Iron Curtain. "We must get the truth through to the captive nations," he had said when he agreed to chair the state's drive.[81]

"Strike a blow for Freedom tonight!" he pleaded on television in February, 1954. He warned viewers that, "in the struggle that is now going on for supremacy between the free world and the Communist world, the Communists never relent and never relax." By contributing money to Radio Free Europe, Americans could "keep the Communists off balance." Two years in a row, on Lincoln's birthday, Church helped Idaho's governor and other officials release "freedom balloons" similar to those that periodically carried millions of anti-communist pamphlets from West Germany into Eastern Europe. The ceremonies in Boise duplicated events in several hundred other cities across the United States.[82]

Church, like most Americans, believed that the Crusade for Freedom and Radio Free Europe were, as he said in 1954, "wholly organized and directed by independent American citizens." Articles and advertisements in *Reader's Digest* and elsewhere portrayed Radio Free Europe as completely nongovernmental. "Sure I want to fight communism—but how?" asked a perplexed and anxious citizen in one advertisement.

The answer was that he could join a huge army of citizen volunteers, whose "truth dollars" counteracted communist lies behind the Iron Curtain.[83]

Actually, Radio Free Europe was far from being an independent, nongovernmental crusade for freedom. It was a covert propaganda operation of the Central Intelligence Agency (CIA). Formed in 1950, it was one of a number of CIA cover organizations, including Radio Liberty, the National Student Association, the Congress for Cultural Freedom, and the Center for International Studies. Only later did a dismayed Frank Church learn that the bulk of Radio Free Europe's budget came from the CIA, not from the nickels and dimes that people like him collected.[84]

In the Fifties, however, Church proudly accepted an invitation from the government of West Berlin to be among sixty Americans on hand to commemorate the fifth anniversary of the Crusade for Freedom's presentation of a "Freedom Bell" to the city's residents.[85] Eventually, when he got in the U. S. Senate, he would learn the truth about the whole operation.[86] But in the 1950s, as he explained later, "I was convinced, as nearly everybody was convinced, that the Cold War policies of the United States were absolutely sound." He tended neither to question Cold War ideas, nor even to examine them carefully: "I merely parodied those concepts." Virtually forgotten for the moment were his insights as a young soldier in Asia, when he had worried that American interventionism abroad resembled the traditional European imperialism against which he had seen young Chinese and Indian nationalists vent their anger.[87]

Church's unreflective Cold War attitudes, along with his cheerleading approach to politics, gave some people the impression that he was mainly glitter and polish with little substance. Associated Press reporters Dale Nelson and Sam Day both initially viewed him as a "typical Junior Chamber of Commerce" person. In the early 1950s, Nelson was decidedly unenthusiastic about the young Boise attorney who seemed little more than "an ambitious young man, a glad-hander." Day, newly transferred from San Francisco to Boise, wandered into an appliance store and happened to see Church on television making a pitch for Radio Free Europe. As Day watched him, he formed "about as negative an impression as I have ever had of anybody." Church, looking "stuffy" and self-satisfied, seemed to represent "the essential problem in the state. The best looking people were. . .just mindless warriors in the cold war."

In Day's opinion at the time, "Church sort of personified the political conservatism of Idaho."[88]

Even members of Idaho's Young Democrats had doubts about Church. After he chaired the group from 1952 to 1954, he himself fell victim to a "Young Turk" movement. At Idaho State College in Pocatello some students who knew little about him personally were nevertheless determined that he not control the state organization. One of them, Dwight Jensen, recalled attending the Young Democrats annual meeting in April 1954 "with the specific idea of keeping him from being the boss at this convention." The convention actually had two parts. One involved a small morning gathering of around fifty Young Democrats; the other was the annual Jefferson-Jackson day festivities, for which some 500 Democrats from around the state were in attendance. Church figured prominently in both. He chaired the larger convention, sitting at the banquet table with the guest speaker, Massachusetts' thirty-seven-year-old senator, John F. Kennedy. And he presided over the Young Democrats' session, one that proved as cloudy for him as the Boise weather.[89]

When the Young Democrats convened, delegates from Idaho State College and the University of Idaho formed an alliance against, in Dwight Jensen's words, "a common enemy": the Frank Church faction. Usually, students from the rival schools had little affection for each other, but this time they stood united. Church's self-assured demeanor, and his frantic "rushing this way and that way trying to get things done," only confirmed their desire to cut him off at the knees. As Jensen remembered the showdown, it reflected "college high-jinks" more than anything else. "We were going to keep Frank Church from winning." And they did, capturing "all but one of the state-wide offices." Church was out as president and Carl Burke as secretary; into their places moved Idaho State College people.[90]

By the end of 1954 the political situation in Idaho was enough to make Church pause. Around the state, despite his best efforts, his status within the Democratic party was still problematic. And within Ada County, where Democrats were "sacrificial lambs," as Dale Nelson described them, he faced a special problem. "I live in 'enemy territory,' " he lamented.[91]

Yet it was in 1954 and 1955 that he, barely thirty, began to talk about running for the United States Senate. He floated the idea with several friends, not all of whom were enthusiastic. Burke, Stan Burns, and Chase Clark were among those who worried that such a race might be premature. After all, the extremely popular Dwight Eisenhower would be running again for president in 1956 and would presumably have long political coattails. Moreover, the incumbent senator, Herman Welker, had won big in 1950 and was a bruising, unscrupulous campaigner with an eye for the jugular. Perhaps the best strategy was to wait a bit longer before taking such a huge political step. But Church, feeling cramped and anxious, was not entirely joking when he told his wife that it might actually be easier to establish a political career by going beyond Ada County and running statewide. The question was when to do so.[92]

During the 20,000-mile Idaho campaign, Frank and Bethine pose with her mother. *Courtesy Boise State University.*

Chapter 3

Going to the Senate: The 1956 Election

"HE'S A FINE KID," remarked an Idaho state Democratic leader of Frank Church in 1956, "but we can't elect him to the U. S. Senate; he's just too young and inexperienced." The remark made sense. After all, Church had never held an elective office and was barely old enough to qualify for the Senate. He looked even younger than his thirty-two years. When, for example, he spoke to a group of high school seniors in Pocatello, Idaho, an enthusiastic teacher found him impressive but believed that he needed to put a little grey in his hair to distinguish himself from the students.[1]

Church's phenomenal 1956 campaign nevertheless had a storybook conclusion. Against what were initially tremendous odds, he leaped from political obscurity to the Senate, defeating former senator Glen Taylor in the Democratic primary and devastating Republican incumbent Herman Welker in the general election. This happened, moreover, despite the fact that Democrats were the minority party in Idaho, and during a year in which Republican President Dwight Eisenhower returned to the White House with more electoral votes than any previous candidate except Franklin D. Roosevelt.

Church's surprising success in 1956 grew partially out of good fortune. Idaho's sputtering economy provided him with a fertile issue, and Welker could not mount an effective campaign because of illness and the declining appeal of his previously successful red-baiting tactics. But Church was no accidental senator. Drawing upon formidable speaking abilities, an affable personality, and an enthusiastic volunteer staff, he staged an imaginative and relentless campaign that blended the new and the old. He explored issues that looked ahead to the 1960s, and he used to superior advantage the emerging political medium of television; at the same time, he relied heavily on old-fashioned grassroots stumping and an "organization" of amateurs whose energy and inventiveness compensated for lack of experience.

I

Richard Church was among those surprised to learn in 1955 that Frank intended to seek a Senate seat. That year, the two brothers talked briefly at Washington D. C.'s National Airport, when Frank happened to be passing through and had a short layover between flights. Richard, still a naval officer, had not seen much of his brother for several years. They chatted for about half an hour. As Frank got up to catch his flight, he announced suddenly that he intended to run for the United States Senate. He explained that working his way up the political ladder would take too long. "If you want something, go right for it," he said. "Shoot for the top. Why not?"[2]

Although Church was willing to take risks, his decision to run in 1956 did not come easily or without considerable thought. More was at stake, after all, than his political future; he had a family to consider. In order to finance his campaign, he and Bethine would have to sell their home and move in with her parents. By 1955, Bethine was well aware that her husband was agonizing over whether to run for the Senate the next year. The personal and family costs of pursuing his political ambitions bothered him considerably. Bethine ultimately placed her own thoughts on paper. In an eight-page, handwritten note to her husband, she conceded that the political odds against him were great: "Yours is the semi-impossible task of getting known and talking to more groups and individuals than you'll ever dream." Nothing was more unpredictable, in her view, than the Idaho voter. "The heartbreaking effort" of a long campaign could end up buried under an Eisenhower landslide. But if Frank decided to run for the Senate, he should know that he had her complete support. "I'm for you honey," she pledged, "a new house worth, a disrupted life's worth and no regrets. . . ." After all, she reminded him, his battle with cancer had raised all too forcefully the philosophical questions of how best to use one's limited time wisely. The financial costs made one pause, but "if it's worth doing it's worth doing without." Moreover, there was always the possibility that he could "entice, and light, and boom this state into a stirring of imagination."[3]

As winter in late 1955 descended, Frank and Bethine Church set out in their battered Kaiser to see if he could muster sufficient support to justify announcing his candidacy. The state's sparse, widely scattered population of some 610,000 made contacts difficult. Except for the capital city of Boise, with around 35,000 residents, there were only several towns of any size: Pocatello (27,000) and Idaho Falls (20,000) in the southeast; Twin Falls (18,000) in the south-central area; Nampa (17,000) in the southwest; and Lewiston (13,000) in the north. In northern Idaho, mining and lumbering were vital, along with some farming. From Nampa across the immense southern section to Twin Falls and beyond, farming dominated. Virtually no large industry existed in Idaho. Identifying the political mood of this geographically diverse region presented a serious challenge for Church; getting people to support him for the Senate would be even more difficult, especially given Idaho's sprawling size and his relative obscurity.

By the time that Church formally announced his candidacy on February 24, 1956, amid a driving snowstorm in Boise, he and Bethine were already well into what turned out to be a nine-month primary campaign that took them over some twenty thousand miles. By mid-August, after weeks of scouring neighborhoods and walking main streets, he had shaken the hands of up to thirty-five thousand people.[4]

Bethine's parents were extremely supportive of their son-in-law's political quest. They persuaded Frank and Bethine to move in with them and took care of seven-year-old Forrest while his parents were on the road. Although the former governor had shrewd political instincts, the only "Clark machine" that existed was, as Bethine's mother put it, "the old Maytag in the basement." The judge nevertheless offered advice and knew people whom Church should seek out.[5]

As Frank and Bethine Church battled icy and snow-covered highways and backroads, Carl Burke assembled a tiny campaign headquarters in Boise. Burke had initially believed that Church would be better off running for the House rather than the Senate, but he was willing to help in any way. Hence he agreed to chair the Citizens for Church Committee, even though it meant slighting his work in his father's law firm. Meanwhile, he anxiously awaited reports from Frank and Bethine, who were very much on the move.[6]

II

Quite literally by a flip of a coin, the couple started in northern Idaho. The choice proved fortunate. State Democrats subsequently chose Lewiston as the site for the 1956 convention. By then, to the surprise of many delegates at the gathering, the Churches had established crucial contacts and the semblance of a political network in the area. "We couldn't have been smarter than to go north," Bethine said wryly as she remembered what came of that flipped coin. But in mid-winter, as the Churches maneuvered without snow tires on the region's slippery roads, almost sliding off a steep hill outside Orofino, they must have questioned the wisdom of the northern strategy. Bethine at the wheel, Frank sat either beside her or in the back seat, pecking out speeches, letters, and press releases on a typewriter resting on his lap.[7]

In mid-February, when Church formally announced his candidacy, he was much aware of the looming possibility that soon Glen Taylor would officially enter the race. If history was any guide, the ex-senator could count on a hard core group of fifteen to twenty-five thousand loyalists. For now, he remained on the sidelines, but he was soliciting funds and obviously waiting to make his move.

Taylor was an enigma. His colorful career called to mind Horatio Alger and P. T. Barnum. One of thirteen children, he had grown up rootless and in poverty, the son of a "hellfire and brimstone" revivalist who preached in mining camps and small towns throughout Utah and the Pacific Northwest. For income, the family performed as a musical and theatrical troupe. Such a life was harsh, but young Glen learned much about grassroots people and, from his father, absorbed a political vision sprinkled with elements of Christian socialism and the Golden Rule. A sixth grade drop-out, he essentially educated himself. By age twelve he was moving from one job to another, working as a sheepherder, a sheet-metal laborer, and, eventually, a member of a traveling vaudeville act. Taylor's background and the economic crisis of the Thirties combined to make him an avowed New Dealer, critical of Franklin D. Roosevelt only for doing too little for the rank and file. In 1938, living in Pocatello, Idaho, he ran unsuccessfully for Congress. In the 1940 and 1942 Senate races, however, he pulled off stunning upsets in the Democratic primaries, only to lose the general elections. Two years later, at age 40, he became a U. S. senator.[8]

Although Taylor was a consummate showman, few people could question his liberal commitments or his political courage. On issues such as civil rights, and eventually as a critic of President Harry Truman's Cold War policies, he was principled and often astute. Wearing a wig that he had fashioned from an aluminum pie tin and human hair, he struck a popular chord among Idahoans by lambasting eastern financial interests and some of the state's most established corporations, including the Idaho Power Company. If these were not sufficient reasons for his opponents to pin the label of "radical" upon him, his decision in 1948 to run for vice-president on Henry A. Wallace's ill-fated Progressive Party ticket was. Two years later, he lost his Senate seat, the victim of vicious red-baiting tactics on the part of Democrats and Republicans alike. Taylor nevertheless made a startling comeback in 1954, capturing the Democratic primary. His 26,591 votes indicated he still had a bedrock following in Idaho. In November, however, a savage Republican attack on his alleged communist connections buried him—this time, it seemed, permanently. Losing by 60,000 votes, he suffered one of the worst defeats of any Democrat in Idaho history.[9]

By 1956 Taylor was a pariah to many Idaho Democrats, yet Frank Church had good reason to worry about him, especially as the number of Democrats in the primary grew, threatening to scatter the anti-Taylor vote. As March ended, there were two other announced candidates: Alvin McCormack, a Lewiston farmer, and Claude Burtenshaw, a political science professor at Ricks College in Rexburg, both of whom Taylor had beaten in 1954. "If this were the field, I would feel more comfortable," wrote Church in late March, "but the fact is that Glen Taylor is merely biding his time, hoping that if he delays his announcement long enough, he will entice one or possibly two more into the Democratic primary." If this strategy worked, it "would tend to spread the anti-Taylor vote very thin and could operate to assure his nomination."[10]

Church's concerns were not misplaced. Four out of five times Taylor had won primaries in which he faced three or more candidates. Moreover, this time Taylor had revenge on his mind. Sweating away as a heavy construction worker, he became obsessed with defeating Herman Welker. On his way to victory in 1950, Welker had made much of Taylor's alleged communist tendencies. With Welker now up for reelection, Taylor was determined to seek retribution. But first he had to win the Democratic primary. And blocking his way, as he later wrote, was the Clark political "dynasty's last hope"—the "baby-faced" candidate, "Frankie" Church, with "his horse grin."[11]

Frank Church hardly sensed that he belonged to any powerful dynasty. To help finance his campaign, he and Bethine had already sold their home, taking the equity of only $6000; and the two of them, not the lieutenants of any tightly organized political machine, went door to door and up and down streets, introducing themselves and shaking hands, trying to convince people to take his candidacy seriously. "We had people," he later recalled, "looking at us and snickering and wondering how this kid who was still wet behind the ears had the temerity to run for the Senate."[12]

Church knew that his only hope was to meet as many people as possible. He thus staged a whirlwind "sidewalk campaign." When people were not at home, he typed brief notes to some of them as Bethine drove him to the next towns. "I am sorry that I missed you," he wrote one individual. "However, I did get acquainted with your granddaughter, Paula. She was riding a stick horse and she told me she never lost a race on it."[13]

While Church worked frantically to increase his public visibility, he worried about the growing Democratic primary field; by mid-April there were six candidates, including Taylor. "Too many candidates have entered the Democratic primary race," moaned Church.[14]

Events now favored Taylor, and Church desperately needed a break. He got one at the Democratic state convention in Lewiston, several days after Taylor announced his candidacy. The keynote speaker, Ray McNichols, a forty-two-year-old Orofino attorney, enjoyed growing political influence, especially in northern Idaho. The popular McNichols had himself expressed interest in running for the Senate, and he had support. Publisher A. L. Alford and editor Bill Johnston of the *Lewiston Tribune*, for example, were eager to back him. But McNichols, who realized as much as anyone that the crowded primary field already favored Taylor, addressed the state convention, intimating that Taylor should drop out and urging the Democrats to rally behind one candidate. It was clear that McNichols had Church in mind, even though he did not specifically name him. Indeed, as McNichols left the convention hall after his speech, he winked at Church.[15]

Like the hills outside Lewiston, blossoming with spring, Church's campaign suddenly found new life. "At the convention," Church wrote elatedly, "the movement to throw the party support behind my candidacy gained a lot of ground." Carl Burke was not alone in viewing McNichols's address as a turning point in Church's campaign. Only after McNichols had clearly moved into Church's camp, for example, did Bill Johnston of the *Tribune* view the young man from Ada County as a serious candidate. And shortly thereafter, two other candidates withdrew from the race.[16]

As the Democratic field narrowed to four, thereby boosting Church's hopes, the Boise attorney rushed around the state, charging "the big-business administration in Washington" with policies that hurt Idaho's workers, farmers, and small merchants. He insisted that he was the only Democrat who could win in November. One of his campaign flyers showed the Democratic donkey virtually prone – ears drooping, eyes dazed, and holding its front hoofs over its head for protection. "Tired of Losing?" the flyer asked. "Well then. . .UNITE behind Frank Church. . .to carry a rejuvenated Democratic ticket to victory. Let's stop losing the general election in our own primary."[17]

Church's exhausting handshaking campaign, which also featured open forums, nevertheless paid political dividends. Both in public speaking and in conversation, the candidate's intensity and energy tended to leave a favorable impression. However, Church was basically shy and often uncomfortable when approaching strangers and asking for their support. In this regard, Bethine's political instincts and judgment were especially important. She was, wrote a family friend who later served on the senator's staff, "as good a person-to-person politician as has ever come down the pike." Laughingly, she told her husband she would help get him started in the morning by pushing him out of the car when she saw the first hand to shake. As soon as Church began talking with people, however, his genuine interest in them became apparent. He was a good listener, sincere and sensitive. At every gathering, no matter how small, he gave a full speech.[18]

Church's eagerness to sway even a few people once continued late into the evening, far beyond what seemed a worthwhile investment of time; only nine or so votes were at stake, and the group was highly skeptical. The discussion of agricultural aid appeared to increase the misgivings of one huge farmer. But when the meeting finally broke up, the farmer, still openly doubtful about Church's arguments, pledged to vote for him anyhow because he had "guts" and the courage of his convictions. Moreover, the farmer suspected that if Church got into office he would not forget individuals such as those at the meeting. Late one night another farmer listened patiently to Church's appeal before saying that he wanted to vote for the Boise attorney but could not: "Because you are in Utah." The Churches had accidentally strayed across Idaho's border.[19]

The sidewalk tour was not only wearisome, it also had its perils. In Malad, a dog bit Church's nose when he leaned too close. A potentially more serious incident occurred on the road back from the Cobalt Mine in the Salmon River country. Aware that Glen Taylor had always done well with the labor vote, the Churches had driven over the rutted and dusty road so that Frank could shake hands with miners coming off their shift. The trip had gone well, providing additional evidence for Church's belief that he was "making excellent progress with labor here in Idaho." The miners, impressed with a candidate so far from the beaten track, invited him to eat with them and applauded his promise to help keep the mine open. But, on the return trip, the car kept slipping out of gear. Bethine fought to hold the gear shift in place as the car bounced crazily down the steep grade, hitting a bump so hard that the trunk flew open.[20]

III

In order to reach a larger audience, Church decided to use the medium of television, still very new across much of the country and especially in Idaho. In 1946 only seven thousand TV sets had been in use throughout the entire United States. But by 1956 Americans were buying some twenty thousand sets daily, and a year later some forty-two million American homes had televisions. In the mountain states by 1958, 73 percent of the families owned TVs. Seldom had a technological marvel so quickly captured the public. Idaho, however, had no television stations until 1953, and the half dozen or so that Church used in 1956 had existed for barely two years.[21]

In the mid-Fifties, moreover, the relationship between television and politics was still in its infancy. In 1952 Eisenhower had huffed when filming scripts, "To think that an old soldier should come to this!" Democrat Adlai Stevenson complained that politics "isn't soap opera, this isn't Ivory Soap versus Palmolive." By 1956, however, with nearly forty million TV sets operating across the country, the major parties turned to television merchandising as never before. Even then, one advertising agent observed that most politicians knew little about the medium: "They need experts to lead them through its labyrinth."[22]

Frank Church and his small volunteer staff knew little about the mechanics of television, and they certainly could not afford to solicit expert advice. Sensing nevertheless the effect that TV could have on politics, they experimented. During the summer of 1956 they made ten political advertisements, each five minutes in length and, of course, in black and white. The budget for the first six of them came to a mere $450. They also filmed a number of twenty-second spots. Scarce campaign funds allowed for few copies of each film, so Church's people urged station managers to return each advertisement by airmail so it could receive maximum use on TV outlets elsewhere in Idaho, eastern Washington, and northern Utah.[23]

Given the relative newness of the medium, and the small budget of the Church candidacy, the amateurish qualities of the productions were hardly surprising. Carl Burke generally ran the productions; Church himself wrote the scripts; Stan Burns, who owned a small photography business, helped plan the settings, and Bethine held the boom microphone. A photographer from the Boise area, who knew how to run a moving picture camera and use sound, was the only member of the production crew who came close to being professional.[24]

The television formats were simple and direct. Each showed Church sitting or standing in front of the camera, discussing issues such as the plight of small businesses, family farms, and public schools in Idaho. Two films were biographical in nature, focusing on him as a person and on why he was a Democrat.

One ad, titled "Idaho's Decade of Stunted Growth," zeroed in on what increasingly became the dominant theme of Church's campaign. The film opened with Church in a dark suit and tie, seated behind a small desk, looking at a chart to his left. "Good evening," he said, turning toward the camera. "For ten years now, the Republican Party has been in continuous control of our state government, and has dominated our congressional delegation in Washington." He leaned forward, serious but relaxed, hands folded in front of him, noting that Idaho as a result had been "wrapped in a kind of economic straight-jacket." Stepping to the chart, he observed that all the other western states were doing better than Idaho. Since 1950, he explained, the state's population growth had been last among the western states and "only one-third that of the national average." His goal was not "growth just for the sake of growth," nor did he want huge businesses to enter the state. People who wanted large corporations could find them in big eastern cities. "No, we have a wholesome, outdoor life here in Idaho," he emphasized, "and all I want is enough growth in this state to make that good life available to our own people." Hence he believed it was "time for a change"—

"time to put an end to Idaho's stunted growth." Smiling broadly, he urged voters to "send a Democrat to the U. S. Senate!"[25]

Despite their amateurishness, the films were generally impressive, especially considering the ways in which they were made and the overall quality of television's political advertising at the time. Limited by time and money, Church relied on only one or two takes of an ad. Although he had thought carefully about what he intended to say, his comments seemed completely extemporaneous. Spurning notes, cards, or anything resembling a teleprompter, he simply looked at the camera and started talking, without hesitating or stumbling over words. "He just started out and just knocked you dead," Burns recalled. Church was extremely photogenic, and his youthful good looks served him well in front of the camera. Confident, self-assured, and friendly, he spoke clearly and in a conversational style.[26]

Some spots worked better than others, of course. The huge Arrowrock Dam outside Boise, completed in 1915, provided a telling backdrop for his discussion of "Build Your Idaho." Leaning close to the camera, talking almost intimately, Church voiced his support for multipurpose dams. Pointing proudly toward the massive structure, he asked with a disarming smile how people could consider such federal dams threats—for example, to farmers' water rights. A film on the problems of agriculture was less successful. Church, dressed in a suit, white shirt, tie, and fashionable hat, looked out of place in a farm setting. He appeared no less incongruous when he removed his hat and placed his foot on a bale of straw. And at the end he was transparently self-conscious about asking the opinion of the farmer, a Mr. Eckard, who stood next to him. Eckard, presumably a better farmer than actor, just as self-consciously shook Church's hand and said he liked what the young attorney had to say.[27]

However contrived some of the film segments were (for example, Church tousling his son's hair or patting Smokey, the family dog), the TV advertisements emphasized ideas and issues as much as images. Mainly, Church used the TV camera to bring the lecture hall into the living room, to take his ideas to people who had not yet met him or perhaps even heard of him.

This was evident in his choice of American foreign policy as the topic for his first TV film. Here was a subject about which he felt strongly, even though it mattered less than domestic problems to Idaho voters. As he stood over a globe, spinning it gently and referring to a rapidly changing world, he assuredly echoed many dominant Cold War themes. "We have a stake," he said, "in preventing the Iron Curtain from being pushed closer to us." Intent upon countering the charges of Herman Welker and other Republicans who blamed the Democrats for "twenty years of treason," he argued that Democrats, through programs like the Marshall Plan, had saved the "sick patient" of Western Europe from "the false appeal of Communism." But, significantly, he addressed as well the need to recognize "the legitimate aspirations of colonial peoples for self-government"– a theme that in the mid-Fifties surfaced only rarely in most discussions of American foreign policy.[28]

Church's television advertisements, abbreviated versions of his stump speeches, also revealed much about his distaste for large corporations. Thus, in defense of small enterprise, Church described the tripling of bankruptcy cases during the Republican "big business administration." Dotting his comments with references to "the big fellow," and accusing Welker of "backscratching for big business," he pledged his support to the small businesses that dominated Idaho's economy– not, he said as he jabbed his finger into the air, to what was good for General Motors.[29]

By midsummer, television was becoming one of the strongest weapons in Church's arsenal. "Judging from the response to my handshaking tours TV is really doing the trick," he wrote. "I am constantly amazed at how many more people instantly recognize me and comment. . . favorably on the TV." He later stressed how crucial the medium had been to his campaign. Without TV, "it would never have been possible for me to become known so quickly to the people." Bethine and Carl Burke agreed.[30]

In 1956 Church was virtually the only Idaho candidate to use television. Welker may have used brief TV spot advertising, but nothing like five-minute films. And Taylor, in the primary, depended upon stump speaking, newspaper ads, and broadsides.[31]

When Taylor and others charged that Church's allegedly lavish campaign spending proved he was the candidate of "the corporations," Church was outraged. In a letter to the *Lewiston Tribune* in early August he wrote furiously that he had "not received a single corporate contribution." Nor had he used any "paid publicity men or professional advertising firms." The voluntary services of friends and supporters had "made it possible. . . to concentrate our money where it counts the most– in carefully planned advertising and five-minute television spots."[32]

IV

By primary election day, August 14, the Democratic race was clearly between Church and Taylor. Indeed, for more than a week after the polls closed no certain winner emerged. As returns dribbled in from around the state, the two men exchanged leads time and again. Carl Burke finally set out on a long overdue vacation to California, convinced that Church had lost, only to learn by telephone in Winnemucca, Nevada, that his friend had squeaked to victory.[33]

By 170 votes, Church, who three weeks earlier had celebrated his thirty-second birthday, edged past Taylor. The two men almost evenly divided up counties and votes in the state's northern panhandle and south-central region. Taylor's greatest strength was in southeastern Idaho, around his home base of Pocatello, although Burtenshaw, who also hailed from that region, carried five of thirteen counties. Church sealed his victory in the ten counties of southwestern Idaho surrounding Boise. There he beat Taylor by nearly two to one, piling up more than 10,000 of his almost 28,000 total votes. In Elmore County, a few miles from the capital, Church impressively captured what had previously been solid Taylor country.[34]

Taylor, convinced that the Clark machine had stolen the election from him by manufacturing votes, especially in counties such as Elmore, cried foul and demanded a recount. Church, though he noted that in 1944 Taylor had been perfectly willing to accept his narrow 216-vote victory without a recount, offered nevertheless to stand by any decision of the Senate Subcommittee on Elections. When both the subcommittee and the Idaho State Board of Canvassers ruled that insufficient evidence existed to justify a recount, Church considered the matter closed. It was time to battle Welker in the general election.[35]

Calling Church "a callow opportunist with no honor or scruples," Taylor persisted. In Elmore County, he canvassed neighborhoods in an effort to turn up evidence of a miscount. When the police arrested him after receiving complaints that he was harassing people, he stepped up his "fight against the corrupt machine that seeks to control the politics of our state." Calling Church a pawn of the "corporate bosses," he decided to keep his own candidacy alive by seeking write-in votes in November.[36]

To finance his write-in campaign, Taylor approached the hated Republicans. He figured they would accept help from any source in order to re-elect Welker. In a bizarre account years later, Taylor described meeting an anonymous Welker supporter in a Boise coffee shop and offering to stage a write-in candidacy in exchange for money. The Republican made a phone call, then drove Taylor in a yellow Cadillac to the city dump. The automobile "was a brand new beauty," Taylor recalled. "I envied the son of a bitch." After some negotiating, the Welker man agreed to give Taylor $35,000 at a subsequent meeting in the dump. With the money the former senator conducted what he described as "the best financed of all my campaigns." There was, in his opinion, no reason for a guilty conscience, because Welker owed him "plenty" for past damages, and Church was part of a "ruthless" conspiracy. After the election, with $7,500 left over from the Welker contribution, he developed a business to make wigs—"Taylor Toppers" as he called them.[37]

Carl Burke and others in Church's camp suspected what Taylor later admitted: Republicans largely financed the former senator's campaign. At the time, however, Church had to move gingerly. The executive director of the National Democratic Committee confidentially described the situation as "very delicate." From the perspective of the committee, "chances of success in Idaho this year will in great measure depend on what happens to Taylor's 27,000 votes." Indeed, the director hinted darkly that Taylor's possible impact on the election was causing some political donors to be "a little hesitant to invest" in Church's campaign. The *New York Times* hardly brightened Church's prospects by observing that Taylor's candidacy "was almost certain to result in the re-election of Senator Welker."[38]

Church had no way of gauging the ultimate effectiveness of an advertising blitz that portrayed Taylor as a wronged man courageous enough to stand up against a corrupt system. Although the advertisements referred to "a 'McCarthyite' " in the race, they focused primarily on the evil deeds of Frank Church, "a 'front man' for a corrupt machine" and "a 'Trojan Horse' to capture another Senate seat for the corporations." Lamenting Taylor's "ability to twist anything we say," Church complained privately that Taylor "is making this just as rough as possible."[39]

Burke pleaded with him not to "be so blasted concerned about Taylor," and to keep his "campaign clean and humble, but hard-hitting. Don't get sucked-in to make some rash statement" about Taylor. "Hell!," Burke encouraged him, "You're running great."[40]

By October 30, Burke was convinced that Taylor posed "less [of] a threat than he did two weeks ago." Visits to Idaho by Tennessee's

Senator Estes Kefauver, the vice presidential candidate on the Democratic ticket, and by Senator John Kennedy of Massachusetts, had boosted Church's cause. The Idaho AFL-CIO leadership had endorsed Church, stirring Taylor to attack the state president of the union as a "phony labor leader." And whereas Church had gone begging for funds during the primary campaign, money now came from the national Democratic party and groups such as the National Committee for an Effective Congress. The amounts were not huge (by October 21, contributions for the general campaign reportedly totaled just under $33,000), but Burke was elated.[41]

According to Boise news columnist John Corlett, however, most people doubted that Church had a chance with Taylor in the race; the big winner would surely be Welker. Even before Taylor launched his write-in campaign, a *Washington Star* columnist described Church as "the underdog," and a *New York Times* news team saw nothing but "an uphill fight" ahead for him. By September 19, the prominent Idaho Democrat Herbert Howe of Lewiston believed Church was "a dead duck" needing a miracle to win. Howe, who had already emphasized that Church could not win without Taylor's votes, advised the Democratic National Committee that "the Taylor, Church situation is going from bad to worse" and that Welker might achieve "a complete rout."[42]

V

With the election only three weeks away, Senate majority leader Lyndon Johnson, carefully monitoring campaigns across the nation, also viewed Church's chances skeptically. One of Johnson's top advisers, George Reedy, urged him to keep his distance from Church's campaign: "We know absolutely nothing about Frank Church and have no indication that a flat, unsolicited endorsement of him would be wise." And some Republicans had already declared that Church's youth and inexperience made him, as the *New York Times* summarized their views, "a made-to-order opponent" for Welker.[43]

The forty-nine-year-old Welker, with his handsome mien and graying hair, personified Hollywood's image of a senator. Moreover, he was a bruising political infighter who kept an eye on the jugular. Again and again he had portrayed his opponents as disloyal radicals. He had won his Senate seat in 1950 by a large margin after promising to "throw out the Commies, pinks, and socialists." In office, he had allied so closely with Joe McCarthy that he had earned the nickname "Little Joe from Idaho." He led the fight against McCarthy's censure in 1954, describing him as "one of the greatest living champions of human liberty."[44]

Entering the 1956 general election as "Idaho's FIGHTING Senator," Welker was not about to change his political style or message. Predictably, he focused on Church's alleged communist connections. Speaking in Blackfoot, Idaho, for example, he charged that "the most radical pinks and punks in the country" were financing his opponent's campaign. He characterized them as "far-off people without faces who represent such different ideologies from the freedom loving West and who are so determined to invade our election in Idaho."[45]

Welker particularly targeted the National Committee for an Effective Congress (NCEC), a small New York-based liberal organization that had formed in 1948 and had subsequently become one of Joe McCarthy's most vigorous critics. In 1956 the NCEC had a special interest in the Idaho election because it involved Welker, "a hard-core specimen of the 'radical right.' " As early as February the NCEC had opposed Glen Taylor's candidacy on grounds that he had no chance of defeating the Republican incumbent. Shortly after Church won the primary, the NCEC's executive secretary, George Agree, met with him, and the organization eventually added $13,000 to his campaign chest. The nonpartisan nature of the NCEC in 1956 was evident in its endorsement of seven Democrats and six Republicans running in House and Senate races. Portraying Welker as "wildly erratic [and] ill-tempered," the committee described Church as "stable, cool, responsible."[46]

To Welker, of course, the NCEC endorsement proved that "Church is just as dangerous a left-winger as Glen Taylor—even more so." Determined once again to make the communist issue a centerpiece for his campaign, the senator also attacked the Supreme Court's 1954 school desegregation ruling as something that communists had not simply influenced: "They wrote it." Clearly, he was not interested in Church's plea that he stop "running against the communists" and focus on "honest issues." Frustrated, Church complained privately that Welker was "spreading more vile stories about me via the whisper route."[47]

With Welker and Taylor both against him, Church tried to play them against each other. He noted that, on the one hand, Welker accused him of being a tool of the communists, while on the other hand, Taylor portrayed him as a Trojan horse for the big corporations. Smiling, he then drove the point home: surely he could not be both of these things. Years later, he credited the opportunity to position himself in the middle as crucial to his campaign.[48]

Taking the offensive against Welker, Church banged away at the senator's record—a record, he charged, that embarrassed President Eisenhower and harmed Idaho. Questioning Welker's Republican credentials, Church emphasized that the senator voted against his own president more than half the time. Church also made good use of an editorial by newspaper editor and Idaho state legislator Perry Swisher, a Republican, stating that an album of Welker's achievements would be full of blank pages.[49]

When Church asked voters to elect a senator in whom Idaho could take pride, he could only hope that they were aware of the shady aspects of Welker's career, because he was determined not to engage in mudslinging. In 1954, for example, national columnist Drew Pearson had accused Welker of the political blackmail that drove Wyoming's Senator Lester Hunt to suicide. The New York *Daily News* a year later had placed Welker in the company of New York gangsters; and in 1956 even arch-conservative columnist Holmes Alexander wrote that Welker "made a sorry spectacle of himself," and was "unwell and unstable." Several times Welker had collapsed in places such as the Senate dining room, leading to speculation that he had a drinking problem. Although Church's staff had compiled a highly charged exposé of Welker's Senate career, Church refused to discuss publicly his opponent's personal conduct. He even ordered the destruction of some sixty thousand pamphlets, the work of a so-called "Non-Partisan Citizens Committee," titled "The Shameful Record of Herman Welker!" Indeed, he instructed an associate to set them afire and to guarantee that they all burned.[50]

VI

Church's campaign kept to the high ground, focusing on issues rather than personalities. And his position on issues was quite progressive, presaging the liberal resurgence of the 1960s. He advocated, for example, a food-stamp plan and an expanded school lunch program. "In this, the richest country in the world," he told one gathering, "it is wrong that one-fifth of our people should remain ill-fed, while surplus food rots in our warehouses." A strong supporter of civil liberties, he resented McCarthy-style hearings in which traditional courtroom protections were absent, and he detested censorship (except for banning obscene literature from the mails) on grounds that citizens were intelligent enough to make their own choices.[51]

Church strongly favored separation of church and state. He pledged to "work wholeheartedly" for passage of the Equal Rights Amendment, legislation he deemed "fine." He recommended expanding Social Security benefits to include disabled workers and the physically handicapped and to reflect increases in the cost of living. For agriculture he urged full parity and government programs designed to save the "family-sized farm." He found price-support programs acceptable on a temporary, emergency basis. But he dismissed the kind of scapegoating that blamed farm workers for agriculture's problems. "With good wages," he reasoned, "the working man is able to pay the high food prices that prevail at the markets."[52]

Regarding labor generally, he condemned "right-to-work" laws as nothing less than "right-to-wreck" organized labor, and he urged replacing the Taft-Hartley law, which in 1947 circumscribed union activities, with "a management-labor law more closely resembling the Wagner Act," the landmark legislation in 1935 that guaranteed labor the right to bargain collectively. In the words of one labor official, Church "was a red-hot liberal, a la CIO-PAC style." He also favored small businesses, which he wanted to protect from "the 'rule of the powerful,' " especially in the form of "giant mercantile establishments" that were monopolizing retail merchandising.[53]

On civil rights, he endorsed the Supreme Court's 1954 desegregation decision and declared he would oppose "any effort to coerce or intimidate . . . minority groups." After Welker had boasted of receiving an endorsement from Mississippi's notoriously racist senator James Eastland, Church stated bluntly: "If I am elected to the Senate, and ever boast of an endorsement by Senator Eastland, that day quit me, for that day I will have proved myself unworthy of your further confidence and support."[54]

His discussions of foreign policy were more firmly rooted in the immediate post-World War II setting. He described the world as a house divided—"half communist and half free"—and warned Americans to "*Keep Up Our Guard!* Always, *Keep Up Our Guard.*" At the same time, however, he hinted at a different perspective, one that suggested he would not be an uncritical proponent of American interventionism abroad. Identifying the end of colonialism as "one of the great events of our times," he urged the United States to be "the natural friend of colonial peoples who aspire to self-government."[55]

For Church, then, ideas and issues were vital to the election. The Hells Canyon Dam was one of the few issues that he ducked, and then only after the primaries. Initially, he (and the Democrats generally) had strongly supported the construction of an immense government dam in the deep Snake River gorge separating Idaho and Oregon. Opposition from the private power companies was fierce, however, and stirred fears among many farmers that the dam would cut off their water supply. Just prior to the general election the Senate, with Welker at the forefront, defeated legislation for a federal dam, and the U. S. Circuit Court of Appeals gave the Idaho Power Company permission to build three small dams. Still, the issue was much alive, but Church preferred to skirt it whenever possible. According to one of his campaign planning documents, the issue was a liability: support for a federal dam could help "in northern Idaho, but in the more populous southern half of the state it will certainly cost. . .votes." Church himself considered the matter primarily a vote-getter for Republicans, and Burke was happy by autumn to declare the matter "dead."[56]

To take his campaign to the public, Church relied on what had served him well in the primaries: a vigorous handshaking tour which took him around the state several times, and television spots. Once again, with Bethine at the wheel and a typewriter often in his lap, he was continually in motion, holding as many as six open meetings in one day. "He has toured 38 counties. . .in 38 days," cheered Burke on October 26. True, the candidate was getting "very little sleep," but Burke believed he was "toughening as he hits the end of the campaign trail."[57]

VII

As the campaign moved to a conclusion, the issue of outside funding and influences took on a dramatic new twist. Welker, bearing down on Church's connections with "communist-front organizations" like the National Committee for an Effective Congress, suddenly found himself on the defensive. Quite by accident, at the end of October his campaign treasurer revealed that Welker had received what at the time was an extremely high amount of contributions—over $88,000—mostly from out-of-state sources. Wealthy families such as the Pews in Philadelphia, the Fricks in Pittsburgh, and the Du Ponts in Wilmington were among the contributors, but most notable were a number of gas and oil companies. Information regarding campaign contributions was supposed to have gone to a special senatorial elections subcommittee, recently formed in reaction to growing public concern about election financing. No national public disclosure laws then existed, and financial reports to the Senate subcommittee were for its review and study, not for open distribution. But when Welker's finance chairman mistakenly mailed his report to the secretary of the Senate, it became a matter of public record.[58]

Church immediately pounced on the revelations, charging that Welker had "been caught with both hands in the cookie jar." Reminding voters that Welker opposed federal regulations of natural gas and favored turning offshore oil deposits to the coastal states, Church accused the senator of being indebted to "the big oil and gas interests of the Southwest." Welker replied indignantly that the disclosures were no accident and that Church should be equally candid with the Idaho public. The senator guessed that "young Church's strange political philosophy" would make more sense once voters learned more about his "faceless, unidentified contributors," especially "a notorious collection of left-wing eggheads" from America's "most radical fringe" and "eastern labor bosses." In the flurry of campaign financing charges that shook the last days of the campaign, Church apparently was the big winner. Looking back, Carl Burke believed that the "bombshell" disclosures of Welker's support from oil companies provided the election's "turning point."[59]

If the general election had a symbolic moment, however, it was perhaps when Church appeared in the Burley High School auditorium on October 27 to debate Welker. Because the senator made the arrangements, Church knew that Welker people would pack the hall. Moreover, because the debate would be broadcast by radio, listeners would hear the reactions of a pro-Welker crowd. Church, a superb debater, was eager to confront Welker; but as Bethine later described it, this was a set-up.[60]

A tight schedule forced the Churches to fly to Burley from Buhl, which lacked an airport. The small plane took off from a field illuminated only by automobile lights. The trip was so cold that, years later, memories of it made Bethine virtually shiver. At the Burley High School auditorium, the decidedly pro-Welker crowd awaited them. The Churches, Bethine still shaking from the trip, took their seats at the front of the room and looked out across the unfriendly audience. Finally, Church asked, "Where is Welker?" The answer was that Welker had already spoken. Confused, Church wondered why the senator had left. When he learned that Welker had been unable to attend and had sent a phonograph record instead, he stood and said impishly that he had debated many times in many places, but never with a phonograph record. As the audience laughed, he seized the moment to talk about "the fighting Senator" who battled with a recorded message. After delivering his own speech he fielded questions, many of the red-baiting variety. At the evening's end, he received considerable applause.[61]

Welker, in a sense, was absent on election day as well, although betting odds in Boise the night before the election favored him 7-5. Church overwhelmed him by a vote of 149,096 to 102,781. Of forty-four counties, Welker carried only three. Gooding County pointed up the dimensions of Church's victory. Heavily Republican, it had strongly supported Welker in the primaries, when Taylor trounced Church by a huge margin. The county GOP, well organized behind Welker, had confidently predicted that he would beat his young opponent by two to one. Yet in November, Church carried Gooding. In light of Church's huge plurality across the state, Taylor's 13,415 write-in ballots, although monuments to the loyalty he still commanded, proved inconsequential.[62]

In Idaho, where Eisenhower easily defeated Adlai Stevenson in the presidential race, the big election story belonged to Church, the political neophyte and underdog whom the *New York Times* described as "pink-cheeked" and looking "scarcely older than a boy out of college." One journalist wrote that Church had already "established himself as the outstanding political personality of the state."[63]

VIII

Several factors contributed to Church's victory. Welker, for example, proved more vulnerable than most observers expected. He was ill, and eleven months after the election died of a massive brain tumor. Moreover, his temperament and ideological rigidity had become serious liabilities. The red-baiting strategies that had once boosted his career were no longer effective. For one thing, Joe McCarthy, with whom he had so fiercely allied, was a diminished political force following the 1954 Army-McCarthy hearings and the Senate's censure vote. For another, Church's boyish appearance and solid Idaho background apparently made him seem an unlikely associate of "pinks and punks." Even among Republicans, Welker's growing rudeness and irascibility had stirred animosities. Significantly, Eisenhower campaigned personally for GOP candidates in Oregon and Washington but left Welker's defense to Vice-President Richard Nixon. By then, the senator's party base was eroding. As a Twin Falls Republican declared, "Hermie's record is O. K. by me. . . . But he hasn't done a damn thing for Idaho."[64]

Idaho's sluggish economy aided Church's cause as surely as it hurt Welker's. Shrewdly, the young Democrat had portrayed the state as a neglected urchin in the midst of plenty. Although the Gem State may not have been suffering terribly, its unspectacular growth contrasted sharply with that of the other western states. Some agriculturalists prospered, but others agreed with a Caldwell resident that "Ike has busted half the farmers in Idaho." Although the state's mining industry was doing rather well, the lumber business had slumped because of tight credit on home building. According to a team of *New York Times* reporters shortly before the election, Idaho was a mosaic "of remarkable prosperity and notable dissatisfaction with conditions." In this setting, Church had forged a viable candidacy.[65]

On another level, Dwight Eisenhower's popularity had not provided the anticipated obstacle to Church's success. Although the president carried forty-one states, including Idaho, his political coattails were short. Republicans across the country, but especially in the West, had their troubles. Idaho Democrats, for example, gained control of the state senate for the first time since 1948. And the incumbent Democrats Warren Magnuson in Washington and Wayne Morse of Oregon returned to the U. S. Senate along with their new Idaho colleague.[66]

Although Church benefitted from a dip in Republican fortunes in Idaho and elsewhere in 1956, and from Welker's own failings, he helped to forge his own success. Indeed, several years later, as John Kennedy prepared to run for the presidency, his staff used Church's 1956 campaign as a model of how to win elections by stressing ideas, by finding themes that squared with the public mood, and by utilizing the media. An agreeable personality also helped Church in 1956. When people said he was too young for the Senate, he laughingly replied, "Well, if that's the only objection you have to me, I'm going to grow out of it." He presented not only a fresh face, as columnist Doris Fleeson described him, but also a forward-looking political agenda that astutely connected his candidacy with state pride. "Our state is like a young giant, still unaware of its potential strength," he told audiences. "Our future is as bright with promise as we choose to make it."[67]

His tireless handshaking campaigns and open forums, combined with his recognition of television's potential, had boosted him from obscurity. Although he would have faced even greater odds in a more populous state, his accomplishment was nevertheless substantial and it highlighted some notable trends in modern American political life. For decades the intense partisan identification of the nineteenth century had been giving way to a politics of individual personality and interest-group concerns. Developments in the mass media, especially with radio and then television, had further focused public attention on individuals, rather than on institutions like political parties. Significantly, Church in 1956 used television to splendid advantage and relied far more upon his enthusiastic and growing volunteer organization, Citizens for Church, than upon the Democratic hierarchy. Even after he won the primary, Citizens for Church remained at the heart of his campaign. As a *New York Times* reporter observed, "he operated out of his own headquarters in Boise, hardly bothering to check in with the Democratic State Headquarters."[68]

Years later, Burke recalled wistfully the enthusiasm and idealism of the Citizens for Church movement. A group of genuine volunteers, it paid no salaries. Indeed, its members paid their own expenses. Over the next several decades, political campaigning in Idaho would reflect the shift across the nation to heavily financed, professional operations in which even volunteers expected some kind of salary. Looking back, Burke described the 1956 Church effort as "a campaign of innocence manned by amateurs." He guessed, with considerable regret, that it might well have been "one of the last campaigns of that kind the state will ever see."[69]

But while Burke praised the volunteers, he emphasized that "the secret of our success" was the candidate himself. Church had staged a remarkable campaign, turning a political gamble into a startling victory. Barely thirty-two and the holder of no previous political office, he had become a U. S. senator—one of the youngest in American history.[70]

Newly elected Senator Church appears on "Meet the Press" in mid-1957 to discuss the Civil Rights bill. *Reni Photo, Courtesy Boise State University.*

Chapter Four

An Auspicious Debut: 1957

"SENATOR MAKING BIG SPLASH," Carl Burke observed happily toward the end of Frank Church's first year in office. Burke did not exaggerate. Few senators have launched their careers as auspiciously as did Church. The considerable attention that he received grew partly out of his youthfulness, his prominence as "the baby of the Senate." But it also had much to do with his abilities, his ambition, his sense of the politically possible, and his pivotal role in one of 1957's most important political developments: passage of the first civil rights legislation since Reconstruction.[1]

During his initial months in office, Church set the pattern for his political career. He gravitated toward big issues and legislative action; he demonstrated his effectiveness as an orator; and he tried to balance his idealistic impulses with political realities. Although his penchant for practical, mainstream politics sometimes tested his liberal instincts, he believed deeply that moderation, accommodation, and respect for political processes constituted America's "real soul." In 1957, his ability to give and take made him a prominent figure in the passage of the Civil Rights Act and won approval from the Senate's powerful majority leader, Lyndon Johnson. But while Church's tendency to compromise emerged as one of his most notable political characteristics, it also provided the basis for criticism that followed him throughout his senatorial life.[2]

I

Church's initial task as a senator was to assemble a staff that understood Idaho and Capitol Hill. His choices were excellent. Partly to compensate for his lack of familiarity with the bureaucratic and political intricacies of Congress, he turned to John A. Carver, Jr. and Verda Barnes. Both had solid Idaho credentials and considerable knowledge of Washington, D. C. Together they set the tone for an otherwise inexperienced staff, which included people who had worked on Church's 1956 campaign but were strangers to national politics.

Carver, the son of a prominent district judge in Pocatello, was only six years older than Church but had worked in the nation's capital in the late 1930s and early 1940s. He had served briefly as a messenger for Montana senator Burton K. Wheeler's Special Committee to Investigate Railroads Financing, and had been close to Idaho senator James Pope. Before entering the Air Force in mid-1943, he had quickly climbed the civil service ranks from Grade 4 to 13 as a personnel specialist. After the war he completed a law degree at Georgetown University and then returned to Idaho, where he served briefly as assistant attorney general before entering private practice in Boise. As an attorney, Carver demonstrated a strong concern for civil liberties and a willingness to defend unpopular causes. A formidable individual—toughminded, exacting, sometimes crusty—he won the respect of Church's other staff members, who admired his intelligence, his fairness, and his abilities. Church named him as staff director and relied heavily on his political knowledge and his administrative talents.[3]

Verda Barnes knew even more than Carver did about Capitol Hill. "A real old pro," as Carver described her, she had moved from Idaho to Washington during the 1930s, been a friend of Eleanor Roosevelt and an ardent New Dealer, worked for organized labor and the Department of the Interior, and served on the staffs of three members of Congress, including Glen Taylor. Harry Wall, an Idaho member of the Democratic National Committee, recommended her to Church. Committee head Paul Butler assured Church that Barnes no longer had any allegiance to Taylor and had, in fact, steered the national committee away from any entanglements in Taylor's 1956 campaign. Barnes ran the day-to-day operations of Church's office, displaying an impressive grasp of detail and Idaho politics. Her rules were firm and clear. Church's staffers were to have "a passion for anonymity," and to avoid saying anything they did not want to read on the front page of the next day's newspaper.[4]

II

Partly because he was so young, Church's Senate debut piqued the interest of the press. "Frank Church Another Borah? Critical Capital Tips Its Hat," read one newspaper headline. *Life* magazine assigned a photographer to follow him around during his first days in Washington, D. C. The city's newspapers showed an interest in him, and twice during his first week in town featured him on the front page. "Everyone wants to do a feature article on Frank," Bethine reported proudly.[5]

Stories abounded about his being the "baby" senator, six years younger than any of his colleagues, whose average age was fifty-eight. When he first walked into his new residence in Bethesda, Maryland, the builder's wife asked him to leave. "Young man, I do not know why you are here," she said, "but I am very busy at the moment getting this house ready for a United States senator who is going to move in tomorrow." At the local country club, a lifeguard requested that he leave the pool because it was the adults' swimming time. Journalists in the press gallery made up a little ditty when he first appeared on the Senate floor: "His name is Church, but if age were the rule, we'd call him Senator Sunday School." Some of his colleagues even mistook him for a page boy. Once, as he waited for an elevator in the Capitol, a woman commented, "I understand that one of you page boys gets mistaken for Senator Frank Church." "Yes, ma'am," laughed Church, "one of us often does." To help distinguish himself from the page boys, he stopped wearing blue suits.[6]

His reputation as an orator quickly attracted speaking invitations. At the Board of Trade's "Welcome to Washington" night for the new Congress, he spoke on behalf of the Democratic Party. Bethine, who had arrived in the city only three days earlier, sat next to House Minority Leader Joseph Martin, who had been in Congress for thirty-three years. She had never before been in the company of such a collection of "fatcats," as she described them. As the other speakers droned on interminably and the audience grew increasingly restless, she worried that her husband faced an impossible challenge once he moved to the microphone. To her relief, his remarks "got a real ovation." Subsequently, after he spoke to the Women's National Press Club, Lyndon Johnson heaped praise upon him: "I know of no member who has entered the Senate since I have been here who has greater promise."[7]

Given all this attention, Church was understandably "divinely happy," in Bethine's words. A series of January receptions and dinners at the homes of senators Hubert Humphrey, Estes Kefauver, and others immersed the Churches in Washington's social circuit. Here indeed was a new and exciting world.[8]

III

It was a serious world as well, with powerful forces converging behind the most important civil rights initiative in almost a century. Socially, groups such as the Congress of Racial Equality and the National Association for the Advancement of Colored People (NAACP) had helped to galvanize a postwar civil rights movement. Legally, the movement had benefitted from a series of favorable Supreme Court decisions. Internationally, the Cold War setting played an ambiguous role, providing civil rights opponents with an opportunity to equate social change with communism, while at the same time spurring federal policies to demonstrate America's commitment to democracy and justice. Economically, the expanding prosperity of the Forties and Fifties aided civil rights by suggesting that individual gains need not come at someone else's expense.[9]

By the mid-Fifties, the building storm over civil rights was too great for America's political parties to ignore. The heavy migration of African Americans to northern cities over several decades had substantially enlarged the number of potential black voters. "In truth," warned Oregon's liberal senator Richard L. Neuberger in 1957, "the Democratic party now confronts the greatest crisis in modern times." Neuberger believed that the Democrats, who had already lost their majority position outside the South, were in deep trouble. If they failed to act on civil rights, or if they tore themselves apart doing so, he predicted that the Republicans would become the dominant party.[10]

Republicans were also attentive to the politics of civil rights, particularly as it bore upon the issue of public order. Violence against blacks was turning the South into a battleground. Partly to avoid involving the federal government directly in civil rights disputes, the administration turned to black enfranchisement. By facilitating ways in which blacks could help themselves through the power of the ballot, the administration hoped both to show the GOP's commitment to civil rights and to reduce the demand for federal intervention.

In April 1956, at the time Frank Church was still fighting his uphill battle in the Idaho primaries, the Eisenhower administration thus presented a moderate civil rights package to Congress. Title I called for a bipartisan civil rights commission; Title II created a civil rights division within the Justice Department; Title III empowered the Attorney General to seek federal court injunctions against violations of civil rights generally; and Title IV focused on federal protection of voting rights. Although the House passed the bill, the Senate adjourned without acting on it.

The 1956 election underlined the importance of the civil rights issue. Some Republicans believed that only by pursuing civil rights more aggressively could they halt Democratic control of Congress. Democrats, meanwhile, noted that Eisenhower's big reelection victory included a higher percentage of black votes than the president had received four years earlier. In ten northern and twelve southern cities, Eisenhower had won a majority of black votes, suggesting that an important shift in party allegiance might be underway. For northern Democrats like Oregon's Neuberger and Illinois senator Paul Douglas, politics as well as conscience dictated an all-out push for civil rights.[11]

Senate majority leader Lyndon Johnson watched these developments closely. Although he had not previously supported civil rights legislation, he recognized that events, the future of his party, and his own ambitions demanded change. A civil rights breakthrough would show Congress's ability to deal with major issues, would help defuse the increasingly explosive situation in the South, and would establish Johnson as a national politician with presidential qualities. As his aide George Reedy advised, "Civil rights legislation is inevitable—the only real issue is whether it will be done reasonably now or unreasonably later." For Johnson, the challenge was not only to get the Senate to act "reasonably," but also to prevent a political war within the Democratic Party. He needed desperately to find people on the Hill who occupied a middle position between northern liberals and southern conservatives. In this respect, senators from the Rocky Mountain states, with virtually no black constituencies, seemed to have more freedom of action. Thus, when Johnson telephoned Frank Church right after the 1956 election, the majority leader sought an ally.[12]

Church, ebullient over his victory the previous day, was enjoying breakfast at his Boise home when Johnson called. He believed that Johnson, who had generally ignored him during the campaign, was trying to make up "for lost time." After congratulating Church and indicating that the future of the Democratic Party rested with its young people, LBJ discussed the historical and political affinities between the West and the South. According to Johnson, a political alliance between Southerners and Westerners had been good for the party as well as the Senate.[13]

During his first day in office, Church got a more direct dose of the famed Johnson treatment. He had just taken the oath of office and was so happy that, according to journalist Mary McGrory, he seemed almost to glow. Smiling up at Bethine and other members of his family in the gallery, he headed toward his back-row seat. Suddenly he felt Lyndon Johnson's long arm around him and found himself in his "first nostril-to-nostril confrontation" with the huge Texan. As Johnson's bulky frame pressed against him, Church struggled to position himself. The majority leader, leaning close, was full of flattery: "Now, Frank, you are the youngest member of this Senate, and you have a great future." LBJ had some advice. "There's lots going for you. But the first thing you ought to learn is that you get along in the Congress by going along." Johnson had a specific example in mind. He was trying to block a motion from New Mexico's Clinton Anderson to enable the Senate to consider a new set of rules.[14]

To casual observers of the Senate, Anderson's move perhaps seemed innocuous enough, but it turned Church's first vote into what Church described as "a baptism of fire." The motion bore directly on possible civil rights legislation. In 1917 the Senate had adopted Rule 22, the filibuster rule, by which two-thirds of those voting could limit debate on a particular issue. Since then, the rule had allowed civil rights foes to block legislation by talking endlessly. Liberals had tried unsuccessfully to revise Rule 22 by making it possible for fewer than two-thirds of the Senate to limit debate; Clinton Anderson's motion represented another attempt. Lyndon Johnson favored some kind of civil rights legislation, but not at a price of alienating his southern colleagues and many Texas voters. In order to table Anderson's motion, he marshalled his forces, among whom he hoped to include Idaho's newly elected senator.[15]

Church, within minutes after taking his oath of office, thus found himself in a "nose-to-nose" encounter with the majority leader. Johnson, eyes narrowed, bore in relentlessly upon him, imploring his young colleague to help set aside Anderson's motion. The matter might not count for much back in Idaho, LBJ conceded, but it was important to the Senate leadership. "It means a lot to us," he emphasized. "It means a lot to me." Johnson clinched the point with flattery and an implied warning: "I like you, and I see big things in your future, and I want to see you get off on the right foot in the Senate."[16]

Johnson mobilized several other southern senators to reiterate the message. Louisiana's Russell Long took Church to his private office and discussed how a bright, young man like the Idaho senator could—with southern support—become vice president. Another senator reminded Church that Idaho's great William E. Borah had vigorously defended the filibuster rule. Years later, in 1979, Church could not recall "ever being pressured within the Senate on any issue as much as I was pressured on Rule 22." He resented the heavy-handed tactics. In his first Senate battle over etiquette and tradition, he instinctively favored change, convinced that Rule 22 had to give way to advance civil rights.[17]

Church's commitment to civil rights was probably more intellectual than visceral. He had grown up in virtually an all-white world; Boise, and Idaho generally, had almost no black population. His attitudes on race flowed less from personal experiences than from basic concerns about equity. He believed genuinely that "the natural goal of Democracy" was to give all citizens, "regardless of social position, of race, of religion, or family wealth, equal treatment under law, and equal opportunity to develop." In his opinion, American history had marked the "inexorable" advance of democratic over aristocratic, exclusionary values. By abolishing slavery and endorsing woman's suffrage and the rights of workers, the nation had rejected discriminatory, restrictive practices in favor of "the basic principles of a free society." The moral was simple: "Restrictions based on race, color, or religion, are morally indefensible."[18]

Not surprisingly, Church initially allied himself with the well-known northern liberal Paul Douglas. A physically imposing man with a shock of white hair and a large, hooked nose, the Illinois Democrat was one of the true civil rights stalwarts on Capitol Hill. In 1957 he organized caucuses of northern and western senators to plan civil rights strategies. Among those who comprised what Douglas liked to call "our group" was Frank Church.[19]

"Inexperienced" and "unseasoned," as he later described himself, Church was not yet thinking in terms of institutional traditions, collegial understandings, or old-boy kinds of arrangements. Over time, he would conclude that exchanges on the Senate floor should be unlimited, "that the rights for extended debate were an institution in the Senate and gave it its unique quality." But in early 1957 that was not his opinion. The issue, as he saw it then, was how to obtain civil rights legislation.[20]

On the evening of January 4, Church thus cast his first Senate vote in defiance of his party's leadership—"a thing I found very difficult to do," he said immediately afterward. Anderson's motion failed, however, when the Senate voted 55 to 38 to table it.[21]

Lyndon Johnson, furious that Church had broken ranks, threw his pen down in anger when he heard him vote against tabling Anderson's motion. For around six months, Church remained in Johnson's "dog house," as his legislative assistant Ward Hower described it. According to Bethine Church, the majority leader treated her husband like "a pariah," refusing even to speak to him.[22]

Church had angered Johnson but delighted civil rights groups. According to the NAACP, senators who voted against tabling the Anderson motion were "the friends of civil rights." The vote on Anderson's motion was actually even more important than the NAACP suspected. Despite predictions that the motion faced a humiliating defeat, support for revising Rule 22 increased dramatically. In 1953, only twenty-one (fifteen Democrats, five Republicans, and one Independent) voted for change; in 1957, the count jumped to thirty-eight (twenty-one Democrats and seventeen Republicans), with three non-voting senators indicating that they also opposed tabling Anderson's motion. The vote jolted the Southerners, who suddenly felt far more vulnerable than before. The most important showdown on civil rights in decades was taking shape.[23]

In June, again with Church's help, the Senate edged closer to enacting civil rights legislation by deciding to circumvent the Judiciary Committee. Time and again, civil rights bills had disappeared in the committee, the domain of Mississippi's James Eastland. "I had special pockets put in my pants," Eastland joked, "and for years I carried those bills around in my pockets everywhere I went and every one of them was defeated." On June 14 Church joined sixteen other Democratic liberals in stating that they intended to evade the Judiciary Committee by bringing the civil rights bill directly to the Senate for debate. Six days later, after the House of Representatives overwhelmingly passed a revised version of the administration's civil rights package, they had their chance. Following some shrewd parliamentary maneuvers, the Senate voted 45-39 to bypass the Judiciary Committee and place H. R. 6127 on the calendar.[24]

By then, however, Lyndon Johnson was trying to split Douglas's group, hoping thereby to regain the civil rights initiative. He brought to the Senate floor a bill to permit government construction of a large dam in Hells Canyon on the Oregon-Idaho border. Douglas correctly viewed this "controlled pause" in the civil rights maneuvering as part of Johnson's strategy to win over western liberals like Oregon's Wayne Morse and Church.[25]

IV

Church's June 19 Senate address on the proposed Hells Canyon dam was thus loaded with political implications. For weeks Church had worked hard on what was to be his maiden speech. The timing and the circumstances in which he delivered it led to conjecture that he was involved in a deal with Lyndon Johnson regarding Hells Canyon and civil rights.

Church opened his remarks by admitting that a government dam in Hells Canyon lacked the support of many of his own constituents. At stake, he insisted, was more than one dam in the massive Snake River gorge. A larger issue concerned whether special interests could thwart public development of the nation's natural resources. In that regard, Church maintained that Hells Canyon dam was "the test case." If its opponents prevailed, they would enhance their chances of blocking other government dams in the United States. Church disputed the claim that the Federal Power Commission had already settled the issue by ruling against a federal dam and in favor of the Idaho Power Company's three smaller structures. The commission, he pointed out, had in fact not chosen between those alternatives because the Eisenhower administration had removed the Hells Canyon dam from consideration. Faced simply with approving or rejecting the Idaho Power Company's application, the commission had granted the licenses.[26]

Turning to more philosophical issues, Church denied that privately owned dams necessarily saved taxpayers' money. In fact, he countered, the Idaho Power Company enjoyed huge public subsidies, through such favors as tax writeoffs. He scoffed at the idea that the company deserved special tax privileges because its electricity helped the nation's defense. Farmers and draftees who also kept the nation secure would have an equal claim to tax breaks.[27]

Zeroing in on the Idaho Power Company, he challenged the claim that free enterprise served the public better and more cheaply than could the federal government. There was a simple, selfish reason why the company favored three small dams rather than one large one. The company was not interested in providing the kinds of multipurpose services that would come from a huge public dam. "There is no market for flood control," Church pointed out, any more than there was for water storage or improved navigation. "The Idaho Power Company is engaged in just one business—the sale of electricity for profit." And precisely because the company considered "its own interests first," the Senate needed to "look to the public interest first."[28]

Church accused the company of perpetrating "a monumental fraud." It had used scare tactics to frighten farmers into believing that a large Hells Canyon dam would take their water. The imagery that the company used in its propaganda was admittedly "poignant. It depicts the farmer, a solitary figure with a shovel, competing with a concrete colossus for his river water." Such imagery, Church answered, was "a ruse." For one thing, Idaho's irrigated areas lay upstream from the proposed Hells Canyon dam. More importantly, farmers benefitted from federal development. In Idaho, for example, thousands of them drew water daily from government reservoirs. The federal government had brought economic growth in the West, including Idaho. Bipartisan support for federal development of America's water system had given life to regional and local economies, not destroyed them. Church pointed to the prosperity that had flowed to Oregon, Washington, and Montana from dams like Bonneville, Grand Coulee, and Hungry Horse. But Idaho, despite the earlier efforts of public power advocate William E. Borah, had limited itself to "small plans for small tomorrows." As a result, the state languished. The Hells Canyon bill "serves no interest, save the people's interest," Church concluded. "It is a good bill. It should pass."[29]

John Carver viewed Church's three-hour presentation as "a hell of a good speech," and the enthusiastic Senate response confirmed his judgment. Paul Douglas described the "truly magnificent" presentation as "the very best analysis" of public power that he had ever heard. Wayne Morse, principal sponsor of the Hells Canyon bill and a difficult person to please, called the speech "the keenest analysis of the Hells Canyon Dam issue which has ever been made on the floor of the Senate." Lyndon Johnson, warming up to Church again, could not recall "any greater contribution that has been made to the debate in the field of conservation since I have been here." Similar praise came from Clinton Anderson, Richard Neuberger, Hubert Humphrey, Texas Democrat Ralph Yarborough, Missouri Democrat Stuart Symington, and others. Even Arizona's conservative Republican Barry Goldwater, who disagreed with nearly everything Church had said, commended him.[30]

Journalists were equally impressed. A. Robert Smith dubbed Church "the boy orator of the Snake," and Barnet Nover of the *Denver Post* concluded that the speech had "catapulted" him "into the very front rank of Senate orators." Radio commentator Edward Morgan of ABC speculated that Church had provided public power advocates with some much-needed Hollywood-style "box-office" appeal for their cause. "If he's not careful," predicted Morgan, "the tall, boyishly handsome national oratorical champion from Boise may develop into something of a legislative matinee idol."[31]

Elated with the way his speech had gone, Church left the Senate floor convinced that he had made a difference in the Hells Canyon fight. As he headed back to his office, Clinton Anderson caught up with him. Church respected Anderson a great deal, especially for his political independence and his refusal to be pushed around. The New Mexico senator complimented him again for his speech, and then asked if he had consulted Lyndon Johnson on the issue. Anderson was undoubtedly surprised at Church's negative reply. The young senator was not being very astute politically. "If this bill gets passed," Anderson told him, "it will be his doing, not yours." Church quickly got the drift of the conversation. "I understood that it was true," he said later of Anderson's assessment of Johnson's role. "But until he said it to me, it hadn't gelled." Church wasted little time. He talked with the majority leader shortly thereafter. And on June 21, when the Senate in a surprising turn of events voted 45 to 38 for the Hells Canyon dam, he praised Johnson (and thanked Anderson for "the word of personal counsel"). "As I told you yesterday," he wrote Johnson in a follow-up communication the day after the vote, "I was so utterly stunned with the success of our efforts for Hells Canyon that I was unable, for a time, to focus upon the great teamwork you organized to make it possible. All credit is due to your leadership. . . ." Although the Hells Canyon bill subsequently failed in the House, its sudden success in the Senate was a striking development.[32]

Church's growing rapprochement with Johnson, the Senate's unexpected passage of the Hells Canyon bill, and new twists in the civil rights battle encouraged speculation that Idaho's new senator had joined western liberals in a deal with LBJ. "Frank," Paul Douglas warned him, "I am afraid that you Hells Canyon folk have been given some counterfeit money." Douglas suspected that the dramatic mid-summer emergence of a coalition between southern and western Democrats on civil rights and Hells Canyon was no accident.[33]

Supposedly, Church and other Westerners had agreed to a trade: Hells Canyon dam for a weakened civil rights bill. Circumstantial evidence for such a bargain was easy to find. Mississippi's Eastland had approached Westerners like James Murray of Montana to see if they would accept the deal. A year earlier, in 1956, the Senate had defeated the Hells Canyon bill 51 to 41. In 1957, with Lyndon Johnson cracking the party whip, forty Democrats had backed it; significantly, five were leading Southerners who in 1956 had voted negatively. Johnson's role in swinging his party behind the bill surprised John Carver, who doubted that LBJ, "down in his guts," felt strongly about Hells Canyon. Utah Republican Arthur Watkins, a fierce opponent of the public dam, claimed that civil rights "had a lot to do with the vote. . . more than most people realize." Johnson had reportedly convinced key Southerners that it might be impossible to block civil rights legislation in 1957, and that they should avoid stirring up northern support for an even stronger law. They had reputedly switched on Hells Canyon dam in exchange for Johnson's building a coalition with western Democrats to water down any civil rights measure.[34]

Interpretations that Church and other Westerners bargained away civil rights legislation overlooked notable considerations, however, among them the genuine desire of senators like Church, Anderson, and Morse to obtain the best civil rights measure politically possible. While Southerners such as Georgia's Richard Russell tried to thwart the civil rights cause, Church and other western liberals worked to guarantee at least minimal progress. Early on, Church concluded that flawed civil rights legislation was better than none at all.

V

The conflict over the 1957 civil rights bill demonstrated Church's bent for the middle ground, for building coalitions, and for what seemed politically tenable. Compromise, to him, was the very stuff of legislation. He revered the Senate precisely because it allowed for debate, rules of proper conduct, moderation. To cynical observers, elaborate rituals of senatorial address were contrived, phony, and hypocritical. But to Church, the inflated etiquette by which senators referred to each other as "honorable" and "esteemed" served a purpose: by the time angry legislators finished complimenting each other, he joked, they had cooled off and no longer wanted to exchange blows.[35]

For Church, the challenge of the 1957 civil rights battle was to advance a moral cause within a political framework. He drew parallels between the era of the Civil War and the contemporary "time of trial for our country." Moral abominations marked both historical periods. Church wanted to avoid the tragedy of the antebellum era, during which demagoguery had replaced reason, and violence had supplanted the rule of law. The abolitionists, in his opinion, had inflamed the issue of slavery, an institution already doomed. And they had successfully crowded out moderates who might have prevented the Civil War. Church's unfavorable view of the abolitionists drew upon scholarly interpretations that prevailed during the 1940s, when he had studied U. S. history under Thomas Bailey at Stanford, and during the 1950s. There was considerable resonance between the senator's predisposition for "rational debate" and the era's larger intellectual climate. Just as Church praised "the calm, dispassionate manner" of the Senate, so scholars celebrated "the genius of American politics" and America's "vital center." Not surprisingly, then, as the civil rights debate moved toward deadlock in the summer of 1957, Church searched for a workable compromise and warned against opportunists who were "more interested in making an issue than in making progress."[36]

Once again Church joined forces with Clinton Anderson. Both men believed the civil rights bill had no chance of passage as long as it contained Part III, authorizing federal injunctions against civil rights violations in general. Civil rights opponents considered it far too sweeping, particularly as it might apply to schools and public facilities. On July 24, Church voted for an amendment, co-sponsored by Anderson and Vermont Republican George Aiken, to excise Part III. The motion carried 52 to 38, much to the dismay of the NAACP and other civil rights organizations. A few months earlier civil rights advocates had given Church high marks. Now he was among those senators whose action against Part III, according to Roy Wilkins of the NAACP, would "be impossible to forget and difficult to forgive."[37]

Church defended his vote on grounds that he had helped clear the way for legislation that would protect the most fundamental of rights, voting. In this regard, he stood in good company. The Reverend Martin Luther King, Jr., emerging as one of the nation's top civil rights leaders, had declared: "Give us the vote and we will do the rest." Moreover, Church hoped that his Idaho constituents would understand his defense of the suffrage. "No one can well represent Idaho," he told them, "where 82.5 percent of our people voted in 1952—the highest percentage in the country—who does not believe in giving effective protection for voting to all citizens. . . ."[38]

Over the next few days, however, Church again disappointed Wilkins and other civil rights advocates by backing a jury trial amendment to the bill. The basic idea behind the amendment was that even violators of civil rights laws had the right to trial by jury, but critics viewed the amendment as a blatant effort to gut the bill.

Few issues proved more complicated, or controversial, than whether jury trials should be required in contempt-of-court cases against individuals who defied civil rights statutes. Clarence Mitchell of the NAACP attacked the jury trial idea as nothing more than "a monkey-wrench" to jam the enforcement machinery of civil rights. History showed that all-white southern juries would not convict whites who killed black citizens, let alone who prevented them from voting. From this perspective, a jury trial requirement would render civil rights legislation meaningless. Liberal commentator Edward P. Morgan of ABC called the amendment "a gambit which under the almost universal southern system of all-white juries would defeat the civil rights safeguards in the very process of their application." Moreover, there was no constitutional right to jury trials in contempt cases. "It is a long-standing rule of law," Arnold Aronson of the Leadership Conference on Civil Rights (LCCR) pointed out, that people who refused to follow court orders opened themselves to convictions without jury trials. Examples ranged from individuals who failed to pay alimony to those who violated labor relations decrees and anti-trust orders. Opposition to adding a jury trial requirement to the civil rights bill was fierce and came from disparate sources, including socialist Norman Thomas and the Eisenhower administration.[39]

But, as Frank Church discovered, the right to a jury trial could not be easily dismissed. When he asked the Library of Congress's Legislative Reference Service for law review essays on the subject, he received an ambiguous reply: although northern and national press coverage of the subject generally "opposed the extension of trial by jury to contempt cases," lawyers and law journals had not yet really explored the matter. In fact, a number of people sympathetic to civil rights favored adding a jury trial requirement to the civil rights bill. Among these were former Secretary of State Dean Acheson, former New Deal brain truster Benjamin V. Cohen, and labor leaders such as John L. Lewis.[40]

In late July, the jury trial amendment became the most important piece in what Roy Wilkins labeled the Senate's "giant chess game" over civil rights. On one side were Southerners who insisted upon the amendment as a quid pro quo for not filibustering. On the other were northern liberals like Paul Douglas who believed the amendment would sabotage civil rights. Meanwhile, Lyndon Johnson applied his considerable talents to finding a middle position—one that would avoid fracturing the Democratic party, produce some kind of civil rights legislation, and boost his national reputation. He found a willing colleague in Frank Church.[41]

Initially, however, Wyoming's venerable Joseph O'Mahoney proposed the jury trial amendment. Small, elderly, and with large, bushy eyebrows, O'Mahoney was an old-style progressive in the tradition of Nebraska's George Norris. Church liked him enormously. O'Mahoney worried about sacrificing "the civil right of trial by jury while pretending to be fighting for the preservation of the voting right." But the first version of his amendment, providing for a jury trial whenever a "fact" was at issue, elicited little enthusiasm. Defense attorneys would invariably claim that facts were in dispute, so all contempt cases would end up before juries. At this point O'Mahoney, who controlled his own amendment, began to accept suggested revisions. As a result, opponents of the amendment were at a disadvantage of having to shoot, in Paul Douglas's words, "at a moving target."[42]

A revised version of O'Mahoney's amendment drew a distinction that Frank Church found persuasive. In an April 29 article in *The New Leader,* University of Wisconsin law professor Carl A. Auerbach had differentiated between two kinds of contempt: criminal and civil. Criminal contempt involved punishment for breaking the law, and thus required a jury trial. On the other hand, judges alone could handle civil contempt because it focused on compliance. In cases of civil contempt, wrote Auerbach, "the defendant 'carries the keys of his prison in his own pocket.' He can open the prison door and walk out any time he pleases by obeying the court's order." When applied to civil rights the Auerbach distinction meant, for example, that a voting registrar who refused to register blacks would be guilty of civil contempt up to the time of the election. He or she could remove the contempt simply by complying with the court order. But after the election was over, mere compliance would be too late. At that point, criminal contempt would be the charge and a jury trial would be necessary to determine guilt and levy punishment. Auerbach privately conceded that he hoped to provide northern liberals with a way to resolve their difficulties over the jury trial issue.[43]

Auerbach's argument definitely appealed to Church, who recognized that the jury trial debate exerted formidable emotional claims. As he explained later, "the tradition of allowing men so accused to be judged by their peers was a very strong one and deeply imbedded in the traditions of the West. I believe in it."[44] Others also found Auerbach's distinction useful. Lyndon Johnson's advisers worked it into O'Mahoney's revised amendment. This version picked up another sponsor, Tennessee Democrat Estes Kefauver, but failed to break the Senate impasse regarding jury trials.[45]

At this point Church made his move, contacting O'Mahoney about co-sponsoring yet another version of the amendment. This version extended the jury trial provision beyond voting rights cases. According to the O'Mahoney-Kefauver-Church proposal, jury trials would be mandatory in all federal criminal contempt cases, including those affecting labor. Here clearly was an effort to sway labor leaders in the AFL-CIO, who vigorously backed civil rights and suspected that the jury trial amendment was a diversionary measure.[46]

Labor leaders were particularly sensitive about events early in the century: courts had typically issued injunctions against strikers, who had then fallen victim to indiscriminate contempt citations. Over the years organized labor had improved upon this situation but still felt vulnerable. In 1957 the dominant labor group, the AFL-CIO, nevertheless informed Church that it would not consent to "crippling" the civil rights bill in exchange for "any possible advantages to organized labor." Fiery James Carey of the International Union of Electrical, Radio, and Machine Workers was more blunt. He described the O'Mahoney-Kefauver-Church amendment as "probably the most dangerous" effort to obscure a fundamental point: jury trials would actually prevent effective enforcement of voting rights. "Labor," pledged Carey, "will not barter away effective protection of the right of a Negro to register and vote in return for the very dubious advantages that Senators O'Mahoney, Kefauver and Church now appear to offer labor." Not all labor leaders felt this way. United Mine Workers president John L. Lewis, one of the most battle-scarred veterans of labor's wars, endorsed the amendment as "wise, prudent and proper." The Railroad brotherhoods agreed with Lewis.[47]

Despite the maneuvering over the jury trial amendment, the Senate remained deadlocked. Minnesota's liberal Democrat, Hubert Humphrey, contended on television's "Face the Nation" that the jury-trial backers "haven't got the votes." Disgruntled LBJ aide George Reedy complained that liberals of the Humphrey-Douglas persuasion were "in a completely unreasoning mood" and could "pull the walls right down over our ears." Something had to happen to rescue them "from their own suicidal complex." Reedy speculated to Johnson that perhaps someone could alter O'Mahoney's amendment by ensuring that southern juries would not be all-white. "A jury anti-discrimination amendment sponsored by liberal Democrats" just might work wonders for the civil rights bill and the party.[48]

Frank Church was already at work on such an amendment. The door was opening for him to become a major player in the civil rights battle, a role he had initially not sought. Indeed, earlier he had told Bethine that he intended to vote for civil rights but not to get embroiled in the legislative disputes. Events, however, had complicated the situation. The civil rights cause was stalled in the Senate and, in Church's opinion, the jury trial amendment seemed to hold the key to its future. Church understood the sensitivity of the jury trial issue. He himself increasingly questioned the wisdom of trying to gain a right (voting) by taking away a right (trial by jury). At the same time, he recognized the difficulties of obtaining racial justice in the South with all-white juries. By helping to resolve this dilemma he hoped not only to ensure the passage of civil rights legislation, but also to make it better.[49]

The challenge was *how* to alter the practice of seating all-white juries in the South, a practice that rendered the original O'Mahoney jury trial amendment unacceptable to civil rights organizations as well as to senators like Douglas and Humphrey. Although Church prided himself on his knowledge of the law and took constitutional arguments seriously, John Carver sensed that he cared less about the legalistic side of the civil rights argument than about finding a way to end the legislative standoff. Church saw the amendment as symbolic, the means by which to pass the bill.[50] He planned to introduce an addendum to the O'Mahoney amendment that would repeal sections of the U. S.

Code barring people who could not meet state qualifications from federal jury duty. This change would presumably open federal juries in the South to blacks.

When Lyndon Johnson eagerly pounced on the idea, Church suddenly found himself back in the majority leader's favor. The Idaho senator had been trying for some time to improve his position with Johnson. In mid-July, for example, when he received a letter from an avowed liberal angry about LBJ's "regressive leadership," Church leaped to Johnson's defense—and then sent a copy of his reply to the majority leader. A "grateful" Johnson applauded Church's letter. Two days later Johnson bubbled over with enthusiasm for Church: "In point of years," he wrote, "you are the youngest member of the Senate but in point of esteem and regard you are moving rapidly into a position that equals any."[51]

When Church formulated his addendum to the jury trial amendment he became Johnson's "young Sir Galahad" again. As Church himself recalled, he had for several months been "absolutely an outcast, a political outcast as far as Johnson was concerned." Suddenly, that situation had changed. Now Johnson talked strategy with him and the two senators closeted themselves with O'Mahoney and Anderson to work out the exact wording of the addendum.[52]

Then and later, Church denied that his work in behalf of the jury trial amendment had anything to do with a deal on Hells Canyon. "That's pure fiction," he said. John Carver concurred. Speaking as a firsthand observer of the Hells Canyon and civil rights battles in 1957, Carver insisted that Church quite independently embraced the jury trial amendment. There was no trade on Hells Canyon: "Frank wanted Hells Canyon, but that was not his method of doing business." Indeed, according to Carver, Church "was pretty damn realistic" about Johnson's tactics and did not want to give anyone the impression that he was in LBJ's pocket. Church conceded in retrospect that Johnson hoped to build political credit with him by helping with Hells Canyon. In that sense, Johnson's support for the big dam was a political chit, with the implied expectation that Church would pay him back. "That's the way that Lyndon Johnson worked." But Church approached the jury trial amendment via a concern for civil rights, not through Hells Canyon.[53]

Although Church's addendum to O'Mahoney's amendment was the Idaho senator's own idea, Johnson seized upon it as the dynamite with which to blast loose the civil rights logjam. According to Church, it was Johnson who determined when he would offer his addendum: "he staged and timed that drama" for maximum effect, like a theater director or "an orchestra conductor with his baton." For example, he did not want Church to come into the Senate chamber until there was a large audience.[54]

Late in the evening of July 31, Johnson told Church that the moment had arrived. He had kept the junior senator waiting in the Senate wings until a maximum audience arrived and the situation seemed ready.[55] By then the decorum that had marked the civil rights debate during the early part of the month had given way to irritability and frustration. Tempers inside the Senate grew as hot as the stifling Washington weather outside. With the decision on the O'Mahoney amendment fast approaching, and with the supporters of the amendment still apparently in need of votes, Church offered his addendum: any U. S. citizen twenty-one years or older who could speak English, was mentally competent, and had no prison record was eligible for federal jury duty. He noted that violations of the civil rights bill would be tried in federal courts. By prearrangement, O'Mahoney and Kefauver accepted the addendum. O'Mahoney took the occasion to praise Church "as one of the ablest" freshman senators whom he had encountered in his several decades on Capitol Hill.[56]

The next day, Church told the Senate he would support the civil rights bill but hoped that it would include the revised jury trial amendment. "If I must choose between an impairment of the right to jury trial, and an extension of the right to vote," he said, "I shall choose the latter, for the right to vote is more fundamental to the processes of a free society." His addendum, however, had removed that choice. By ensuring the eligibility of blacks for jury duty in federal courts, the Senate would block discriminatory all-white juries. Church indicated that he felt special anguish when his fellow liberals attacked the jury trial amendment. Describing himself as "an adherent to the cause of liberalism and an advocate of civil rights," he pleaded for legislation that did not depart from "hallowed" legal procedures. "Liberals," he contended, "should know that proper procedure is the heart of liberty." The importance of grounding the civil rights bill on sound, traditional procedures was particularly important because, he surmised, "in the future this bill may need to be enlarged to cover other civil rights that local law enforcement is failing to protect."[57]

Technically, Church conceded, "there is no Constitutional right to a jury trial in criminal contempt proceedings." At the time the Constitution and the Bill of Rights were ratified, court injunctions were rare. Over time, however, "as the contempt power began to grow outside of its historic bounds, it became apparent that jury safeguards should grow with it." Church had nothing against expanding the injunctive power, as the civil rights bill would do. He simply wanted Congress to remain vigilant "of the hard-won, long-fought-for procedures of Anglo-American law that have made us the freest nation on earth."[58]

A little more than twenty-four hours after Church added his addendum to the jury trial amendment, the Senate voted, with the result in doubt to the end. The anti-amendment forces even brought in two senators who had just gotten out of the hospital, Missouri Democrat Thomas Hennings and Maine Republican Frederick Payne. Around midnight, following a last round of heated debate, the amendment nevertheless passed, 51 to 42.[59]

Church had been the "bellwether," according to LBJ aide George Reedy: "Once he had broken the trail, the others were willing to go along." Among those who switched their support to the revised amendment was Massachusetts Democrat John F. Kennedy, whom Roy Wilkins of the NAACP had thought would vote against it. Washington's two Democrats, Warren Magnuson and Henry Jackson, also moved behind the jury trial amendment once it contained Church's addendum. The addendum may have directly gained the support of other senators as well; ten had joined Church in requesting its inclusion. At the least, Church unquestionably facilitated the decision of several northern and western liberals who voted affirmatively. As John Kennedy explained, "Everyone agreed, whatever his position on the jury trial question, that the Church addition marked an improvement." When Kennedy left the Senate following the vote, he encountered Bethine Church coming through a revolving door. Grabbing her arm, he swung her to the side and said, "Your man pulled it off." A disappointed Roy Wilkins allowed that Church's addendum had in fact provided the margin of victory.[60]

In the early morning hours of August 7, after twenty-five days of debate, the Senate passed a civil rights bill for the first time in almost a century, 72 to 18. Paul Douglas and Wayne Morse summed up the anger of the dissenters. The real winners, Douglas guessed, were "the advocates of segregation and of white domination." Looking sadly at his colleagues, the Illinois senator warned that the distinction between civil and criminal contempt would prove meaningless: voting rights cases would invariably be matters of noncompliance, and thus become matters of criminal contempt. Nor would the presence of blacks on federal juries encourage enforcement of civil rights. Did anyone really believe, he asked rhetorically, that a southern jury would unanimously find "a white election official guilty for depriving a Negro of the right to vote?. . . A hung jury is almost as good as an acquittal." Morse furiously dismissed the amended bill as "a sham"; without Part III and ways of genuinely enforcing the voting-rights section, the legislation did not even constitute "half a loaf" of civil rights.[61]

On September 9, Eisenhower nevertheless signed a slightly revised version of the civil rights bill. The final product, after clearing the House and Senate, eliminated jury trials in cases involving less than forty-five-day jail sentences and $300 fines.[62]

VI

Church proved instrumental in passing the 1957 Civil Rights Act, but not everyone approved of his role. "Some of his liberal friends," recalled John Carver, "thought it was the damndest sell-out in history." Their bitterness welled up at a party when Clayton Fritchey engaged Church in what Bethine described as a "brutal, brutal argument." Fritchey, a journalist who headed the Democratic National Committee's Public Affairs Division, was certain that Paul Douglas had taken the honorable position. Even on Church's own staff, there was dissension. Ward and Phyllis Hower, staunch civil rights supporters, believed that this time their boss was wrong. Phyllis became, in her words, "very emotional about it" and barely spoke to Church for several weeks.[63]

Bethine Church also worried that her husband was wrong in supporting the jury trial amendment. "I only hope and pray that the Star that Frank has moved under politically holds up," she wrote her parents. She wondered if his concern for fine legal points, or what the NAACP viewed as "flights of legal philosophy," was appropriate in this instance. Perhaps the angels also had "an illogical side"; if so, she regretted that "we aren't on it."[64]

Letters of praise from avowed racists were hardly reassuring in this regard. "Am extreemly [sic] pleased that you stepped forward like a man having pure Caucasian heritage," wrote one person who feared white citizens were falling under "the heel of a yet primitive, throat slitting, raping group." A Cleveland man thanked Church for the jury amendment: "Let's have White Supremacy." Applauding Church, a Mississippi school superintendent expressed anger at "darkies" and "the malignant powers of communism and mongrelization." A series of congratulatory letters from Augusta, Georgia, assumed that the senator had opposed the civil rights bill.[65]

From civil rights supporters came charges of betrayal. "Who the hell are you trying to fool with this amendment of yours?" asked an angry Pennsylvanian. "You know damn well, no Negro will ever get a fair trial by jury anywhere in the deep south." Someone else wondered how much Church had received "to sell out to the racist bigots." And a New Mexico resident expressed disgust that "another pro-South, anti-Negro Senator" had appeared in Idaho. "We might just as well have continued with Welker. At least *he* was honest in his obtuseness. *You* campaigned as a liberal. Now we know you as a phony and a charlatan."[66]

Perhaps the most stinging rebuff to Church came when a group of Minneapolis civil rights workers objected to his speaking at the First Annual Roosevelt Day Dinner, scheduled for September 28 in the Twin Cities. In mid-summer the Minnesota Young Democratic-Farmer-Laborites (YDFL) had invited Church, "one of the most aggressive liberal senators," to be the featured speaker. The uproar that followed Church's selection caught the organization off guard and threatened to ruin what was supposed to be "the biggest single project that the state YD's have ever undertaken."[67]

By mid-August the *Minneapolis Tribune* carried large headlines, "Jury-Trial Senator Sparks State Civil Rights Tornado." Civil Rights advocates in the Minneapolis-St. Paul area threatened to picket the dinner, a protest "not to be taken lightly," according to the local Committee for Integration in Minnesota. "We do not want Church here." Indeed, one woman believed that those responsible for inviting Church were lucky that "no ambassadorships are open in Outer Mongolia this season." A Minneapolis attorney, L. Howard Bennett, thought that Church's appearance would be "a gratuitous insult" because the senator was among those who had weakened civil rights with "cunning gimmicks." Minnesota, argued Bennett, should not provide "a national forum for those who are out of tune with the liberal and progressive tradition of this state." The controversy over Church placed Minnesota's Democratic-Farmer-Labor party in an awkward position. A demonstration against the Roosevelt Day gathering would embarrass the party as well as Idaho's senator.[68]

On August 21, Church said that he would not deliver the Minneapolis address after all. He described the incident as "another symptom of the emotional frenzy over the racial question that now grips the country." Privately, he was hurt that Hubert Humphrey had deserted him. After all, he had agreed to speak at Humphrey's behest.[69]

Humphrey felt badly about the YDFL incident, even though he did not publicly defend Church. Behind the scenes, he urged Church's critics not to judge the Idahoan unfairly. He pointed out, for one thing, that many western senators felt strongly about the jury trial amendment, as did top attorneys like Abe Fortas and Thurmond Arnold. For another thing, Humphrey was convinced that "this fellow Frank Church is a friend of civil rights. He is sympathetic to civil rights. His heart is good. He is intelligent. He is liberal. . . ." The civil rights movement had nothing to gain, and much to lose, Humphrey warned, by turning Church into a pariah. Additionally, the Minnesota senator resented the damage that the local "squabble" had inflicted on his relationships with some of his Senate colleagues. Certainly his association with Church had suffered. According to Bethine Church, her husband "could never understand Hubert's embarrassing him like this and knuckling under." By September 1957 Church had decided that he could not trust Humphrey.[70]

The YDFL incident also made Church wonder about the reliability of some civil rights leaders. He found a good deal of irony in Roy Wilkins's request that he work for a stronger civil rights bill in subsequent sessions of Congress. "While you are writing to solicit my support," he answered Wilkins with some bitterness, "the NAACP and allied organizations in Minneapolis are threatening to picket my appearance. . . ."[71]

Church could not understand why civil rights groups were unhappy with him. As he saw it, the jury trial amendment had prevented a southern filibuster and thus "made the difference between a minimal law on the statute books and an extremely strong bill dying on the Senate floor." It thus marked a significant "first step" in the field of civil rights. John Kennedy agreed, arguing that Church's addendum had created "a new civil right," one that guaranteed the right of blacks to serve on federal juries. In Kennedy's opinion, critics overlooked this major accomplishment. The specific contributions of the addendum aside, Church pointed out several times that he would have voted for the civil rights bill even without the jury amendment.[72]

Especially perplexing to Church was criticism of the civil rights law as a compromise measure. He did not share Wayne Morse's view "that a liberal should go down in defeat on an issue" rather than compromise on fundamentals. As Church told one audience, "There is nothing wrong with 'compromise,' when it is based upon valid principle." Indeed, "our history demonstrates that moderation in great moral causes has often proved more of a virtue than a deficiency." Although Church had nothing against moral indignation, he worried that fanatical, doctrinaire, unyielding positions all too often resulted in violence and tragedy. He noted that even the great Puritan revolutionary Oliver Cromwell, assuredly a man of conviction, recognized the dangers of forcing moral judgments upon other people. Church quoted Cromwell's admonition, "Think, I beseech ye in the bowels of Christ, that ye may be mistaken." Such advice was particularly instructive, according to the Idaho senator, when people faced "stupendous moral issues. . . . It is excellent advice to give ourselves before condemning compromise as moral weakness." Church wanted progress in civil rights without explosive confrontations, like those that by the fall of 1957 rocked Central High School in Little Rock, Arkansas. He was convinced that the only way to rectify the nation's terrible racial problems was through forbearance, an awareness of human frailties, and a lack of moral arrogance.[73]

In his eyes, the 1957 act proved that the system worked. The law represented a middle alternative to those on each extreme, some screaming "Never," others shouting "Right Now." With moderation, accommodation, and consensus, the legislative process had taken "a one-step-at-a-time approach." The Civil Rights Act, admittedly minimal, nonetheless represented a breakthrough—the first since Reconstruction. A limited breakthrough was better than no progress at all.[74]

Ironically, Church critic Roy Wilkins used many of the same justifications in his own defense. When Wilkins and black leaders such as Clarence Mitchell and Martin Luther King, Jr. urged passage of the amended civil rights bill, they received sharp rebukes from their more militant colleagues for giving in too quickly. " 'A job' is being done on me," complained Wilkins. He wished that his attackers would try to understand the "hard political realities" of the civil rights fight. Granted, the Civil Rights Act was imperfect, but it was "a workable and serviceable instrument for securing an increase in registration and voting." It was certainly better than nothing, which was the alternative. Wilkins lamented that many people overlooked the gains that had occurred within "the terribly complex game of power-politics being played." He hoped that he and other civil rights leaders, who had tried to secure the best legislation possible, would eventually receive proper credit for their efforts.[75]

Church, of course, wanted the same recognition. He believed genuinely that the jury trial amendment had "cut the Gordian knot that had long tied the arms of the Senate." For some time, however, his reputation among civil rights groups for having "voted wrong" in 1957 would continue to haunt him. So, also, would the charge that he was too willing to negotiate. A disillusioned Ohio resident, who had contributed $6 to Church's 1956 campaign, could not believe that already Church had joined "the professional compromisers. . . . And at so young an age too!"[76]

VII

While Church dismayed some civil rights advocates, he won the approval of Lyndon Johnson. The majority leader had walked a political tightrope over the civil rights issue. The 1957 civil rights "miracle" that national political observers attributed to him had boosted his presidential ambitions considerably.

Church, for his role in that miracle, now enjoyed Johnson's affection. "I was almost stifled in his embrace," he recalled. At the end of the civil rights fight, the large Texan hugged him warmly. "He would pick you up and wrap his arms around you and just squeeze the air out," Church remembered. Johnson's praise was lavish. No one, he claimed, had "a finer and more precise understanding of the issues than the junior Senator from Idaho. You proved that the vitality and the courage of the West is still a living reality." In wirephotos following passage of the civil rights bill, Johnson beamed at Church like a proud father. "Welcome to the club," his expression suggested. According to George Reedy, Johnson viewed Church as his "protégé," and although Church "was something of a novitiate" in the Senate club, still on probationary status, "there was no doubt that he would make it."[77]

Within the next several months, Johnson provided tangible evidence of his gratitude. A few days after the vote on civil rights, he appointed Church to represent the Senate at a conference of the Organization of American States in Buenos Aires, from August 15 to 24. Johnson had not forgotten Bethine Church's comment at a cocktail party earlier that year about her hopes of someday visiting South America. The assignment was, in Frank Church's words, "a kind of indication of his new friendship and embrace." According to columnist Drew Pearson, Johnson had deliberately passed over the logical choice, Wayne Morse, a member of the Foreign Relations Committee and chair of the subcommittee on Pan-American affairs. Morse, by voting against the jury trial amendment and the civil rights bill, had earned no favors.[78]

In contrast, recalled Church, "Nothing was too good for me." He received Johnson's blessings throughout the following year. "First, he put me on the McClellan Rackets Committee, and that was getting front-page billing. Then, when the first vacancy occurred, he put me on Foreign Relations, when I had been in the Senate less than two years." The seat on the Senate Foreign Relations Committee was a special plum. William E. Borah had been a powerful force on the committee for years, chairing it for a while, and Church desperately wanted to follow his footsteps. Church's legislative assistant, Ward Hower, was convinced that his boss's contribution to the jury trial amendment "was what got Frank on the Foreign Relations Committee." Estes Kefauver and Henry Jackson were senior to Church, and both wanted the assignment, but LBJ shunned them. "Frank didn't hesitate to let Lyndon Johnson know that he wanted on the Foreign Relations Committee, and Johnson didn't hesitate to let Frank know that he wanted the jury trial amendment," according to Hower. "I am morally certain that there was a tacit *quid pro quo*."[79]

VIII

Church's first eight months in office had been remarkably fruitful. In a very short time the young senator had made a strong mark. The *Washington Daily News* placed him among a half-dozen "Front Page Senators of 1957." Describing him as serious and eloquent, the newspaper credited him with providing "the final successful fillip that put the civil rights bill over without a filibuster." "Rarely have members of the Senate 'club,' " wrote a news service reporter, "been as impressed with a freshman colleague as they have with the thirty-three-year-old legislator from Boise, Idaho." Some Democrats were reportedly already placing him in the liberal tradition of Borah, George Norris, and Wisconsin's Robert M. La Follette. Thomas O'Neill, a close observer of Capitol Hill, believed that Church—in less than a year—had attained what some senators never received in a lifetime: "acceptance into the inner circle of the United States Senate." An Associated Press wirephoto had shown him standing jubilantly, arms upraised, between Paul Douglas and Hubert Humphrey in a victory pose after the Senate passage of the Hells Canyon dam bill. Other wirephotos featured him clasping hands with O'Mahoney, Johnson, Kefauver, and Georgia's Richard Russell, celebrating adoption of the jury trial amendment.[80]

Bethine Church observed correctly that her husband was impressing liberals and conservatives, Northerners and Southerners alike. According to Florida senator George Smathers, "young Frank Church" had been "outstanding" during the civil rights debates. Smathers, who had entered the Senate in 1951 as a notorious red-baiter, was one of only five Southerners to vote for the Civil Rights Act. He was sufficiently impressed with his new Idaho colleague that he nominated him to the U. S. Junior Chamber of Commerce's list of ten outstanding young American men for 1957—an award that Church received. And when Paul Douglas, one of the Senate's premier liberals, wrote an article on "The Bright Young Men of Politics," he placed Church "first, of course," and anticipated that his new colleague might eventually be as influential as Borah. "We've got something here," said an unidentified Democrat. "He's a real thinker. Watch him go."[81]

Church had every reason to feel good about his political debut. "I enjoy being a Senator," he told his constituents in September. "I like the work."[82]

Church presents a photograph of William E. Borah to Foreign Relations Committee chair J. William Fulbright as Mike Mansfield and Wayne Morse watch. *Senate photo, courtesy Cleve Corlett.*

Chapter Five

Getting "Out Front": 1958-1960

FROM THE MOMENT Frank Church entered the Senate, he aspired to be a national figure. According to his first administrative assistant, John Carver, he wanted to be "out front" in American politics. Church was well aware that no Democrat from Idaho had ever served more than one term. His only hope of breaking that tradition was to tend his home grounds with particular care, establishing himself as someone to whom Idahoans of various political persuasions could look with pride, as they had with the legendary William E. Borah. His own ambitions fed this political imperative. He was determined to be a senator who made a difference, not one who simply occupied a seat for a single term.[1]

Certainly Church's whirlwind entry into the Senate during the debates over the 1957 Civil Rights Act suggested that he had exceptional political promise and savvy. Over the next several years he continued to demonstrate that he was no ordinary senator. In the late Fifties, although he was in some respects a resolute Cold Warrior, he clearly began to question some of the Cold War's basic premises, especially regarding nuclear weapons, military aid, and governmental secrecy. He was also in the forefront of the debates over Hawaiian and Alaskan statehood. A visible critic of the Eisenhower administration's policies, he helped to block confirmation of several presidential appointments. Although still the youngest member of the Senate, he won an assignment that he actively pursued: that of keynote speaker at the 1960 Democratic convention.

I

Dilemmas were nevertheless inherent in his quest to be "out front." He had to balance his interest in foreign policy issues against the more locally focused expectations of his Idaho constituents. Other tensions were of a more personal nature as he constantly juggled the demands of public and private life.

Early on, Church made a crucial decision: he would not sacrifice his family on the altar of politics. He consequently spent little time in cloak-room socializing, or in chatting with colleagues late into the evening. As much as possible, he protected his time at home. He typically rejected weekend party invitations with the simple explanation that he needed to be with his family. Bethine later speculated that her husband's family commitments might have impeded his career because he had not gotten to know many senators as well as he might have. Forrest Church agreed. His father was not "a political buddy" who spent much time with Senate cronies. Nor was he willing to travel much by himself, giving speeches or participating in political gatherings. "Rather than go out on the road for a week, he would take us to the beach," Forrest recalled.[2]

By all accounts, Church never judged family time a sacrifice. It was a given, a necessity, something from which he personally drew great support and satisfaction. Forrest recalled "nothing austere or forbidding about him." Indeed, shortly after taking office, Church mortified the ten-year-old by sliding down a bannister in a public building, losing control, and crashing against an office door. A woman who rushed to help ended up offering an embarrassed apology, "Oh, excuse me, Senator, I didn't know it was you." Nor would Forrest ever forget his father's inevitable "moooo" as he cut into a rare steak, even in restaurants. "My father was one of the happiest men I have known." He was also accessible, although not in the sense of playing catch with a baseball—something which he and Forrest did only once to the embarrassment of both. Dinners were typically a time of playful banter. Forrest fondly remembered these discussions, which were perhaps similar to what Frank Church had enjoyed with his own father. In all of this, Bethine remained a forceful and vigorous presence. "For my mother particularly," Forrest has said, "having fun was almost an article of faith."[3]

In the rumor mill of the nation's capital, Church's family relationships seemed almost too good to be true, more appropriate to the idealized domestic settings of Beaver Cleaver's television household. In early October 1957 the Churches adopted a new-born baby, Chase, whom they nicknamed "Spud," after the famed eastern Idaho potato. "We are doing a reasonably good job with both boys," Bethine wrote her husband proudly several years later. "Neither of them are cry babies or tantrum throwers. They are both sympathetic and thoughtful." Moreover, "they know that we're happy together and they seem to feel very sure of their family." In late summers, when Bethine and the boys visited her parents' ranch while the Senate was still in session, the letters between her and Frank left no doubts about the strong bonds between them.[4]

Some people worried that Bethine was too visible in the senator's life. But she said there was no way she could be the kind of wife "who just sits in the background with her hands folded in her lap and her ankles crossed and speaks only when spoken to." She believed that too many political wives had personal problems because "they're left outside, like a dirty shirt." Someone with a less ebullient and warm personality could have created a big problem in the senator's office. Her phone calls came with sometimes irritating frequency, not because she tried to boss his staff or check up on her husband, but because of her unlimited interest in what he was doing. At least once, good-naturedly, the secretary told her that she had used up her quota of calls for the day. To some observers she seemed to hover too much over her husband, suffocating him with attention. One journalist described her as "a gushy wife," always plucking lint from the senator's jacket or straightening his tie. But Church firmly defended her when a friend urged her to be less intrusive. He needed her as she was, he said. When she jokingly wondered if he would prefer that she ask him if he wanted his slippers rather than how he had voted that day, he replied that if he wanted a wife to wait on him he would have married one like that in the first place. He laughingly told an audience that yes, indeed, he had to check everything with his wife: "The people of Idaho have an extra senator in Bethine and they're lucky to have her."[5]

By all accounts, the Churches were exceptionally close. One staffer described their relationship as "the longest-running high school romance in history." They were openly affectionate, even cuddly. She was more than the senator's spouse; she was his closest friend, advisor, and political partner. In some respects she was an even better politician than he, more natural and outgoing. No hint of romantic scandal ever touched them, even though in 1957 a reporter described him as one of the "Capitol's Most Kissable Men." Ward Hower, a member of Church's staff from 1957 until 1963, knew personally "that there were some women really after him, but they didn't get him." A number of people concluded that the Churches' marriage was among the enduring institutions in Washington.[6]

Church's family values were thus anything but packaged clichés, served up for public effect. He believed genuinely in the strengths of a closely knit, caring home. As a child he had known the advantages of such a setting, and as a spouse and father he worked conscientiously to establish a loving environment.

His conduct and values unquestionably served him well with many Idaho voters, especially the substantial number of Mormons in the southern and eastern parts of the state. One of his most potent political weapons was his family-oriented life style. It was something that even people who disagreed with his politics could appreciate and admire.

But Church was not as prudish as reporters and many of his peers believed, or as his "Frank Sunday School" nickname suggested. He enjoyed drinking socially, having a cocktail before the evening meal, and smoking a good cigar, even though he preferred not to publicize such behavior among Idaho's voters. In fact, he carefully avoided photographs that showed him with a cigar or glass in hand. When campaigning in the eastern part of Idaho he smoked his cigar and sometimes had a nightcap in his aide's room, lest the cleaning maids know the next morning that someone in Church's quarters had been smoking or drinking. When a friend sent him a cigar catalogue, he instructed his secretary to file it where he could find it. She humorously filed it under "Vices." Church played poker, even though Carl Burke laughed that he could barely distinguish "between a full house and a straight." Certainly he had a playful side, was easy going, tolerant, witty, and good-natured. He told one aide that the Democratic Party had attracted him because of its reputation for "rum, Romanism, and rebellion." And, after seeing the film, *La Dolce Vita*, he responded to a comment that the movie was decadent by laughing, "I could enjoy life like that." Vibrant, charming, and a skilled storyteller, he could be the life of the party.[7]

Among his Senate colleagues, however, Church had the reputation of being stiff, distant, aloof, a little too earnest, even "prissy." In many respects he was a loner, uncomfortable with bear hugs and close, face-to-face encounters. To some individuals he was more than a little pompous. A few senators reportedly chafed at his rather florid oratorical style. Occasionally he seemed to be lecturing them, a tendency that gave rise to the comment that he would have been better off had he not won the national debate contest when he was sixteen. Even during informal conversations he spoke carefully and precisely, with measured tones and complete sentences in which the commas, periods, and paragraphs seemed to be in place. He lacked any kind of "aw shucks" mannerisms. "He really aggravated a lot of his colleagues in the Senate,"

John Carver recalled. Carver speculated that, at first, Church found it difficult to relax around well-known associates many years his senior. Certainly the Senate had to be an intimidating place for a person in his mid-thirties. Still, one individual noted that over the years even Church's whispers took on a pontifical ring.[8]

Forrest believed his father was basically shy but balanced this shyness against his "rhetorical, old-fashioned, forensic" training. As a youth, Frank had developed a public side, one that was mature and serious, ready suddenly to take the debater's platform and speak formally about an important issue. Individuals who came to know only his public side seldom suspected that he had a folksier dimension.[9]

II

To achieve his goal of national prominence Church needed to find an acceptable mesh between his personality, his ambition, and circumstances. During his first months in office he talked candidly with John Carver about strategies. He quickly ruled out trying to work his way up the Senate's administrative ladder. He lacked the disposition for it. Senatorial business, in Carver's words, "always bored the hell out of Frank" and would cut drastically into his family time. He also rejected a second option: trying to become a dominant political force in Idaho. Given Idaho's Republican leanings, it seemed advisable to stay outside the state's internal political disputes. Embroilment in local Democratic Party feuds would be divisive and distracting. Whereas Hubert Humphrey in Minnesota had the advantage of working from a solidly established partisan base, Church did not. With rare exceptions he thus avoided factional infighting. Over the years his aloofness frustrated some Idaho Democrats, who wanted him to be more active in shaping the party; but Church remained as detached as possible. The option that appealed to him was what Carver described as the "Foreign Relations track." In many respects, this was the course William E. Borah had followed. Church's boyhood hero had persistently avoided becoming a party functionary, staying "above" state factionalism. And he had become a power on the Foreign Relations committee, ultimately enjoying a reputation as "statesman."[10]

Shortly after entering the Senate, Church thus had a political script in mind. The question was whether events would help him. He had quickly proven that he could gain respect. Journalist Bill Hall guessed that even senators who did not like him personally "had to admit that the son-of-a-bitch had brains." But Church nevertheless had to move carefully, remaining alert to senatorial politics and choosing his issues well.[11]

Complicating this, of course, was the fact that issues in the forefront of national debate did not necessarily count for much at home. Civil rights, for example, was hardly a burning question in Idaho and engendered more animosity than support. And the "foreign policy track," although it assuredly stirred Church's own interests, evoked little local enthusiasm.

In that regard, Hawaii's Daniel Inouye guessed that Church's push in the late Fifties for Hawaiian and Alaskan statehood was "not a popular position with his constituents." The admission of Alaska, according to John Carver, was less controversial in Idaho, but Church vigorously promoted the addition of Hawaii as well. His interest in the statehood issue had developed in the mid-1940s, when he debated the subject at Stanford. Ironically, the debate format once required him to argue against Hawaiian statehood at the University of Hawaii, where his opponent was Inouye, eventually one of his Senate colleagues. But upon entering the Senate, Church strongly advocated admitting Hawaii and Alaska as states. On April 12, 1957, he hand-delivered a letter to the White House, asking that Eisenhower back the statehood bills. In 1958, he wrote Lyndon Johnson at least three times, urging the placement of the statehood issue high on the agenda. And on May 5, 1958 he gave a lengthy Senate speech on the subject.[12]

To Church, the right of self-government was a given, but he also viewed the statehood issue as an ideological weapon in the Cold War. By admitting Alaska and Hawaii the U. S. could both reaffirm "its anticolonial heritage" and ally itself with the "militant nationalism" sweeping the world. United States history, from Church's perspective, offered a timely model for people seeking self-determination. Americans had built a nation, not an empire; and, as Church told one audience, "statehood has been the method of its construction."[13]

Americans were less enthusiastic about Alaskan and Hawaiian statehood than Church would have wished, however. Politics was a key reason. According to George Sundborg, who in the mid-1950s edited a Fairbanks newspaper and championed Alaskan statehood, Republicans worried that Alaska would be a source of liberal Democratic votes. When the Eisenhower administration chose to link the admission of Alaska and Hawaii, it was essentially trying to stall the statehood movement. Hawaii's chances were already problematic, given racial fears within both political parties about the islands' non-Causcasian population. The administration-backed joint statehood bill was, as Church pointed out, a strategy to unite "the opponents of statehood for either Territory."[14]

A counter-strategy that Church endorsed was to consider Alaska and Hawaii separately, thereby splitting the coalition of individuals who opposed statehood for only one of the territories. His May 5 Senate speech focused on immediate statehood for Alaska, but he emphasized that Hawaii would follow soon because "the barrier will have been broken." In an impressive two-hour presentation he dismissed the argument that the territories should not become states because neither was contiguous with the existing forty-eight states. Such an argument would have kept California, Oregon, and Louisiana from the Union. Church talked mainly about America's historic ideals, particularly that of "government by consent of the governed." When Alaskans paid taxes to the federal government they were victims of "taxation without representation," colonists in a nation that opposed colonies. Their status was an anomaly in the larger world setting as well, as empires melted away. Church argued fervently that America's traditions, ideals, and history combined with world conditions to demand statehood for Alaska.[15]

His speech won profuse praise from some of his colleagues and helped to jar the Alaskan statehood bill from the Senate calendar and bring it to the floor. "Long may you reign!" said Paul Douglas of Illinois. Oregon's Richard Neuberger called Church "the foremost champion of Alaskan statehood," and Texas Democrat Ralph Yarborough believed that the young senator had delivered "one of the greatest speeches" in the 85th Congress.[16]

That summer Alaska became America's 49th state. "Alaskans will always be grateful to Frank Church for the valiant support he gave our statehood struggle," George Sundborg said thirty years later. "He was one of the energetic young Western liberals who led the way for us."[17]

Over the next few months he pressed just as ardently and as successfully for Hawaiian statehood. Indeed, Montana Democrat Mike Mansfield claimed that no senator had "worked harder or with greater enthusiasm" for that cause than Church. In early 1959 Hawaii entered the Union. Church reassured his constituents that Idaho was now better off, because power on Capitol Hill was tipping westward. More importantly, the nation had erased "the last major vestige of our adventure in colonialism," sending a message around the world that the United States stood for freedom and self-government. Church assumed that other Idaho citizens were equally proud of this blow for liberty.[18]

When the newly admitted states turned to the nitty-gritty political details of electing their congressional delegations, Church and Massachusetts senator John Kennedy stumped throughout Alaska for Democratic candidates. Vice President Richard Nixon and Secretary of Interior Fred Seaton were the leading Republican voices. A particularly close senatorial race developed between Democrat Ernest Gruening and Mike Stepovich, an Eisenhower appointee who had been Alaska's last territorial governor. Gruening eked out a victory, which he attributed in part to Church and Kennedy. He had already developed a friendship with Church, with whom he had worked during the statehood fight. Subsequently, the two men remained close in the Senate.[19]

III

Although Church's role in the statehood debates may have boosted his image in Idaho as a Senate leader, his direct challenges to the Eisenhower administration placed him on softer political ground. In mid-1958 he took the lead in blocking confirmation of Bernard Flanagan as civil service commissioner. And a year later, during a landmark collision between the president and Congress, he voted against the appointment of Lewis L. Strauss as Secretary of Commerce.[20]

Within Idaho his opposition to Flanagan was probably less controversial than his anti-Strauss vote. Although Church took issue with the popular Eisenhower over Flanagan, he did so because the appointee had lied. A Washington columnist had discovered that Flanagan's civil service job application was packed with misinformation. John Carver conducted his own investigation of Flanagan with bulldog tenacity. Carver later downplayed his role, but Ward Hower remembered clearly that Carver had persuaded Church to take the offensive against Flanagan. According to Hower, Carver put the case together and then "pressed it on Frank, who probably wasn't very interested in it in the first place."[21]

By the time the thirteen-member Post Office and Civil Service Committee held its three sessions on Flanagan's confirmation, Church was deeply involved. Armed with information, he bore down on the hapless Flanagan with what *Newsweek* described as "rigorous cross-examination." Flanagan, sweating profusely and shifting his chunky frame uncomfortably, attempted to explain the "honest mistakes" in his civil service application. Church, resembling a trial attorney, pressed on relentlessly, wondering how the mistakes could have been "honest." Flanagan had, for example, claimed falsely that he held a bachelor's degree from a Vermont university. He had inflated his number of undergraduate hours from 73 to 120 and his semester hours in law school from 52 to 73. Columnist John Cramer reported that Church's "documented, airtight case" had turned up more than two dozen Flanagan misstatements. During the first hearing Church did most of the questioning. Subsequently, other committee members rallied to his side. Although the Eisenhower administration reportedly exerted enormous pressure on the committee, by the end of the third hearing six senators had joined Church. Eisenhower, at Flanagan's request, withdrew the nomination. Church carefully explained to his constituents that the incident involved truthfulness, not partisanship. Flanagan's deceptions had clearly rendered him unfit to preside over the nation's civil service system.[22]

A year later Church would find it more difficult to justify in Idaho his vote against Lewis Strauss. Whereas the Flanagan appointment had been relatively minor, Strauss was Eisenhower's choice for a major cabinet spot. The Strauss case, moreover, did not involve anything as clear cut as dishonesty. Instead, it resulted from politics, conflicts over ideology and personality, and a shift within the Senate.

When Eisenhower, on October 24, 1958, announced Strauss's appointment, he could hardly have guessed that he would soon receive what *Time* magazine described as a "stinging personal slap" from the Senate. For one thing, history was on the president's side. The Senate had rejected only eight cabinet choices since 1789, the last in 1925. Since then, Congress as a whole had increasingly deferred to presidential authority. For another thing, Strauss, a rear admiral in World War II and a Wall Street banker, had an impressive governmental record in several administrations. An authority on nuclear energy, he had helped to plan the development of the hydrogen bomb. President Harry Truman had appointed him to the newly formed Atomic Energy Commission in 1947, and Eisenhower had elevated him to chair it. Looking back, Eisenhower wrote that Strauss's credentials were so good that "it should not have taken the Senate more than minutes to confirm his appointment as Secretary of Commerce."[23]

But Eisenhower had not taken into account the damage that Strauss would inflict upon himself. Secretive, vain, dogmatic, and seemingly anxious to offend, Strauss, as chair of the Atomic Energy Commission, had already alienated New Mexico senator Clinton Anderson. And as committee hearings proceeded on his appointment, his arrogance angered other senators. Some worried as well about his hard-line anticommunism. He had been a key figure in labeling Dr. Robert Oppenheimer a security risk, even though the physicist was one of the heroes of the Manhattan Project. Moreover, he was anxious to employ the Commerce Department in "economic warfare" against the Soviet Union. Public power advocates, such as Church, had additional reasons for disliking him: Strauss was an unyielding supporter of private power development.[24]

Strauss might have surmounted the difficulties of ideology and personality, but the recently transformed Senate was another matter. The body that in 1959 considered his appointment was significantly different from its immediate predecessors. Following the dramatic 1958 elections the Democratic majority had jumped from slight to overwhelming. When Eisenhower first named Strauss there were forty-nine Democrats and forty-seven Republicans in the Senate. By 1959 the numbers were sixty-four to thirty-four, with the Democrats claiming their first senator from Maine, Edmund Muskie, as well as both senators from the new state of Alaska. The famous "class of '58" tilted the Senate away from the G. O. P.; it also tipped the Democratic Party from the South to the North and West. Many of the younger Democrats were anxious to take the offensive against the Eisenhower administration, which seemed to be stumbling in the wake of an economic recession and recent Soviet successes in space. Some of them also resented Lyndon Johnson's leadership. They considered him too dictatorial and too soft on the administration.[25]

Pennsylvania's Joseph Clark was already putting together a liberal bloc, which included Frank Church. Clark hoped to coordinate the energies of the liberals, in part by getting their staff members to meet on Friday afternoons. Besides Church, other senators who participated in this loosely organized effort included Paul Douglas, Michigan's Pat McNamara, Colorado's John Carroll, and Minnesota's Hubert Humphrey. In March 1959 Clark warned Johnson "of a very real problem": "the younger men in the Senate, plus those most recently elected, are getting more restless and frustrated week by week because they have no real chance to be heard on questions of party policy." Clark worried that "an angry row" was emerging "between the past and the future in the Senatorial Democratic Party."[26]

Unfortunately for Strauss, the fate of his nomination thus rested with a Senate full of Democrats, groping for their own identity, and resentful of domination from either the executive branch or the majority leader. What Eisenhower had assumed would be an easy confirmation turned instead into a raging battle. While Lyndon Johnson withheld judgment on Strauss, Clinton Anderson methodically set out to sink the admiral. Anderson's major charge was that Strauss, as chair of the Atomic Energy Commission, had not kept Congress fully informed. As Anderson forged a growing opposition, LBJ realized that he could help Strauss only by further endangering his own leadership position among restive young Democrats. Eisenhower, meanwhile, became increasingly angry at the "childish" efforts of Anderson and his followers. The administration mounted an all-out push to confirm Strauss. Eisenhower said privately that, if the nomination failed, the 1960 "Republican presidential nominee ought to campaign on one point–'If elected, I'll appoint Strauss.' " By all accounts the forthcoming confirmation vote was going to be razor-close and would draw a good deal of political blood.[27]

Back in Idaho, a worried Judge Clark feared that his son-in-law would make a major political mistake by opposing Strauss. Clark guessed that Idaho residents would not understand the rejection of Eisenhower's choice for the cabinet. Moreover, Strauss would be Secretary of Commerce for only another eighteen months. If Church intended to vote against him, he needed to have some good answers to the question, "Is it worth it?" Church conceded that a negative vote would be very unpopular back home. He also granted that eighteen months of Strauss as Secretary of Commerce mattered little. Although it was thus "very difficult" to reject his father-in-law's counsel, he was going to do so anyhow. For one thing, he simply did not believe that the admiral should join the cabinet. Yet he admitted that "political considerations" also influenced his thinking. Chief among these was Clinton Anderson's vehement dislike of Strauss. "Clint feels very strongly about this matter, and has the support of nearly all of the Democratic Senators from the West," Church explained. "As Chairman of the Reclamation and Irrigation Subcommittee of the Interior Committee, he has much to say on Idaho projects." Already, the New Mexico senator had been a powerful ally in Church's fights for public power. Church did not wish to alienate him. Anderson aside, he was unwilling to desert other of his "closest friends," including Oklahoma's Mike Monroney. "Since they are on the right side of the case, in my judgment, I think I should not break with them, even though it would be politically wise to do so."[28]

On June 19, Church helped to provide the narrow 49 to 46 victory against Strauss's nomination. At one point during the roll call Arizona Republican Barry Goldwater expressed the administration's frustration. "Goddamn," he said, smashing his fist down on his desk. Church had no way of knowing how many Idaho voters shared that sentiment.[29]

IV

His assignment in 1958 to the Senate Select Committee on Improper Activities in the Labor or Management Field, better known as the McClellan Committee, could only have complicated his situation in Idaho. The Senate had established the committee in January 1957 to investigate corruption and racketeering in labor and industry. Organized labor was understandably nervous. Divisions tore its own ranks, and anti-union sentiment was on the rise. Labor leaders such as Walter Reuther of the United Auto Workers continued to draw upon the idealistic working-class movements of the Thirties. Others, such as Teamster president Jimmy Hoffa, were corrupt and dictatorial. Some observers worried that investigations of Hoffa-style corruption could easily turn into a labor-bashing crusade. George Meany, president of the AFL-CIO, looked upon Arkansas senator John L. McClellan as "an anti-labor nut." Although the committee as a whole was not necessarily anti-labor, it had a definite pro-management tilt. Over the next several years, moreover, its revelations about labor hoodlums and racketeering fueled efforts to produce reform legislation—some of which had a decidedly anti-union caste. On March 31, 1958, Michigan's Democratic senator and former trade unionist Patrick McNamara angrily resigned, complaining that the committee had "outlived its usefulness."[30]

Partly because the committee generated widespread media attention, Lyndon Johnson asked Church to replace McNamara. "I've got a vacancy there to fill," Church remembered Johnson saying, "and it will give you some good exposure. . . . I think it will be good for you." Church recalled that he was by now "strongly in his [Johnson's] embrace again and nothing was too good for me." If he had doubts about the assignment, he withheld them. His inclination at the time was to follow Johnson's lead. The majority leader typically stood at the Senate door with his thumb up, or down, indicating how he expected Church and other Democrats to vote on particular bills. Once, when Church knew that he disagreed with Johnson, he waited to enter the Senate until Johnson had his back turned, then slipped by him, and voted contrary to the majority leader. For several weeks afterward, LBJ refused to speak to him. Having gotten back on Johnson's good side, Church was reluctant to displease him again. Moreover, Church himself apparently saw the McClellan Committee as an opportunity. John Carver got the distinct impression that he was "genuinely pleased and gratified" with the appointment. Again, "it was a matter of being out front."[31]

The assignment nevertheless constituted a potential challenge to Church's convictions as well as to a key group of his Idaho supporters. He sympathized with organized labor. More than a decade earlier, at Stanford, his instinctive appreciation for unions had helped him win a debate in which he argued against more federal control over unions. He had not felt well going into the competition and found himself falling back reflexively on his own sentiments. As a matter of principle, he personally opposed greater control of unions. In what he described later as "a purely impromptu address," he had vigorously defended union activities as better in many respects than those of many other U. S. institutions. The unions had, for example, been among the most active organizations in America in combatting racial discrimination. And the practice of closed membership was as defensible for labor as it was for professions such as law and medicine. Church told the debate audience that Americans could easily decide to legislate particular union abuses out of existence. The difficulty, however, was in doing so without violating the rights of workers. A decade after the debate, when Church campaigned for the Senate, he strongly backed the right of laborers to organize and bargain collectively. Although Idaho's organized labor movement was relatively small, including only 18,000 of the state's 280,000 voters, it controlled about a quarter of the nonagricultural work force. In 1956 Church had relied heavily on its support.[32]

By the late Fifties a major corporate drive for "right-to-work" laws (outlawing union shops) gathered force in several states, including Idaho. In 1957 the Idaho legislature almost passed such a law. A year later, "right-to-work" literature inundated the state with the appeal: "Let Freedom Ring for Idaho." In California, where a similar advertising blitz was underway, movie producer Cecil B. deMille applauded the McClellan committee investigations for popularizing right-to-work laws. In 1958 Idaho unions barely beat back such legislation again.[33]

Given the Idaho situation, as well as his own beliefs, Church had to move circumspectly on the McClellan Committee. To individuals who believed he was in labor's pocket, he explained that he was helping to "expose the cancerous abuses of Hoffa and his ilk"–the "gangsters, thugs, and hoodlums" who were "feasting like maggots upon the earnings of honest working men and women." When a union official in Coeur d'Alene rebuked him for "so blindly" following McClellan, he offered assurances that he would in no way "be a party to an assault upon the union movement." He also stressed that he favored "anti-racketeering," not "anti-labor," legislation. To people who noted only the McClellan committee's exposure of labor corruption, he served a reminder that the committee had uncovered managerial abuses as well: "Employers appear to me to be at least equally implicated." He also liked to point out that the findings of the McClellan Committee applied to conditions outside Idaho, which was still primarily rural. It "makes one appreciate Idaho," he said.[34]

All in all, Church's two years on the McClellan Committee were a mixed blessing. "Frank didn't like that job much," John Carver recalled. "The whole thing was rather distasteful to him." Church, the young innocent from Idaho, discovered a seamier, more vicious and immoral side of American life than he had known. At one point he clashed angrily with Jimmy Hoffa. When Hoffa claimed to be cleaning up the Teamsters and talked of the importance of majority rule, Church impatiently snapped, "I don't want a lecture from you. I've read the history of the United States and certainly don't consider you an authority on morals."[35]

But for Church there were benefits to serving on the committee, partly because he got to know John and Robert Kennedy much better. He often sided with the Massachusetts senator, a committee member who apparently shared his discomfort with the labor investigations. Church backed a Kennedy-sponsored bill that guaranteed secret elections as well as publicly disclosed financial reports within unions. The bill, with the endorsement of the AFL-CIO, twice passed the Senate overwhelmingly, only to fail both times in the House. Church also liked the committee's counsel Robert Kennedy, and praised his "maturity and judgment." Robert, in turn, congratulated him for bringing "a needed breath of fresh air to the committee." In his best-selling account of the investigations, *The Enemy Within*, Kennedy described Church as "absolutely fearless, asking some of the most astute and penetrating questions that I heard put. I envied his articulateness." As an example of Church's integrity, Kennedy quoted the Idaho senator's response to an A & P Company attorney. When the lawyer said he saw nothing wrong with a secret deal between the corporation and one of the unions, Church retorted, "Well, I do."[36]

V

Church's conscientious but unenthused work on the McClellan Committee resembled his contributions to the Senate's Interior Committee. His request to join Interior when he took office was no surprise. It was the premier western committee, one that had much to do with issues important to Idaho's economy. Except for environmental issues, however, Church seemed to view the committee's activities as an obligatory distraction. Utah's Frank Moss and North Dakota's Quentin Burdick, both liberal Democrats with a passionate interest in the committee's broad agenda, believed he was basically bored with questions involving irrigation, range management, and agriculture. At one point Moss was flabbergasted when Church asked him what a sugar beet looked like. Church, an Idaho resident, was surely kidding. "No," Church replied, "I don't remember that I ever saw a sugar beet." "He was dead serious," Moss remembered. "I don't think he had ever been out in the fields and ever seen a sugar beet." Moss admired Church greatly, but regretted his apparent disinterest in the Interior Committee. From the Utah senator's perspective, Church sat on the committee primarily "to keep his powder dry politically at home."[37]

Certainly Church did not relish his early assignment to the Interior Subcommittee on Indian Affairs. He initially had high hopes that he could improve Native American conditions, which he described as "the shame of our Nation." But after several years his hopes gave way to frustration. Not only did Indian problems seem insoluble, but he also had difficulty understanding his inability to build, in John Carver's words, "any real rapport with the Indians."[38]

Part of the problem probably grew from his own confidence in acculturation. When he took office he basically supported the policy of termination, which Congress instituted in 1953 to phase out reservations and federal responsibilities for Indian tribes. He had no quarrel with the policy's goal of assimilating Native Americans into the larger national culture. "Our technological progress in the United States will not allow any minority group to languish in past glories," he wrote. "The sooner all Indian tribes and their members realize this fact, and prepare to stand on their own feet, the better it will be for all of us." Such words perhaps sounded harsher than he intended, because he ultimately chose not to mail the letter that included them. Certainly, as he made clear, he did not believe that Indians should sell their lands or abandon either their culture or their tribal organizations. He wanted simply to end their isolation from the mainstream culture and their treatment "as a dependent racial group." In 1959 he took a middle position between advocates of rapid termination and people who rejected termination altogether. He favored moving more slowly with termination, and always with tribal consent. Also, to raise the economy of Indian areas, he backed federal programs to provide more development loans, more money for vocational training, and better health services.[39]

Because he viewed himself as a friend of Native Americans, he could not understand why many of them apparently disliked him. Perry Swisher, a Pocatello newspaper editor/politician, guessed that he never really accepted bi-culturalism and perhaps viewed the Indians' distance from him as a display of intransigence or ingratitude, rather than an expression of independence. Church may have known "intellectually" why they were suspicious of him, Swisher said, but "it was not a bridge he ever crossed emotionally." Increasingly, he viewed Indian issues as intractable, mired in bureaucratic resistance to change and Indian politics. His disenchantment was evident by 1960, when he became chair of the Indian Affairs Subcommittee, a job that John Carver said he "really hated" and left as soon as possible. Hal Gross, a lobbyist for Indian legislation, sensed that the senator had "soured" somewhat on issues involving Native Americans. When Gross sought his help in breaking loose a bill to help Indians on reservations resolve problems regarding heirships to land, he was initially unresponsive. Disappointed, Gross told the senator that he had expected better of him. He had thought Church would be willing to stand up for something that was right. Church said nothing for a moment, then smiled. He subsequently supported the legislation.[40]

For the most part, however, he concluded that he did not know how to help Native Americans. He said he had attempted to effect reforms, only to find himself "in danger of being labeled an enemy of the Indian people." He took no pride in that admission. His expectations had been higher.[41]

VI

Frank Moss suspected that Church had troubles with the Subcommittee on Indian Affairs partly because his real interests rested elsewhere—with the Committee on Foreign Relations. Moss conceded that the Indian subcommittee was full of difficulties. Still, according to the Utah senator, Church's "whole life was that damned Foreign Relations, and I suppose he circled around that all the time." John Carver agreed.[42]

Church's zeal for the Foreign Relations Committee was hardly surprising. Intellectually and emotionally he had pointed himself toward it since at least the eighth grade. His desire to follow in William E. Borah's footsteps; his letter in 1938 to the Boise newspaper about American isolationism; his early aversion to colonialism; his wartime experiences; his 1950s involvement in the Crusade for Freedom organization; his attention to foreign policy themes during the 1956 election—all attested to his deep interest in foreign relations.

Shortly after his appointment in 1959 to the committee he dropped by the office of the staff director, Carl Marcy. "From the first day he walked into my office," Marcy believed, "it was clear he wanted to be chairman." Church was surprised that Borah's picture was not hanging on the wall alongside those of others who had chaired the committee. When Marcy explained that the hanging of the pictures started after Borah, Church volunteered to provide a photograph of Idaho's former senator. According to Marcy, Church then added wistfully, "Maybe someday I'll be there."[43]

When Church joined the Foreign Relations Committee he was particularly anxious about the testing of nuclear weapons. A few months earlier, on October 31, 1958, a gathering in Geneva, Switzerland, had raised hopes of a test ban. The Conference on the Discontinuance of Nuclear Weapons Tests had brought together representatives from the United States, Great Britain, and the Soviet Union. It had quickly reached an impasse, however, raising the possibilities of renewed testing. Already in 1958, before a temporary moratorium went into effect, the three major nuclear powers had exploded at least sixty-three nuclear bombs—almost half as many as in the previous thirteen years. The threatened resumption of tests ignited a full-scale debate within the Eisenhower administration and on Capitol Hill between advocates and opponents of a test ban.[44]

Church quickly emerged as a strong proponent of a limited test ban. On February 25 he wrote to Acting Secretary of State Christian Herter urging that the United States offer a last-ditch proposal in Geneva to halt at least atmospheric tests. The Geneva talks had bogged down over the means of policing underground testing, so Church hoped it was still possible to prohibit atmospheric tests through some kind of international control system. On March 2 he presented this idea to the Senate, with the strong support of Mike Mansfield, J. William Fulbright of Arkansas, Joseph Clark, and Ernest Gruening. Time was running out, he warned. He doubted that the Soviets wanted a shooting war. The problem, instead, was that small conflicts might escalate into a nuclear catastrophe. Given this horrific prospect, it was essential to take a minimal first step toward international controls. His "eleventh hour proposal," as he called it, represented a middle position between Tennessee's Albert Gore, who had urged a three-year unilateral American ban on atmospheric testing of nuclear weapons, and a few senators who favored an immediate ban on all nuclear testing, below and above ground. Leaders of the newly-formed National Committee for a Sane Nuclear Policy (SANE) were unhappy with Church's recommendation, which they feared would divert attention from a comprehensive test ban. Church also wanted to stop all testing, but was convinced that a series of smaller steps was the only way to reach that goal and insisted that a compromise might save the Geneva talks.[45]

Columnist Drew Pearson claimed that Eisenhower's "vitally important note" to Nikita Khrushchev in late April bore Church's imprint. The letter basically followed Church's recommendations in calling for an agreement that would end atmospheric tests. According to Pearson, the president's communication had captured the headlines, but the real credit belonged to Idaho's junior senator. "The unassuming baby member of the Senate" had maneuvered quietly behind the scenes, pressuring the State Department. Consequently, in the words of the *Christian Science Monitor,* it was Church's plan that was "now offered by the West." *Newsweek* columnist Ernest K. Lindley described the Church approach as attractive on all fronts: it was a valid idea in its own right; it placed the United States on the diplomatic offensive; it addressed the issue of atmospheric pollution; and it outlined a strategy that would be relatively easy to police.[46]

Pearson and others may have conceded too much influence to Church. The senator was not alone in pressuring the administration for a Geneva initiative that would ban atmospheric tests. John McCone of the Atomic Energy Commission and a March 6 preliminary report from a presidential panel of scientists offered much the same recommendation. Still, Church helped to make the point.[47]

Unlike some of the other advocates of a limited ban, however, Church was less concerned with Soviet duplicity than with the dangers of nuclear fallout. Reports in early 1959 of increased radioactivity stirred new fears of nuclear testing's dangers to public health. By spring SANE and other groups sponsored public protests. At a SANE rally in Brooklyn, for example, Nobel Prize-winning scientist Linus Pauling warned that a hundred thousand children faced death from higher levels of strontium-90. Frank Church added his voice to the outcry. In April he pleaded in *The Reporter*, a liberal journal, that "we must stop poisoning the air." If negotiations over nuclear testing failed, the "invisible rain" of radiation would become ever more lethal. Writing separately to his Idaho constituents, Church warned grimly of recent news that the presence of strontium-90 in some Minnesota wheat and Dakota milk had reached alarming levels.[48]

Although a Soviet-U. S. agreement to ban atmospheric tests was not yet attainable, Church was already in the Senate vanguard on that critical issue. He addressed vigorously the dangers of atmospheric pollution, the escalation of armaments, and the threat of nuclear war, "with the end of man coming ignominiously through vomiting fits from radiation." In early 1959 *The Atlantic* placed him among "that little band of senators, including Humphrey and Gore, who pay some attention to disarmament." On February 11, 1960 Senator Mansfield pointed out how closely a new State Department proposal on ending further nuclear tests—in space, the atmosphere, and the oceans—resembled Church's suggestions to Secretary Herter several days previously. Mansfield described Church as "brilliant," and complimented the administration for accepting his advice.[49]

While Church pressed the case for arms control, he also took the lead in limiting U. S. military assistance to Latin America. On May 28, 1959 he submitted three amendments to the pending Mutual Security Act. The first proposed to lift some of the secrecy from U. S. military aid to Latin America. In forceful language, Church described such secrecy "as an affront to the whole philosophy of a free society." He objected to subordinating "the people's right to know to the desire of bureaucracy to avoid embarrassment or harassment." Indeed, he believed that secrecy usually had more to do with concealing "bad judgment, incompetence, and corruption" than with protecting national security. His second amendment cut the administration's proposed military assistance program to Latin America by almost $30 million, holding it at existing levels. Church argued that expanded military aid lacked grassroots support in Latin America and was not necessary for U. S. security. His third amendment stipulated that military assistance to Latin America should protect the U. S., not meet the "internal security" needs of the recipient countries. Church was worried, as he phrased it several weeks later, about arming "military dictators against their own people." Ernest Gruening and Oregon's Wayne Morse especially appreciated Church's attack on excessive government secrecy. In Gruening's estimation, it helped to signal "that the time has come for Congress to reassert its prerogatives" regarding foreign appropriations.[50]

Church's amendments survived the Senate debates and the conference agreement with the House, ending up in late July on Eisenhower's desk for the president's signature. One newspaper carried the headline, "Sen. Church's Big Week." The accompanying article marveled that he had just turned thirty-five.[51]

A year later Church attempted to place a lid on the military assistance program as a whole. He offered an amendment to reduce the administration's request by 10 percent, thereby keeping the program at its existing level. Already, he said, the United States was sending military aid "to 39 countries—to almost half the countries of the world." This tendency to use "military nostrums" for world problems threatened disaster. Church shuddered at the prospects of more and more weapons going to volatile countries in Africa, Asia, and the Near East. The United States was, in effect, contributing to an arms race that could only intensify problems between nations such as India and Pakistan. The Idaho senator emphasized that he had no quarrel with foreign aid itself. "I may be the first elected representative from my State ever to vote for foreign aid," he guessed, even though aid programs were assuredly not popular in Idaho. He objected to excessive military assistance, however. His was "a moderate amendment," he claimed, one he had purposely limited in order to gain its passage. This time, however, Church failed to get his way. The amendment failed, 32 to 27.[52]

VII

Midway through Church's first term, a mixture of orthodox Cold War assumptions and revisionist views thus continued to mark his thinking on foreign policy. Some of his more bellicose Cold War statements may have been for political effect. He was, for example, quick to blame only the Soviets for blocking an arms control agreement, even though the Eisenhower administration was badly divided on the issue, had repeatedly altered the U. S. position, and often seemed interested primarily in scoring public relations points. But criticism could hardly have opened the administration to Church's recommendations.[53]

Strategy aside, in basic ways Church was a typical Cold Warrior who believed the United States had avoided war with the Soviets only by holding the upper hand. He complained that the Eisenhower administration had lulled the nation to sleep with false assurances about American superiority. "The present danger," he told Arizona State University's graduating class in 1958, "is the danger we may lose the cold war." This was a war that Americans never wanted. Indeed, he said, "We resent it." But it was a cruel reality, and the free world was "on the defensive." With the launching of the Soviet space capsule Sputnik, "the Red Star has been catapulted aloft."[54]

In a Reno, Nevada, speech in 1959 Church pulled no punches: "Well I say it is time for America to wake up!" If Americans failed to recognize that they were in "a fateful duel with Russia," they would soon invite a Soviet attack. "Two ways of life are. . .contesting for supremacy," he told another audience in early 1960. "It is a mortal competition. . . .We will either *win* it or *lose* it. . . .They have seized a third of the world in 15 years!" Church worried that America's military strength was declining and the nation was "ill-prepared to fight brushfire wars—the kind that are most likely to occur." From this perspective, the developing nations in Africa and Asia were up for grabs. To yield ground in those areas to the Soviets would be to assure "eventual Communist dominion over all the world." According to Church, America waged the Cold War precisely to prevent such dominion. And he could not say with confidence that the United States was winning. Fidel Castro's takeover in Cuba, for example, had brought "a Communist beachhead" to within ninety miles of American shores.[55]

When Frank and Bethine Church visited the Soviet Union in late 1959 they found the experience chilling. On a rainy Sunday they filed past the glass-covered sarcophaguses of Lenin and Stalin, on display in what the senator described as a "pagan mausoleum which is the Cathedral of World Communism." They attended a church service in which only a few old people were present, and they predicted that within a decade the church would no longer exist. They were appalled at the enforced conformity, "the 'organization man' carried to the ultimate extreme," as Church described it–"an *ant society* in human form." Moscow depressed them as "a mustard colored city of massive monotony–the stores, the merchandise, the apartment houses, all bear the stamp of the state upon them." The Churches came away from the Soviet Union reminded of what they detested about communism: its atheism, its authoritarianism, and its aggressiveness. It was, in Church's words, "tyranny in a red cloak."[56]

As he moved into the 1960s, Church thus believed that America's large defense expenditures were not the product of unwarranted hysteria. "The Communists now control the lives of more than one billion people," he wrote, "and they don't seem to be showing any signs of letting up in their determination to dominate the world." Nor was the United States threatened simply from outside its borders. "I suggest to you," he warned a Pennsylvania audience, "that the greatest totalitarian triumphs of the Twentieth Century have come from within the countries" themselves.[57]

Although Church echoed fundamental Cold War assumptions, he nevertheless qualified them substantially when he looked at the revolutionary ferment in Africa, Asia, and the Middle East. Convinced that anti-colonialism, not sympathy for communism, was the driving force in those regions, he believed the U. S. needed to help emerging countries by encouraging domestic reforms, rather than by propping up dictators who were supposedly America's allies. At a minimum, he argued, American ambassadors should be able to empathize with "the poor and the average citizens," not just the wealthy, social elites.[58]

Church also warned against rigid thinking when dealing with the Soviet Union and other nations. He worried about efforts to impose grand conceptual schemes upon a messy world. Progress in foreign relations came "fitfully, in little steps." Abstractions, such as "liberation" or "massive retaliation," too often ended up buried under historical realities.[59]

Invariably, Church cast his lot with reasonability, civility, and the power of education. He feared that an obsession with national security was already jeopardizing American freedoms. "If we must prepare endlessly for total war," he admonished one audience, "we must be prepared, ultimately, for total government!" When he discussed the threat to America from within its own borders, he did not focus on spy rings or enemy collaborators or critics of the United States. That was the error, he believed, of Joseph McCarthy's followers. As "zealous patriots waving the Stars and Stripes," they would destroy freedom in order to save it. Church, ever the civil libertarian, believed firmly in open discussion. That was one reason why he championed a broad education in the liberal arts. "Freedom can live and grow only in intimate association with the humanities," he said. "Do not trifle with the humanities, for to do so is to strike at freedom in its most vulnerable place." Good education encouraged creative thinking, not conformity. For a democracy to survive, it needed independent-minded people who could govern themselves. For Church, education's primary purpose was to enlarge understanding. "An educated person must always be, by definition, a foe of intolerance and bigotry." He worried that the Cold War imperiled American education by encouraging censorship, loyalty oaths, anti-intellectualism, and an overemphasis on purely technical and scientific training.[60]

VIII

Church's concerns about anti-intellectualism and his absorption with foreign policy matters did not necessarily count for much among his constituents, however. The senator took great pride in his position on the Foreign Relations Committee. But, as staff director Carl Marcy once observed, the public tended to think that its members spend their time flying "from world capital to world capital and forget their domestic constituency." Idaho was far from immune to such perceptions. In 1960 a Louis Harris poll documented strong isolationist sentiments in the state as well as "resentment against centralized government because it is necessarily enmeshed with foreign affairs." An Idaho attorney warned Church that the state's residents were interested primarily in domestic matters. Carl Burke thus urged his old friend to devote more newsletter space to local issues, less to foreign policy.[61]

Hoping to be more than another one-term Democratic senator from Idaho, Church deliberately adopted a strategy which, according to Ward Hower, focused "attention on his appearance, his personality, his decency, his reasonableness." He made sure that his staff was extremely attentive to constituent requests, complaints, and general correspondence.

Letters from his office invariably had a personal touch, and many reflected a painstaking effort to address all of the points that constituents raised. Church himself helped to monitor the correspondence. "Please redo this letter. Tone it down," he advised Carver at one point, after the administrative assistant had drafted a curt reply to a religious bigot. "Just because it makes you mad, John, there's no use making him mad. He lacks your tolerance, but that's a common failing." Years later an aging, white-bearded man spoke emotionally about how Church had several times assisted him when "the bureaucracy didn't bureau." "God, how I loved that man," he added with a choking voice.[62]

When Frank and Bethine Church returned periodically to Idaho they assiduously sought out local residents. Early on, he started a regular series of courthouse tours which took him for at least a full day to each county seat in the state. He talked with anyone who showed up. Bethine was "just absolutely fabulous" on the stump, according to staffer Tommie Ward. "That woman could just charm the birds off the trees." She would "set down and talk to farmers' wives about anything: legislation, what was happening, children, recipes—you name it."[63]

One of the senator's favorite grassroots strategies was to deliver high school commencement speeches. Always his most effective when giving a set speech, he could make well-rehearsed and oft-delivered lines seem extemporaneous. "When the commencement speeches were over and you walked out with parents," recalled Ward Hower, "you heard them talking about what a wonderful man he was, not about issues" or his political affiliation. Church's messages typically celebrated the pleasures of Idaho—the joys of fishing in cold, mountain streams, of backpacking, of sleeping under the stars. He also articulated things that, in Hower's words, "parents wished they knew how to say to their kids about old-fashioned virtues, hard work. . . how to make something of their lives." His appearance was as eloquent as his words. His well-shined shoes, his neatly combed hair, his boyish good looks, his nicely fitted suit invariably made a good impression, offering a model of proper conduct and success. Certainly his presence made local people feel important, especially in small towns and schools where they typically felt ignored. Once, when he spoke to a graduating class of seven in a remote valley town in central Idaho, people drove as far as fifty miles from their sheep and cattle ranches to hear him.[64]

Church's commencement speeches were legendary, even among his colleagues. Frank Moss guessed that Church's graduation addresses, sometimes as many as three in a day, had a powerful impact on "those little communities. He was the big senator, and a handsome guy that came in and made a great speech.... It stood him in good stead, even though he was more liberal than the general populace out there."[65]

While Church stood politically to the left of many of his constituents, he shrewdly avoided getting on the wrong side of highly charged issues such as gun control or regulations on farm labor. He refused in 1959, for example, to identify himself too openly with efforts to protect farm workers. He accepted John Carver's advice that the cause of migrant workers might evoke his "humanitarian considerations" but "would stir up an awful hornet's nest in Idaho." Similarly, when Michigan's Pat McNamara tried to apply child labor laws to farms (excluding children who worked on their own families' property), Church agreed with Carver and Ward Hower: the legislation might be a good idea, but he should not be one of the sponsors.[66]

At every opportunity he portrayed himself, in contrast to the Republican administration, as the true defender of Idaho's interests. He had to be somewhat careful in this respect, however. As one friend warned him, Eisenhower was almost a protected species in the state. Although the president was well-liked in Idaho, residents were nonetheless uneasy with the state's stagnant economy and the rising cost of living. This provided Church with an opening.[67]

Time and again he reminded his constituents that he was aware of the state's problems in mining, timber, and agriculture. In his newsletter he recounted the sad joke of the farmer who kept buying and selling hammers at $3 apiece. "You don't make any money doing that," noted a storekeeper. "I know," said the farmer, "but it beats farming!" In the Senate, Church criticized the administration's farm program as "a monumental failure" and joined Minnesota Democrat Hubert Humphrey in sponsoring the "Food for Peace Act." The idea behind Food for Peace was to export surplus agricultural goods to starving people around the world, thereby helping American farmers as well as countering the hunger and despair that encouraged communism. In a Senate speech which he mailed to constituents, Church expressed the frustration of farmers who did not wish "to be driven to a city job," and who, at the same time, did not like subsidies that paid them for not farming. "There is a nagging reproach," he contended, "in the sight of sun and rain falling unheeded on fields left barren of seed."[68]

Although local issues like agriculture did not especially appeal to Church, he could not ignore them. He doggedly watched out for Idaho's economic interests. Sometimes he engaged in clever public relations gambits. In early 1960, for example, he poked fun at the idea of a congressional "pork barrel," and at the same time scored some points for his state's limping mining industry. He sent each senator a small paperweight, in the form of a pig, from the Bunker Hill Company in north Idaho. "Remember," he said, "it is a symbol of a weighty problem confronting the mining states of our country." On other occasions, he sought immediate results. Thus in the late Fifties he cooperated with the state's senior senator, Republican Henry Dworshak, in arranging for public hearings to keep open a Pocatello naval ordnance plant that employed almost 450 people. He supported a small subsidy program for mining, which Eisenhower vetoed. To help Idaho's lumber industry he co-sponsored legislation that directed the Small Business Administration to earmark some timber sales for smaller companies. And he opposed temporary excise taxes placed on freight and passenger service. He disliked such taxes in principle but also, as he remarked in the Senate, because they discriminated against remote states, such as Idaho: the farther the goods traveled, the higher the tax.[69]

IX

Although Church conscientiously defended the interests of his constituents, he remained convinced that he needed to develop a reputation of being larger than the issues if he hoped to win a second term. Otherwise, Idaho's political history and the growing number of Republican voters might be too much to overcome. The larger his shadow, the more he might stir grassroots pride, just as Borah had done for so many years.[70]

As early as 1958 he thus started campaigning actively to be the keynote speaker at the 1960 Democratic convention. As Carver said, this was a way of "getting a national reputation working toward his own reelection." Television coverage of the 1956 political conventions had captured public attention, suggesting that the role of keynoter could provide enormous national exposure. Harry Wall, Idaho's representative on the National Democratic Committee and one of Church's closest Idaho allies, emphasized this point when he recommended that Church deliver the 1960 address. Wall reminded the head of the national committee, Paul M. Butler, that Idaho had never reelected a Democrat to the Senate. But if Church could become nationally well-known, like Borah, he might gain a second term. "Idahoans remember the Borah tradition," Wall argued, "and national recognition accorded to Frank represents his best chance for breaking the jinx and winning in 1962." Idaho newspaper editor Bill Johnston observed that even rumors about Idaho's junior senator as the keynoter had in themselves enhanced his reputation.[71]

National columnist William S. White believed that the Democrats might choose Church, in part because they needed to pick up support in the western states. White, a long-time Senate observer, described him as "perhaps the most widely respected of the young Democrats of the Senate—for general ability, for fairmindedness and. . .for oratorical powers." Moreover, according to White, Church would present a good television image of youthful vigor, which was exactly what the Democrats wanted; and he was not himself linked to any of the presidential candidates.[72]

White's last point was crucial. Church had to appear nonpartisan. He could not afford to antagonize any of the Democratic presidential aspirants. By October 1959 John Kennedy had become "very interested" in Church's delivering the keynote address. Church could not, however, align himself with the Kennedy candidacy lest he anger Lyndon Johnson, who also had his eye on the White House. "Oh man, that was the greatest tightrope walk in history," laughed John Carver, when he recalled Church's effort to move between Kennedy and Johnson.[73]

Privately, Church favored Kennedy. Kennedy's Idaho contact, Robert Wallace, passed the word along to the Massachusetts senator, indicating that "Church has said he can take no public stand now because he is running for Keynoter." Wallace sensed that Church did "not want to antagonize Lyndon Johnson, yet." Church successfully walked the tightrope. He and Carver suspected that the Kennedy people had much to do with Church's eventual selection as the convention's keynoter. Johnson, in turn, apparently offered no opposition because he assumed the Idaho senator was in his camp.[74]

Church, however, doubted that Johnson could win a national election. And he worried that the Texan, despite his formidable abilities, knew far too little about international questions. Kennedy, in contrast, "thoroughly understands our predicament abroad." Church's appreciation for the Massachusetts senator went back at least to 1956, when

Kennedy had campaigned in Idaho on his behalf. On Capitol Hill the two senators had teamed up in opposition to loyalty oaths and in favor of many kinds of legislation. Church believed that Kennedy's last three years in the Senate had been "brilliant," and he was confident that Kennedy would make an outstanding president.[75]

When Church flew to Los Angeles in mid-1960 to deliver his party's keynote speech, he was thus already primed for the "New Frontier." Indeed, he had used that very terminology himself over two years earlier when speaking to a meeting of Young Democrats. In Los Angeles, however, his audience would be much larger than a non-televised gathering of Young Democrats. "I worried for six months about not getting to make this keynote address," he wrote his brother just before the Democratic convention, "and now I'm worrying about having to make it!" He had wanted to be "out front." Soon he would get his wish.[76]

Church delivering keynote address at the 1960 Democratic convention. *Courtesy Boise State University.*

Chapter Six
The New Frontier: 1960-1963

When Frank and Bethine Church arrived at Los Angeles International Airport on July 6, 1960 with their four-year-old son Chase, they had every reason to smile. They had exchanged eastern heat and humidity for a glorious California day, the sky a brilliant blue and the temperature in the mid-70s. Clearly, the Churches enjoyed their celebrity status. Cameras clicked as the press turned out to greet the young senator who, in five days, would open the Democratic convention. He told reporters he had finished writing the speech the day before and that all the candidates would find it acceptable. Actually, he had been practicing the speech for weeks and, as Bethine later observed, it was almost as if he had written it with John Kennedy's candidacy in mind.[1]

Temperamentally and ideologically, he was already a Kennedy partisan. For the next several years he identified strongly with the crisis-oriented, activist approach of Kennedy's New Frontier and talked enthusiastically about a "new liberalism." That new liberalism, for Church as well as for Kennedy, nonetheless contained much that was old, especially concerning the Cold War. Like Kennedy, the Idaho senator believed the Soviets were testing the United States and that the U. S. needed to shake itself from the Eisenhower doldrums and rise to the challenge. But, also like Kennedy, he displayed a willingness to measure Cold War tenets against what he was discovering about the world. This flexibility was particularly true regarding Africa, where in late 1960 he witnessed confrontations between nationalism and colonialism, as well as between grassroots movements and autocratic regimes. His capacity to change was also evident when he approached a domestic issue such as the environment. Despite the political risks in Idaho, he supported wilderness legislation. His role in 1961 as floor manager of the controversial wilderness bill, along with his political alliance with Kennedy's New Frontier, provided the backdrop against which he sought a second Senate term.

I

In mid-1960, however, Church was understandably preoccupied with his upcoming keynote address. Spurning help from his staff, he had labored on the speech for months, revising and rehearsing it endlessly. His secretary guessed that she had typed at least three dozen versions of it. Through an adjoining wall, Minnesota senator Eugene McCarthy heard Church holding forth in his office again and again. McCarthy kept thinking that no one should practice a speech that much. But Church was determined that the address would be a real barn burner, reminiscent of William Jennings Bryan's famed "Cross of Gold" speech in 1896.[2]

He also hoped to awaken the nation to the perils facing it. Despite his cheerful demeanor when he arrived in Los Angeles, he was genuinely anxious about the state of the union. "All is not well in the world for the United States," he wrote a friend shortly before the convention. "Unless we have the gumption to face up to the hard truths, we may be headed toward catastrophe." America's problems, he said, were internal as well as external. Too many citizens were smug and self-satisfied, oblivious to their own country's growing social problems and the misery of other nations. Church viewed the 1960 election as a watershed event, crucial to the U. S. and the world. America, he was convinced, desperately needed new leadership and a new agenda.[3]

Headlines in mid-1960 conveyed a sense of building crises. News of Soviet belligerence, troubles in Fidel Castro's Cuba, and violent upheaval in Africa provided daily reminders of a dangerous and rapidly changing environment. "The world is living on a banana peel," a New Jersey pipefitter's spouse told pollster Samuel Lubell. Columnist James Reston believed the United States was experiencing a profound political shift as it moved from "the old Model-T" world of earlier days to "the Jupiter-C political rocketry of the 60s." Church agreed with these assessments, as his speech made clear.[4]

Despite his high hopes, his keynote address turned out to be a nightmarish experience. For one thing, the pressure to do well was immense. "Expect Church to Wow Dems," read a *Los Angeles Times* headline. The accompanying story promised that he would "revive the lost art of keynoting." At the Sports Arena, the convention site, an unprecedented electronic blitz awaited him. The three television networks had about a thousand people on hand. NBC alone had thirty-two cameras; CBS had twenty-eight more, plus eighty-two microphones.

The estimated TV audience ranged from seventy to ninety-two million. Understandably, before Church left for the convention hall on the afternoon of July 11, he was too nervous to eat.[5]

When he delivered the keynote address, however, his nervousness quickly gave way to frustration. The audience was relatively sparse and rudely inattentive. As Church looked across the sprawling arena, he saw many empty seats and people milling around. With the exception of the Idaho delegation, most of the delegates on the floor were more interested in the carnival spirit of the convention than in listening to him. "The noise down there was crazy," recalled journalist John Corlett, "just crazy. . . . It was just god awful. I don't know how he stood it, really." The discourteous behavior infuriated Carl Burke. Then he relaxed somewhat, noting that Church seemed to be focusing on the TV cameras, aiming his remarks at the millions of viewers outside the hall.[6]

While Church tried to concentrate on his television audience, he kept encountering technical difficulties on the platform. One problem concerned the three teleprompters, new to a political convention. Church did not wish to use them, but they were operating anyhow, scrolling his sentences on the screens. Whenever he made adjustments in his speech, the operator quickly rolled the script forward and backward, trying to find the place. One distraction led to another. The huge platform on which Church stood was multi-decked and included a device that adjusted each speaker's height to a uniform 11 feet, 4 inches above the floor. When the teleprompter operator decided that Church was having difficulty reading from the screens, he began to elevate and lower the platform. Church was agonizingly aware of the whirring gears, the rolling words on the screen, the moving platform, and the noisy arena. He struggled on, trying to keep the TV viewers in mind.[7]

He spoke alarmingly of both domestic and foreign crises. First, he discussed the "urgent needs at home," needs the Eisenhower administration had left "untreated like festering sores." These included the rising cost of living, the spreading slums in America's "rotting cities," the increase in juvenile delinquency, and the troubles besieging farmers and small entrepreneurs. The Republicans had offered nothing more than "a pitch-man prosperity. . . run by hucksters." By what rationale, he wondered, could the nation spend more money on alcohol and tobacco than on public education? "To sweeten private life, our stores display a billion bottles of deodorant, yet a modest bill to reduce the stench from our polluted public rivers was vetoed." Gesturing with both hands, he asked: "Are we to become a modern Babylon of public want amidst private glut?"[8]

Focusing the second half of his speech on foreign policy, he delivered a ringing Cold War call to arms. Contrasting America's "showcase of Democracy" with the expanding "Red Empire," he contended that nothing less than "the fate of Western civilization is at stake." He warned that, "if we yield Europe, Asia and Africa to the Communists, the balance of power will fatally shift against us, thus assuring eventual Communist dominion of all the world." He claimed that the U. S. lagged behind in the "mortal competition" between freedom and communism. He asserted that America was slipping in scientific knowledge and military strength. And he accused the Republicans of simply scowling while "the Communists have seized a third of the world in fifteen years!" Stridently, he declared that the American people did not want to replace Theodore Roosevelt's old adage, "Walk softly and carry a big stick," with "Talk tough and carry a toothpick." Only "an awakened and rededicated America," he concluded, could "make history's verdict ours."[9]

Church's conclusion provided the opportunity for the convention's first floor demonstration. It lasted about five minutes. The Idaho delegation led a parade and waved placards, "Idaho is Proud of Frank Church." Someone handed him a large Idaho potato.[10]

Overall, however, his address had been a big disappointment. "It was like a caricature of a speech," recalled Idaho journalist Sam Day. "It just fell flat as a pancake." Day remembered one network television commentator joking afterward that Church resembled singer Pat Boone ready to burst into song. Columnist David Broder later dubbed the speech an embarrassment, a "rhetorical, arm-waving" effort that summoned up images of Claghorn, the blowhard politician in the Li'l Abner comic strip. Eugene McCarthy was somewhat more charitable, but believed Church's oratory raised "too much sail, more sail than the ship can carry." Even the senator's close friends and staffers realized that Church had not enjoyed one of his finer moments. He had been histrionic, stilted, forced. Verda Barnes watched the speech on TV with Harry Wall, Idaho's National Democratic Committee representative. At one point they gave each other discouraged looks and shrugged helplessly.[11]

Church knew he had not done well. "All I can say in my defense," he said much later, "is I didn't know any better." He concluded ultimately that he had squandered a great opportunity and set his political career back by perhaps ten years.[12]

At the time, however, he was unwilling to dub his effort a failure. The reaction from the Kennedys was positive. Immediately after the speech, he learned that he had impressed Joseph Kennedy and his guest, the publisher Henry Luce. The information came from Ted Kennedy, who seemed to agree. Subsequently, when Church was leaving the Biltmore Hotel, someone hailed him, "Frank! Frank!" It was John Kennedy. The Massachusetts senator had stopped his car in the middle of the street to congratulate him. While the police frantically tried to deal with backed-up traffic, JFK waited for Church to get into the auto. Kennedy told him that Luce had not only liked his speech, but had also asked why Church had not previously gotten more attention. Over the next few days the Idaho senator was surprised at how many people recognized him. In restaurants, on sidewalks, at the beach, they greeted him and asked for his autograph. He marveled at television's power to provide such status. Certain that "we never have known anything before quite like it," he predicted that TV would determine the outcome of the 1960 election.[13]

After the keynote address Church no longer had to mask his preference for John Kennedy's candidacy. He and Bethine guessed later that his endorsement of JFK shocked Lyndon Johnson, who still hoped to receive the nomination. As Church admitted, LBJ had been his "benefactor" in the Senate and had every reason to expect his support in Los Angeles. In recent months, Johnson had praised him effusively. During a Foreign Relations Committee meeting he had handed him a note predicting that Church was going to accomplish great things and might even become president some day. In 1960, however, Johnson wanted that position for himself. He shrugged off Kennedy's pre-convention lead, saying that it would not hold up beyond the second ballot. To Johnson's chagrin, Church was among the people who climbed on JFK's bandwagon.[14]

The day after the keynote speech, Church urged the Idaho delegation to back Kennedy. He fared less well than he had hoped. Several delegates strongly favored LBJ. At the last moment, Church at least persuaded them to postpone a straw vote on the presidential candidates. Political editor John Corlett guessed that Church's prestige would suffer if he could not unify the Idaho delegation around Kennedy.[15]

On July 13, Kennedy and Johnson made separate appeals to the Idaho people in Church's Biltmore Hotel suite. Kennedy told them that any candidate could run and win on Church's keynote address. He then spoke briefly about his commitment to developing the state's natural resources. When Johnson made his appearance, the room was thick with tension. Church introduced him as "the greatest majority leader the Democratic party has ever had." Ignoring any reference to Johnson's presidential qualities, Church praised the Texan for his personal help and friendship. Johnson's response was cool. Stepping onto a coffee table to address the delegation, he said that he had endorsed Church as the keynoter at a time when the Idahoan was not the frontrunner for that honor. Glaring at Church, he reminded the delegates that no Democratic senator had been reelected in Idaho. He hoped in 1962 to campaign for Church, but he wanted to do so as president. Moreover, as president he would be able to help Idaho because the state had more in common with Texas than with Massachusetts. When Johnson talked privately with several of the delegates, he was bitter about Church. "Who does that little pipsqueak think he is?" LBJ asked. "After all, I made him and now he's biting the hand that fed him."[16]

After the candidates had met with the Idaho delegation, Church pleaded Kennedy's case on grounds that JFK had a better chance of winning the election. His plea was unsuccessful. Several delegates were openly resentful, refusing to give in to Church, despite his status as senator and the convention's keynoter. When the Idahoans cast their first ballots a few hours later, they were badly divided. Six votes went to Kennedy, four-and-a-half to Johnson. Missouri senator Stuart Symington picked up two votes, and two-time presidential nominee Adlai Stevenson got half a vote. Despite his failure to win a majority of the Idaho delegation, Kennedy became the Democrat's presidential candidate on the first ballot. Johnson subsequently received the vice-presidential nomination.[17]

That fall Church campaigned actively for the Democratic ticket in a dozen states, from Massachusetts to Oregon. He canvassed Idaho, guardedly optimistic that Kennedy might overcome what seemed to be a slight edge for his opponent, Richard M. Nixon. Kennedy barely won the election, but without Idaho's help.[18]

Idaho remained Republican territory. Nixon carried the state by a comfortable margin, Senator Henry Dworshak won another term, and both branches of the state legislature contained slight GOP majorities. The governor was still Republican Robert E. Smylie, who had not been up for reelection.

The Democrats were not without hope, however. Ralph Harding, a thirty-one-year-old attorney, captured the House seat of Republican Hamer Budge, who had served ten years. Gracie Pfost, very popular in the northern First District, won a fifth congressional term. And Church's office came up with some encouraging statistics: the 46 percent of the vote that Kennedy received in Idaho represented a 12 percent jump over Adlai Stevenson's showing in 1952.[19]

An influential Idaho Democrat nevertheless had a cautionary message for Church. Lloyd Walker, an original Church volunteer who would soon chair the state party, advised him not to identify too closely with Kennedy-style Democrats. There was simply too much suspicion of the East among the state's rural population. According to Walker, Kennedy and his people had "very little in common with Gustav Schultz who raises beets on the south forty." Kennedy's Idaho backers, including Walker himself, tended to be "either the city type or the smart aleck college type in the eyes of the old dirt scratcher." Walker feared that Church, if he were not careful, might fall victim to the wide cultural gap that separated the New Frontier's eastern, urban, Ivy League ilk from the life styles of rural Idaho.[20]

II

Church did not immediately see Walker's letter, however, because on November 16 he and Bethine commenced a dizzying five-week tour of Africa that covered more than twenty-two thousand miles. He was the Foreign Relations Committee representative on a Senate study group that included Utah's Frank Moss and Wyoming's Gale McGee. Ted Kennedy, the president-elect's brother, joined them for part of the trip.

When Frank and Bethine departed the nation's capital on a crystal clear morning in mid-November, they headed for a continent in massive flux. During the past eleven months, seventeen African nations had won independence and there was talk about 1960 as the "Year of Africa." For some time Church had predicted the shattering of Europe's empires. Now he had an opportunity to see firsthand vast sections of that post-colonial world.[21]

After a two-day stopover in Spain he was even more inclined to view the African independence movements with sympathy. A cold drizzle added to his gloomy sense of President Francisco Franco's oppressive Spanish government. He learned from a U. S. reporter that Franco was deliberately avoiding the visiting senators, partly because he was angry that Church's speech at the Democratic convention had mentioned him as a dictatorial ruler. Church left Spain more convinced than ever that the U. S. had made a mistake by backing Franco.[22]

Almost symbolically, the weather brightened when the Americans left Spain. They flew over the Rock of Gibraltar and landed several hours later under a brilliant sun in Morocco. For the next four weeks they moved through a world of stunning geographic and economic contrasts—a world in the throes of one of the great modern political transformations. In Morocco, Church fell ill and when he reached Egypt was too sick to visit the Aswan Dam or the pyramids. The group flew next over incredibly barren terrain into Ethiopia, which Church characterized sadly as a "feudal state." His mood improved when he entered the lovely uplands of Kenya. "Kenya is the first African country I have left without a feeling of depression," he wrote. Tanganyika kept him in good humor, despite the heat and mosquitoes. He found Chief Minister Julius Nyerere "the most impressive African leader I have yet met." Southern Rhodesia, with its sprawling black ghettos and segregation, was a dreary place—"a symbol of white domination of the Africans." In the highlands a carload of young blacks shouted "Freedom!" at the Americans.[23]

On December 5 the Americans circled over majestic Victoria Falls, taking aerial photographs of the mile-wide river plunging 350 feet down sheer cliffs. A few hours later they were in the conflict-riddled Congo, an area in which the new and the old jostled for position, with a nuclear reactor only minutes away from primitive mud huts. They moved on to Nigeria and Togo, where the heat and humidity seemed almost unbearable; then to Ghana, where they swam in a powerful surf along a lovely, palm-lined beach, visited the Volta Dam site, and talked to a political opponent of Marxist president Kwame Nkrumah; and then to the Ivory Coast, where they enjoyed cooler temperatures, rides through dense rain forests, and a dinner performance that, according to Moss, resembled a Cecil DeMille Hollywood production.[24]

In Liberia they learned that the United States had abstained from supporting a United Nations resolution calling for an end to colonialism. "Cannot understand such an abstention," Church jotted in his diary. "Resolution passed 89-0. We joined with the notorious dictators,

Spain, Portugal, South Africa." Stunned and discouraged, he wrote, "If we don't wake up soon, all of Africa will slip away." A question nagged at him as the group entered the last five days of the trip, traveling to Mali, Guinea, and the Senegal. Was the United States going to end up on the wrong side of one of the great struggles of history? Huge amounts of American aid to Africa would be meaningless if the U. S. failed "to take sides with the Africans on the *colonial issue*. It is here where friend and foe are first separated in the African mind."[25]

Just before Christmas, the Churches returned to the United States. The trip had been frantic, including twenty-five stops in sixteen African nations. But the senators had learned a great deal. Moss was certain that "nothing can now stem the tide of freedom and independence." Church concurred. Many Africans had told him that they hoped the new U. S. president would alter American foreign policy, aligning it more with the independence movements. "If he doesn't," Church predicted grimly, "the reaction will be dangerously adverse."[26]

Like Church, John Kennedy very much recognized the need for a new African policy. Indeed, he had asked the Idaho senator to make the trip. Both men disliked America's implied endorsement of European rule. The Eisenhower administration, except for a brief flurry in its last two years, had not been particularly sympathetic to the independence movements, worrying more about what it called "the new imperialism" of the Soviets than about old-style colonialism. Former Secretary of State John Foster Dulles had criticized the emerging nations for their declarations of diplomatic neutrality; he believed they were in fact moving toward communism. But even after Dulles's death, the Eisenhower administration had rejected the United Nations resolution advocating an end to colonialism. In contrast, the Kennedy administration sought quickly to demonstrate its interest in African nationalism, its respect for neutralism, and its willingness to disassociate the United States from European imperialism. Despite these intentions, Cold War anti-communism proved a strong vice from which to pry America's African policies. The need to maintain a united front with western European nations against the Soviets imposed its own imperatives. Again and again, Cold War diplomacy dictated the administration's African policy.[27]

Frank Church also had difficulty seeing Africa in terms other than those of the Cold War. In his travel notes he emphasized that the U. S. had to keep Africa "from being pulled behind the Iron and Bamboo curtains." Back in the United States he spoke ominously of the "Red Empire" trying to unfold its "red flag. . .from Cairo to Capetown" and imposing "a Red hammerlock" on the world.[28]

III

Mixed throughout Church's observations on Africa, however, was another theme, one that questioned the relevancy of the Cold War model for the emerging world. "We see the world as divided between two great contesting camps, the free nations against the communist nations," Church told an Idaho audience. "Africa sees the world divided between the 'haves' and the 'have-nots.' " In his African travel notes he repeatedly stressed the need to understand the perspectives of other nations. A statistic that especially bothered him showed that Americans and Canadians, who together constituted less than 10 percent of the world's people, reaped over two-thirds of the world's income. In Africa he had observed some of the remaining 90 percent of the population. Their plight was one of grinding poverty. Children wandered the streets with bellies bloated from malnutrition, bodies covered with running sores, and eyes whitening from trachoma. Church used a telling anecdote to dramatize his point before American audiences. He described Forrest's first visit to the Capitol. The youngster had roamed with him through the majestic rotunda and the marble hall and had eaten in the Senate dining room. When he subsequently climbed into the old family car to return home with his mother he asked, "Mommy, why is it that Daddy is so rich when we're so poor?" That kind of question, Church suggested, was exactly what the "have-nots" of Africa, Asia, the Middle East, and Latin America asked when they compared their poverty to the staggering wealth of the United States.[29]

Although Church still tended to place issues of poverty, disease, and hardship in a Cold War context, he became more and more aware that the East-West rivalry scarcely concerned millions of people. In his African notes he found great wisdom in Abraham Lincoln's advice: "We must disenthrall ourselves." Church applied this wisdom to the 1960s. Americans simply had to see the world from the perspectives of other people. In that spirit, Church attempted to understand the thinking of a pan-Arab revolutionary. He also told several American audiences that "Africa can be no one's prize. . .it belongs to Africa." The United States, he believed, should align itself with independence movements, such as Algeria's against France. He urged Americans to be tolerant of the emerging African nations. Most of these new countries, lacking private capital, would probably choose a socialist course. Moreover, their declarations of neutrality in the Cold War were hardly surprising. The United States had offered similar declarations during its formative years.[30]

Long-time Senate observer William S. White claimed that Church was falling into an isolationist trap, like William E. Borah earlier. In the 1930s Borah had inadvertently encouraged the German Nazis by opposing "entanglements" with "colonialist" Britain; in the 1960s Church was helping the Soviets by siding with Algerian revolutionaries against the French. "Will Church of Idaho, in his honest zeal, become the Borah of this generation?" White wondered. White hoped that Church would not weaken the cause of freedom against totalitarianism.[31]

Church's impassioned Senate speech on June 29, 1961 was an implicit response to White's criticism as well as an endorsement of Kennedy's African policies. The Idaho senator applauded the new administration's willingness to approach Africans on their own terms, independent of European needs. Unaware that the Central Intelligence Agency was fighting a covert war against the Congolese rebel Patrice Lumumba, he applauded JFK's "positive new policy toward Africa." He denied that it was foolish to sympathize with anti-colonial movements. The simple reality was that the era of Western colonialism had ended. "Should we," he asked, "now permit ourselves to be linked with it in its death agonies?" He disagreed that support of African independence would undermine the North Atlantic Treaty Organization (NATO), a bulwark against Soviet expansion in Europe. NATO, he argued, would prevail out of self-interest; there was no reason to make Africa its hostage.[32]

Although Church sometimes placed African independence in the context of America's struggle with the Soviets, he was more and more skeptical about a Cold War model of foreign policy. His letters and speeches indicated a growing suspicion that Cold War interpretations were too doctrinaire to fit the experiences of the people he had encountered in Africa. His evolving, sympathetic perspective contrasted sharply with popular treatments of the African upheavals. *Time* magazine, for example, portrayed the Belgian colonists as heroic civilizers, and even the *New York Times* depicted the Belgians as having "set out to substitute the carpenter's hammer for the tribal drum." The cartoonist of the *Indianapolis Star* showed Soviet premier Nikita Khrushchev in the jungle with savage-looking Africans. The caption read, "Bingo, Bango, Bongo, I Don't Want to Leave the Congo." Key U. S. policy makers, from the State Department to the CIA, all too often shared, and reenforced, these popular sentiments.[33]

By mid-1961 Church's growing skepticism about a Cold War-driven foreign policy departed markedly from most popular and official thinking. In a closed session of the Foreign Relations Committee he warned of impending doom in Iran, where Cold War policies had bound the United States ever closer to the iron-fisted Shah. "All I know about history," Church stated firmly, "says he is not long for this world, nor his system. And when he goes down, boom, we go down with him."[34]

Following his African trip, Church more than ever worried that American foreign policy was the prisoner of dangerous myths. He outlined these myths in a proposed article for the *New York Times Magazine*. Americans, he wrote, tended to believe that their own revolution of 1776 was transportable, and that their kind of democracy and economic development provided the logical script for other peoples. They thus overlooked the special characteristics of their own history, which ranged from the accessibility of natural resources to protective oceans. Americans also erroneously viewed the Cold War as a struggle between freedom and communism when, in fact, many of the nation's allies were dictatorships. All too often the United States ended up defending a "dying order of Shahs and Potentates" in the face of a "rising tide of internal revolution and reform." The overriding question, Church argued, was whether "a country grown conservative and content," like the U. S., could "make common cause with radical and violent upheavals elsewhere in the world." If Americans could not shake free of their myths about that world, they would stumble through endless disasters—"*including a dangerous over-commitment in Asia*."[35]

IV

When the editor of the *Times* magazine found the proposed article too long, Church volunteered to discuss another important topic, "Where are the liberal voices?" The senator was increasingly eager to champion liberalism in various public forums. For some time he had proudly described himself as a liberal—someone, he said, who believed ardently in civil liberties, supported government's role as a public servant, and tended to look "forward rather than to the past." The biographical sketch which his office released in mid-1960 indicated that he had "consistently supported and voted for liberal legislation." By the 1960s he advocated "a new birth of liberalism," a "genuine liberalism" that would help the elderly and the infirm while fighting social ills in the nation's decaying cities and elsewhere.[36]

In some respects, however, Church's liberalism drew more from the early twentieth century progressivism of a Borah than from post-World War II interest group pluralism. Like a good progressive, he invoked a communitarian ideal that elevated "the general interest above all special interests." In the spirit of a latter-day Borah or William Jennings Bryan or Woodrow Wilson he warned of "the scourge of giantism in business and politics." Perhaps remembering his father's modest business, he worried that small entrepreneurs were finding it ever harder to compete with huge corporations. He wanted to protect the independent merchants whose contacts with communities were more intimate than those of "a remote corporate hierarchy" or "organization men." One way to do this, he said, was to impose a graduated tax on corporate profits that gave "preferred treatment to small business."[37]

Church embraced a core liberal idea that had expanded over the course of the twentieth century: government should be a powerful force for economic and social good. The lesson that Church and other liberals drew from the Great Depression, World War II, and the emerging civil rights movement was that government, as an agent of the people, could solve problems. Government's duty was to protect citizens from economic adversity, enlarge opportunities, and ensure fairness.

An activist government was essential in Church's opinion, especially given the growing complexity of society. The senator told several dubious constituents that people courted disaster by expecting government to do nothing while the gap widened between "the privileged few and the rest of the population." He refuted arguments that an activist state would lead to communism. Indeed, he believed that a democratic government, responding to the people's needs, was "the best and perhaps the only defense against communism." Communism had triumphed in societies that were illiberal, not liberal. Americans, Church argued, should not fear the federal government as an "alien creature." Given the growth of the modern media, the central government was probably under greater scrutiny, and thus more responsive to grassroots needs, than many so-called local governments.[38]

Church's view of government undoubtedly placed him at odds with many of his more conservative constituents, but it helped him feel at home in John Kennedy's New Frontier. He shared the new administration's confidence in a practical, problem-solving approach and its determination to "get the nation moving again." He also appreciated its reliance on a new generation of political leaders, many of whom were his own age.

V

Kennedy had been in the White House only a short time when the phone rang in Church's office. A relatively new staff person asked who was calling. "The President," said a voice. "The president of what?" she inquired. There was a brief pause before the reply: "The United States." The staffer, finally realizing that John Kennedy was at the other end of the phone, hurriedly placed Church's secretary on the line. "I want to talk to Frank," Kennedy told her. She was unable to find him, however, until later that afternoon. When Church finally returned the call, he learned that Kennedy had wanted him to come to the White House that day for a private lunch. Terribly disappointed that he had missed the opportunity to talk with the president, Church berated his staff for not having tried harder to find him.[39]

The missed lunch in no way symbolized the communications between the Kennedy administration and Church, which were open and fairly close. Although the senator was not part of John Kennedy's inner circle, the White House people viewed him as a gifted, dependable ally. In turn, Church admired Kennedy greatly. Their relationships in the Senate had been comfortable and relaxed. After Kennedy became president, the contacts between them remained friendly, albeit more formal. Church told one staffer that once Kennedy became president it was no longer possible to think of him as "old Jack." In a very real sense, the Kennedy political mystique captivated Church. He liked not only John Kennedy, but also Robert, with whom he had worked on the McClellan Committee, as well as Ted, who had impressed him greatly on the African trip. Church identified strongly with the Kennedy brothers and in some respects patterned himself after them.[40]

The senator's confidence in the new administration muted his rare disagreements with the president's policies—during the 1961 Berlin crisis, for example. In mid-1961 that divided city again became a Cold War focal point. Nikita Khrushchev had described it as "the testicles of the West. When I want the West to scream, I squeeze in Berlin." In the summer of 1961 Kennedy feared that Khrushchev's renewed squeezing, in the form of a threat to limit access to the city, represented yet another test of American resolve. Khrushchev, in turn, hoped that East German control of all of Berlin would staunch the flow of refugees from east to west and codify the permanent division of Germany. On July 25 the president told the nation that "we cannot and will not permit the Communists to drive us out of Berlin." He called up military reserves, tripled the draft call, discussed the need for "fallout shelters in case of attack," and asked Congress for more defense money. Across the nation, anxieties about a possible nuclear war galvanized the construction of fallout shelters. Ironically, the walling off of East Berlin in mid-August eased tensions. "Why would Khrushchev put up a wall if he really intended to seize West Berlin?" Kennedy asked his aides. Privately, Kennedy conceded that "a wall is a hell of a lot better than a war." The wall represented a tacit compromise: Khrushchev had stopped the flight of refugees into West Berlin, and Kennedy had reasserted Western access to the city. For a few weeks in mid-1961, however, until the wall helped to calm the situation, a full-fledged crisis had existed.[41]

In the midst of the crisis, Church had the terrifying sense that events were rushing out of control. He left a July 17 meeting between Kennedy and a group of congressional leaders shaken and upset. Bryce Nelson, who drove him home afterwards, had never seen him look so distressed, pale, subdued. Finally, Church said quietly, "It is very chilling to hear the president of your country say, 'This bill [foreign aid] will be very useful to us next year, if there is a next year.' " Church was apprehensive that Kennedy and Khrushchev were engaged in a deadly face-off over a largely symbolic issue. Cold War rituals and expectations seemed to demand posturing and a tendency to see military force as the immediate answer to problems. Writing to Lester Markel of the *New York Times*, Church indicated the need to break from "current orthodoxy" when evaluating Berlin. But the national obsession with presenting a united front to the world limited discussion of foreign policy options. It also encouraged a tendency to brand dissenters as irresponsible or guilty of appeasement.[42]

Church's own experience several days later in the Senate illustrated the point. On August 16 he offered an amendment to restrict military aid to Western Europe. He considered foreign aid indispensable, but saw no reason for American taxpayers to subsidize nations strong enough to pay their own way. J. William Fulbright, chair of the Foreign Relations Committee, took the lead in rebuking Church for the timing of his proposal. "I violently object to the psychological effect this amendment would have at this time," said the Arkansas Democrat. With the Berlin crisis in mind, Fulbright objected to any action that might imply the U. S. was backing away from its European allies. The administration was also clearly against the proposal, which failed 22 to 70.[43]

On August 21 some of Church's frustrations spilled out in a conversation with United Nations ambassador Adlai Stevenson. After dinner at pollster Elmo Roper's home, the two men discussed the administration's decision to abstain on an upcoming United Nations resolution concerning Tunisia. Fighting had broken out in that north African nation when French troops refused to evacuate a naval base at Bizerte, a base the French continued to occupy even after granting Tunisia its independence. Thirty-two countries, mainly African and Asian, introduced a UN resolution denouncing French violation of Tunisian sovereignty. But the United States, unwilling to offend the French, was not going to vote for it. Church and Stevenson agreed that the U. S. abstention was wrong. Discouraged, Church told Bethine that "it looks like I got my speech in on 'Our New African Policy' just in time—while we still have one!"[44]

He seldom expressed publicly his occasional misgivings about the administration's policies, however. Even though he realized that Idahoans must never view him as a Kennedy lackey, he usually defended the president's actions, even regarding Berlin. Kennedy, he told constituents, was showing that the United States would not "be bullied or pushed around by the Russians."[45]

Although Church sometimes spoke candidly with the administration, he was for the most part reluctant to challenge the president directly. For one thing, he shared the prevailing confidence in the presidency. "It was generally thought in those days," he said in retrospect, "that Presidents were infallible, particularly where foreign affairs was concerned." Certainly this was the message of Theodore White's smash best-seller, *The Making of the President, 1960.* The book, which dominated the sales charts for months following Kennedy's election, concluded that the world looked to the White House "for miracles."[46]

Church may not have expected miracles from the Kennedy White House, but he overwhelmingly applauded its spirit and agenda. He believed that Kennedy, like Franklin D. Roosevelt, had shaken the nation's capital "back to life again." People of ideas again had influence: "The egghead—not the fat head—is welcome once more."[47]

Among Idaho constituents Church made much of his own access to the administration. "It pays to have the ear of the President," he said, and his Washington newsletter showed him talking intently with Kennedy. At least twice his personal discussions with Kennedy aided Idaho farmers. In 1961 Church rescued wheat and barley growers by threatening to "camp on the White House steps." The target of his anger was a proposed limit of 25 percent on the amount of wheat and barley in mixed-feed grains. Idaho's feed-grain producers insisted they needed a 50 percent allowance to remain competitive. When the Department of Agriculture refused to modify the regulation, Church went directly to Kennedy. Within an hour, at the president's request, Agriculture Secretary Orville Freeman exempted twenty-four Idaho counties from the regulation. On January 19, 1962 Church was back at the White House, objecting this time to proposed acreage controls on potatoes, a major Idaho product. His appeal to the president made a difference. Kennedy's farm message a few days later omitted any mention of potatoes. Idaho voters apparently took note. According to a Louis Harris poll in mid-1962, 70 percent of them believed that Church's access to the president benefitted the state.[48]

VI

Church's constituents were far less enthusiastic, however, about his prominent effort in the Senate's passage of the 1961 wilderness bill. On this issue he challenged Idaho's powerful lumber and mining interests, opening himself to charges of betraying the state's economy. Although he had hoped to play an inconspicuous role during the wilderness debates, he displayed political courage once circumstances forced him to the front.

His thinking on the environment had been evolving for some time. Throughout much of the 1950s he had leaned toward the development of natural resources. His zeal for the Hells Canyon dam reflected this tendency. In the Hells Canyon fight, the main lines of argument were over who would build dams, not over whether they should be built. By the late Fifties, however, Church thought more about preservation. His growing interest in turning parts of Idaho's spectacular Sawtooth area into a national park marked this transition. Although publicity photos of Church plunging through clear mountain streams were largely for effect, he enjoyed mountain scenery and the outdoors. He was no hunter or dedicated backpacker, but his intellectual appreciation for nature ran deep. Among his staff, John Carver and Verda Barnes fretted that his concern for saving the Sawtooths would take him over a political cliff. Idaho residents were still overwhelmingly oriented toward developing the state's resources. "We were a state that needed dams, and needed income from cattle, and needed income from mining, and needed the loggers," said Carver. Towns such as Grangeville and Cottonwood, for example, depended on lumber for their existence.[49]

Across the nation, however, a subtle transformation was taking place. In Carver's estimation, a new conservation movement emerged in 1958, when "anti-wilderness hard-heads" such as Utah senator Arthur Watkins met defeat. In 1961 environmentalists found an additional ally in Secretary of the Interior Stewart Udall. By then, legislation that a few years earlier had seemed extreme was finding support beyond the Wilderness Society. Carver himself was instrumental in this development. In 1961 he left Church's office to become an assistant secretary of Interior.[50]

Early that year, as the Senate's Interior Committee considered wilderness legislation that New Mexico's Clinton Anderson had introduced, Church received a wave of reminders that Idaho's economy was in jeopardy. "Timber is a crop, and shouldn't be locked up to rot," one constituent told him. "We should expand, not stagnate," advised another individual, who thought the wilderness plan was communistic. A Grangeville citizen drew a cartoon showing "Out of State 'Wilderness' Committees" peering over a fence at a contented Idaho resident and saying, "We neighbors have decided to make a park of your yard."[51]

Although Church's replies were non-committal, the senator was in fact by then firmly committed to wilderness legislation, if not to a particular plan. He studied the wilderness issue carefully, and did not depend upon aides to feed him information. Invariably, he tried to avoid useless personal confrontations and to find a practical, balanced approach. Still, as his staff continually warned him, he was courting political danger.[52]

In early 1961 he attempted to block Henry Dworshak's strenuous opposition to Clinton Anderson's bill. Idaho's senior senator wanted to open national forests to extensive mining, but Anderson's proposed measure prohibited commercial activities within wilderness areas. Church worked for a compromise. He successfully got the Interior Committee to accept language that allowed for mining surveys in forest areas, by means "not incompatible with the preservation of the wilderness environment." Anderson mistakenly assumed that Church was himself trying to thwart wilderness legislation, and at one point snapped irritably at him.[53]

Soon, however, the New Mexico Democrat realized that he had misjudged his young colleague. Following a rigorous full-day session on the bill in mid-July, Anderson could not praise him enough as a valued ally. "You were wonderful!" he said. He placed Church among "the loyal souls" who had gotten the bill on the Senate calendar, despite the odds. The situation had been "tough," but Church had demonstrated that he had real fortitude.[54]

Once the bill moved to the Senate floor, Church was prepared to let others lead the fight. Events decided otherwise. When Anderson suffered a gall bladder attack just before the floor debate, he asked Church to take charge. The Idaho senator, expecting a tough reelection battle the following year, was not enthusiastic about the assignment. As Anderson recalled, "He was willing enough to support the bill because he believed in it, but he was not happy at the prospect of offending his constituents gratuitously by leading the floor fight for it."[55]

On September 5 and 6, Church nevertheless guided the bill through the Senate debate. The purpose of the proposed legislation, he explained, was to set up a coherent, rational policy by which to establish a national wilderness preservation system. What lands, in other words, would constitute the system? Who would make the decisions and on what basis? Much of the time Church assailed misconceptions about the bill. Contrary to what opponents claimed, it would not place additional land in the control of the federal government: "All the land involved is already owned and managed by the federal government." Moreover, the legislation would not cause economic dislocation. Existing grazing and mining rights would continue. Lumbering had already been excluded from the lands covered in the bill. Individual states would still have jurisdiction over fish, wildlife, and water laws. The proposed bill would of course protect certain federal lands from development, but Church argued that such legislation did not signify creeping socialism. For one thing, through democratic processes a designated wilderness area could be reopened. For another thing, wilderness legislation was simply a manifestation of the time-honored procedures by which towns and neighborhoods reserved certain zones for residential or playground use rather than industrial development.[56]

Church denied that the bill was an example of class legislation, aimed at sealing off beautiful areas for rich outsiders. In Idaho, for example, "the great majority of people" who went into the mountains were state residents, "and not wealthy ones either." He granted that a majority of travelers might prefer paved roads, motels, and organized campgrounds. But they had such things already. What about the rights of others who wanted a more pristine setting? What about the need to save some parts of the country for posterity? "Wilderness is not a renewable resource," Church noted. "Once occupied, cut over, or exploited, it is lost forever." And that would be tragic. Church did not want the entire nation confined to "the domesticated life of congested cities and clipped countrysides," or the U. S. would "become a cage."[57]

During the debates Church tried to reassure some of his own constituents. He said that he would not support a bill that threatened their livelihoods. Nor would he approve of legislation that took away what was already theirs. He reminded Idahoans that "the federal government, which once owned all of Idaho, still owns nearly two-thirds of it." The wilderness bill would allow Congress, representing the people, to administer those lands more thoughtfully than before. Existing mines were not endangered, nor was lumbering where it was currently permissible. In order to emphasize this point to Idaho residents he sent many of them a map with information that the "maximum possible" acreage involved would be "5.7 percent of Idaho's total area. Actual inclusion would probably be less." In other words, at least 95 percent of the state would be unaffected.[58]

On September 6 the Senate passed the bill, 78 to 8. Among the dissenters was Idaho's Dworshak. The real credit for the bill's overwhelming victory belonged to Clinton Anderson, as Church himself emphasized. More than anyone, the New Mexico senator had prepared the way. Still, Church had managed the floor debate exceedingly well. An appreciative Anderson believed he had been nothing less than "brilliant." The director of the Wilderness Society applauded him for providing "the needed rescue work at the last." Other conservation groups, such as the National Audubon Society and the National Wildlife Federation, were equally grateful.[59]

Church's fight for the wilderness bill involved considerable risk. Wilderness legislation was still highly controversial, as the House demonstrated in 1962 by rejecting the Senate's proposal. Church himself felt that he had thrown a shovel of dirt on his political grave every time he spoke during the Senate debate. Clinton Anderson had no doubt that "Frank had character and guts." Because the Idaho senator had stood up against "the local timber and mining barons," columnists Drew Pearson and Jack Anderson included him among their congressional "profiles in integrity."[60]

Chase Clark feared, however, that his son-in-law's integrity had given way to folly. "Tell me, Frank, how do you expect to win?" he asked as he looked ahead to the 1962 election. "All the organizations that count are against you: the cattlemen, the woolgrowers, the mining association, the forests products industry, the newspapers, the chambers of commerce. . .and for what? For wilderness." The former governor knew something about the power of Idaho's user groups. "You don't just have rocks on your mind," he told Church with exasperation; "you've got rocks in your head!"[61]

By the fall of 1961 rocks were also flying at him from Idaho. The mining industry attacked him over television and radio, contending that state residents needed to worry more about their so-called friends than their enemies. "You are selling Idaho down the river," an angry constituent charged. Others accused him of being "an 'Idahoan last,' " a "dumb bunny," and a betrayer. "Just who do you think you are anyway, Mr. Krushchev [sic] personally?" asked one furious individual. When Church ventured into some of Idaho's mountain communities, the crowds were so angry that they reminded him of lynch mobs.[62]

In important respects the wilderness issue provided anti-Frank Church groups in Idaho with exactly the weapon they needed. It allowed some of the larger corporations to make common cause with working-class people. Broadcasts, advertisements, and letters from mining and timber companies suggested that employees might lose their jobs because of wilderness legislation. "You, or your children's, future employment is involved," one lumber company wrote to its employees. The mining industry warned that "the obsession over recreation" and bird watching would wreck the economy. "It may be true that all work and no play makes Jack a dull boy, but by the same token, all play and no work makes Jack a bum and welfare recipient." Such arguments found an audience among at least some Idaho laborers. One union local of the International Brotherhood of Pulp, Sulphite, and Paper Mill Workers informed Church that all of its 380 members viewed the wilderness bill as a threat to their community. Even some prominent Democrats criticized the senator. A. M. Derr, who had run for governor in 1958, wondered how Church could ever support a bill that would so damage Idaho's already depressed businesses.[63]

Church rightly worried that his political opponents intended to defeat him "with scare arguments over the Wilderness Bill." The *Idaho Statesman*, for example, claimed the bill symbolized Church's larger liberal agenda and his determination to be "a proponent of so-called great experiments." According to the newspaper, the real issue in the 1962 election would be that of the federal government versus states' rights. Church, who the *Statesman* said had "consistently worked for more federal government in Idaho," stood on the wrong side of that battle. A "conservative uprising" reportedly awaited him.[64]

To lead the uprising, Idaho Republicans settled on Boise attorney John T. Hawley as Church's challenger. Hawley, four years older than Church, was the grandson of former Idaho governor James H. Hawley. In 1952 he had defeated Church badly in the race for a seat in the state legislature. Subsequently, he had served as Idaho's assistant U. S. District Attorney. Politically conservative, he was a Republican in the mold of Arizona's Barry Goldwater. Carl Burke predicted that Hawley would be a tough candidate, hard-hitting, forceful, and well-financed. The campaign might also be dirty. Burke told Church that he had just spoken with Hawley's brother, Jess: "They're going to use every means short of criminal means to get you out of office. . . .This is a battle for your political life."[65]

Hawley made clear from the outset that his quarrel with Church was ideological. When he announced his candidacy he accused the senator of pushing legislation that would shift power from individuals to the federal government. Church was presiding "over the obliteration of the sovereign rights of the state of Idaho." The senator had "promoted almost every egghead spending plan and bureaucratic power-grab measure that has come along." His support for government spending and controls would "take our nation and Idaho down the path to economic socialism." Idaho voters, according to Hawley, had not intended for Church "to attempt to become a profound expert in international affairs."

Rather than looking out for his home state, the junior senator had traveled to distant places such as Africa. "He's talked endlessly about spending billions overseas," Hawley charged. "This may be fine for communist Yugoslavia but it doesn't put one pay check in an Idaho worker's pocket." Hawley presented himself in his campaign literature as "an *Idaho Man!*" He pledged to fight back against the government centralization that "the New Frontier is jamming down our throats." He would not be a senator who "merely parrots what the master planners of the New Frontier think is good for us," or who would "rubberstamp the visionary theories of the administration's experts."[66]

Hawley had more than a distinct message; he also ran an impressive, well-organized campaign. His workers seemed to be everywhere, handing out literature in hotel lobbies, canvassing neighborhoods, organizing counties systematically. "Hawley has taken a leaf out of our book," Burke lamented. At the grassroots, his campaign was nothing less than "terrific."[67]

Burke noticed something else. The dynamics of the campaign seemed almost light years removed from that of 1956. Serving again as Church's campaign manager, Burke was "stunned" at the spiraling costs of television and radio advertising. To place fifty billboards in Idaho for four months would cost almost $8,000, a price that did not include the charges for making them. In March, Burke estimated that Church would need to raise at least $75,000 in Idaho alone—an amount that probably exceeded by far what any previous Democratic candidate had gotten in the state. "Our opponent has twice that much."[68]

Equally troubling was the fact that the Democrats' gubernatorial candidate, Vernon K. Smith, was saddling his party with a volatile issue: legalized gambling. Smith had emerged victorious from a pack of six in the primary election, campaigning on that issue alone. He believed that local-option, legalized gambling would energize Idaho's economy just as it had Nevada's. Church rightly suspected that the idea was a loser. A Louis Harris poll showed that 65 percent of Idaho voters opposed gambling. Many saw it as a threat to families and children and a magnet for gangsters. The poll also indicated that the gambling issue could hurt Church's campaign, eroding some of his bases of potential support.[69]

No group was more important than the Mormons in that regard. Significantly, in mid-1962 their overwhelming support for Church surpassed that of any other religious denomination. According to one

Church staffer, some Mormons reportedly believed that the senator was one of them, and even referred to him as "Brother Church." Church did nothing to disabuse them of that notion. He avoided any formal listing of his religious affiliation and periodically delivered Senate speeches on Mormon achievements. In July 1962 the Harris poll showed that the Latter Day Saints backed him by a whopping 76 percent; but they were incensed about Smith's gambling plan. As the pollsters warned, "the legalized gambling issue could do irreparable damage to Frank Church and the Democratic party this November."[70]

Church made a rare move. He plunged into internal state party politics. Ordinarily, he avoided involving himself in intraparty feuding. Idaho in effect had two Democratic parties, the official one and the senator's. Usually, they got along well and cooperated with each other. A few Democrats nevertheless worried that Church was pulling the party too far leftward. Others groused about his aloofness but recognized that he was, in Carl Burke's words, "the only game on the block." In 1962 Church realized that he could not remain detached from the gambling issue. When he heard that the Democrats, at their mid-July platform convention in Idaho Falls, were ready to approve an unequivocal pro-gambling plank, he was irate. He had understood that the party would adopt a neutral position. Immediately, he telephoned Burke. Alarmed at the news, Burke and Ray McNichols quickly departed the bar convention at Sun Valley, raced to Idaho Falls, and closeted themselves with Smith for a whole night. For a while Smith clung tenaciously to his pro-gambling plank. Finally, however, Burke and McNichols prevailed. The Democratic platform ultimately included a compromise plank that Church favored. It credited both sides of the gambling issue with worthy intentions, but left the matter with individual candidates to champion or oppose as they saw fit. Church himself subsequently reminded voters that he had consistently backed federal anti-gambling laws. He thus dodged a political bullet. "You can't imagine running on a ticket with Vernon K. Smith," Burke later sighed.[71]

With the gambling issue out of the way, the election appeared to be in Church's control. Burke remained nervous, but the mid-1962 Harris poll was extremely encouraging. There were potential trouble spots, of course. The poll showed that opinion was evenly divided on the wilderness bill, with 25 percent still withholding judgment. Moreover, Church received strong negative marks regarding the role of the federal government, taxes, and foreign aid. Overall, however, he was "well ahead" of Hawley, who could not stir much excitement. A substantial 62 percent of Idaho voters gave Church a favorable job rating, as opposed to 38 percent who found his work unfavorable. The senator enjoyed a lead over Hawley among every occupational, income, religious, and social group in the state – except for retired people. Granted, Church's lead was better among some groups than others: 77 percent among laborers as opposed to 57 percent among business and professional people, for example. The Harris pollsters nevertheless had no difficulty interpreting the evidence: "However it is sliced, Senator Church is easily the strongest Democrat in the state, including President Kennedy." The explanation for this phenomenon was Church himself. Voters approved of his record by a 3-2 margin; but they liked him as an individual by a huge 6-1 count. In their opinion, he was a person of integrity genuinely interested in helping them.[72]

Church's campaign themes facilitated such conclusions. "Idaho is Stronger with Church in the U. S. Senate" and "I'm Proud of Church" appeared on flyers, decals, matchboxes, an eight-page newspaper advertisement, and over radio and television. A series of 60-second TV spots opened and closed with a "Keep Idaho strong" appeal.[73]

Most effective, however, were Church's personal appearances. With Bethine accompanying him, he scoured the state. Residents of each county knew that at some point he would be at their courthouse, his feet sometimes up on a desk, chatting for hours with people who dropped by. One registered Republican recalled sitting in a "crummy little cafe" in a small town when a tall, black-haired man walked over and struck up a conversation about the state's problems. The man was Frank Church. She voted for him that November, and liked him thereafter: "To me, he's Idaho." As John Carver later emphasized, ranchers might disagree with the senator on the wilderness bill, but at least they sensed that he understood their needs and their frustrations and did not see them as a bunch of robber barons.[74]

VII

In October, however, the Cuban missile crisis suddenly threatened to derail Church's campaign. Cuba had been growing as a national issue for several months. Republicans hammered away at John Kennedy for not upholding his 1960 campaign promise to diminish the threat of Fidel Castro's regime. New York senator Kenneth Keating charged him with ignoring a Soviet military buildup in Cuba that included offensive missile sites. The administration insisted that such charges were groundless, and that the Cuban situation was under control.[75]

Church agreed. In late September he spent two days with a congressional delegation inspecting the American military base at Guantanamo, Cuba. At one point, in fact, he and Wyoming senator Gale McGee postured somewhat when each of them defiantly stuck a foot across the boundary separating the base from Cuban territory. He returned to the U. S. confident that the administration had the situation well in hand. "If Castro takes a punch at us at Guantanamo," Church told the press, "he'll be flattened faster than you can say Floyd Patterson," the name of the world's heavyweight boxing champion. Church also quoted a Marine who told him, "Senator, if Castro meddles here, we'll clobber him." The senator's lengthy newsletter to Idaho residents was equally reassuring. It emphasized that, if Cuba indeed posed a threat, Church would know about it because of his place on the Foreign Relations Committee and his friendship with the president.[76]

Church subsequently wished that he could have jerked that newsletter from the mail. It arrived in his constituents' mailboxes on October 22, the very day that President Kennedy announced over television that the Soviets were indeed putting offensive missiles in Cuba. Idaho's junior senator suddenly appeared uninformed and out of touch.[77]

When Bethine Church first heard about the missiles she broke into tears, convinced that nuclear war was imminent. Her one consolation was that at least her children were in Idaho, not Washington, D. C. Church, equally alarmed, refused to conclude that war was inevitable.[78]

Certainly there was little to cheer. The Cold War was turning deadlier than ever. Even if the Cuban crisis cooled off, Church might be left with only a few more weeks in the Senate. The recent newsletter had shattered his image as a knowledgeable expert close to the president. "The campaign is over," he told Bethine and his administrative assistant Ward Hower as they drove somberly through northern Idaho. As they dropped down a long grade into the Clearwater Valley, Hower predicted that Church would lose the election if, in forty-eight hours, he was still driving around Idaho. They stopped at the side of the road. A pouring rain and the darkening late afternoon skies seemed all too symbolic. "There is one chance," Church said. "I have to find a phone."[79]

At a service station pay phone along the Clearwater River, Hower finally reached Harlan Cleveland at the State Department. Cleveland, an assistant secretary of state and a friend of the Churches and the Kennedys, "understood exactly" the purpose of the call, Hower remembered. "You didn't have to draw him a picture." Cleveland then talked with Church about the arrangements by which the administration would bring the senator back east for a briefing. Church also spoke with Bobby Kennedy at the White House and found him equally helpful.[80]

Within twelve hours Church was in Boise boarding a military jet that would whisk him eastward. Newspeople looked on, with cameras clicking and TV tapes rolling. It was a dramatic moment. In retrospect, Bethine conceded that the pictures of her kissing her husband good-bye may have appeared "sort of schmaltzy." But she was in fact terrified at the time that she might never again see him if the crisis disintegrated into nuclear war. At high altitudes, the sleek government jet rushed Church and Hower to New York City. There, the senator supposedly helped United Nations ambassador Adlai Stevenson prepare a report. Church indeed talked briefly with Stevenson but, according to Hower, not about policy; by then the Cuban crisis seemed to be winding down. "Stevenson knew exactly what was going on," Hower recalled. "He knew why Frank was there"–namely to get some much-needed publicity as an important leader dealing with a national emergency.[81]

Events could not have worked out better for Church. The missile crisis ended and he finished his campaign with a show of strength. On television after his return to Idaho, for example, he discussed the crisis and reassured viewers about the future. Representative Ralph Harding, also seeking reelection, happened to be at the studio. A TV person noted that, while Harding had been campaigning in Idaho, Church had wrestled with national problems. Church was rather embarrassed at such a perception, although it helped his cause. He was convinced that he would have lost the election had he not been able to turn the missile crisis in his favor.[82]

A few days later voters returned him to the Senate by a solid majority. He captured almost 55 percent of the vote, beating Hawley 141,657 to 117,129. More impressively, he carried over three-fourths of Idaho's counties. Hawley, who had run an aggressive but clean, decent campaign, claimed that he had been "Cubanized."[83]

The Democratic Party, which had done well nationally, at least held its own in Idaho. True, Republican Robert E. Smylie had clobbered Vernon Smith to become the first governor in Idaho history to win a third term; and the GOP had maintained slight majorities in the state legislature. But Democrats Ralph Harding and Compton White, Jr., had captured both congressional seats, Harding as an incumbent and White replacing Gracie Pfost. Pfost narrowly missed joining Church in the Senate. The mid-1962 death of Henry Dworshak had unexpectedly left open the remaining four years of his term. Pfost barely lost to Len Jordan, a staunchly conservative former governor.[84]

Although the *Idaho Statesman*'s John Corlett believed that the Republican Party was weakening, the larger election message appeared to be that Idaho voters preferred the status quo. One of them explained why he had voted for Church the Democrat and Jordan the Republican. Church, he said, could help Idaho through his contacts with John Kennedy. "So I voted to send Frank back there to continue to work on our behalf on these national issues and items where Idaho's welfare is at stake. And I sent Len back there to watch" him and Kennedy.[85]

Frank Church emerged from the election as Idaho's most powerful Democrat and, at age thirty-eight, its senior senator. Eleven months before the election an internal memo within the state's GOP had described him "as a heavyweight." In November he earned that label. He would be returning for at least another six years to Washington, D. C., the "Rome of the Modern World," as he described it to one reporter.[86]

Church visiting a strategic hamlet north of Dalat in the Tuyen Duc Province, South Vietnam, December 1962. *U. S. Army photo, courtesy Boise State University.*

Chapter Seven
Liberal in the Middle: 1963-1964

"ACTUALLY, I PRETTY much stand alone," Frank Church said in the early 1960s, "out in the 'no-man's land' between. . .warring camps." Although he referred specifically to the battle over wilderness legislation, he instinctively sought a middle position on most issues. An avowed liberal, he avoided political extremes, sought to build a consensus from competing points of view, and assumed that a healthy American democracy could deal effectively with the nation's problems.[1]

His early enthusiasm for the Kennedy administration bolstered his confidence in the nation's policies and political processes. Church still believed that Americans must not relax their opposition to the communist threat abroad, but he was certain that the path to victory rested with continued trust in democratic procedures and "the integrity of our leaders." With fresh, creative leadership, the United States seemed ready again for the challenges that confronted it. Church was convinced that John Kennedy was maturing in office, even "showing signs of becoming a great President." During the Cuban missile crisis, for example, Kennedy had avoided a bloody conflict and yet still inflicted, in Church's words, "the most humiliating setback the Communists have suffered since the beginning of the cold war."[2]

Following Church's reelection in 1962, however, the Idaho senator found the middle ground increasingly difficult to hold. The growing presence of the radical right disturbed him, as did the violent backlash against the civil rights movement. To combat the spreading virulence in American life, he championed liberalism with renewed zeal and spoke out against the rising conservatism of Arizona senator Barry Goldwater and his followers. He also worried about America's involvement in Southeast Asia. Not surprisingly, he sought a middle course on the issue of Vietnam, hoping that the U. S. might be a positive force there without enlarging its military commitment. But the tumultuous events of 1963 and after battered his centrist faith in compromise, civility, and reasonableness.

I

In late 1962 Church got a hint of bad times ahead when he visited Laos and Vietnam. A few months earlier he had written optimistically that it appeared "possible to encourage and sustain effective military resistance to the Communists in South Vietnam." After he toured that region as part of a Senate study mission he was less certain.[3]

Accompanying him on the trip were Utah's Frank Moss and Wyoming's Gale McGee, the same senators with whom he had toured Africa two years before. On a cold, rainy November 18, they embarked on a thirty-two thousand mile journey. Over the next thirty-five days they enjoyed occasional respites—hunting pheasants along the demilitarized zone in Korea, riding elephants and visiting the huge towers of the Anghor Wat shrine in Cambodia, and shopping in Singapore. But their mood was gloomy as they flew across the Mekong Delta region into Laos. In the city of Vientiane, red dust rose from the unpaved streets to blanket everything. The abject poverty reminded Church of Africa. Moss described the area as "sad and dirty"—"a problem without a sure solution." To Church it was "a forlorn place." All three senators were frustrated that the U. S. investment in Laos of almost a half-billion dollars over the past decade had not yielded better dividends.[4]

They found the situation in South Vietnam almost as discouraging. "A protracted struggle, at best, can be the only realistic forecast," they concluded. In their official report they endorsed the American commitment and strategies in Vietnam, but sensed that the government of Ngo Dinh Diem was making little progress in building popular support.[5]

The brief report omitted some of the historical reasons for Diem's predicament. In 1954, despite massive U. S. financial assistance, the French had lost a bloody guerrilla war when they tried to regain their former Vietnamese colony. American policy makers insisted that the Vietnamese rebels were part of a world-wide communist offensive, rather than nationalists seeking their country's independence from colonialism. The Geneva settlement that ended the French-Vietnamese conflict established a provisional line at the 17th parallel—a line, according to the agreement, that "should not in any way be interpreted as constituting a political or territorial boundary." In 1956 a unified Vietnam was supposed to hold national elections, yet they were never held because the United States rallied behind Diem, who in the mid-1950s began to construct his own government in Saigon. Contrary to the

Geneva agreement, the U. S. helped to create a legal fiction: that South Vietnam was a separate nation.

From the American perspective, the Diem regime offered a base from which to block communism in Southeast Asia. Diem's government had little to do with democracy, however: "I don't care what the people think," said Diem's brother, Ngo Dinh Nhu, who fashioned the Saigon government into a police state. Diem, moreover, confiscated huge chunks of land from the peasants and returned it to the original Vietnamese landlords who had aided the French. By 1958 the pattern of land ownership in the Mekong Delta resembled what it had been under French rule, with only 2 percent of the owners controlling 45 percent of the land and around half of the farmers owning none. The United States nevertheless backed Diem, considering his regime a sovereign state that would keep the other "dominoes" in the region from falling to communism.[6]

On December 6, 1962, Church, McGee, and Moss visited some of the "strategic hamlets" that the U. S. was building in South Vietnam: fortified villages in which Vietnamese peasants were supposed to find protection from communist guerrillas. Some four thousand out of a prospective fourteen thousand hamlets had already been constructed. Church later said that the hamlet program struck him as "insane." The dense jungle area around the villages provided ideal cover for guerrillas. The people inside the hamlets looked "wretched." And a Catholic priest, who had lived in the area for years, noted bitterly that the program only made things worse for the residents. Church's travel notes nevertheless indicated that he at least found America's advisory team in Vietnam "first rate."[7]

Church was considerably less happy about Ngo Dinh Diem. As the senators drove from the Saigon airport into the city they encountered a huge military escort taking Diem to his palace. Troops pushed people back, window shutters were closed, and the avenue resembled an armed camp. Diem's remoteness from the people was painfully clear. Church was visibly upset, more so than the other senators. He observed disdainfully to Moss that Diem resembled a monarch from some ancient period and that Saigon was like a police state. Moss was less shocked at the situation because violence in the area seemed to justify Diem's concerns with security. The senators themselves drove with their car windows only partly open, lest a communist guerrilla throw a grenade inside.[8]

Although Church left Vietnam with considerable misgivings about America's involvement, his travel notes indicated that he still believed the U. S. faced its "greatest test" there. And the report that he, Moss, and McGee submitted to the Senate referred to "the battlefronts of the cold war"–none of which was uglier than that along Asia's Pacific rim. All three senators emphasized the need for Diem to advance economic and political democracy in South Vietnam; at the same time, they saw few alternatives for the U. S. except to back him. By December 20, when Church headed home, he had even found some encouraging trends. The "fighting has taken a favorable turn," he said.[9]

II

For a while in 1963, however, events within the United States pulled Church's attention from Vietnam. The swelling right wing movement alarmed the senator. Radio and television commentators, pamphlets, books, and speakers unleashed a flood of frightening messages that the United States was falling victim to alien, communistic influences.

Church's mail reflected the trend. From the "Christian Brotherhood" came "highly confidential" news that Jews, blacks, and the United Nations were seeking "satanic world domination." The Cinema Educational Guild, certain that "the Reds are back in Hollywood," advocated boycotting a long list of actors and writers (including Lucille Ball, Kirk Douglas, Rita Hayworth, Groucho Marx, and Sidney Poitier) as well as impeaching Chief Justice Earl Warren for "giving aid and comfort to the COMMUNIST CONSPIRACY." Students at one Idaho high school informed Church that they had viewed a film, "Communism on the Map," showing communists in control of the Pentagon.[10]

When constituents questioned Church's own patriotism, he typically replied that he was alert to the dangers of the international communist conspiracy. Sometimes he added that his work on the Senate Foreign Relations Committee allowed him a special opportunity to deal with the problem. On other occasions he attempted to allay fears through reminders that the Federal Bureau of Investigation carefully monitored the activities of Soviet agents. He occasionally also suggested that individuals should be more careful about conspiracy theories; the groups from which they got their information were all too often using "the classic fascist technique: tell a lie so big that its very grotesqueness will deceive some people." Sometimes Church specifically criticized the John Birch Society, which had formed in 1958 out of fear that communists had already taken over the U. S. government with the help of none other than Dwight Eisenhower. Church warned that "not everyone who says 'He is a communist' is really serving the cause of Americanism." The senator emphasized, however, that he would do nothing to halt the dissemination of propagandistic materials, no matter how untruthful they were. "I subscribe to the Jeffersonian principle," he said, "that error can be tolerated so long as there is freedom for truth to compete with it. . . in the marketplace of ideas."[11]

The spread of right wing paranoia in Idaho particularly disturbed the senator. Shoshone County, for example, had its own "Anti-Communist Association." From across the state constituents wrote frantically to Church about communist control of the National Council of Churches, the Air Force training manual, the Central Intelligence Agency, the State Department, Radio Free Europe, American public schools and universities, the Kennedy administration, and a host of other organizations, agencies, and individuals.[12]

John Birch Society members were increasingly antagonistic when Church spoke in Idaho. On one occasion, as he anticipated a sizable turnout of Birchers, Bethine assured him that he could deal with them by staying calm and answering them politely. As expected, many Birchers were present and, at the end of his speech, wasted no time expressing their displeasure with him. After fielding a number of questions, he started out of the hall with his administrative assistant Ward Hower. Suddenly they heard Bethine, across the room, explode with anger. "You're what! What! How dare you call my husband a traitor!" The senator smiled knowingly at Hower and said, "You'd better go get hold of Bethine."[13]

"Sometimes Idaho scares me," Bethine admitted in the early 1960s. Her affection for the state was virtually unlimited, but the rancor that increasingly marked its politics bothered her. The senator, equally fond of his place of origin, conceded that it had more than its share of "crackpots." By 1963 he was convinced that right wing organizations were targeting Idaho and other mountain states for a major promotional campaign. "The traditional conservatism, rugged individualism and scarcity of population of the Intermountain West," he wrote, "is looked upon by the 'far right' as ideal territory from which to establish a national base." The challenge, he told one aide, was how to meet this threat without getting into "a pissing contest with a skunk."[14]

Church resorted to his usual strategy of trying to educate the public. In the early Sixties he used speeches, letters, and articles to present the case for liberalism and against the right wing. On May 6, 1963 he published a spirited defense of liberalism in the *U. S. News and World Report*. A few weeks earlier, South Dakota senator Karl Mundt had used the pages of that journal to attack liberalism. Church countered that Mundt and other conservatives were redefining liberalism so that it could be the villain "for their well-oiled political spook show."[15]

The Idaho senator took aim at conservative allegations that "do-gooders" were taxing hard-working citizens in order to aid lazy people and build a socialistic bureaucracy. He countered that, in fact, "Big Government on the Potomac is chiefly the product of the warfare state, not the welfare state." Eighty percent of the federal budget related to the military and national security. Only seven cents of every tax dollar went to programs for education, public health, and needy people.[16]

Church turned to "another hobgoblin": the growth of the federal bureaucracy. The national government was actually not even keeping pace with the growth of the rest of the country. The number of federal employees for every one thousand Americans had dropped from sixteen in 1952 to thirteen in fiscal 1964. Between 1952 and 1962, state and local government personnel had grown by 63 percent; federal civilian employment dropped 3 percent. Church granted that the federal government had expanded substantially over the decades. Its expansion did not represent an insidious conspiracy, however. Government had grown in response to public needs, and at the public's insistence, as Americans devised practical solutions to the problems within their changing society.[17]

"The last hobgoblin in the political spook-show version of liberalism," he wrote, was the supposition that the federal government opposed individual freedoms. American history belied such an assumption. From the abolition of slavery to recent battles to end voting restrictions, the government had been an ally of individual rights. Because of government, the lives of most Americans had become "longer, fuller, and easier." Church granted that citizens paid more taxes and faced more regulations than in the past. But society itself had changed dramatically through technology, urbanization, and industrialization. "The form of the free life known to the old frontier is disappearing, and there is no way to recapture it." Who, then, were liberals? They were, Church contended, people who tried to adjust to changing times while keeping

America "open and free." And their preferred strategy was practical and moderate—a "middle course" between radicals on the right and the left.[18]

In other forums, Church pressed his campaign to show that fears of Big Government in the United States were exaggerated. He joked before one audience about the Nevada farmer who criticized government programs generally, but liked those that helped him. "This is a *good* program for *me*!" the farmer said about agricultural research.[19]

Elsewhere, Church reminded Idahoans of the days when railroad monopolies had victimized them, or when unregulated stock market speculation had brought on the economic crash of 1929. Government regulation existed to protect the public "from concentrated economic power." Moreover, the social and economic development of the nation was not a product of private industry alone. The federal government had built "freeways" that competed with toll roads, as well as dams for reclamation and flood control. It was thus inaccurate, Church contended, to generalize wildly that government competed with private enterprise. "We must ask, 'What is the purpose?' and 'What are the alternatives?' " of government actions. Church had difficulty understanding the argument that Idaho taxpayers should not have to help pay for a mass transportation bill that benefitted residents of eastern cities. Why then, he wondered, should people in Boston and elsewhere pay to build roads in Idaho? According to Church, Idaho received approximately $3 in federal funds for every $1 collected in the state for federal taxes. He emphasized time and again that the United States was a *nation*, dependent upon the cooperation of citizens in all its states.[20]

In the fall of 1963 Church criticized Arizona Republican Barry Goldwater for encouraging "the frantic voice of fanaticism." Goldwater's simplistic view of America, he said, repudiated the legacy of responsible Republicans such as Abraham Lincoln and Theodore Roosevelt and led "inevitably to extremes." Church stressed that his quarrel was not with Goldwater, whom he considered a personal friend, but with the Arizonan's budding presidential candidacy. "It is the Goldwater brand of Republicanism against which we western Democrats must prepare to wage the coming campaign," he predicted. In Church's opinion, liberals had a particular responsibility to educate the individual who looked "into a Goldwater pot" and saw "the world as the world is not." Goldwater, Church said bluntly, "simply doesn't live in the real world." He had asserted, for example, that he feared Washington, D. C., more than he feared the Soviet Union. And he advocated an increasingly belligerent foreign policy.[21]

According to Church, the West bore a special burden for Goldwaterism. Goldwater drew upon the West's "nostalgic romance with the lawless, trigger-happy days, the careless exploitation, the get-rich-quick temperament of the old frontier." Church countered that there was another side to the region's history—one that had moved beyond fast-on-the-draw "gunmen, black-jack dealers, and the flash of gold in the pan." The West also included farmers who understood the importance of caring for the land, and people who had built cities in the desert. Americans should not forsake this community-oriented, cooperative aspect of their past "for a pot of fool's gold," Church argued.[22]

As his comments made clear, Church rejected the tendency of Goldwater and his followers to find easy answers to complex problems, to deal with issues abstractly rather than in their historical contexts, and to favor extreme statements and solutions. When the conservative Americans for Constitutional Action gave Church a zero approval rating for the first session of the 88th Congress, he was delighted. In his estimation, the world of the political right was not one of reasoned debate, logic, historical facts, and mutual respect for institutions and individuals. It was instead nostalgic, paranoid, and given to the violent, quick response of the mythic gunfighter. Church worried that the radical right was poisoning national debate and substituting rancor and suspicion for a shared civic culture.[23]

III

The increasingly ugly and vicious backlash against the civil rights movement only confirmed his fears. The South in the 1960s resembled a war zone. In 1960, when African Americans tried to integrate lunch counters, they encountered epithets, threats, and physical attacks. Violence against civil rights activists quickly escalated. The desegregation of the University of Mississippi in 1962 required federal troops and claimed two lives. During the spring of 1963 the police in Birmingham, Alabama, used dogs, cattle prods, and fire hoses against civil rights demonstrators. On June 12 a sniper in Jackson, Mississippi, assassinated Medgar Evers, field secretary of the National Association for the Advancement of Colored People. A few days later President Kennedy, who had moved very cautiously to protect civil rights, submitted an omnibus bill to Congress. This might be his "political swan song," he told his brother Robert; but, "if we're going to go down, let's go down on a matter of principle."[24]

Church agreed that fundamental principles were at stake. He cosponsored the civil rights bill, which called for voting protections, equal access to public facilities, the end of federal funding to discriminatory programs, and more federal leverage to desegregate schools. Six years earlier Church had helped to remove the public accommodations section (Title III) from the 1957 civil rights bill in order to gain passage of at least some legislation. This time around, however, he was unwilling to concede that section.

Despite his strong support for the civil rights movement, he was nevertheless uneasy when tens of thousands of demonstrators converged on the capital for the August 28, 1963 March on Washington. Like the Kennedy administration, he worried about the potential for violence. At the least, the march might galvanize a huge political backlash. According to pollsters, 63 percent of the public opposed the demonstration. Church became nervous when he learned that some of his own staff planned to join the march. He worried instinctively about taking politics out of formal governmental channels and into the streets. Too much could go wrong. An outbreak of violence could undercut the civil rights movement and feed the fires of extremism. Still, he made no effort to dissuade his staff from participating. Several aides thus joined the quarter of a million demonstrators who filed peacefully down Pennsylvania Avenue to the Lincoln Memorial on that clear, warm, summer day. Although Church never encouraged any of them to march, he ultimately offered a kind of tacit approval by letting his fourteen-year-old son Forrest join them.[25]

IV

That summer, in South Vietnam, another kind of public protest erupted with shattering consequences. In the afternoon of June 11, a seventy-three-year old Buddhist monk calmly assumed the lotus position at an intersection in downtown Saigon and burned himself to death, protesting a May 8 incident in the city of Hue. On that bloody day, government troops had fired into crowds of Buddhists opposing a ban on the display of flags to celebrate the anniversary of Buddha's birth. Nine people were killed, some of them children. When the Diem government shrugged off the incident as a product of communist trouble-making, more Buddhists took to the streets or began hunger strikes. The Buddhist demonstrations quickly evolved from protests against religious persecution to a powerful political movement, a magnet for Vietnamese who opposed the stranglehold of the Ngo family. The June 11 self-immolation vividly marked that transition. On August 21, after three more monks and a Catholic nun immolated themselves, government forces raided the pagodas in major cities and arrested hundreds of Buddhists. The government's clumsy and brutal response to the demonstrations was bad enough; but Diem's sister-in-law, Madame Nhu, added to the horror by saying she would applaud if more Buddhist burnings occurred.[26]

By late August, the Kennedy administration's Vietnam policy had reached a crisis. Without informing Congress, the administration veered toward supporting a coup. The plot fizzled, however, when Vietnamese military officers had second thoughts. As the Vietnam situation deteriorated, Kennedy and his advisors searched frantically for options. At an August 31 policy meeting, Paul Kattenburg, a Foreign Service officer who had served in Vietnam in the 1950s, watched disapprovingly as key officials discussed a country about which they appeared to know virtually nothing. Kattenburg, who had just returned from another visit to Vietnam, grew increasingly depressed. "God, we're walking into a major disaster," he thought. He remarked abruptly to Vice President Lyndon Johnson and others in the room that the United States should simply seek an honorable withdrawal from Vietnam. They quickly dismissed his advice. The United States simply could not leave Vietnam, they said; it was essential to win the war against the communists.[27]

Frank Church worried deeply about Vietnam but, like the administration, he focused more on how to salvage a bad situation than on a fundamental reassessment of American policy. In a September 5 executive session of the Far East Subcommittee of the Foreign Relations Committee he criticized the United States' identification with the repressive Diem regime. At one point he asked icily what the administration hoped to do with "this Mandarin," Diem. "There has been nothing like him since the Borgias." Church threatened to introduce a resolution to end U. S. aid to South Vietnam if repression there continued. When Assistant Secretary of State Roger Hilsman pleaded with him not to act without first consulting the administration, he agreed, but only if the executive branch moved quickly.[28]

The administration had already considered the advantages of such a resolution. On August 30, Ambassador Henry Cabot Lodge, Jr., had suggested that the House of Representatives might threaten to cut off foreign aid unless the Diem government carried out reforms. A few days later, Lodge reiterated the importance of having some "leverage" when he spoke with Diem. From the administration's point of view, a resolution from Church offered real possibilities, if it were correctly worded and timed. Everyone knew that Church was close to the president, Hilsman recalled. "When a guy like that does something it sends a message all around the world." Hilsman told Lodge that the ambassador might be able to make good use of "this Congressional storm-warning." In the meantime, Hilsman's instructions from the State Department were to contact the senator about the resolution's wording: ". . .This is more likely to (a) get us what we want and (b) cement relations with Church."[29]

In early September Church cooperated so closely with the administration that he became, in Hilsman's words, "a major collaborator in our policy. He was the co-author." Church's draft resolution, which he submitted to Hilsman, indicated that the American people could not back a government that "oppresses the people and religious sects," and warned that Diem's regime would have to make "a determined and effective effort to regain the support of its own people" if it hoped to maintain American support. Church's foreign policy assistant remembered a telephone call coming from Kennedy's national security advisor, McGeorge Bundy, urging the senator to "keep it up." Bundy sent Church his own suggestion about how the resolution should read. Church nevertheless had to move discretely because rumors had already surfaced that he was putting together a resolution at the behest of the White House. "We feel," wrote Carl Marcy, the Foreign Relations Committee chief of staff, "that any implication. . .that you are acting at the instigation of the Administration would diminish the effectiveness of a Senate resolution."[30]

Church thus worked quietly with the White House. Hilsman, the president's personal liaison with the senator, appreciated his willingness to forgo headlines or attempt to preempt the administration. "He had a huge sense of responsibility and integrity." Hilsman recalled. "He held off until we said 'go.' "[31]

On September 10, Hilsman and Church talked candidly. Hilsman stressed that the resolution needed almost unanimous backing in the

Senate. A defeat would "do us in," he said. Church, confident that the Senate would rally behind the resolution in order to help the president, reassured him. Hilsman and Church considered possible changes in the draft resolution. The senator wanted to say that a continuation of religious persecution in South Vietnam would jeopardize U. S. support. Hilsman, more tentative, noted that former ambassador Frederick Nolting denied that such persecution had occurred. Church held firm, insisting that it had. Finally, Hilsman suggested alternative wording such as " 'repression of Buddhists,' " but he was willing to work with Church on the language.[32]

Later that afternoon Hilsman told the National Security Council (NSC) that the Idaho senator "would be fully responsive to suggestions as to the wording of the Senate resolution and to the timing of its introduction." National Security Council members were nevertheless somewhat nervous. McGeorge Bundy sensed that the prevailing view of Church on the Hill was that he was too junior, too much the "grownup boy orator," to play a "heavyweight" role. A larger, strategic problem was that any effort to use congressional criticism of Diem might get out of control, turning into an attack on the issue of foreign aid itself.[33]

When the NSC met the next evening with Kennedy, the president concurred that Church's resolution could be helpful, but only if it did not jeopardize the foreign aid bill. Kennedy wanted simply to send Diem a signal of America's displeasure, not to do anything that would in fact reduce U. S. aid to Vietnam or elsewhere. Bundy and Secretary of State Dean Rusk were among those who thought that Church could introduce the resolution with the understanding that the Senate should delay action on it.[34]

On September 11, while Church awaited word on the resolution from the White House, he spoke in the Senate in behalf of the administration's nuclear test ban treaty. Here at last was the first step toward arms control that he had been advocating since 1959 – an end to nuclear testing in the atmosphere. Following the scary days of the Cuban missile crisis, the mood in both the United States and the Soviet Union had become more receptive to such an agreement. On August 5 the Soviets signed the treaty and within three days it came before the U. S. Senate. Church eloquently defended the treaty. He conceded that the agreement was "a small step, and it comes very late." But it would protect people physically and psychologically from nuclear fallout, and it might also divert more money to pressing domestic problems, such as unemployment, industrial competitiveness, and urban renewal. Almost two weeks later, on September 24, the Senate ratified the treaty 80 to 19. Although polls showed that 80 percent of the public approved, the opposition had been vigorous. "The right-wing crowd has really been moving into gear," observed Hubert Humphrey's administrative assistant. Church himself received warnings that, by supporting the treaty, he was signing America's death warrant, bringing it ever closer to the burial that Nikita Khrushchev had promised.[35]

Church's Vietnam resolution also drew fire. He introduced it on September 12, following Hilsman's meeting the night before with Kennedy and the NSC. Among Church's critics was columnist Joseph Alsop, who categorized the resolution as a "ridiculous" move that undermined America's efforts in Vietnam and served the interests of Mao Tse-Tung.[36]

The administration was pleased, however. The sense-of-the-Senate resolution was precisely what the White House wanted. The proposed resolution threatened that, "unless the government of South Vietnam abandons policies of repression against its own people and makes a determined and effective effort to regain their support, military and economic assistance to that government should not be continued." Church also tailored his introductory remarks to fit the administration's wishes. In his original draft, for example, he asserted that the military situation in Vietnam had "worsened." He altered this to say that the war effort had "gradually improved," but that the Diem regime's "acts of political folly" had "gravely undermined" such progress.[37]

According to Roger Hilsman, the resolution "was very important" for the administration, allowing it to apply additional pressure on Diem. Equally important, Kennedy's people were able to ensure that the resolution never reached a vote. The administration concurred with the aims of the resolution, but wanted no action on it lest the president lose some flexibility regarding Vietnam.[38]

V

The White House was equally committed to protecting presidential influence over foreign aid. That concern, of course, had accounted for the administration's desire to keep Church's resolution separate from the aid debate. As Robert W. Komer of the NSC noted, the president worried less about foreign assistance "cuts in any given year than the secular trend toward annual slashes" in the program.[39]

In the fall of 1963 the executive branch encountered resistance on foreign aid, partly because of Church. Although he endorsed foreign assistance in principle, he again tried to amend the foreign aid bill by eliminating wealthy countries from it. By his count, American subsidies went to all but eight nations outside the Soviet bloc. The legitimate purpose of foreign aid, he said, was to help struggling, undeveloped nations resist communism and raise their living standards. Rich countries that could take care of themselves "ought to be taken off our dole." If they were not, Church predicted that public backing would disintegrate and foreign aid would "collapse like a house of cards." The senator went out of his way to emphasize that he was not criticizing Kennedy, but rather the programs that came "wrapped in a uniform," pushed along by military and bureaucratic imperatives. Still, as one Kennedy adviser lamented, the "hydra-headed foreign aid monster" faced trouble enough in the House of Representatives without the Senate making the situation worse.[40]

By October the administration had a bleak outlook on its foreign aid package. The threat of restrictive amendments remained a problem. On October 7 members of the Foreign Relations Committee spent two hours venting their frustration about Vietnam and growing turbulence in Latin America. Every committee member except Fulbright and Alabama's John Sparkman complained about the aid program. Meanwhile, in a heated debate that week over a developing crisis in the Dominican Republic, Church joined a half-dozen senators in demanding an absolute end to American aid until that nation restored democracy.[41]

In an essay for United Press International, Church applauded "the liberal revolt against foreign aid." He reiterated his point that rich nations should not receive U. S. aid. He chastised the military assistance program as "both wasteful and excessive." He wondered why America spent billions of dollars "to sustain a garrison state in South Korea," and "to indulge an old man's dreams" by propping up Chiang Kai-shek's army in Formosa. He questioned the wisdom of giving military aid to African and Latin American nations. "We understand that Kennedy inherited these excesses, and we don't blame him for them," he insisted. "But it is now within his power to come to grips with them." He hoped that liberals like himself, who had backed the foreign aid program "at considerable political risk," would receive the hearing they deserved.[42]

The battle in 1963 over foreign aid ended with an authorization of $3.6 billion, but the actual appropriation was "$3.2 billion—the largest cut in the history of the program" to that point, according to Kennedy aide and historian Arthur Schlesinger, Jr. An elated Church complained only that the "liberal revolt" had received insufficient credit for altering the aid program. He and senators such as Wayne Morse, Ernest Gruening, Hubert Humphrey, and Albert Gore had been able to "force revisions" that led to major reductions in funding.[43]

VI

Church's record on Vietnam was more cautious. In hopes of pressuring the Diem government to reform itself, he had cast his lot with the administration, despite a growing sense of futility about Vietnam. As he pushed his "no reform, no aid" resolution, he gathered evidence suggesting that reform was, in the words of the *New York Times*' David Halberstam, "one of the myths of Vietnam." According to Halberstam, whose reporting Church described as "brilliant," the power structure of Diem's government was impervious to change. Other clippings that Church collected made the same point. Ed Meagher of the *Los Angeles Times*, for example, doubted that American-style tinkering and horse-trading would ever influence Diem and his family; they ruled by edict and "could not act like popular democrats if they tried."[44]

Church was inclined to agree, particularly after his late-1962 visit to Vietnam. The situation in that strife-torn nation was "ambiguous" at best, he wrote one constituent. South Vietnam was itself locked in civil war, and Church was not hopeful about the outcome. He related a story about an American Confederate officer who had boasted, "We can beat those Yankees with cornstalks." Later, in defeat, the chastened officer had said, "The trouble was, those dam' Yankees wouldn't fight with cornstalks."[45]

Compounding Church's unease about Vietnam was his suspicion that the U. S. government was not being truthful. The senator was especially skeptical about official claims that U. S.-trained South Vietnamese troops enjoyed grassroots support. He guessed that a late-September tour of Vietnam by Secretary of Defense Robert McNamara and General Maxwell Taylor had resulted in a "whitewash." Church's assessment convinced one of the senator's staffers to be less quick "to attribute admirable motives to the Administration in the future."[46]

On November 1 the Vietnam situation changed dramatically. A coup toppled the Saigon government and led to the assassinations of Diem and his brother Nhu. The Kennedy administration had unquestionably encouraged the coup, even though news of the murders upset Kennedy greatly. Superficially, at least, Diem's overthrow offered the administration what it wanted: an opportunity to effect reforms and bring some political stability to South Vietnam. On the other hand, the U. S. role in establishing the new Saigon government meant that, more than ever, the South Vietnamese fit Kennedy's earlier description of them as "our offspring."[47]

Church tried to put the best face on the altered situation in Vietnam. In the Senate he complimented Kennedy for following "the correct course." There would have been no coup, he believed, had the Vietnamese people themselves not favored change. Church regretted the deaths of Diem and others, but he cited a *Washington Post* article claiming American innocence in the coup. Writing subsequently to his new Senate colleague George McGovern of South Dakota, he hoped that "the initial promise displayed by the new Vietnamese government will permit a rapid victory over the Viet Cong and a withdrawal of American soldiers from that country."[48]

His guarded optimism about the future flowed mainly from his confidence in John Kennedy. Although Kennedy had enlarged the U. S. presence in Vietnam by sending around seventeen thousand military advisors, Church remained convinced that the president viewed the war as South Vietnam's to win or lose. In other words, JFK would not directly involve American combat troops. Church sensed, moreover, that Kennedy was "having second thoughts" regarding America's commitment in Vietnam. But the senator later conceded that he based such a conclusion on his own impressions. He never talked personally with the president about Vietnam, and he was aware that Kennedy's public statements suggested no fundamental rethinking of America's role in Southeast Asia. Indeed, in the late summer and fall of 1963 the president had reaffirmed his belief that the fall of South Vietnam to communism would knock other Southeast Asian nations into the Soviet bloc. He had told newscaster Walter Cronkite that it "would be a great mistake" to withdraw from Vietnam. And a speech that he was supposed to deliver in Dallas on November 22 stressed that "we dare not weary of the test."[49]

Eight-year-old Frank and his brother Richard with their mother. *Courtesy Boise State University.*

Father and son, Frank Church II and III. *Courtesy Bethine Church.*

Frank Church and Carl Burke as high school buddies, c. 1941. *Courtesy Bethine Church.*

Bethine and Frank Church on their wedding day, June 21, 1947. *Courtesy Boise State University.*

Recuperating from radiation treatments, Church poses in mid-1949 with Forrest, Bethine, and her parents. *Courtesy Boise State University.*

Church on the air in behalf of Idaho's Crusade for Freedom organization, 1954. *Courtesy Boise State University.*

Church's staff in crowded office space shortly after Church became a senator. Administrative assistant John Carver talks in the back with Verda Barnes while, on the right, Ward Hower looks on. Barnes and Hower later served as Church's administrative assistants. *Courtesy Boise State University.*

As a member of the Labor Rackets Investigating Committee in the late Fifties, Church worked with committee chair John McClellan and counsel Robert F. Kennedy. *Courtesy Boise State University.*

In 1959, Idaho's congressional delegation (Church, Representatives Gracie Pfost and Homer Budge, and Senator Henry Dworshak) greet another Idaho product, Harmon Killebrew, Washington Senators' third baseman. *Courtesy Boise State University.*

Church campaign poster, 1962. *Courtesy Barry Kough*.

Church visiting with President John Kennedy, their expressions correctly conveying the good relationship between them. *Courtesy Boise State University.*

Church gets some of the Lyndon Johnson treatment. *Courtesy Boise State University.*

Church's opposition to gun control laws was a constant, puzzling and frustrating many liberals. But in 1967 such opposition served him well in his battle to survive a movement to recall him. *Courtesy Boise State University.*

Church, with senators Charles Goodell, George McGovern, Mark Hatfield, and Harold Hughes, during the May 12, 1970 television program in support of the Amendment to End the War in Vietnam. *Courtesy Boise State University.*

Church with Idaho's junior senator, Len Jordan, around 1970. Although different in many respects, the two men got along well together and respected each other. *Courtesy Boise State University.*

Church fishes an Idaho stream, early 1970s. *Courtesy Boise State University.*

Church backpacking through the Idaho wilderness in the Seventies. *Courtesy Boise State University.*

Church addressing a Democratic rally in Lewiston, Idaho, in 1974. *Courtesy Barry Kough.*

Idaho's top Democrats, Governor Cecil Andrus and Church, both campaigning for re-election, huddle at a labor picnic in Idaho in 1974. *Courtesy Barry Kough.*

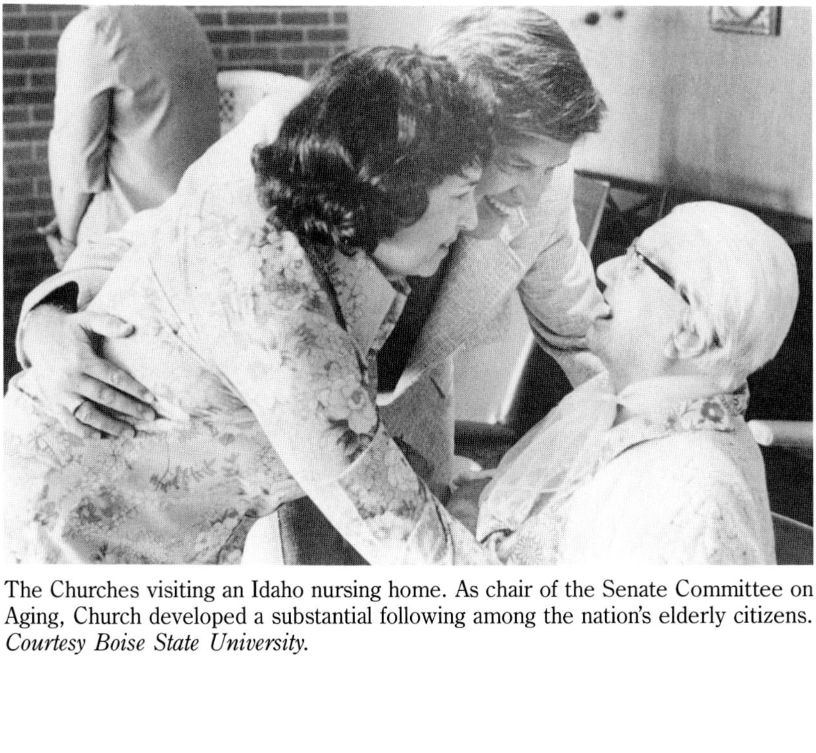

The Churches visiting an Idaho nursing home. As chair of the Senate Committee on Aging, Church developed a substantial following among the nation's elderly citizens. *Courtesy Boise State University.*

Church talking with Idaho gradeschoolers. *Courtesy Boise State University.*

Church believed nonetheless that Kennedy was engaged in "some soul-searching" about America's Vietnam commitment. In a private conversation at the White House the president told Church that he intended to revise America's China policy, but would not be able to do so until after his reelection in 1964. Church doubted that Kennedy would have considered sending troops to Vietnam at the very time he considered softening the U. S. position on China. In retrospect, Church admitted that Kennedy's position on Vietnam was "clouded"; but the senator's gut-level notion was that Kennedy would not have involved the U. S. more deeply in Southeast Asia. In the fall of 1963 the senator found considerable reassurance in that assumption.[50]

VII

In late 1963, Church worried far less about Kennedy's intentions in Vietnam than about political extremism in the United States. On November 22 he was discussing the radical right with veteran diplomat Averell Harriman at a State Department luncheon when he received an emergency phone call. Church excused himself from the small group of senators and State Department people who were honoring a Filipino official. Stepping next door he tried to call his office but, because the circuits were busy, had considerable difficulty getting through to Capitol Hill. Suddenly, his press secretary came on the line with the shocking news that Kennedy had been shot in Texas and was apparently dead. Ashen and shaking, Church burst back into the dining room, just as the guests were starting dessert. "The President has been shot—and is dead," he announced. Gasps of disbelief gave way to confusion as people headed in different directions. Stunned, Church returned to the Senate with Alabama's John Sparkman, hoping that somehow the president might in fact still be alive. The official news brought no comfort: John Kennedy had been assassinated in Dallas.[51]

"It was often said of me," Church told the Senate a few days later, "that I was a 'Kennedy man.' " With pride, he acknowledged the truth of that label. He doubted that he would "know his equal again."[52]

Kennedy's assassination confirmed Church's fears that extremist hysteria was ripping the nation apart. To friends and Idaho constituents the senator sent a letter pleading for a return of "reason and decency against the councils of ignorance, bigotry, and hate." With his letter he included three newspaper columns that placed Kennedy's death in the context of what columnist Walter Lippmann described as "a searing crisis within the American spirit," a crisis that fed on hatred, suspicion, and intolerance. Church could only hope "that a national revulsion against every kind of fanaticism will wash the land clean."[53]

On December 16, Church consoled Robert Kennedy and expressed a wish. "I so admired John F. Kennedy," he wrote, "that I grieved his passing almost as though he had been my own brother." Church was reluctant to offer advice, but he hoped that Robert would not step down as attorney general: "Finishing the work for civil rights that you have so well advanced would be a living monument to your brother's memory."[54]

VIII

Church threw his own energies behind the passage of the martyred president's civil rights bill, which had suddenly found new life. On November 20, California congressman Don Edwards had lamented that the bill, H. R. 7152, "was running out of gas." Following John Kennedy's assassination, however, a substantial number of Americans seemed anxious to commemorate the thirty-fifth president by passing his legislative proposals. By the end of 1963 a solid 62 percent of the public favored his civil rights measure. And 79 percent backed his successor, Lyndon Johnson, who was determined to secure a civil rights law. Incredibly, less than a month after Congress reconvened, the House passed H. R. 7152. On February 7 the bill went to the Senate. By then, a Harris poll indicated that public support of the bill had grown to 68 percent; a Gallup poll showed a somewhat lower approval rating of 61 percent, but even this figure was a notable jump from that of 49 percent seven months earlier.[55]

The signals from Idaho were far less encouraging, however. Indeed, the civil rights issue seemed primarily to tap fears of big government and racial minorities. Such alarm mystified Church. There were few racial minorities in the state, and almost no African Americans. Moreover, in 1961 the Idaho legislature had passed a civil rights law that in some respects was more rigorous than the proposed federal act, especially regarding discrimination in public places. (The law had passed easily, 44 to 10 in the House and 29 to 14 in the Senate.) Church tried to reassure critics that the proposed federal measure would simply extend elsewhere what Idaho and several dozen other states were doing already to uphold the Constitution. Letters to him in late 1963 and early 1964 were nevertheless fearful, often resentful, even ugly and threatening.[56]

Literature from organizations such as the Coordinating Committee for Fundamental American Freedoms seemed to find a receptive audience in Idaho. The committee, combatting "total federal regimentation" and receiving funds from the Mississippi legislature, poured anti-civil rights advertisements and pamphlets into mountain states such as Idaho, Montana, and Wyoming. Letters to Church in late 1963 demonstrated the corrosive effects of the committee's misrepresentations and exaggerations. He found particularly disturbing a lengthy resolution from the Hailey, Idaho, Chamber of Commerce claiming that the civil rights bill was communistic. Shortly thereafter, the Sandpoint Chamber of Commerce took a similar position. An editorial in the *Lincoln County Journal* maintained that "there will be a federal agent at the door" ordering people what to do with their private homes: " 'civil rights' is only the cover up for a giant instrument of federal control. . . ." Church regretted the fanatical tones that often characterized opposition to civil rights. In exasperation, he told one constituent that the John Birch Society was a greater threat to American freedoms than proposed civil rights legislation.[57]

As the civil rights battle heated up in the Senate, Church worried that "the voice of those who favor the bill is not being heard in Idaho." By April his constituent mail was running ten-to-one against the bill. In the face of fierce resistance, the senator moved on several fronts. He sent dozens of letters to Idaho ministers, chapters of the League of Women Voters, journalists, and sympathetic constituents, pleading for assistance in advancing a "fundamental moral issue." He, and the cause of civil rights, desperately needed their help. "I believe civil rights is one area in which morality can be directed by proper legislation," he said.[58]

Church also stepped up his campaign against the radical right. He sent information to radio and television stations in Idaho about the gross distortions that filled the broadcasts of Carl McIntyre, Dan Smoot, Dean Manion, Gerald L. K. Smith, and other far-right commentators. Programmers, he insisted, should consider their own responsibilities for airing the falsehoods of these announcers. The response to his appeal was mixed. Several stations dropped the broadcasts. But mainly Church evoked anger. A number of postcards from "Alert Americans" repudiated him "as another example of our drunken slobs, mentally debauched Communist Jew loving authorities." Incensed at this "sordid response," the senator fired off a letter to McIntyre, questioning exactly what kind of minister would cultivate such a following.[59]

While he sparred with McIntyre he also intervened in behalf of a young woman from Idaho whose civil rights activities had landed her in a Mississippi jail. Lois Chaffee, daughter of a Kellogg, Idaho, family, graduated from college in 1962, taught in a racially integrated private school in Jackson, Mississippi, and volunteered as a field worker for the Congress of Racial Equality (CORE). On June 13, 1963, the day after the murder of civil rights leader Medgar Evers, she was arrested for allegedly disturbing the peace in a demonstration. After she told the court that she had seen white police officers beating up black children, she was charged with perjury, which carried a prison sentence of up to ten years. While she awaited trial, Jackson authorities refused to let her speak over the telephone to her parents and blocked efforts to bail her out of the county jail. Her family attorney in Kellogg called Church about the matter and got immediate action. The senator instructed Verda Barnes on his staff to concentrate on the Chaffee matter. Following Chaffee's eventual release on bond, the young woman's attorney praised Church: "There is no doubt in my mind that if you and Verda had not been as aggressive as you were, she would still be in jail." Chaffee's parents concurred. While Chaffee awaited trial Church continued to monitor the situation closely, making sure that she had good counsel. He also used her case as an illustration of why people in Idaho, far from Mississippi, had an interest in civil rights legislation.[60]

In the Senate, Church joined the front lines of the most important civil rights battle since 1957. This time, however, the proposed legislation was more substantive. And this time the stakes were higher for both sides. As southern senators launched the longest filibuster to that date, their opponents prepared to do what the Senate had failed to do eleven times previously when considering civil rights: invoke cloture (or halt debate with a vote of two-thirds of the membership).

"You liberals will never deliver," Lyndon Johnson had chided Hubert Humphrey, the floor manager of the civil rights bill. "Liberals will be off making speeches when they ought to be present in the Senate." The president's challenge had the desired effect. It stung the Minnesota Democrat, whose unspoken response was, " 'Damn you, I'll show you.' " Humphrey joined California Republican Thomas H. Kuchel in setting up an organizational system to combat the filibuster. They appointed team captains—Church among them—who were responsible for getting their colleagues on the floor for quorum calls as quickly as possible. Without a quorum, a majority of the membership, the Senate faced adjournment. For the filibusterers a quorum call was a favorite tactic because it allowed them a respite and wore down their opponents. When a quorum call was announced at the opening day baseball game, Humphrey and others scurried back to Capitol Hill, while Georgia's Richard Russell stayed at the stadium, relishing the plight of the civil rights advocates.[61]

Day after day, Church helped to round up his colleagues for quorum calls. Working with him was Jerry Brady, who, in his mid-twenties, was a newcomer to the senator's staff. Years later, Brady recalled the difficulties of tracking down senators like Ohio Democrat Frank Lausche, "who really wanted to be on the golf course instead of defending the civil rights bill."[62]

Church also helped to defeat crippling amendments, including, ironically, several that resembled the jury trial amendment of 1957. On April 30 he told the Senate he had modified his earlier views. In 1957 he had favored jury trials in all criminal contempt cases. But he now believed that a similar proposal "would go too far." Judges needed reasonable power to sustain their rulings. In lieu of mandatory jury trials in all criminal contempt cases, Church voted for a compromise measure that provided the right to jury trials in cases where fines were more than $300 or sentences exceeded thirty days. Here, said Church, was a healthy balance: it allowed judges some flexibility in enforcing court orders while guarding against "arbitrary or abusive extension of judicial power." Out of more than five hundred proposed amendments, the jury trial measure was one of only twelve that the Senate accepted.[63]

As the Senate moved toward final action on the civil rights bill, the efforts of Church's staff to mobilize sentiment in Idaho began finally to pay off. By the end of April the mail that had been running ten-to-one against the bill had evened out. From May into June, the letters tilted clearly in favor of the bill.[64]

June 10 was a historic day in the Senate. With the temperature outside at 100 degrees and the clock approaching high noon, the vote on cloture finally took place. Every senator was present, including California Democrat Clair Engle, who was dying and so weak that he could only point feebly to his eye to signal his affirmative vote. By a 71 to 29 count, four votes more than the required two-thirds, the Senate accepted cloture. The longest filibuster ever—more than 534 hours—had ended. Eight days later, the Senate passed the civil rights bill, 73 to 27. On July 2, Lyndon Johnson signed the bill into law, marking a major civil rights achievement. Although the voting sections of the law were bland, relying primarily on case-by-case proceedings, the sections dealing with public accommodations, employment, and education were strong.[65]

The fight for the 1964 civil rights act had many heroes. Humphrey had excelled. Everett Dirksen's surprising switch in favor of the bill had been crucial. Engle's last, mute votes had demonstrated great commitment. But Frank Church could take pride in his own role. As a floor captain, he had been in the thick of the fight. And he had helped to effect a dramatic reversal of opinion in his home state. "I pray that this bill will open a fissure in the glacier of racial prejudice which overburdens us," he said, "and that a prolonged thaw in racial tensions may follow its enactment." Otherwise, he feared that hatred would spawn more violence and political demagoguery.[66]

In order to reduce passions, he hoped also that the civil rights movement would itself seek a season of quiet. Continued protests at this point would endanger civil rights, rather than advance them. Church thus urged people such as John M. Bailey, head of the National Democratic Party, to speak with black leaders about curtailing public demonstrations. The senator personally contacted James Farmer, the national director of CORE. In Church's estimation, CORE's demonstrations would only strengthen the white backlash. And that backlash would benefit Barry Goldwater, who had recently locked up the Republican presidential nomination by winning the California primary. By voting against the civil rights bill, the Arizona senator had further endeared himself with many white Southerners. According to Goldwater, the new law would "require the creation of a federal police force of mammoth proportions"; this, combined with "an 'informer' psychology," could in turn reduce America to a police state. Church urged Farmer to help ensure that civil rights groups did not jeopardize Lyndon Johnson's reelection in November by encouraging racial turmoil.[67]

Church's plea for moderation was understandable, given his worries that a white backlash would boost Goldwater and right wing extremism. But to many civil rights workers the terrible summer of 1964 rendered meaningless the very idea of restraint. The state of Mississippi, for example, was like a battlefield. "Hate and viciousness seemed to be everywhere," recalled Cleveland Sellers. At age nineteen, Sellers was registering black voters for the Student Non-Violent Coordinating Committee (SNCC). He knew that "death could come at any time in any form: a bullet between the shoulder blades, a fire bomb in the night, a pistol whipping, a lynching." Never had he "experienced such tension and near-paralyzing fear."[68]

In Mississippi alone, racist terrorism resulted in at least thirty-five burned churches, thirty burned homes and buildings, eighty beatings, and six murders. Lyndon Johnson's administration nevertheless hesitated to send federal protection. The White House specialist on civil rights, Lee White, believed it "incredible that those people who are voluntarily sticking their head into the lion's mouth would ask for somebody to come down and shoot the lion." When searchers in August found the bodies of three civil rights workers in a shallow Mississippi grave, the movement shook with renewed fury. David Dennis of CORE had spoken earlier against violence. But at the funeral of the three young men he sobbed, "I've got vengeance in my heart tonight. . . . If you go back home and sit down and take what these white men in Mississippi are doing to us. . . then God damn your souls." That kind of anger, prompted by searing personal experiences, countered Church's desire for a cooling-off period in American politics.[69]

IX

New developments in Vietnam added to the senator's uneasiness. The overthrow of Diem had produced more instability, and the war in the countryside was going badly. In Saigon itself, as General William Westmoreland later said, the "atmosphere fairly smelled of discontent."[70]

The deteriorating situation boded ill for Lyndon Johnson. As a tough-minded Cold Warrior, he was certain that the Soviets and Chinese were taking his measure. He thus wanted to hold the line in Vietnam. Yet he preferred to do nothing that might jeopardize his standing with the American people, thereby imperiling his dreams of winning the November election and building a Great Society. During the spring of 1964 he avoided enlarging the U. S. commitment while looking for ways to answer Barry Goldwater's charges that "the architects of defeat" were shaping America's policies. According to Goldwater, "American back-downsmanship" dominated the administration, rendering it "cross-eyed with our friends, wide-eyed with our enemies, . . . glassy-eyed in

Southeast Asia." On March 2 Johnson told Senator Fulbright over the phone that a moment of truth was approaching: "We've got to decide whether to send them [troops] in or whether to come out and let the dominoes fall."[71]

Church fretted that the administration was considering a more substantial U. S. presence in Vietnam. "I would hope that we don't make South Vietnam a launching pad for another Korean war," he told a reporter in mid-March during a lengthy interview. He said that he had "always had grave misgivings over the original decision which took us into Vietnam." Indeed, he would protest "strongly" if the U. S. were to make that choice again. Perhaps trying to signal the Johnson administration, he recalled John Kennedy's distinction "that the war in South Vietnam was their war, not ours." Over the next several months Church worked on what he viewed as a major Senate speech on Vietnam.[72]

On June 23, although his remarks were not yet ready, an extemporaneous exchange with Fulbright suggested what he had in mind. In retrospect, one publication described the occasion as "the day Frank Church became a dove." When he took the Senate floor he intended to commemorate the twentieth anniversary of the founding of the United Nations. Almost as an aside he suggested that the UN might help to effect a negotiated settlement in Southeast Asia. Fulbright challenged him on this point, arguing that the time was inopportune to involve the UN in that region. Perhaps, Fulbright speculated, the UN could play an effective role at a later date—but only after the United States had helped to stabilize the situation by halting North Vietnamese aggression. Church expressed concern that the United States might be looking too much toward a military solution. Fulbright replied that America, as the strongest free world nation, had a special obligation in Vietnam: "They will either go down the drain or we must step in."[73]

Church hesitated momentarily, admitted that he was still trying to organize his thoughts on the subject, and then plunged on to discuss why he was deeply anxious about Vietnam. As he reflected for about ten minutes on the war in Southeast Asia, a hush fell over the chamber. The only movement in the room, according to one observer, was Church's pacing back and forth. The Idaho senator noted that recent talk about retaliating against North Vietnam bothered him greatly. If "a political war" in the South was unwinnable against twenty-five thousand communist soldiers, how sensible was it "to take on the army of North Vietnam?" The point seemed elementary: "Expanding the war is not getting out," he said. "It is getting further in." And if the Chinese sent troops, the U. S. would be in a conflict resembling the Korean war. Dispatching American soldiers into the jungles of Vietnam would be futile. "Do we think," Church asked, "that the history of the last twenty years means that a white nation is going to be upheld in fashioning the destiny of Asia?" The Idaho senator had no quarrel with the administration if it intended simply to continue giving aid to the South Vietnamese government. But he wanted to plant "some warning posts" for those who might be considering an enlarged, bloodier trail into Vietnam. He conceded that sometimes a nation must fight a war to defend its vital interests. "But let us be sure," he pleaded slowly and emphatically. "Let us be sure."[74]

About five weeks after Church's exchange with Fulbright, troubles surfaced in Vietnam with a vengeance. On August 1, in the Gulf of Tonkin, North Vietnamese torpedo boats fired on a U. S. destroyer, the *Maddox*. The Johnson administration, determined to show its resolve, sent the destroyer *C. Turner Joy* to accompany the *Maddox*. On August 4 both ships reported being under attack. Despite a "flash" update that the attack might have been a false alarm, Johnson wanted to retaliate quickly by giving the North Vietnamese "a real dose." He immediately ordered air strikes against their torpedo boat bases and some oil storage dumps. The next day he sought a congressional resolution authorizing the president "to take all necessary measures to repel any armed attack against the forces of the United States and to prevent further aggression." Subsequent scrutiny of these events would raise doubts about what had actually happened in the Tonkin gulf. The initial attack on the *Maddox* had in fact been a retaliatory response to provocative actions. A day earlier, South Vietnamese gunboats had attacked North Vietnam, and the *Maddox* had been conducting electronic surveillance off the North Vietnamese coast. The August 4 attack on the U. S. destroyers remained unverified.[75]

But in the heat of the moment, Congress rallied around the president. On August 7 the Gulf of Tonkin resolution passed the House unanimously and the Senate 88 to 2, with Wayne Morse and Ernest Gruening the only dissenters. J. William Fulbright piloted the resolution through the Senate.

Church, like most of his colleagues, concluded that this was not the time to quarrel with the administration. During the brief ten-hour

Senate debate on the resolution, he noted his "serious misgivings about the correctness of American policy in Southeast Asia." Indeed, he believed that the policy reflected America's "addiction to an ideological view of world affairs." He nevertheless added quickly that the incident in the Gulf of Tonkin demanded a response. "There is a time to question the route of the flag, and there is a time to rally around it, lest it be routed."[76]

Looking back, Church judged his support of the resolution a terrible mistake. It became, one of his staffers said, his "scarlet letter." But, at the time, his basis for judgment was the administration's claim that the North Vietnamese had attacked U. S. ships on the high seas without provocation. The resolution was simply a means by which Congress approved of retaliatory steps that the president had already taken. Church never viewed the resolution as doing more than that—certainly not as giving implicit approval for Johnson to send U. S. troops to Vietnam. Indeed, in August 1964, LBJ was portraying himself as the peace candidate, in contrast to the hawkish Goldwater. Johnson emphasized that he had no intention of sending American soldiers to fight Asian wars.[77]

Church conceded later that he desperately wanted to believe Johnson because Goldwater's candidacy seemed so scary. Bryce Nelson, who had become Church's foreign affairs assistant the previous fall, sensed that the senator voted for the Tonkin resolution "with a lot of reservations." But Church kept his doubts to himself. His worries about Goldwater, and his perceived need to stand behind the president in a time of crisis, dictated nothing less.[78]

In this respect, the Idaho senator was not alone. In words that echoed Church's, Fulbright later explained that he had not been "in a suspicious frame of mind" about Lyndon Johnson's intentions: "I was afraid of Goldwater." Looking back, Fulbright allowed that the Foreign Relations Committee should have conducted extensive hearings and shaped a somewhat different resolution. But the committee had not, thus facilitating what turned out to be "a disaster; a tragic mistake." Wisconsin Democrat Gaylord Nelson concurred.[79]

X

Like Fulbright, Church was so worried about Goldwater's candidacy that he gave Johnson the benefit of the doubt. In several speeches,

Church described Goldwater as "the Arizona Kid," a man with a quick-on-the-draw temperament more suited to the old frontier than to the 1960s. Goldwater's thinking was simplistic; his methods extreme and militant; his charges of "socialism," "subversion," and "sell-out" unfounded and incendiary. "This country of ours," Church reassured audiences, "is not an old Victorian haunted house, creaking with insolvency, its foundations being eaten away by Red Termites, about to be betrayed to the enemy." Using another analogy, Church quipped that "our times are not some kind of spook show filmed by 19th Century Fox." With so much racial ferment in the nation, Church believed it imperative that people of moderation prevail. Goldwater's brand of "right-wing fanaticism" could only encourage extremist actions and violence.[80]

Goldwater's stance on foreign policy, particularly Vietnam, upset Church. The Arizona senator seemed to view belligerency as the foundation of a foreign policy. In Vietnam, he apparently believed there was "a quick and easy solution." Church warned that "when passion governs policy, catastrophe will readily follow." And he resented Goldwater's claim that Democrats were afraid to stand up to communism. Ironically, Church struck a militant note of his own, responding that "Lyndon Johnson isn't cringing in South Vietnam today. He doesn't know the meaning of the word."[81]

During the last several weeks of the 1964 campaign Church stayed in Idaho, trying to help Congressman Ralph Harding stave off a strenuous right-wing challenge from George Hansen. The John Birch Society was fueling an intense anti-Harding movement. Hansen, an arch-Goldwaterite who had recently passed out Birch Society literature in Pocatello, relished conspiratorial themes. He claimed, for example, that Harding was receiving support from a "secret international pacifist society," the Council for a Liveable World. Church wanted to do everything he could for Harding, and believed also that he might be able to pull Idaho behind Lyndon Johnson.[82]

To Church's relief, Johnson won a resounding victory, capturing a record-setting percentage of the popular vote and carrying 44 states. Idaho ended up in the Democratic column for the first time since 1948, although just barely. The public had not only rejected Goldwater, but had provided Johnson with overwhelming majorities in Congress. With the economy booming, the president seemed able now to fashion the Great Society that he envisioned—an America that benefitted all groups, including the poor and minorities.

Church nevertheless recognized that troubles lurked beneath these encouraging developments. Race relations were increasingly volatile. Vietnam remained a burning issue. And the rancor in American politics had hardly disappeared. In Idaho, the malicious campaign against Ralph Harding ended in victory for Hansen; and the Goldwaterites seized control of the Republican Party from the moderate wing that Governor Robert Smylie had dominated since 1954. Goldwater did better in Idaho than in any other state outside of Arizona or the five in the deep South that he carried. As pollster Peter Hart later discerned, 1964 marked a pronounced rightward shift in Idaho politics. Frank Church's decision to step up his campaign against the radical right thus reflected his awareness of trends within his own state as well as elsewhere. But he could not ignore what was happening thousands of miles across the Pacific, in a place called Vietnam.[83]

Significantly, although he still rejected extremist positions, he complained when a constituent accused him of occupying a "dead center" position on Vietnam. "I do not think I am at 'dead center' on this question," he replied, "and I am certainly not regarded as being a 'middle of the roader' on the issue." The war in Southeast Asia was beginning to challenge his faith in centrist politics.[84]

A happy moment with LBJ. *Courtesy Boise State University.*

Chapter Eight
Up and Down with LBJ: 1965

"HOW ARE LYNDON relations!?" Although Bethine Church had asked that question following the 1960 Democratic convention, it took on special relevancy for her husband after Johnson's election to the presidency.[1]

Like Lyndon Johnson, Frank Church valued political consensus and compromise. Church's main quarrel with the radical right was that it was intolerant of other opinions and would choke democratic processes with the rope of ideology. In contrast, the senator respected Johnson in large part because the huge Texan instinctively understood the give-and-take of the political arena. In 1964 the president had fulfilled Church's expectations by helping to unify the nation following John Kennedy's assassination, by using his persuasive talents in behalf of social legislation such as civil rights, and by showing restraint in foreign policy. But as the year 1965 unfolded, Church took issue with the president on foreign policy matters, especially regarding Vietnam. On that subject, "Lyndon relations" quickly became stormy and ultimately disillusioning.

I

Right after the 1960 election, relations between Church and Johnson had improved markedly. At one point, Church had flown with the new vice president to the Pacific Northwest to dedicate a dam on the Snake River. LBJ, although suffering from laryngitis, had been very cordial. Church asked him why he had surprised so many people by agreeing to occupy the bottom half of the ticket with Kennedy. Johnson, trying to save his voice, jotted down on a small piece of paper that he had done so for one, simple reason: his Texas colleague, House Speaker Sam Rayburn, had told him that if he did not join the ticket, Richard Nixon would become president. "I suspect," Church said later, "that was as straight an answer as anybody ever got to that question." Following

John Kennedy's assassination, Church had strongly supported Johnson, helping to construct the early phases of the Great Society in 1964 and actively backing civil rights and wilderness legislation. He had, of course, enthusiastically endorsed Johnson during the 1964 election.[2]

But, deep down, he was nervous about the possible implications of the Tonkin Gulf resolution. In September 1964, a few weeks after passage of the resolution, he aired his concerns in an interview that he knew would not be published until after the election. The occasion was a visit from a former Stanford schoolmate, Ed Keating, editor of the liberal Catholic magazine, *Ramparts*. When Church privately expressed misgivings about Vietnam, Keating coaxed him into granting the interview. Bethine listened to the conversation with growing bewilderment and trepidation. She had not realized the extent to which her husband's doubts about the U. S. role in Vietnam had developed, nor had she been aware of the depth of his feelings on the matter. His growing dissatisfaction "just scared me to death," she said later. She feared that in Idaho and elsewhere people "would just really blow him out of the water." Over the next several months, in fact, she argued with her husband, sometimes heatedly, about the risks of breaking with the president over an explosive issue such as Vietnam.[3]

Despite Bethine's resistance, Church remained on a collision course with the administration. Adamant that the U. S. not stumble into policies and commitments because of a lack of public debate, he had a lengthy discussion shortly after the election with J. William Fulbright about the best course to follow in Southeast Asia. They agreed that the administration's position on the expanding Vietnam conflict rested on "precarious assumptions"—assumptions that the president could control the escalation, that China would not react, that the public would obligingly accept an enlarged U. S. presence, and that victory would be easy. Even a "victory" could saddle the U. S. with a massive aid program. While the two senators resisted any enlargement of the American role, they suspected that the existing policy was also flawed. All indications were that the political situation in South Vietnam would remain volatile. Even if that beleaguered area found stability, it would more than likely be through a dictatorship that would reflect badly upon the United States. Church and Fulbright settled on a more promising option: "a planned, phased contraction of United States military assistance, neutralization and ultimate withdrawal." For the moment, however, the thoughts that came out of the meeting between Church and

Fulbright constituted nothing more than a draft memo. A member of Church's staff hoped that, at the least, the Idaho senator could use it as the basis for a speech.[4]

In the meantime, *Ramparts* in late December published Church's interview. By then, Congress had adjourned for the Christmas break, and the Churches were visiting in Idaho. The interview might have gotten little national attention, except for a *New York Times* reporter who spotted it and called the senator. Suddenly, as Bethine remembered, the situation "hit the fan."[5]

The *Ramparts* interview was a warning shot across the administration's bow. The senator took issue with strategists who believed the war in South Vietnam could be won by bombing the north. China might well respond, as it had done earlier in Korea. Even if the war remained local, the South Vietnamese needed themselves to win it: "The only answer to Communist subversion. . . is to be found within that country itself." Church conceded that the South might lose the war. If that happened, he hoped Americans would accept the result: Vietnam "is not our country and never has been." Insofar as the U. S. took over the war, it would be fighting "the tides of history." Asians would shortly forget America's honorable motives and see nothing more than another white, western nation using force to get its way. In this regard, the U. S. could fall victim to "an imperial attitude," convinced that it had the power to determine what happened in other countries. If America's Asian policy was flawed, it might be because the U. S. refused to recognize the limits of its power.[6]

Although the administration greeted these comments "with a riot of silence," as Church later put it, surprising encouragement came from "your number one fan," Hubert Humphrey. On down the line, the new vice president would be more circumspect about applauding public critiques of America's Vietnam policy. But, for now, Humphrey judged Church's interview as "excellent. You have performed a great service for American foreign policy." J. William Fulbright agreed, placing the *Ramparts* interview in the *Congressional Record*.[7]

The *New York Times*, praising the senator's "fresh voice on Vietnam," gave the interview front-page attention. According to the *Times*, Church's effort to prepare the way for U. S. extrication from Vietnam deserved a wider hearing. With that in mind, the editors of the *New York Times Magazine* solicited a feature article from him, "We Are In Too Deep in Africa and Asia."[8]

By this time, Church was actively formulating his thoughts on Vietnam. In December he lunched with David Halberstam, whose coverage of the war for the *New York Times* had won a Pulitzer prize. He talked at length with John Mecklin, editor of *Time,* who had served with the American embassy in Saigon and was publishing a book on the turmoil he had observed there. And he asked University of Chicago political scientist Hans Morgenthau for his assessment of America's choices in Southeast Asia.[9]

The senator continued to view the war primarily in practical terms. He admired the courage of the Senate's only two consistently outspoken critics, Ernest Gruening of Alaska and Oregon's Wayne Morse. Both had labored virtually alone in opposition to the war for a number of months. But Church knew that their legalistic and moralistic arguments had little effect on their colleagues. Morse suffered a gadfly's reputation; and Gruening's tendency to blame the U. S. as the aggressor struck most listeners as harsh and strident. Church's decision to emphasize the pragmatic side of the matter came easily. He was not yet thinking of the war as a moral issue. That would come later. For the moment, his inclination was to consider America's involvement in Vietnam not as systemic, but as an unintended slide into a quagmire. As always, Church's approach was coolly analytical.[10]

In early 1965 the quagmire deepened. Another coup shook South Vietnam in January, along with renewed Buddhist demonstrations and Vietcong victories in the field. Most of Lyndon Johnson's advisers now agreed: the U. S. would have to bomb the north in order to avoid defeat. Vietcong attacks on a U. S. army barracks in Pleiku on February 6 provided the opportunity to set this plan in motion. Reprisal strikes against the north immediately devolved into "Operation Rolling Thunder," a program of sustained bombing.[11]

On February 14, as the administration intensified air attacks on North Vietnam, Church's article, "We Are In Too Deep in Africa and Asia," appeared in the *New York Times Magazine*. To the senator's delight, Walter Lippmann judged the essay "splendid." "I am happy," Lippmann told him personally, "that we have another Borah from Idaho." Church decided to use the article as a speech in the Senate, despite Bethine's demurrals.[12]

His Senate remarks on February 17 opened what developed into a major debate on Vietnam. "We evidently think that everything which happens abroad has become our business," declared Church, adding the stinging comment that "we have plunged into these former colonial regions as though we had been designated on high to act as trustee in bankruptcy for the broken empires." Contrary to the prevailing theory, he insisted that the southeast Asian nations were "not so many dominoes in a row." And he pleaded for a negotiated settlement, perhaps policed by the United Nations.[13]

Toward the end of his Senate speech he departed briefly from the text of his *Times*' article to comment on recent developments. Careful not to criticize the air strikes, he said that the bombing of military installations in North Vietnam "may persuade Hanoi and Peiping that the United States is not, and has never been, a paper tiger." But he emphasized again the need for a negotiated settlement, even though he realized that "cries of 'appeasement' " already awaited anyone who urged such a course. He then predicted ominously that, without negotiations, "the next step will be to send American land forces into battle, thus converting the struggle into an American war on the Asian mainland."[14]

Coincidentally, on February 17 South Dakota's George McGovern also addressed the Senate and urged negotiations—a word the administration did not wish to hear. In Lyndon Johnson's opinion, the U. S. had nothing to negotiate in Vietnam. America's objective, he told a group of business leaders that same day, was to defend and protect the "freedom of a brave people who are under attack that is controlled and that is directed from outside their country."[15]

On February 18 the press was full of stories of clashes between "hawks" and "doves" in the nation's capital. That afternoon, Johnson sent national security advisor McGeorge Bundy to the Hill to contain the debate. Church, McGovern, Wisconsin's Gaylord Nelson, Minnesota's Eugene McCarthy, Ohio's Stephen Young, and Wyoming's Gale McGee (who had vociferously defended the administration the previous day) received invitations to meet with Bundy in the vice president's office. Humphrey was also present. When Church arrived, Bundy looked up from reading the February 17 debate and commented that the press seemed to have exaggerated the differences between Johnson and various senators. In fact, Bundy was surprised to find how constructive the speeches had been. Neither McGovern nor Church, he noted, had urged U. S. withdrawal from Vietnam or even criticized the retaliatory bombings. Nevertheless, he made it clear that Johnson hoped the Senate debate would end lest the North Vietnamese misconstrue America's resolve. "Americans have to present a united front," he said.[16]

Church countered that a debate over war or peace in Asia would, in the long run, be of service to the president. The other senators also stood firm. When Bundy left, Humphrey broke into a smile. The vice president had sent a lengthy memo to Johnson a few days earlier objecting to a larger war. But he had also pledged support for whatever decision Johnson made. That was why, in Bundy's presence, Humphrey had occasionally interjected comments in the administration's behalf. Now, alone with the senators, he beamed, "You boys don't scare easily, do you?"[17]

When Church and McGovern returned to the Senate they discovered that they were under attack from their colleagues. Illinois Republican Everett Dirksen tossed his wavy white hair defiantly and warned against running up a flag of surrender in Vietnam. Talk of negotiations would simply lead to "a really big war" and leave the United States "facing the enemy on the inner line from Alaska to Hawaii." Massachusetts Republican Leverett Saltonstall agreed, along with Democrats George Smathers of Florida and Frank Lausche of Ohio.[18]

That evening Frank and Bethine Church joined a group of around two dozen senators and their spouses as guests at the White House, where Johnson had scheduled a briefing on Vietnam. The gathering started on a pleasant enough note. Lyndon and Lady Bird Johnson posed with each couple for photographs in front of the fireplace and offered cocktails in the East Room. Then came the briefing. While spouses gathered to see a film on White House paintings, the senators joined LBJ in an office.[19]

At the outset, Church knew he was in trouble. Johnson fixed "a burning gaze" on him. Then, in an obvious reference to William E. Borah, Johnson spoke of a senator who had once believed that he knew more about foreign policy than did the president. The senator had foolishly predicted that there would be no war in Europe. Church sat uncomfortably, well aware that he was the target of Johnson's jab. During the rest of the briefing, as Church recalled shortly afterwards, LBJ was highly agitated, "talking with the speed and gestures of a carnival barker." When Mississippi Democrat James Eastland asked why the U. S. could not keep a government in power in Vietnam, Johnson answered that he could not even control "such matters right here in the United States." Church, tempted to respond, decided that this was neither the time nor the place.[20]

Downstairs, meanwhile, Bethine Church grew more and more anxious. The briefing was lasting much longer than expected, and she knew her husband had left the afternoon meeting with Bundy expecting a chilly reception at the White House. Several times she asked Lady Bird's assistant if there was any news about why the briefing was continuing so long. "Is it Frank?" she inquired nervously at one point. Finally, to her relief, she saw her husband coming down the stairs with the other senators. Mike Mansfield, walking alongside Church, wondered why his Idaho friend had remained quiet during the briefing. "Mike," Church answered, "the President was in such a high state of excitement, I felt a question from me might cause him to blow a fuse."[21]

The evening was not over, however. A few minutes later, while the guests enjoyed refreshments in the State Room, Church looked up to see Johnson coming "through the crowd like a dreadnought parting the destroyers left and right." Suddenly, Church found himself "in one of those nose-to-nose encounters" with the president for about thirty minutes. Johnson, cordial but relentless, talked virtually non-stop while downing several scotches. Now and again, when Johnson drew a breath, Church interjected some replies. He hoped, for example, hat the press had not given Johnson the wrong impression. He was not advocating withdrawal from Vietnam; indeed, he too believed that the U. S. should honor its commitments. Nor was he critical of the retaliatory bombing raids. He simply hoped to keep the war from expanding.[22]

Johnson became increasingly exercised. Across the room, Texas senator Ralph Yarborough sensed that the president was "bawling out" Church. More and more animated, Johnson wrapped one arm around Bethine's shoulders and seemed oblivious to the fact that he was bearing down on her so hard that she thought her heels would go through the floor. Then, without realizing what he was doing, he pushed her away and almost to the floor. When Lady Bird and others approached anxiously, Johnson waved them off. "Frank and I are old friends," he said. "We want to talk this thing out." On another occasion he noted that "Frank helped me to pass the civil rights bill of 1957. He and I know how to get along together." Somewhere in the very spirited conversation, Church noted his great respect for columnist Walter Lippmann. The president concurred that Lippmann was very astute, and the exchange ended shortly thereafter. As the guests walked out the door,

Eugene McCarthy joked, "If Frank Church had just surrendered, we all could have gone home half an hour ago."[23]

Church left the White House convinced that the lively discussion was "without rancor or belligerence on either side." Bethine felt differently, and cried all the way home. In her opinion, Frank was making a terrible mistake. She knew that her cousin, D. Worth Clark, had fallen on bad times politically in the early 1940s after shrugging off the possibilities of World War II. She worried also about hurting Lady Bird Johnson, with whom she was quite close. The senator downplayed the incident at the White House, suspecting the matter was closed.[24]

It was not. To his surprise, a story soon circulated in the press and in social gatherings that Lyndon Johnson had cleverly reminded the young senator about who was in charge. The president had reportedly told him that, next time he wanted a dam in Idaho, he could go to Walter Lippmann. Church concluded subsequently, after talking with several colleagues and newspeople, that Johnson himself was the source of the account. He personally found the LBJ version amusing, and suspected that the president hoped "such a story would help to tamp down further criticism of his policy in Vietnam from Capitol Hill." What galled the senator were the inferences that some observers drew from Johnson's rendition. Supposedly, LBJ had taken the forty-year-old senator to the woodshed and, with the famed Johnson treatment, shown him the error of his ways. Columnists Rowland Evans and Robert Novak especially infuriated Church by portraying him as a kind of White House puppet who had mistakenly delivered his February 17 speech.[25]

Such interpretations were "preposterous," Church angrily shot back in a press release. "I wouldn't knuckle under on Vietnam for all the dams in the Northwest, and the President knows it. He would be the last man to attempt to silence me with such a threat." As evidence, Church repeated his speech, "We Are in Too Deep in Africa and Asia," in Detroit on February 22 and at Stanford University on March 2.[26]

He recognized, at the same time, the need for caution in dealing with the president and Idaho constituents. In a letter to Johnson on February 19 he expressed affection as well as support. "Believe me, Mr. President," he wrote, "when I say that I care very much about you, and that I see in you those qualities of greatness which few of your predecessors have possessed." He emphasized that he would certainly not want to limit Johnson's effectiveness in handling Vietnam. The newsletter sent to Idaho residents at the end of February made this same point, while also articulating his own concerns about Southeast Asia. On the one hand, he indicated that he backed the president: "He has talked to me about the problem, and we have had a cordial, intimate exchange of views." Church also expressed sympathy for LBJ's predicament, comparing it to that of "trying to unscramble an omelet twelve years in the baking." On the other hand, the senator expressed alarm about where the U. S. seemed to be headed. He entitled his newsletter, "Viet Nam: The Burning Fuse," and raised the possibility that America was slipping into another Korean-type war. "Before we go down that road again, I want to be sure there is no better alternative," he explained. He enclosed a reprint of his *New York Times* article on U. S. over-involvement in Africa and Asia.[27]

II

These were clearly difficult days for Church. "It was the hardest period we've ever lived in Washington," said his wife almost fifteen years later. Members of his staff also wondered nervously if he was going too far. "Boy, he is really asking for it," thought aide Jerry Brady. Church's secretary, Tommie Ward, remembered that the nagging question in the office was " 'How is this going to play in Idaho?' It's a conservative, rock-ribbed state." There was every reason to worry. Verda Barnes, by then Church's chief administrative assistant, expected that his actions would cost him his Senate seat.[28]

Church, too, feared he was cutting his own political throat. Idaho "is a hawkish state to begin with," he reflected subsequently. "We still live close to the legends of the western frontier and people in Idaho are inclined to believe that the way to deal with an enemy is to shoot it out in western style." As one constituent reminded him, "The people of Idaho are not lilly livered liberals. They are red blooded Americans with great pride in the country." The writer, a World War II veteran, was convinced that Church did not reflect the mood of Idaho. A dentist from Hayden Lake concurred, claiming that Church spoke instead for people in "double-breasted suits" who favored welfare and gave in to communists. According to the head of Idaho's Republican party, John O. McMurray, Church represented "a small group asking for American appeasement of the Communist Vietnamese."[29]

Even Church's father-in-law could not understand why he would question the president's policy. To Chase Clark, an old-line Democrat, it made no sense at all for Frank not to support a Democratic president. Nor had the judge forgotten how his nephew Worth Clark had stumbled into political oblivion by taking a strong isolationist position on the eve of World War II. "A major rift," as Forrest Church described it, developed between his father and grandfather. They got along only by carefully avoiding the subject of Vietnam during the judge's last two years.[30]

Certainly the administration hoped to impress upon Church the need to rally behind the president. In early 1965 the Central Intelligence Agency informed him that North Vietnam was publicizing his *Ramparts* interview. According to a radio broadcast in Hanoi, he had "protested against the U. S. war of aggression in South Vietnam" and taken issue with "the U. S. ruling circles' myth" concerning the war.[31]

The administration signaled its displeasure with Church in other ways as well. Bryce Nelson, the senator's foreign policy assistant, had a bitter experience in this regard. He attended a dinner in early 1965 sponsored by the Council for a Liveable World. Assistant Secretary of Defense John McNaughton was the featured speaker. During the question-and-answer session, White House aide Douglass Cater strongly implied that opposing the war effort was virtually treasonous. As Nelson remembered it, Cater then said, "I'll let Senator Church's foreign affairs assistant speak on this because Senator Church has been one of the most irresponsible people on Vietnam." Stung, Nelson snapped back that the U. S. might already be too deeply into Southeast Asia to get out easily, but Church and others on the Hill were trying to warn against other Vietnams. Nelson found the incident "chastening." "Never before or never since have I been, in effect, called a traitor to my country, and to have it done by an aide to the President of the United States just really shocked me." From the administration's view, nothing less than loyalty was on the line—loyalty to one's president, loyalty to the nation.[32]

As the situation in Vietnam disintegrated, Lyndon Johnson felt trapped. If he "lost" Vietnam to the communists, he feared a conservative backlash at home. If he mobilized the nation for a wider war, he would jeopardize his Great Society programs. If he sent more Americans, U. S. casualties would mount. In early 1965 he chose to escalate America's military involvement in a piecemeal fashion, using deception and secrecy. Step by step, he redefined U. S. policy, turning "their" war into "our" war. Looking back on those critical months, he lamented that he knew he would "be crucified" whatever he did: "If I left the woman I really loved—the Great Society—in order to get involved with that bitch of a war on the other side of the world, then I would lose everything at home." In that context, it became increasingly difficult for him to tolerate dissent or suggestions of disunity.[33]

Johnson thus gave little attention to the merits of what critics such as Frank Church were saying. That was unfortunate, because Church provided precisely what presidential aide Richard Goodwin later believed key policy makers lacked: historical perspective, an appreciation of the need for information and informed debate in a democracy, and insights into some of the revolutionary transformations that were remaking regions such as Southeast Asia. But Johnson and his advisors tended to place the Idaho senator among what Secretary of Defense Robert McNamara described as the "no-win group who doesn't want another Korea." Johnson wanted support, not what he viewed as niggling suggestions from people who did not understand the big picture. He had no patience with suggestions that the war was getting out of control. "I'm going up Ho Chi Minh's leg an inch at a time," he told George McGovern. And when McGovern, like Church, expressed reservations about the administration's policy, Johnson angrily replied, "Don't give me another goddamn history lesson. . . . I don't need a lecture on where we went wrong. I've got to deal with where we are now."[34]

Church nevertheless continued to voice doubts about Vietnam. On March 4 he hosted a dinner so that the noted political scientist Hans Morgenthau could discuss the issue. Present were several Senate staff people, Alaska senator Robert Bartlett, radio commentator Edward P. Morgan, and a group of reporters, including David Broder, Chalmers Roberts, and Richard Strout. Morgenthau argued that the American position in Vietnam was untenable, in part because policy makers assumed erroneously that European-style containment would also work in Asia. Church was soon actively involved in the discussion. Years later, David Broder remembered how Morgenthau and Church had struggled to convince "a largely skeptical group of reporters" that the war in Vietnam flowed from an indigenous revolution, not aggression from the Soviet Union or China. If the United States persisted on its present course, they had argued passionately, it would repeat the awful mistake of the French: trying to beat back an anti-colonial revolution by military intervention. That policy had not worked for the French in the early Fifties; it would not work for the United States in the Sixties.

"I went home thoroughly unconvinced that night," Broder later wrote, "but had many occasions in the next dozen years to recollect that warning."[35]

On March 8, 3,500 U. S. Marines splashed ashore in Vietnam. They joined 23,000 "advisers" already there. General William Westmoreland had requested the Marines in order to protect the U. S. air base at Danang.[36]

As the troops settled in, Church completed an article for the "Speaking Out" section of the widely popular *Saturday Evening Post*. Entitled "We Should Negotiate a Settlement in Vietnam," the essay had an almost desperate tone. "The war hawks are putting on the heat," Church wrote. "Debate is discouraged; dissent is condemned," and "talk of a negotiated settlement in Vietnam is equated with Munich" and European appeasement of Hitler in the 1930s. Bluster about war threatened all rational discussion. "We may have invested prestige in Vietnam, but by no stretch of the imagination does this struggle threaten the life of our country." In answer to arguments that South Vietnam was "the testing ground" for communist guerrilla warfare, he replied that insurgency could not flourish without a popular base. Again he emphasized that Vietnam's was a civil war. Other nations could not change that fact, however interested they might be in the outcome. Church repeated his conviction that the U. S. simply had to work for a political settlement. He admitted that pro-communist elements might ultimately prevail, but this result would be even more likely as the war dragged on. A favorable settlement would surely be among "the first casualties of a widening war."[37]

It would be a month before Church's essay appeared in print, but there were signs across the country that a growing number of Americans shared his anxieties. On March 24, the first Vietnam "teach-in" occurred at the University of Michigan when three thousand students braved bomb threats inside and freezing weather outside. Over the next few weeks the teach-ins spread to dozens of campuses. A Gallup poll in early April showed great public ambivalence about Vietnam, with 41 percent favoring negotiations and 42 percent calling for more troops and planes. On Capitol Hill, the murmurs of discontent continued.[38]

In an effort to gain control of the situation, the administration took several steps. It sent speakers to college campuses to counter the teach-ins. The president tried to mollify some of his congressional critics through White House meetings and, on April 7, with a major address at Johns Hopkins University.

Johnson anticipated that his Baltimore speech would forestall another round of debate on Vietnam in the Senate. But aide Douglass Cater informed him a few hours before the address that "Church and his cohorts" intended to talk about Vietnam as soon as the Senate convened the next morning. McGeorge Bundy promptly called the Idaho senator and asked him to come to the White House at 5 p. m. Church arrived to find McGovern and McGee already there. McGee's presence was curious. The Wyoming senator had no quarrel with the escalating military involvement in Vietnam, and in that sense was not an ally of Church and McGovern. Perhaps the administration assumed that he, as a Westerner and a friend of both men, might help persuade them. In any case, Bundy gave them copies of the speech that Johnson would soon deliver. "We sat there like three school boys," Church recalled, reading the text. Church and McGovern were pleasantly surprised that Johnson now seemed willing to negotiate a settlement.[39]

Bundy took them upstairs to a little study next to the Oval Office to meet with the president. Johnson looked up with an icy stare and asked, "How's the dam building program coming out in Idaho?" Without thinking, Church replied quickly, "Mr. President, the next dam we finish, we're going to call the Walter Lippmann dam." The room suddenly became deathly silent. Johnson's aide Jack Valenti, who was also present, and Bundy had stricken expressions. The tension virtually crackled. Then Johnson threw back his head and laughed heartily. "Who do you suppose circulated that story anyway?" he asked impishly. When Church said that he did not know, Johnson smiled broadly and said, "Some Republican, I suppose."[40]

The next twenty minutes belonged almost entirely to the president. "Now, I'm doing exactly what you fellars wanted me to do," he said. "I'm going to offer to negotiate." He hoped that his forthcoming speech would satisfy his Senate critics enough that they would not follow through on their proposed debate the next day. His goal, he explained, was to get his education bill through the Senate and help to complete a huge legislative record in the first hundred days of his term. Earlier in the day, Church had told Douglass Cater that he would not agree to postponing discussion of the Vietnam issue. But the senator had learned subsequently that McGovern was willing to wait. So now, as LBJ talked anxiously about the fate of his education bill, Church offered a compromise. "I'll make you a deal," he said, because he was so pleased with the President's upcoming address. "I will cancel my speech in the Senate tomorrow if you will agree to read it." The president quickly accepted the offer.[41]

It was perhaps a somewhat relieved Johnson who spent the next few minutes talking about the challenges he faced in Vietnam. He claimed to be in agreement with the three senators because, like them, he wanted neither to "cut and run" nor to engage China in a war. As much as anyone, he insisted, he wanted a peaceful settlement in Vietnam. But he emphasized that he would never repeat Neville Chamberlain's mistake at Munich in 1938, when the English prime minister had deferred to Hitler. Church, turning to flattery, expressed confidence in Johnson. "I'm just as willing to trust in your judgment at the conference table as I am willing to trust your judgment on the battlefield." "Good," replied the president, slapping his knee. "This is where I think we should stop the conversation. I'm going to quit while I'm ahead." McGovern and Church left the room with a real sense of accomplishment, convinced that Johnson had yielded on their central point—the need to negotiate.[42]

The morning after Johnson's Johns Hopkins address, Church canceled a press conference that he had scheduled for 11 a. m. He also announced that he would not deliver his Senate speech on Vietnam because the president's remarks "much encouraged" him. Clearly, he was putting much stock in the fact that, in Baltimore, LBJ had expressed willingness to engage in "unconditional discussions."[43]

At the time, Church found heartening Johnson's perceived openness to negotiations. "I thought that he had really embarked on a bonafide effort to bring the war to a close," the senator said later. Bethine recalled how excited her husband had been the evening of the Johns Hopkins address. Subsequently, he learned that Johnson had in fact attached a number of conditions to the proffered "unconditional discussions." The president's idea of a "balanced approach," as McGovern later summed it up, was to appear to give ground to his Senate critics ("Okay, I'll offer to negotiate") and then to render such negotiations impossible.[44]

Johnson's strategy in that regard increasingly pushed Church to conclude that the administration's effort to find a middle ground between hawks and doves was inherently flawed. Building a political consensus had worked for LBJ as majority leader, but that tactic proved tragically less viable for a president making foreign policy. ". . .This was a matter of policy that could not be cut down the middle," Church subsequently recognized. Johnson ended up hedging on what the military wanted, yet slipping more and more toward greater military involvement. "The question was whether the policy itself was correct or wrong," Church recalled. "And if it was wrong, it had to be changed." In 1965, the president had no such thoughts in mind.[45]

Indeed, according to his advisor William Bundy, Johnson "was in a very intense He-who-is-not-with-me-is-against-me kind of mood in that period." An anti-war demonstration of more than fifteen thousand people in the nation's capital on April 17 hardly improved his disposition. McGeorge Bundy had recommended "a strong peaceloving statement" from Johnson "that might cool them off ahead of time." But the president's words were probably counterproductive in that regard. He pledged America's presence in Vietnam "as long as is necessary. . . .There is no human power capable of forcing us from Vietnam."[46]

The administration perceived the antiwar protests as damaging the U. S. abroad. "Every student anti-U. S. policy demonstration is priceless gold for the Viet Cong," aide Jack Valenti told the president. The White House asked the Federal Bureau of Investigation to check the extent to which communists had influenced the April 17 protests. Johnson also wanted the FBI to run "name checks" on the war's critics. Presidential aides Richard Goodwin and Bill Moyers worried that LBJ was acting more and more paranoid and irrational. Although Johnson seemed in control of the situation most of the time, his behavior grew increasingly erratic and susceptible to extremely bizarre outbursts. In the Oval Office on June 22 he suddenly told Goodwin and Moyers, "I am not going to have anything more to do with the liberals. They all just follow the communist line—liberals, intellectuals, communists. They're all the same. . . .I can't trust anybody anymore."[47]

Had Frank Church known about such comments he would have been even more apprehensive. Instead, he continued his efforts to accommodate the administration even as it moved, crab-like, along the military course he feared. His reaction to a crisis in the Dominican Republic reflected this ambivalence.

On April 28 the president dispatched twenty thousand Marines to the Caribbean nation to halt a perceived communist takeover. Here, again, was a resort to force, without discussion or debate. Yet Church initially offered Lyndon Johnson "the strongest praise" for "a venture well begun." The president's quick response, Church told the Senate, had helped to prevent "a calamity." By supporting Johnson's intervention in the Dominican Republic, Church sought to legitimize further his dissent about Vietnam. He explained that, just as he would continue to "speak up" when he disagreed with LBJ over Vietnam, so he would applaud policies that deserved it. "I have accepted his judgment that the landing was necessary to save American lives and prevent a communist takeover," he wrote an Idaho reporter. But he nevertheless left the door open to change his mind: "There is a possibility that the facts on which the judgment was made are mistaken; only time will tell."[48]

Similarly, he hedged when the Foreign Relations Committee met in executive session with Secretary of State Dean Rusk on April 30 to discuss the Dominican Republic and Vietnam. By then there were already some 34,000 troops in Vietnam. Fulbright noted that the Tonkin Gulf resolution had endorsed only a limited action at that time. The Arkansas senator objected that the administration was waging war without congressional consent. "A lot of us have been quiet," he said. "We do not want to embarrass the administration." Clearly, he was hinting at the possibilities of bringing the Tonkin Gulf resolution up again for discussion. Although Church favored additional debate on the subject, in order to inform the public about alternatives in Vietnam, he advised against formulating another resolution. Church's position was more moderate than that of Wayne Morse, who a few hours later on the floor of the Senate urged his colleagues to reexamine the Tonkin resolution and decide forthrightly whether the president could continue to use it as the basis for military action.[49]

Church's hesitancy during these weeks perhaps exhibited his continuing hope, however dim, that the administration was still seeking a way out of the Vietnam imbroglio. It probably also revealed much about his perceptions of the Senate. He may have suspected that the Senate, given the chance, would reaffirm Johnson's interpretation of the Tonkin Gulf resolution as a "blank check." This did not mean that there was great sentiment among his colleagues for escalating the war. Indeed, an Associated Press poll of eighty-three senators early in the year had shown that only seven favored sending U. S. combat troops to Vietnam or bombing the north. Church later said, moreover, that "many" senators had privately expressed their general agreement with his dissent. But, for a variety of reasons, they were reluctant to oppose the president. A prime example was Georgia's powerful Democrat, Richard Russell. One of the most respected senators, he was convinced Vietnam was "a mistake" and "a bottomless pit." Yet he also believed that the issue had moved beyond debate: "Our flag is committed and,—more important,—American boys are under fire. . . ." To the extent that most senators were inclined to rally around the president, they were implicated in Johnson's policies: it was their war as much as his. Johnson, of course, applied his own talents to assure that they were on board. He used cajolery, flattery, threats, rewards, and the famed "Johnson treatment." Hence his outspoken critics on the Hill were few in number, and, according to McGovern, "unorganized."[50]

Church was himself swept along, although he kept trying to trail an anchor. He supported, for example, the president's May 4 request for $700 million to use in Vietnam. As LBJ defined the request, it would have been hard to refuse without seeming to endorse communist aggression and to deny U. S. soldiers essential resources. Around ten of the eighty-eight senators who voted for the funds, Church among them, also expressed doubts about the policy. He indicated that, although he backed America's soldiers and "the present policy of the President," he in no sense wanted anyone to interpret his vote as offering a "blank-check endorsement" for future decisions. It was imperative, he said, to aid troops already in the field, but it was equally important to recognize that "the greatest possible calamity" could flow from engaging U. S. forces in an Asian land war. Wayne Morse, who (with Ernest Gruening and Gaylord Nelson) voted against the bill, castigated Church and the other "reservationists." "Whom do you think they are kidding?" he asked angrily. Of course the administration would view the affirmative vote as an endorsement for its action. "I think the White House must be laughing at their 'reservation.' "[51]

Peter Fenn, a close friend of Forrest Church, recalled asking the Idaho senator why he did not simply vote to cut off the funding for Vietnam. "You know," Fenn observed during several lengthy talks, "you continuously vote for funds." Frank Church conceded that Congress could stop the war by refusing to finance it. But, he insisted, the votes for such a step simply did not exist. If any kind of opportunity developed for even a close vote, the senator vowed he would be on the side of Morse and Gruening. Otherwise, he was not about to join a few senators in a futile stand that would open him to criticism for betraying American soldiers in battle. To do so would prove only that he could cut off his own political head.[52]

Instead, he continued to urge more public debate of the Vietnam issue. On June 24 he exhorted his Senate colleagues once again to expand the dialogue about the nature of American policy and the means of negotiating a settlement. "To remain silent," he said, "would be to behave like a mock parliament of a totalitarian state." Dramatically punctuating his speech several times by saying, "Yet the war goes on," he wondered if the U. S. was trying to be "a kind of global policeman" intent on "imposing a Pax Americana." Twice he emphasized that his criticisms of U. S. policy in Asia did not constitute a reproach of the president, with whom he sympathized. Three weeks later he was back in the Senate, imploring the president to ignore appeals to step up the bombing in North Vietnam.[53]

In fact, however, the president was on the verge of sending more combat troops. Nervous about his impending decision, as well as about key Great Society bills still lodged in Congress, Johnson was in no mood for criticism. On July 5 he shocked Richard Goodwin by suddenly remarking in the middle of a discussion of domestic policy: "You know, Dick, the communists are taking over the country." Johnson then produced an FBI file on the noted journalist Theodore White and said, "He's a communist sympathizer." A few days earlier Johnson had suggested that the *New York Times* reporter, Tom Wicker, was conspiring to destroy him. Although presidential aide Jack Valenti was struck by how reasonable and disciplined LBJ was during these months, Goodwin and Bill Moyers viewed the president's "increasingly vehement and irrational outbursts" with alarm. More and more he was personalizing the war, seeing himself engaged in a lonely, principled fight against the communist conspiracy. Padding about late at night in the White House situation room, he gathered the latest reports from Vietnam. "I don't let those planes hit so much as a shithouse without my personal approval," he told George McGovern.[54]

III

On June 24 Frank Church got a disturbing taste of Johnson's frustration and anger. Late in the evening he joined the president on Air Force One for a flight to San Francisco to commemorate the twentieth anniversary of the United Nations. As chair of the subcommittee that dealt with UN affairs, he was a logical choice to make the trip. Otherwise, LBJ might have preferred to have someone else along. Only a few hours before, Church had questioned America's Vietnam policy and encouraged negotiations in a Senate speech—a copy of which he had previously sent to the White House.[55]

Right after Church got on the plane with Republican senator Frank Carlson from Kansas and Glenn Seaborg, the head of the Atomic Energy Commission, Johnson began regaling them about Vietnam. He became extremely agitated as he described staying up all night to receive the results of bombing attacks. Church was startled to learn how extensively the president himself was involved in the details of the war: "I thought it meant that he was losing his capacity to render an objective judgment by losing his detachment and becoming emotionally a part of the war itself." Johnson, clearly very tired, tried to impress his guests with the weight of the terrible burden he carried. He spoke almost non-stop during dinner on the plane, holding forth excitedly about how he was going to handle Ho Chi Minh, that old man in North Vietnam with the scanty beard. Church listened uncomfortably, not agreeing with Johnson but reluctant to say anything.[56]

Suddenly a young lieutenant delivered a radio message that had just arrived. Johnson read it, flushing angrily. He threw the message at Church, demanding, "Read that." It contained news of a plastic bomb explosion in Saigon that had killed several U. S. soldiers, including two American women. As Church read, Johnson stared at him coldly. "What would you do?" the president snapped. "I suppose you would turn the other cheek." This jab was too much for the usually mild-mannered senator. He did not have to take that kind of abuse, even from the president. As his wife later said, "His fuse was not easily lit, but I guess this hit him." Incensed, Church shot back a reply. He expressed his own sadness at the deaths of the Americans, and then tore into Johnson directly: "We're the ones that sent them out there. And we did so knowing the danger, the risk. Plastic bombs are terrible things but that's all the Vietnamese have to fight back with. They don't have big bombers to drop napalm on villages from 35,000 feet." His own emotional juices now flowing, he added a comment. If he were a Vietnamese, he said, "fighting on their side, I'd be fighting that way too, making plastic bombs." Johnson spun away, talked briefly to Carlson and Seaborg, and then stomped off to bed.[57]

The plane stopped over in Kansas City so that Johnson could meet with former President Harry Truman the next day. Church rode in the front seat of the car, while LBJ and Truman chatted in the back. Johnson ignored the senator. Later, back on the plane, LBJ continued to snub him until the presidential photographer started lining up everyone for a picture. Only at that point did Johnson speak to him: "Come on, Frank. I think it would be good for me to have my picture taken with a peacenik." The president had little to say after that.[58]

IV

Church remained hopeful nevertheless. He interpreted as a good sign the July 27 appointment of Arthur Goldberg as the late Adlai Stevenson's successor at the United Nations. "Goldberg feels, as I do," Church wrote a friend, "that the UN has fallen into a serious decline. . . partly by a tendency to turn away from it, as we have done in Vietnam." The senator appreciated the fact that Goldberg would be an advocate within the administration for using the UN to help negotiate an end to the war.[59]

By then Church was almost desperately seeking favorable interpretations of the administration's Vietnam policy. Press speculation that the Senate doves were coming around to Johnson's position had it all wrong, he said. As a matter of fact, the president was joining the doves. "Actually," Church assured an Idaho friend, "Johnson has come out for most of the things I have advocated, including unconditional discussions and negotiated settlement. . . .The position of the administration is now much closer to my own than was the case a year ago."[60]

He said this even as he recognized America's growing military intervention. On July 24 aide Douglass Cater reported to the president that Church, Fulbright, and Vermont Republican George Aiken expressed concern the U. S. was sliding into a land war in Asia, a slide doomed to failure. National Security Advisor McGeorge Bundy tended to discount such information. He categorized Church, Fulbright, Mansfield, and several others as " '*reluctant realists*' whose viscera says get out but whose heads tell them the present policy is unavoidable." Bundy's interpretation was assuredly not what the senators wished to convey to the White House.[61]

Unfortunately, Church himself seemed to illustrate the accuracy of Bundy's assessment. So desperately did he wish to "exert some moderating influence upon the future course of events," as he put it, that he downplayed his own differences with the president. As the administration accelerated U. S. involvement, Church appeared to be backpedaling, saying, in effect: okay, but no more. He, for example, left presidential aide George Reedy with the impression that he was willing to approve of more troops in Vietnam. In a long talk with Reedy in late June, he continued to make the case for keeping the war in the south and not escalating the bombing; he felt "in my bones" that increased strikes against the north would bring in the Chinese. Yet, on the issue of troops, he appeared more flexible. "The only activity that he can recommend," Reedy informed Johnson, "is to continue putting in more ground troops in South Vietnam as you are now doing."[62]

On the July 18 "Issues and Answers" television program, Church sounded much like the president: "I have always held to the position that we can't 'cut and run' in Southeast Asia. We have committed American prestige. . . .we have to stay the course in Vietnam." Although he stressed his opposition to more bombing in the north (something which the other guest, Representative Gerald Ford, advocated), and although he warned against turning the Vietnam conflict into another Korean war, he seemed amenable to the president's sending more troops. When asked specifically about this he answered flatly: "This is a stage in the war where we have to demonstrate that we are in South Vietnam and won't be driven out. . . ."[63]

He was disappointed to hear that some viewers believed he had resembled a hawk more than a dove in his television appearance. "Actually, I have grave misgivings about any new movement of troops into Vietnam on such a scale or with such a mission as would result in the Americanization of that war," he wrote. "If this is what the President is about to propose, then I might have to break entirely with the Administration on this issue." Ironically, the very day that Church said this, Johnson forced his hand.[64]

On July 28, at a televised press conference during the lunch hour, Johnson made a historic announcement. He was committing fifty thousand additional combat troops to Vietnam and would send more later. Although he was transforming the war into an American conflict, he did everything possible to disguise that fact. He insisted that U. S. policy in Southeast Asia remained unchanged. He slighted the consequences of his decision for the American people. And he refused to demonstrate that this was no "two-penny military adventure," in the words of General Earle Wheeler, by putting the nation on a war footing. Instead of mobilizing the reserves and National Guard and raising taxes, he gave the impression that it was possible to have guns and butter. The last thing he wanted was to undercut his Great Society programs.

Even the timing of his announcement suggested how much he wished to minimize his decision; the television audience was smallest at midday.[65]

To the small group of Senate "doves," and to a growing number of antiwar protestors, the meaning of Johnson's announcement was nevertheless clear. "We are going deeper into the war," Mike Mansfield told Johnson. "Escalation begets escalation." Mansfield warned, prophetically, that congressional and national support for the president did not indicate a deep commitment to the Vietnam conflict.[66]

In retrospect, Frank Church considered Johnson's Americanization of the war as nothing less than "a betrayal." Johnson had campaigned in 1964 as the peace candidate. He had then proceeded to "do one thing and say another," eventually transforming Vietnam into "a kind of Asian Alamo."[67]

Like Mansfield, Church saw bad days ahead. By the middle of 1965, as the U. S. moved inexorably into "the big muddy," Johnson's domestic political consensus was in jeopardy and ugly tears were appearing in the social fabric. For Church, who invariably stressed the virtues of comity and civility, and who opposed the spiraling military intervention in Vietnam, the future looked cloudy indeed.

With J. William Fulbright looking on, Church asks a question during the 1966 Senate Foreign Relations hearings on Vietnam. *Courtesy Boise State University.*

Chapter Nine

A Dove Encounters Trouble and a Dogcatcher: 1965-1967

AT THE END OF July 1965 a "sorely troubled" Frank Church contemplated the future of the Vietnam war. If matters there worsened, he was not sure which path to follow. "I may wash my hands of the whole affair, as Wayne Morse has done," he threatened, "and enter the 'Never-Never-Land' of radically ineffectual dissent."[1]

He did not do so, of course, for that option went against his very nature and would have required that he step completely out of character. His own disposition was too optimistic, too resilient, to succumb to periodic setbacks. As usual, he tried to make the best of the situation, to act as a moderating force, to seek ways of shaping and influencing policy. In foreign relations he continued as one of the foremost Senate "doves," gradually extending his critique of the Vietnam war into an overall assessment of the American role abroad, yet trying to work with the administration as much as possible. At home he prominently supported Great Society legislation, even as the political backlash against such support grew. He was hardly surprised that the radical right continued to attack him; indeed, in that regard he launched some offensives of his own. He was nevertheless startled in 1967 when a small-town dogcatcher initiated a movement to recall him, suddenly endangering his political career. Perhaps even more difficult for Church to understand was the growing criticism within the civil rights and antiwar movements that liberals like him were the source of America's problems.

I

By 1965 the United States had reached a turning point. Domestic discontent escalated rapidly as the Johnson administration plunged into the jungles of Vietnam. Racial violence heightened. Early that year blood flowed in Selma, Alabama. Several people were killed, and television news carried chilling scenes of white police officers brutalizing civil rights demonstrators. Malcolm X, the most powerful voice in northern, black ghettos, was assassinated in February. In August, shortly after Lyndon Johnson signed a major voting rights act, the Watts section of Los Angeles erupted into a devastating riot, lasting several days. Governor George Wallace continued to tap the fury of enraged whites, north and south, who saw the civil rights movement as a terrifying symbol of unwanted change while significant rifts developed between white and black civil rights workers engaged in the Student Non-Violent Coordinating Committee's Mississippi projects. "If you don't like the way we do it, get the hell out of the state," one angry black organizer shouted at northern white members of SNCC who had come to Mississippi that summer. And Martin Luther King, Jr. spoke out against the Vietnam war in August, arguing that it was "inextricably bound together" with racial injustice and poverty within the United States.[2]

King's words indicated that the antiwar movement was spreading. Although antiwar protests remained small, sometimes drawing more hecklers than participants, they were nevertheless finding a larger audience. Just as significantly, a broad-based critique of the war was taking shape—a critique full of portent for Frank Church.

On November 27 in the nation's capital, some twenty-five thousand people demonstrated peacefully against the war. One observer said that, in appearance, they "would not have been out of place at the Army-Navy game." But the last speaker of the day, Carl Oglesby of the Students for a Democratic Society (SDS), signaled the direction at least some protestors were moving. Why, he wondered, was the United States fighting such a ghastly war? The presidents and policy makers who had involved the U. S. militarily in Southeast Asia were "not moral monsters." Indeed, they were "honorable" individuals. They were also something else, Oglesby observed: "They are all liberals. . . .To understand the war, then, it seems necessary to take a closer look at this American liberalism." After discussing the characteristics of a nation "of beardless liberals," well-intentioned but basically unable to understand a world of revolutionary change, Oglesby answered critics who might believe he was "anti-American. To these I say: Don't blame *me* for *that*! Blame those who mouthed my liberal values and broke my American heart." He then appealed to "humanist liberals" to recognize that their "own best hopes" rested with the antiwar movement. "Help us risk a leap," he pleaded.[3]

Frank Church was willing to leap, but ultimately not nearly as far as Oglesby and others wished. He opposed the Vietnam war, often eloquently; but he was reluctant to stray too far from the administration. In addition, the line from which he kept trying to jump shifted ever rightward. As the administration stepped up U. S. military actions in Vietnam, he ended up accepting conditions that he had once opposed vigorously, such as using combat troops. From his perspective, this was the sad reality with which he had to deal. From the point of view of the emerging "new left," however, this was the inevitable fate of reformers. The establishment or ruling class co-opted them, making it more and more difficult to distinguish a good "humanist liberal"—such as Church—from the bad liberals, the can-do technocrats who helped to stoke the engines of an unjust and exploitive "system."

Todd Gitlin, for example, came to see the Frank Churches of America as well-meaning but ineffectual. In 1965 Gitlin, an early SDS president, had watched with dismay the televised reports of U. S. Marines entering the Dominican Republic. For the first time he found himself identifying with "them"—those on the other side who were victims of America's military might. "Four months earlier," he recalled, "I had signed my name to an SDS resolution that referred to the United States government as 'we.' From now on, whenever I spoke of my country and its government, the pronoun stuck in my throat." Gitlin had met Church in 1962, indeed had helped drive him to the Baltimore airport, along with a friend who worked on the senator's staff. Church's participation a few months later in a Harvard study session on Vietnam, and his subsequent critique of U. S. foreign policy in the *New York Times*, had confirmed Gitlin's favorable impression of him. The senator was "an honorable man." But by the late Sixties Church had become simply "one of the right-minded liberals who knew better and was defaulting."[4]

II

From the outset, Church had an ambiguous relationship with the antiwar protestors. In many respects, he understood and even sympathized with them. He refused in October 1965, for example, to add his voice to those of Democratic senators such as Thomas Dodd of Connecticut and John Stennis of Mississippi in chastising the antiwar movement as pro-communist and un-American.[5]

Sometimes his frustration with U. S. interventionism touched a moral nerve, jolting him towards an assessment of his country that was as bleak as that of its angrier critics. In a conversation with White House aide Harry McPherson at a dinner party in early August 1966, Church expressed despair at the United States' terrible penchant for violence. Indeed, Church asserted sadly, America's violent propensity made the nation a threat to the rest of the world. This was too much for McPherson. "I got very angry," he recalled, "and we got into a sharp, short argument." It was one thing, McPherson believed, to contend that U. S. policy in Southeast Asia was foolish or a mistake; it was another thing to suggest that "we liked to crush little brown people as we had crushed little red people and we would crush other kinds of people"–but that "was essentially what Frank was saying."[6]

In some ways, Church's emerging critique of U. S. foreign policy was thus as sharp as Carl Oglesby's. The SDS president, in his November 27 speech, criticized America's counter-revolutionary tendencies. Armed with the ideology of anti-communism, Oglesby said, corporate liberals opposed revolutions and allied with right-wing dictators in defense of an unjust, unpopular, status quo. Church made basically the same points in late 1965 and early 1966 in two trenchant assessments in the *New York Times* and *Washington Post*, "How Many Dominican Republics and Vietnams Can We Take On?" and " '. . .the Basic Flaw in Our Asian Strategy.' " The ideas in these pieces were not new to him, but he was now even more forceful, more impassioned. Here was Church at his best–thoughtful, informed, eloquent. The Vietnam war, as he later recognized, was pushing him to reexamine the basic premises of a "highly simplistic notion of the world," one which he himself had articulated on many occasions.[7]

With prose that sometimes sparkled, he portrayed the United States as trying to hold back history itself. Nationalism, in the forms of revolution and guerrilla warfare, was demolishing the old colonial empires. Americans had trouble understanding this massive transformation, partly because their obsession with communism trapped them in a "rigid and doctrinaire" time warp, but also partly because of their conditions. "Sober and satisfied and comfortable and rich," the United States was close "to being the most unrevolutionary nation on earth." Unable really to understand revolutionary ferment, Americans attempted to deal with hunger and oppression abroad through doses of foreign aid, thus trying "to buy a little reform. . .as a substitute for revolution." Church worried that the U. S. was mounting a futile crusade to produce American solutions for other countries' problems. But, he warned, "Lyndon Johnson can no more protect the world from insurrection than Woodrow Wilson could make it safe for democracy."[8] Church's portrait of an opulent, counter-revolutionary America had much in common with that of Oglesby and others in the emerging new left.

Turning specifically to Vietnam, Church viewed it more as a test of America's folly than of its resolve. "We are an alien in Asia," he argued, "a suspect, rich power, the only one that remains after the others have fled." He disputed the administration's contention that the war in South Vietnam was a product of aggression from the north rather than a revolution. Vietnam, he emphasized, was supposed to be one nation, as the 1954 Geneva agreement had stipulated at the end of the Vietnamese-French war. "The North Vietnamese are not foreigners," Church insisted; "they are Vietnamese." Church also took issue with the interpretation that Vietnam was the "final test of our capacity to resist Communist aggression." No matter what happened in Vietnam, other revolutions would continue to break out, and most probably not in ways that Americans preferred. It was essential that these struggles not turn into American wars.[9]

"The hour is late," Church warned, but perhaps not too late for the United States to learn from history and to place events in a broad perspective. In this regard, he assessed the dangers of drawing the wrong lessons from America's post-World War II containment policy in Europe. Containment, after all, had not really kept communism out of Western Europe; the Communist Party was strong in Italy and France, for example. Although containment had kept Soviet troops out of those countries, only one West European nation had been involved in a civil war: Greece, to which the United States had sent aid, but not soldiers. There were thus real dangers, Church suggested, in using the analogy of Western Europe to justify U. S. military intervention in Asia.[10]

Church, like political scientist Hans Morgenthau, accepted the traditional concept of international spheres of influence. He rebutted policy makers in the administration, such as George Ball, who judged the spheres of influence argument as an outdated excuse by which great powers justified their greed. This, responded Church, was "sheer sophistry." Powerful nations, like huge geopolitical magnets, exerted massive influence over smaller countries around them. The U. S. could no more keep China's giant shadow from extending across Asia than could Chinese military forces in Guatemala proscribe the U. S. from Latin America. In that regard, America's effort to build an enclave in Southeast Asia could only be "an expensive and protracted adventure." Church worried that Lyndon Johnson was falling victim to "the siren songs of the new crusaders" who believed it possible "to impose a Pax Americana upon an unwilling world." He hoped this would not happen. If it did, the president might "well forfeit the great place in history he desires."[11]

Church's comments, which he repeated in various ways in addresses and on television news programs, heartened critics of the war, just as J. William Fulbright did with a series of speeches in 1966 that he published subsequently as *The Arrogance of Power.* Church, Fulbright, and other Senate doves helped to legitimize protests against the administration's foreign policy, providing a public forum and respectability for dissent.[12]

This was especially so in late January 1966 when the Senate Foreign Relations Committee commenced public hearings on the war. Fulbright later described them as "an experiment in public education," exactly the kind of undertaking that Church approved. As Church enthusiastically put it, "the long slumbering" committee had finally awakened in a surprising "show of Congressional independence." In early February the networks provided live television coverage, much to Lyndon Johnson's chagrin.[13]

The administration scrambled frantically to assess public reaction. Some staff members reported that the hearings were confusing the American people. Others found signs of public disapproval of the committee's actions. One aide informed Johnson of Texas Governor John Connally's opinion that people were "not questioning the U. S. foreign policy: Their real worry is that the U. S. Senate has such men among it's [sic] membership." Political commentator William S. White sent the president a copy of his television critique of the "screeching anti-Vietnam war bloc"–"a little band of willful men," "a telephone booth bloc" that had "long since passed the outermost limit of tolerance." The administration seemed nevertheless to concur most with Ohio Senator Frank Lausche's fear that "the 'wild Turks' " on the committee were damaging America's war effort and "prolonging Ho Chi Minh's will to resist."[14]

Wyoming Senator Gale McGee, a strong supporter of the administration's Vietnam policy, viewed the hearings as an effort to "stage a spectacle" rather than an educational forum. He found irritating the contrast between the genteel behavior of some committee members in executive session and their more histrionic appearances on TV, where they made their speeches and then exited without listening to the rest of the session. Some seemed invariably to speak "with their finger in the political winds." But McGee had no quarrel with Church in this respect. "I have *no* recollection of his playing any kind of a game at the hearings," McGee said later. "He was most conscientious," and "was *always* willing" to hear the other point of view.[15]

The administration, however, was no more inclined than *Time* magazine to applaud even fair-minded critics on the committee. "*Time* magazine," Church observed, "true to its war-hawk frenzy, fairly frothed over in print, spanking the nervy Senators for their impertinence. Goebbels's old propaganda ministry couldn't have done a more thorough job of twisting the news." The administration, meanwhile, tried both to upstage the committee and to scold it. In what presidential aide William Bundy described as a "preemptive act," Johnson distracted news attention from the hearings by flying to Honolulu to meet with military advisors and South Vietnamese officials. Here, as two scholars later described it, "was a star-studded cast designed to put the low-budget Fulbright production in shadow." A few days later, on February 4, Johnson irritably told several members of Congress that public criticism of the administration fortified the enemy's will to resist. The president failed to "understand why Americans who dissent can't do their dissenting in private" or "why prominent men in the United States continue to criticize our policy." In mid-May Johnson lashed out at the " 'Nervous Nellies' " who "will turn on their leaders, and on their country, and on our own fighting men." On October 21 he warned the Vietnamese, Soviets, and Chinese not to "misjudge our speeches in the Senate."[16]

Church nevertheless believed that, once the hearings commenced, "the jig was up" for LBJ. Johnson could try to disguise that fact by traveling to Honolulu or anywhere else; but, deep down, he had to know "that he was in a very different kind of political struggle." Once the committee moved its discussion from behind closed doors, it was less a prisoner of the White House and State Department. In a sense, Church may have been correct. Johnson knew and understood the Senate.

"Dove" speeches there hardly shaped his policy in a major way, but they reminded him of the fragility of his political consensus. Just as Johnson later thought that the antiwar comments of CBS anchorman Walter Cronkite meant he was losing the support of Middle America, so he must have paused when former Senate allies – such as Fulbright and Church – vigorously protested his war policy.[17]

III

For Church, the challenge was to use such leverage, however limited, as effectively as possible. He knew that Johnson took personally much of the criticism of his policies. The president thus privately referred to Fulbright as "Half-bright," and said that George McGovern should be in jail. In that regard, Church was encouraged when Adlai Stevenson, shortly before dying in 1965, indicated that he had never heard Johnson refer to the Idaho senator in similarly uncomplimentary ways.[18]

During the summer of 1966 a display of presidential friendliness and gratitude again reassured Church. Johnson had invited him to join several African diplomats and U. S. government officials on the executive yacht. After dinner, when movies were shown on deck, Johnson called Church over next to him. The senator sat on a cushion beside the president and they talked about Texas, Idaho, and the West. Johnson was very congenial. He avoided the subject of Vietnam, stressing instead his conviction that Congress had boosted American foreign policy by passing the recent civil rights law.[19]

Johnson's friendly disposition may have reflected his appreciation for Church's help in obtaining Great Society legislation. In 1965-66, for example, the senator voted for the civil rights voting act, the poverty program, the education act, housing and urban affairs legislation, and consumer and environmental protection.[20]

Church had the impression that LBJ was more tolerant of him than of other administration critics: "He would blow hot and cold with me for some strange reason." At one point, for example, Church went to the White House in search of federal assistance to deal with huge forest fires in Idaho. Johnson initially resisted, showing him that the national disaster emergency fund specifically excluded fire damage and that a number of states had unsuccessfully made requests for such aid. Moreover, the president noted that Idaho still had not repaid the federal government for previous firefighting expenses. Church conceded that his case was weak and, in effect, threw himself on Johnson's mercy. Surprisingly, Johnson approved $250,000—"more," according to Church, "than had ever been spent for any fire on previous occasions."[21]

Johnson may indeed have been fond of Church in important respects, but the senator nevertheless read far too much into his displays of affection. Behind the scenes, the president was considerably less cordial toward him. In mid-1966, for example, Johnson rejected Church's recommendation regarding a Department of Interior position. As an aide wrote after talking with Johnson, the president "was inclined to feel that any appointment for anyone connected with Frank Church at this particular point in time would not be particularly pleasurable." A year later, Johnson's collection of malicious gossip included a story about Church. Ohio senator Frank Lausche, one of the administration's staunchest defenders on the Foreign Relations Committee, told White House staffer Mike Manatos, "It's frightening to see Senator Church arrogate unto himself a wisdom which no man in history has ever had, including Socrates." Manatos believed the president would enjoy "this gem."[22]

Johnson's generous response to Church's urgent request for funds to deal with Idaho's forest fires was as much manipulative as it was obliging. "Nothing points out more forcibly than this request of Frank's," Manatos told the president, "the realities of politics—that he needs the President much more than he might have realized." Help from Johnson would thus be instructive. "For once Church is here hat in hand," chortled Manatos, "off cloud nine and back to reality."[23]

In sum, Church enjoyed less favor at the White House than he believed. The view there reflected Harry McPherson's derogatory remark to Bill Moyers that Church "would give his life to be thought a statesman." Indeed, Church would have found devastating a comment that Johnson made privately when commenting on the senator's position on Vietnam. As McPherson recalled, the president said something to the effect that "Idaho sent me the dumbest guy I have."[24]

In March 1966 columnists Rowland Evans and Robert Novak reported that Church, "the most reluctant and cautious member of the Senate peace bloc," was unpopular at the White House. Opinion of him, "never very high," had reportedly "hit a new low" when he failed to go on record against Wayne Morse's effort to rescind the 1964 Tonkin Gulf resolution. Morse's proposal claimed only five votes, with 92 opposed to it. Church, in Idaho at the time of the vote, had remained silent on the matter. As a result, wrote Evans and Novak, he stood "as low or even lower with the President than the five Senators backing the Morse amendment."[25]

Church, enraged at the columnists' account, viewed it as a "mean-minded smear, vicious even by Evans and Novak standards," yet another example of "the abuse being dished out against the handful of senators who have had the temerity to question American policy in Vietnam." He said he would have opposed Morse's motion had he been present, and he noted that for two years he had spoken out on the Vietnam war. Sometimes he had angered the president, sometimes the larger public. But he had never sought to hide his opinions.[26]

When Church cited ABC television commentator Joseph McCaffrey's explanation for the Evans and Novak attack, he implicitly conceded that the administration had planted the story with the journalists. "It is almost as if the trained seals among the columnists were given the word from on high to work over the Senate's minuscule minority," McCaffrey stated in an editorial. "Never have so few caused so much comment." Here, Church assumed, was surely evidence of the impact that he and the other doves were having on the White House. The Washington columnist for the respected *London Observer* provided additional encouragement, claiming that Church "alone has probably done more than all the demonstrators" to push the president toward negotiations.[27]

Insofar as Church hoped to exercise such influence, he had to maintain an aura of respectability. He must never join Wayne Morse in "Never-Never-Land," holding forth in the Senate late in the afternoons with only his wife listening. Morse's lonely five o'clock orations had earned the irascible Oregon senator a reputation as "the 5:00 shadow." Church wanted a more substantive role, and to play it he needed credibility with his colleagues, the administration, and the public.[28]

It was damnably difficult, however, to be part of the loyal opposition, however moderate, in a time of war. As Church told one audience, the Vietnam conflict seemed to relegate people to one flock of birds or another: hawks and doves. "If you get in between, you are fair game for the snipers from both sides—like a sitting duck!" But, as the nation polarized, and as public demonstrations for and against the war mounted in number and intensity, the middle was precisely where Church tried to situate himself. "He wasn't a hard-liner dove," recalled

Utah senator Frank Moss. "He didn't come down hard and just hammer in any place. He was always watching that middle ground."[29]

There were gratifying signs of his success in that regard. Wayne Morse praised his *New York Times*' article, "How Many Dominican Republics and Vietnams Can We Take On?" Fulbright lauded his "absolutely first-rate" piece in the February 20, 1966 *Washington Post*. And that same month, presidential advisor Clark Clifford raved about Church's appearance on Eric Sevareid's television program. Clifford, who was then "one of the biggest hawks in town" according to Secretary of State Dean Rusk, extolled Church's "exceedingly impressive," "outstanding" presentation. "I was tremendously impressed," wrote Clifford. "What an impact it had upon me."[30]

But none of this prepared Church for the phone call he received late in the evening of July 14, 1966. Suddenly he had electrifying proof that his kind of dissent could make a difference. On the other end of the line was Undersecretary of State George Ball with an urgent request. The North Vietnamese government was reportedly ready to put on trial, and then execute, downed American fliers. The Johnson administration had attempted, with no apparent success, to dissuade the Hanoi officials from taking such a step. The situation was desperate. Ball implored Church to solicit from other Senate doves a plea to Hanoi not to execute American prisoners of war. Ironically, as the *Boston Globe* observed, the administration which had snubbed the senator was now asking him to pull some of its "most agonizing chestnuts from a perilous fire."[31]

Church acted immediately, alerting his staff within a matter of minutes. Even before the sun came up, he and his assistants were in his office, trying frantically to locate other dove senators. They hoped to gather as many of their signatures as possible for a petition that Church had quickly drafted. Time was crucial. The executions could occur at any moment. By early afternoon Church had gotten fourteen colleagues to join him, including Pennsylvania's Joe Clark, on vacation in Wyoming. In order to get the message to Hanoi as quickly as possible, Church called a 2 p.m. press conference, making sure to invite as many foreign correspondents as possible, especially those with the Soviet press. He also made sure that the "Plea for Sanity," as he named it, was translated into French in order to facilitate communications with Hanoi.[32]

An hour before the press conference, Church garnered three more supporters, pushing the total to twenty-one. They were all on record as critics of the war. Included were Morse, Gruening, McGovern, Fulbright, Clark, Moss, Robert and Ted Kennedy, Mike Mansfield and Lee Metcalf of Montana, Gaylord Nelson and William Proxmire of Wisconsin, Minnesota's Eugene McCarthy, North Dakota's Quentin Burdick, Stephen Young of Ohio, Indiana's Vance Hartke, Connecticut's Abraham Ribicoff, Maurine Neuberger from Oregon, Alaska's E. L. Bartlett, and Harrison Williams, Jr. from New Jersey. The five-paragraph statement was largely Church's and, according to the *Boston Globe*, rang "with mountain-state Old Testament rhetoric."[33]

In the glare of television lights, Church grimly read the appeal, warning that U.S. reprisals would inevitably follow the executions of American airmen. "We have publicly criticized the mounting involvement of our country," Church and the other senators told the North Vietnamese. The killings of American prisoners of war "would drastically reduce the influence of all those in the United States who have tried to curtail the fighting. It would incite a public demand for retaliation swift and sure," thereby enlarging the war. A few days later came evidence that the appeal had not been in vain. The North Vietnamese government announced it had postponed bringing the U. S. prisoners to trial.[34]

"Church was a good one to call," George McGovern said later about the administration's choice. As a member of the Foreign Relations Committee and a well-known critic of the war, he conveyed a message that may have carried special weight in Hanoi. United Nations ambassador Arthur Goldberg agreed. Appreciative of what Church had done, Goldberg was "profoundly convinced" that the appeal had influenced the North Vietnamese to spare the Americans. The incident also sent an important message to the senator's Idaho critics. "Church's Role Saves Airmen," read one editorial.[35]

For Church himself the moment was sweet. He had apparently been able to help protect the prisoners of war. The administration, moreover, had turned to him and the other Senate doves for critical assistance. They, in turn, had not only demonstrated their loyalty, but had presumably shown that moderate, reasonable dissent could serve patriotic purposes after all.

A more cynical interpretation might have given Church pause. Later, historian William C. Gibbons found hints that the administration had used the prisoner of war issue to muzzle domestic protests. The North Vietnamese, after all, denied charges that they intended to execute the downed airmen. From this perspective, the POW issue may have provided the administration mainly with a potent political weapon against critics of the war. Americans, rather than the government in Hanoi, were perhaps the intended audience for the administration's warnings about the fate of U. S. prisoners.[36]

If this was indeed the case, Church was apparently unaware of it. He believed the administration had used him in the best sense, to save American lives, not to sharpen the POW issue as a political knife against the growing antiwar protests. Indeed, he worried quite genuinely that his own criticism of the administration might send the North Vietnamese the wrong message. A James Reston column in the *New York Times*, indicating that Ho Chi Minh believed the United States would eventually give up, bothered him greatly. Ho "does not understand the United States," Church reportedly told Johnson aide Harry McPherson. "He does not know we are a proud and powerful country with a history of winning military engagements. He does not know what a proud and determined man the President is." Insofar as Ho believed otherwise, he was making a terrible miscalculation. And if that were true, Church hoped that the recent "Plea for Sanity" might serve as a warning to Ho. According to McPherson, Church speculated that perhaps he and the other doves could be most effective by emphasizing America's unwillingness to back down.[37]

However unintentionally, Church's comments to McPherson facilitated his role in any administration ploy to use the POW issue for political purposes. Such were the possible dangers of being both critic and ally—the loyal opposition. In this regard, a memorandum of presidential advisor Mike Manatos would have disheartened Church. Manatos noted that some of the Senate doves had been "brutally" critical of the Vietnam policy, but he emphasized that most, including Church, had "*supported* the President by their votes." Johnson, in turn, found those votes reassuring. The "best poll is a roll call vote in Congress," he said.[38]

The senator did not want to be in anybody's pocket, certainly not Lyndon Johnson's on the Vietnam war. Yet it was difficult to ignore the routine CIA reminders to him and the other doves that communists around the world made much of their dissent. In that regard, as his conversation with McPherson suggested, he concluded that the doves needed to reaffirm American resolve in Southeast Asia.

This was perhaps why he agreed, in the late spring of 1967, to an administration request to gather signatures for yet another message to Hanoi, this one warning the North Vietnamese not to expect a unilateral U. S. withdrawal. As George McGovern later explained, the signers also hoped to undercut the assumption that the Senate doves were aiding the enemy. Here, as one Church aide put it, was an opportunity for the dissenters to take "a cheap hawk position."[39]

Church had been working on the message, "A Plea for Realism," for several weeks, but brought it before the public shortly after receiving a CIA translation of a radio broadcast in the Soviet Union saying that he, McGovern, Fulbright, and Robert Kennedy had launched "one of the sharpest attacks ever on official U. S. policy." According to the Soviets, this attack signaled "a growing crisis of trust" and "danger for Washington's top officialdom." The "Plea for Realism" contained sixteen signatures, including many that had appeared almost a year earlier in behalf of the American POWs. The main point of the new message was that, whatever their individual reservations about the war, the senators "steadfastly opposed. . .any unilateral withdrawal of American troops from South Vietnam." Hanoi simply must not misconstrue the nature of antiwar dissent in the Senate. Moreover, it was imperative to realize that the bulk of American opinion favored a tougher military policy, not disengagement.[40]

At a 1 p. m. press conference on May 17, Church distributed copies of the plea, which someone had already leaked to the Baltimore *Sun*. Emphasizing that he personally had written the statement and gathered the signatures, he denied collaborating with the administration. He conceded having given an advance copy to Secretary of State Rusk to ensure that the wording would not jeopardize any ongoing negotiations; but he disputed press reports that Rusk had elicited the statement from the antiwar senators on grounds that it would have special credibility. When a reporter asked if Rusk had told Church that the "Plea for Realism" might help the administration, he nevertheless hedged. He answered vaguely that he would, of course, do nothing to harm the administration's efforts to find peace. In fact, however, he had already informed Kentucky Republican John Sherman Cooper that "Secretary Rusk believes the declaration would be helpful."[41]

Eugene McCarthy dubbed the letter a "retreat," while Ernest Gruening denounced it as a "betrayal." Both senators had endorsed the earlier plea in behalf of American POWS, but refused to sign the "Plea for Realism." Despite the disavowals of the White House press secretary, they suspected that the statement bore the administration's imprint. They also guessed correctly that it was partly an "election cover" for their dove colleagues who soon faced reelection; a Church aide later conceded that the appeal was not without political motivation. *Time* magazine agreed that Church and the other signatories were trying to protect "their own political flanks," but nevertheless also praised the Church document for speaking "to Hanoi with candor." Beneath a photograph of a stern-looking Church, index finger pointed at someone, the magazine's caption indicated that Church's words hardly comforted the enemy.[42]

None of this meant that Church saw the doves as pawns of the administration. Indeed, few things made him angrier than that perception. In May 1967 he denied the administration a key vote in the Foreign Relations Committee after a White House aide asked threateningly, "Where do you think you are going to get financial support for next year's campaign except from us?" The administration apologized to Church, after he explained that someone on the president's staff—he would not say who—had made the remark at a social function. "According to Frank," Mike Manatos reported to Johnson, the statement "might have been meant to be a quip and in jest, but the whole process and attitude which produced that sort of comment was not tactful and really quite insulting."[43]

Church was equally unhappy with speculation that he was tempering his criticism of the war because of pressure from the administration. In print, over radio and television, in lectures, and in the Senate, he continued to disagree emphatically with the fundamental premises of U. S. involvement in Vietnam. Indeed, during his May 17 press conference, he underlined once again his misgivings about the war. "The original intervention was a mistake," he said bluntly, just as the war's continued expansion was also wrong. "But the war exists," and the challenge was how to negotiate its end while recognizing that U. S. troops were already there and would not leave unilaterally.[44]

As always, Church stressed the role of dissent and debate in a democracy. Just as he hoped Hanoi would not misjudge the doves' critique as an indication of United States softness, so he wanted Americans not to construe it as unpatriotic. He despaired of U. S. government efforts to propagandize the war. "Sometimes," he wrote political scientist Hans Morgenthau, "it seems to me we are more than half way into 1984."[45]

At the same time, he worried about public protests against the war. When constituents complained that the demonstrations of "beatniks and pro-communists" aided the enemy, he expressed a shared concern. "The danger of such protests," he wrote, "is that the Communists in Vietnam could take the demonstrations as an indication of American failure to support the administration's Vietnam policy." This was, of course, precisely the criticism that "hawks" aimed at him. But he drew an important distinction between lawful dissent and the right of free speech, as opposed to violent protest or the visits of Americans such as Stokely Carmichael to Hanoi. Church was well aware that the antiwar demonstrations made his own position more difficult to defend, especially among many of his own constituents who saw little difference between his actions and those of protesters in the streets.[46]

For a variety of reasons he thus kept distance between himself and the demonstrations. When Dr. Benjamin Spock, one of the better-known critics of the war, implored Congress to provide "a persistent, aggressive leadership to rally to," Church's reply was as detached as it was brief: "I will continue trying to do my part, as you keep on striving to do yours."[47]

IV

The senator's differences with the growing antiwar movement were philosophical as well as tactical. He was more inclined than some of the protestors to see America's military involvement in Southeast Asia as tragic rather than malevolent. The old saying that "the road to Hell is paved with good intentions" seemed particularly applicable to him when he viewed Vietnam. "Our intentions have been good enough, but the policy has been wrong," he wrote. "Now we find ourselves trapped in a situation where. . .we are 'like a giant being bled to death by Lilliputians.' " Ironically, America's strength had become its weakness.[48]

To some critics of the war—and, increasingly, of American culture generally—such faith in the nation's good intentions was badly misplaced. American history, from their perspective, was bathed in blood. Church, as he demonstrated in his heated exchange with Harry McPherson, could entertain such thoughts himself; but his comments reflected momentary frustration and not a sustained critique. Whereas he generally leaned toward a tragic reading of events, people with a more radical disposition believed that such an interpretation diffused blame and responsibility. To them, "tragedy" seemed an intellectual euphemism for masking the horrors of slavery, imperialism, racism, sexual discrimination, genocide, and an expansionist, exploitive culture at war with elemental justice, genuine pluralism, and a nonacquisitive, cooperative ethos. The problem, some began to say, was with "Amerika."

"To be white and radical in America this summer," wrote one young man in 1967, "is to see horror and feel impotent." Another explosion of urban riots produced the most violent of "the long, hot summers" to that point. Following the worst American riot in a century, Detroit Mayor Jerome Cavanaugh said of his city: "It looks like Berlin in 1945." Frantz Fanon's *The Wretched of the Earth* (1961), which had become a kind of primer for anticolonial movements everywhere, found an American audience. "You'd better get this book," one black writer advised fellow journalists. "Every brother on a rooftop can quote Fanon." In August, the *New York Review of Books* stirred considerable controversy with a cover that showed how to make a "Molotov cocktail."[49]

Meanwhile, across the Pacific, almost half a million U. S. combat troops were in Vietnam by 1967, and the war was costing $2 billion a month. That year, American air sorties against North Vietnam leaped to 108,000, including massive strikes against designated areas around Hanoi. Bombing in the South was far more extensive. Since 1965, the United States had dropped more bombs in Southeast Asia than it had in all the sectors of World War II. It had also dropped tons of herbicides in an effort to destroy jungle cover. "Puff the Magic Dragon" airships, capable of firing eighteen thousand rounds a minute, and napalm bombs took a terrible toll on the civilian population. And still the war escalated. "The solution in Vietnam is more bombs, more shells, more napalm," said General William Depuy, "till the other side cracks and gives up."[50]

Within the United States, the growing protests moved along political and, increasingly, cultural fronts. San Francisco's Haight-Ashbury district and other urban areas became symbols of rebellion against familiar American values and conventions. Considerable media attention went to the "hippie"—who, in the words of newly elected California governor Ronald Reagan, "dresses like Tarzan, has hair like Jane, and smells like Cheetah." While some counterculture advocates celebrated the "summer of love" in 1967, more militant protestors urged flexing muscles against the dominant society. "We live in the belly of the monster," announced black power advocate H. Rap Brown. "So it's up to us to destroy its brain." "Liberals!" recalled Todd Gitlin. "The very word had become the New Left's curse. . . .Carl Oglesby's distinction between 'corporate' and 'humanist' liberals was getting murkier."[51]

Frank Church's son, Forrest, was also having difficulties making that distinction. Enrolled at Stanford, where his father had studied twenty years earlier, he was feeling disillusioned and alienated. "As far as I could see it," he recalled, "everything my parents were involved in, belabored as it was with inevitable compromise, was a sham." It was more and more difficult for him to talk with them. Forrest immersed himself in Russian novels and books about the Russian revolution and considered dropping out of college, where he had little interest in his grades. Talking with his father was "almost hopeless," he remembered. "Everything that he had devoted his life to struck me as superficial." Over the next few months, the differences between father and son would grow considerably.[52]

As the upheavals and turbulence of the Sixties drove wedges between Americans, splitting even family members from each other, Frank Church continued to seek solutions through what he viewed as reasoned dissent. He tried to organize the Senate doves into a more coherent and potent force. They held sporadic and informally organized "caucuses." As George McGovern recalled, "Frank was one of those who thought there should be more effort of that kind." A problem in this regard, as McGovern pointed out, was that "senators are almost impossible to organize."[53]

Still, the Senate doves enjoyed some sense of camaraderie and shared purpose. McGovern and Church became fairly close, for example. In 1966 Church voted with the South Dakota Democrat 85 percent of the time, more than he did with any other senator. A historian by training, McGovern particularly appreciated Church's sense of the past and his ability to place events in a broad context. McGovern also found consolation in his colleague's wit. "It would kind of save the day," he remembered fondly. "I think there is such a thing as being so absorbed in public issues that one loses his sense of balance. That never happened to Frank," who had a tremendous "capacity to laugh at himself." According to McGovern, Robert Kennedy was also "especially high on Church" and said so several times. Kennedy, who did not identify very much with the antiwar senators until around the middle of 1966, indicated that he believed Church and McGovern were two of the more perceptive doves on the Hill.[54]

On one occasion Kennedy invited the two senators to his Hickory Hill home for dinner, along with veteran diplomat Averell Harriman. McGovern recalled arriving about thirty minutes late, and "walking into a battlefield," with Harriman and Church engaged in "the bitterest kind of argument" over Vietnam. The former New York governor, still an ardent hawk, had recently rebuked war critics such as Walter Lippmann for giving Hanoi the wrong impression. McGovern promptly sided with Church. The discussion was blunt and harsh, resulting in what McGovern described as "a pretty rough evening." Church was quite distressed to find Harriman, a battle-scarred veteran of diplomacy, so vehemently supportive of the war.[55]

Sometimes Church, as he told columnist Arthur Hoppe of the *San Francisco Chronicle*, felt "a little like a Volkswagen sitting on a railroad track not knowing when the train is coming around the bend." Hoppe had once considered the senator a "shallow-seeming boy wonder" who would have made a good model for the 1930's Arrow Collar advertisements. But, as he interviewed him in the mid-sixties, Hoppe found comfort in Church's integrity and willingness not "to go along with the crowd" on Vietnam, despite pressure from the administration and his home state. Church seemed somewhat resigned to his relatively lonely predicament, but he fretted that some incident could easily provoke the public into equating any kind of opposition to the war with treason. Hoppe left the interview feeling good that the Idaho senator was in office. As the reporter walked out into the wilting District of Columbia heat, however, he spotted headlines about yet another crisis in Vietnam. "And for a chilling moment," he wrote, thinking of Church's vulnerability, "I thought I could hear a train whistle around the bend."[56]

V

Hoppe would have been even more alert to that train whistle had he visited Idaho in 1967, when events threatened suddenly to knock Frank Church off the political track. The events developed largely out of the senator's ongoing quarrel with the radical right. In his estimation, the 1964 defeat of Barry Goldwater had in no sense lowered the "fever" of extremism in American politics. Idaho was proof of this, but other examples abounded. A *Washington Post* article following the election indicated that Goldwater's twenty-six million votes had only "emboldened" the radical right in communities such as Bartlesville, Oklahoma.

In that prospering, "All-American" city, study groups of the Sooner Freedom Forum pondered such subjects as "Communist brainwashing" via television. A full-page ad in the local newspaper claimed that the Communist Party supported Lyndon Johnson. In this setting, the give-and-take of traditional politics had turned ugly, punctuated by anonymous telephone threats and refusals of office mates to speak to each other.[57]

To Church, it was essential to understand the social and cultural roots of political paranoia in the United States. It would not do, he insisted, to dismiss the radical right as America's lunatic fringe. Hence, when one individual warned him that the communists were taking over and would soon liquidate many Americans, he wanted to know why "this honest, deeply disturbed woman" felt so threatened. Why, also, would a Boise man believe that he needed to give a pistol and knife to his wife as Christmas presents so that she could protect herself against local communists? Church's reading of political commentators such as Walter Lippmann and Eric Sevareid, as well as of scholars like Hans J. Morgenthau and Daniel Bell, persuaded him that the radical right was tapping an overpowering fear of the modern world—a world that was complex, interdependent, rapidly changing. People on the right were susceptible to "Big Scare purveyors," like the Reverend Carl McIntyre, because they felt adrift. Their spiritual needs found little sustenance in the dominant commercialism all around them; and a sense of alienation from big government, cities, and the seemingly endless Cold War overwhelmed them. Ironically, their suspicions led them to declare war on freedom itself.[58]

It was time, Church had decided, to expose "the delusions of the Radical Right." This required a willingness to speak out in defense of democratic processes and political civility, and to provide balanced, informed perspectives on the modern world. To that end, in 1965, Church published an essay, "Conspiracy, USA," in the popular magazine, *Look*, and urged his Senate colleagues in the new 89th Congress not to underestimate the menace of right-wing extremism. "We have had our know nothings before," he told the Senate, but the contemporary radical right was even more ominous: it raged not just against particular minority groups, as had previous backlash movements, but the "entire prevailing American establishment." In that sense, it drew directly upon the precedents of McCarthyism.[59]

Church's speech so impressed Wayne Morse that the Oregon Democrat urged reprinting copies for other senators to send their constituents. Oklahoma Democrat Mike Monroney, who had encountered the "filth and hate peddlers" in his home state, praised the speech as "splendid, courageous and timely." On NBC's televised "Today Show," host Hugh Downs recommended the *Look* essay to everyone; it was "the best thing" he had recently read. Positive responses came from around the nation, from intellectuals such as Stuart Chase in Connecticut to a frightened Louisiana housewife, who had received anonymous phone threats that she could "pick up her son in pieces" unless she ceased advocating curriculum reform in the local school.[60]

Within Idaho, Church set out to organize what aide Jerry Brady described as "a kind of counter right wing network." The senator encouraged what he called local "watchdog" committees, not to silence extremists, who enjoyed the right of free speech as much as anyone, but to answer them via letters to editors and over radio and television. These small groups needed to be bipartisan, intent on building coalitions. Rather than serving as liberal havens, they should offer "responsible conservatives" an alternative. Meanwhile, liberals themselves should expound their ideals "in a proud, aggressive way." The strategy would be to use "positive, democratic methods" to combat extremism. "There is really very little precedent for this type of public education in a small town," Church believed. The radical right had, in effect, moved into a political vacuum; the way to answer it was with local action and local voices. "We really went on the war path in a very aggressive fashion," recalled Brady. Church "went way out in front on this, nationally." When several political fanatics called his press secretary Rick Raphael a son-of-a-bitch, Church reassured him: "You must be doing something right."[61]

By that criterion, Church was doing quite well himself, increasingly becoming a pariah to the radical right, whether in the form of a John Birch Society "section leader" in Nampa, Idaho, or national conservative columnist Ralph de Toledano, or Dean Manion, who broadcasted weekly from South Bend, Indiana. According to de Toledano, Church was one of "the anti-anti-communists" who damned the enemies of "Red subversion." A guest on the "Manion Forum" believed that "the deadly error in Senator Church's confused thinking is that he does not seem to fear Communism." Manion concurred, adding that the senator was one of the reasons the U. S. was losing "everywhere in the world." In February 1965 Manion published Father Daniel Lyons's speech which heaped considerable blame on Church for America's apparent willingness to accept defeat in Vietnam. "One shudders to think that he is on the Foreign Relations Committee," said Lyons, who believed that the senator preferred "the old, muddy, liberal line" to recognizing the threat of communist enslavement.[62]

By 1967 Idaho seemed increasingly susceptible to such thinking as the state moved right with a vengeance. In Ada County, for example, there was fierce resistance to a proposed zoning ordinance, "the closest thing to communism," in the eyes of one angry resident. Robert Smylie, the three-term, moderate Republican governor, fell victim to the gathering conservative forces, losing the 1966 primary election to Don Samuelson, who advocated a "Kick a Beatnik in the Seatnik" week. That fall, Samuelson became governor; archconservative George Hansen won reelection by a wide margin; and Payette attorney James McClure, who endorsed the "Liberty Amendment" to abolish income taxes, handily defeated Democrat Compton White to capture the other congressional district. Republicans, mostly ultra-conservative, controlled every major office in the state, except Church's.[63]

Even within his own party Church had problems. He had angered some of the old guard in 1966 by intervening in a factional battle for the first time since his confrontation with Vernon Smith over the gambling issue. On September 14 a small plane carrying the Democratic candidate for governor, Charles Herndon, crashed in a rugged mountain area. Herndon's death threw the party into turmoil. Cecil Andrus, a one-time logger who had run second to Herndon in the primary, was his logical replacement. But Andrus had refused to close ranks with Herndon after the primary and seemed more sympathetic to Perry Swisher, a Pocatello publisher and state legislator who had filed as an independent. Tom Boise and several other veteran Democrats were furious with Andrus and endorsed the more conservative Max Hanson, a state legislator from the Republican-leaning farm and ranch area of Camas County.[64]

The eighty-one-year-old Tom Boise was one of the state's political legends, an old-fashioned wheeler-dealer from Lewiston who had never held elective office. Slight and quiet-spoken, he was the heart of the Democratic Party in northern Idaho, but his behind-the-scenes influence extended clear across the state. A close friend of Chase Clark, he had been an important and early backer of Frank Church. In 1966, while guiding Herndon to victory in the primaries, he had developed an aversion to Andrus and his followers. "Those young men haven't been kind to me," he complained in June at the state Democratic convention. When Democrats gathered in the state capital in September to choose Herndon's successor, Tom Boise was in a Spokane, Washington, hospital with heart trouble. By phone he nevertheless continued to direct the pro-Max Hanson forces.[65]

At this point, Church broke from Tom Boise, entering the fight in behalf of the more liberal Andrus. "It wasn't necessarily the wisest political move," Carl Burke said in retrospect, "but Frank felt strongly that his future was tied to a strong gubernatorial candidate. Besides, he and Cece were friends." In some ways, as journalist Sam Day observed later, Church's split with Boise over the gubernatorial candidate resembled his breach with Lyndon Johnson over Vietnam: he disagreed each time with people who had been very important to his early career. To some observers, he had turned against his political mentors. But Day believed that, in both cases, Church had demonstrated political courage and a willingness to stand by his principles.[66]

When the state central committee met in Boise to determine Herndon's successor, Verda Barnes flew in from Church's office. Barnes, by then the senator's chief administrative assistant, was one of Idaho's most astute political operators and, according to another member of the staff, "probably the best administrative assistant on the Hill. Hell of a woman." She, Burke, Myrna Sasser, and several other Church allies went head-to-head with Hanson's backers. As Burke remembered, "It was very hard. Wee hours in the morning. That was old-time politics." When the vote finally came, Myrna Sasser's hands were shaking so hard that she could barely keep count. Andrus squeaked to an 84-82 victory, with one abstention. Church had prevailed in his effort to push the party in a more liberal direction. But some old-line Democrats were incensed. "Why did you do this to us?" raged a thirty-year political veteran. Andrus lost in November to Samuelson, partly because some of the Herndon/Hanson faction worked for him only half-heartedly, if at all.[67]

Against that backdrop of political infighting, Church's opposition to the Vietnam war assumed even larger significance. It elicited a "violent reaction in local Democratic circles," according to Byron Johnson, Church's friend and a future Idaho Supreme Court justice. "It was hot and heavy." "Every place I went," said Church's long-time supporter, George Klein, "I had to defend him." Some Democratic legislators told Klein, "You've got to get Church off that Vietnam business." A public opinion poll that Church's office took in early 1967 was downright discouraging. Verda Barnes informed the senator that his political stock was so low he could not be elected dogcatcher. Ironically, in the spring of 1967, it was a dogcatcher in northern Idaho, Gene Mileck, who spearheaded a drive to oust him from the Senate.[68]

Mileck, a short, muscular forty-two-year-old, had flirted with the John Birch Society, and then left it because he "got sick and tired of waiting for them to do something—other than write letters." The organization was "like a kindergarten," too ineffectual for his taste. He saw himself as a loner, an "independent son-of-a-bitch," fighting for his rights against virtually everyone. "I'm no lawyer," he said, "but I'm no damn fool either." After working in numerous jobs, ranging from embalmer to seaman and logger, he had settled as a house painter in the small town of St. Maries, along the St. Joe river. There, his anger at unleashed dogs had motivated him to sign on as dogcatcher, collecting $3 for every dog he caught. He grew increasingly unhappy with Frank Church, whom he saw as betraying American soldiers in Vietnam. Mileck himself did not favor the war; but he believed that, because the United States was already there, it needed to win. "There's only one way to do battle," he said, "do it. If you are going to be married, be married. If you are going to get divorced, get a divorce. But don't mess around."[69]

It was to Mileck that Ronald Rankin looked when he wanted someone to chair a drive to recall Church. Rankin, a thirty-eight-year-old ex-Marine, had moved in 1965 from California's deeply conservative Orange County to Coeur d'Alene, Idaho. His interest in politics dated from 1954, when he stayed home from his job as a machinist to watch the televised censure hearings of Wisconsin senator Joe McCarthy. "I think my wife and I both sat on the floor, and watched the old black and white and cried," he recalled. In 1964 he had helped manage the successful campaign of an avowed Bircher, John Schmitz, to the California state Senate. After moving to Idaho he was covering the Washington state legislature for the right-wing Yakima (Washington) *Eagle* when he received a call from the office of the Liberty Lobby in Washington, D. C., asking him to organize a drive to recall Church. According to state law, a recall petition required 10 percent of the votes in the last gubernatorial election. At that point the officeholder had five days in which to resign, or seek reelection on a simple yes or no ballot within thirty days. In 1967 the petition would need 25,538 signatures.[70]

Rankin gathered that spring with at least seventy-five people in Boise to discuss strategies. They agreed they could not count on the Republican Party to defeat Church the following year. The state's GOP seemed too oriented toward country club politics. It included people – in Rankin's words – "who didn't have the resolve. . .the stamina, or knowledge, or the know-how, or the ability to unseat" Idaho's senior senator. It lacked a Gene Mileck.[71]

Rankin had met Mileck at a conservative meeting in St. Maries. In his opinion, the housepainter had the right stuff. "I felt Mileck was enough of a political barroom brawler," he recalled, "that a few extra jabs wouldn't bother him that much." Rankin approached Mileck about heading a movement to recall Church. He told the combative dogcatcher that he could provide seed money if Mileck could gather the required signatures. In April the two men formed a Victory in Vietnam Committee and drafted a recall petition.[72]

The petition charged that Church "had consistently opposed military measures which would help win the war in Vietnam," and had supported a pro-Soviet treaty at the very time that Russian weapons were killing American soldiers. The Soviet consular treaty, to which the petition referred, allowed the United States to build a consulate in Leningrad and the Soviets to open another one of their own, probably in Chicago. Church had voted for it, but so had sixty-nine other senators, including minority leader Everett Dirksen. On America's right, however, the treaty betokened yet another Soviet intrusion on American soil. The eight-page tabloid that the Committee for Victory in Vietnam distributed included a comic strip, "The Communists Next Door." It showed Soviet agents, under the cover of diplomatic immunity, smuggling "into our cities atomic demolition munitions. . . .Suitcase-sized A-bombs. . .can be scattered throughout the U. S. A.!"[73]

To finance the printing of the petitions and the recall literature, Rankin turned to wealthy conservatives in southern California. Since moving to Idaho he had reportedly received over $15,000 from a small group of millionaires, including William Penn Patrick, director of Holliday Magic Cosmetics, Inc. Patrick claimed to have spent over $500,000 on conservative causes in the last eighteen months. He was vice chair of the new Committee to End Aid to the Soviet Enemy (CEASE) and he chaired the Support Our Servicemen Committee (SOS), which urged, among other things, "unchaining" Chiang Kai-Shek to help win the war in Vietnam. In 1966 he had run for governor of California, but

Ronald Reagan had overwhelmed him in the Republican primary. Undaunted and still determined to save "the American way," he was ready to underwrite the movement to recall Church.[74]

Quite fortuitously, Church stumbled across the recall plans. The brother of a Church aide happened to work at the San Rafael, California, company printing the recall petitions and literature. He leaked that information back to the senator's office. Church promptly contacted columnist Drew Pearson, who agreed to look into the matter. On May 8, Pearson's widely circulated column revealed "one of the most significant political developments in the nation": the effort of a California-based movement to recall Church and "scare other senators into adopting a right-wing voting course." It thus turned out that, on the very day that Rankin and Mileck announced the beginnings of the recall movement in Idaho, Patrick appeared before television network news cameras in southern California to claim credit for bankrolling it.[75]

VI

Suddenly the recall effort became national news. Over the next few weeks it received attention on the TV networks and in the major newspapers and magazines. *Newsweek* portrayed the senator as "the fighting dove," and *The New York Times Magazine* featured a cover story about Frank Church "in trouble." As Seattle reporter Shelby Scates observed, Church looked like "a pushover" to the right wing. After all, his constituency had the reputation of thinking like John Wayne. Radio commentator Edward P. Morgan noted that Idaho was the target of "one of the heaviest concentrations of rigid, right-wing propaganda seen anywhere in the republic." Of the eighty or so weekly newspapers in the state, he found that a majority of them circulated "aggressively right-wing views." Only one of the thirteen dailies was Democratic. With fewer residents than the District of Columbia, and occupying twice the space of Virginia, Idaho was suspicious, insular, and vulnerable to the hate that rained on the state through the mails, radio, and television.[76]

"Fighting for his political life," as *Newsweek* put it, Church made a series of trips back to Idaho. In one week alone he barnstormed fifteen hundred miles by car, rickety airplane, and even an old-fashioned, cable-guided, side-paddle ferry which carried him across the swollen Kootenai River. In small cafes, on street corners, in courthouses, in grange halls, and high school auditoriums he tried to bank the threatened fires of the recall movement. He emphasized that he had voted for every military appropriation for America's troops in Vietnam. And while he seemed to hedge somewhat on his dovish position by saying that he favored keeping "the war within manageable limits," he also described U. S. involvement in Southeast Asia as "self-defeating" and completely out of proportion with America's own national interest.[77]

At a Coeur d'Alene press conference he momentarily lost his temper. He had been up well past midnight attending meetings on the other side of the state. Out of bed by 5 a. m. to catch a flight to northern Idaho, he was already exhausted when he met with the reporters. When an unidentified newsperson fired a series of leading and highly critical questions at him, dismissed his answers, and refused to give up the floor to other reporters, Church shouted back angrily in frustration. "I did lose my cool," he admitted afterward. The hostile journalist turned out to be the editor of the Yakima (Washington) *Eagle*, which Church described as nothing less than "a house organ for the John Birch Society."[78]

As Church defended himself up and down the state, he also seized the initiative against his adversaries, proving he could play very hard political ball. This seemed an appropriate time, for example, to remind his constituents that he was with them in opposition to federal gun control laws. His staff drew up an anti-gun control petition and placed it throughout the state, in sporting goods shops and grocery stores. "It looked a hell of a lot like the recall petition," remembered Church aide Rick Raphael, "except the answers were absolutely the opposite. If you wanted Frank to vote against gun control, you said 'yes.' If you wanted him recalled, you said 'yes.' " Raphael heard that some people "signed the gun petition, thinking they were signing the recall petition."[79]

Church made much of his anti-gun control fight. On July 21 a ninety-second news film showed him with several staff members on the Capitol steps with boxes of petitions bearing an estimated 44,000 signatures. The petition from one community, population 447, contained 213 names. "Senator Frank Church, the western states' most outspoken opponent of federal firearms legislation," said the narrator, "this week took his fight into Senate hearings on proposed control bills." Church believed that gun control was a state—not a federal—matter. In the West, the narrator explained, guns were "the equipment of sportsmen, not criminals or rioters." According to the film, members of the Senate subcommittee had laughed uproariously when Church told them that almost everyone in one north Idaho town had "signed the anti-gun control petition with the exception of the town dogcatcher."[80]

Years later, Church's actual sentiments on the gun control issue remained a mystery. Feelings in Idaho ran so strongly against controls that his opposition to such legislation was quite simply a political imperative. Church's first administrative assistant, John Carver, never discussed the matter with him because there was nothing to discuss. Subsequently, aides Neal Parsell and Jerry Brady still were uncertain about the senator's real opinion on the issue. "He never let on how he truly felt about this," said Brady. "I think that he just took it as a political fact of life." A close friend and staffer, Bryce Nelson, was nevertheless convinced that the senator's statements on controls were purely for consumption back home. "I can't believe that he really believed what he said about gun control."[81]

Other people who knew the senator well (Myrna Sasser and Mike Wetherell, for example) concluded nonetheless that he genuinely believed the issue was local in nature. Anti-gun legislation might be necessary in some urban areas, but not in rural Idaho. According to Sasser, Church did not see the necessity "to tell some cowboy out here that he couldn't wear a six-gun on his hip." Patrick Shea, who worked for the senator in the 1970s, suspected that Church felt this way only initially. Early in his career, Church had sincerely opposed federal controls. Such thinking was part of the cultural baggage that he carried from his youth; after all, his father had run a sporting goods store. The senator himself was a quite capable trapshooter, and handled a twelve-gauge shotgun very effectively. Shea guessed, however, that Church began to change his mind about gun control following the assassinations of Martin Luther King, Jr. and Robert Kennedy. But, even then, Church recognized the futility of endorsing firearm regulations in Idaho.[82]

Certainly that was true in 1967, a year in which Church felt special pressure to demonstrate his political toughness to his constituents. He unquestionably employed the anti-gun control issue to political advantage against the recall movement. The extent to which his use of it jarred with his own conscience was problematic.

As the anti-gun control petitions gathered signatures and momentum for Church, the Committee for Victory in Vietnam must have wondered about its lack of good fortune. The committee was even less lucky than it realized. Once again, inside information about its strategies ended up in Church's possession, this time courtesy of Ron Rankin himself. Church aide Jerry Brady happened to be at the Boise airport when he encountered Rankin. Brady approached him, saying that he recognized him from pictures in the press and liked what he was doing. They ended up discussing the committee's plans for over an hour, with Rankin never realizing that he was talking to a member of Church's staff. "We could not have picked better caricatures for adversaries," Brady recalled. "They were just wonderful. . .so dizzy."[83]

But Church's most important weapon was the fact that California money was subsidizing the recall movement. "I think the people of Idaho have too much sense," he told local audiences, "to allow this state to be taken over politically and economically by carpetbaggers from California." Here was an issue that resonated from the northern panhandle to the Utah border. An influx of transplants and tourists from California was already stirring animosities and uneasiness in the Gem State. People in northern Idaho, as one resident recalled, were suspicious "of anything south of the Salmon river," let alone from out-of-state. In the words of journalist Alice Dieter: "In the first place, southern Idaho hardly speaks to northern Idaho. In the second place, nobody speaks to a Californian." "Flush back to California," read the restroom graffiti in one small-town restaurant.[84]

In that context, the recall movement seemed yet another manifestation of the California plague. "The Carpetbaggers Are Coming," warned the *Lewiston Tribune* as it lambasted individuals who considered "the citizens of this state an easy mark for glib pitchmen from the big city." "Church Is Right, We 'Cannot Be Bought,' " editorialized *The Coeur d'Alene Press*. A Republican woman at a breakfast in the sawmill town of Riggins objected to "this outside power, these insidious people," who wanted to tell Idaho what to do. "There's got to be some way of stopping 'em from buying so much property in the state," she said. A retired Marine sergeant agreed. He saw the recall movement as "a smokescreen" to get Idaho's water, something which Frank Church was protecting. The irony was strong. As one reporter noted, those who suspected the senator of being an enemy of Idaho were now themselves under suspicion.[85]

By summer the recall effort was in far more trouble than Church. Top Idaho Republicans, including Senator Len Jordan and Governor Samuelson, denounced it. "Before the recall, Church was dead," observed one Republican district attorney, but now "the people feel this way, 'We like the independency here. Somebody is picking on Frank Church.' " Even one of the signers of the recall petition ended up feeling so badly about hurting the senator that he apologized profusely to him and removed his signature. Church "was virtually unelectable," snorted one GOP official, until the recall effort made a martyr of him. "Church may be a son-of-a-bitch, but he is *our* son-of-a-bitch"– such, according to the senator's speechwriter Rick Raphael, was popular wisdom. Grangeville's Fred Boynton perhaps summed it up best. "The people of Idaho voted him into office," said the seventy-eight-year-old Republican, "and the people of Idaho will vote him out of office when they damned well please."[86]

In July the recall attempt disintegrated. A few weeks earlier the Committee for Victory in Vietnam had planned optimistically to erect thirty large billboards, ten of them illuminated, calling for Church's ouster. But its plan had gone aglimmering. Recall supporters collected fewer than two thousand signatures on the petitions. And they seemed to have earned the displeasure of almost everyone, even conservative columnist William Buckley. The *National Review* editor said they were attempting "a most un-conservative thing." Buckley had no stomach for Church, but even less for such "populist" exhibitions of direct democracy. Cosmetics millionaire William Penn Patrick decided to quit underwriting the effort. He explained that California's conservative Republican senator George Murphy had persuaded him of the recall's capacity to provide "undeserved support" for Church. Moreover, by now he had other things on his mind. The militantly right-wing Minutemen Party had endorsed him as its vice-presidential candidate for 1968, and he was considering whether to accept.[87]

In frustration, Ron Rankin and Gene Mileck turned on each other. Rankin concluded that Patrick was investing little in the recall movement while trying to gain publicity from it; but Mileck, ever the loner, suspected that his colleague was secretly receiving large sums of money from the millionaire. When thugs beat up Mileck in Spokane, he was certain that Rankin and Patrick were responsible. He fired Rankin, who in turn accused him of having "a Don Quixote complex. He blew it." Mileck disagreed. "My allies became my enemies because I wouldn't let them use me," he said later. His battle now "was to stay alive, for Christ's sake, and oppose these sons of bitches." Pressing ahead on his own, he tried unsuccessfully to resuscitate the dying recall movement.[88]

VII

The political situation turned sharply in Church's favor. The collapse of the recall effort, he remembered, "got me up off the canvas after about an eight count or a nine count. . . ." He had beaten back his challengers and gained an even wider audience in and outside Idaho. And he had done so without relinquishing his role as a critic of American foreign policy.[89]

He continued to express regrets about both "the imperial virus" that had driven the United States into Vietnam and "the brutalizing effect this war is having upon the American character." He spoke openly about "the dissipation of the 'American ideal' which was to be an example to the world, and was never to be imposed abroad by force of arms." In an *Esquire* magazine article, "From the U.S.A. to All the World With Love," he noted sadly that the United States had become "the principal arms dispenser of the world," and was apparently more devoted to "furnishing swords than plowshares." As a result, America too often sided with military elites against change in underdeveloped nations. This, he said, was the mistake that the U. S. had made in Vietnam, when it had bolstered the unpopular Diem regime.[90]

In an interview in late 1967 with television commentator Joseph McCaffrey, he argued that the Johnson administration's policy of escalation had failed. Indeed, he said, "there's been something rather wrong, maybe something immoral, about the proposition that we can fight a tidy war that the theoreticians and geo-politicians say is necessary. . . and that we can do it without costing anybody anything here at home." It was time "to begin a policy of de-escalation." And he pointed to a theme that was increasingly on his mind: the need for Congress—especially the Senate—to reassert itself, reclaiming constitutional powers that it had steadily relinquished since the 1940s to the Executive branch.[91]

The 1968 election still lay ahead, giving people such as Grangeville's aging Fred Boynton the chance to vote him out if they damn well pleased. But going into that year, Church sensed that the recall effort had boosted his chances of winning a third term. A few months earlier, during the last phases of his fight against the recall movement, he had been in a reflective mood as the car in which he was riding sped across a high valley between McCall and Boise. Coatless, his sleeves rolled up, he had sought comfort against the ninety-five-degree heat as well as America's misdirected policies in Vietnam. Why, asked the reporter who sat with him in the back seat, had he decided "to 'fly like a dove' rather than 'screech like a Hawk' "? Pushing his hair back from his forehead, Church replied, "This notion that we are somehow going to settle everything by teaching the Communists a lesson in Vietnam is a grandiose self-delusion." It was the terrible consequence of antiquated Cold War attitudes–"frozen patterns of thought." The State Department premise that Ho Chi Minh was simply an agent of some large conspiracy was "the denial of wisdom," reminding Church of the Bourbon kings who had reputedly learned nothing and forgotten nothing.[92]

As the parched grazing land flashed by on that blistering summer day, he wished that more of his Senate colleagues would make public the doubts that they expressed to him privately; but their instinct for political survival silenced them. In that regard, he could take pride in his own conduct. Perhaps he recalled a letter he had received more than a year earlier from sociologist David Riesman. The Harvard professor had complimented him for speaking out against the Vietnam war. "I remember a comment you made, a very just one, a few years ago," Riesman wrote, "mainly that if your constituents in Idaho knew where you really stood, they would throw you out." But they knew as never before where he stood in 1967 because of all the recall publicity. And that year they had decided overwhelmingly not to throw him out of the political ring. He had survived for yet another round.[93]

Stressing his courage and independence, a photo used in Church's 1968 campaign literature portrays him walking alone. *Courtesy Boise State University.*

Chapter Ten
"Time of Reckoning": 1968

"THIS YEAR WOULD appear to be the time of reckoning," Frank Church guessed in early 1968. Six weeks later, following the North Korean seizure of the U. S. S. *Pueblo* and the opening of the Tet offensive in Vietnam, he delivered a spellbinding speech in the Senate. Entitled "The Torment in the Land," it portrayed a nation mired in trouble at home and abroad, and emphasized themes that increasingly agitated the senator: the need for a fundamental reordering of national priorities, and for Congress to reassert itself within the constitutional system of balance of powers. "The hot summer looms ahead," he prophesied, indicating that the U. S. was in a race with the clock. Had he known of the terrors still to come over the next few months, he would have been even more somber. The year 1968—the worst yet in what journalist Richard Rovere described as "this slum of a decade"—brought extraordinary anguish to the United States, and plenty for Church himself. But even slums sometimes have their bright spots; Church's came with his reelection to a third term.[1]

I

Going into that fateful year the signs were far from encouraging. In 1967 the expanding Vietnam war had claimed 9,400 additional American lives and countless numbers of Asians. America's cities and college campuses had themselves taken on features of combat zones. An apocalyptic mood seemed to be settling over the country. According to *New York Times* columnist James Reston, "Nineteen sixty-seven had a bad press and even the obit writers weren't sorry to see it go."[2]

Although Church had survived the recall attempt in Idaho, he had much to ponder. The 1968 election still lay ahead, and it was apparent that right wing groups were determined to block the reelection of Church and other Senate doves. "Nationally," he observed, "they are concentrating their efforts in states like Idaho – small states, where their money can be concentrated in the most telling effect. . . .They'll concentrate their fire and fanaticism against me."[3]

He worried also that the nation was locked on a disastrous course. "The great need in this country is to re-order our priorities," he told one reporter as they drove toward Boise late in the summer of 1967. Twenty percent of the American population lived in economic misery. "We want to take the Great Society to Southeast Asia," he observed sadly, but "we don't even have the Great Society here." The war in Vietnam was coming full circle, crippling America's own economy at the same time that it devastated the Vietnamese. Exasperated with his congressional colleagues, he accused them of becoming "calloused." They were "unwilling to pay for rat eradication, which could be paid for by just four hours of the war in Vietnam."[4]

A few weeks later, on October 29, he expanded his critique of Congress, asserting that its pronounced deference to the executive branch in foreign policy was generating a constitutional crisis. Speaking in Boise to the Idaho Press Club, he discussed a dreadful irony: to protect itself against perceived foreign dangers, the U. S. was destroying its own system of government. The Constitution provided for separate branches of government, checked and balanced against each other. Starting around 1940, however, the nation had increasingly turned to the president to determine foreign policy. According to the Constitution, war-making power rested entirely with Congress. But Congress, like the larger public, had rallied around the president during the emergencies of World War II and the Cold War. Recent presidents had arrogated to themselves the power to define the national interest and to direct military forces as they saw fit. Accelerating this trend were specialists and experts in foreign policy. Church had no quarrel with the need for competent, informed presidential advisors. But some of them had "demonstrated a certain arrogance" he complained, "purveying the belief that anyone who is not an expert, including Congressmen, Senators, and ordinary citizens, is simply too stupid to grasp the problems of foreign policy."[5]

Church told his audience that he agreed with diplomatic historian Ruhl Bartlett, who had testified before the Foreign Relations Committee a few months earlier: " '. . .There is nothing in the realm of foreign policy that cannot be understood by the average American citizen.' " The senator applauded the Foreign Relations Committee for its recent demonstrations of independence. Of late, it "was exhibiting a new but well-founded reluctance to grant the executive any more blank checks." The previous spring, for example, it had rejected an urgent request for more aid to Latin America—a request that the president thought would strengthen his hand at an upcoming meeting with other Latin American leaders. But the committee, by a nine to zero vote, had consented only to consider in due time any such financial requests. Although presidential aide Walt Rostow had judged this action "worse than useless," Church thought that the results "were salutary. Having no gifts to dispense, the United States was obliged to deal with the Latin Americans as a friend rather than as a patron." Church found especially encouraging an "unusual resolution" that the committee was considering. It called for a sense of the Senate that the president could not dispatch troops to any foreign soil—except in response to an attack—without acquiring the constitutionally mandated consent of Congress. To Church this meant, quite simply, that "the executive is being put on notice that its account with Congress is overdrawn. . . ."[6]

Had Church known about the advice that Lyndon Johnson was receiving in late 1967, he would have been less hopeful. A "draft speech for the Senate," which National Security Advisor Rostow submitted to the president on October 3, conceded virtually nothing to Congress in foreign policy. In response to senators questioning the administration's Vietnam policy, Johnson would fire off some queries of his own: to what extent did they presume to have better information than the president? What of the expertise of the Secretaries of Defense and State who had been in office for seven years? What kind of message were the senators sending to the enemy? Rostow then advised Johnson to quote from a North Vietnamese prisoner who had found antiwar dissent in America heartening, and then to tell the senators that they "ought to think twice before" assuming that their information was "better than that available to the President of the United States. . . . And, once in a while, too, we should think about that old-fashioned phrase: 'giving aid and comfort to the enemy.' "[7]

A few days before Rostow drafted the speech, Johnson had told several aides: "The major threat we have is from the doves." The president set out to undercut the antiwar movement. He requested that the Federal Bureau of Investigation, for example, run security checks on individuals who wrote letters and telegrams critical of a speech he had recently delivered. And he also mounted a public relations campaign to show that the war was going well. "We are pleased with the results" in Vietnam, he informed the press on November 13. "We are inflicting greater losses than we are getting." Two weeks later, Vice President Hubert Humphrey said on television that the U. S. was progressing extremely well "on every front in Vietnam." That same month, General William Westmoreland was equally optimistic, even suggesting that within two years the U. S. might begin to withdraw troops.[8]

To Church, such rosy predictions failed completely to recognize the casualties that the war was inflicting on the American economy and spirit, let alone on the Vietnamese. Johnson's Great Society was coming apart, as a number of commentators had already observed. But the president seemed unwilling, or unable, to reconsider his policies—to wrestle with the crucial matter of priorities. As historian Paul Conkin later said, "Johnson hated subtraction and division; he loved addition and multiplication."[9]

The president was a man divided, as Church discovered once again in the fall of 1967. On September 21 Johnson hosted a small gathering of several Democratic senators who were up for reelection the next year. During most of the dinner LBJ held forth on the war almost non-stop. After the meal the group moved upstairs to the balcony, where Johnson continued to speak with bravado about the war and what he had in mind for Ho Chi Minh. Church felt increasingly uncomfortable. He was determined not to spoil the evening or create an incident, but he could not bear to listen to the descriptions of how wonderful the war was and how it would soon be over. He finally moved to the other side of the porch. Brandy and cigar in hand, he looked out over the White House garden, trying to lose himself in thoughts about the physical beauty of that clear, star-filled night. Johnson, noticing that he was no longer with the group, suddenly pushed his way through the other senators and moved toward Church. "I thought," Church said later, "well here it comes again." The president threw a big arm around his shoulder. "I notice, Frank, you've been looking at the garden," he commented. "Did you ever hear the story about how Thomas Jefferson first planted this garden?" No, Church replied, he had not. Johnson proceeded to tell him the story. "He couldn't have been gentler or nicer," Church remembered. After about fifteen minutes, LBJ said quietly, "Let's go back and join the crowd." Not once had the president mentioned the war to Church. And afterward, he shifted the discussion to domestic politics, a conversation in which the senator engaged "with relish."[10]

In retrospect Church believed that the incident demonstrated "much more sensitivity than [Johnson] is normally credited for. He understood that I was discomforted by the conversation, and . . . he undertook to bring me back again into the party." The occasion illustrated, as Church noted, how complicated and complex Johnson was. But it also symbolized LBJ's preference for the politics of inclusion, not exclusion—"a no-losers game," as Paul Conkin later described it, in which all claimants in society received something.[11]

It was precisely the no-losers premise of the Great Society that shattered in the late Sixties. The fiscal demands of both massive military spending and LBJ's domestic programs did not lend themselves to fine economic tuning. Guns and butter proved an unworkable combination. As different groups sensed that they were losing ground to others, or that their expectations would go unrealized, discontent turned to rage. It fueled the third party presidential candidacy of Alabama governor George Wallace as well as the cries of "Black Power," the walkout of some fifteen thousand Chicano students in 1968 from Los Angeles high schools, the wrath of Native Americans, and the swelling ranks of right wing organizations such as the John Birch Society.

II

Convinced that a drastic reordering of national priorities was essential, Church by the end of 1967 was formulating his "Torment in the Land" speech. He had already informed his constituents that he would oppose the president's request for a 10 percent tax hike to help pay for the war. In a newsletter he tried to suggest how mammoth the costs of the Vietnam conflict were, and to answer critics of the War on Poverty who blamed it for the nation's economic troubles. Chopping "off every limb on the Administration's anti-poverty tree, the Job Corps, Headstart, Vista, Appalachia, the manpower retraining program, slum clearance, urban renewal, all of it," he wrote, would produce an amount insufficient to pay for one month of the Vietnam war. He personally preferred to pare back "that bloated boondoggle, the moon shot" program, but even a $500 million cut would cover only one week's worth of fighting in Vietnam.[12]

As Church prepared to argue that a mistaken war abroad generated ugly conflict at home, there was little evidence that his comments would strike a popular chord. Louis Harris polls in December 1967 showed that 58 percent of the public wanted to increase U. S. military pressure in Vietnam; 63 percent opposed stopping the bombing in the North; over 75 percent thought the antiwar protests encouraged the enemy; and 70 percent judged the demonstrations as "acts of disloyalty." As Church had observed earlier that year, "In all of our past wars, I can recall no contact between 'hawks and doves' in which the hawks failed to prevail. I see no basis for anticipating a different outcome at this time." Indeed, he said, "if political expediency were my purpose, I would have been a screeching hawk from the start."[13]

In late January 1968, as he worked on his speech, two jarring events occurred. On January 23 North Koreans seized a U. S. intelligence-gathering ship, the *Pueblo,* claiming that it had violated the twelve-mile limit off their coast. They took the commander and eighty-two crew members prisoner. To Church, the North Korean act was nothing less than piracy, but he wondered if it was yet another indication of the price of the Vietnam war: "perhaps we have spread ourselves militarily too thin to protect our interests elsewhere."[14]

On January 30, a week after the seizure of the *Pueblo,* a huge communist offensive rocked South Vietnam. Suddenly, the communists were everywhere, momentarily occupying even the American embassy in Saigon. When CBS News anchor Walter Cronkite saw the first bulletin, he burst out, "What the hell is going on? I thought we were winning the war!" Over the next several weeks the network evening news shows portrayed South Vietnamese cities that were anything but secure, and a war in which the United States was a long way from victory.[15]

In his newsletter following the start of the Tet offensive, Church struck a patriotic note, emphasizing the dilemmas that U. S. soldiers faced in such a futile war. He drew parallels between himself and a Marine officer who had helped to retake the city of Hue, and who had then replaced the Viet Cong flag with the stars and stripes. When the officer received orders that he could not raise the American flag over a South Vietnamese city, he angrily took it down but refused to put the banner of South Vietnam in its place. "It must be maddening," Church wrote, to defend a country "that has so little stomach to defend itself" and was so corrupt. So, too, he speculated, "the Marines must have scorned the rosy reports still emanating from our own officialdom." How many Americans, Church wondered, were going to die in Southeast Asia? He pledged his continuing support for the Americans who were there, but reiterated his opinion that U. S. military intervention in

Vietnam was a horrible mistake. He reminded his constituents that he had first spoken out against the war four years earlier, at the time that it had shifted from a program to aid the anti-communist Vietnamese to a war that Americans fought themselves. And he had done so despite warnings that he should keep quiet and "go along" with dominant opinion. "Well, sometimes," he said firmly, "a man just can't go along—like the Marine in Hue who hauled down the American flag, when ordered, but refused to raise Saigon's in its place!" However strained the analogy of the Marine officer was, it highlighted the image that Church wanted to project in Idaho as the 1968 election neared: the independent-minded, courageous individual, willing to stand outside the crowd.[16]

That image was no mere pose, as Church proved again in his "Torment in the Land" speech. On February 21 he offered his own State of the Union address, as he described it, a penetrating indictment of America's Cold War foreign policy as well as a gloomy assessment of a society at war with itself. His main point was that the nation simply had to reorder its priorities.[17]

The well-crafted speech was vintage Church; it was his own creation and reflected his passion for language. He wrote most of his own material anyhow, partly because of his continuing reluctance to delegate authority—a tendency evident in his need to see every press release and to monitor constituent mail. But he did so also because of his abiding faith in words and the power of speech. He had an old-fashioned orator's confidence in his ability to persuade, as well as an editor's eye for precise expression and careful sentence structure. Whenever a staff member had to draft one of Church's speeches, the experience was invariably humbling. One aide recalled the sense of jubilation that came with learning that the senator had kept several of the original sentences. Pride of authorship was something that a staff person could ill afford. All of Church's speeches bore his own imprint; and in many cases he had reworked his own prose time and again. "To speak well," he contended, "you *have* to be the author of the text itself."[18]

Interestingly, although Church as a teenager had wowed the national debate judges with his extemporaneous remarks, as a senator he spoke from a text. "The press always wants a handout," he explained. "You've got to have something to give them if you expect decent coverage." Moreover, to find the largest possible audience, he usually prepared major addresses for publication in newspapers or journals.

Although he relied on a text when speaking, he attempted to avoid the appearance of simply reading it.[19]

After spending considerable time preparing a speech, he was typically nervous about its delivery. He rehearsed again and again in his office and before coming to the Senate floor practiced it one more time. If he arrived in the chamber only to learn that the moment for his address had not yet arrived, he sometimes retreated to a stall in the Senate restroom, where he continued to read over his comments. "I had to know what shoes he had on," recalled one of his aides. "When he had to be back on the floor, I'd have to go in there and say, 'Sorry to bother you, Senator, but it's time. . . .' "[20]

In early 1968 Church was particularly anxious about his "Torment of the Land" speech. He intended from the outset for it to be a major address, and the text was his alone and took hours to prepare. As usual, he sat at the typewriter, talking as he wrote. After typing a sentence or two, he would stop and speak to the empty room, trying to get a sense of the way the words sounded. Meticulously, he tested phrases for their cadence, searched for dramatic metaphors, and imagined himself delivering the speech to his colleagues.[21]

He took the floor on February 21 with the Tet offensive in its third week, the crew of the *Pueblo* still imprisoned in North Korea, and the presidential primary election in New Hampshire fast approaching. Church entered the Senate chamber, opened the black binder containing his text, paused for effect, and began speaking. He was in his preferred element, not wheeling and dealing behind the scenes, but standing in the Senate with a painstakingly prepared address in hand. Speaking very deliberately at first, with the tips of his fingers in his jacket pockets, he became more animated and expressive as he proceeded. One reporter noted what "a good, strong baritone voice" he had. It was "resonant, beautifully modulated"–"trumpetlike" in its "clarion projection," tone, and marvelously exact articulation.[22]

Church told the Senate that something was "seriously wrong" with the United States. The evidence was everywhere. Responsible citizens had concluded that the nation had somehow lost its bearings. Some of America's brightest young people had repudiated their own country. However one might deplore the emergence of "hippies," the senator emphasized that it was impossible to dismiss them. It was equally misleading to focus on violent demonstrators and to ignore a huge number of peaceful college students who felt "profoundly disturbed about their country." Another sign of domestic discontent existed in the seething cities. In Church's opinion, the nation's "marathon dance with war" was finally taking a ghastly toll. The conflict in Vietnam "pervades and brutalizes our culture." Its awful images were ubiquitous, filling everything from the evening's television news to children's comic books. "Violence begets violence," he admonished. The war was circling back to America's own streets, as some returning veterans transferred the "arts of guerrilla warfare" to the festering slums. Driving home the point, Church quoted a Vietnam veteran who had looked down on the burning buildings of Detroit and said, " 'It's here, man, that the real war is.' "[23]

America's post-World War II bipartisan foreign policy had not prepared the nation for that "real war," Church argued. It had skewed attention toward problems abroad, rather than at home. Consequently, almost 75 percent of the 1967 budget was for "war or war-related programs, while only 12.2 percent went for health, education and welfare." The United States had become the world's largest munitions supplier. It had also built a massive nuclear arsenal, sent its troops around the world, and distributed billions of dollars of aid to 124 foreign governments. "We have wrapped our arms around the world as if it were our oyster," said Church. And for what purpose? Not security, and not peace, because "the dangerous delusion of American omnipotence" had produced one military conflict after another. The real source of America's "global intervention" was a deep-seated fear—fear of communism, fear of the future, fear of an inability to control events. "Like other nations before us that drank deeply from the cup of foreign adventure," Church noted with a memorable phrase, "we are too enamored with the nobility of our mission to disenthrall ourselves."[24]

It was time, he insisted, for Americans to turn their attention to their own troubled land. Military spending in Vietnam and elsewhere was draining the nation's economy, throwing its budget badly out of balance. Efforts to help fund the Vietnam war by imposing a proposed tourist tax struck the senator as "grossly unfair," an additional "harassment of our citizenry by a government increasingly immersed in a foolhardy endeavor to bestow liberty abroad instead of insuring its blessings here at home." The senator's words were searing counterpoints to Lyndon Johnson's dreams of a Great Society. Church also chastised Congress for its willingness to yield on budget issues rather than face up to the need to alter the nation's priorities. "The baited trap" in Vietnam loomed on one side, America's flammable slums on the other.

Another hot summer of discontent lay ahead, the senator warned. While the nation continued to spend billions of dollars to squash a revolution in Vietnam, "insurrection smolders in every major city in America." Church's question was chilling: "Must it come to guerrilla warfare on our own streets before we begin to put first things first?" With both arms raised, he concluded his speech by quoting from John Quincy Adams of the dangers that faced the U. S. if it went in search of monsters abroad: " 'She might become the dictatress of the world. She would no longer be the ruler of her own spirit.' "[25]

The speech, according to one observer, had an "electrifying effect." Church sat down to stunned silence, but applause soon cascaded from the galleries—despite the pounding of the presiding officer's gavel. Several senators rushed to congratulate him and their praise far exceeded the typical compliments that followed a colleague's presentation. Alaska's Ernest Gruening believed he had just heard "one of the great speeches of all time. I believe it ranks with the classics, with the addresses of Daniel Webster and other distinguished orators of the past."[26]

Several days later Church advocated the suspension of the foreign aid program "for the duration of the war in Vietnam," and at the end of July he voted accordingly. "The time of giving has been foreclosed by the war in Vietnam," he said when opposing the $1.9 billion foreign aid program that the Senate nevertheless approved. He also favored bringing home half of the U. S. troops in Europe. "The time is over for tap-on-the-wrist adjustments in foreign spending," he charged. The nation was over-extended abroad. Moreover, until the U. S. reduced costs of its Vietnam involvement, he planned to support across-the-board reductions in domestic spending.[27]

Some critics found Church's actions greatly disturbing. Columnist Crosby S. Noyes viewed his February 21 speech as signifying a growing trend toward isolationism. The result, predicted Noyes, would mean nothing less than "the abdication of the United States as a world power." Church and other doves, according to Noyes, refused to face up to the terrible consequences of their recommendations: the abandonment of Asia to communism and the violation of American commitments. "The effect would be precisely the same as if American power had ceased to exist." Such criticism ignored a crucial distinction that the senator had made. Church rejected an "ostrich-like isolationism" along with international commitments that exceeded the nation's resources. As always, he tried to stake out "the rational middle ground," as he described it.[28]

For a brief moment in March, however, that middle ground suddenly seemed more than a dream. On March 12, Senator Eugene McCarthy shocked the political world by compiling 42 percent of the primary vote against the incumbent Lyndon Johnson. "Perhaps all is not lost," wrote a jubilant Church. "There are stirrings in the land."[29]

Church himself had been one of the doves whom antiwar people had hoped might challenge Lyndon Johnson in the primaries. The previous fall, liberal organizer Allard Lowenstein had asked George McGovern to head a "dump Johnson" movement. McGovern refused because he had to worry about his own Senate reelection in 1968. Church's name came up as an alternative, although McGovern guessed that the Idaho senator would be equally concerned with his own election problems. Such was indeed the case. Church declined Lowenstein's invitation, partly because he doubted that he had the kind of national recognition that any presidential challenger required. As a result, Lowenstein, bespectacled, intense, and driven, eventually turned to McCarthy who, in late October, agreed to enter the race. The only alternative, the Minnesota senator had said that summer after listening to yet another Johnson advisor defend the president's Vietnam policy, was to take the war issue "to the country."[30]

Neither McGovern nor Church expected McCarthy, or any protest candidate, to get more than 10 to 15 percent of the New Hampshire vote—a token showing. Both senators were astonished and elated with McCarthy's performance. In retrospect, Church judged McCarthy "the most important political figure of that year." By challenging Johnson so closely in New Hampshire, "he wounded the President," and wounded him severely.[31]

How severely became evident the evening of March 31 when the president stunned a nationwide television audience with the announcement that he would not accept a nomination for another term. In choosing not to seek reelection, LBJ nevertheless emphasized that his administration still sought an independent, non-communist South Vietnam. He did, however, announce a partial bombing halt of the north and indicated a willingness to go anywhere, anytime, to talk peace. Church's response to LBJ's speech was grateful. "It was Lyndon Johnson's finest hour," he told the press over the phone right after the president's speech. Johnson was sacrificing his political future in order to enhance the prospects of peace. When Hanoi responded positively several days later to Johnson's declared willingness to negotiate, Church's hopes lifted even more: "I can now see a glimmer of light at the end of the tunnel," he said.[32]

III

Trying to interpret the rapidly changing events of 1968 was, however, a little like trying to grasp quicksilver. The administration in fact held to terms that virtually guaranteed the failure of peace talks with North Vietnam. And McCarthy's surprising performance in the New Hampshire primary hardly attested to strong antiwar sentiments. People who voted for him were mainly opposed to Johnson; indeed, over half of the Democrats who voted were not even sure how McCarthy stood on the war.[33]

Politics became even murkier on March 16 when Robert Kennedy announced his candidacy for the Democratic nomination, threatening to divide the antiwar wing of the party. In an interview with *Washington Post* reporter Haynes Johnson, Kennedy conceded that his entry into the race would place pressure on many of his friends. "I understand how it is for [Robert] McNamara, or Church or [Lawrence] O'Brien. . . . I feel sorry to make them have to choose." Church initially found Kennedy's candidacy distressing. "My sympathies were with McCarthy because he had made the fight against Johnson," he said later, "and I thought that Bobby really muscled in when he saw the opening." In that regard, Church spoke for many disgruntled antiwar liberals. Over the next several weeks, however, Kennedy's belated campaign burst with energy as the New York senator began to galvanize his audiences. Church's position on Kennedy softened, and he concluded that he could support either him or McCarthy. In contrast, he was extremely unhappy when Hubert Humphrey entered the race on April 17. The vice president extolled the virtues of "the politics of happiness. . . and the politics of joy," but Church had little stomach for his publicly exuberant support of the Vietnam war.[34]

By May the Idaho senator seemed to be edging toward Kennedy's camp. In response to a query from Kennedy advisor Theodore Sorenson, Church indicated that Kennedy had virtually no organization in Idaho. Humphrey, on the other hand, was "moving fast" and McCarthy was starting to have an imprint in some counties at the precinct level. "Things seem to be going better in neighboring Utah," he said, intimating whose side he was on; there, Kennedy had done well in mock elections at the University of Utah. Church also suggested some contacts who might be helpful in Idaho. However much he might have begun to favor Kennedy, he decided to avoid the presidential contest as much as possible and to concentrate on his own reelection campaign. Local politics dictated as much. When he heard that rumors of his impending bolt to Kennedy were hurting him in southern Idaho he emphasized that he was not taking sides. "Any other course would be a serious mistake for me."[35]

But, as Secretary of the Interior Stewart Udall recollected, the events of 1968 were "like a Greek tragedy": the fates had set the stage and "there was really little choice left." Unexpected events battered the best-laid plans again and again. On April 4, in Memphis, Tennessee, an assassin's bullet brought down Martin Luther King, Jr. Riots broke out in more than 125 cities. At Church's Senate office, the staff heard endless sirens blaring in the nation's capital before receiving word that trouble was spilling into the downtown area. It took over three hours for Verda Barnes and Rick Raphael to maneuver several miles through the massive traffic jam, their eyes anxiously on the fire and smoke billowing up from the ghetto area several blocks away. As the frenzy of burning and looting intensified, federal troops surrounded the White House and installed a machine gun post on the steps of Congress. On "the dark day of Dr. King's funeral," Church struggled to put his thoughts on paper. He reminded his constituents that the overwhelming majority of black Americans had not participated in the riots. And he urged people, regardless of their race, to commit themselves to King's standards of "decency, justice and nonviolence."[36]

Two months later, on June 4, an assassin's bullet claimed Robert Kennedy, minutes after he had won the California primary. Church was stricken by the news. He had been fond of Robert; indeed, he liked immensely all three of the Kennedy brothers with whom he had worked. In 1961 he had joked about why Ted Kennedy's photographs of the African trip had not turned out well. The fault, he had assured Ted, "was not yours. As I recall, you were using Bobby's camera. It was an overbred camera, and doubtlessly suffered from the same anemia that often afflicted the royal families of Europe." Now, seven years later, Bobby was yet another victim of the rising violence of the Sixties.[37]

After Frank and Bethine Church attended the funeral in New York City, they rode the train bearing Kennedy's casket to Washington,

D. C., and then crossed the muddy Potomac River to Arlington Cemetery, where Robert was buried near his brother John. The train procession from New York City was as instructive as it was emotionally wrenching. "For eight agonizing hours," Church viewed the faces of thousands of people lining the tracks. The train moved, not through wealthy urban areas, but through dilapidated and ugly tenement districts. "I see fury and I see fright," Church wrote in his notes of that sorrowful journey. "There are no grand vistas to look upon, only cluttered shop yards, grimy warehouses, dumps and slums." The poor residents nevertheless signaled their affection for a man whose sentiments and ideals, if not his background, mirrored theirs. People were on their knees crying; others held up scrawled signs, "Robert Francis Kennedy–Farewell!" "We are passing through the Baltimore station," Church wrote. "The people are singing the Battle Hymn of the Republic. . . . It is growing dark." For the Churches, it was "the longest day of our lives."[38]

Shortly thereafter, a still-grieving Church addressed the state Democratic convention in Idaho Falls. "It is a time for searching our souls," he told the gathering as he focused on Robert Kennedy's assassination. He expressed admiration for the New York senator's ability to step beyond the ordinary bounds of politics. Kennedy was a "rich man who cared passionately about the plight of the poor," and he refused to follow the political dictum of going along in order to get along. Church noted bitterly that most politicians were only "animated mirrors." Unfortunately, he said, referring to King and Kennedy, America seemed determined to strike down its few genuine leaders.[39]

He blamed the killings upon a continuing state of war that placed a premium on force. Americans "have been steeped in violence," he said. "It is the curse of the land." Verging toward a radical indictment of American culture, he chastened people who were quick to condemn ghetto rioters and student demonstrators. "Remember," he cautioned, "the moral climate we have furnished, and the example that we, ourselves, have sometimes set." But as much as Church tried to understand the roots of the nation's domestic violence, he could in no sense condone it. "The maintenance of liberty depends," he insisted, "upon the maintenance of order." The right to dissent did not include the right to break the law. He conceded that in the urban riots and on some campuses, the situation had "gotten seriously out of hand." It was thus imperative, he argued, to take certain steps: to deal with the source of grievances, ranging from discrimination to poverty; to enforce the law; and to end expensive and counterproductive military adventures in foreign lands. Those were goals to which he said he was committed as he sought a third senatorial term. He hoped that his fellow Idaho Democrats would work for him in trying to see that the United States fulfilled its promise.[40]

Church perhaps had Hubert Humphrey, among others, in mind when he referred to politicians who resembled "animated mirrors." Although Church and his former Senate colleague agreed on many issues, Church had been wary of Humphrey for over a decade and disapproved of the vice president's cheerleading support for the administration's Vietnam policy. The fact that the vice president was now likely to get the Democratic nomination galled him. His anger boiled up during a heated exchange with Byron Johnson, one of Carl Burke's younger law partners and a rising Idaho Democrat. Johnson planned to support Humphrey at the Democratic national convention in Chicago but also to vote for an anti-Vietnam war plank in the party platform. Church "got on me pretty hard that I was supposed to be a young liberal and here I am voting for Humphrey," Johnson recalled. "What he was really trying to say was, 'Here I've pinned a lot of hopes on you. You are going to be this great liberal, and now you go off and support Lyndon's guy. What the hell is going on here?' " Stung by what he viewed as "a real putdown," Johnson snapped back, "Tell me again about gun control, Frank." Church said nothing more. "It was one of the few times that I ever saw Frank at a loss for words," remembered Johnson, who took no pride in the exchange. He looked to Church as a model, and the senator's comments had "cut a little bit." As much as anything, the incident demonstrated Church's frustration with Humphrey.[41]

IV

By summer, Church felt cornered. He was uneasy about attending the Democratic convention in Chicago, partly because he had premonitions of trouble there, partly because of the demands of his reelection campaign, and partly because Eugene McCarthy and George McGovern both wanted his support. In early August, McGovern decided to declare his own candidacy for president as a kind of stand-in for Robert Kennedy. He wanted Church to deliver his nominating speech. But McCarthy also sought Church's help, asking if he would at least offer a seconding speech in his behalf. One of McCarthy's key people, Harvard lecturer

Martin Peretz, communicated several times with Church. Given the delicate political situation in Idaho, Peretz understood why Church might refrain from committing himself publicly to a seemingly "vain effort." He nevertheless wondered if Church would provide behind-the-scenes help by talking to Senator Robert Bartlett about the important convention role that Alaska could play. By leading off the convention's roll call with an endorsement of McCarthy, Alaska could strike an important symbolic blow in behalf of the Minnesota senator.[42]

Church agonized over the situation. He and Bethine talked about his dilemma as they drove across the sweltering desert of southern Idaho. If he went to the convention, he would have to choose between McGovern and McCarthy. He found them both acceptable candidates and was reluctant to offend either. Moreover, it was a moot decision because Humphrey clearly was going to win the Democratic nomination. In Idaho, meanwhile, Church negotiated a political minefield. Already vulnerable because majority opinion seemed overwhelmingly to favor a more aggressive war in Vietnam, his hopes for reelection depended on how much the voters respected his independence and judgment. There might be a limit to their tolerance, especially if he seemed to be getting "too forward" by endorsing a candidate whose credentials were suspect among local citizens. Even within his own party, Church had to be careful. As he commented later, some Democrats were not about to crown McCarthy for beheading their king, Lyndon Johnson. Church wanted to do nothing more that might mute their enthusiasm for him. Complicating the matter was his suspicion that nothing but trouble awaited the Democrats in Chicago. What was he to do? Bethine replied that he should "take a leaf out of Wayne Morse's book." Meaning what? he asked. "When in doubt, attack."[43]

Embracing Bethine's suggestion, Church took the offensive. He announced that he would not attend the Democratic convention because it was, in effect, rigged. The nomination was already decided, even though it would not reflect the opinion of many Democrats across the nation. To attend would be a waste of the senator's time. He had his own political race to think about.[44]

In one stroke, Church thus avoided alienating either McGovern or McCarthy. He also telephoned McCarthy, apologizing for not being able to help his candidacy. The Minnesota senator understood Church's position and appreciated the call. In retrospect, McCarthy could not remember that any other senator had privately expressed regrets for not being more helpful.[45]

By avoiding the convention, Church also placed himself some fifteen hundred miles from the violence that indeed erupted inside and outside the Democratic convention. Chicago turned into an armed camp. For several bloody days, police clashed with demonstrators, who chanted, "The whole world is watching."

The convention damaged the antiwar movement. Sam Brown, a young divinity student who had helped organize McCarthy's New Hampshire campaign, believed that the violence repulsed many Americans who had previously sympathized with the peace efforts. "Instead of nice people ringing doorbells," he said, "the public saw the image of mobs shouting obscenities and disrupting the city." Moreover, the Democrats had rejected the peace plank. Hubert Humphrey later explained why he had not backed it: Lyndon Johnson had told him "that the plank did not meet with the policies of this government." Although 80 percent of Democrats in the primary elections had voted for either McCarthy or Kennedy, the plank failed, 1,567 to 1,041. Some delegates put on black arm bands; some stood in the aisles shouting, "Stop the war"; some knelt in prayer. The nomination was Humphrey's, but he had missed the opportunity to build a bridge to the doves in the party.[46]

Half-way across the nation, Frank Church sadly monitored the convention. He believed that Humphrey had botched a chance to redeem himself. It would have been possible for him to say that, as vice president, he had to support Johnson; but now that he was his party's nominee, he would seek peace. Church assuredly preferred Humphrey to Richard Nixon, the Republican nominee, but he emphasized that he did "not intend to give Hubert Humphrey a 'warm embrace.' " Instead, he wrote, "I'll be stressing my independence as a Senator." To Eugene McCarthy he expressed gratitude for putting up the good fight. "Yours was the first crusade I have witnessed in American politics," he wired him. "The outcome was predestined as we both knew. But your imprint on the conscience of the country not only will endure, it may well shape our future."[47]

V

For Church, 1968 was turning into a painful year. As one shock after another pounded the nation, he increasingly betrayed a sense of moral outrage at what Americans were doing to themselves and to others. And his critiques of the Vietnam war and America's social problems broadened.

His willingness to work the margins of political acceptability in Idaho was often remarkable. He was assuredly cautious about patently unpopular developments such as the Poor People's March in the late spring of 1968, when some three thousand people lived in A-frame plywood shacks for several weeks near the Lincoln Memorial in Washington, D. C. He deemed it "tragic" that the march's leaders made unreasonable demands, including a guaranteed annual wage. "Jobs and education, not more welfare, is where the answer lies," he said. He also was displeased to learn that Office of Economic Opportunity (OEO) funds had helped to subsidize anti-white plays in New York City's Harlem Youth Program. Yet, he was otherwise very supportive of the OEO, especially its Job Corps component, which he compared to the popular Civilian Conservation Corps of the Depression era. When a Nampa, Idaho, group attacked it as constituting a "Hitler Youth Program," he gave a spirited response. He wished "the self-appointed saviors of Nampa" would get their facts straight: the program was entirely voluntary; around one hundred youths benefitted from the job training camp in the national forest east of Kooskia; and women did not live in camps near men nor wear " 'unfeminine' marching shoes." He continued to defend the Job Corps, despite warnings that his political opponents in Idaho were "beating [it] to death."[48]

In many respects, however, he was worlds apart from the social ferment boiling up across the country. Culturally, there was virtually no resonance between him and the new consciousness that surfaced in myriad forms, from underground newspapers to fashion. In matters of life style, etiquette, values, and taste, Frank Church was essentially conservative. "In the best sense of the word," recalled Ward Hower, who worked for him during his first seven years in office, "he would have been a Tory." Patrick Shea, another staff member, agreed, noting that Church had a kind of "patrician attitude." Even much of the senator's dissatisfaction with U. S. foreign policy was conservative in the classical sense. He accepted such concepts as balance of power and spheres of influence, for example. Temperamentally, "he liked old things and antiques, and manners," according to Hower, and he "valued stability—institutional stability, marital stability."[49]

Perhaps as close as Church got to a "countercultural" expression was around 1962, during a trip to Harvard. He had gone there to participate in some informal study sessions on Vietnam. The meetings, which were in effect precursors of the teach-ins, had no official university sponsorship. No dean or other Harvard officers welcomed the senator to campus. He was there at the behest of David Underhill, a former aide and Harvard undergraduate. Although the event focussed on the growing war in Southeast Asia, a few of the students decided to have some fun with an arts festival exhibit that was underway. Church joined them in the basement of one of the campus residence buildings, where they playfully engaged in "action" art, throwing paint randomly on a canvas. The senator got in the spirit of the moment, seeming to have "a fine time" as he swished some bright paint across the creation. Laughingly, he told Underhill that this was the one thing upon which his constituents agreed with Nikita Khrushchev, who had recently compared an exhibition of modern art to what a dog would deposit on a canvas. In the basement of Harvard's Quincy House, Church thus defied his constituents' aesthetic taste and struck a humorous blow for "modern" art. But having helped to create the "action painting," he refrained from parading it around the streets and campus with the students.[50]

Church was in fact uncomfortable with much about the emerging American culture, ranging from pornography to the growing use of profanity. Moderate in temperament, he had little tolerance for the extravagance that more and more characterized conduct and language. All around him was disconcerting evidence of what cultural commentator Benjamin DeMott described as "overkill." The excesses of the radical right had bothered the senator for some time. John Birch Society founder Robert Welch, for example, had declared that the United States was "one vast asylum" and "the worst patients" were running it. And, in 1964, Barry Goldwater had told the Republican national convention that "extremism in defense of liberty is no vice."[51]

By 1968, however, this penchant for the extreme, the excessive, seemed overwhelming. "On every side," recollected Students for a Democratic Society activist Todd Gitlin, "extremity was the commonplace style. . . .The rhetoric of showdown and recklessness prevailed." Black novelist James Baldwin labeled the United States the "Fourth Reich." Writer Susan Sontag declared that "the white race is the cancer of history." Black Power militant Rap Brown asked, "How many white folks you killed today?" "The family is the American fascism," insisted social commentator Paul Goodman. The Berkeley *Barb* advocated closing down or abandoning the universities: "The professors have nothing to teach. . . .We can learn more from any jail than we can from any university." Timothy Leary, a leading advocate of the drug LSD, told Yale university undergraduates that the leaders of American government were "for the most part impotent old men riding on youth. . . . Laws are made by old people who don't want people to do exactly those things young people were meant to do—to make love, turn on, and have a good time." "The world belongs to politics," asserted historian Theodore Roszak, "which is to say the world belongs to death."[52]

Such stridency and hyperbole grated on Church, just as surely as the increasingly confrontive nature of American politics alarmed him. "Confrontation politics," as the New Left called it, appealed more and more to protestors bent on provoking the mainstream society. They hoped to reveal the ugly realities that lay behind official posturing and to awaken people to the nation's moral failures and shortcomings. The civil rights movement had pointed the way. By taking direct action, whether in parades or sit-ins, civil rights demonstrators had shaken the larger society, stirring consciences and precipitating long-overdue change. Antiwar groups, and others who hoped to influence policies and reshape politics, found the strategy ever more alluring. It appeared in numerous forms, including the tumultuous student protests at Columbia University in the spring of 1968. Irving Howe, a democratic socialist, found the tactics as chilling as did Church. "Confrontation politics" was a dangerous game because it divided society and encouraged a repressive backlash. "Polarization helps, not the left," warned Howe, "but the right; not those with grievances, but those with guns." Howe believed that American politics had reached "a bad moment" because the war, inequities, and social conditions demanded radical protest; yet such protest, if not restrained, could well end up strengthening the opponents of justice and damaging democratic processes as well.[53]

These were precisely Church's concerns. The susceptibility of American culture to "overkill" encouraged tendencies that jeopardized democracy. When people insisted on shouting—and, eventually, shooting—each other down, democracy itself became the victim, and the victors were those with no other claim to success than raw power. Confrontation politics, the senator feared, ultimately destroyed the middle ground, reasonability, and the art of democratic persuasion.

Thus he added his voice to the cries for law and order and against "crime in the streets," themes which had risen steadily in American politics since Barry Goldwater's 1964 presidential campaign. "Like yourself," Church wrote an angry constituent, "I have no sympathy for those who desecrate the flag, and I am currently supporting legislation to make flag-burning a federal crime."[54]

A catch-all phrase, "crime in the streets" had come to stand for many things. For some it was little more than a convenient charge to hurl at the civil rights movement, thereby clothing an essentially racist backlash with respectability. For many citizens, however, it was an anguished scream of terror and resentment, articulating fears that their country was disintegrating in the face of riots, unsafe streets, delinquency, drugs, social permissiveness, changing rules and standards, and disrespect for authority and traditional values. By 1968, George Wallace had placed "law and order" high on the agenda of his presidential candidacy on the American Independent Party ticket. He promised to make Washington, D. C., safe "for your children to visit," and he rebuked psychologists, sociologists, and other "pointy-headed intellectuals" who blamed society, not the criminal, for murder and rape. "We Want Wallace," cheered thousands of followers as he scoffed at a legal system in which a criminal could knock "you over the head" and get "out of jail before you're out of the hospital," while the arresting officer ended up on trial. Richard Nixon, the 1968 Republican presidential nominee, similarly seized upon the law and order issue – blaming the Johnson administration and the Supreme Court for an increase in street crime; praising "the non-shouters, the non-demonstrators," "the silent majority" that worked hard, paid taxes, and obeyed the law; and promising to appoint judges who were not soft on crime. Frank Church also made much in 1968 of "the rising tide of crime and lawlessness." He wanted policies that would provide real, not token, protection for frightened citizens.[55]

This objective, however, did not make Church's position comparable to that of Wallace or Nixon. Indeed, from the senator's perspective, any failure to distinguish between him and them simply attested to the polarizing tendencies of the era. It reflected the affinity for extreme positions and judgments, the cultural "overkill" that encouraged quick categorization and labeling. It discounted what to Frank Church, ever the debater, was crucial: nuance, shadings, fine points. He had no doubts, for example, that there were significant differences between himself and the architects of the Vietnam war, and he could not understand the New Left's assumption that all politicians were basically alike. By his own admission he had once subscribed uncritically to cold war doctrines. But he had altered his thinking over the years, sometimes at considerable political risk. His "Torment in the Land" speech represented his growing readiness to challenge an axiom of his own earlier political faith: the belief that containing communism abroad and reforming America at home were achievable. No, he was not simply another member of the "Establishment."

Similarly, his calls for law and order typically had a different inflection than those of a Wallace or a Nixon. He, too, expressed displeasure with the Supreme Court's rulings against public prayer and reading from the Bible in the schools; and he had "serious reservations" about recent Court decisions that, according to critics, tipped the scales of justice too much toward the rights of the accused. He favored a constitutional amendment to reverse the Court's prayer decision. As he interpreted the matter, the First Amendment prohibited the establishment of an official state religion, not the practice of "customary religious observances which are so much a part of our traditional life." But, unlike Wallace and Nixon, he avoided using the Court's controversial rulings as issues to inflame public resentments and passions. Instead, he attempted to assuage worries and provide a source of reassurance. He thus emphasized that, historically, "the opinions of the Court tend to balance out in the long run." And, when telling a constituent that he, too, sometimes disagreed with the Court, he added, "I am sure you would not want to deny those freedoms guaranteed in our Bill of Rights to others, which we claim for ourselves." Even though he favored a prayer amendment, he was attentive to the difficulties of wording it so that it would still protect religious freedom.[56]

Like Wallace and Nixon, Church talked about the need for law and order. Unlike them, he used that issue as a fulcrum for defending the war on poverty and for criticizing the Vietnam war. He observed, for example, that punishing the guilty and enforcing the law against rioters were entirely necessary but, in themselves, ignored larger social problems. As long as the slums remained, they would breed new violence. Hence he favored the anti-poverty program. While some critics attacked it for allegedly rewarding rioters, Church saw it as a way "to help slum inhabitants break out of a vicious circle in which so many of them are now entrapped." Putting his own spin on the law and order issue, Church thus pointed out that in 1968 "we will dish out nearly eight times as much on a war in Vietnam as we will spend in the United States for all police, all courts and all correctional institutions." Was it not time, he asked, "to start putting first things first in this country," rather than squander billions of dollars abroad?[57]

VI

Church's 1968 reelection campaign would test how carefully he could deal with volatile issues such as law and order without engaging in demagogic tactics. In this "year of reckoning," issues and events seemed to conspire against moderation, restraint, tolerance. Seldom in the nation's history had so many social forces collided with such fury. Seldom had there been such bitterness, despair, and rage. Idaho, in this respect, was anything but protected ground for Church. A poll in October 1968 showed that the Vietnam war and social unrest were overwhelmingly dominant issues in the state. A whopping 97 percent of the Idaho electorate judged the law and order issue "very important." Moreover, Church could expect no help from the Democratic presidential ticket; it was in fact a liability. In a September poll, Nixon claimed 42 percent of Idaho's voters while Humphrey limped along with only 16 percent, four points behind George Wallace. Church would have to surmount a huge swell of opinion for Nixon.[58]

He would also have to deal with a formidable challenger: George Hansen, the Republican senatorial candidate. The congressman from Idaho's second district was physically imposing, six-feet-six-inches tall, lanky, and with a Marine-style brush haircut. Ideologically, he was decidedly conservative; the Americans for Constitutional Action gave him a 100 percent rating for his two congressional terms, in contrast to Church's 11 percent. He enjoyed the blessings of Richard Nixon, who told one of the largest political crowds in Idaho history that Hansen was "one of the bright new stars in Congress." Moreover, the Idaho branch of George Wallace's American Independent Party backed him, support which he eagerly accepted. "None of our organization is for Church," said one Wallace organizer. "They know that he's been soft on communism and law and order." Hansen hoped to make the most of the ideological differences between himself and Church. He contended that the senator was "a 100 percent supporter of the Great Society" and "the second wildest spender in the Senate. . . . His philosophy is not consistent with that of the people of Idaho and mine is." Moreover, Hansen said, "he may be more suave but I'm more direct." A natural campaigner, ambitious, friendly, and hard-working, the 38-year-old Mormon wanted, as someone quipped, to "separate Church and state." He appeared to have the means to do just that. As Church viewed the situation, he faced his "hardest campaign" yet, "with an opponent who is not only extremely well-financed by all the right-wing organizations, but a well-known and vociferous hawk, in a State filled with conservatives."[59]

What one eastern reporter described as "a titanic political battle" threatened to become vicious as well. An Idaho Democrat who favored Hansen called Church a "socialistic & communistic loving left winger. . . . After twelve years of radicalism, who can trust you—you big blabber-mouthed spoiled brat." The senator suspected, correctly, that Hansen would do everything possible to encourage such sentiments. "Church's dislike of Hansen was basic," said Mike Wetherell, who worked on the senator's staff for a decade. "He simply considered Hansen to be dishonest and manipulative," a politician "who appealed to the worst in people rather than the best."[60]

Hansen's capacity for mischief surfaced early when he attacked Church's support for civil rights. Race was a particularly sensitive issue in Idaho in 1968, even though only some two thousand of the state's seven hundred thousand residents were black. Following Martin Luther King's assassination, for example, there had been fierce resistance to plans for a march and memorial service on the capitol steps in Boise. The city's population of seventy-five thousand included no more than three hundred blacks, yet nervousness about the event had been considerable. Authorities had finally granted permission to hold the services, but had banned the march. At the mayor's request, black youths at the nearby Job Corps center were denied passes until the "emergency" had passed. Playing on these fears of racial violence, George Hansen urged an end to civil rights legislation on grounds that it encouraged riots. He raised questions about the loyalty of black leaders and suggested that King's assassination had been deserved—"the chickens coming home to roost," as he put it. He advocated that police shoot to kill black looters as a way to discourage further riots; indeed, he said, a few deaths now would save lives in the future. The comment about King's death elicited absolute disgust from Church, who became as angry as his aide Mike Wetherell had ever seen him.[61]

Refusing to downplay his support for civil rights, Church instead helped to integrate the Kenwood Country Club in Bethesda, Maryland. The club had recently barred Walter Washington, the District of Columbia's black mayor, from speaking at a luncheon. In response to that incident, Church had joined CBS reporter Robert Pierpoint and others on a neighborhood committee aimed at breaking the club's racial barriers. After failing to elicit support from such influential local residents as congressmen Melvin Laird (R-Wisconsin) and John Rhodes (R-Arizona), the committee decided to take its cause to the public via a story in the *Washington Post*. Pierpoint, reluctant to use Church's name in the story without permission, called the senator's office. Church was campaigning in Idaho, however, and his legislative assistant objected that news about the Kenwood fight would give Hansen more ammunition. At Pierpoint's insistence, the staffer nevertheless agreed to contact the senator. Church replied quickly that, certainly, the committee could use his name. "It was a risk for him," recalled Pierpoint, who admired his willingness to place principle ahead of votes.[62]

Meanwhile, Hansen blasted away at Church's position on Vietnam as well as on civil rights. To Hansen, the Vietnam war was yet another chapter in the Soviet plot to communize the world. In order to achieve a quick and necessary victory, he favored abandoning Lyndon Johnson's "appeasement" policy and bringing "North Vietnam to its knees," if necessary by using nuclear weapons and invading China. He emphasized that he was no dove like Frank Church, whose dissent provided "aid and comfort" to the communists. Instead, he was a superhawk. "When you live by the sword, you don't shorten the blade," he said, "you sharpen it."[63]

To counter this barrage, Church engaged in some "gunslinging" himself, as aide Neal Parsell put it. He attacked federal gun control laws with renewed energy, presenting sixty-five thousand Idaho signatures to the Senate in order to limit restrictive legislation. "Who fired the shots that counted against federal gun controls?" asked one of his newspaper advertisements. "Frank Church did." According to the narration of one of his television spots, Church opposed blanket gun controls "because this is Idaho, the heartland of the open West." In the video clip the senator discussed urban crime problems, indicating with a shrug of his shoulders that cities such as Chicago could deal with their problems as they saw fit. "But," he said, jabbing his finger in the air with conviction, "I'm not for them telling us what kind of laws we should have in Idaho." Another of his television commercials reminded one reporter of a scene from the popular TV series *Bonanza*: "It depicts him in cowboy clothes, galloping up to the camera on his trusty steed and delivering a few homespun remarks on 'Western independence.' " The reporter half expected him "to whip out a six-gun and scare off any Californians who might be fixin' to raid an Idaho water hole." Another TV spot showed Church standing in front of beautiful peaks in the Sawtooth range. "I come from mountain country," he said. "And I know that sometimes a man must stand alone." As the picture faded to a view of the mountains, a narrator indicated that "Frank Church is his own man. Maybe that's why he's Idaho's."[64]

The central motif of Church's campaign was that of the robust, autonomous Westerner. The senator, according to his campaign ads, was "Idaho's voice of independence." The cover of a particularly striking brochure portrayed him in denim jacket, blue jeans, and cowboy boots, sitting casually on a wooden wagon. Still youthful looking, smiling broadly, his thick hair coal-black, "Church of Idaho" exuded a relaxed, but commanding demeanor. Another photograph showed him with a backpack; in yet another he sat at his desk with the figure of an eagle to one side and a picture of Idaho's celebrated political maverick, William E. Borah, on the wall. One page featured the word "INDEPENDENCE" six times to describe his position on various issues and quoted Montana senator Mike Mansfield saying that Church stood "for rugged Western independence." On the back of the brochure a photograph showed Church in his suit, hands in pockets, head tilted slightly upward, strolling away from the camera and up a hill toward the Adams County courthouse. An American flag fluttered in front of him. The caption read: ". . .sometimes a man must walk alone."[65]

By portraying himself as a man apart, Church put distance between himself and the unpopular Johnson administration. From this perspective, his early opposition to the Vietnam war was anything but unpatriotic; instead, it represented a courageous willingness to think and act as a tough-minded individual. In one television ad Church recalled General Douglas MacArthur's warning not to engage American soldiers in a war on the Asian mainland. "I agree," he said. And, he reminded the viewers, he had made himself clear on that point, even though initially he "was pretty much alone." He hoped, as well, that Idaho citizens would not forget his consistent support for American troops once they were in battle.[66]

Similarly, the senator separated himself from the administration's farm policy. According to Idaho Democrats such as John Glasby and Lloyd Walker, Secretary of Agriculture Orville Freeman's agricultural programs were "very unpopular." Freeman seemed interested primarily in helping large wheat and corn farmers in the Midwest rather than aiding Idaho's more diversified and smaller-scale operations. In Church's office, as aide Neal Parsell recalled, "our approach was to do what the farmers wanted us to do ('I am not a farmer, so I have to listen to what farmers tell me. . .')." Although some of the demands were of doubtful consequence—for example, a state-of-origin labeling requirement on potatoes—the senator's tendency was to be supportive. Deep down, however, Church's staff people suspected that there was little chance to save the small family farm, so common in Idaho. Perhaps, thought the senator's good friend and campaign manager Carl Burke, "the family farm is deader than a doornail." Even within Idaho, guessed Burke, the 75 percent of the population that constituted towns and cities was more interested in developing the land than saving it for modest tillers of the soil. Parsell thus believed that "our efforts amounted to handholding and empathy, little more."[67]

This did not mean that Church had abandoned Idaho's small farmers. He supported legislation, for example, to protect agricultural land from the purely speculative ventures of large, diversified, non-farming corporations seeking tax write-offs. And his newsletter, *Idaho Farm Roundup*, was full of newspaper clippings in 1968 attesting to specific steps he was taking in behalf of his agricultural constituents. Philosophically, as a campaign advertisement indicated, he hoped "to free the farmer from government controls." Price supports had not worked. He hoped somehow to help farmers improve their bargaining position in the larger economy. In his correspondence he admitted that he had no real solution to agriculture's difficulties. But he urged farmers themselves to organize more effectively so they could seize the initiative. "Action has to begin with farmers, and the government can only support them." In that regard, Church could play a role. A thirty-second campaign ad emphasized this as a rancher described how the senator had saved his land from the federal government.[68]

During the 1968 campaign Church attempted to focus on Idaho issues as much as possible. That spring, prominent local Democrats such as Lloyd Walker had encountered "an awful lot of heat" because of worries that Church was "abandoning Idaho in favor of foreign relations." Walker urged him to "get away from the foreign policy thing and back to the business of Idaho." In this regard, the senator stressed his actions to preserve the state's natural beauty. "It is possible to live the good life here," he said in one television ad, as he talked about wilderness legislation that protected the state's water and air. Chatting in another video spot about "the kind of wholesome life" that Idaho provided, he compared the state's streams with the Potomac River, "one of the most polluted in the world." The Potomac was so much "like an open, flowing sewer" that his son Chase had worried about somebody decaying in the river, rather than drowning in it.[69]

Indeed, protecting Idaho's water became a battle cry that rivaled Church's defense of the state's right to determine how it wanted to deal with guns. "Keeping Idaho Water Out of California's Reach"–this was how a campaign pamphlet summed up the issue. In a television spot, Church stood alongside the Snake River, indicating that California wanted this water. A narrator then stated solemnly, "Frank Church is running so Idaho water can keep running in Idaho." The point was that Idaho, with its small population, needed all of the clout of an established senior senator to protect its holdings. In a state whose economy had historically been extractive, such concerns were more than symbolic.[70]

George Hansen's supporters struggled to show that Church might be from Idaho, but he was not of it. Some, in fact, suggested that Church was not even a good American. The senator "says he's for Idaho water," snorted one of the leaders of Wallace's American Independent Party and a Hansen backer. "So what? If we lose the Constitution what good is Idaho water?" Trying to cast doubt on Church's Idaho credentials, Hansen's people charged that Easterners were financing the senator's campaign. "Can They Buy Idaho's Senate Seat?" asked a four-page Hansen tabloid. According to the tabloid, Church was receiving money from the Council for a Liveable World and the Committee for a Sane Nuclear Policy (SANE). Church, perhaps remembering that Hansen had earlier defeated incumbent Ralph Harding by linking him to the Council, countered that he in fact refused contributions from both of these groups.[71]

The National Committee for an Effective Congress (NCEC) was another matter. As in 1956, the organization supported Church; and Hansen, like Herman Welker before, attempted to hammer him with this fact. The committee in 1968 endorsed Church along with Democrats Joseph Clark, J. William Fulbright, Ernest Gruening, John Gilligan,

George McGovern, Mike Monroney, Wayne Morse, and Gaylord Nelson, as well as Republicans George Aiken, Thomas Kuchel, and Charles Mathias. Letters soliciting contributions went out from the NCEC over the signatures of prominent historians Barbara Tuchman and Henry Steele Commager. "America is a house divided," they said, and among its victims might be this "small band" of nationally minded politicians who had courageously confronted the issue of Vietnam. "They placed their political fortunes on the line for us," wrote Tuchman and Commager, "and now we must not lose them." Working closely with the NCEC was Pulitzer Prize-winning poet and playwright Archibald MacLeish. The Massachusetts resident was particularly interested in reelecting Church and McGovern, solid liberals who were the "first two and most consistent Senate advocates of a negotiated political end to the Vietnam war."[72]

MacLeish, interestingly enough, initially hesitated to support Church because he found the senator's position on gun control "deeply" troubling. "As you surmise," Church answered him, "I am faced with a condition, not a theory. In Idaho, a gun connotes sport, not a crime." He conceded that some anti-gun control people used the issue in hysterical and misleading ways, but he did not count himself among them. Beyond that, Church would not go. "If my position on Federal gun controls is a disappointment to you," he wrote, "I hope I will make up for it in other ways." MacLeish apparently found the response acceptable. By the time of the election, Church and McGovern had received $72,500 in contributions via MacLeish's personal appeal.[73]

In Idaho, George Hansen zeroed in on the NCEC, "an ultra-liberal organization," and MacLeish, "a poet and attorney with a background of involvement with Communist organizations." According to Hansen's evidence, MacLeish had associated himself with some two dozen procommunist groups, including his defense of the "Hollywood Ten" and contributions to *Partisan Review*, in Hansen's view a "Communist publication." Why had the NCEC and other "out-of-state groups" endorsed Frank Church? Because, the Hansen people answered, Church was a self-proclaimed internationalist not really interested in "guarding the citizens of our own country"; because he was a "dove" on Vietnam, "one of the early peace-mongers," according to conservative columnist Holmes Alexander; and because of his liberal voting record. "Whom will Frank Church represent—the people of Idaho or his outside financial supporters?" wondered Hansen's backers.[74]

VII

Church himself worried far more about a problem much closer to home. The relationship with his son Forrest had continued to deteriorate, a source of considerable personal grief as well as a possible political swamp. A closely knit family was something that Frank and Bethine Church valued personally and needed politically. In campaign materials, and in newsletters, they had always included evidence of domestic bliss. And they had done so proudly, knowing that it was no masquerade. Literature for the 1968 campaign showed them sitting in their Maryland living room, or standing by a rail fence in the Sawtooth valley, with Forrest and Chase. Idahoans could certainly be proud of this handsome, still-young couple and their two sons, hair neatly trimmed, shoes shined, smiling. These were portraits in which defenders of the beleaguered American family could find reassurance, especially in a time of intense social stress and generational conflict. But the photographs were more pose than the Churches would have liked.

At Stanford, Forrest had grown a beard and let his hair grow long. He had changed intellectually as well as physically. Although not interested in politics in high school, during his freshman year in college he had driven nonstop to Boise with several friends to protest directly to his father about the Vietnam war. Subsequently, his discontent moved along channels that were more cultural and personal. "After his freshman year," recalled one of his classmates, he "sort of dropped out and lived up in the hills and was very antipolitical and very anti-everything his father stood for."[75]

Communications between father and son broke down almost entirely. Bethine also had trouble understanding her son's transformation, but one of his peers sensed that she was more open, more tolerant. Frank and Forrest, on the other hand, seemed unable to agree upon anything. The Vietnam war was an example. Although the senator opposed the war, he found his son's declaration of pacifism troubling. Citizens had obligations, in his opinion. Forrest, however, adamantly rejected military service; he placed his commitment to the human race ahead of what he deemed as narrow patriotism. There was no way that he would participate in the immorality of Vietnam. The senator argued the case for working within the system, not abandoning it. "At the time," as Forrest recalled, Frank Church "felt his position was undercut by irresponsible elements which outflanked him to the left." It hardly helped to believe that his own son was among them.[76]

More than specific issues divided father and son, however. As Forrest struggled to make sense of the chaotic world around him, and to define who he was, his father seemed an adversary. It may have been, as Ward Hower suspected, that the generation of the Sixties perplexed Frank Church greatly and he was not very tolerant of it. Or perhaps it was more a matter of personal dynamics, a product of the chemistry of personalities in turbulent times.[77]

For whatever reason, the father and son could not agree upon even the rules of evidence. As Forrest recollected later, "There comes a point where you feel things very deeply but you can't yet express them." Frank Church, in contrast, had always appeared able to articulate his thoughts. He was, in his wife's words, "very cerebral about things." Logical, precise, fastidious in speech and conduct, he was virtually tone deaf to arguments that favored intuition over intellect—that substituted amorphous feelings and subjectivity for objective data. If you asked him the time, two aides later joked, he would give you the history of the clock; another aide noted that he tended to think in terms of how many sides there were to a cube. Against that coolly analytical mind, Forrest, the young college student, collided. He recalled having "a moral certainty, emotional certainty, a deep feeling about something," but being unable to put it effectively into words. But his father believed that something not articulated had little worth. In one particularly heated exchange, Forrest thought that his father was toying with him, showing off intellectually. "He wasn't," Forrest believed in retrospect. "He was just trying to convince me with the only way he knew how to convince me, with logic and I was responding with emotion." At the time, however, Forrest exploded in frustration; tears running down his face, he objected to what seemed to be an attack on his very being.[78]

Forrest sensed that his father viewed him as "a frivolous and ineffectual and somewhat self-indulgent person. He never had any experience at that." Had the senator known about an incident in California when he was up for reelection in 1968, he would have been even more certain of Forrest's irresponsibility. On a date with Amy Furth, a Stanford freshman whom he later married, Forrest stole two pumpkins from a field. Although his action was purely an act of bravado, a demonstration of daring, a few minutes later he was under arrest, riding in the back of a police car. What, the officer asked, did his father do? Worked for the government, huh? "What level? GS 13, GS 14?" "Oh," Forrest answered, "about GS 20, I think." His escapade with the law, minor though it was, could have been greatly embarrassing to his father; but the victimized farmer, enterprising as well as forgiving, agreed not to press charges in exchange for $15 for the pilfered pumpkins.[79]

Meanwhile, in Idaho, Frank Church was emphasizing "that lawful authority be upheld and orderly processes preserved." It was a free country, he told audiences, which meant that people had "the right to change the law, but no one has the right to break the law." A television spot for his campaign showed him addressing the law and order theme. "The maintenance of liberty," he said, "depends first of all upon the maintenance of order," and this applied to cities and college campuses as well. A narrator's voice praised such "plain talk like this."[80]

In that context, news of a wayward member of the Church family would have been welcome indeed to George Hansen's backers. Someone had already been creative enough in that regard: shabby-looking individuals with long hair walked the streets of northern Idaho towns, soliciting votes for Frank Church and identifying themselves as members of Forrest's San Francisco "Hippie Club."[81]

In the summer of 1968 the senator needed displays of family solidarity and rectitude, but his staff people worried that Forrest, as he later put it, was "a ticking time bomb, George Hansen's secret weapon." Speaking to Forrest largely through intermediaries such as Carl Burke and Jerry Brady, Church asked his son for help. To the senator, the request seemed innocent enough: come to Idaho but without the beard and the long hair. To the son, it was "a painful abridgement" of his personal freedom. He did not view it as his business if his father was, or was not, reelected to the Senate. Ultimately, Brady persuaded him to shave his beard, trim his hair, and return to his home state. But, back in Idaho, he chose mainly to retreat to the basement of his parents' Boise house, which, in his words, he "turned into a romantic ghetto, a kind of good-guys hideout from the outside world." There he wrote poetry, read about the Russian revolution, and listened to the music of the Jefferson Airplane and Frank Zappa's Mothers of Invention.[82]

These were terribly distressing days for Frank Church personally. On a trip to Idaho Falls to appear in a parade, he confided to Peter Fenn, an old friend of Forrest, that his son's disinterest in the campaign hurt deeply. "He was very angry at Forrest," recalled Fenn. As he saw it, his son, by not enthusiastically helping him, had in effect joined the other side. Church wondered if Forrest loved him. He questioned whether he had been a good father. Fenn tried to reassure him, explaining that Forrest's conduct flowed from his search for an identity, not from disrespect or a lack of love for his parents.[83]

A few weeks later, a reconciliation of sorts took place. The Churches were at the Robinson Bar Ranch filming campaign advertisements. One evening, the senator asked Forrest and Peter Fenn to walk with him by the river. The night was clear and crisp, and the aspen leaves rustled gently. Church confronted Forrest with the differences between them. He said he was hurt. Forrest explained that he was not personally angry with his father. Well then, the senator wondered, did it matter to him who won the election? Forrest assured his father that, of course, he wanted him to win. Moreover, he knew that his father was doing all that he could to end the Vietnam war, especially given the realities of Idaho politics. For a poignant moment, Frank and Forrest Church embraced. Forrest cried. Tears welled up in his father's eyes. "It was the kind of thing that a lot of people wish they had done with their fathers at some time," Fenn recalled. Difficulties between the father and son were not yet over, but for precious minutes that night alongside the Salmon, they faded against the star-filled mountain sky.[84]

VIII

The campaign had its lighter moments. Rick Raphael remembered stumping with Church across the state. At one point, Bethine was "driving like hell" along the Bitteroots. As the road twisted and turned, Raphael sat in the back seat trying to type material for a speech that the senator would soon deliver. The old portable typewriter had a broken spring. "I am typing while he is dictating," Raphael recalled, "and every time that we went around a sharp curve, my carriage would go off. I'd scream to get Bethine to slow down because I couldn't keep the damn thing writing." Ultimately, they broke out laughing. There was a good deal of comradeship during the campaign. "Frank liked to sing," Raphael recollected wistfully, "and Bethine liked to sing. We'd sing old songs, and he always liked burning a camp fire."[85]

As the campaign moved into its last weeks, there was increasingly more to sing about. Church was still aware of possible dangers ahead. "I am caught in a pincer between the Nixon hook and the Wallace hook," he wrote in mid-September, a fact that made his reelection look impossible. But on the circuit, people seemed "exceedingly warm and responsive." An October poll confirmed what Church sensed. Nixon's huge lead in the presidential race was not benefiting Hansen much. Only 41 percent preferred Hansen to Church's 52 percent. Moreover, the "undecideds" of a month earlier were turning primarily to the incumbent. Church enjoyed a lead among males and females as well as every age group. Although his lead was smallest among voters under age thirty-four (44 to 31 percent), two-thirds of those over sixty-five preferred him to Hansen. His support from the elderly constituted a dramatic reversal from six years earlier. One measure of difference between his and Hansen's support was economic class. Among the highest income group, he trailed Hansen 46 to 50 percent; but he moved ahead 48 to 40 percent among people in the middle and lower middle economic brackets; and he completely outdistanced Hansen within the lower income group, 77 to 17 percent. Geographically, he was strongest in rural areas (56 to 36 percent) and in towns (51 to 39 percent); but the few cities such as Boise belonged substantially to Hansen (55 to 35 percent). Although the congressman also dominated the Mormon constituency (59 to 39 percent), other denominations favored Church heavily by a count of 59 to 28.[86]

Hansen, who at one point had seemed such a formidable challenger, kept stumbling. His effort to show that Church was "one of the chief architects of chaos we are experiencing" never found much of an audience. Some voters may have resented the low level upon which he moved his campaign. About a week before the election, his efforts to suggest that Church was an irresponsible leftwinger finally touched the senator's political nerve. "It was the first time we saw the senator really blow up," Rick Raphael said later. "He wanted to respond immediately." Subsequently, the Church people aired a short television commercial showing a large poster of Church. The only sound resembled a wind whistling. After fifteen to twenty seconds, someone from off camera threw a huge glob of mud against the poster. With a splat, it struck Church's face, then dripped down. After a few more seconds of silence, an announcer's voice urged voters not to let such mud-slinging defeat Frank Church. "It worked," recalled Raphael. Carl Burke was less sure of the ad's salutary effect. Like Church, he was nervous about using it, lest they engage in some campaign excesses of their own. But Burke had no trouble identifying the Hansen campaign as "the dirtiest we had up to that time."[87]

Hansen's stridency appeared to alienate some possible supporters. Boise's *Idaho Statesman*, the state's largest newspaper and solidly

Republican, objected to the "smear attacks" and twisting of facts that marked Hansen's campaign. On October 13 the *Statesman* broke precedent by endorsing Church and even comparing him to Borah.[88]

As before, Church himself proved the difference. Idaho voters might disagree with him, but they respected his independence and integrity. And they believed that, in Washington, he was their advocate. Cleve Corlett spent two months in 1968 accompanying Church across the state. In town after town, Church drummed away on the theme that sometimes an individual simply must walk alone. And he appealed to his audiences to let him continue doing just that.[89]

Although Church and his staff were "running scared" initially, Jerry Brady recalled that the campaign turned into "a kind of lark." Carl Burke, whose law practice by the late Sixties demanded about sixty hours of his time each week, came through again for his old friend. According to Byron Johnson, one of Burke's partners, his dedication placed "a severe stress" on the law office, because he was so important to the firm. But every noon, for up to two hours, Burke met with campaign staff people in Church's headquarters in the Hotel Boise. When he was in his office, he spent considerable time on the phone, talking with Democrats across the state, or with Church. The senator trusted him, sought his opinion, relied on him. Sometimes, recalled Johnson, tensions developed between Burke and Bethine Church, who was exceptionally savvy about politics in her own right and sometimes had different ideas about strategy. The two generally got along well, however, and Church himself invariably made final campaign decisions. Meanwhile, a host of other Church loyalists, such as Stan and Marylu Burns, turned yet another version of Citizens for Church into a daunting political force. Watching from nearby Utah, Senator Frank Moss was so impressed that he asked to use Church's campaign materials as models for his own reelection effort in two years.[90]

Apparently, many Republicans were also impressed, even though a joke after the election held that Church could not have won because no one admitted voting for him. One Republican who backed Church was a former county chairman in Payette, a solid GOP town near the Oregon border. He co-hosted a Church reception for around 150 people, mostly Republicans. "He's the best senator we've had in years," said the local publisher. The reason: "Water, primarily," and the fact that "he has some national stature."[91]

Ironically, even Gene Mileck had second thoughts about Church. The much-publicized housepainter and dogcatcher, who a year earlier had led the recall movement, agreed with George Hansen on most issues. But he concluded that the huge congressman was basically selfish, more concerned with his own advancement than with the people of Idaho. Mileck ended up endorsing Church, whom he saw as responsive to Idaho's citizens and someone who had maintained "the stature of a rugged individual and gentleman in the face of great stress."[92]

A week before the election two of Church's aides went to a popular skidrow bar in downtown Boise, where there was an odds board on the election. They were pleased to see that no one was betting on Hansen. A drunk who had passed out face-down at the bar reared back and belched. He had an "I'm for Church" button pinned to his cap. After looking through blurry eyes at the two aides, he rested his face again on the bar. The aides smiled at each other. People, no matter what their status, seemed to be staying on at least one wagon: that of Church.[93]

IX

On election day, the count was not even close. Church carried all but four of Idaho's forty-four counties and won 61 percent of the vote, 173,482 to 114,394. He even carried staunchly conservative Canyon County, where Nixon almost tripled Hubert Humphrey's presidential vote, and where Congressman James McClure beat his Democratic opponent, Compton White, Jr., two to one. Idaho was unquestionably Nixon country; his 165,000 votes left Humphrey far behind with 89,000, and George Wallace a distant third with 36,000. But Idaho was also Church country, as his ads had proclaimed. The senatorial election was, as Cleve Corlett later described it, "a referendum in which the people of Idaho decided that they were going to give the senator the leeway he needed to be an independent voice and to stand on the world stage. That's what it was all about."[94]

For Church, the moment was bitter-sweet. The bad news was that Richard Nixon, a man whom he had always viewed as "a menace," was president. Moreover, Ernest Gruening and Wayne Morse, the original Senate doves who had provided the only two votes against the Tonkin Gulf resolution in 1964, had met defeat. Their break with Lyndon Johnson may have cost them their seats, but, in retrospect, Church was certain that his own rupture with the administration had helped him win a third term. "If I had been just another Democratic senator supporting the Johnson administration," he said later, "I would have never been elected." Idaho, the hawkish state with the conservative reputation, had once again demonstrated some of the ironies of history. It had sent Frank Church—the dove and the liberal, according to his opponents and the popular media—back to the Senate. William Shannon of the *New York Times* believed that 1968 was "the year that failed to turn." Church had reason to believe otherwise.[95]

Church talking with Majority Leader Mike Mansfield, a key figure in the emerging dove coalition. *Courtesy Boise State University.*

Chapter Eleven
Fighting Back: 1969-1970

"YOU SURE ARE a big failure," Bethine Church commented ruefully to her husband not long after Richard Nixon took office. "You have been talking against this war for six years or seven years now and we are still involved in it." The senator perhaps smiled sadly at her observation, but he otherwise found the tragic conflict in Southeast Asia grimly depressing. In his book of anecdotes and political humor for speeches, the page marked "Vietnam" was conspicuously empty.[1]

As the war deepened and broadened in the early years of the Nixon administration, Frank Church helped take the lead in what was fast becoming an epic constitutional struggle. Foreign policy provided the occasion for this conflict, but the larger, underlying issues spun out of the growth of the national security state and, with it, the "imperial presidency." The Nixon administration's quest for even more power in the White House, when combined with the spreading war in Southeast Asia, heightened the political crisis. Increasingly, with Church much in evidence, a bipartisan coalition of liberals and moderates began to fight back against an aggrandized executive branch and an unpopular war.

I

The general calm that marked the opening months of the Nixon administration was misleading. Initially, an easing of public tensions signaled the arrival of a "new Nixon," one who was conciliatory, dedicated to ending both the Vietnam war and national disunity. He promised to establish a truthful, open administration, to be a "peacemaker," and "to bring the American people together." But the outbreak of new political storms was a virtual certainty given the persistence of the Vietnam war, the Senate's revived interest in its constitutional prerogatives, and the character of Nixon and his advisors.

In retrospect, Nixon blamed his opponents for the outbreak of troubles. All of his "enthusiasm and determination," he said, had not been able to offset a political fact: "I was still the first President in 120 years to begin his term with both houses of Congress controlled by the opposition party."[2] Although he overemphasized the purely partisan aspect of the opposition, he was indeed in some respects a prisoner of circumstances, for he took office at a time when some of the most fundamental Cold War assumptions were beginning to erode.[3]

Those assumptions included the importance of secrecy in a hostile world, the centrality of the presidency in shaping national policy, and the responsibilities of the U. S. in combatting communism around the globe. In 1947 such assumptions had taken clear statutorial and intellectual form. That was the year of the Truman Doctrine, in which President Harry Truman insisted the U. S. would go anywhere to meet the communist challenge. It was also the year of the National Security Act, which established both a National Security Council to advise the president on defense and foreign affairs, and a Central Intelligence Agency to gather information on perceived foreign threats to national security. And it was the year in which a federal loyalty program went into effect. Here were the crucial ingredients of the modern American national security state, forged out of the fears and crises of the early Cold War.

Over roughly the next two decades, those fears and crises also deepened the growing mystique of the presidency. The erosion of traditional party politics, the decline of political patronage, and the rise of the media—especially television—sharply tilted the balance of power in favor of the executive branch. But the primacy of foreign affairs exerted the greatest influence. In dangerous and uncertain times, it seemed, the necessity for quick action and unified responses required a powerful president. The logic of World War II and, subsequently, the Cold War left little room for alternatives. In the Oval Office, pontificated veteran *Time* reporter Hugh Sidey in 1963, lay "the very heart of this nation's meaning, the very core of freedom, thirty-five feet long by twenty-eight feet, four inches wide."[4]

Although by the end of the Sixties Frank Church lamented the growth of executive power, he recognized that it had developed largely as the product of congressional default. He himself had once championed the role of a strong president in guiding U. S. foreign policy, and he had not been immune to the dazzling spell of John Kennedy's

Camelot. But Lyndon Johnson's interventionist policies abroad had stung him and a number of his colleagues on Capitol Hill, especially in the Senate. Angry at Johnson's deceptions and his apparent "Senate be damned" approach to foreign policy, they had become increasingly suspicious of presidential claims to power, more jealous of congressional prerogatives. This tendency was evident on the Senate Foreign Relations Committee, certainly as early as mid-1965, and increasingly influenced Church's criticism of the Vietnam war. "It is the return of the Caesars I think we are seeing enacted here," he warned as he watched the expanding powers of the White House. As Richard Nixon soon discovered, senatorial restiveness about what Church described as "a new Caesardom" was extensive and cut across party lines.[5]

But Nixon was not about to give ground to a resurgent Congress. Early on he revealed his taste for an imperial presidency. A man of modest, even pinched, origins, Nixon loved the trappings of office. The Nixon White House was even more obsessed with presidential imagery than were the John Kennedy and Lyndon Johnson administrations. The White House mess chief thus fretted that "the President does not like ice cubes with holes in them." Nixon wanted trumpets to herald his entry at public events and, for a while, he had a ceremonial guard unit that wore Prussian-style hats and white tunics with gold braid. "The President's greatest political asset is the Presidency," speechwriter Patrick Buchanan advised him. "We are selling personality." This meant, among other things, cultivating the myths and mysteries surrounding the office. "We go seriously astray," warned aide Raymond Price, "if we think too much of 'issues' as traditionally defined and not enough about the Presidency itself—its aura, its mystique, the almost religious way in which Americans respond to it." Convinced that "politics is much more emotional than it is rational," Price believed that the idealized President resembled a "leading man, father, hero, pope, king," someone "larger than life, a living legend." To cultivate this mystique, according to Buchanan, the president should not become too "familiar" a person; it was essential to maintain "*distance* between the Presidency and the people. . . ."[6]

Nixon sought more than public aloofness; he also wanted distance from potential critics, other governmental institutions, and even most of his own cabinet. Dominant power was to reside in the hands of the president and a select few people around him. Meeting on November 25, 1968 with Henry Kissinger, his choice for National Security Advisor,

Nixon put in motion plans to consolidate even more authority at 1600 Pennsylvania Avenue. "He was determined to run foreign policy from the White House," Kissinger recalled, rather than through the State Department, whose bureaucrats he judged insufficiently loyal to him.[7]

He wanted to centralize power in the White House for both temperamental and ideological reasons. Nixon had always been inclined to view his political opposition with almost paranoid suspicion. Instinctively combative, he liked to compare politics to war: a dirty business that required a passion for the jugular. "You don't know how to lie," Nixon had once counseled a friend. "If you don't know how to lie, you'll never go anywhere." When challenged, Nixon could be ruthless. Over the years, he had developed the smoldering resentments of a snubbed and unappreciated outsider against "them"—his political enemies, liberals, Democrats, members of the news media, representatives of the eastern, Ivy League, privileged class. He had doggedly fought his way back from political oblivion to capture the presidency, but in the process had accumulated a huge reserve of grudges and suspicions. His advisers, often new to politics and typically worried and outraged at the apparent breakdown of morality and old certitudes in the 1960s, shared his siege-like view of the world. "You were either for us or against us," recalled one aide who described the "us vs. them" mood.[8]

The Vietnam war rubbed these feelings like a new shoe on a blister. Although Nixon publicly struck a "peacemaker" image, he in fact followed the thinking that he had outlined in a *Reader's Digest* article in 1964: "all that is needed, in short, is the will to win—and the courage to use our power—now." As president, Nixon hoped to win the war quickly by demonstrating his ruthlessness to the enemy. "I call it the madman theory," he told his aide Bob Haldeman. "I want the North Vietnamese to believe I've reached a point where I might do *anything* to stop the war." To that end, in March 1969 the administration commenced secret bombing strikes against Cambodia. Nixon from the outset thus moved his Vietnam policy along two tracks, one for the public record and one that he tried to hide from Congress and even from key officials in the military and his own administration.[9]

The president's apparent relish in defying Congress led Frank Church to wonder if the nation was witnessing the decline of representative government and "the rise of 'executive hegemony.' " Nixon in 1969, for example, according to a top executive aide, did not want "*any* Presidential consultation with Congressional leaders prior to submission of the Foreign Aid Message." This cavalier disregard for congressional opinion marked the Nixon presidency from its beginnings.[10]

II

A showdown with Congress consequently loomed early in the Nixon administration. It came during the spring and summer of 1969, not over Southeast Asia, but over what presidential aide Bryce Harlow identified as "the developing *Big Issue*": the proposed Anti-Ballistic Missile System (ABM). A few years earlier, the ABM had been anything but controversial on Capitol Hill. "We arm to parley" had summed up Congress's approach to the Soviets. Appropriations to help deploy the ABM had gone virtually uncontested through 1967. But by 1968 the economic and psychological costs of the Vietnam war had planted doubts in the scientific community, the public, and the Senate about the wisdom of the ABM. Nixon had thus scaled down Johnson's earlier system, focusing on one that would protect selective missile bases in the U. S., rather than cities. Even then, as Harlow advised him, the prospects of the ABM's passage were "bleak" and would require a "maximum effort, including all-out Presidential participation." Nixon was willing to go all-out. "I knew," he later wrote, "that the vote on ABM would reverberate around the world as a measure of America's resolve." In the Senate, however, a growing coalition became convinced not only that the ABM represented bad national security policy, but also that it was time to stand up to the president and say so.[11]

Frank Church belonged to this coalition. Whereas some of his colleagues objected to the ABM on economic and technical grounds, he placed the issue within the larger context of power, its limits and restraints. In this regard, he mirrored the thinking of the foremost Senate critics of Vietnam, such as J. William Fulbright of Arkansas and Tennessee's Albert Gore, Sr. The ABM, from this perspective, was not an isolated issue, but part of a flawed approach to foreign policy. As Church wrote Gilbert Harrison of *The New Republic*, "One can argue in chicken-or-egg fashion which came first, our vast foreign commitments or the huge military machine necessary to maintain them. It really doesn't matter, for the two are inseparably linked."[12]

Nixon, aware of this larger dimension to the ABM battle, still agreed with columnist Stewart Alsop's description of the opposition to the ABM as " 'essentially emotional – it is the liberals' way of getting back at the generals for Vietnam.' " In Nixon's estimation, "the liberals had deluded themselves: America would not make the world safer by acting dishonorably." Here was all the more reason for him to order his congressional liaison people to "fight to win." "Make sure that all our guys are there" to vote, he instructed Bryce Harlow. "Don't let anyone go to the bathroom until it's all over."[13]

The ABM contest thus lumbered toward a mid-summer vote fraught with symbolic meaning. At issue were competing versions of foreign policy, as well as Congress's role in making it. Church, ever more protective of senatorial prerogatives, judged the ABM proposal as costly, dangerous, and downright "goofy." His major objection, however, was that it was symptomatic of virtually everything that had gone wrong with U. S. foreign policy. A "policy of compulsive interventionism, conducted on a global scale," he told Gilbert Harrison, had dictated an ever larger military budget. That budget, including its proposed provisions for ABM deployment, could not shrink as long as the nation's "foreign policy goals remain so swollen."[14]

More and more, Church noted how closely U. S. foreign policy resembled that of the Soviet Union. The sad ironies of the situation nagged at him, broadening his examination of U. S. policy, pushing him toward a comprehensive critique at once moral and historical. Starting in March 1969, Church sketched out his thinking in speeches before the Senate and a conference of the United Methodist Board of Christian Social Concerns.[15]

He raised a question that increasingly bothered him: could the United States learn to live in a world of revolution? In Church's opinion, the history of the twentieth century provided an answer that was anything but reassuring. Neither the U. S. nor the Soviet Union seemed able to recognize that nationalism drove "the engine of change in modern history." Both nations were obsessed with order. Ideology motivated American policy as surely as it did that of the Soviets. Both countries sought to preserve "ideological purity" in their perceived spheres of influence. Soviet tanks thus rolled into Czechoslovakia and the U. S. suppressed revolutions in Latin America, all in the name of self defense and protecting national interests. A perverse definition of national interest had allowed America to turn Vietnam into "a showcase of bankruptcy, a hopeless war fought for insubstantial stakes." By aligning itself with the forces of order, Church lamented, the U. S. had placed itself against its own oft-stated ideal of self-determination—

meaning "the *right* of the peoples of smaller countries to settle their own affairs without interference by the great powers."[16]

There was indeed a danger to the United States, Church warned, but it came from within, from the nation's own policies. Ultimately, "a foreign policy of intervention" clashed with democratic values. By ignoring domestic needs, by feeding "a burgeoning military/industrial/academic complex," by resorting to deception, hypocrisy, and secrecy, the nation smothered its own values, its own ideals. "The greatest danger to our democracy," Church insisted painfully, "is not that the communists will destroy it, but that we will betray it by the very means chosen to defend it."[17]

Increasingly, Church also found U. S. policy morally offensive. The aid that America gave to developing countries too often bound "millions of people to live under a feudalism which fosters ignorance, hunger and disease. It means blighted lives, children with bellies bloated. . . ." Church offered some poignant advice to foreign policy makers who relied upon abstractions about power and diplomacy: "Go to a Brazilian slum, or to a devastated village in Vietnam."[18]

In the Senate on July 11, after making a passing reference to the follies of the ABM policy, he elaborated on his earlier comments to the Methodist conference. Describing the United States and the Soviet Union as "two sentinels of the status quo," he criticized America's "proxy war" in Laos and its efforts to manufacture a favorable U. S. image abroad. "All this, we are told, is influence, and influence is power. But is it really power?" he asked. "The real stake. . .is not power at all, but a shadow that calls itself power, nourishing an egotism that calls itself self-interest."[19]

During the opening months of the Nixon administration it would have been hard to find an elected official whose judgments of American foreign policy were harsher than Church's. Similarly, no one was more determined to reclaim Congress's voice in articulating a new foreign policy. On June 19, in defense of "the survival of constitutional government," he delivered a fiery Senate speech on the imperial presidency.

The occasion for his speech was a renewed debate over William Fulbright's National Commitments Resolution, the fate of which demonstrated a remarkable turnaround in Senate thinking. In 1967, Fulbright had introduced a sense-of-the-Senate resolution reaffirming "the role of Congress, particularly of the Senate, in the determination of national security policy." Specifically, no executive could make a "commitment" to a foreign power without the Senate's approval. At first, however, Fulbright was not able even to bring his resolution to a vote. In the spring of 1969 he reintroduced his non-binding resolution. The Arkansas Democrat, convinced that Nixon's search for an "honorable peace" in Vietnam represented "the calm before the storm," believed "we face a bad time."[20]

Speaking for the resolution, Church contended that nothing less than "the survival of constitutional government was at stake." He also took the occasion to puncture the myth of executive wisdom, a myth, he said, that "today lies shattered on the shoals of Vietnam."[21]

On June 25 the Senate approved Fulbright's resolution, 70 to 10. The resolution was purely symbolic, in no sense binding on the administration. That accounted for Nixon's decision not to fight it, and for the substantial margin of victory. But, in Church's mind, the meaning was clear: "the Executive branch must uphold its end of the Constitution."[22]

Nixon viewed the opposition to the ABM system as a much more serious threat than Fulbright's resolution. And on this issue the administration barely prevailed. On August 6, an amendment to halt all spending for ABM deployment failed by a 51-50 vote, with Vice-President Spiro Agnew casting the tie-breaker.

III

For Church and other critics of the Vietnam war, the ABM vote suggested the limits of their power. The Senate "doves" by 1969 numbered around thirty-five, perhaps a few more. The ABM fight had allowed them to garner additional support, but not the kind that might translate into majority opposition to the war. The doves simply lacked the votes to reverse America's involvement in Southeast Asia in any vital way, a discouraging fact given their worries about Nixon's policy. They were increasingly aware of the administration's secret bombing raids in Cambodia, but hesitated to speak out lest they endanger U. S. troops. On May 16, Church took an indirect approach by claiming that Nixon was pouring "the same old Johnson wine." He quickly backed off, however, expressing hope that the president was indeed rethinking his policies. But Nixon gave little reason for such optimism. Angry about opposition to the ABM, the president lashed out publicly at the "new isolationists" who lacked vision and thought only in negative terms. "When the first vessel set out from Europe for the New World," he said, "these men would have weighed the risks and they would have stayed behind."[23]

While the ABM confrontation ultimately underlined the difficulties in challenging the administration on foreign policy, the doves nevertheless found it instructive. Out of that fight emerged, more than before, the semblance of an organization as well as a strategy. The organization was largely at the staff level, where people such as William G. Miller, an aide to Kentucky Republican John Sherman Cooper, began to build an informal network. But there were also important movements toward bipartisan cooperation among the senators themselves. The initial strategy was elementary enough: contain the war.[24]

Church and a small group of Senate doves had already discussed this strategy, late in Lyndon Johnson's administration. They had gathered one day with Majority Leader Mike Mansfield, in the Montana senator's office. Church was there, along with Republicans John Sherman Cooper, Vermont's George Aiken, and New York's Jacob Javits, as well as Democrats Stuart Symington of Missouri, Phil Hart of Michigan, and a few others. Their discussion, according to Cooper's top aide, had been oblique, indirect, and lacking specifics. But the meaning had been clear enough: if the doves could not stop the war in Southeast Asia they would do the next best thing—prevent it from spreading. Then, by carefully choosing issues, and by emphasizing the Senate's constitutional obligations regarding foreign policy, they hoped to start squeezing the war, working its margins in an effort to compress it. In this context, the ABM battle of mid-1969 hinted at real possibilities. If the doves chose the right issues, it might be feasible to enlarge the antiwar coalition, and thereby to shrink the war.[25]

Most immediately, however, simply containing the war loomed as an urgent challenge, especially because the administration claimed—falsely—that it was already extricating the U. S. from Southeast Asia. In June 1969, Nixon had formally announced his policy of "Vietnamization," aimed at gradually turning over more of the war to the South Vietnamese. To that end, the president had withdrawn twenty-five thousand American troops. But reducing the troops was a far cry from removing America's military presence. Indeed, the administration was in fact escalating a policy of force.[26]

While the Vietnam war appeared to be winding down, it was in fact steadily spilling into neighboring Cambodia and Laos. Suspicions about growing American military involvement in Cambodia had been confirmed on May 9, when *New York Times* reporter William Beecher broke a story describing the first of Nixon's bombing strikes there. Laos also showed signs of escalating U. S. activities.[27]

Since the early Sixties, Frank Church, like most senators, had been aware of the hidden war in Laos, but he knew little of its details. In the fall of 1969 a Senate subcommittee under Stuart Symington began to provide information. Symington, a former hawk, lashed out at U. S. involvement in Laos: "I have never seen a country engage in so many devious undertakings as this."[28]

Church worried that the war was also moving into Thailand. On August 13 he angrily walked out of a Pentagon briefing when Secretary of Defense Melvin Laird refused to discuss U. S. military contingency plans there. "What is the Pentagon concealing?" he asked in a press release the next day. If America's plans regarding Thailand were as truly innocent as the administration claimed, why were they secret? Perhaps, he stated acidly, the Pentagon needed "an elementary civics lesson," a reminder of Congress's role in ratifying foreign commitments. The basic issue, he insisted, came down to "the sovereignty of the people. But, more and more, the Executive Branch of government behaves as though it were the master—not the servant—of the people." Church wondered about the administration's intentions in Thailand. Were deception and secrecy leading the U. S. into another Vietnam war?[29]

IV

By late summer 1969 Church and other Senate doves questioned what they should do next. The Vietnam debate was ready to burst forth again, in public demonstrations and in the legislative arena. But the administration, fresh from its narrow victory in the ABM battle, hardly seemed open to debate, let alone criticism. It preferred to tar the Senate doves as uninformed, meddling obstructionists, if not worse. On July 1, for example, Vice President Agnew had told the Midwestern Governors' Conference that "self-professed experts" on Vietnam were "undermining our negotiations and prolonging the war."[30]

The situation appeared to confirm Church's penchant for caution. Intellectually and morally, of course, he had no doubts about what the

United States must do in Southeast Asia. "What we really must decide, with respect to South Vietnam," he said succinctly, "is whether we are going to stay or leave. I think we should leave." His political instincts nevertheless continued to monitor his increasingly radical critique of American foreign policy.[31]

Thus when Senator Charles Goodell of New York approached him about co-sponsoring a proposal that would end the war within a year, he demurred. There was much about Goodell that Church could like. The moderate Republican, whom Governor Nelson Rockefeller had appointed to complete Robert Kennedy's term, was quite willing to stand up to the Nixon administration. He had, for example, voted against the ABM. And, like Church, Goodell believed that the only sensible policy in Vietnam was to get out. To that end, Goodell talked to Church about an amendment to cut off all funding for U. S. troops in Vietnam after December 1, 1970. Church, however, refused to sign on, indicating that such legislation had no chance of passage and that he was working on an alternative plan. Goodell, unable to find any co-sponsors, acted on his own, introducing his end-the-war amendment on September 25.[32]

Church's approach was more circuitous, aimed at keeping up pressure on the administration while avoiding direct confrontations. This tactic seemed even more prudent after journalist Jack Anderson reported that Nixon, in a meeting with presidential aides, had lambasted "bug-out resolutions." His mood belligerent, the president had indicated that Hanoi's intransigence might cause him to stop withdrawing U. S. troops and even to step up the war.[33]

In the fall of 1969, Church tried in several ways to persuade the administration without boxing it in. He co-sponsored a bipartisan measure aimed at conveying a sense of the Senate's impatience, and he supported what turned out to be the largest antiwar protest to that date, a huge national "Moratorium" against the war on October 15.

The bipartisan measure was a sense-of-the-Senate resolution that he introduced on October 8 with Oregon Republican Mark Hatfield, an ardent opponent of the war even before entering the Senate in 1967. Far more moderate than Goodell's amendment, it simply urged a more rapid withdrawal of American troops from Vietnam, eventually leading to complete disengagement. There was no mention of a time table, no threat of cutting off funding.

Five days later, a correspondent on ABC's televised news program, "Issues and Answers," suggested that Church now seemed "almost a conservative" in contrast to Goodell. Church disagreed, defending his and Hatfield's resolution as one that would put the Senate on record in favor of complete disengagement from Vietnam. Moreover, the resolution's purpose was to build "broad bipartisan support so we can get some action, which takes votes, a majority of votes." What bothered Church was the political wisdom of Goodell's amendment, not the idea behind it. In fact, he agreed with Goodell that another year was surely enough time for the South Vietnamese to prepare to stand alone. If the vast army of South Vietnam could not win on its own, the government did not deserve to survive.[34]

In sum, the mildness of the Church-Hatfield resolution belied the Idaho senator's building outrage against the war. This was evident even in the lengthy speech with which he introduced the resolution. At one point, he argued that an admission of failure and a quick exit from Southeast Asia would in fact constitute a kind of victory—"a victory of principle over pride and of intelligent self-interest over messianic delusion." He rebuked Vietnam strategists for their misplaced faith in technology and " 'scientific' theories of warfare." In fact, "the Vietnamese turned out not to be scientists," and the strategists displayed a "disastrous insensitivity to the thought processes of an alien culture." There was simply no defensible reason to stay in Vietnam. The United States was not physically threatened; "Saigon does not stand guard over Seattle."[35]

While the Hatfield-Church resolution complimented the president for bringing some American troops home, Church's speech was much less friendly. He accused Nixon of stalling, of using talk about an "honorable settlement" and Vietnamization as cover for remaining in the war. Moreover, he suggested that Nixon was playing politics with the war, trying to find scapegoats for a failed policy. A "spurious, jingoist 'patriotism' " marked the administration's efforts to label the war critics as virtual traitors. In response to Henry Kissinger's comment that it was difficult to play chess with twenty kibitzers at your elbow, Church shot back: "Long may they 'kibitz.' . . ." Indeed, he lauded the war protestors for having kept the war from escalating even more than it had. "Whatever hope of peace there is now, it is the 'kibitzers' gift to the architects of failure."[36]

During the October 15 Vietnam Moratorium Day, Church did more than praise the protestors; he joined them. Sam Brown and David Hawk, veterans of Eugene McCarthy's 1968 campaign and staunch antiwar activists, originated the idea of the moratorium. To their surprise, "it caught on like wildfire," as Hawk later recalled, eventually capturing the attention of the press, galvanizing grassroots enthusiasm, and eliciting a wave of endorsements from the United Automobile Workers, former Supreme Court Justice Arthur Goldberg, several dozen members of Congress, and others. On October 9, forty-seven members of the House and seventeen senators, including Church, commended the moratorium committee for "attempting to change policies through protest" that was "peaceful, lawful and non-violent." That same day, Church and Hatfield organized a pro-moratorium television news conference in the Capitol Hill reception room. The Idaho senator applauded the renewal of dissent and urged "all like-minded citizens to join us." He hoped for wide-ranging participation in the moratorium, "marked by mounting demands for disengagement in the Congress, by prayers for peace in the churches, by peaceful demonstrations on the campuses." According to *New York Times* reporter John Finney, he and Hatfield were fast becoming leaders of the Senate's Vietnam war critics.[37]

On television a few days later, Church took issue with the president's response to the moratorium. "Under no circumstances," Nixon had said, "will I be affected whatever by it." Church doubted that this was true. Dissent, he insisted, had already helped reverse America's involvement in Vietnam, and he guessed that it would continue to do so. "If we fall silent about it now, we take the pressure off."[38]

The massive, one-day moratorium had, in fact, placed considerable pressure on the administration. Held on a weekday, it nevertheless involved millions of Americans in thousands of towns and cities. Historians at the Library of Congress estimated that there had never been a larger national public protest in the U. S. Students and nonstudents, adults and youths gathered in silent vigils, torchlight parades, church services, and other meetings. In New York City, 90 percent of high school students stayed away from classes.[39]

Church encouraged his office staff to participate in the moratorium, although he hardly needed to do so. The redoubtable Verda Barnes, the senator's chief administrator and a veteran of labor's battles in the 1930s, had already marched in front of the White House with another Church aide, Marty Peterson. Wearing a mink coat and a black arm band, she had tossed her head defiantly and shouted with the other, mostly younger, demonstrators, "One, two, three, four,/ We don't want your fucking war." The night before the moratorium, she and Peterson stayed up until midnight, fixing sandwiches for the protestors.[40]

The next day, members of Church's staff joined aides from other House and Senate offices for a forty-five minute silent vigil at the Capitol. "I want to go with you," Church told them. As they stood on the east front steps, it was apparent that not all of the photographers were from the press. "People kept coming up real close and taking our picture," recalled Myrna Sasser. Leaning toward Church, she remarked nervously, "We are getting our pictures in a lot of files, I think." "Don't worry about it," he shrugged.[41]

Church continued to hope that peaceful demonstrations would send a chastening message to the administration. Unlike most elected officials, he did not turn his back on the November 15 "Mobilization" march, or "Mobe," on Washington, D. C. Despite covert and overt government efforts to stymie the march and chilly, threatening weather, the demonstration drew perhaps a half million participants. Members of Congress overwhelmingly kept their distance, however. "The Mobe scared the congressman away," organizer Sam Brown said later. Church was not there, but he joined Senators Goodell, Hatfield, George McGovern, Harold Hughes (D-Iowa), and Edmund Muskie (D-Maine) in appealing to area residents, universities, schools, and churches "to open their facilities, their hearts, and their homes to their fellow Americans who come in peace to their capital." The "Mobe" constituted the largest single political demonstration to that point in American history.[42]

Four days later, Church tried to use the Mobilization as leverage against the war. "We have just had the largest public demonstration in the history of our country in Washington," he told Secretary of State William Rogers. "Opposition to the war is really out of our hands. It is just there and it is very big."[43]

The administration, however, saw war opponents only as disloyal or cowardly. Years later, Nixon described the protestors as mainly "pampered kids" who "really wanted to avoid fighting, to keep from getting their asses shot off." At the time, Vice President Agnew contended that politicians who backed the antiwar movement were "intellectual eunuchs."[44]

In his November 3 television address, the president threw down the gauntlet to his critics. The speech took weeks to prepare. After completing it early one morning, Nixon jubilantly telephoned his top aide: "The baby's just been born." Later he judged the speech as belonging to the very few that "actually influence the course of history." Its point, he said, was clear: "we were going to keep our commitment in Vietnam." He intended "to stand and fight." Speaking sternly from the Oval Office, he said that he was bringing more troops home but was opposed to a "precipitate withdrawal" that would only destroy America's credibility abroad. Nearing his conclusion, he castigated a "minority" that was "mounting demonstrations in the street." To that group he had a special message: "North Vietnam cannot defeat or humiliate the United States. Only Americans can do that." He then appealed to "the great silent majority" for continued support. According to a Gallup poll, 77 percent of the national audience liked the speech.[45]

In the Senate and in several published essays, a disappointed Church took issue with the president. Nixon, he said, was engaging in "political theatrics" when he voiced his opposition to "precipitate withdrawal." This was a phony issue, a dragon that the president had conjured up for the television audience. "Nobody in Congress is urging the President to preside over a Dunkirk-type evacuation." When Republican senator Karl Mundt asked Church to define what he meant by precipitate, Church snapped back impatiently, " 'Precipitate,' as defined by Webster, means sudden, unexpected, impetuous, reckless." Church had little faith in the policy of Vietnamization, which could keep U. S. troops in Southeast Asia for at least several more years. He favored yet another alternative, one that Nixon had not mentioned but which was embodied in the Hatfield-Church resolution: the rapid removal of U. S. troops, leading to complete and total disengagement.[46]

Convinced that the Nixon administration had little interest in that goal, Church focused again on an effort to keep the war from widening. At the end of 1969, he teamed up with Kentucky Republican John Sherman Cooper to provide the most notable victory yet in the doves' strategy to contain the Vietnam conflict.

V

Ten days before Christmas, the Senate passed what turned out to be the first of a series of Cooper-Church amendments. This version prohibited the use of American combat troops in Laos or Thailand. It also inaugurated a remarkable partnership in the effort to wind down the Southeast Asian war.

Although age, party, and region separated Church and Cooper, they constituted a remarkably effective legislative team. Cooper, a product of Kentucky's foothill country, had graduated from Yale a year before

Church was born. Tall and courtly, he was the model of a southern gentleman. With an expression that reminded some observers of a basset hound, he was thoroughly without pretension. Despite his good ol' boy mannerisms on the stump, he was thoughtful and learned. His judicious handling of legislation, as well as his experiences as ambassador to India and, intermittently, as senator since 1947, made him one of the most respected people on Capitol Hill.[47]

In some respects, Cooper and Church were a study in contrast. Whereas Church was an orator, Cooper was a mumbler. According to one story, a young reporter had almost fallen from the press gallery while leaning over the edge in an effort to hear the Kentucky senator. And whereas Church had a very orderly mind, Cooper was notoriously absent-minded.[48]

The two senators nevertheless had their similarities. Both were somewhat anomalous in their home states. Church was a Democrat from largely Republican surroundings; Cooper was a Republican from a state so staunchly Democratic that the famed agnostic Robert Ingersoll once quipped that he would believe in Hell if the GOP ever captured Kentucky. And Cooper, like Church, had demonstrated a willingness to take issue with his party's leadership. To some of his GOP compatriots, Cooper seemed too much of an "emotional New Dealer." His independent streak had been evident in his early criticism of Joe McCarthy, his opposition to segregation in schools and public places, and his co-sponsorship of Lyndon Johnson's Medicare legislation. Temperamentally, Cooper and Church were skilled negotiators who disliked confrontation. And, although both had voted for the Tonkin Gulf resolution, they had been early critics of the Vietnam war.[49]

In 1967, when Church had authored the "Plea for Realism," warning the North Vietnamese not to expect a unilateral U. S. withdrawal, Cooper played a key role. Because Church recognized that any effective action needed Republican as well as Democratic support, he had turned to Cooper. In effect, he had left the fate of the document in the hands of the chain-smoking Kentuckian. Cooper had promptly signed the petition.[50]

In the fall of 1969 Church, not surprisingly, again looked to Cooper, this time as a possible co-sponsor for the Hatfield-Church sense-of-the-Senate resolution. But this time Cooper would go no further than to compliment Church for trying to keep the war's opposition on a bipartisan level. He believed the resolution was the best he had seen, but for the moment he preferred "to work in another way—at the White House." This did not mean, however, that Cooper was in the administration's camp. Openly skeptical of Nixon's Vietnamization policy and deeply worried about the secret air war in Laos and Cambodia, he joined Mike Mansfield in drafting an amendment to the Defense Appropriations bill prohibiting U. S. combat involvement in Laos and Thailand. His original intention had been to include Cambodia, but Mansfield had not wanted to offend Prince Norodom Sihanouk, who was maintaining Cambodia's neutrality.[51]

There were some ironies in the Senate's mid-December passage of what became the first Cooper-Church amendment. Cooper, absent because his mother had just suffered a stroke, did not vote on it. And Church attached his name to it late, via a substitute amendment.

On a chilly, windy December 15, with a hint of snow in the air, the Senate went into a rare secret session to debate Cooper's proposed amendment. For three hours, the session remained closed so that senators could obtain the first detailed White House information on the bombings in Laos. When the Senate finally turned to the amendment, discussions immediately broke down. There was confusion over the intent of the legislation. Would it cut off the ongoing air combat missions in Laos, or merely prevent the introduction of U. S. ground troops there and in Thailand? Some senators wanted to do nothing that would tie the president's hands. Others feared the amendment would go too far if it applied to the air war. Church worried that the amendment's ambiguities would not prevent U. S. forces from spilling out of Vietnam into neighboring countries. Thus he turned his attention to writing a compromise measure that would specifically ban only ground combat forces. "We are not trying to make any changes in the status quo," he assured colleagues who expressed concern about giving aid and comfort to the enemy. As the debate continued, he was in constant motion—speaking to the issue; huddling with Republicans Gordon Allott of Colorado and Jacob Javits of New York, as well as California Democrat Alan Cranston, over the wording of his motion; and interviewing, just outside the Senate door, a prospective new staff member, Tom Dine. Shortly before Church introduced his substitute motion, Allott made sure that it was acceptable to the White House. By a 78 to 11 vote, the Senate adopted Church's revised amendment.[52]

The White House claimed a victory. Press Secretary Ron Ziegler considered the Cooper-Church amendment an "endorsement," not a "curbing," of administration policy. And Senator Robert Griffin (R-Michigan) said that the amendment's language was "in line with the expressed intention of the President of the United States." Church, on the other hand, saw the amendment as primarily a "reassertion of Congressional prerogatives" in foreign policy.[53]

Church began immediately to work with Cooper on another, stronger amendment. This time, the two senators kept close contact with each other, as did their office staffs. Two of their staff people proved indispensable—Thomas A. Dine, whom Church had just hired, and Cooper's top aide Bill Miller.

Dine, brash and energetic, had just turned thirty when he became Church's top foreign affairs assistant in January, 1970. A New Yorker, he had never been to Idaho. He had received an M. A. in South Asian history at the University of California-Los Angeles and had served in the Peace Corps, first as a volunteer in the Philippines and then as director of its congressional liaison office. After working as a personal assistant to Ambassador Chester Bowles in India for two years in the late 1960s, he had signed on briefly as Senator Cranston's legislative assistant. Knowledgeable, friendly, and with a forceful personality, he enjoyed Church's confidence. "I find him extremely affable and accessible," Dine reported after several weeks on the job. "I like Senator Church very much." Dine gave little thought to the politics of the senator's home state. His attention was almost wholly on international issues, and he brought to his job considerable understanding of South Asia.[54]

Significantly, within several months after hiring Dine, Church added two other Easterners to his staff, Wes Barthelmes and Wendell Pigman, both of whom had worked for Robert Kennedy. More and more, Church was separating national from Idaho politics, working carefully on two levels. In fact, according to another member of his staff, Lynda Clark, some press releases regarding the senator's efforts in foreign affairs were for release in the Washington, D. C., area but "purposely" not distributed in Idaho.[55]

As relationships grew between Church and Cooper, Dine and Bill Miller became close friends. Miller's mind was as impressive as his boyish good looks. A graduate of Williams College and Oxford University, he had been an instructor in Elizabethan literature at Harvard before joining the Foreign Service and the State Department. When John Sherman Cooper, whom he had met in India, hired him, Miller was elated. "For me," he said, "it proved to be a liberation after the State Department, where so much had been a lie and a deceit." Temperamentally a teacher and a poet, Miller also demonstrated a knack for the wheeling and dealing of politics.[56]

In early 1970, Miller and Dine worked on drafting legislation to block the administration's stealthy expansion of the war. The *New York Times* confirmed in mid-February, for example, that recent B-52 bombing strikes had pushed U. S. involvement into northern Laos. Senate doves pondered how to alert yet again a weary public. The enthusiasm of the October moratorium had quickly faded. As columnist Mary McGrory put it, "Dissent seems to have gone the way of the dance marathon. The President has made it unfashionable." A National Democratic Committee white paper concluded that Nixon had successfully handled popular opinion, tailoring his Vietnam policy to fit the national mood, which was "glum and tired, but unwilling to accept outright defeat." Church sadly agreed. "In one fell swoop," he said, the president's troop withdrawals and Vietnamization policy had "declawed the hawks and placated the doves."[57]

In late January and throughout February, Church tried to sound an alarm about "the danger of the baited trap" in Laos and Thailand. After reworking a speech that Tom Dine had drafted until it had, in Dine's words, "that Biblical ring of Church's to it," he spoke to the Senate. Bit by bit, he warned, America was expanding its military presence in Laos. This was evident in stepped-up bombing raids, which had resulted in the shooting down of several U. S. aircraft, and in increased combat operations by U. S.-supplied Laotian troops. More trouble was brewing in Southeast Asia, Church contended, and it was time for Americans to hear the truth from their own government.[58]

As fighting spread in Laos, the Cambodian situation fell apart. On March 18, perhaps with prompting from some U. S. military officials in Vietnam, Sihanouk's anti-communist prime minister, General Lon Nol, conducted a coup. Disorder quickly engulfed the beleaguered nation. Rival Cambodian gangs fell on each other, and vigilantes massacred local Vietnamese, including children. Although Nixon and Kissinger insisted that the coup surprised them, the administration quickly backed the new ruler. "From day one," according to the State Department's East Asia chief, "Nixon was insisting on building up Lon Nol." Lon Nol's cry for help on April 14, and the administration's apparent determination to rescue his government, sent anxious tremors through the ranks of the Senate doves. Not surprisingly, Church sought out Cooper—"the strongest possible ally I could find on the Republican side of the aisle," as he later explained.[59]

VI

The renewed Cooper-Church alliance was a complex creation, and among its key architects were Vermont Republican George Aiken and, especially, Mike Mansfield. Aiken and Mansfield, both representing the liberal wings of their respective parties, and both early critics of the war, more than gave their blessings to the Church-Cooper team. As Bill Miller subsequently said, they provided a kind of "laying on of hands."[60]

Over the years, Mansfield had influenced Frank Church considerably. John Kennedy's advisors had noted this, but during the Sixties the bonds between the two Northwest senators had strengthened. According to Utah Democrat Frank Moss, Church's Senate visibility increased after Mansfield succeeded Lyndon Johnson as Majority Leader. "Mansfield was very friendly to him," Moss recalled. Church aide Pat Shea was even more emphatic: "Mansfield was really a protector of Church." Shea sensed that Mansfield, a former college history teacher, especially appreciated Church's awareness of historical nuance and context. Church, in turn, as his speechwriter Bill Hall remembered, viewed the Montanan as "a wise old owl, a good adviser." Lyndon Johnson had believed that Mansfield was too much of an isolationist, but Church predicted that the future would "prove Mansfield more correct than Johnson." Church was overly generous in attributing most of what he knew about foreign policy to Mansfield; still, his admiration was genuine. He found especially appealing Mansfield's commonsense perspectives and his aversion to evangelical and ideological causes.[61]

It would have been difficult not to like Mansfield, "a Senator's Senator," as columnist Jack Anderson described him. Starkly thin, and with a serious, almost morose, demeanor, he was not an imposing or colorful figure; but few people exuded more strength of purpose or character. Never one to seek the spotlight, he graciously accorded his colleagues both credit and opportunities. In the late spring and early summer of 1970, Mansfield, more than anyone, ran interference for the Cooper-Church initiatives regarding the Southeast Asian war. His crucial ally in that respect was the Republican "dean" of the Senate, the white-haired, grizzled, seventy-seven-year-old Aiken. Aiken, who had a kind of cracker-barrel aura, once dedicated a book on wildflowers to Peter Rabbit; less whimsically, he had suggested in 1966 that the United States should simply declare a victory in Vietnam and then leave.[62]

With the backing of Aiken and Mansfield, Church and Cooper prepared to enlarge their amendment of December 1969 to include Cambodia. For several months they had been moving in this direction, but Sihanouk's overthrow and the prospects of U. S. intervention to "save" the Lon Nol government made the matter even more urgent. On April 12 they indicated they would soon offer an amendment to the military appropriations bill blocking U. S. combat troops from Cambodia. Less than three weeks later, on April 30, they reiterated their intention, warning the president not to open "a new front" and jeopardize "his declared policy of de-escalation." By then, Church had already prepared a lengthy Senate speech on the matter.[63]

There was more reason for alarm than Church, Cooper, and other doves suspected. Four days earlier, Nixon had already decided to send U. S. troops into Cambodia. "We would go for broke," Nixon wrote in his memoirs. Convinced in part that he had to act to save his Vietnamization policy, Nixon indulged what he called his "big play philosophy" and went "for all the marbles." Intent on sending a forceful message to Vietnam, he was also determined to defy the predicted domestic backlash and his Senate critics. Chafing because of the Senate's recent rejections of two of his Supreme Court appointments, Clement F. Haynsworth and G. Harrold Carswell, he told Henry Kissinger over the phone that "those senators think they can push Nixon around. . . .Well, I'll show them who's tough." On the phone again to Kissinger, he said angrily, "The liberals are waiting to see Nixon let Cambodia go down the drain the way Eisenhower let Cuba go down the drain." And he reportedly told his advisors that his decision to invade Cambodia was partly to let the Senate know that he was nobody's patsy.[64]

As Church and Cooper prepared to exclude U. S. combat troops from Cambodia, Nixon announced that he was sending the soldiers anyhow. Over the next few searing months, while America shook with renewed violence and protest, the White House and Senate once again squared off over the powers of the presidency and Congress. In this highly charged setting, the new Cooper-Church amendment moved onto the historical stage.

John Sherman Cooper and Church discuss their proposed amendment on television.
Courtesy Boise State University.

Chapter Twelve

The Battle Over Cooper-Church: 1970-1971

ON APRIL 30, 1970 FRANK CHURCH watched the television screen with growing wrath as Richard Nixon informed the nation he had ordered U. S. troops into Cambodia. Pointing to a map, the president explained that the tactical objective was to wipe out "the headquarters for the entire Communist military operation in South Vietnam." This was not an invasion, he said, because the troops would withdraw after demolishing the communist sanctuaries in Cambodia. Nixon placed the Cambodian offensive within a grand context: "If, when the chips are down, the world's most powerful nation, the United States of America, acts like a pitiful, helpless giant, the forces of totalitarianism and anarchy will threaten free nations. . .throughout the world." According to Nixon, "It is not our power but our will and character that is being tested tonight."[1]

As the president finished his speech, Church smacked the table sharply with his hand. He was irate, really seething, recalled Tom Dine, who was with him. But he quickly reined in his emotions, spurning obscenities or an emotional diatribe for a simple, clipped description of Nixon as "unctuous." It was a typical Church response, controlled and cerebral. Out of his anger leaped what Dine described as a Standardized Student Test word: "unctuous." There was no doubt, however, that the senator was furious and obviously struggling to contain himself. As he and Dine walked out of the local NBC affiliate where they had watched the address, they heard a smiling television reporter remark blithely about an interview he had just finished with Spiro Agnew. The reporter's cheerful demeanor and references to Nixon's "great speech" pushed Church to the limit. He muttered to Dine that Agnew's response to the president's address was probably "Sieg Heil!" Dine had never seen Church so livid. Clearly the senator was fighting mad.[2]

Over the next several months Church emerged more than ever as a national politician, resisting the expansive nature of the war and the Nixon White House. As embittered citizens again took their frustrations into the streets, and as the White House squared off against a perceived assault on the powers of the presidency, he moved into the center of the political storm. His natural bent toward compromise collided again and again with his growing sense of moral outrage, anguish, and urgency. Fighting off his own growing despair about his country's conduct abroad and at home, he continued his attempts to smother the war by legislative means, especially via several versions of the Cooper-Church amendment. His efforts threw into sharp relief his reputation for trimming and compromise, but also drew criticism from constituents and the administration that he was unpatriotic.

I

Following Nixon's April 30 television address, Church stepped up his attacks on the administration. He joined several other leading Senate doves in garnering television time to encourage a peaceful, nationwide movement to end the war. He tried, with John Sherman Cooper, to cut off the funding for U. S. combat in Cambodia. And he seized every opportunity to denounce Nixon's Vietnam policy.

Before hushed and crowded Senate galleries on May 1 he accused Nixon of continuing to pursue America's earlier, and sadly discredited, objectives in Vietnam. His speech had been ready for some time, but he reworked it overnight in light of the Cambodian invasion. "Vietnamization," he asserted, was nothing more than a repackaged edition of an old policy, bent on maintaining an anti-communist regime in a divided Vietnam and "preserving an American bridgehead on the mainland of Asia, next door to China." The policy, inherently flawed, rested upon the myth of a monolithic communist conspiracy "of which Mr. Nixon himself was one of the principal perpetrators." It sustained the delusion that the U. S. was obligated to protect any anti-communist government, "however decadent." Church downplayed the president's claim that an American departure from Vietnam would lead to the massacre of South Vietnamese. The war itself, he argued, was "the real bloodbath," and its continuation reflected the logic of the U. S. army officer who had said, " 'We had to destroy Ben Tre in order to save it.' "[3]

His voice ringing out clearly, Church asserted that "we keep fighting in Vietnam because we are not yet willing to acknowledge that we should never have gone there in the first place." By widening the Indochinese conflict, he believed, the administration was creating a war without end. He suspected that the American search for communist sanctuaries just over the Cambodian border was a hopeless venture. In that regard, he agreed with Tennessee Democrat Albert Gore, Sr., who had spoken a few hours earlier: the enemy sanctuary stretched from the Cambodian border to " 'all of Asia behind it.' "[4]

Church moved to his main point: Congress should use its constitutional power over the purse to halt the war. "If the executive branch will not take the initiative, then the Congress and the people must." To that end, Church said, he and John Sherman Cooper, along with Mike Mansfield and George Aiken, would soon introduce an amendment to prohibit U. S. troops from fighting in Cambodia. He emphasized "the bipartisan character of our dissent. . . . In a matter of war and peace there is no party aisle that divides the Senate."[5]

On May 1, as Church and his colleagues debated Nixon's invasion of Cambodia, the nation simmered restlessly. Trouble had already broken out on some campuses, although with relatively little violence. Nixon, meanwhile, visited the briefing room at the Pentagon and decided, on the spur of the moment as he recalled, to order that "*all* the sanctuaries" in Cambodia be wiped out. "Just do it," he ordered. "Knock them all out so that they can't be used against us again. Ever." Increasingly agitated and using obscenities, he shouted, "Let's go blow the hell out of them." He resembled "a college coach giving a pep talk," according to a senior Pentagon official. "He was a little bit out of control. It scared the shit out of me." In a subsequent pep talk Nixon advised his staff to stand fast. "He had a few rough things to say about certain Congressmen," recalled presidential speech writer William Safire. And then he issued what Safire called "a rough charge to his own troops": " 'Don't worry about divisiveness. Having drawn the sword, don't take it out—stick it in hard. . . . Hit 'em in the gut. No defensiveness.' "[6]

By May 2 widening campus and community protests were turning violent. Students at a growing number of universities declared strikes, the ROTC building at Kent State was burned, clashes occurred between protestors and police, and a student was wounded at Ohio State. "Cry, the Beloved Country," grieved *New York Times* columnist Anthony Lewis. He had trouble understanding how a government could urge demonstrators to act reasonably, and with moderation, when it spurned diplomacy and negotiation in favor of violence. Lewis despaired for his nation. "Nothing for years has cast so dark a shadow on America's future" as had the Cambodian invasion, he wrote.[7]

Over the next few days the situation worsened dramatically. On May 4, Ohio National Guard troops at Kent State shot four students to death and wounded nine. Ten days later, Mississippi police killed two students at Jackson State. Throughout early May, protests jarred over 50 percent of the nation's campuses; more than five hundred schools canceled classes. Firebombings and vandalism increased. Thousands of protestors poured into Washington, D. C., where protective buses ringed the White House. Nixon's top aide, H. R. Haldeman, slept in the White House bomb shelter. Not all demonstrators opposed the Cambodian invasion, however. On May 8, hundreds of helmeted construction workers waded into an antiwar demonstration in New York City's Wall Street district, injuring dozens of people. "The very fabric of government was falling apart," recalled Nixon's National Security Advisor Henry Kissinger.[8]

Frank Church's attention was torn between the Senate and the turbulence in the streets. Across the country, his own son Forrest had taken to the barricades in the worst riot Stanford had ever seen, closing the university down. The senator sent telegrams to all Idaho colleges and universities, urging an end to violent protests. Violence, he said, would only fan "the fires of those who practice the politics of hate." He pleaded with students and other citizens to spurn disorder and, instead, to support the forthcoming Cooper-Church plan to extricate U. S. troops from Cambodia. Worried that scheduled demonstrations in Washington, D. C., would turn ugly, he suggested that Maryland Democrat Joseph Tydings, as chair of the Senate's District of Columbia Committee, establish "a bipartisan Congressional 'monitoring team' " that might "serve as a needed dampening buffer between the two contending forces," law enforcement authorities and protestors.[9]

These were days that tested Church's political faith. *New York Times* columnist Anthony Lewis perhaps articulated the anguish of liberals such as Frank Church as well as anyone. "It has been hard for most of us middle-class, middle-aged Americans of liberal instinct to accept the apocalyptic vision of many students," wrote Lewis. "We believed in reason. But the President's course in Cambodia would make the most optimistic rationalist despair for his country." Like Lewis, Church struggled to make sense of the situation.[10]

Church's gloom was almost overwhelming by the time he delivered a college commencement address in Nampa, Idaho. His speech was uncharacteristically grim for the occasion. Although he tried to strike an optimistic note by reaffirming America's historic ideals, the bulk of his message cataloged national woes. Indeed, his perspective on America had perhaps never been bleaker.[11]

"I find a great and powerful nation that has wandered so far from its historic ideals that it has almost lost its way," he said. With considerable rhetorical effect, he started eight sentences in a row with "I find an America. . . ." In each case, the America he found contrasted starkly with its traditional beliefs. The United States that valued life was building "a daily body count like so many baseball scores" in Southeast Asia. The nation that had once expressed " 'a decent respect for the opinions of mankind' " was acting "in open defiance of the common sense of most of the civilized world." The country whose Constitution gave Congress the power to declare war had turned over "that power to the CIA, the Pentagon, and closeted chief executives who now commit American forces across foreign frontiers without so much as a glance at the Congress." This was a nation, Church remarked sadly, that still discriminated against people on the basis of race, that polluted "the fragile ecological balance of our environment," that was afflicted with rising crime, and that was obsessed with armaments and "absolute power."[12]

"So today," he told the graduates, "I call upon my country to come home from the distant battlefields of Asia to the healing of our own troubled land." By now, Church was drawing upon the format and, in places, the exact wording of George McGovern's "Come Home, America," speech. Several months earlier the South Dakota senator had brought applauding Democrats to their feet in Denver, Colorado, with an impassioned appeal that Church now used as his own. "Come home, America," Church begged in five consecutive sentences—home from racism; home "from boasts of a silent majority to the higher ground of conscience and responsibility"; home from "the hunger of little children, from the loneliness of the aging poor." "Come home, prodigal America. . . ."[13]

On that warm spring day Church implored the American people to reclaim their power over war and peace. In Congress that meant an end to hand-wringing and a willingness to regulate military spending. It was time to act.[14]

In Idaho, as elsewhere, the climate for such a message was not very nourishing. Vice-President Spiro Agnew's visit to Boise right after the Cambodian invasion illustrated the prevailing mood. When Governor Don Samuelson learned that students planned a demonstration, he declared a state of emergency and summoned the National Guard. Some four hundred antiwar demonstrators marched peacefully on the Rodeway Inn, where Agnew spoke. "The Cossacks were there in force," newspaper editor Sam Day wrote scornfully, "ready to be unleashed on the rag-tag army of dissidents." The protestors remained orderly – singing, praying, and making speeches as a gentle rain fell. Day guessed that many of the well-clad guests inside the Inn did not even know of the demonstration. They had paid $100 a plate to hear Agnew defend U. S. policy, and he did not let them down. Americans, he said, intended "to reaffirm our credibility and decisiveness when these qualities have been sharply questioned not only by Hanoi but by others." Agnew did not have to name Frank Church for Idaho listeners to recognize at least one person whom he had in mind. Some people in the audience, as Sam Day observed, occasionally "peeped through the windows at the unwashed proletariat" outside the Inn. When the demonstrators faded away after a while, one member of Agnew's audience, bourbon and water in hand, muttered, "Christ, I'd like to get my hands on those sleazy bastards."[15]

While Church moved ahead with his and Cooper's amendment to remove American troops from Cambodia, he received many reminders of the treacherous political ground he was walking in Idaho. Some constituents charged him with cowardice, appeasement, aiding the communists, even treason. A letter in one newspaper reported that people in Idaho Falls were talking about "Tokyo Rose" Church. Printed cards, warning against the Cooper-Church amendment, as well as "the naive doves of Socialism and the outright agents of Communism cursing our American way of Life," flooded the senator's office. A cartoon in the *Idaho Statesman* portrayed Church sawing off the branch from which President Nixon dangled. The Cooper-Church idea "stinks," charged a letter writer from Rexburg, articulating the opinion of more than a few Idaho residents.[16]

The Nixon administration agreed. It watched anxiously as the Senate Foreign Relations Committee on May 11, by a nine to five vote, added the amendment to the Foreign Military Sales Act, which controlled cash and credit arms sales abroad. The House had already approved the measure. According to the amendment, funding to retain U. S. ground forces (as well as military advisors and instructors) in Cambodia, or to allow "any combat activity in the air above Cambodia in support of Cambodian forces," would be illegal without specific congressional approval. Church conceded that the amendment did "not attempt to undo what has been done." It would take perhaps eight weeks to become law, and by then the president should have completed what he himself had said was a temporary action. The point of the amendment was to guarantee that the action was no more than temporary, and that there would be no repetition of the attack on Cambodia. To mollify indignant defenders of the administration, Church and the other sponsors altered the amendment to say that it targeted only funds spent after 1 July 1970.[17]

As the Senate prepared to commence its debate, White House strategists discussed a counter-offensive. H. R. Haldeman scratched out in his notes, for example, the importance of getting "the labor boys [to] go to work on Senate re Cooper-Church."[18]

This was no trivial matter to the administration. Tom Charles Huston, a young attorney with growing White House responsibilities, believed that the Cooper-Church amendment represented nothing less than an "Assault on the Constitutional Powers of the Presidency." In a lengthy May 23 memo, he advised Haldeman, John Ehrlichman, Henry Kissinger, and other administration leaders that, "unless we meet this assault directly and rebuff it, we will have presided over a constitutional revolution." The stakes could not be higher. "We will make a momentous mistake – the ramifications of which will extend far beyond the Nixon Presidency –" he warned alarmingly, "if we fail to recognize that what we are witnessing is not a limited revolt against Cambodia, it is a major revolution against the foreign policy powers of the Presidency." Huston's tone was grave. "Every day the maneuvering room of the President is being circumscribed." There was a real danger to the "constitutional legitimacy of his role as Commander-in-Chief" and, indeed, to "the moral foundation of the Presidency itself." It was thus essential to recognize the Senate challenge for what it was and to "mobilize a broad-based campaign" against it.[19]

That broad-based campaign moved along several fronts. On Capitol Hill, the administration determined to "line up rip snorters" against Cooper-Church. At a May 2 White House meeting, for example, Haldeman jotted down notes about the importance of finding "inflammatory types to attack Senate doves—for knife in back disloyalty—lack of patriotism." A few days later, Haldeman's notes called for "3-4 good gut fighters," senators such as Arizona's Barry Goldwater and Robert Dole of Kansas, "guys that will really ram them." It would be good to "use stab in the back line," accusing the amendment's supporters of selling out American troops. One possible strategy that the president discussed with his advisors in mid-May would attach an amendment to Cooper-Church that included Israel. The idea here was to send a message that the Senate could hardly deny the president military powers in Vietnam and still expect him to use those powers to defend Israel. "Put the hook into the Jewish boys," wrote Haldeman, in hopes of making pro-Israeli senators uneasy about Cooper-Church.[20]

As the administration set up legislative obstacles to Cooper-Church, it also launched a huge public relations effort, including mass mailings from veterans' groups aimed at mobilizing a huge letter-writing campaign to Congress. Working with White House counsel Charles Colson, the commanders of the American Legion and the Veterans of Foreign Wars wrote to tens of thousands of their organizations' members. "We must not permit the President's hands to be tied by the Cooper-Church amendment," insisted J. Milton Patrick of the American Legion, using words that Colson himself had suggested. Ray Gallagher of the VFW charged that opposition to the Cambodian military operation was "the result of a cleverly organized campaign by dissident elements." He described the Cooper-Church amendment as representing "the first time the Senate has debated a 'declaration of surrender.' " Put pressure on Congress, he begged. "This is urgent. The enemy within our country have [sic] a long head start in opposing our President."[21]

By May 16 the administration was beginning to show signs of panic. Presidential aide Bryce Harlow guessed that Cooper-Church had enough support for Senate approval. "We must amend it," read Haldeman's notes from a White House meeting. The challenge was how to give ground without appearing to do so. Somehow, the resolution had to appear supportive of the president. But the matter was delicate, especially because Nixon's official position was one of no compromise. Some staunch White House supporters in the Senate thus backed the administration "so hard. . . .that they hurt us," wrote Haldeman. They "won't take any amendment at all so we lose them—and still have doves against."[22]

Nixon himself sought to take the initiative by saying that he intended to remove the troops from Cambodia by June 30. When he had first announced the Cambodian offensive he had set no date, indicating simply that U. S. forces would withdraw "once enemy forces are driven out of these sanctuaries, and their military supplies are destroyed." On May 4, however, the day of the Kent State killings, he briefed several members of Congress that U. S. troops would move no more than nineteen miles into Cambodia and would be out by July 1. Four days later at a news conference he moved the date to June 30. In neither case did he preclude returning troops to Cambodia.[23]

White House strategists did not want it to appear as though the president were bending to Congress. They took great care to counter any such perceptions. A "talking paper" for a May 20 White House meeting stressed that "we must sell strongly the success of the operation—not the defensive line that 'we'll be out by June 30.' " Celebrations of the president's success had to accompany "a strong attack on the opponents. We should hit Cooper/Church. . . .We've got to pull out all the stops on this." The main objective, as Haldeman's May 19 notes indicated, was to delay action on Capitol Hill until the president could take his message of victory to the country: "Don't let Senate get credit for results." Appropriately, the president in a June 3 televised press conference declared that the Cambodian incursion "has been the most successful operation of this long and very difficult war." Indeed, "all of our major military objectives have been achieved."[24]

Over the next few weeks the White House set up road blocks to stall the Cooper-Church amendment. Bryce Harlow was confident that pro-administration senators could sustain a debate for several weeks. In fact, "our leadership apparently is willing to try to continue the debate up to at least the middle of June," Harlow told Haldeman. "At that point, we may have to own up to the fact that Republicans, with Administration approval, are definitely engaging in a filibuster." On the Foreign Relations Committee, staff director Carl Marcy informed J. William Fulbright that top administration people such as Henry Kissinger and Melvin Laird had met with the Republican caucus, urging it to fight the amendment as discrediting the president. The administration was turning the Cooper-Church amendment into "a partisan issue," complained Marcy, thereby "polarizing the Senate in the field of foreign policy."[25]

The delays and the political fencing frustrated the Senate doves. Wherever they turned, they encountered obstacles—off as well as on Capitol Hill. Confronted with the immense White House public relations effort, they looked for ways in which they could more effectively take their case to the American people.

South Dakota's George McGovern came up with the idea of buying a half-hour of national television time. CBS and ABC both turned him down; NBC agreed, but only if he could deliver $60,000 in three days. McGovern, stymied at one point, considered mortgaging his home to help produce the money. Through contributions and a loan, however, he was able to provide NBC with the required check—fifteen minutes before the deadline. The program was scheduled for Tuesday, May 12. Not surprisingly, McGovern asked Oregon Republican Mark Hatfield to appear on TV with him. On April 30 he and Hatfield had introduced an "End the War Amendment," calling for the systematic withdrawal of all U. S. forces in Vietnam, Cambodia, and Laos by at least the end of 1971. Charles Goodell, the New York Republican who the previous September had introduced a similar proposal, found the McGovern-Hatfield maneuver somewhat perturbing. In his mind, the two senators were basically appropriating his bill. But he was nevertheless willing to support them and, to that end, he also wanted to appear on the television program. Iowa Democrat Harold Hughes was equally interested, so the television team soon included these four.[26]

Church wanted to make it five. "He really sort of persuaded us that he should be on it," recalled Goodell of the TV panel. The proposal to include him came from McGovern, but Goodell had no doubt that the Idaho senator had planted the idea. Goodell initially was not enthusiastic. Although Church had recently signed on as a co-sponsor of the Hatfield-McGovern amendment, he was, in Goodell's opinion, "sort of a latecomer" to any effort that would impose an actual deadline for ending the war. Goodell attributed Church's interest in the TV show to his "good political sense" and recognition that the program would attract a wide audience. The New Yorker remembered that he and the other three senators had "quite a debate" about whether to include Church, but they ultimately did so because he was eloquent and would help the cause.[27]

At 7:30 p. m. on May 12, the NBC situation comedy "I Dream of Jeannie" gave way to a less humorous message. Viewers watched what the panelists described as the first nationwide broadcast produced by a congressional group. A narrator's voice reminded the viewing audience that the nation was more divided than it had been in over a century because of the Southeast Asian war. "Not since the days of the Civil War have Americans treated each other like this." The narrator indicated that the bipartisan Amendment to End the War would return to Congress the decision of whether to commit Americans to battle. "Through protest. . . petition. . . and an act of *law*, we shall have at last ended the Vietnam war." McGovern opened the panel, which had rehearsed several times before the program's final taping. When Church first spoke, he referred to his and John Sherman Cooper's other amendment, one aimed at imposing limits on the Cambodian situation. "But this End the War Amendment takes the full step," he said, "and provides an orderly method for the extrication of the United States from the war in Vietnam, itself." The senators collectively touched on a number of themes: the weaknesses of the president's Vietnamization plan, which could allow the war to drag on for years; the reasonability of allowing a year and a half to complete U. S. withdrawal from the war; the war's terrible toll on America's resources, psyche, and ideals; the damage to Vietnam; and the need to relinquish the role of policeman of Asia in favor of addressing America's own festering problems. At the conclusion of the thirty-minute program each senator urged citizens to send letters and petitions to Congress in support of the End the War Amendment. "Remember," said Church, who also asked for contributions to help pay for the telecast, "that 66 cents of every tax dollar now goes for the war."[28]

The public response to the telecast was even better than the five senators anticipated. Almost half a million dollars in contributions allowed McGovern to pay off the loan and raised the prospects of subsequent advertising and broadcasts. Church's own office almost ground to a halt trying to keep up with the deluge of letters and telegrams. A photograph showed him at his desk with two bulging postal sacks that constituted one day's mail. He happily reported that "much" of the correspondence backed the Cooper-Church and End-the-War amendments.[29]

In May and June the Senate doves and the administration fought over a series of proposed revisions to the Cooper-Church amendment.

The administration was clearly trying to buy time while attempting to bolster presidential powers. Church, in turn, was anxious to preserve the amendment and bring it to a favorable vote.

II

Once again, the charge surfaced that Church was too quick to compromise. To some antiwar protestors, the Cooper-Church initiative attested to the characteristic tendency of established politicians to dabble in legal niceties, fencing rhetorically rather than taking a firm stand. What Mark Hatfield tagged as "a lawyer's approach" left some critics cold; delivering speeches, negotiating alternatives, allowing for options, conceding points to the opposition seemed more suitable for courtroom plea-bargaining than for ending a protracted and morally offensive war. Erwin Knoll of *The Progressive* magazine faulted Church for being too much "a man of the system," always trying "to be part of the respectable center." In Knoll's opinion, this proclivity invariably got in the way of Church's "decent instincts." Other observers shared Knoll's impatience. On at least one tense occasion, aides Tom Dine and Cleve Corlett had to stand on the receptionist's desk in Church's office, trying to quiet a large group of demonstrators who were chanting, "You are not doing enough." Even Forrest Church was not impressed with his father's oh-so-reasonable efforts to deal with an "insane war."[30]

Within the Senate, as well, came talk about Church's tendency to settle for too little. One detractor believed that Church was on an "ego trip," so anxious to see his name on legislation that he rushed to compromise. Arkansas Democrat J. William Fulbright, among the skeptics, suspected, in the words of his top aide on the Foreign Relations Committee, Carl Marcy, "that Senator Church was likely to waffle." Fulbright once informed Marcy that Tennessee's Albert Gore or Missouri's Stuart Symington were people upon whom he could count. But he believed that, in Marcy's words, "Frank may switch" because he was "a bit of an opportunist." Charles Goodell regarded Church as less opportunistic than cautious when dealing with legislation. The New York senator nonetheless found unpersuasive the argument that such caution was simply being "practical." "That's the kindest way of interpreting it," he said.[31]

Church's penchant for compromise sometimes even irritated people who generally admired him. George Ashworth of the Foreign Relations

Committee staff, for example, found him "impressive" and believed that he did not merit the criticism he received. Still, Ashworth himself ultimately hedged his opinion of the Idaho senator.[32]

At the time of the Cooper-Church debate Tom Dine also worried that his boss was compromising too much. Sometimes he told him so. On other occasions he kept his frustrations to himself. Once when the senator was discussing possible changes in the Cooper-Church amendment with *New York Times* reporter John Finney, Dine stood helplessly in the background. Finney recalled that the young aide was "rolling his eyes to the ceiling and shrugging his shoulders as if to say, "What can I do?"[33]

Finney had the sense that Church was playing his alliance with John Sherman Cooper "to the hilt, really," pushing the legislation partly to add to his own prestige. The *Times* reporter likened him to a puffin bird: "he would puff up a little bit every time you approached him." But Finney conceded that "the toga complex" was not unique to Church and even had its political uses. Whereas a Cooper or a Mansfield felt awkward and uncomfortable going before television cameras, Church flourished under the kleig lights. "In a way Church was one of the first television creations in the Senate," reflected Finney. "He knew how to use television."[34]

Publicity, moreover, was an indispensable aspect of the fight over the Cooper-Church amendment. Whereas the battle eventually put an exhausted Cooper in the hospital, Church relished the pressure, rising to the occasion when he met with the press, spoke on the Senate floor, and appeared time and again on television. When Cooper and Church rehearsed for TV shows, Cooper fumbled along. Church, in contrast, was articulate and dramatic, compensating precisely in those areas where Cooper was weakest.[35]

Church garnered such publicity because he identified and dealt with big issues such as the constitutional role of Congress in shaping foreign policy, the domestic implications of the national security state, and America's role in a revolutionary world. He also took a prominent role in shaping the legislative agenda and he spoke with special effect. From the moment he entered the Senate he had spurned a quiet backbencher's role. That determination, his defenders pointed out, was what made him an exceptional senator. Insofar as he resembled a puffin bird, the press was partly responsible. "Hell, I told him what makes a good picture," laughed George Tames, longtime photographer on Capitol Hill for the *New York Times* who "always made a point of getting a picture of Church." The senator was an appealing subject because he photographed well and was in the thick of legislative battles. Church did not just puff, Tames insisted; he also produced. Dine, Miller, and others suspected that some of the criticism of Church as a headline hunter came partly out of envy. "Frank Church was no more a headline grabber than anyone of his contemporaries," according to Ross Baker, a political scientist who studied the Senate carefully and also worked for several senators, including Church. "He was just ever so much better at choosing the issues," huge ones, such as "war and peace, freedom and government accountability."[36]

While Church had a keen eye for substantive matters, he nevertheless also had a performer's love for the limelight. "He wasn't very subtle about it" either, according to Idaho journalist Sam Day. "He was very conscious of his image and cultivated the press." One person who worked with him on the Foreign Relations Committee found his quest for favorable publicity "almost unseemly." Another, Pat Holt, asserted that "some senators have bigger egos than others, and Church had one of the bigger ones." Dwight Jensen, an Idaho journalist and politician, believed that Church's headline hunting blemished an otherwise admirable career. Jensen was convinced that Church's finest moments came when he wanted to *do* something. But, Jensen recollected, "I don't think he ever quite got over wanting to *be* something."[37]

Church had always sought publicity. He urged his first press secretary, Porter Ward, to attract press coverage aggressively. Sometimes he even rewrote press releases about himself. Ward joked that the best way to get the senator to read a memo would be to set it in newsprint. When Bryce Nelson worked in the senator's office in the early Sixties, he gathered piles of clippings about Church from newspapers in Idaho and elsewhere. "Frank would spend hours each week reading them," recalled Nelson. "It was almost as if he couldn't measure the effect of what he was doing unless he could read about it in the press."[38]

But Church's fascination with the press was not a mere reflection of vanity, of wanting documents over which he could preen. He recognized the power of the press as a shaper and mirror of public opinion. On the one hand, the press provided a vehicle by which he could get ideas and information to the people, thereby countering official White House and other government stories. In the era of the Vietnam war and the imperial presidency, this strategy was essential. On the other hand, the press tapped public opinion regarding Church himself. And in this regard, Church was not interested only in adulation. Bryce Nelson once removed from the office mailing list the names of columnists Rowland Evans and Robert Novak because they were relentlessly critical of the senator. "Oh no, put them back on," Church instructed Nelson. "Don't ever cut anybody off the mailing list, whatever they say about me."[39]

While some critics accused Church of pursuing headlines, members of his staff sometimes groused among themselves that he was insufficiently attentive to publicity. Despite advice that he should act quickly on "newsworthy" items, recalled aide Mike Wetherell, he occasionally frustrated his staff by seeming to drag his feet, gathering more information, and thinking through the situation. Some staffers thought he had his priorities askew when, with Bethine and Chase, he left town for periodic weekend retreats to a cabin in the Pennsylvania woods that lacked a telephone. To these aides, Church was missing opportunities to cultivate important political and social contacts in the nation's capital. His unwillingness to linger around the Senate in the off hours, as well as his inaccessibility at the cabin, suggested that he was putting family above career, undercutting his potential as a mover and shaker, denying himself important publicity. Church, from this angle, hardly seemed obsessed with promoting himself.[40]

From another angle, of course, publicity was not always a political boon. Much of the media attention that Church received during the Cooper-Church fight did not augur well for his future as a senator. Constituents sent numerous clippings of articles, cartoons, and letters to the editor that were anything but flattering. Some Idaho critics, for example, forwarded copies of columnist William S. White's rebuke of Church as one of the "new isolationist senators" who would hurt the United States. Others mailed columnist David Lawrence's essay lambasting Church and his dove colleagues as the first legislators in American history who, during a war, interfered with the movement of troops and supplies. Syndicated cartoonist Reg Manning portrayed Cooper and Church in the act of tying the hands of the president. A published letter to Church from a University of Idaho student warned against "the yellow hordes" and accused the senator of aiding the communist conspiracy and promoting a "Pearl Harbor" kind of policy. When constituents clipped and sent to Church these articles and cartoons, they typically wrote comments such as "Shape up or Ship out."[41]

If the charge that Church sought headlines thus missed some of the nuances of the situation, so did the complaint that he "caved in" too quickly, and was too anxious to compromise. He may have moved tentatively and cautiously; but on an issue such as the Vietnam war his path over the long haul was clear. Year after year, from late 1964 on, he spoke consistently against the war, not circuitously but directly and passionately. With growing fervor and authority he attacked its root assumptions. As columnist Mary McGrory recalled, "He was out there, he was doing what he could, he was standing up to pressure, he never wavered, he never failed." In retrospect, Tom Dine concluded that Church was rightly concerned with the number of votes he could muster, especially on controversial issues. "My experience with him," Dine recalled, "was that to get from here to there you had to do certain things. And we always got to there." Aide Garry Wenske agreed: "Above all, Church knew how to count votes." An incremental approach, chipping away, made sense. Church never lost sight of the ultimate goal: getting America out of Vietnam. The question was *how* to get out, how to build a Senate majority and how to pass legislation that the more conservative House would sustain. The Cooper-Church amendment, after all, also needed the ratification of a House that was still, in Bill Miller's words, "saluting the President left and right." On the dominant issues, such as the Southeast Asian conflict, Church was steadfast and principled. Wisconsin Democrat Gaylord Nelson described him as downright "gutsy."[42]

Regarding the Cambodian invasion, Church was determined that the doves not lose a showdown with the administration. No message could be worse. Although he backed the End-the-War amendment (the Cambodia operation "finally got him off the dime," said Charles Goodell), he was certain that the McGovern-Hatfield initiative had no chance. The real hope rested with Cooper-Church, around which it seemed possible to build a winning coalition. Mike Mansfield, George Aiken, Cooper, Fulbright, and other prominent doves shared his opinion. Most of them also endorsed Hatfield-McGovern and viewed it as a stalking horse essential to the passage of Cooper-Church. The very existence of the more extreme End-the-War amendment made Cooper-Church seem more moderate. McGovern and Hatfield emphatically preferred their own measure but, in the name of a united front, supported the more equivocal Cooper-Church proposal unstintingly.[43]

According to colleagues such as George McGovern, Church was a skilled tactician. Carl Marcy recalled at least once when the Foreign Relations Committee should have followed Church's advice. When the Nixon administration withheld some foreign policy documents on the grounds of executive privilege, a furious J. William Fulbright urged cutting one budget item by 50 percent, thereby sending a message to the White House. Church objected, recommending a far more modest cut of 10 percent. Although Fulbright prevailed in the committee, the Senate restored the full budget. In this instance, Marcy believed that Church had been correct in advocating "a small nibble" rather than a big bite. "If we had taken a small bite we probably would have made it," Marcy conjectured. The smaller cut might have survived the Senate and transmitted the desired warning to the White House. Instead, there was neither a cut nor a warning.[44]

Even colleagues who found Church quick to compromise were generally forgiving. As the Ralph Nader Congress Project pointed out in the early 1970s, "It is hard to find critics of Frank Church." Charles Goodell wished that Church had been quicker to endorse a deadline on leaving Vietnam, but the New York senator recognized the "very thin line" that Church had to walk back home in Idaho. Mark Hatfield believed that Church "was so far ahead of his constituency" regarding Vietnam "that anything he did on this subject was a stand of courage." The assumption in the Senate, according to Hatfield, was "that Frank may have kept his options open a little more because of his constituency," and this was understandable.[45]

If Church often tested the limits of Idaho politics, he nevertheless invariably adhered to his conception of politics as "the art of the possible." This caution had been clear since the 1957 civil rights fight. "I've always had the pragmatic view that you ought to legislate," he told one interviewer, "and to legislate you have to remain in the realm of the possible." Without a majority vote, a proposal in itself was basically meaningless. Church realized that it would be ludicrous, as well as counterproductive, to fight to regain Congress's constitutional powers, only to have Congress again defer to the executive branch.[46]

By 1970, no legislative test was more politically sensitive, volatile, and complicated than that of the war in Southeast Asia. Even friendly social gatherings and dinner parties disintegrated into screaming matches. In the Senate, doves endured criticism as "sunshine patriots" or as friends of Ho Chi Minh. Tempers flared during the debates after the Cambodian invasion. When Mark Hatfield commented on the tiny flag that one of his conservative colleagues wore in his lapel, the other senator snapped, "It's too bad you can't wear one. I support our boys over there."[47]

White House strategies only exacerbated the situation. When discussing "the offensive against Congress" with President Nixon, speechwriter Patrick Buchanan advised that Spiro Agnew "and his hired guns" should launch "partisan, iron-booted, hob-nailed assaults on the Congress. . . . Let's cut loose and see how much blood we can spill."[48]

Frank Church, in contrast, viewed himself as a liberal who could converse with conservatives, a Democrat who could negotiate with Republicans. "Frank was a peacemaker in terms of his colleagues," recalled George McGovern. William Miller observed that Church—like Cooper, Mansfield, Aiken, New Jersey Republican Clifford Case, and others—kept looking for something that might encourage "a healing situation." In the estimation of these senators, the Cooper-Church amendment offered the most realistic chance of moving substantively toward that goal.[49]

III

Trying to build a coalition around the Cooper-Church proposal was nevertheless, according to Tom Dine, "god-damned difficult, period." In retrospect, Dine joked that it was a good thing that his wife became pregnant before the long debates started: "It would not have happened afterwards because we spent twenty hours a day on this from April 30 until the end of June. It was tense and rugged." Although Church and Cooper made a splendid team, neither felt comfortable pressuring or twisting colleagues' arms. Dine remembered that Church avoided talking to other senators about their votes, and several aides recalled their boss's aversion to the telephone. The Idaho senator was so reluctant to engage in Lyndon Johnson-style political hardball that Dine occasionally despaired: "It drove me crazy sometimes."[50]

Church was assuredly not opposed to political bargaining and trades, but his wheeling and dealing tended to be indirect and far from flamboyant. This pattern was apparent during the vote in early 1971 over funding the supersonic transport airplane (SST). From the outset, Church opposed the SST, largely on environmental grounds but also because he thought it an expensive toy. The Nixon administration backed the project, but so did Washington's Democratic senator Henry Jackson, who wanted to boost the aircraft industry in his state.[51]

At the time of the SST vote, Church had not yet returned from a speech he had given the previous day in New Mexico. Rather than rushing back to Capitol Hill, he had delayed, stopping off in Missouri. His legislative assistant, Mike Wetherell, urged him to return to the Senate as soon as possible. The vote, Wetherell emphasized, was important to environmentalists, who had been counting on Church to oppose the project. Church indicated simply that he would not be present. Subsequently, back in his office, he told the puzzled Wetherell what had happened. He had determined that his vote was not necessary to block the SST, which failed 51 to 46. "Scoop Jackson wanted that vote, and I couldn't give him the vote," Church explained. "So he asked me at least not to be present to vote as a favor to him." Church reminded Wetherell that Jackson chaired the Interior Committee, which handled resources that were often vital to Idaho. Not to honor Jackson's personal request might be asking for trouble. He told Wetherell that he did not feel particularly comfortable with what he had done, but he defended his decision as realistic. Wetherell sensed that Church's discomfort came from his having acted on personal grounds, rather than on the merits of the issue. "I did not see him do that very often," Wetherell said.[52]

On Cooper-Church, the Idaho senator had no doubt that the merits of the issue were at stake. "Make no mistake about it," he said, "the Senate as an institution is on trial here." At risk was the constitutional expectation that Congress was "the people's bulwark against one-man rule." More than usual, Church thus engaged in the difficult process of trying to corner votes, especially within the Democratic caucus and among his western colleagues.[53]

He might have been more effective had other senators feared him. Temperamentally, however, he resisted going for the jugular and trying to intimidate them. His reputation as someone bent on accommodation, not confrontation, plagued him in this respect. On the Hill, reporter George Lardner discovered that some of Church's colleagues viewed him as "a pussycat," someone who lacked the stomach for a fight. Church aide Jerry Brady drew an interesting analogy: the senator resembled an "English barrister; he got the business but needed someone else to make the deal."[54]

True to form, Church relied primarily on his Senate speeches, press releases, and media appearances to make the case for his and Cooper's amendment. He knew that the Cambodian invasion had prompted unprecedented amounts of mail to the government. Mail to elected officials was, as one of Church's aides observed in *The New Republic,* "part of the calculus of decision, and when it is extraordinary in size, intensity, and spontaneity, its impact cannot be ignored." As the final vote on Cooper-Church neared, Church believed that constituent mail had converted several " 'swing state' Senators" to the amendment, a possibility that some of the Nixon people at least privately discussed. Church thus continued to look to public opinion as a fulcrum with which to move the Senate.[55]

While Church was reluctant to play hardball politics, the White House was not. Quite willing to use pressure and leverage, the administration "got around with much more facility than we did," according to Tom Dine. In a series of moves, the president and his allies tried to delay and weaken the Cooper-Church amendment. They hoped to show that the Senate was acting like a fool, Bob Haldeman wrote in his notes. Their strategy against the Senate was simple: in Haldeman's words, "keep screwing it up." At the same time that Nixon's people worked to postpone the vote, they portrayed the ongoing debate as evidence of the Senate's inability to act with dispatch. White House appeals to loyalty were also effective. Although Republican senators such as New Hampshire's Norris Cotton privately opposed the Cambodian invasion, they were willing to be "good soldier[s] when the chips are down," as one White House memo put it. Even John Sherman Cooper was reportedly uncomfortable with his role as critic, according to Bryce Harlow who talked with him at length. Cooper was "troubled over his own amendment" and relationship with the president, Harlow reported. He "feels things have a way of getting out of hand," and "he wants to be coop[erative] and not *hurt* P[resident].[56]

In early June two votes tested the strength of the Cooper-Church forces. Both involved amendments that the administration backed, at least behind the scenes. The first came from Kansas Republican Robert Dole and would have invalidated Cooper-Church if the president learned that enemy forces were keeping American prisoners of war in Cambodia. The second was even more open-ended. Sponsored by West Virginia Democrat Robert Byrd, it would allow the president to keep U. S. forces in Cambodia as long as American lives were in jeopardy in South Vietnam. The Byrd proposal would in effect vitiate the Cooper-Church amendment, while Dole's would hold it hostage to a presidential claim that even one U. S. prisoner was in Cambodia. Tom Dine informed the staffs of Senate doves that the Dole/Byrd initiatives represented "*the* tests." It was imperative that no senator miss the votes.[57]

Church kept an anxious eye on these developments for personal reasons as well. On May 30 his son Forrest would marry Amy Furth in northern California, and the senator worried that he might miss the ceremony. He was delighted that Forrest had discovered the Stanford sophomore, an intelligent and attractive young woman, although he was uncomfortable with some of the circumstances. The previous November, on a speaking tour in California, he had learned that Forrest and Amy had been living together in what Forrest later described as "a commune of sorts, complete with a dog, two cats, and a goat." Frank Church looked at the twin bed and asked point blank if Forrest and Amy shared that small space. When Forrest answered affirmatively, the senator gave him some money with which at least to buy a double bed. Bethine, a rather stern traditionalist around whom it was best to avoid even off-color jokes, was dismayed that her husband encouraged illicit relationships. He was apparently more amenable to the situation but, as Forrest's good friend Peter Fenn recalled, he was generally "prudish" about such things.[58]

Despite the tense situation in the Senate surrounding the Cooper-Church amendment, Frank and Bethine Church caught the last possible plane westward in time for Forrest's wedding. Even at the ceremony, however, not all was peaceful. Forrest showed his parents the wedding vows that he and Amy had written. "My mother was audibly appalled," he remembered. "My father just got a little quieter than usual." The problem from his parents' viewpoint was a section in which Forrest joined Amy in a declaration of pacifism, with Forrest pledging never to serve in the military. Frank Church huddled with his son. He had no intention of trying to tell Forrest or Amy what their wedding vows should say. "Your pronouncement of pacifism, however, could not be more poorly timed. All I ask is that you do not release it to the press." To Forrest, here was further evidence of the moral purity of his generation in contrast to that of his parents. His mother and father were concerned about the political dynamite of the vows, not the sentiments they expressed. Again, he felt like an "outsider" from his parents' world, someone whose love was not "riddled with compromise." He and Amy exchanged the vows they had written. "Reluctantly," however, they withheld copies from the guests. Even then, the vows were reprinted in some Idaho papers as well as *Stars and Stripes*, the armed forces publication.[59]

Rushing back to the Senate, Church was on hand for the showdown over Robert Dole's proposed alteration of the Cooper-Church amendment. By then, Dole had become the administration's chief advocate on the Hill, in effect taking over the role of minority leader Hugh Scott. A year older than Church, Dole had also escaped a brush with death as a young man. Badly wounded in Italy during World War II, he had barely survived. The price had been high: excruciating pain, damaged hands, and the loss of a kidney. The tenacity he brought to the Cooper-Church battles was that which had characterized much of his life, best summed up in his mother's advice, "*Can't* never did anything." He had used that tenacity in the service of a political philosophy that one colleague described as "somewhere to the right of Genghis Khan." By 1970 he had formed a one-person "Dole Patrol" in defense of the president and had earned the nickname, "Nixon's Doberman pinscher." Whatever the label, Dole was a fighter who could, in the words of Tom Dine, "slash and burn with the best of them." As a Dole aide said, "He won't quit."[60]

Church was not about to quit either. He tried to turn upside down the administration's argument that the Cooper-Church amendment would tie the president's hands. The operative date in the amendment, he pointed out, was July 1, 1970, the day after U. S. forces were supposed to be out of Cambodia according to the president's own timetable. The amendment would not force anything on the White House; it would merely preclude returning troops to Cambodia. "By enacting the amendment," he argued, "we would be strengthening the President's hand, helping him overcome evasions and footdragging by his own bureaucracy and foreign allies. . . ." The Congress, moreover, would be helping to shoulder "the responsibility for bringing the war to a close." The administration's backers were not persuaded, but Dole's proposal nevertheless failed. On June 3, by a 54 to 36 vote, the Cooper-Church forces held off a major threat.[61]

The fight over the Byrd initiative still lay ahead. Dole described it as "the main event" and the White House stepped up its pressure.

Urging his Senate troops to keep up their good work, President Nixon told minority leader Hugh Scott that Byrd's proposal went "a long way" toward easing his dissatisfaction with Cooper-Church. White House advisors, viewing the upcoming vote as "crucial" for the president, discussed yet another possible public relations blitz from the American Legion and Veterans of Foreign Wars, this one threatening that the veterans would "organize against the Senators who do not vote to protect our boys in Vietnam." On June 8, with the vote only several days away, the administration nervously counted forty-four senators on each side, with nine undecided and three absent.[62]

Frank Church did not much care for Robert Byrd, whom he viewed as petty and unprincipled. In retrospect, however, he believed that the dapper West Virginian had marshalled formidable constitutional arguments against restricting the powers of the commander-in-chief in wartime. In early June 1970, Church thus plunged again into the constitutional thicket of executive/legislative powers. Byrd's initiative, he contended, would tilt the scales too much in favor of the presidency, in effect giving Nixon a blank check resembling that of the Gulf of Tonkin resolution. Church conceded that, of course, the president as the commander-in-chief could protect U. S. troops without a vote from Congress. The real issue was Congress's ability to restrain the executive branch from committing troops and money abroad. Byrd's motion would be "an open-ended invitation" to enlarge an undeclared war. Church's response to Byrd resembled his reaction to a Henry Kissinger comment. Kissinger, when insisting that only the president could get America out of the war, had pleaded for the public to give Nixon support and "even an act of love." Church had other advice: "What we need is not an act of love, but an act of Congress."[63]

On June 11 the Senate rejected Byrd's proposal by a close 52 to 47 vote. Church hailed "an historic watershed." Although Dole and other administration supporters signaled their intentions of engaging in debate through the end of the month if the president wanted, Bryce Harlow informed Nixon that "the troops are tired," willing to settle for some cosmetic changes in the Cooper-Church amendment. After that, they believed the administration could "proclaim victory and get a lopsided vote. . . in favor of the amended Cooper-Church proposal, thus (they argue) washing out any political gain for the Democrat leaders." In this regard, they eventually did very well.[64]

IV

On June 30, the day upon which Nixon indicated that the last of the U. S. troops had left Cambodia, the Senate approved a somewhat revised Cooper-Church amendment, 58 to 37. After July 1, 1970, without specific approval from Congress, there could be no funding for U. S. troops in Cambodia, nor for military instruction or air combat activity in support of Cambodian forces. Among the changes to the initial proposal was an important disclaimer of any intention to question the president's constitutional powers to protect the lives of U. S. forces. According to Carl Marcy, Pentagon lawyers were "elated" by the disclaimer. "They believe it nullifies what Senators Cooper and Church sought to do," Marcy informed Fulbright. As the military attorneys interpreted the revised amendment, it prohibited Congress from denying funds to the president when he was acting to protect troops anywhere. Presidential aide William Timmons agreed, and informed Nixon that the Senate's disclaimer constituted a White House victory.[65]

Nixon speechwriter Patrick Buchanan thus believed that "our people bollixed up the dove operation nicely." He was equally pleased that television's handling of the vote conveyed a sense that the results of Cooper-Church were " 'murky and unresolved.' " White House briefing statements suggested that Nixon should describe Cooper-Church as "a highly confusing document," and then state his skepticism about Congress dabbling with military tactics that might endanger troops in the field. In an hour-long news conference, Nixon took exactly this approach. He claimed also that he did not see how the amendment would have any effect on him or his policies. Later, in his memoirs, he castigated this "first restrictive vote ever cast on a President in wartime" as both "meaningless, since all Americans had already left Cambodia," and replete with "serious" symbolic meaning.[66]

Church, of course, was overjoyed that the amendment had cleared the Senate. At the least, he believed, the vote would discourage the president from taking the war into Cambodia again. Perhaps the amendment was the hinge upon which the door would finally start swinging shut on the war. The Idaho senator also found personally gratifying the praise that he received from John Sherman Cooper and George Aiken about his role in the long debate: "No one could have done better."[67]

A few hours after passage of the amendment, the Churches and the Dines went to the Senate dining room to celebrate. Robert Dole happened to be eating at another table. They took the opportunity to compliment him for putting up such a tenacious battle. Dine joked, "We've got a new amendment prohibiting the use of U. S. combat forces against Burma!" Dole countered with some appreciation of his own: "Put me on as a co-sponsor!"[68]

There were nevertheless problems in claiming too much for the Cooper-Church amendment. Journalist I. F. Stone, one of the most astute observers of American politics, correctly observed that the summer's debate had not really addressed fundamental issues: "the nature of our foreign policy and the size of our military establishment." He found the Cooper-Church people "too busy splitting. . .constitutional hairs." Sometimes, in fact, he had difficulty distinguishing the doves from the hawks. The amendment left untouched, for example, the air war over Cambodia, except to say that bombing could not be in "direct" support of the Cambodian government. In the whole affair, Stone saw the influence of Wimpy, a character in the Popeye cartoon strip who talked tough and then said, "Let's you and him fight." Stone much preferred the McGovern-Hatfield amendment, which would impose a firm date on U. S. withdrawal from Southeast Asia.[69]

The Senate's 55 to 39 rejection of the McGovern-Hatfield motion on September 1 was a reminder, however, of the constraints under which Church and the doves had worked during the tense and volatile summer. The White House had gone after the amendment with a vengeance, establishing outside groups to lead in the attack. "Americans for Winning the Peace" was the designated "high level group." "The Tell It to Hanoi Committee," headquartered in New York City, took the lower road, claiming that Congress would give the communists what they could not win on the Southeast Asian battlefield. The committee used the suggestions of White House advisor Charles Colson, who described McGovern, Hatfield, and the twenty-two other sponsors of the amendment as "apostles of retreat and defeat," "unilateral disarmers," "neo Neville Chamberlains," and "salesmen of surrender, selling the 'sell-out' like some sell used cars or potato chips." According to the hard-hitting "Tell It to Hanoi" literature, the twenty-four Senate doves "would swim the Mekong if the price was right." This "band of carping critics" refused to recognize the "major military success" of President Nixon's Cambodian operation. Indeed, their "Damn the consequences, full speed for home!" approach to foreign policy would destroy America's credibility abroad. "It is the President, and the President alone," insisted the Tell-It-To-Hanoi group, "who is authorized to conduct the foreign policy of the United States."[70]

The fate of the End-the-War amendment confirmed Frank Church's sense of what was politically feasible in the summer of 1970. He had voted for the amendment but, as he had suspected, the doves lacked the numbers to get the whole loaf of McGovern-Hatfield. They had at least gotten part of a loaf. With Cooper-Church, the Senate finally took aim at the economic life blood of the war–its funding. Even the thirty-nine votes in the losing cause of the End-the-War amendment provided evidence, in Hatfield's words, that the doves were becoming "a decisive political force."[71]

Church went a step further, declaring that the doves were now *the* decisive political force. On September 6, 1970, over CBS television, he aired a theme that he repeated in a variety of forums: the doves had won the debate over the war, even though they did not yet realize it and the hawks liked to pretend differently. His point was that the Nixon administration was publicly committed to two central dove positions, withdrawing U.S. troops from Vietnam and seeking a negotiated settlement of the war. No longer was the debate over whether to withdraw, but when. Ironically, said Church, "the less there is to argue about, the hotter the argument gets!" Hence Vice President Agnew had castigated congressional critics of the war as " 'architects of surrender' " and the administration had resorted to every possible trick to make the critics look bad. Although the doves had won the argument, Church urged them to keep up the pressure on the administration to prevent detours on the road out of Vietnam. Theirs, he said, represented the epitome of patriotism–"not the patriotism of conformity" but that of an earlier American, Carl Schurz, who had insisted, " 'Our country right or wrong. When right, to be kept right; when wrong, to be put right.' "[72]

Later that month Church elaborated on these comments at Colorado State University, urging students not to despair about the prospects of ending the war. He asked them to remember the time when "ferocious hawks" swooped down on the few doves in the country. But now the hawks were less fearsome. "They perch on strange new standards which proclaim: 'No *Precipitous* Withdrawal.' 'No *Humiliating* Defeat.' 'Peace *With* Honor.' " Such slogans were as cynical as they were phony and politically contrived, their purpose "to give protective cover to the hawks," who had in fact lost the debate. No more was there talk from the administration about military victory or the dangers of a falling Southeast Asian domino crushing Seattle. Richard Nixon's secret plan to end the war had turned out to be what? "*Withdrawal*!" Church guessed that "the President has decided that the care and feeding of the restive hawks obliges him to keep flailing away at the doves, even as he occupies their premises." The "well-plucked hawks" were, from this perspective, an endangered species.[73]

Church's "the doves have won" message was largely for rhetorical effect. Not all the signs were hopeful. Carl Marcy observed, for example, that by mid-1970 the Foreign Relations Committee " 'security' briefings" had become a grotesque joke. Again and again came depressing evidence that, on matters of national security, "a non-elected bureaucrat, or a Presidential consultant," had more power than any number of senators together. The White House obsession with secrecy had reached absurd proportions. Agents from the Departments of State and Defense, the CIA, and the National Security Agency "swept" the hearings room looking for electronic bugging devices. "All they assure the Committee," wrote Marcy "is that there are no Russian or foreign bugs in the room. But we do not know whether these agencies may have left their own bugs behind!"[74]

Such suspicions were not altogether unfounded, according to Church and William Fulbright. In late July the two senators worried that within the military were the makings of a coup. Alarmed, they took to the Senate floor to denounce the 1970 prize essay of the U. S. Naval Institute, "Against All Enemies," by Navy captain Robert J. Hanks. Hanks had done more than accuse the Senate doves of endangering American security. He had also recommended that "we in the military cannot stand idly, silently by and watch it done." The essay obviously did not reflect one officer's opinion, or it would not have won recognition from the U. S. Naval Institute. Presiding over the institute was none other than the chair of the Joint Chiefs of Staff, Admiral Thomas H. Moorer. Here, according to Church, was "the very stuff of which military coup d'etats are made." The essay was "dangerous," reflecting the view that the military needed to stage what Church described as "a desperate, rear-guard action" to protect the nation against internal enemies. Church saw echoes in Hanks's article of Spiro Agnew's attacks on the doves. "Perhaps we have reached a point where unprecedented things are going to become commonplace," the worried Idaho senator told his colleagues. "If that is so, we are in for serious trouble in the United States."[75]

At the White House, such trouble was brewing. Presidential aide Bob Haldeman's notes described talk of building up a "chamber of horrors" in which "to hang the Dem[ocratic] left." Tom Huston was supposed to develop a front organization, resembling Students for Democratic Society, and have it endorse possible 1972 presidential candidate Hubert Humphrey, thereby tarring him with a radical brush. The president himself "wants to see the research on this," wrote Haldeman. There was also discussion about the need for the Internal Revenue Service to conduct field audits of leading Democrats. Some presidential aides hoped to find "a Commie" in the membership of the Council for a Liveable World, an organization with which Church was associated. "We simply have got to keep the label of radical sympathizers on the Democrats," advised Charles Colson. Whereas Church, in one of his "Doves are Winning" speeches, had called for "a broad, bipartisan consensus" uniting Congress and the White House, plans at the White House pointed elsewhere. "Now we don't work *w/* Cong[ress]," Haldeman jotted in his notes. "Go against them." Indeed, the White House viewpoint was that the president "must *never* get along" with the legislature during the second half of his term.[76]

Moving into the fall of 1970 the administration's mood was upbeat, reflecting a sense that it now controlled events. It had not only successfully blocked the McGovern-Hatfield amendment, but also was even contemplating ways of taking legal steps against the "Amendment to End the War Committee." The committee, constituted of the amendment's twenty-four Senate sponsors, including Church, had appealed through television and newspapers for citizens to write Congress in support of the amendment. In the eyes of the administration, the senators had formed an illegal lobby. One White House document concluded that "the committee's activities appear to raise a number of very serious questions as to possible violations of Federal Criminal Statutes."[77]

A Louis Harris poll showing that the public approved of the Cambodian operation by a two-to-one margin also buoyed the administration. According to H. R. Haldeman, this provided an opportunity to go after the "radical liberals" who had opposed the president. Charles Colson detected a sudden, remarkable tractability on the Hill. Senators now seemed to have more respect for the administration; indeed some senators who had defied the president were scrambling to make amends. Colson could not recall within the past fifteen years such a huge shift in political opinion. He guessed that most senators now recognized the commanding position of the president. When Colson recommended that uncooperative senators "should still get the cold shoulder from us," Nixon scrawled "Right" in the margin. In this context, the White House staff put together "Action Request P-606" to "hit back at Frank Church's comment that 'the doves have won.' . . ."[78]

That fall the House of Representatives eliminated the Cooper-Church amendment from the Foreign Military Sales Act. The Nixon administration had made clear to House members that the president would otherwise not sign the measure. Columnist Joseph Alsop wrote gleefully that "the Senate's passage of the Cooper-Church amendment has now turned out to be the super non-event of 1970."[79]

V

The amendment still had some life, however. On December 22, after several failed attempts, Church and Cooper finally attached a modified version to a Cambodian supplemental aid package that the administration wanted badly. The amendment addressed only the land aspects of the war, however, prohibiting funding either U. S. ground personnel in Cambodia or Cambodian military forces. It did not prevent using planes over Cambodian air space, nor bombing strikes necessary to protect U. S. troops in the field. "What a loop-hole," moaned one antiwar person who believed that the administration was "making an *ASS* of Cooper-Church by repeatedly saying 'We're not using *ground* troops.' " Church admitted that "the omission of airpower restrictions was not an oversight," but explained that there were insufficient votes to halt the air war. As Cooper put it, "We tried our best."[80]

Despite the amendment's weaknesses, it represented "one of the most significant aspects of the 91st Congress," according to the *Washington Post*. "It is the first time in our history that Congress has attempted to limit the deployment of American troops abroad in the course of an ongoing war." Church, who took the initiative in drafting the revised amendment, had tried to keep as much of the original format as possible. "Otherwise," as he told Cooper, "it could easily be concluded that we have thrown in the towel." A strength of the amendment was that it restricted any legislation, not just a specific aid package, from funding Cambodian ground operations.[81]

A problem, of course, was how to prevent the White House from simply disguising its actions. Church knew that the administration was in fact providing "direct tactical support for the Lon Nol government" in Cambodia. Although U. S. planes were supposedly acting only to interdict supply lines into Cambodia, they were actually providing aerial cover for the Lon Nol forces. Official claims to the contrary, the administration was giving U.S. military assistance to yet another Southeast Asian regime and venturing deeper into the quagmire.[82]

In early 1971, convinced "that the President doesn't really intend to bring the United States out of the war," Church again approached John Sherman Cooper with a rather simple idea. The two senators would place in the form of a congressional resolution Nixon's own oft-declared intentions to extricate the U. S. from the Southeast Asia. The resolution, as Church described it, would declare that America's policy was "to achieve the full and complete withdrawal of all our armed forces—land, air, and naval—from Indochina, including all American Prisoners of War." There would be no timetable, no effort "to cover the whole waterfront" of the war's issues. Church believed that, if Nixon signed the resolution, it would "remove all basis for doubt that he harbors some hidden purpose to preserve an American foothold in Southeast Asia." It would, however, be essential to force the administration's hand on the matter, confronting it "with a resolution, which it must either support or oppose." When Cooper hesitated, on grounds of an unfavorable mood, Church persisted. He did not wish "to lean on" the Kentucky Republican, but he was confident that the resolution had a reasonably good chance of passage because it allowed the president some maneuvering room.[83]

By March, Church's appeals to Cooper were urgent. He worried that Cooper's "reluctance to move," although understandable, might well mean they would miss their opportunity. News that South Vietnamese troops had just launched a major ground assault into Laos had jabbed "a spur in the flanks of the Senate," as Church phrased it. In response to rumors that the South Vietnamese might also move northward, Walter Mondale (D-Minnesota) and William Saxbe (R-Ohio) were already working to extend the Cooper-Church amendment to North Vietnam. "In short," said Church, "they have grabbed the ball and intend to run with it." Nor were they alone. Jacob Javits (R-New York) was trying to spell out more clearly the war-making powers of the president and Congress. Mike Mansfield and Maine Democrat Edmund Muskie planned to sponsor a resolution calling for a "total withdrawal" of American troops within nine months after North Vietnam's release of U.S. prisoners of war. And the McGovern-Hatfield amendment was surfacing again. Cooper and Church, once in the vanguard of the Senate antiwar movement, were in danger of falling behind. "We are fast being preempted," Church warned his Kentucky colleague. If the two did not take action that went at least as far as the Mondale-Saxbe initiative they would appear to have retreated from their own previous position regarding Cambodia, Laos, and Thailand. Even worse, they might seem to be disavowing their own earlier commitments.[84]

More than ego was at stake: Cooper and Church sought to protect the middle ground that they had tried so hard to cultivate. As Church explained, "Events could easily push us to a choice between extremes we are unwilling to espouse or no action at all"; other senators simply must not "cut the ground from under us." Church thus sent Cooper a modified version of the resolution that he hoped the two of them could sponsor. It would subsume the Mondale-Saxbe bill under a larger legislative umbrella, "extending the Cooper-Church formula to North Vietnam while affirmatively establishing an orderly but complete withdrawal from Indochina as our overriding national purpose." Moreover, by not imposing deadlines on the president, and by assuring the release of America's POWs, it might provide the foundation of a new political consensus: "a legislative limb on which 'hawk' and 'dove' could perch together." Indeed, Church believed, "this resolution could become the focal point of the Congressional effort to bring this war to an end." Church anxiously awaited Cooper's response, reminding his friend that "time is of the essence."[85]

Over the next four months the two senators worked out what Church unveiled to the press on July 7 as "a new end-the-war amendment." Its purpose, he explained, was to spell out national policy, a total U. S. "disengagement from hostilities" in Southeast Asia, "not continued American involvement in some new form." Once enacted, the amendment would stop all funding for U. S. forces in North and South Vietnam, Cambodia, Laos, and Thailand, "except to the extent necessary to withdraw said forces and to protect them from imminent danger as they are withdrawn." This was no "mere sense-of-the-Senate resolution," Church emphasized. It would be a law applied to "the use of public money from every source." The proposed amendment nevertheless stopped short of imposing a date for total withdrawal upon the president. Instead, it urged the president to set the deadline for completing the removal of U. S. forces.[86]

To people in the antiwar movement, Church's preoccupation with spelling out national policy could easily seem inconsequential, another example of empty legislative word games. To the senator, however, the matter was anything but frivolous. For some time he had argued that the U. S. really had no clear policy in Southeast Asia. Explanations for America's military presence there kept shifting or, worse, were deliberately confusing and deceptive. The word "policy" had become a sad joke on Capitol Hill, as Bill Miller discovered shortly after he started working for Senator Cooper. When the Foreign Relations Committee turned its attention to a section of the military assistance bill entitled "Policy," members started laughing. Miller was startled at how "bitter" they were. The senators finally decided, as Miller recalled, "to strike the entire section as meaningless and hypocritical." They could no longer even maintain the pretense of believing the words.[87]

Church hoped that his and Cooper's new amendment would clarify and guide America's Southeast Asian policy. By letting the president control the date for removing all U. S. fighting forces, the amendment would provide Nixon with leverage to negotiate the return of American POWs. And, by uniting the executive and legislative branches, Republicans and Democrats, hawks and doves, it might prevent "a post-war era of bitter recrimination," such as the country had suffered during the days of Joe McCarthy.[88]

Once again, Mike Mansfield and George Aiken co-sponsored Cooper-Church. The first Cooper-Church proposals had focused on halting the spread of the war; the 1971 version, which was attached to the Foreign Aid Authorization bill, was oriented toward getting out of it. "The pattern was clear," Henry Kissinger later observed irritably. "Senate opponents of the war would introduce one amendment after another, forcing the Administration into unending rearguard actions. . . ." In Kissinger's estimation, the Senate encouraged the North Vietnamese "to stall, waiting to harvest the results of our domestic dissent."[89]

The administration thus had no use for the latest Cooper-Church initiative. The White House wanted to concede nothing to Congress that, as presidential aide William Timmons told Nixon, "appears to force your hand on future Vietnam withdrawals."[90]

This resolve was abundantly clear in the president's reaction that autumn to Mike Mansfield's much watered-down amendment to the military procurement bill. In its original form, Mansfield's non-binding resolution had urged the total withdrawal of U. S. troops within nine months after the return of American POWs. The version that finally received House approval on November 10 referred only to a "date certain" following the prisoners' release. Even this was too much for Nixon. He signed the bill but announced that he would disregard the Mansfield amendment because it infringed upon his role as commander-in-chief. The president, as Cooper's top aide observed, "had in effect rejected the Senate's view that foreign policy should be made jointly by the two branches."[91]

Frank Church was incensed at Nixon's rebuff. "What is he going to do next?" he asked. "Dispatch Henry Kissinger, his foreign policy advisor, to Capitol Hill to disband the Congress?" Church again urged Congress to take control of the purse-strings: "I favor such legislation. I shall sponsor such legislation, and I hope that Congress passes such legislation."[92]

The Senate doves were momentarily in disarray, however. Mansfield saw no alternative but to regroup and forge ahead. But along what course? Missouri Democrat Thomas Eagleton privately indicated that the Mansfield amendment, lacking a date, was "mush." Eagleton, Ted Kennedy (D-Massachusetts), Philip Hart (D-Michigan), Gaylord Nelson (D-Wisconsin), Charles Mathias (R-Maryland), and others considered pressing ahead with the Cooper-Church amendment, but ultimately backed off. Mathias told Cooper's aide that there were probably enough Senate votes to pass the amendment, but some senators were having second thoughts about such action. By throwing down the gauntlet to Nixon, they might seem to be engaged in a vindictive power struggle that placed personalities above issues. Cooper himself was unwilling to push the amendment, but for another reason. He believed that the continuing efforts to alter it, especially regarding the POW issue, shifted attention from the main point: whether the U. S. sought total withdrawal of its military forces or intended to keep residual troops there. Church, at least initially, had been ready to revise the amendment to make it more palatable to some of its foes. He had suggested to Cooper a change that would have made the release of the POWs, rather than the enactment of the amendment, the mechanism for cutting off funding for anything other than withdrawal of U. S. troops in Southeast Asia.[93]

By the end of 1971, what David McReynolds of the War Resisters League described as a "down mood" had settled over the Senate doves and the antiwar movement. John Sherman Cooper concluded in late November that there seemed to be no way in which Congress could block Nixon's apparent commitment to maintaining a long-term residual force in Southeast Asia. Frank Church had no reason to be more optimistic. The legislative momentum behind the Cooper-Church amendments had dissipated.[94]

Church fishing with son Chase along an Idaho stream. *Courtesy Boise State University.*

Chapter Thirteen
Against the Tide: 1970-1972

FRANK CHURCH'S growing bitterness toward the ongoing Southeast Asian war drove him further from the political center. By the 1970s, events pummeling his deeply felt political beliefs forced him to make agonizing choices. While he labored to pass legislation to end the war, the administration defiantly used greater and greater force, ruthlessly bombing to oblivion tens of thousands of Asians. Moreover, the White House still summoned up huge public support by waving the flag and portraying presidential critics as disloyal and unpatriotic. Church wavered between feelings of futility, outrage, and a continuing desire to work within traditional legislative channels. For him, it was a dispiriting and even frightening time.

Occasionally, he seemed almost ready to break loose from his mainstream political moorings. He conceded in a December 1970 speech that Americans had every reason to worry about their country, "the decency of its purposes, the virtues of its shared ideals and the soundness of its institutions." He understood why many of the nation's young people believed that "the system is rigged for war, not peace," and in favor of powerful, monied interests. The United States, aspiring to "take charge" of the world, had assumed the role of global "policeman, banker and judge." By dropping napalm bombs on defenseless Vietnamese villages, it had forfeited its claims to moral leadership. As Church contemplated the U. S. reliance on military solutions, and as he sadly considered the nation's serious injustices and misplaced priorities, he knew why many disaffected Americans were defying "the establishment." "If it won't yield," he said, as he summed up their deep feelings of frustration, "at least it can be discomforted. Why not?"[1]

Church's own bouts of alienation radicalized him somewhat, pushing his egalitarian and democratic instincts more forcefully to the surface. His frustrations with the ongoing war, the "imperial presidency," and the persistent inequities of American life prodded him to brave the political tide. He tried even more doggedly to turn the tide, not just on the war but on such issues as foreign aid, the environment, treatment of the nation's elderly citizens, and the administration's backing of the brutal Pakistani regime. Although he remained in many ways cautious and attentive to the political constraints of Idaho and Capitol Hill, he became increasingly impatient with power relationships that favored economic, political, and intellectual elites, or that damaged the environment. "God damn it, I've become a senator," he told one aide. "If I hedge my view, and if I can't say what I really believe, . . . then it isn't worth being here."[2]

I

He repeatedly stressed that Americans needed to turn their attention to their own domestic problems. "Above all," he said, "the American foreign policy tail must stop wagging the American dog!" When he listened to the words of the popular folk song, "This land is our land," he was reminded of the troubles that blanketed the country, from decaying cities to declining family farms, unsafe streets, poverty, racial tensions, and a deteriorating environment. He applauded environmentalists who were trying to improve the quality of life by cleaning up the air and water, resisting the "endless clutter of billboards and neon signs," and rejecting "shopping centers as the hallmark of American culture." These Americans deserved all the support they could get.[3]

Church considered himself their ally. After the successful fight in the early Sixties over the Wilderness Act he had continued his risky political move into the environmentalist camp. In March 1965 he had introduced the National Wild Rivers bill, designed to protect sections of six of the nation's scenic rivers from human development. Included were stretches of the Salmon and the Clearwater in Idaho. When Lyndon Johnson had encouraged such legislation in his State of the Union address in early 1965, Colorado's powerful Congressman Wayne Aspinall had dismissed the idea as downright crazy. Secretary of the Interior Stewart Udall had known immediately that environmentalists faced a repeat of the battle over the Wilderness Act, which had finally become law in 1964. Once again, they had to deal with Aspinall, a zealous promoter of land and water reclamation projects who virtually ruled the House Interior Committee. Environmentalists despised him. One claimed that he had done "more damage to the American earth than any other human being in this century." In turn, Aspinall had declared war on the "conservationist extremists," as he called them. The only hope for the Wild Rivers bill had been, as Udall recognized, to repeat the strategy that produced the Wilderness Act: put enormous pressure on the spunky Coloradan by rolling up huge margins for the bill in the Senate and by demonstrating that conservation issues had substantial public support.[4]

This had eventually happened. After passing the Senate several times by large votes, the bill had finally gotten through the House in 1968. According to Udall, Frank Church had been as responsible as anyone for the bill's success. Indeed, Udall believed that Church was one of the two or three people in Congress who most deserved credit for "the monumental pieces of conservation legislation of the 1960s," the Wilderness and Wild Rivers acts.[5]

In Udall's estimation, Church's importance in the development of conservation issues on Capitol Hill went far beyond his taking the lead on the Senate floor. Church also sent a strong signal that the West was in transition. For years, environmental legislation had been a very shaky issue in the western states. Idaho, as Udall remembered, "was really a state which all of us considered pretty much in the grip of the user interests—the timber, mining and other interests. . . ." Church demonstrated that public opinion was turning on the conservation issue, and that support for conservation need not be a political liability in the mountain and desert regions. The votes of sports and outdoor people had the potential to offset the opposition of mining and timber interests.[6]

Idaho journalist Bill Hall once joked that in all of Idaho there were probably only about nine hundred environmentalists, but virtually "everybody is a hunter or a fisherman. . . . At one time we had 700,000 people in the state and something like 450,000 hunting and fishing licenses." When Church spoke to this outdoor constituency he emphasized that protecting the environment made good economic sense. "Tourism is Idaho's fastest growing industry," he wrote one constituent in the mid-Sixties. Appealing to local pride, he noted that people came from miles away to try their luck in the state's fabled trout streams. Wild Rivers legislation, from this perspective, would boost Idaho, not hurt it.[7]

By the late Sixties and early Seventies, Church was an outspoken advocate of what he and others called the "new conservation" movement, one which reflected a rising popular interest in ecological issues. A central concern of the movement revolved around the burdens and liabilities of technological progress. In several forums, Church voiced this concern, noting that pesticides, herbicides, automobiles, airplanes, nuclear installations, and other modern creations were poisoning the water and the air.[8]

"Today, we asphalt Americans, our eyes smarting, are rocketing men to the moon while standing knee-deep in our own litter," Church told an Idaho audience on the first "Earth Day," April 22, 1970. Wisconsin senator Gaylord Nelson had conceived Earth Day as a nationwide "teach-in" about the endangered planet, and the huge response to it indicated that ecology was an idea whose time had indeed arrived. Perhaps more than twenty million Americans joined the day's events, attending speeches, planting trees, and picking up litter. Helping to mark the event in Pocatello, Church described a grim situation: "Our rivers are clogged with filth; smog is the 'air apparent' in our large cities. Our eyes are assaulted by unrelieved urban ugliness. . . . Much of our land is hideously defaced." The problems, he said, grew out of an uncritical acceptance of technology, an exploitative temperament, and "a mania for growth." Drawing upon the example of recent antiwar demonstrations, he urged citizens to form a "moratorium movement" to save the environment.[9]

Church's eloquent words demonstrated again his ability to articulate serious problems. In this regard, journalist George Lardner, who followed national politics carefully, judged the Idaho senator as one of the brightest people and perhaps the best speaker on Capitol Hill. Ironically, however, Church's eloquence created dilemmas of its own by raising expectations. As Lardner said, Church's sympathetic audiences could "listen to him espouse this or that position in unvarnished form and think, 'That's good, that's great.' " It was then hard not to disappoint them, especially given Church's preference for compromise.[10]

Environmental issues were, in that respect, particularly difficult to handle. They stirred heated controversies in which the stakes were painfully high. Short-term economic needs typically vied with long-range ecological imperatives. Few issues were as complex, inflammatory, or as serious, especially as the twentieth century wound down.

It was an environmental matter that elicited from Frank Church one of the angriest responses that Mike Wetherell observed in ten years of working for him. A group of southeastern Idaho ranchers had been having trouble with large concentrations of wild horses. Finally, they had resorted to driving them off a cliff. Wetherell informed Church of the incident, explaining in a memo that the actions, admittedly reprehensible, were perhaps understandable given the ranchers' economic necessities. Church's handwritten reply said simply, "They should hang the sons-of-bitches." Wetherell was somewhat surprised at the intensity of Church's reactions. Seldom had he heard his boss swear, and never in writing. When he asked Church about the matter, the senator said that there was simply no excuse for what had happened. Other solutions existed than killing "helpless animals."[11]

As with most of the environmentalists, Church wanted the federal government to take a more active role in protecting wild animals and natural resources. Although he conceded that the government had itself contributed to the mounting ecological crisis, he wanted it to battle more aggressively such problems as pollution.

He even went so far as to discuss a potentially very sensitive issue for Idaho—the worldwide population explosion and the proposed antidote of family planning. As a lapsed Catholic speaking in the strong Mormon country of southeastern Idaho in early 1970, for example, he knew the issue of family planning placed him on treacherous political footing. With notable courage he plunged ahead anyhow. "Every 24 hours," he informed his audience, "a city the size of Salt Lake is being added to the population of the world!" The "swarming human horde" pointed to environmental catastrophe. He backed U. S. efforts to provide other nations with technical assistance to curb the burgeoning population; at the same time, he regretted that the federal government had not allotted money for family planning within the United States. Well aware that he was already encroaching on religious and cultural sensibilities, he deferred to voluntary and local standards. He sought a passive federal government role in this area, helping to provide family planning services in accordance with prevailing local wishes. Only when "a given community freely chooses to set up strictly voluntary" services would federal funds be available. In communities whose dominant religious groups opposed artificial methods of controlling birth, he said, "any federal intrusion would be devoutly resisted."[12]

In this instance, Church placed the rights of the local community ahead of those of the individual, or the larger society. He nevertheless also took the side of population control, recommending federal funds for family planning services, at least where such services did not violate dominant local beliefs. By categorizing the population explosion as yet another example of the "runamuck willfulness" that was destroying the environment, he hoped to alert people to the consequences of their choices, and then to provide some legislative alternatives for change.[13]

Church's recognition of issues, and his stand on them, won praise from environmental groups. This was true in 1969 when Richard Nixon nominated Walter J. Hickel as Secretary of the Interior. Not since Dwight Eisenhower's choice of Lewis Strauss for Secretary of Commerce had there been such controversy over a cabinet nominee. Hickel struck a political nerve that Nixon's other cabinet nominations did not. As governor of Alaska, he had displayed a speculator's mentality by enthusiastically supporting the development of public lands. To people who constituted the "new conservation" movement, his kind of go-getter thinking was anathema. During the confirmation hearings, Frank Church joined George McGovern in grilling Hickel. "With reluctance and grave doubt," Church ultimately voted for Hickel. There was, he said, insufficient reason to deny the president his cabinet choice. If nothing else, Church hoped that the Senate's interrogation had raised Hickel's sensitivity to environmental issues and put him on notice that "we. . .will be literally looking over his shoulder." One national environmental leader, Thomas E. Dustin of the Izaak Walton League of America, applauded Church "in the strongest terms" for conducting one of the "sharpest" interrogations that Dustin had ever heard. "I think we owe you a great deal."[14]

Conservationists generally agreed that they had a friend in the Idaho senator. "We've worked with Church a lot," said the lobbyist for one national group, "and we note him as first class on environmental issues." Even a conservationist who believed that Church did not go far enough on ecological matters conceded that, "if you consider his constituency, he's doing pretty well." In 1970 the League of Conservation Voters, an organization that cooperated with the Friends of the Earth in compiling congressional votes, gave Church a respectable 73 percent rating. Another ecologist went so far as to describe Church as "the best we have" on environmental issues, precisely because his experience "with the realities of Idaho politics" had sharpened his awareness about what was politically possible.[15]

Church himself believed that most of his constituents were sympathetic to conservation as long as they did not view it as a threat to their livelihood. If they had to choose between their jobs and conservation, they would quite understandably opt for their jobs. "Farmers, miners, ranchers – that's how people make their living in the state," he said, "so I try to support their legitimate interests." Balancing those interests with environmental needs was, of course, the heart of the issue and a severe political test. Church found hope in his perception that the old arguments of the user groups no longer had the hold they once did. The political challenge was to take advantage of this subtle transformation in constituent attitudes.[16]

Within Idaho, a defensive strategy and buying time sometimes seemed the best course. To that end, Church struck a bargain with the state's junior senator, Republican Len Jordan. Church and Jordan were an unlikely combination. The Republican rancher, a product of hardscrabble life in remote Idaho regions, including Hells Canyon, had been a staunchly conservative governor in the early Fifties. He had slashed the public school budget by a third; indeed, his funding of state institutions had been so paltry that at one hospital a lone physician cared for four hundred mental patients. An adamant opponent of raising taxes, Jordan had left his successor with a substantial state debt. He had also been a leading advocate of private power development, including the right of Idaho Power to build a dam in Hells Canyon. Jordan had entered the Senate in 1962, upon the sudden death of the equally conservative Henry Dworshak. In 1966 he had won a big reelection victory. By then, however, he had begun to moderate his views, and within the next few years he even started to question the Vietnam war.[17]

By all accounts, Church and the elderly Jordan grew rather close. Church perhaps recalled the advice of John Carver, his first administrative assistant, who had once advised against getting "in a spitting contest with Henry Dworshak," Jordan's predecessor. Carver's advice was elementary: sitting senators do not run against each other, so they have little to gain by engaging in political combat. More than good politics informed the Church/Jordan relationship, however. Despite their differing political philosophies, they came to respect, trust, and even like each other. Their staffs got along well enough that at one point they had a joint softball team in the Capitol League.[18]

Church and Jordan compromised on dam-building in Idaho. Jordan worried that the state needed more water for irrigation. He viewed the Snake as a working river whose water and power were essential to the state's economy; and he wanted to dam parts of the Salmon river as well, diverting it to southern Idaho through a series of reservoirs. Church worried, too, but by now about the huge environmental price that dams exacted. The two senators decided on a temporary solution. In 1968 they co-sponsored a ten-year moratorium on building more dams on the Middle Snake to allow for additional study. Jordan assumed that further investigation would prove the need for development; Church believed that time was on the side of preservation. Politically, each hoped to gain from putting a hold on dam-building. "He understood my position," Church recalled. "I understood his. It happened to serve both our purposes at the time to vote for a moratorium." For the next several years they tried to get the moratorium bill through Congress.[19]

While preservationists initially saw the moratorium as a way to block the development of Hells Canyon, through which flowed the last free-running stretch of the Middle Snake, many soon judged it a liability. Continued study held up the possible inclusion of the Middle Snake under the Wild and Scenic Rivers Act, and it did nothing to prevent commercialization of land alongside the river. By the 1970s the Hells Canyon Preservation Council decided that Church, "in the past a good conservationist," was wrong on the moratorium. The council now turned to political allies from outside Idaho, especially Senator Robert Packwood (R.-Oregon) and Representative John Saylor (R.-Pennsylvania), sponsors of a National Rivers bill which would protect the Snake's turbulent 120-mile rush through the deep, rugged canon.[20]

Church fretted that impatient preservationists were about to destroy the "delicate balance" that he had worked out with Jordan. Events, he was convinced, would show the wisdom of maintaining that balance and buying time for conservation.[21]

A controversy in the craggy mountains of central Idaho turned up the political heat. In the late Sixties a New York firm, the American Smelting and Refining Company, proposed a huge open-pit molybdenum mine in Idaho's stunningly beautiful White Clouds area, where jagged peaks, studded with glacial lakes, soared to almost twelve thousand feet. Church quickly rallied to the preservationists, introducing legislation to turn the contested federal lands into a Sawtooth-White Cloud national park and recreation area, and drawing fire from constituents who believed he favored, in the words of one indignant citizen, "the so called flower sniffers, bird watchers, mother nature lovers and the hippies." Jordan's support of Church underlined the importance of the two senators' working relationship. Although their bill won Senate approval without opposition in mid-1969, it remained stuck in the House Interior Committee, partly because of the opposition of Idaho Representative

James McClure, no friend of environmentalists. Governor Don Samuelson was likewise an opponent. He defended the mining company's plan as a way of creating new jobs and businesses. "They are not going to tear down mountains," he reportedly said. "They are only going to dig a hole." Church, still trying to get something of value from the deteriorating situation, eventually agreed to drop the more comprehensive national park idea in favor of a national recreation area, which would be less restrictive regarding multiple purpose usage.[22]

As the national park proposal bumped to a halt, in part because the Forest Service sided with the mining and timber interests, some environmentalists criticized Church for not fighting hard enough. One of them complained that he had "failed to stand by his initial convictions when the heat was put on him." Such comments piqued the usually unflappable senator, who countered that "some avant garde conservationist groups in Idaho" were "purists." They reminded him of what Oregon senator Wayne Morse had once said about unions. "Wayne Morse always voted for unions," Church explained, "but he crossed them one time and they said he sold out!"[23]

In 1970 the White Clouds issue continued to agitate Idaho's politics and became a centerpiece of the gubernatorial campaign. The Democratic candidate, Church's old friend Cecil Andrus, loudly protested against mining in the White Clouds area and campaigned on a "quality of life" theme. Governor Samuelson began to waver as mail flooded his desk in opposition to eastern mining interests who would savage Idaho's scenic areas. Presenting himself as a defender of the environment, Samuelson moved his television advertising into the great outdoors. Using sky and stream backdrops, he pledged "Clean air and clean water in a clean state." His bid for reelection fell short by ten thousand votes. That fall, environmental issues helped to make Cecil Andrus Idaho's first Democratic governor since 1946. Four years later Church helped to make the Sawtooth/White Cloud National Recreation Area a reality.[24]

Although the political pendulum seemed to be moving toward environmentalism, Church in the early Seventies nevertheless continued to stand by his dam-building moratorium agreement with Len Jordan. He watched anxiously in mid-1971 when a new Idaho environmentalist group, the Coalition to Save the Snake, endorsed immediate passage of the Packwood-Saylor National Rivers bill. Len Jordan, incensed because the Packwood-Saylor proposal jeopardized Idaho's access to irrigation water, dubbed it the "Snake River Water Export Bill of 1971." Determined to protect their moratorium compromise, Church and Jordan were clearly unhappy with Packwood.[25]

The Oregon senator nevertheless persisted, threatening in mid-1971 to offer his bill on the Senate floor as a substitute for the moratorium proposal, which the Interior Committee had unanimously approved. Although he suddenly became the hero of many conservation groups, especially the Hells Canyon Preservation Council, and although he gathered more than two dozen co-sponsors for his bill, cynics attacked him for grandstanding and needlessly dividing the conservation cause. Members of the Interior Committee were furious at what Jordan described as a legislative "end run." Church countered Packwood's parliamentary move by helping to forge a unanimous front among the other Pacific Northwest senators—Mark Hatfield, Henry Jackson, and Warren Magnuson—and by lobbying other senators. According to one newspaper account, the campaign against Packwood's bill was so successful that co-sponsors "peeled off in droves."[26]

Church's efforts to dissuade Packwood's co-sponsors reaped dividends, reportedly in the specific case of Minnesota Democrat Walter Mondale, but sparked rumors that the Idaho senator was treating Packwood "vindictively." Aide Mike Wetherell, speaking for Church, sharply rejected such accusations: "To say that it is vindictive to attempt to defend a long-held position, worked out carefully over years of negotiation, is a serious distortion." In Church's estimation, if anyone was vindictive it was Packwood, whose unyielding tactics had jeopardized the dam-building moratorium in Congress. Underlying the substantive issues was something else: Church's integrity. As long as Jordan remained in the Senate, Church wanted to respect their agreement on a moratorium. That agreement was basic to the working relationship that made possible Jordan's assistance on a variety of state-related concerns, including the battle for the Sawtooth/White Clouds National Recreation Area. In Church's estimation, keeping his word to Jordan did not constitute a betrayal of the conservationist cause. After all, he insisted, the moratorium would help preserve Hells Canyon by keeping dams out of it.[27]

Under pressure, Packwood on June 25 chose not to substitute his bill for the moratorium. He nevertheless claimed a victory because the Interior Committee agreed to hold hearings that fall on his proposal. Ironically, Packwood owed a lot to Church: the Idaho senator had prevailed upon Henry Jackson to schedule the hearings. Church's quarrel had never been with Packwood's ultimate objective of saving the Middle Snake. But in the interim, Church was fiercely determined to protect the moratorium, both to gain time for Hells Canyon and to honor his agreement to Jordan.[28]

Caught between ardent environmentalists and Idaho's mining, logging, and private power interests, Church was hard pressed to please anyone. His sympathies, however, were clearly much more with the environmentalists. One environmentalist, in fact, claimed that Idaho's mining industry regarded the senator as "an enemy" and had placed him on its "blacklist." However true that may have been, Church was indeed basically suspicious of natural resource developers. In 1970 he supported federal clean water and clean air legislation as well as the establishment of the Environmental Protection Agency. Believing that environmental questions seldom yielded simple answers, he nevertheless thought the debate belonged essentially to the conservationists. Significantly, the organizations outside Congress that he considered most knowledgeable on environmental issues included no representatives of business and industry. Instead, the sixteen groups that he listed as his main sources of information ranged from the National Wildlife Federation and Sierra Club to the Wilderness Society and Friends of the Earth. And, although environmentalists sometimes quarreled with him, there was no doubt that he had their backing. In 1972, for example, the National Wildlife Federation recognized him as its "outstanding conservation legislator."[29]

By then, his impatience with corporate land users was increasingly apparent. During a set of hearings in April 1971 he sharply questioned representatives of the timber interests. Thumbing skeptically through a brightly colored, glossy booklet that the Weyerhaeuser company had prepared in defense of clearcutting policies, he asked Weyerhaeuser's senior vice president, F. Lowry Wyatt, if clearcut forests really resembled the lovely regions in the booklet's photographs. Wyatt conceded that it would take a while for them to appear that way. "In other words," countered Church, "your forests don't actually look like this." Wyatt admitted that they did not, but he hoped they would soon. Church warned that multiple use environmental policies could all too easily become a polite cover for actions that in fact foreclosed more than one use. "Show me an open-faced mine and then show me another use of the area," he said. Clearcutting presented a similar problem.

As Church put it, "A large piece of clearcut land has obviously usurped other uses. Logging has become the dominant use." Gary Eisler, testifying on behalf of the Friends of the Earth, found Church's behavior a welcome contrast with that of other senators who deferred to the timber industry's advocates and either walked out or lost interest when conservationists testified. According to Eisler, Church won "the approval of conservation-minded witnesses."[30]

II

Church also displayed a growing impatience with the plight of the nation's elderly citizens, and in their defense he collided with the Nixon administration. By the 1970s older Americans had become one of Church's strongest constituencies. Such had not been the case a decade earlier, when polls had showed him doing least well with the aged. Verda Barnes may have been partly responsible for the change. The most knowledgeable person in the senator's office about day-to-day developments back home, she spent considerable time contacting people in Idaho, using the telephone "like a maestro," as Mike Wetherell recalled. It was Barnes who convinced Church to get on the new special Committee on Aging. Starting in 1959, it had been a six-person subcommittee of the Labor and Public Welfare Committee; in 1961, it had become a large special committee with a purely investigatory mission. When Barnes advised Church to seek one of its fifteen positions, he had not been enthusiastic. Years later, he laughingly described how he had told her, "I don't think I'm that interested." Tossing her dyed, reddish-blond hair, she had responded, "You will be." She was right. Church never regretted joining the committee, and his interest in it genuinely grew.[31]

The appearance in 1961 of one of the Senate's youngest members on the new committee struck some observers as paradoxical. An elderly, outspoken Senate elevator operator asked Church why he was going to a particular floor. Church explained that he was a new member of the Committee on Aging. The puzzled operator stared at the senator, in his mid-thirties, and then sighed that only the government could think up an arrangement like that.[32]

Of Aging's seven subcommittees, Church served on the one that investigated the consumer interests of the elderly. Starting in 1968 he presided over it, looking into the prices and quality of such things as prescription drugs, hearing aids, and nursing homes. In January 1971 he stepped up to the chairmanship of the entire Committee on Aging, thus becoming the first Idaho senator in almost four decades to chair a full committee.

Politics and conscience fused nicely for Church on the committee. When he endorsed legislative ideas springing from it, Verda Barnes was anxious to get out a press release. "This is potent stuff for oldsters!" she remarked. But the committee assignment was no mere public relations ploy for the young senator. This was abundantly clear to Pat and William Oriol, who knew as much about the committee as anyone. Pat Oriol had been its first staff employee, starting in 1959 when it was still part of the Labor and Public Welfare Committee; Bill Oriol had come to it in 1961, as an aide to chairman Harrison Williams (D-New Jersey), and by the late Sixties he was staff director. Church, upon taking charge of the committee in 1971, met with Bill Oriol to discuss the coming agenda. Oriol was dazzled. Church emphasized that his overriding goal was to eliminate poverty among older Americans. To do this, he wanted to make adjustments in the Social Security system, an area that his predecessor Harrison Williams had generally left to the powerful Senate Finance Committee. As Church summed up his views on Social Security and on ending poverty among the aged, Oriol sat transfixed. "I looked at him. We were the only ones in the room, but the way he was telling me this—well, it was inspiring." Oriol "kept looking to see if there was anybody else in the room, and there wasn't." Church was expressing his own sentiments, not speaking for public effect. Over the next few years the senator turned the Aging Committee, despite its purely advisory capacity, into a significant force on Capitol Hill.[33]

As the committee's new leader, Church clashed immediately with the Nixon administration, charging that it was trying "to balance the budget on the backs of sick old people." He castigated the administration for opposing an increase of slightly more than 6 percent in Social Security benefits, a sum that barely matched the overall cost of living and ignored the huge jump in fees—medical, rental, and transportation—that especially hurt the elderly. Church's criticism came as the *New York Times* warned, in a headline, "Many Aging Face an Economic Nightmare." In southern Florida, for example, police arrested a sixty-nine-year-old widow who had stolen a twenty-five cent can of soup; older citizens rummaged through garbage cans; and a group known as "Save Our Seniors" emerged. According to the Committee on Aging, poverty had declined in the late 1960s among all age groups—except for citizens over sixty-five, where it had increased.[34]

Church was able in 1971 to help push into law a 15 percent increase in Social Security benefits, despite President Nixon's threats to veto anything over 10 percent. *Washington Post* columnist Colman McCarthy wrote that "the administration was again kicked from a position of initial stubbornness to a reluctant concession, like a mule being kicked in the rump to a new pasture." Church believed that McCarthy had accurately summed up the situation.[35]

One of Church's boldest moves was to call for an income supplement program. On April 26, 1971 he introduced legislation to boost Social Security payments (through general Treasury revenues) so that no elderly citizens fell under the poverty line. He pointed out that 25 percent of Americans over age sixty-five lived below that level. "In this richest of nations," he told the Senate, "it is unnecessary and unpardonable that five million older Americans should be forced to endure poverty. We have the capacity to end this dreadful condition, and we must do it."[36]

In the summer of 1972, Church successfully led the way in enacting one of the most important reforms in the history of the nation's Social Security program. On June 30 his amendment to the debt ceiling legislation passed the Senate 82 to 4, and the House 302 to 35. Nixon, facing huge congressional majorities, signed it into law the next day. It raised Social Security benefits by 20 percent, the largest dollar increase since the program had started in 1935. Although Church had not gotten his proposed income supplement program for the aged (and the blind and handicapped as well), his amendment boosted above the poverty line almost one-third of the individuals over sixty-five who had been below it. Over the long term, the amendment did something more influential than raise benefits substantially: it provided for automatic cost-of-living adjustments to help protect the elderly against inflation. Those automatic adjustments ultimately fell under fire for helping to fuel inflation and contributing to what became a staggering federal deficit. But as Church aide Cleve Corlett emphasized, the senator viewed the amendment as fiscally conservative because it would regularize the Social Security system, making it more streamlined and predictable. It would tie raises in benefits to the pace of inflation and thereby help to remove them from the vagaries of politics.[37]

Although Church believed that older Americans suffered most from insufficient income, he worked also to extend a variety of federally funded services to them, including legal aid, home repairs, low-cost meals at conveniently located centers, reduced airline fares, and more protection against fraud. He recommended establishing an Office on Aging at the White House level. He also addressed the controversial problem of using artificial means to keep terminally ill patients alive. In August 1972 the Committee on Aging conducted hearings on the subject of "death with dignity." Church raised the fundamental question, "When is an illness truly so hopeless that no fight should be made against it?" Although there was no agreement on the answer, the hearings were symbolically important. Never before had the Senate addressed the issue of "death with dignity," let alone listened to a preponderance of professional witnesses who favored it. A month later, Church advocated the establishment of a World Assembly on Aging to grapple with the "retirement revolution" that was already shaking the social and economic foundations of many nations.[38]

On the Aging Committee staff, Bill and Pat Oriol watched all this with delight. In their view, Church was "a masterful legislator"–"eloquent, determined, and skilled." He effectively set the committee's agenda, worked hard, and made his own commitments clear. Many times he told the Oriols that nothing gave him more pleasure than helping the elderly, especially in his home state. "He did not hesitate to use the word love," recalled Bill Oriol. Nor did Bethine Church, whose visits to Idaho nursing homes became legendary.[39]

Around the country as well as in Idaho, the senator's reputation grew rapidly among groups of older Americans. In 1973, the newly established Senior Advocates International named him as its first "Senior Advocate," credited him with "almost single-handedly" securing the increase in Social Security payments, and featured him on the cover of its magazine. And a year later, the National Council of Senior Citizens gave him an Award of Merit as a "leading voice in Congress" for the elderly. The citation said that he had demonstrated "massive" concern for America's aged.[40]

III

His concern for the elderly reminded him once again of the terrible social costs of the Vietnam conflict. "We could abolish poverty among the elderly for what it costs to run the war in Southeast Asia for just three months," Church informed the Senate in early 1972.[41]

Bitter at the war's skewing of national priorities, Church also worried that the Vietnam conflict imperiled democracy within the United States. He was alarmed, for example, when the U. S. government, for the first time in American history, used the power of prior restraint to block the publication of information. In mid-1971, President Nixon ordered the Justice Department to stop the *New York Times* and other newspapers from publishing the "Pentagon Papers," the Defense Department's secret history of U. S. involvement in Vietnam before 1967. "Critics of the war would use them to attack my goals and my policies," Nixon later explained. The president was also responding to National Security Advisor Henry Kissinger's warning that publication of the papers threatened national security and the administration's ability to conduct foreign policy. "It shows you're a weakling, Mr. President," Kissinger reportedly told him. To Frank Church's relief, the Supreme Court ruled against the administration and allowed publication of the "Pentagon Papers." Church had vociferously criticized the Justice Department's injunction as censorship and as a threat to the fundamental freedoms of speech and press.[42]

By the 1970s the dangers of concentrating too much power in any one individual or institution had perhaps never been more evident to Church. It was thus not surprising that he seemed preoccupied with thoughts about power and democracy when an aspiring young Delaware politician, Joseph Biden, stopped by his office in 1971. Biden, only twenty-nine years old, was thinking about running for the Senate the next year. He looked upon Church as a kind of model, someone who fifteen years earlier had done exactly what Biden hoped to do: defy the odds and become a "boy senator." The conversation surprised Biden somewhat. Church talked less about winning and holding office than about power and responsibility in a democracy. His message had a strong Jeffersonian twist, as Biden recalled, reflecting both a "happy disrespect for power" and a great concern about its misuse. It seemed to Biden that Church was "sort of like the conscience of the Senate when it comes to power."[43]

IV

Increasingly, Church's thinking resonated with that of the "movement" side of the 1960s and early 1970s—moralistic, skeptical of privileged elites, and anxious to deliver "power to the people." He had always been somewhat more radical in private than in public, and that side of him stirred restlessly as he contemplated the seemingly endless war and recent American politics. "I sometimes think that the Senate resembles a fudge factory, where we shape each piece, slicing a little here, adding a little there, but where the recipe never changes and the candy stays the same," he said cynically in 1971. The beneficiaries were not the masses of people, but "the big interests. . . by which I mean big government, big business, and big labor." These huge interests, he said, "seem always able to command a majority, no matter how unprincipled or outrageous their legislative proposal might be."[44]

"To a certain extent there were two Frank Churches," recalled Jerry Levinson, an aide who worked closely with the senator in the early 1970s. One of them reflected what the senator's friend Bryce Nelson described as the "prairie radical tendencies" of a George Norris or William Jennings Bryan. "He had a gut-level response," remembered aide Garry Wenske, "to any sort of domination of one person over another." In this regard he perhaps recalled with distaste his own childhood experiences, when bullies had driven him out of St. Joseph's grade school. Correspondingly, his brother Richard suspected that he had left the Catholic Church partly because he disapproved of its authoritarian nature, its efforts to tell others what to do and think. Whatever the sources of his conviction, Frank Church as a senator still chafed at the efforts of powerful nations, groups, or individuals to impose their will on those who were weaker. Levinson remembered driving Church to work through the heavy traffic on MacArthur Boulevard, listening to him inveigh against big business and the power brokers of the East Coast elite. Another aide recalled Church's comment that a well-known adviser to John Kennedy and Lyndon Johnson was "just too Ivy League." Then, with embarrassment, Church realized that the aide was a Harvard graduate. He smiled and said apologetically, "You know what I mean." The Frank Church who criticized someone for being too Ivy League occasionally struggled with himself—a self that had establishment leanings and that, as Levinson and others pointed out, courted approval from some of the very elites that he otherwise disliked.[45]

Speechwriter Bill Hall believed that Church fell "between two worlds." In Idaho, the senator had to contend with charges that he was "a fancy pants, eastern sort." But back East there were reminders of the snobbish disdain with which some people viewed a product of the mountain West. Early in his Senate career Church heard that *Washington*

Post publisher Katherine Graham had reportedly described him as "that cowboy from Idaho." Years later, the alleged comment still rankled. When Hall once expressed admiration for Graham, Church snapped, completely out of character, "She's a bitch." According to Hall, the senator resented slights that he was "a western hick."[46]

He was proud of his modest background and origins. After almost two decades of living in the Washington. D. C., area he could still say that he had "no feeling of belonging to this city." His sense of who he was never really changed. Although he enjoyed dealing with important people, he remained basically "the kid from Idaho" who never lost sight of his roots. His speaking mannerisms and what some friends recognized as shyness made him sometimes appear pompous, but he was in fact remarkably free of concerns about status.[47]

Even during the heady days when he first entered the Senate as a kind of political whiz kid, he kept his success in proportion. David Underhill, who later joined his staff, remembered walking as a young teenager into the senator's Boise office to introduce himself. Church made the youngster feel entirely at ease, chatting at length with him. Underhill ended up at Church's home that afternoon, helping the senator paste green stamps in a coupon booklet.[48]

By the Seventies, Church regretted that he was becoming "the Senator," even to people who had known him for years. When a former high school classmate apologized with some embarrassment after using his old nickname of "Frosty," Church laughingly reassured him: "Call me anything but 'the Boy Orator.' " Political scientist Ross Baker believed that, "of all the members of Congress I worked for, Frank Church was the most accessible and approachable." According to Baker he "shunned and abhorred snobs and people who traded on social connections."[49]

Bill Hall agreed. By the time Hall joined Church's staff in 1975 the long-time reporter was one of the most knowledgeable observers of Idaho politics. Himself an Idaho product, Hall loved the state even as he infuriated many of its residents with a biting satire in the tradition of the best journalistic humorists. A medium-sized, quick-witted man with a zest for letting the air out of inflated egos, Hall later described himself as a kind of plague that beset Idaho's senior senator. He remembered getting lost when driving Church to an interview and ending up as perhaps the "only aide in Washington who was regularly chauffeured about the city by a United States senator." Church, in Hall's estimation, was "the least of the Senate's many prima donnas."[50]

Church invariably treated his staff with respect, consideration, and graciousness. Granted, he tended to be formal and somewhat reserved. "Other senators I have worked for or been around would use a little bit of profanity and describe their real inner feelings," said Patrick Shea. "Church, from my perspective, rarely did that." Moreover, as Mike Wetherell observed, he "did expect his staff to be solicitous of him. He was not called by his first name," for example. Yet many people who worked for him felt they were more than mere employees; they were people about whom he seemed genuinely to care. Even staff people who considered themselves at the bottom of his office's administrative ladder appreciated his interest in "us little folks," as one put it.[51]

By the 1970s, more than ever, Church displayed a growing wariness of elite "experts," whom he increasingly saw as constituting a modern "priesthood." Unlike senators such as J. William Fulbright, he tended to remain apart from academics and the various foreign policy "think tanks" in Washington, D. C. A curious staff member in the mid-Seventies once checked the senator's Rolodex to see which foreign policy experts it included. The name of only one academic appeared, and even here the Rolodex card contained a parenthetic note: "old Idaho friend." Church's aides guessed that he simply trusted his own expertise in foreign policy. As usual, he remained the loner, keeping to himself, relying mainly upon his own judgments, his staff, and the advice of his best friend and critic, Bethine. "He used to say that there is nothing very complicated about foreign policy," remembered Bill Hall. "It's treating other people the way that you would like to be treated." Certainly Church was not much impressed with the way in which the "expert" makers of foreign policy had led the U. S. into the Vietnam war. "When one considers the shambles in Asia," he told journalist Sam Day regarding U. S. policy, "we might have done better with Mickey Mouse than with Dean Rusk." Church liked America's faith in representative government because, as he informed a group of high school students, it rested on the premise "that the rank-and-file citizen, and not just the 'big-shot,' is capable of passing judgment on major policies. . . ." Tom Dine suspected, however, that something other than ideology was at work here; he sensed that Church felt uncomfortable with the tiny circle of the foreign policy elite.[52]

This discomfort was evident in Church's relationship with the prestigious Council on Foreign Relations, into whose ranks he had been invited in 1963. Since its emergence in the aftermath of World War I, the privately-funded Council had favored leaving American foreign policy in the control of a small group of informed experts—like the Council's self-selecting members, who were mainly well-established bankers, lawyers, academics, and journalists. Following World War II it helped to provide the rationale for the activist, international U. S. foreign policy of the Cold War. Its defenders portrayed it as "the school for statesmen," or as a public-spirited "post-graduate academy of political science." But right-wing critics placed its five-story headquarters in New York City's fashionable Park Avenue district at the center of a dark conspiracy to deliver America to domestic subversives and foreign control.[53]

Frank Church laughed off the conspiracy theories. When his friend, Bayless A. Manning, the dean of Stanford University's law school, became the Council's president in 1971, Church jokingly congratulated him "for becoming a Captain of the imperialists!" By then, however, Church counted himself "a rebellious member of [the Council's] crew."[54]

The rebellion with which Church identified was part of a larger democratic assault on many organizations and institutions. The "movement" culture of the Sixties was continuing to spread, despite the disarray, disillusionment, and internal discord that wracked its various parts. Its challenges to the traditional distribution of power were both social and intellectual, jeopardizing customary "old boy" networks and the legitimacy of modern "experts." From professions such as psychiatry and medicine, to academic disciplines such as history and anthropology, dissenters rejected conventional formalities and elitism.[55]

The winds of change also buffeted the Council on Foreign Relations. This was hardly astonishing, given the foreign policy establishment's role in the Vietnam war and also the Council's membership—mainly, as one reporter said, "rich guys with a passion for respectability." Harvard's liberal economist John Kenneth Galbraith resigned, describing the organization as "the seat of boredom." When the board voted narrowly in 1969 to admit women, one member said it was equivalent to the conservative "Union League taking in Communists." Another member left the stormy meeting in tears. Over the next several years the Council wrestled with how much it should accommodate change. Some members urged the organization to open its doors to a diversity of opinion and people; others warned against rushing to reform. "Contrary to the theology of radical chic," groused one member who was suspicious of some of the proposed changes, "the issue of 'democratic governance' is a phony. . . ." Another skeptic resented "the disaffection with the Establishment" that had given rise to "every kind of minority group" and to "bad taste"; he urged the Council not to fall victim to "fads": "A non-Establishment Council would be a contradiction in terms."[56]

After initially aligning himself with the Council's reformers, Church resigned in early 1973. He objected to the rigidity of the organization's perceptions and its elitist composition. In his opinion, the group suffered "from far too much in-breeding," from the old guard's continuing control, from unrepresentative membership, and from an aversion to dissent and "revisionist" points of view. Although his letter of resignation indicated only that he no longer had the time for membership, he subsequently explained that he had left the Council because it was "too Presidentially-oriented."[57]

V

Far more consequential than Church's departure from the Council was his celebrated break, in late 1971, from the Cold War wisdom about foreign aid. Foreign aid had been one of the foundations of U. S. internationalism since World War II. It was both a humanitarian response to help nations in need and, increasingly, an economic weapon in the Cold War struggle for influence over developing countries. From the 1940s into the 1970s, critics of foreign aid typically had to fend off charges that they were isolationists, oblivious to America's responsibilities in a larger world. Some of the critics believed simply that foreign aid was a waste of money, or was a diversion of money abroad that should instead go toward assisting Americans at home. Other critics were more ideological. The aid program smacked of imperialism to those on the left, while the more dominant right-wing opponents viewed it as an international plot to bleed America's economy in behalf of communistic, or one-world, causes.

Church had entered the Senate as a strong supporter of foreign aid, despite its unpopularity in Idaho. A Harris poll showed that 55 percent of Idaho's citizens in the early 1960s opposed sending aid abroad, while only 29 percent favored it and 16 percent were unsure. "I believe I am the first elected representative from Idaho who has ever supported foreign aid," Church told one constituent in mid-1961. "This involves a very serious political risk on my part, which I would not take if I did not feel that the country's vital interests did not require it." Although he conceded that the program had weaknesses, he believed that it was essential "for our own national survival."[58]

Early on, however, he had voiced reservations about the continuation of aid to wealthy countries and about military assistance programs. In the mid-Sixties his growing doubts about foreign aid brought him into momentary conflict with Bethine. Over dinner one evening she objected furiously upon learning that he might vote against a foreign aid bill. She "went through the roof," as Forrest Church recalled. "She exploded." In her opinion, cutting off foreign aid would be a foolish retreat to pre-World War II isolationism. Her husband's reply, which he articulated in numerous speeches over the next several years, was that U. S. foreign aid had become a huge pork barrel from which petty military dictators were feeding, rather than a source of aid to peasants who truly needed support. By the end of the Sixties he was completely disillusioned with the ideological base upon which U. S. foreign aid rested. He concluded that, insofar as America offered economic assistance abroad, it should do so to save people from want, not from communism. It was time, he told Carl Marcy on the Foreign Relations Committee in 1968, to stop using foreign aid as an instrument of Cold War foreign policy.[59]

On October 29, 1971, Church bade a formal "farewell to foreign aid," helping to lead the Senate to a surprise 41 to 27 defeat of the foreign aid authorization bill. The vote was more a product of circumstance than anything else. Conservatives were still unhappy about a United Nations vote several days earlier expelling Nationalist China (Taiwan) and admitting the People's Republic of China. Many delegates from third world countries, some of which had been receiving U. S. aid dollars, had celebrated the occasion by cheering and dancing in the aisles. Senators who were eager to punish such displays of ingratitude thus joined their "dove" colleagues who were still steaming about the removal of the Cooper-Church amendment from the aid bill. While some senators were concerned mainly with penalizing disloyal foreign allies, others, such as Church, hoped to send a message to the White House.[60]

In his long Senate speech, Church said goodbye not only to foreign aid, but to the central assumptions that had guided U. S. foreign policy in recent years. Americans, he remarked, had confidently believed presidential adviser Walt Rostow's assurance "that we are the greatest power in the world—if we behave like it." But, unfortunately, "behaving like it" had meant that the U. S. had thrown around its power and money, fighting a war to keep the peace, and backing military dictatorships in the name of freedom. The deficiencies of the aid program mirrored the larger failures of U. S. foreign policy; the flaws were systemic, products of faulty concepts and poor politics. Church shrugged aside the theories of Rostow and others regarding economic development. He predicted that the coming revolutions in Third World nations would "bear no resemblance to the kind of benign, gradual 'takeoff' into self-sustaining growth envisioned by American aid officials and private investors." Such faith in stable development overlooked the sad realities that U. S. aid mainly supported corrupt and oppressive dictatorships, while the wounds and grievances of the dispossessed masses festered. "However much we may have wanted reform and development," he charged, "we wanted 'stability,' anti-communism and a favorable climate of investment more." Indeed, he said, "Our foreign aid program has become a spreading money tree under which the biggest American businesses find shelter when they invest abroad."[61]

It was time, Church pleaded, to cut through the abstractions to some unlovely truths. There were two real beneficiaries of U. S. aid programs: repressive foreign governments, not their citizens; and American corporations, not the American people. Church had no quarrel with a real foreign aid program, one that truly helped people in impoverished countries. But he wanted nothing more to do with a "program which has been twisted into a parody and a farce." In a moving peroration, he told the Senate that "the dilemma of aid lies not abroad, not in the slums of Calcutta or in the rural backlands of Brazil, but in ourselves." The challenge, he said, was to recognize that the United States could not reshape other countries in its own image or permanently hold back revolutions.[62]

Church's speech received considerable attention. The *Washington Post* reprinted most of it on the front page of its Sunday "Outlook" section, and *The American Legion Magazine* paired him in a debate with Senator Charles H. Percy (R-Illinois) over ending foreign aid. Church also gave a lengthy explanation, "Why I Voted No," in the liberal *New Republic* magazine.[63]

Church chose not to circulate the full text of his Senate speech in Idaho. There was, of course, no problem within the state regarding his opposition to the foreign aid bill. It was the nature of his argument that might stir controversy. As he told Carl Burke, "I think you'll agree that it's much too radical." He expressed surprise that the bill had failed.

"The administration collectively must have turned 10 shades of green," he wrote. There was no doubt that Richard Nixon placed a high priority on the aid programs, which he described as basic to "the whole conduct of our national security policy." The Nixon Doctrine, the president informed Senate minority leader Hugh Scott, meant that the U. S. would protect its interests abroad "*less* by direct involvement and *more* by supporting the efforts of others." Without the aid programs, America's interests and allies would be "left high and dry." Here, certainly, was reason enough for the White House to resent Church's role in the Senate's October rejection of the foreign aid authorization bill.[64]

Church continued to bore in on the administration, attacking with special fury its response to the war that broke out in 1971 between Pakistan and India. Since 1947, Pakistan had been a geographically and culturally divided nation. Political and economic power rested in West Pakistan while, a thousand miles on the other side of India, East Pakistan seethed with resentment and unrest. When 97 percent of the voters in East Pakistan indicated in December 1970 that they favored autonomy, President Yahya Khan in West Pakistan sent troops. An incredible bloodbath ensued as the attackers cut off women's breasts and gouged out children's eyes. The West Pakistan army slaughtered perhaps as many as three million people in unbelievably brutal fashion. Around ten million refugees fled for safety into India. On December 3, 1971, Yahya Khan launched air strikes against Indian airfields, bringing India into the war.[65]

Kenneth Keating, the U. S. ambassador to India, pleaded that America keep its distance from this "reign of military terror," but the Nixon administration was determined to inflate the horrific regional conflict into a Cold War confrontation. Nixon, already privately laying the groundwork for a groundbreaking trip to China, viewed Yahya as a crucial player in the administration's secret negotiations with Peking. The president also despised India's Prime Minister Indira Gandhi, whom he believed was plotting with the Soviets to take over Pakistan. Nixon and Henry Kissinger thus insisted on turning the situation into a global showdown with the Soviet Union. As Kissinger advised the president, "We can't allow a friend [Pakistan] of ours and China's to get screwed in a conflict with a friend of Russia's." Despite the unspeakable atrocities of the Yahya regime, Nixon instructed his National Security Advisor "to tilt toward Pakistan," a comment that news columnist Jack Anderson made public.[66]

Frank Church was incredulous and charged the administration with "gross ineptitude." His opinion rested in part on information that the former U. S. ambassador to India, Chester Bowles, wrote him about the Pakistan-India conflict. But, primarily, he drew upon his own observations. In late November he and Ohio Republican William Saxbe visited India to gather information for the Senate Foreign Relations Committee. The suffering and horror that he encountered were so devastating that, for several weeks after his return to the U. S., he could "think of little else." Unlike the administration, he complimented India for its compassionate treatment, over eight months, of some ten million refugees—fourteen times as many people as resided in Idaho. He also came away convinced that the heartrending tragedy's immediate cause was the refusal of Yahya Khan to accept the results of the December 1970 elections. Looking ahead, he predicted that Pakistan could "never be put back together again." A crowd of young East Bengalis, shouting "Recognize Bangla Desh," had driven this point home to him as they surrounded his car on a road into the refugee camps. The Nixon administration must have found especially galling Church's sympathetic portrait of Indira Gandhi, with whom he had talked. As if that were not enough, Church also rebuked the U. S. government for not speaking out against the deplorable actions of West Pakistan's military junta and called for a policy of complete neutrality, in which the U.S. would aid neither side.[67]

Church's December 6 Senate speech, which the speaker of India's parliament said "could not have been a better, more accurate and objective assessment," blamed the administration for misreading the situation completely. By favoring Pakistan, Church contended, "we have ended up siding with a loser, once again." America had no business taking sides in this war: indeed, the U. S.'s quick judgment that India was the aggressor "comes with ill grace. . . . How long could we have waited to strike back had a bloody massacre in Mexico led to the influx of 10 million Mexican refugees into southern California, New Mexico, and Arizona?" In fact, he added, "the United States should be the last in the world" to cast aspersions on India for its alleged aggression. "If India has intervened in the civil war of her neighbor, we did the same in Vietnam with far less provocation."[68]

Henry Kissinger had already warned the Indian ambassador to Washington "that no matter how much you succeed in influencing important senators, you have to deal with this administration and that means the President." In fact, Kissinger dismissed the opposition of congressional leaders such as Church on grounds that they were simply looking for "any excuse for attacking the President." This was not the view in India, however, according to A. K. Dutta Chowdhury, who helped to run the refugee relief camps. Writing to Church in early 1972, as the war ended and Bangladesh emerged as a new nation, he praised the senator: "We in India consider you as a great American leader who upholds human values and the cause of human liberty."[69]

VI

For Church, the administration's reckless handling of the India-Pakistan war constituted further proof that the nation desperately needed new leadership. He had collided with the Nixon White House again and again since 1969 over domestic as well as foreign policies. He had, for example, helped to block the confirmation of two Nixon appointees to the Supreme Court, Clement F. Haynsworth and G. Harrold Carswell, both of whom had raised the ire of civil rights groups. "I don't suppose either one of those [votes] flew very well in Idaho," guessed Indiana Democrat Birch Bayh, who led the fights against Haynsworth and Carswell. "Yet Frank was there," as he had promised he would be.[70]

Church also attempted, although unsuccessfully, to stop Nixon's nomination of Earl L. Butz as Secretary of Agriculture. Church was normally inclined to approve a president's cabinet appointees, but he believed there were sufficient reasons to vote against Butz. In his opinion, Butz spoke for large corporate farms and "efficiency" at the expense of small family farms. Church feared that Butz would continue to push America down the road toward "giantism," helping further to bury rural America under an economic system of "huge fiefdoms," worked "by hired hands, on behalf of absentee stockholders, interested only in maximizing their dividends."[71]

Nixon's impoundment of appropriated funds also drew Church's fire. By simply choosing not to expend funds that Congress had designated for certain programs, Nixon was thumbing his nose at the principle of representative government. Church objected as well to the administration's effort not to repeal the excise tax on pickup trucks, as well as on cars. "The Nixon Administration wants to give a tax break to the man who buys a new Cadillac," read one of his reports to Idaho farmers.

"Senator Frank Church thinks the same break ought to also go to the farmer who buys a pickup truck."[72]

During the early 1970s, Church's voting record became even more liberal. In 1971 the American Security Council (a coalition of military leaders, defense industry executives, and other advocates of stronger defense measures) gave him a zero approval rating; and the Americans for Constitutional Action, a conservative group, gave him only 17 percent. In contrast, the liberal Americans for Democratic Action, with whom he had a cumulative 79 percent approval rating going into 1971, jumped him up to 93 percent. He was by then voting against the Nixon administration more often than before, 77 percent of the time in 1971 as compared to 68 percent in the previous two years.[73]

The Senate colleague with whom he voted most often from 1969 through the early Seventies was George McGovern. It was thus no surprise that in 1972 Church aligned himself with the "McGovern revolution" that was transforming the Democratic party.[74]

Church and George McGovern talk in a Senate corridor. *Courtesy Boise State University.*

Chapter Fourteen
"New Politics" and War's End: 1972-1973

LIKE MANY AMERICANS by the 1970s, Frank Church was ready to leave behind the politics of what journalist Theodore White called "the Old Country," a brand of politics that historically had revolved around powerful local groups and bosses, party loyalty, and dividing the spoils of office. The upheavals of the Sixties had suggested the possibilities of a "new politics," committed to issues rather than keeping people in office, and dedicated to what the Students for a Democratic Society (SDS) called "participatory democracy." From SDS to the civil rights movement and the emergence of the counter culture, the struggle had been to open up the system, to break down social and racial barriers, and to encourage grassroots insurgency. Protests against the status quo had spread quickly across the political spectrum, from the New Left's community-organizing campaigns to Alabama governor George Wallace's ringing assaults on liberals and government bureaucrats. In this context, American liberalism itself turned a major ideological corner by emphasizing more than ever rights for the previously disenfranchised and by stressing cultural, or "life style," issues.[1]

Frank Church likewise hoped to open the corridors of power and end politics-as-usual. The Vietnam conflict and domestic crises had fueled his disaffection with the Cold War agenda, with presidential power, and with "experts" who seemingly cared more about technology and numbers than about people. It was imperative, he told Maine Democrat Edmund Muskie in 1971, that the Democrats renounce the "*status quo* politics" that benefitted powerful economic groups and responded far too meekly to prevailing injustices.[2]

Church resembled a rejuvenated New Dealer more than an emerging "life style liberal," however.[3] At heart a cultural traditionalist, he was less attentive to cries for personal liberation than to the growing anguish of middle- and working-class people who felt that mainstream politicians had abandoned them. He continued to endorse civil rights-related issues and, far more than most senators, sided with environmentalists. But he also warned his liberal colleagues not to overlook the economic needs of blue collar and middle-class voters, many of whom were turning to George Wallace, who as a third-party presidential candidate in 1968 had received over 13 percent of the vote, and Richard Nixon. Hoping to expand America's political processes, to enlarge the nation's social and economic agenda, and to steer the country from military adventurism, Church in 1972 backed the presidential candidacy of his friend and ally George McGovern. At one point it appeared that he might even join McGovern on the Democratic ticket. And, in 1973, Church helped to end American combat in Southeast Asia.

I

By the early Seventies, Church sensed that American politics was undergoing a profound transformation. He regretted what he called "the balkanization" of the United States. People seemed unable to communicate with each other, except through intolerant slogans and " 'non-negotiable' demands." Church also lamented the decline of "old-fashioned patriotism" that had once pulled Americans together, even amid the travails of the Great Depression. Many citizens, he observed sadly, no longer believed in their country.[4]

Church understood their discontent. He sympathized with much of the left's critique of Cold War liberalism. Indeed, he himself faulted liberal internationalism for its role in turning the U. S. into a global watchdog. He also recognized that, within the United States, government programs had too often fallen victim to the traditional pork-barrel politics of the status quo. Although he agreed with the left on key points, he empathized as well with the "middle Americans" whom Wallace and Nixon were courting.

Rarely had the media and public officials discovered a group as quickly as they did the middle Americans, a term that typically applied to disgruntled whites. Portrayed as "troubled" and "forgotten," these whites provided the momentum for the political backlash that at the end of the Sixties suddenly captured wide attention. Although middle America contained large numbers of business and white collar people, the media focused primarily upon its blue collar constituency. Even more misleadingly, the media then tended to caricature working-class people as uninformed, bigoted, authoritarian reactionaries. The best-known symbol of this group of middle Americans was Archie Bunker, the prejudiced and narrow-minded character in "All in the Family," the popular television series that began in 1970.[5]

A working class upheaval was in fact underway in the United States, but it was far more complex than the Archie Bunker stereotype allowed. Real grievances fueled the growing resentment of white, working-class families. The Vietnam war, inflation, racial changes, and social policies such as affirmative action appeared to come primarily at their expense. Adding to their political estrangement was a sense that their government had rejected them. In George Wallace's words, the government had fallen into the hands of "pointy-headed, intellectual morons" who were unable "to park a bicycle straight." Wallace capitalized upon working class anger by attacking these "theoreticians and the bureaucrats," and "the liberals, intellectuals and long-hairs [who] have run the country for too long."[6]

Church had no use for Wallace's liberal-baiting or racist demagoguery, but he realized that the Alabama governor had tapped a deep rage and despair in America's lower ranks. "I agree," he wrote a Wallace supporter in Idaho, "that the workingman in the middle is getting the worst of it these days. I don't think it was planned that way, but that is the way it has worked out." Church suspected that blue collar Americans were turning to Wallace largely because they believed their government no longer represented them. In this regard, Church faulted the Democratic Party for having increasingly ignored the working class that had been so vital to the New Deal's liberal coalition. In Church's opinion, the Democrats could stop the social hemorrhaging of their party only by again responding to common citizens.[7]

To rebuild the party's popular base Church believed the Democrats needed " 'Populist' candidates" who would reshape the national agenda. The federal government had to concentrate on the demands of its own people rather than on "which faction should govern some little country on the fringes of China." One of its primary tasks should be to revamp the nation's welfare system, which large numbers of working class Americans viewed as an unfair raid on their hard-earned incomes.[8]

Church was certain that no Democrat could defeat Richard Nixon in 1972 except by substituting a populist strategy for business-as-usual politics. In December 1971 he passed along this advice to Democratic presidential aspirant Edmund Muskie. He warned Muskie that Nixon had captured the nation's middle ground. The Idaho senator liked almost nothing about Nixon, whom he described as "a wooden personality, a conniver, a dissembler; a man without basic conviction, and a vindictive man with a streak of meanness in him." Church insisted nevertheless that Nixon's political achievements had been substantial. Playing the devil's advocate, he told Muskie that Nixon might in fact be the best of the four presidents under whom the two senators had served, going back to Eisenhower. "He is the first President to recognize that we are no longer a market economy," said Church, noting that Nixon had broken somewhat from the usual Republican reliance on market solutions to economic problems. Nixon had, for example, advocated a national growth policy and adopted wage and price controls. As Church viewed the situation, any Democrat who ran a "me-too" campaign in 1972 would have no chance of defeating the president.[9]

Church had simple advice for Muskie: instead of being a status quo candidate, he should help to mobilize the forces of "really significant change." The Maine senator needed to attack the massive outlays to the military, foreign aid, and the space program. "What you have to do," Church urged him, "is to convince people that it is possible to change our spending habits in such a way that the problems at home will be solved." To make his case, Muskie would need to rely heavily on television and demonstrate that he presented a real alternative to Nixon.[10]

When Muskie inquired if his candidacy would have Church's support, the Idaho senator hedged. He preferred George McGovern, who, as president, "would make the most difference in terms of changing directions." McGovern, for example, was determined not to repeat the mistakes of 1968, when Democrats and Republicans alike had succumbed to politics-as-usual with devastating results: a continuing war in Southeast Asia and mounting social crises at home. Church admitted that he felt particularly close to McGovern because of their antiwar battles. The Idaho senator nevertheless conceded that political urgency might push him into Muskie's camp. He was concerned that, as time elapsed, either Hubert Humphrey or Henry Jackson might become the frontrunner. Church decided to endorse no one until McGovern had more time to demonstrate his national strength.[11]

A political waiting game was risky, however, given McGovern's seemingly lost cause. By the start of 1972, McGovern appeared to have little chance of blocking either Humphrey or Jackson, let alone winning the nomination. Jackson's hawkish position on the Vietnam war and on defense spending was unacceptable to Church, even though he otherwise got along well enough with the Washington senator. Church had no enthusiasm for Humphrey, who he believed now epitomized the old politics of narrow interest groups and the status quo. Additionally, as vice president, Humphrey had publicly defended the Vietnam war. "It's not that I don't trust Hubert," Church told an aide, "but I don't."[12]

That left Muskie in the event McGovern should falter. By early 1972 Muskie appeared to be the frontrunner. There was much about the lanky Maine Democrat that Church respected. He too was a survivor in a largely Republican state, and he and Church voted together most of the time. Muskie had, moreover, finally joined the ranks of the Senate doves on Vietnam. Church was nevertheless still concerned that Muskie, a moderate, running against Nixon as a centrist candidate, would turn the election into a tweedledee/tweedledum affair that the president would easily dominate.[13]

Church tried in several ways to push Muskie deeper into the reform camp. He applauded Muskie's speech in late 1971 to the National Farm Organization, for example, and used the occasion to recommend a sharper critique of the existing farm program. "The tide toward giantism has not been stemmed," he told Muskie, pointing to the need "to prevent corporate farms from gobbling up the land." He counseled Muskie to defend small farmers and to help end the federal "gravy train for the larger operators." His own suggestion in this regard was that only individual farmers, not corporations, should qualify for price supports and other government subsidies. This approach would protect family farms and also curtail corporate expansion.[14]

As the primary elections drew near, Church agonized over whom to endorse. He still favored McGovern, but political momentum seemed clearly to favor Muskie. Torn, Church discussed his dilemma with several members of his staff. "His heart was for McGovern," recalled Mike Wetherell, but he worried about alienating Muskie, who might be the next president. When he finally decided to back Muskie it was, Wetherell believed, "for political reasons. You could tell that he didn't feel comfortable doing it."[15]

On February 19, 1972, Church and Governor Cecil Andrus both endorsed Muskie at the Democratic Party's annual Jefferson-Jackson dinner in Boise. The Maine senator was in attendance and had every reason to smile. Church's glowing comments included praise for Muskie's new-found opposition to the Vietnam war and for his capacity to grow "in stature, in knowledge, and in the strength of his convictions." A Muskie candidacy, Church predicted, would provide the public with a genuine choice in November, in part by bringing the war back into the national debate. Already, he noted, the administration was trying to silence Muskie. But the Maine senator "refused to be hushed," despite presidential aide H. R. Haldeman's recent accusations that his criticism of Nixon's policies was helping the enemy. After Church turned the podium over to Muskie, he perhaps listened uncomfortably as his colleague delivered an address that journalist Sam Day described as a "bromide of silken, unspecific reassurances about bringing the people together and healing the nation's wounds–new Nixonisms in Democratic vernacular." This was precisely what Church had warned against. He presumably breathed easier when Muskie criticized Nixon's Vietnam policy. "I acknowledge that Senator Church has been wiser than I have been with respect to the war," Muskie said, indicating that he too was now dedicated to ending America's involvement in Southeast Asia.[16]

A few days later, however, Muskie's candidacy floundered in the snows of New England. Tired from campaigning in California and elsewhere, Muskie arrived in New Hampshire to find his early lead in the state slipping. Voters were reportedly not sure what he stood for. On February 26, standing in a blizzard on a flatbed truck, the exhausted Muskie lashed back at the right-wing *Manchester Union Leader* for its scurrilous and dishonest attacks on him and his wife. Calling the newspaper editor a "gutless coward," Muskie seemed to break into tears several times. Although he had no way of knowing it at the time, he had fallen victim to a series of "dirty tricks" on the part of the Committee to Re-elect the President. Using phony documents and planting rumors, the committee was determined to drive the Democratic front-runners from the race. Although Muskie won the New Hampshire primary, his emotional performance on February 26 reduced his margin of victory and turned the campaign's momentum against him.[17]

Frank Church again found himself in a quandary. He thought about switching to McGovern, who was doing remarkably well in the primaries and emerging as a real contender. But he worried about seeming inconsistent and breaking his commitment to Muskie. When Muskie ran last in Pennsylvania's April 24 primary (behind Humphrey, George Wallace, and McGovern), Church acted. He telephoned Muskie, who had decided to leave the race, to say that he was shifting his endorsement to McGovern.[18]

As much as any national politician, McGovern symbolized the new politics. He had not only picked up the mantle of the Eugene McCarthy/Robert Kennedy Democrats, but had also chaired a party commission that, after a series of hearings in 1969, issued a ringing *Mandate for Reform*. The McGovern Commission, calling for "popular control of the Democratic Party," recommended guidelines that would bring seriously underrepresented groups of blacks, women, the young, and the poor into the party's structure and selection processes. The Democratic national committee adopted the guidelines, including a rule that convention delegates needed to win their seats through some kind of an election, not through automatic bids because they held political office or represented traditional power groups. As a leading advocate of such changes, McGovern enjoyed the support of people who viewed him as an anti-establishment alternative to the old-style party bosses. His candidacy in 1972, according to historian Herbert Parmet, "was essentially the new-politics revenge for 1968, the culmination of reformist, new-breed activism that represented the mobilization of the antiwar movement" in another bid to capture the presidency.[19]

II

Frank Church demonstrated an affinity for the new politics in several ways. He too preferred an expansive political process that was inclusive, not exclusive; open, not closed; public, not secret; and the territory of common Americans, not the special preserve of the economically and socially privileged. He thus applauded consumer advocate Ralph Nader and his "Nader's Raiders" as prime examples of an aroused and active populace. Starting in 1964, he voluntarily disclosed his annual income and assets on grounds that citizens should know about the economic status of their representatives and possible conflicts of interest. In 1970 he advocated the abolition of the Electoral College, a step that he said would advance "the historic trend toward broadening the role of the people in their government." He favored an end to the military draft because conscription, except in the most dire national emergency, contradicted the ideals of a democratic society. He also pushed for the constitutional amendment, ratified in 1971, that lowered the federal voting age to eighteen. And from 1969 to mid-1972 he was one of only seven senators who, according to the Leadership Conference on Civil Rights, had voted "correctly" on all sixteen designated civil rights issues.[20]

Concerned also about women's rights, he viewed equal pay, equal job opportunities, and equality before the law as nothing less than imperatives. His initial uneasiness about the Equal Rights Amendment (ERA), after he first entered the Senate, had raised suspicions in the National Woman's Party and elsewhere that his 1956 pledge to "work whole-heartedly for its passage" was disingenuous. What made him pause, however, was not the principle behind the amendment. Instead, he had been mulling over information from the American Federation of Labor and the Congress of Industrial Organizations that some anti-women's rights groups would seize upon the ERA to roll back state laws protecting women against substandard wages and working conditions. Despite these reservations about the amendment, he ended up as one of its co-sponsors.[21]

On the issue of women's rights he did not limit himself to favorable speeches and votes. In 1964 he appointed one of the first women ever to be the chief administrator of a senator's staff, Verda Barnes. Although her views on gender issues were in many ways traditional, she had been a kind of feminist role model for her generation. In the 1930s she had served as a labor organizer; and, as a divorced, single parent, she had raised her daughter alone. Church by all accounts depended greatly on her, valued her advice, and awarded her complete confidence.[22]

His admiration for Barnes as an individual, and his respect for her intelligence, were in character. He spurned gender stereotypes and regarded women as social and intellectual equals. Karin Lissakers, whom Church appointed as staff director of a subcommittee that he chaired, considered his attitudes on gender "remarkable," especially on the Senate Foreign Relations Committee, where a "retrograde" view of women prevailed. At the time he chose her there were perhaps only two other women in the entire Congress who served as staff directors. In retrospect, Forrest Church was struck by how his father never appeared to see women as sex objects. "He never would joke," let alone use condescending language or mannerisms, "if a beautiful woman went past." One female journalist doubted this until she interviewed him. "Some of these old bastards in the Senate aren't safe to interview alone in a private office," she said. Church, in contrast, was a model of decorum. "I'm not suggesting I'm irresistible," the reporter told Church's press secretary after the interview, "but I usually get some reaction." From Church, however, she had gotten no such "man-woman reaction, if you know what I mean."[23]

Church's attitudes toward women were anything but paternalistic. He was not given to macho posturing, nor did he think about male prerogatives. Instead, he and Bethine pressed the Democratic Party to include more women in leadership roles—and they did so at least five years before the McGovern Commission's *Mandate for Reform* made a similar recommendation.[24]

III

Church thus moved easily into the camp of the new politics and George McGovern, whose campaign was defying all predictions. For antiwar activists, McGovern's candidacy represented the last best hope. They had been so discouraged by the end of 1971 that one dissident had lamented, "We stand in the antechamber of a dying antiwar movement." Even a five-day U. S. air barrage of North Vietnam in late December failed to stir much protest, and the war began to lose the media's attention. In this context, the more radical wing of the antiwar movement began to collapse into a kind of political black hole, "isolated, self-enclosed," as SDS leader Tom Hayden put it. McGovern's candidacy exerted a different kind of political gravity, pulling the liberal, even moderate, wing of the antiwar movement into mainstream politics and encouraging what the *Guardian* described as "the normalization of dissent."[25]

Richard Nixon, declaring that "the Presidency is what is on the line," shrewdly countered his opposition. His landmark summit meetings in China and the Soviet Union during the first half of 1972 suggested that his innovative leadership was reducing Cold War tensions. "With the T. V. spectaculars of Peking and Moscow pre-empting the airwaves," J. William Fulbright wrote Muskie, "what you and I or anyone else has to say is going to be difficult to bring to the notice of the public." Moreover, Nixon's Vietnamization policy, by bringing American troops home, diverted attention from vastly escalated bombing raids. By March 1972 the number of U. S. troops in Vietnam had dropped to ninety-five thousand; the air war, in contrast, jumped dramatically in the first three months of 1972, matching its scale for the entire previous year. Meanwhile, in January, Nixon instructed his top aides "to sustain a massive counterattack" on his domestic critics, assailing their lack of patriotism. "Keep nailing them," he ordered, keep accusing them of "consciously giving aid and comfort to the enemy. They want the enemy to win and the United States to lose. They want the United States to surrender."[26]

Like other opponents of the war, Church found the bombing morally repellent. For some time he had tried to remind the Senate that the war's "wasted people" included far more Indochinese than Americans. He anguished that Nixon's Vietnamization policy was causing the "indiscriminate slaughter" of Southeast Asians. But because of the wide perception that the war was winding down, the American public seemed oblivious to the horrific human costs of the air war, a conflict that Church believed was as "Orwellian" as the proposition, "War is Peace."[27]

The air war exploded with new fury at the end of March 1972 after the North Vietnamese suddenly staged a massive invasion of the South. The administration struck back with a vengeance. Claiming that he did not need congressional approval to protect U. S. troops, Nixon ordered bombing strikes against Hanoi and Haiphong for the first time since 1968. Civilian as well as military targets fell under siege. Suddenly, the antiwar movement reemerged in America's streets and on Capitol Hill.[28]

In the Senate, Church quickly dusted off the Cooper-Church end-the-war amendment of the previous year. This time, however, he had a new legislative partner, New Jersey Republican Clifford Case. John Sherman Cooper, Church's ally in so many earlier battles, was no longer interested in fighting for the amendment, but not because of any disenchantment with Church. Looking back several years later on his relationship with the Idaho senator he was moved to tears, describing him as "a good man. He was honorable and he was truthful. . . . He followed his convictions." The seventy-one-year-old Kentuckian had simply worn down, to the point that he had decided not to seek reelection in 1972. "I have been in the lead too much," he reportedly told Case, whom he urged to take over. Still, he was uneasy about Church's rewording of the amendment, which would set a December 31, 1972 date for cutting off all funds, contingent upon an agreement to release American prisoners of war. All along, Cooper had championed the constitutional right of Congress to stop funding the war, but not to issue orders to the president.[29]

Clifford Case, a tall, gangling minister's son, was twenty years older than Church. His background and sober demeanor inspired the joke that his wardrobe included a hair shirt. One of the most liberal Senate Republicans, he had voted against Nixon time and again. Like Church, he was a member of the Foreign Relations Committee and had been committed for some time to reasserting congressional powers. Moreover, he looked upon Church as "able, considerate, understanding," and principled.[30]

Church saw much to gain in an alliance with Case. The fact that Case, like Cooper, was older, independent-minded, and a highly respected Republican might help Church's legislative initiatives "sell better," as Tom Dine put it. "We will call this Case-Church," not Church-Case, the Idaho senator instructed Dine about the new amendment. Dine personally found Case "a hell of a lot easier to work with than Cooper." The New Jersey senator was more decisive and moved quickly once he had made up his mind.[31]

Once again, however, the administration held the upper hand. In April the White House announced the removal of twenty-thousand more U. S. troops within the next two months and stepped up the bombing. On May 8, Nixon ordered the mining of North Vietnamese ports and river systems. Convinced that the Pentagon bombing plans were "timid," Nixon told Henry Kissinger that "we should go for broke. . . .we must *punish* the enemy in ways that he will really hurt at this time. . . .I intend to stop at nothing to bring the enemy to his knees." The president wanted "the military to get off its backside" and reach that goal. "What distinguishes me from [Lyndon] Johnson," Nixon wrote in a long memorandum to Kissinger, "is that I have the *will* in spades."[32]

As bombs rained down on North Vietnam, Frank Church pleaded with the Senate to add the Case-Church amendment to a bill authorizing funds for the State Department. In a May 5 speech full of historical and literary allusions, he rejected the administration's charge that the recent North Vietnamese offensive constituted a new war. "The mind boggles at our seemingly limitless capacity for self-deception," he said. "The reasons for our intervention, grown hollow over the years,. . .have fallen of their own rotten weight." North Vietnamese regulars had been fighting in the South for years; in fact, by 1969 they had constituted 70 percent of the enemy force. For reasons that Church said he could not understand, the administration seemed incapable of learning from the errors of the past. It thus continued to repeat those mistakes. "The strategic bombing will fail again, as it failed before," Church predicted. "Darken their skies with clouds of bombers, rain down destruction upon them, spread the carnage far and wide, and they may scurry for cover but they will not yield." The purpose behind the Case-Church measure was to make binding the Mansfield amendment of the previous fall, which the president had said he would ignore. Was the Congress so supine that it would roll over and "suffer the President's rebuke?" Church hoped not. The amendment that he and Case were co-sponsoring would allow six months in which to remove the remaining U. S. troops, assuming that the North Vietnamese agreed to release American POWs.[33]

The Case-Church amendment was in trouble from the outset, however. It suffered from the early defections of Cooper and Vermont's George Aiken. Aiken, a key supporter of the Cooper-Church amendments, had decided that Church was "prone to criticize the Nixon Administration, with or without cause." Although Aiken himself disapproved of the U. S. bombing raids, he believed that the Case-Church proposal would in effect give South Vietnam to the North for "a small price" of returning the POWs. On the Senate floor the crusty Vermonter startled Nixon's critics by urging them not to "take the side of the enemy." Even more stridently, Mississippi Democrat John Stennis attacked the Case-Church proposal because it would force the U. S. out of Vietnam "like a whipped dog." Michigan Republican Robert Griffin wondered why anyone in the Senate would want to contribute to the possible defeat of South Vietnam. These attacks on Nixon's critics as unpatriotic fit perfectly with the president's own recommended scenario. The strategy was emblematic, according to *New York Times* columnist Tom Wicker, of "the self-serving doctrine the imperial Presidency and its political courtiers are trying to impose." It was working, moreover. "The Democrats are beginning to cave," Tom Dine observed unhappily; "the liberal-moderate Republicans are seeking sanctuary within the White House walls."[34]

On May 16 the Senate voted 47-43 to substitute an amendment from Robert Byrd (D-West Virginia) for Case-Church. The Byrd amendment made the removal of U. S. troops conditional on an internationally supervised cease-fire, as well as the release of American prisoners.

To Church, it made no more sense than a British proposal would have during the American Civil War to conduct an international plebiscite in the Confederacy on the issue of secession. The defeat of the Case-Church amendment constituted a major victory for the White House and a stunning setback for the Senate doves.[35]

IV

For Frank Church and many antiwar activists, George McGovern's candidacy, following the Senate defeat of Case-Church, took on even greater urgency. On May 25 the senator sent a letter to more than a thousand Idaho Democrats stating that the party could "no longer afford status quo politics" and that he was campaigning for McGovern. Three weeks later, at the state's Democratic convention, he took dead aim at "the 'old' politics" of Hubert Humphrey, who had become McGovern's chief challenger, as well as at Richard Nixon.[36]

By then, young and well-organized McGovernites, many of them relative strangers to organized politics, were shouldering aside the Democratic Party's old guard. The pattern at Idaho's Sun Valley gathering resembled that of many other state conventions across the country. Anti-establishment leanings were so strong at the Idaho meeting that Carl Burke wondered if even Church would emerge as a delegate to the national convention in Miami.[37]

The surge of middle- and upper-middle-class reformers into the McGovern movement both pleased and bothered Church. He liked the activists' commitment to "participatory democracy" and their strong antiwar convictions. Yet he was well aware that they tended to drive away the working and lower-middle classes. He recognized that "the unyoung, unblack and unpoor" held the preponderance of political power in 1972. To make them feel unwelcome in the Democratic Party seemed hardly sensible. Despite Church's satisfaction at the influx of McGovern enthusiasts, he worried that they were too youth-oriented. Basically, he was uncomfortable with those aspects of the new politics that focused heavily on cultural, or life style, issues.[38]

At Idaho's state Democratic convention, he observed uneasily "all kinds of looney movements," as he later described them—"far out movements of every sort." An enraged Governor Cecil Andrus repudiated the convention immediately afterwards for having alienated old-line Democrats. In retrospect, Church deemed Andrus's action "good sense."[39]

At the time, however, he aligned himself wholeheartedly with the reform element at Sun Valley. As Carl Burke observed, Church needed to convince the reformers that he was one of them, "a good guy," or face the embarrassment that he might not be a delegate from his own state to the national convention in Miami. In this regard, Church at least knew that McGovern had promised to do everything possible to assure his selection as a delegate. After the convention, Church was pleased that the Idaho delegation to Miami included a strong McGovern component, perhaps half, and that he was part of it. He was thus not about to disavow the Sun Valley proceedings.[40]

Just as importantly, he was swept up in the political fervor of the new politics at Sun Valley. He was instrumental in making the Idaho delegation its most representative ever. Of the twenty delegates (seventeen of whom had votes), half were women, two were blacks, and two were Mexican-Americans. Several were in their late teens. Verda Barnes indicated that an effort to include a Native American had failed because no Indian had wanted to seek a spot on the delegation. A petition to nominate Shirley Chisholm, the first black female member of the House of Representatives, for vice president at the national convention received Church's support. Although Chisholm's nomination would be largely symbolic, it would underline the party's commitment to racial and sexual equality. In a move that subsequently haunted Church's 1974 reelection bid, the senator may also have signed a petition pledging support for the California lettuce boycott, inspired by Cesar Chavez. Although he said later that he could not remember signing any such document, some of his staff were certain that he had.[41]

Addressing the enthusiastic throng at Sun Valley in behalf of McGovern, Church described his friend as a champion of the new politics. A McGovern presidency, he said, would end the national "crisis of faith" in government. "The *status quo* is the problem!" Church told the cheering crowd. Over the next few minutes he jabbed at the status quo in a series of cadenced references: "a *status quo* war in the jungles of Southeast Asia"; "a *status quo* military budget so bloated it devours two out of three Federal tax dollars"; "a *status quo* tax system which leaves manifold tax havens for men of leisure but picks the pockets of men who work." Warming to his subject, he attacked the status quo for polluting the environment and for discriminating on the basis of race and sex. "It is the *status quo* that helps the bigs get bigger," he stated angrily.[42]

Church, who a few years earlier had proudly described himself as a centrist politician, now heaped scorn upon those "who insist on driving right down the middle of the road." There were, he complained, too many "*status quo* politicians" treading the well-worn path of privilege and favoritism, unable to deal with America's real problems—its injustices, its poverty, its racism and sexism, its failed foreign policy, its befouled water and poisoned air.[43]

Having identified the source of the nation's incapacities, Church told his audience that it was time for "a different breed" to replace the old-style politicians. He left no doubt whom he had in mind: "There's only *one* man who never was, and never will be, a *status quo* politician—and that man is George McGovern!" McGovern, he said, would bring a new set of priorities to the White House. A McGovern presidency would work to close tax loopholes, expand the corporate tax base, cut defense spending (the nation's "biggest scandal"), and demolish the illusion that "the United States must stand as a self-anointed sentinel for two-thirds of the world."[44]

By the time Church delivered his ringing Sun Valley address he was a prominent figure in McGovern's camp. He had already stumped vigorously for McGovern in the California Democratic primary. In turn, McGovern had turned to him for campaign advice and had intimated that, if he became president, he would like to have Church in his cabinet. Church, he said, "would make a great secretary of state."[45]

At the national Democratic convention in July, there was even a brief moment when it seemed that Church might be McGovern's running mate. Columnist Jack Anderson and Las Vegas oddsmaker "Jimmy the Greek" both thought so; and two members of McGovern's staff, Henry Kimelman and Mike Feldman, discussed the possibility with the Idaho senator. Ironically, Church's "boomlet" fell victim to old-style politics. "Too many of the old staffers are thinking in terms of the old politics, ticket balancing and that sort of thing," Kimelman told Church.[46]

This tendency was evident in the frantic, behind-the-scenes search for a vice-presidential candidate after McGovern had nailed down the top spot on the Democratic ticket. When McGovern learned that his first choice, Ted Kennedy, was not interested in running for vice president, he asked his chief advisers for recommendations. McGovern was somewhat surprised to find that the list did not include Church. When he discussed the list with his staff, Church's name came up but encountered resistance. As McGovern later wrote, the argument against a McGovern-Church ticket was that "it would combine two antiwar senators from sparsely settled Western states." In retrospect, McGovern judged such thinking as "superficial" and "silly." Actually, there were some other objections as well. As McGovern recalled, the complaint had surfaced again that Church was "too much of an orator and not enough of a mover and shaker." Connecticut senator Abraham Ribicoff was particularly emphatic in saying that Church lacked depth. "I felt that [Ribicoff] judged him unfairly," McGovern remembered, "but he weighed in pretty heavily."[47]

Although Church was unaware of the complaints that he was a political lightweight, he was not surprised when Missouri senator Thomas Eagleton got the vice-presidential nod. Church had not really expected to get the position, had not sought it, and even had doubts about his own administrative abilities. The speculation about his candidacy had nevertheless added an extra dose of excitement for him at the convention. All of the attention had been great fun. He was flattered, too, when top McGovern aide Frank Mankiewicz assured him, "If we were not running George, we'd be running you. You know we couldn't run two George McGoverns on the same ticket." He also felt good about the large number of delegates who had thanked him throughout the week for opposing the war and championing the elderly. "This gave me a feeling of having a constituency of my own at the convention, which pleased me very much," he wrote following his return from Miami.[48]

On July 19, less than a week after the convention, McGovern talked confidentially with him over the phone about his prospects of becoming secretary of state, if the Democrats won the election. McGovern was neither making a commitment nor expecting one. He simply wanted Church to put the idea "on the back burner and let it simmer for a while." McGovern said that he found the Henry Kissinger style of diplomacy a disgrace. If he became president, he hoped to bring the conduct of foreign policy out of the White House basement and to restore the authority of the State Department. Church sympathized with this view, indicating that it was time to "put an end to the succession of tough professors." He also told McGovern that the U. S. needed to stop holding domestic issues hostage to foreign policy. Looking ahead, McGovern guessed that the only obstacle to Church's nomination as secretary of state might be resistance from some members of the Jewish community who somehow had the impression that the Idahoan was "soft on

Israel." Perhaps, Church ventured, this would be an appropriate time for him to visit Israel. McGovern quickly picked up on the idea, urging him to make the trip before the November election.[49]

V

As Church prepared to go to Israel, the air war in Vietnam intensified. "The bastards have never been bombed like they're going to be bombed this time," Nixon informed his aides at the end of June. By mid-July, North Vietnam alone was the daily target of over three hundred air strikes.[50]

On July 24 the Vietnam issue sparked a bizarre series of Senate clashes between the administration's critics and defenders. The Capitol was still wilting under hot, muggy conditions and a dense cloud of pollution—the kind of setting, George Aiken guessed, "that warps one's judgment and intensifies one's emotions." Aiken also sensed that some Democrats, just back from their Miami convention, were "disgruntled and belligerent."[51]

For old-line party professionals, the convention had turned into a circus. A comment by movie star Shirley McLaine, who had been a delegate, pointed up all too vividly the reign of the new politics. Her California delegation, she said approvingly, had resembled "a couple of high schools, a grape boycott, a Black Panther rally, and four or five politicians who walked in the wrong door." Many dedicated professionals had in fact played major roles in Miami. Church, Gaylord Nelson, and Stewart Udall had been among McGovern's floor leaders, for example. But Congressman James O'Hara (D-Michigan) said afterwards that the proceedings had encouraged the public to associate "McGovern and gay liberation, and welfare rights and pot-smoking and black militants, and women's lib, and wise college kids." Following the convention, some Senate Democrats were still seething about the proceedings and the party platform, which included planks calling for immediate U. S. withdrawal from Vietnam, amnesty for draft evaders (after the troops and POWs had returned), the abolition of capital punishment, and the right of Americans to choose freely "their own choices of lifestyles and private habits without being subject to discrimination or prosecution."[52]

Perhaps as a reflection of the agitated political scene, the Senate's July 24 performance was unexpected and unpredictable. The day started with a surprise when John Sherman Cooper, his patience apparently exhausted, proposed a new, stringent amendment to cut off all funding of U. S. forces in Indochina in four months, without conditions. "Good God!" a startled Nixon said to Kissinger after discovering Cooper's intentions. "What does *this* do?" The administration, not about to wait for an answer, rallied its troops for a showdown.[53]

The next few hours were a study in confusion, as sides switched bewilderingly. Before the day had ended, the Senate doves delivered the administration a stunning blow and then fell victim to a White House ploy that left them defeated and divided against themselves.

Church, while in the thick of the battle, tried desperately to contact McGovern, lest the new Democratic presidential nominee miss the rapidly developing historic moment. But McGovern was out of reach in the Black Hills, and his absence quickly caught the media's attention. Church fretted that his friend might be politically wounded by missing a major vote on the Vietnam war. The Republicans indeed tried to turn McGovern's absence to their advantage. Minority leader Hugh Scott observed that the South Dakota senator had botched a leadership opportunity by failing "to put his vote where his oratory is."[54]

Meanwhile, the Senate's July 24 maneuvering became more intricate. Massachusetts Republican Edward Brooke tried to alter Cooper's amendment with wording that virtually replicated the recently defeated Case-Church initiative, calling for cutting off funds for U. S. military operations in Indochina in four months, contingent upon the release of U. S. POWs. Surprisingly, the Senate adopted Brooke's motion with dispatch, 62-33. Amazed, Church could only guess that many senators were "relieved" to have an alternative to Cooper's proposal, with its stark requirement of unconditional withdrawal. There was no time to rejoice, though, because Mississippi's John Stennis moved to strike the Brooke amendment. Stennis was a Democrat, but his strong hawkish views qualified him to lead the administration's desperate, last-ditch effort to undercut the end-the-war initiative. Church, at the request of Mike Mansfield and John Sparkman (D-Alabama), managed the floor debate for the next eighty minutes and delivered the summary argument against Stennis's motion. To his astonishment, the Senate then voted against Stennis, 49-46. Church was jubilant. For the first time the Senate had adopted a mandatory end-the-war amendment, voting to cut off funding in Southeast Asia and thus to force out U. S. troops, contingent upon a settlement of the POW issue. Here, as *New York*

Times reporter John Finney wrote, was "the strongest, most binding amendment yet passed by the Senate to require the withdrawal of U. S. forces from Vietnam."[55]

But the day was not over. As Church praised the Senate at a televised press conference, he heard that the administration intended to sacrifice its entire military assistance bill, rather than have it pass containing the end-the-war amendment. The bill included nearly $300 million in military and economic aid to Cambodia. Dumbfounded, Church hurried back to the Senate floor where he learned that Mansfield and J. William Fulbright embraced the opportunity to help the administration vote down its own military assistance program, which they detested. Church shared their antipathy for the program, but saw the administration's apparent willingness to forfeit it as a trap. He tried to convince his two dove colleagues that the military assistance bill would ultimately survive, just as a foreign aid bill the previous year had eventually passed despite the Senate's rejection of the original. Attaching an end-the-war amendment to such an important bill constituted a real victory, in Church's opinion. Mansfield and Fulbright disagreed. In their view, the end-the-war amendment had no chance of surviving, either in conference or on the president's desk. Why not, they reasoned, use the administration's own votes to block the military assistance bill? Church begged them to recognize that by defeating the military bill with the accompanying amendment, "we were only voting against ourselves."[56]

As Church watched helplessly, Fulbright, Mansfield, and several other doves helped squash the military assistance bill, 48-42. The administration, knowing that it would be able to revive the bill minus the end-the-war amendment, had in Church's estimation "snatch[ed] victory from the jaws of defeat." On a day full of twists and turns, wrote Church, "we marched all the way up the hill and conquered the summit" by passing the end-the-war amendment, "and then turned around and marched back down again" by giving up the amendment. The effort may have taken an even greater toll on the doves. John Finney sensed that "much of the energy and organization had gone out of the antiwar effort in the Senate." The administration had foiled the end-the-war maneuver, and Hugh Scott took the opportunity to excoriate the Senate doves for having tried to hand over to Jane Fonda the president's ability to negotiate. At the White House, meanwhile, the word was out to warn Republicans on the Hill that their lapses during "the end the war effort" only helped McGovern and constituted "unacceptable behavior." A dispirited Church could only hope that the media coverage of the Senate's rapid reversals would at least divert attention from McGovern's absence. Perhaps, too, his forty-eighth birthday on the day after the Senate's see-saw battle would bring better news.[57]

VI

It did not. At a press conference in South Dakota, George McGovern and Tom Eagleton revealed that Eagleton had a history of emotional difficulties and had been hospitalized three times for rest. McGovern nevertheless expressed full confidence in him as a running mate and said that even knowledge of the Missouri senator's medical background would not have altered the decision to place him on the ticket. "It's not happy news," wrote Church. He predicted, correctly, that the revelation about Eagleton would inspire "gossip, rumor and alarmist talk. It places the ticket on the defensive from the opening gun of the campaign and thus constitutes another hurdle for McGovern to overcome."[58]

As McGovern struggled over the next few days with the Eagleton problem, going so far as to say that he backed his running mate "a thousand percent," Church retreated to Idaho's mountains. With Bethine and Chase, he took a float trip down the Middle Fork of the Salmon River, the spectacular "River of No Return." They emerged four days later to find that the Eagleton matter had deteriorated even more.[59]

McGovern called Church in Boise. When McGovern indicated that Eagleton would have to leave the ticket, Church agreed that no option existed. The conversation turned to Church's availability as a running mate. Church was unenthusiastic, saying that he could not provide the kind of diversity the ticket needed. Like McGovern, he was a Westerner from a thinly populated state. He was, moreover, a lapsed Catholic. If McGovern linked up with someone who had left the Catholic Church, a crucial constituency might desert the Democrats in November. Church advised McGovern to choose a Catholic, preferably Muskie, or maybe Sargent Shriver, Ted Kennedy's brother-in-law who had directed Lyndon Johnson's War on Poverty. McGovern asked Church point blank if he was interested in the vice presidency. "I said neither yes nor no to him," Church recorded in his diary, "I simply reiterated the reasons why I felt he should look elsewhere."[60]

Once again, a Church "boomlet" developed. Over the next few days the press pursued him for interviews and information. On CBS television, Walter Cronkite mentioned him as a frontrunner. *Time* and *Newsweek* magazines took photographs of him for possible cover stories.[61]

On August 2, Church huddled in the Senate with McGovern about the vice-presidency. Again, Church explained why he would not be a good choice. This time, he added that he had already heard jokes that he was not man enough for the job because he had lost his left testicle during his bout with cancer. Laughing, McGovern replied, "Sometimes I think the problem downtown is that there are too many balls." Serious once again, McGovern pressed Church about how he would respond to a request to join the ticket and Church repeated once again the reasons he believed it was a bad idea. But whomever McGovern chose, Church hoped that it would not be Hubert Humphrey, who "would go down very badly with the new politics people."[62]

The next afternoon, Church ruminated on McGovern's dilemma with three staff members, Tom Dine, Cleve Corlett, and Wes Barthelmes. He was worried that he had hedged too much about his own availability for the ticket, so much so that McGovern appeared to see him as "a kind of security blanket," someone who would be around to accept the vice-presidential spot if others refused. The more Church thought about the vice-presidency, the less he wanted it. He did not want "to be relegated to the banquet circuit as a huckster to support all the policies of the Administration. . . ." If by chance McGovern asked him to join the ticket, Church said that he would insist on a more substantial role.[63]

As he sipped on a drink, Church confided to his aides that the whole issue of his ever being vice president was probably moot anyhow. McGovern's campaign had gotten off to a terrible start, and not just because of the Eagleton fiasco. A worse problem, in Church's opinion, was the Democratic Party's rapidly eroding base.

In recent months Church had spotted danger signals among his Democratic constituents in Idaho, especially over the welfare issue. The owner of a small-town gas station, for example, had quipped that he was going to stop working so hard and retire on welfare. An embittered worker in North Idaho had expressed similar views, saying that he was tired of busting his rear end in the mills while many people got paid for doing nothing.[64]

Church believed the Democrats desperately needed to respond to such grievances by revamping the welfare system. He, along with Abraham Ribicoff and Gaylord Nelson, had made this point in early June to McGovern, arguing that many working Americans resented welfare as a free ticket, a government handout, a dole. Even Nixon had made himself vulnerable on this issue when, during his first year in office, he had recommended a guaranteed minimum annual income. Frustrated, Church worried that liberals had botched the opportunity to turn the welfare controversy to their advantage. "We should have stuck by the old work-relief concept of the New Deal, which made me a Democrat," he told his aides. "We should have insisted that all able-bodied recipients work and that the government should supply the work to do." Public works projects could, for example, help to clean up the environment. Even mothers of dependent children could work if government provided day care centers.[65]

To salvage the Democrats' position among working-class and other middle American voters, Church also wanted McGovern to inject more economic populism into the campaign. Prior to the Democrats' Miami convention, he had urged his colleague to press for a minimum tax upon wealthy people who were using loopholes to avoid paying taxes. He had agreed as well with Gaylord Nelson's advice that McGovern should chastise the huge corporations that were driving out small businesses and dehumanizing the economy.[66]

As Church watched McGovern's search for Eagleton's replacement in early August, he became increasingly "downcast" regarding Democratic hopes in 1972. Several people had already turned down McGovern's offer of a place on the ticket, and the press had made much of this. According to one joke, McGovern had posted a sign in the Senate cloakroom: "Anybody willing to serve as my vice-presidential candidate please call the following number." Church wondered why McGovern was making the refusals public, "thus creating the impression that no one wants to run with him." The Idaho senator was sadly convinced of one thing–"It sure is a new way of running for the Presidency."[67]

In the meantime, Church's own possible vice-presidential candidacy continued to attract attention. Idaho governor Cecil Andrus volunteered to "break his ass" in Church's behalf, but hoped that the senator would not end up on the ticket, which more than likely faced defeat in November. Carl Burke felt differently. He believed that Church could help the McGovern ticket and, even in a losing cause, the exposure would not hurt Church's 1974 reelection. Within Church's family there was predictably much excitement. Church kept daily contact with Bethine, who was still in Idaho. Chase obviously hoped that his father would end up on the ticket. And Forrest, living in California with Amy, was enthusiastic enough about his father's prospects to have shaved off his beard. Church greeted this as a considerable concession. He was pleased that Forrest was "showing much more mature interest in politics." If nothing else, all the talk about Frank Church for vice president had provided an opportunity for family unity, following the strains of recent years.[68]

Church nevertheless still hoped that McGovern would not turn to him, even as he watched the vice presidential situation disintegrate further into a comedy of errors.[69] On August 4, McGovern told Church that he had given Muskie the most recent offer. Church called Muskie that day, urging him to accept. The conversation went well, and Church was encouraged. When he returned to his office, however, he found a curious note from McGovern, requesting that he not "push too hard" for Muskie after all. Immediately on the phone to McGovern, Church learned that Muskie had wanted a task force of three of his people and three of McGovern's to try to work out an understanding. McGovern's aides had come back irate, convinced that they had never seen so incompetent a staff as Muskie's. Their reaction had startled McGovern. He told Church that his people had been so disturbed that he had not known whether they needed electric shock treatments or martinis. Church quipped that, considering the Eagleton fiasco, martinis were preferable. More seriously, Church asked McGovern if he was perhaps relying too much on his staff.[70]

Although Church slept that night with his "fingers crossed," hoping Muskie would join the ticket, he discovered when he awakened that the Maine senator had rejected McGovern's offer. "This threw a blanket over my mood for the morning," he wrote. He was afraid that McGovern would now turn to him. "I suggested a few minutes later in a telephone conversation with Verda [Barnes] that perhaps I should go into hiding." That day calls from the press flooded his office and home. Church finally worked out a code with his staff whereby he would not pick up the phone unless it had the correct combination of rings. The suspense ended that evening when McGovern announced that Sargent Shriver would be his running mate.[71]

The "grim week," as Church called it, had finally ended. He was pleased with the choice of Shriver, whom he had recommended to

McGovern a few days earlier. Church spent Sunday, August 6, swimming in a neighbor's pool and doing yard work. But he was distressed about the considerably diminished chances of a McGovern victory. "We are now on our own three yard line with our backs to the goal with 97 yards to go between now and November."[72]

Further stacking the odds against McGovern was the public mood, which Church viewed as jaded, even indifferent. He was appalled at the lack of indignation about either the bombing in Vietnam or the reputed activities of the Committee to Reelect the President. News reports had suggested that the committee might have been responsible for a failed effort to burglarize and bug the Democratic headquarters. The public silence constituted "a travesty," Church believed, perhaps reflecting the war's brutalizing influence. But he attributed it also to "the character of the political leadership that has afflicted this country for the past decade or more."[73]

His disenchantment had perhaps never been greater. The distance he had traveled since his initial attacks upon the Vietnam war was particularly striking. He now viewed the war less as a quagmire, previously one of his favorite analogies, than as a moral abomination. Indeed, he classified himself in 1972 as one of those people for whom the war was nothing less than "a monstrous immorality."[74]

Because most Americans nevertheless seemed inured to the barbaric nature of the war, Church fretted that Nixon—not McGovern—was taking advantage of Vietnam as an issue. Polls were suggestive in this regard. By 1971 around two-thirds of the public had concluded the war was a mistake; but of that number a substantial majority abhorred "the peace movement" as unpatriotic and radical. A University of Michigan sample poll of the residents of Detroit and its suburbs showed that only 11 percent of the general population who opposed the war did so on moral grounds. If the polls were correct, opponents of the war were not necessarily "doves" at all. They might want the U. S. out of Vietnam, but not at the inference that thousands of Americans had died there in vain. And they were apparently willing to allow the president to take a "stronger stand" in order to win what he described as "peace with honor."[75]

The message was clear to Church. "The people you must reach, the Middle Americans who will determine the outcome of this election," he advised McGovern on August 16, "*favor* the bombing. They see nothing wrong in bombing the hell out of an enemy." In their estimation, Nixon was "hanging in tough." He was "winning the war and leaving it too!" It was thus counterproductive, Church dejectedly told McGovern, to talk about the immorality of the war. The only possible way to defeat Nixon was by emphasizing the war's "frightful cost and uselessness." McGovern could perhaps also note the contradictions of Nixon's policies. Why, for example, was the administration making peace with China and the Soviet Union and still fighting in Vietnam? Church suspected that Nixon hoped to strike some settlement in Vietnam just before the election. "Against this possibility," he urged McGovern, "you must begin right away to build a backfire." The Democrats needed to ask why the president was suddenly exploring a possible settlement with such zeal. Why had he not done so earlier, before sacrificing twenty thousand additional American lives? Even as Church made these points to McGovern, he felt uncomfortable. "I'm struck by the cynical character of my observations," he wrote. It seemed so utterly wrong to be focusing on the politics of the war, rather than on its terrible immoralities. "If I have become a cynic on Vietnam," Church explained, "three Presidents turned me into one. I need a President I can believe in again."[76]

On August 20, Church tried to boost the spirits of a "somewhat discouraged" McGovern. There were assuredly reasons for dejection. A Gallup poll had just shown the Democrat trailing Nixon by a whopping 26 percentage points. Yet, sitting by the pool with McGovern at a small get-together, Church tried to be optimistic. He recommended that McGovern stage a massive television campaign that would point up the discrepancies between the image that Nixon projected and the realities of the administration. McGovern could, for example, document the huge social and economic costs of the war. He could show that the price of one laser bomb was equivalent to that of a comfortable American home. He could also try to counteract the White House portrait of him as a big welfare spender. Under the administration, tax loopholes constituted a kind of welfare program for the very rich. By attacking these loopholes McGovern could indicate that he was seeking a more equitable system, one more protective of working people. As Church talked to McGovern he was probably also trying to lift his own spirits. "This was kind of a bad day," he admitted when it was over.[77]

VII

Shortly thereafter, Church left for Israel. Although officially on a study mission for the Foreign Relations Committee, he also hoped to aid McGovern's cause. He tried to do this, for example, in an August 23 conversation with Abba Eban, at the Foreign Minister's home in Jerusalem. For one thing, he stressed that no one should discount McGovern's chances of winning the election. The polls could be quite misleading. After all, McGovern had "come on like a prairie fire" to win the Democratic nomination, despite polls that six months earlier had placed him near the bottom of the presidential candidates. Church also told Eban that Israelis worried unnecessarily if they believed that McGovern, as president, would desert them. McGovern not only fully supported a free and independent Israel, but also had no intentions of reducing the U. S. Sixth Fleet in the Mediterranean. Delicately, Church touched on the matter of the Jewish vote in the U. S. He mentioned the apparent comments of Yitzak Rabin, Israel's ambassador to America, that the Israeli government backed Nixon. Such statements could have "unfortunate consequences," Church indicated, especially because McGovern was as much Israel's friend as was Nixon. "Discussion of the Jewish vote as a 'block vote' and of the Israeli Government favoring one candidate as against another," Church informed Eban, "wouldn't serve the best interests of Israel in the United States in the future." In this respect, Church believed he had made progress. Eban agreed that U. S. friendship for Israel crossed partisan lines.[78]

That evening Church spoke informally at a dinner that Eban gave for him. Although he mentioned neither Nixon nor McGovern by name, the intent of his comments was clear. Americans, he said, were engaged in "a lively debate" concerning the U. S. role in the world. One side of the debate—by inference that of Nixon—approached "foreign policy as though it were played on a global chessboard, where the countries of the world are so many pieces, moved from square to square by the superpowers." From this perspective, only strategic and economic concerns seemed important. The dangers of such an approach for a nation such as Israel were that "economic and strategic considerations shift with events." There was, however, an opposing school of thought, one that placed ideology first. Church placed himself—and by inference McGovern—here. This school celebrated the principles of free government and individual liberty in the U. S., and looked for friends who had the same goals for their countries. Precisely because this school genuinely valued free governments, it represented Israel's better hope. By making freedom "a changeless ingredient in our foreign policy," Church said, "we will best serve the future interests of small countries like Israel."[79]

Ironically, Church, the former opponent of ideology, now appeared to be its advocate. There was, however, a major distinction between his new references to ideology and his earlier, disparaging remarks. This distinction manifested once again the impact of the Vietnam war upon him, as well as upon other critics of U. S. foreign policy.[80]

Early in his career Church had drawn his foreign policy assumptions primarily from the "realist" school, whose proponents dominated intellectual discussions during the two decades after World War II. Church especially admired Ambassador George Kennan and political scientist Hans Morgenthau. Both of them argued forcefully that the zealous moralism of Woodrow Wilson's foreign policy had resulted in tragedy. Under Wilson, they said, the U. S. had become a kind of global Don Quixote, crusading against "evils" with disillusioning results. The historical lesson was clear: practical self-interest, free of moralistic and ideological baggage, should be the basis of American foreign policy.

The Vietnam experience had put this assumption under a new intellectual microscope. Although Kennan, Morgenthau, and a number of other realists spoke out against the war, some critics of U. S. foreign policy concluded that realism was part of the problem. Faith in "objective," empirical solutions was badly misplaced, they insisted; indeed, "realism" was itself laden with ideology. In the case of the United States, as historian Christopher Lasch observed in the mid-Sixties, this ideology protected "the interests of the privileged, educated, white Americans who subscribed to it." As the Vietnam war continued, Lasch and others began to ask what moral people could do to halt barbaric and unthinkable policies, despite their cloak of rational practicality. Lasch called for an "unremitting attack" on the assumption "that napalm, the destruction of crops, the destruction of villages, the 'pacification' of peoples are justified under any circumstances at all."[81]

Church may not have read those particular words of Lasch, although they appeared in *The Nation*, a liberal journal with which he was quite familiar; but he was alert to the shifting intellectual emphasis in favor of morality as a proper gauge for foreign policy. In Israel he thus used the word ideology in reference to a set of moral and political values that he believed U. S. foreign policy had forsaken. By placing himself with what he called the "ideological school," he was in effect moving onto moral ground.

For similar reasons, he espoused the new politics in 1972. Still primarily a consensus politician, he now, perhaps more than ever in his life, worked strenuously to change the nature of the prevailing consensus—a consensus that, at home and abroad, seemed disturbingly at odds with the nation's historic ideals. In George McGovern's presidential candidacy he saw a genuine alternative to a political system much in need of moral uplift.

Church returned from Israel confident that he had given McGovern's cause a boost. He had sensed, for example, that the questions about McGovern from the Israeli press had grown friendlier and less critical. Also, the Israeli government seemed determined to remain neutral about the presidential race, rather than endorse Nixon.[82]

For Church himself, the Israeli trip had been edifying and politically beneficial. He had long held a romantic view of Israel, found the popular 1960 movie "Exodus" deeply moving, and since entering the Senate had supported Israel as a democratic nation and an American ally; but his first visit there made him even more respectful. The booming economy and the resolute, determined citizenry impressed him. He particularly liked Prime Minister Golda Meir. Her modest residence and lack of pretension offered a welcome contrast to Nixon's imperial U. S. presidency, which so aggravated Church. When Meir took refreshment orders from him and other guests at her home, he expected her to summon a servant. Instead, she excused herself and went to the kitchen. Curious, Church found her personally preparing a tray with coffee, tea, and orange juice. The incident underlined "the egalitarian character of Israel's society," he subsequently told the Senate. Several years later he was still telling the story.[83]

What he had seen in Israel made him an even more vocal champion of that country. To that point, as Tom Dine later observed, he had not been conspicuously pro-Israel. The Israelis whom he had encountered on his visit reminded him of the pioneers who had settled his native Idaho. "These are fiercely independent, strongly motivated people," he said. "They have built a society from scratch in a period of only a quarter of a century." Not surprisingly, he filed a glowing report with the Senate Foreign Relations Committee on September 21. "I found in Israel a spirit of accommodation," he wrote, "a spirit I hope will also emerge in the Arab countries. Israel wants peace and is willing to compromise to achieve it." Because the report was so unabashedly pro-Israel, Church's aides worried that anti-Israeli terrorists might send bombs through the mail. They handled unusual boxes and packages with care, especially in light of the recent murders of Israeli athletes by Palestinian terrorists at the Olympic Games in Munich.[84]

VIII

With the Israeli trip behind him, Church threw himself energetically into the presidential campaign. "I know I did you some good," he told McGovern, following a road trip through five eastern states. He pointed out to older people, for example, that Nixon had opposed all three of the Social Security increases that had passed after he became president. Stumping in Idaho and elsewhere, Church claimed that a McGovern victory "would mean a government for the little guy instead of the big guy." He promised that McGovern would cut wasteful government spending, including that of the military. Why, he asked, should the U. S. keep enough troops abroad to form "an American colony in the heart of Europe, bigger than the population of four American states?" Turning to the subject of Vietnam, Church insisted that McGovern, not Nixon, had remembered the advice of General Douglas MacArthur that the U. S. should never fight land wars on the Asian mainland: "Unlike President Nixon, Senator McGovern has opposed this foolish, futile war from the start." Church focused as well on the scandals that had rocked the administration. "If the capacity for moral outrage still lives," Church exhorted his audiences, angry citizens would "turn the rascals out" and choose new leadership.[85]

On November 7, however, voters overwhelmingly reelected Richard Nixon. The results were never in doubt. A White House aide had quipped at one point, "We're really running scared, for about an inch." In a speech afterwards McGovern said, "For years, I wanted to run for President in the worst possible way—and I'm sure I did." Battling public perceptions of him as a radical who favored drugs, abortion, and amnesty—or "grass, ass, and amnesty"—he had posed no threat to the incumbent president. The vice-presidential debacle had hardly helped.[86]

In retrospect, McGovern believed that he had made a significant mistake in not choosing Church as his running mate in Miami. "The irony is that he was honest about telling us about a possible trouble area"–his break from Catholicism. "Eagleton, who had a much more serious skeleton in his closet, so to speak, never told us about it, never even hinted at it." McGovern had no illusions that a ticket with Church could have beaten Nixon; but he suspected that, with Church as their vice presidential candidate, the Democrats would have run a much more respectable race. They might have carried twelve to fifteen states, thereby at least making the McGovernites less vulnerable in the Democratic Party after the election.[87]

The McGovernites were instead buried under a Nixon landslide. Nixon had campaigned as a defender of stability and orderly change at home, and as a statesman who was bringing Americans home from Vietnam and achieving "peace with honor." The president not only received a near-record 60.7 percent of the vote, but won all but the seventeen electoral votes from Massachusetts and the District of Columbia.[88]

After the election many old-line Democrats declared open season on the "new politics." Determined to regain party control from the McGovernites, they struck back with a vengeance in what columnist James Wechsler characterized as "a kind of ideological holy war." With fliers and full-page advertisements, the newly-formed Coalition for a Democratic Majority (CDM) urged Democrats to "Come Home." Describing themselves as "Cold War or labor liberals," CDM's founders claimed that the new politics had failed miserably in 1972 because it was isolationist, elitist, oblivious to the common citizens' desire for law and order, and viewed America as morally bankrupt and corrupt. The *New Republic* observed skeptically that the CDM was, at root, nervous about participatory democracy and the insurgent role of amateurs and activists in the Democratic Party. Certainly a fear of grass-roots activism marked the comment of one labor leader who believed that the Miami convention had included "too much hair, and not enough cigars."[89]

Frank Church liked cigars and was pleased when his son shaved off his beard, but he was not yet ready to return to what he had called status quo politics. A few weeks after the election he published a letter in the *Washington Post* defending McGovern for giving millions of voters a voice and for trying to "shape our institutions to serve the American ideals of individual liberty and shared institutional power." For Church, the fight for these goals was not over.[90]

IX

The prospects for success nevertheless appeared bleak, especially when the president in December ordered the most extensive bombing raids yet against North Vietnam. "I don't want any of this crap about the fact that we couldn't hit this target or that one," Nixon warned the chairman of the Joint Chiefs of Staff. "This is your chance to use military power to win this war, and if you don't, I'll consider you responsible." The bombing represented what Senator George Aiken gloomily described as a "sorry Christmas present for the people of America," but it was even worse for the North Vietnamese. In twelve days starting on December 18 the U. S. dropped a greater tonnage of bombs than it had during Nixon's first two years in office.[91]

Once again the administration had acted without consulting Congress. A discouraged George Aiken noted that he "might as well be on another planet" as to try to learn what the White House had in mind. As public outrage resurfaced, and as Senate doves threatened to challenge the administration following the Christmas recess, Nixon and his advisers, according to aide Charles Colson, "knew we were racing the clock." At the end of December, in exchange for the North Vietnamese returning to the negotiating table in Paris, the bombing stopped.[92]

On January 16, Tom Dine excitedly called Frank Church's office with news that a cease-fire agreement was apparently imminent. "AT LONG LAST?" wondered Verda Barnes, as she passed along the message. A week later it was official. Nixon told a television audience of an arrangement "to end the war and bring peace with honor in Vietnam and South Asia." A cease fire would begin on January 27. Within sixty days America's 23,700 remaining troops, along with American prisoners of war, were to be out of Vietnam.[93]

Church was relieved but wary. "We have fought the war with so many illusions," he cautioned the public, "let us have no illusions about the peace." Although grateful about the scheduled removal of U. S. forces, he believed that American policy had not changed. Indeed, he warned that the White House was "busily engaged in designing new ways to keep us involved." What, he asked, would the administration do once the fighting between the Vietnamese resumed, as it inevitably would? To guard against a renewed commitment of American forces in such a situation, he and Clifford Case introduced a bill on January 26 barring any kind of U. S. reentry into hostilities in Vietnam, Laos, or Cambodia without congressional authorization.[94]

The tentative nature of America's withdrawal was immediately evident in the opposition to the Case-Church initiative. Arizona Republican Barry Goldwater saw such legislation as jeopardizing Nixon's "monumental achievement" in defeating communist aggression. Goldwater believed that the administration's peace agreement "should put an end to the Senate 'doves' and the so-called anti-war activists in this country." In his opinion, these people had only prolonged the conflict. Senator John Tower (R-Texas) agreed, charging that the doves' "cut and run plans" had constituted one of America's sorriest chapters. According to Robert Griffin (R-Michigan), the Case-Church proposal signaled Hanoi that it could violate the peace agreement with impunity. Once again, he claimed, Congress raised enemy hopes that the victory it could not win on the battlefield would arrive "on a silver platter."[95]

Church sharply rejected the accusation that he and Case were encouraging Hanoi to do whatever it wanted. Their bill said simply that, if fighting erupted again, the president could not reinstate America's military presence without congressional approval. The issue, he reminded his colleagues, was that of constitutional processes.[96]

Actually, the threat of renewed U. S. involvement was quite real. Since October the Pentagon had been working on contingency plans for the support of the Thieu government in South Vietnam after any cease fire went into effect. The plans included the use of U. S. air power to enforce any agreement. A U. S. military command post would operate out of the American embassy in Saigon to coordinate military and intelligence operations.[97]

A more immediate problem remained in Cambodia, which the Paris peace agreement did not affect. The Paris accord called upon the U. S. and North Vietnam to respect the neutrality of Laos and Cambodia, but it did not provide for a specific cease fire in those countries. For years, under the pretext of cutting off communist infiltration into South Vietnam, the White House had sent U. S. bombers into Cambodia. With the final withdrawal of American troops from Vietnam in late March, the Cambodian bombing stood exposed for what it was: a way of bolstering the Lon Nol government. American B-52s could hardly be protecting American troops in Vietnam if there were no more troops there to protect. Yet the bombing intensified dramatically. In April 1973 alone, U. S. bombers dropped almost as many explosives on Cambodia as they had in all of 1972.

Church, furious at the continued bombing, shuddered at the fate of thousands of uprooted Cambodians in shanty towns outside Phnom Penh. Poignantly, he quoted one young woman who had sought nightly shelter in a deep bunker: "When the noise was so loud that I couldn't hear if I was screaming or not, I knew the Americans had come."[98]

Although the administration wanted the bombing to buy time for what Nixon described as an effective negotiated peace in Cambodia, domestic political events suddenly overwhelmed the White House. By mid-April, the Watergate scandal was breaking through the administration's barriers to contain it. The term Watergate, which grew from a June 1972 break-in at the Democratic National Committee headquarters in Washington, D. C., came to signify the vast range of illegal activities and corruption within the Nixon administration. After a 77-0 Senate vote on February 7 to establish a Select Committee on Presidential Campaign Activities to investigate some of the crimes, White House aides scrambled to come up with a viable "game plan." Initially, Nixon remained confident, telling presidential counsel John Dean on March 13 that the Senate hearings would "peter out quickly." There was no crisis, Nixon maintained, except "among the upper intellectual types, the ass holes, you know, the soft heads." He dismissed all the talk about Watergate as "the last gasp of. . .our partisan opponents." Over the next few weeks, however, he became more apprehensive. Worried that the situation was "breaking so fast," an increasingly distracted Nixon spent hours discussing the crisis with his top aides. "Everything is likely to blow around here!" he fretted. A Gallup poll at the end of April showed that half of the American public suspected the president himself was involved in a Watergate cover-up. "It's all over," Nixon commented to his press secretary, "do you know that?. . .Well, it is. It's all over."[99]

As the Watergate crisis spun out of Nixon's control, his leverage over Congress weakened dramatically. "Watergate is the bursting of the boil," J. William Fulbright told a television interviewer on May 19 when discussing presidential powers.[100]

Church urged his colleagues to seize the moment. In an exclusive interview with the *Chicago Tribune* on April 9, he described the bombing of Cambodia as "an utterly illegal act," proof "that the administration has refused to quit this war." He had little confidence in the Vietnam cease fire because it left untouched the issues that had divided the Vietnamese for decades. The administration, in his opinion, was still pursuing a misbegotten policy, albeit in another guise, one which could embroil the U. S. in Indochina yet again. "Saigon has been given the tools to defend South Vietnam," he said. "From now on, it's up to Thieu." On May 8 he urged the Senate Foreign Relations Committee to cut off funds for the bombing. Mere resolutions were no longer adequate, as Nixon had demonstrated when he repudiated the earlier Mansfield resolution. Taking the Senate floor on May 14, Church announced that he and Case now had thirty-eight co-sponsors for their bill. The American Air Force, he argued, had "become an arm of the Lon Nol government" in Cambodia—and had done so through "the unrestrained use of Executive power."[101]

On June 14 the Senate overwhelmingly adopted the Case-Church amendment, 67-15. It passed so quickly that Church and Case did not even have an opportunity to debate it.

The embattled administration responded, even as additional Watergate revelations detonated around it. On June 27, two days after John Dean commenced his damaging testimony against Nixon before Congress's newly formed Watergate Committee, the president vetoed legislation to cut off the bombing in Cambodia. Unlike the Case-Church measure, which had not yet passed the House, this legislation focused only on Cambodia. Thomas Eagleton had sponsored it in the Senate and the House had approved it on June 25. Nixon attacked the bill for denying him "the means to enforce the Vietnam peace agreement." He knew what Congress did not: he had secretly told Nguyen Van Thieu that the U. S. would resume bombing in North and South Vietnam if necessary. Indeed, a mid-March entry in Henry Kissinger's office journal indicated that the only unresolved issue was when to renew the air strikes.[102]

The spreading Watergate scandal was quickly denying Nixon room in which to maneuver, however. Painfully aware that his presidency was endangered, he reluctantly decided to strike a compromise on the bombing cutoff. Although the House of Representatives had upheld his June 27 veto that same day, he recognized that other bills would soon follow. "I could not win these battles forever," he wrote later. He thus agreed to halt the bombing of Cambodia on August 15, after which he would need to get congressional approval for any military action. "With every passing day," Henry Kissinger remembered bitterly, "Watergate was circumscribing our freedom of action." Kissinger, along with Alexander Haig and other White House advisers, thought it was essential to continue the bombing. Otherwise, he protested, Congress was "going to throw everything down the drain for nothing." Nixon, in retrospect, described Congress's decision to enforce the August 15 deadline as "tragic and irresponsible." Like Kissinger and other defenders of the administration, Nixon was convinced that Watergate and a vindictive, short-sighted Congress had "fatally undermined the peace we had won in Indochina."[103]

This interpretation turned history upside down, according to Frank Church. Speaking in Delaware on June 6, 1973, he argued that the Vietnam war had begat Watergate. The war itself had been a grotesque creation of a foreign policy based on secrecy, deception, and an arrogant refusal to let Congress play its rightful role. "Under the Nixon administration, we have come full circle," Church said. "If 'dirty tricks' were acceptable in foreign policy, why, in the view of the White House Chiefs-of-staff, were they any less so in domestic affairs?" In Church's opinion, "Watergate could not have happened but for the moral and political perversion generated by Vietnam."[104]

The June 29 passage of a modified Case-Church amendment was a bitter-sweet moment for the Idaho senator. By a 63-26 vote the Senate approved a Fulbright amendment to a continuing resolution that had already passed the House. Like the original Case-Church amendment, it cut off funding for all U. S. military action in North and South Vietnam, Cambodia, and Laos without further congressional approval. But, per the president's demand, it now allowed the bombing to continue until August 15. Church was not happy about the bombing extension, but believed there was no option. Nixon, through his congressional liaison people, had made it clear that he would not veto a bill containing the August 15 deadline. To some irate doves, however, Nixon's "concession" amounted to nothing less than a moral abomination. They refused to agree to the continuation of the dreaded bombing for another forty-five days.[105]

Even Tom Dine wondered if his boss was correct in accepting the compromise. He and Church debated the issue at length the day before the vote. "I state my view and F. C. states his," Dine wrote in a memo for his own record later that day. "If I don't like team position to point where I am unable to play in cooperative manner and support the position, then option open to resign." By the day of the vote Dine had decided that Church was correct; to reject the compromise would only lead to a stalemate with the administration. In the back of the Senate chamber, Dine ended up in a heated exchange with Senators Ted Kennedy and Thomas Eagleton and their aides. How, they demanded angrily, could Church agree to a continuation of the bombing for another six weeks? Firmly in Church's corner by now, Dine argued back, "We've got them [Nixon and his people]. We've got them by the short hairs. We had to give something." The intensity of the exchange indicated the high level of emotions as the Senate moved toward a vote.[106]

Inferences that Church was caving in to the administration stung him deeply. That he resented such insinuations was clear in the impassioned address that he delivered to the Senate on June 29. By then, Mark Hatfield had said fiercely that "one does not compromise about the slaughter of innocents." Ted Kennedy, in a fiery statement, had predicted that congressional approval of the Nixon compromise would "go down in infamy in American history." To the Massachusetts senator "this cruel and calculated pact" amounted to nothing less than "amnesty for the slaughter of the past, and a license for six more weeks of slaughter in Cambodia." Mike Mansfield had declared that accommodating the president's request constituted "an abdication of the constitutional powers of the Senate. . . .The bombing must stop—not next month, not on August 15, but now."[107]

Church was obviously distressed by the nature of the rhetoric. By the time he rose to his feet to defend the modified amendment, it was evening. The long, emotion-packed day was wearing down. He opened his speech by conceding how uncomfortable he felt by aligning himself against the likes of Kennedy, Mansfield, and Hatfield, with whom he had long stood in opposition to the war. But he found "somewhat repugnant" the inference that supporters of the compromise were "impure, while those who oppose it somehow stand on the side of conscience. I have a conscience, too." He was willing to match his credentials as a war critic with those of anyone else in the Senate. No one needed to remind him "that the war in Cambodia is an abomination. It does not have to be emphasized, insofar as I am concerned, that it is an unconstitutional exercise in Presidential power."[108]

What, Church asked, suddenly justified the charge that agreeing to a deadline constituted an endorsement of an immoral, unconstitutional war? The Cooper-Church amendments contained deadlines. So did the McGovern-Hatfield amendment. So did Mansfield's amendment. Yet Church could not recall that anyone had viewed these as endorsements of the war. "This is not a contest of conscience, in which the side of the pure stands arrayed against the impure," he insisted. "This is a stark and simple matter of how we bring this awful war to an end." And in this regard there was an undeniable reality: without the president's signature, no cutoff of funds was possible. Just a few days earlier, the House had sustained a veto. To block the proposed compromise would not end the war. The conflict would continue, perhaps for months. "The bombing will go on, and the young, the old, the sick, and the innocent will die—in larger numbers and for a longer period of time than if we adopt this proposal tonight." Voting for the compromise agreement was no sell out, no "cave-in." Instead, the opportunity had arrived at last to accomplish what Church assumed "the opponents of the war always wanted to do, namely to cut off funds and force an end to our part of the war." In "good conscience" Church voted for the resolution.[109]

Although the resolution carried substantially, Church undoubtedly left the Senate that evening with mixed emotions. After years of trying to build a dove coalition to end the war, he had voted against some of his old allies: Kennedy, Mansfield, Muskie, and Eagleton. The rancor that had suffused the last hours of debate, with the inferences that supporters of the compromise measure lacked conscience, had unquestionably pained Church.

At least the war was finally ending. The June 29 vote had driven the final nail into the coffin of the Vietnam conflict. For the United States, military involvement in or over Indochina would end August 15.

Upon close reflection, Church could even have found evidence that perhaps the "new politics" had prevailed in notable ways after all. True, McGovern's campaign had been full of disappointments and setbacks. As Church had feared, McGovern's support sagged badly among middle- and lower-income whites, who increasingly viewed the Democratic party as the voice of cultural radicalism rather than economic reform. There were encouraging political signs nevertheless. Not only was the Vietnam war ending, but the Nixon presidency was also on the defensive, fighting for its very survival as the Watergate revelations poured forth. After a long, long time, Congress was finally reasserting its powers. In fact, the passage of the modified Case-Church amendment on June 29, 1973 constituted what two scholars later described as "the Bastille Day of the Congressional revolution." In the words of historian William

Berman, "After suffering through more than one hundred roll call votes since 1966, the doves had finally prevailed." Several months later, on November 7, Congress overrode Nixon's veto of the recently passed War Powers Resolution, which limited the president's use of military troops in an emergency to sixty days without explicit congressional authorization. Church had co-sponsored the resolution. Although he doubted that the resolution would in fact work, he saw it as "a symbol of the effort of Congress to regain its place in the constitutional scheme of things."[110]

Church had no intention of relinquishing his role as a leader of that effort. Indeed, he was already working on ways to limit the emergency powers of the president. The fact that the Watergate hearings were again raising political consciousness seemed also to bode well for another of his major projects, an investigation of the influence of multinational corporations on U. S. foreign policy. Moreover, with the end of the Vietnam war, overdue attention could go to the nation's domestic needs. The new politics might yet have an opportunity to reshape the national agenda.

Church presiding over the multinationals investigation of the oil industry. *Courtesy Boise State University.*

Chapter Fifteen

Fighting the National Security State and Big Business: 1972-1974

ALTHOUGH SOME OBSERVERS disliked his "Sunday School" demeanor, Frank Church was at his best as a kind of "moral lightning rod." By the 1970s his moralistic tendencies were increasingly apparent, challenging his innate caution, distracting him from his favored middle ground. The moral clarity of issues jolted him more and more, pushing him to take political risks. His criticism of the Vietnam war had become more searing and uncompromising once he saw it as a moral abomination. Similarly, U. S. assistance to repressive Latin American regimes elicited a "gut level" outrage from him. Costa-Gravas's disturbing 1973 movie "State of Siege," about U. S. complicity in Uruguay's brutal military rule, moved him profoundly. His anger at the abuses of U. S. power abroad only heightened his fears that, at home, America's democratic principles and processes were also in jeopardy.[1]

His growing suspicion of concentrated power, whether in the White House, big business, or elsewhere, became strikingly apparent in 1972 when he took command of two of the most important congressional committees in post-World War II America. He co-chaired the Special Committee on National Emergencies and Delegated Emergency Powers, which dealt with troubling issues of governmental authority in American life. And he chaired the Subcommittee on Multinational Corporations, whose highly publicized investigations of relationships between U. S.-based multinational corporations and American foreign policy illuminated shocking corruption and the arrogant misuse of power.

His targets were formidable. He battled the national security state on one front, while on another he took on the world's largest corporations, each of which was wealthier than most nations.

I

The Special Committee on National Emergencies represented a major effort to rein in the national security state. For several decades, in the name of protecting America, the U. S. government had built an immense but virtually unnoticed structure of emergency powers constituting what the committee's staff director, William Miller, described as a "national security loophole" which jeopardized constitutional processes and vastly strengthened presidential authority. No senator was more determined than Church to close this "loophole."[2]

In mid-1970 Church had listened incredulously when Secretary of Defense Melvin Laird claimed that President Nixon had the legal authority to keep U. S. troops in Cambodia, even if Congress cut off funding. That authority, Laird told the Foreign Relations Committee, was in the form of the Feed and Forage Act of 1861, an obscure Civil War statute that permitted the cavalry to buy feed for its horses if it ran out of funds and Congress was no longer in session. According to Laird, Nixon could use that act to override Congress and continue paying the U. S. troops in Cambodia. Shocked at the testimony, Church wondered "what other laws were on the books which might be construed as permitting the President to govern without leave of Congress."[3]

Church subsequently joined Maryland Republican Charles "Mac" Mathias in calling for a Senate investigation of presidential emergency powers. On June 13, 1972 the Senate established an eight-person special committee, equally divided between Republicans and Democrats, to conduct the investigation. Because of Church's well-known interest in restoring the balance of power between the legislative and executive branches, Majority Leader Mike Mansfield appointed him as chair.

In a unique move, Church suggested to Mansfield that Mathias should be co-chair. The idea had considerable merit. Mathias had been the chief sponsor of the legislation that formed the committee, for one thing. Moreover, a dual chair made good political sense: it would underline the bipartisan nature of a committee that might well recommend trimming presidential powers. Church, much in character, was already building a coalition, turning to Mathias just as he had allied with John Sherman Cooper on the Vietnam issue. Church knew there was little chance that Mathias would attempt to protect the Nixon administration. The Maryland Republican had already demonstrated his political independence by opposing the Vietnam war and backing the Cooper-Church amendment. Mathias nevertheless believed that Church and Mansfield had shown "unprecedented" generosity by asking him to share the committee's leadership.[4]

Church sometimes viewed the committee's task as hopeless. Even the Justice Department did not have a listing of emergency powers that Congress had historically conferred on the president. Moreover, as Mathias recalled, the Pentagon and National Security Council were suspicious of the committee and "not at all happy with what we were doing." There was also every reason to suppose that the president would resist any move to diminish executive authority.[5]

Unexpectedly, the committee received a much-needed break. When the staff in 1973 started a laborious hand search of existing laws, it discovered a legislative gold mine. The entire U. S. Code was on an Air Force computer in Colorado. "We've got it, we've got it," Church excitedly told Bethine after the discovery. He was so happy with the breakthrough, she recalled, that he virtually jumped up and down. It was now possible to conduct a computer search for emergency statutes. Using key words such as "security" and "crisis," the committee eventually identified hundreds of existing emergency laws.[6]

By October 1973 the shocked committee had learned that four declared states of emergency were still in effect: Franklin Roosevelt's 1933 declaration to manage the banking crisis, Harry Truman's in December 1950 to deal with the Korean war, and Nixon's on March 23, 1970 to counter a Post Office strike, and on August 15, 1971 to enforce restrictions on currency and foreign trade. Equally disturbing, the committee also identified no fewer than 470 special statutes the president could use during a declared national emergency. Never before had the extent of the president's emergency powers been so startlingly apparent. "We were faced," Church said, "with literally hundreds of laws that the chief executive could invoke even though no real emergency existed." The president's "virtually unlimited power" included the authority to seize property, institute martial law, take control of transportation and communication, and even suspend publication of the *Federal Register.* "These emergency powers," in Church's words, "were like a loaded gun lying around the house, ready to be fired by any trigger-happy president who might come along."[7]

In the context of the unfolding Watergate investigations in 1973 and 1974, this information revealed chilling possibilities. The committee had uncovered "the blueprint for an American dictatorship," according to the *Washington Post*. "Even more sobering than the scope of these emergency powers is the fact that they could be invoked at any time, even today. . . ." Tom Dine recalled wondering with Bill Miller, "Jesus, what have we created here? We are telling Nixon that he could legitimately exercise power here and stay in power by turning us into a police state." Church himself worried that Nixon might launch some "diversionary action abroad" as a pretext to strengthening his position at home.[8]

By mid-1974 Church and Mathias were ready to introduce in the Senate a National Emergencies Act to terminate the four existing declared emergencies, repeal many of the 470 statutes, and establish procedures to cover future national crises. Under the procedures that the Church/Mathias committee recommended, any presidential declaration of national emergency would automatically end after six months, unless Congress by joint resolution terminated it earlier or extended it. Although the proposed legislation was ready for Senate consideration by July 1974, Church and Mathias held back on introducing it during the last days of the collapsing Nixon administration. They undoubtedly agreed with Mike Mansfield, who reportedly told Bill Miller that "it is too good and important a bill to let those Nixon people get at it."[9]

They did not have long to wait. In late July the House Judiciary Committee approved three articles of impeachment, including the charge that Nixon had abused his powers. As one Republican, Hamilton Fish, Jr., sadly summed up the evidence of Nixon's guilt, "There was no smoking gun. The whole room was filled with smoke." A Gallup poll revealed on July 26 that the president's public support had plummeted to 24 percent. By August 2, according to a Louis Harris poll, 66 percent of the public favored impeachment. On August 9, Richard Nixon resigned as president and a relieved Senator Church lifted a glass of champagne in celebration.[10]

In Church's estimation, the Watergate scandals represented the Cold War's revenge on America's domestic life. The methods that U. S. policy makers had used to combat communism abroad had ultimately circled back home. "Imitating the methods of opponents is what got us into trouble in the first place," Church observed. For more than a quarter of a century the patterns of "secrecy, divisiveness and intrigue" had spread like an ugly web across America as political leaders tried to defend democracy with undemocratic tactics. In that context, the Gulf of Tonkin resolution had been a kind of " 'dirty trick,' a foreign policy precursor, and something of a precedent, to the domestic dirty tricks of Watergate." Determined to centralize executive power even more, the Nixon administration had used secrecy, deception, and a willingness to ignore the Constitution. Watergate, Church believed, was the grotesque culmination "of a foreign policy broken loose from its domestic, democratic moorings," and of a tendency to clothe the American presidency with "an aura of imperial infallibility."[11]

On August 22, soon after Nixon's resignation, Church and Mathias brought their proposed National Emergencies Act to the Senate. They did so after an encouraging conversation that morning with the new president, Gerald Ford, who conceded the importance of returning to normal government. Although Ford agreed with the bill's general idea, he carefully avoided endorsing the bill itself. Upon the advice of his aides, he at least hoped to buy time. A recommendation from the attorney general's office had warned him, for example, that "the actual enactment could have dire effects on many agencies, particularly Defense."[12]

For more than two years Church and Mathias struggled to secure legislation that Ford would not veto. Theirs was a losing cause, they suspected, because the president was reluctant to give any appearance of executive weakness. At the White House, worries ran high that the Vietnam war and Watergate had resulted in what Ford described as an "imperiled presidency." Already convinced that Congress was going too far in challenging presidential authority, the administration eyed emergency powers legislation nervously.[13]

Ford ultimately signed the National Emergencies Act, however, after it passed the House overwhelmingly, in September 1975 and the Senate, without objection, on August 27, 1976. But even as he did so he questioned the constitutionality of the section that permitted Congress to terminate a national emergency by a concurrent resolution, and he ordered his attorney general to challenge it. Mathias was convinced that Ford had been under pressure to veto the bill right up to the end.[14]

Determined to downplay the act's significance, Ford turned the September 14, 1976 signing into a nonevent. Mathias, caught by surprise when he learned that Ford was going to sign the bill, rushed to the White House, arriving there only to discover that no one had bothered to notify Church. At Mathias's insistence, White House aides called the Idaho senator. When Ford signed the bill, without ceremony,

Church and Mathias were the only other officials present. It was "a very rare thing," Mathias believed, for a president to give up that much authority.[15]

Almost no publicity surrounded the National Emergencies Act. "We didn't get much coverage," recalled Tom Dine. The law "wasn't sexy enough." Too legalistic to capture much attention, the act was profoundly important nonetheless. Church viewed it as one of his proudest accomplishments. It had, he wrote, "more to do with returning our government to normalcy—after 43 years of emergency rule—than anything that has occurred during my twenty years of service in the Senate." He considered it one of the landmarks in "the historic redemption of Congress that has gone forward in this decade." Mathias agreed, noting later that it returned "an enormous inventory of powers to the Congress."[16]

II

Church correctly believed that the Watergate scandals had facilitated the congressional reassertion of authority. Indeed, he said, "it is scarcely to Congress' credit, but it took Watergate to embolden the legislators to put a final end to American participation in the Indochina war."[17] Just as surely, the National Emergencies Act owed its existence to the political fallout from Watergate.

Watergate also spurred the Senate to investigate multinational corporations. In late February and early March 1972, newspaper columnist Jack Anderson published three startling stories charging the Justice Department with settling its antitrust suit against the International Telephone and Telegraph Company (ITT) in exchange for the company's $400,000 contribution to the Republican National Convention. On March 22 and 23, Anderson jarred the public with additional information. He accused ITT of plotting in 1970 with the Central Intelligence Agency (CIA) to block the election of Chile's president, Salvador Allende, a Marxist who had threatened to nationalize ITT's 60 percent interest in the Chilean telephone company. Anderson also claimed that ITT president Harold Geneen had offered the Nixon administration a contribution of "up to seven figures" to keep Allende out of power.[18]

Anderson's revelations immediately jolted Frank Church and the Senate Foreign Relations Committee into action. Vermont Republican George Aiken suspected that politics accounted at least partly for the committee's response. "The Democrats have built up the ITT to make it look as if it were almost the Republican party itself," he wrote irritably. Aiken did not count Church among the "cooler heads of our Committee," especially when the Idaho senator insisted that the committee investigate ITT's efforts to influence the Chilean election. On March 24, Church offered two motions. He wanted the committee to "undertake an in-depth study of the role of multinational corporations and their relationship to the foreign policy of the United States," and to "obtain forthwith all ITT documents concerning Chile between September 1 and November 1, 1970." The committee overwhelmingly adopted both motions, although Aiken recorded that most members did not favor turning the investigation into "a major project."[19]

Public reaction to the committee's highly publicized decision to investigate multinational corporations such as ITT apparently caught the senators by surprise. According to the committee's top staff people, Carl Marcy and Pat Holt, the largely favorable response was nothing less than "astonishing." Indeed, Marcy and Holt warned William Fulbright, Clifford Case, and Church that the committee was now on the spot. If it appeared to waver, or conducted a half-hearted inquiry, it would "acquire the public image of a paper tiger, to the despair of its friends and the glee of its adversaries." Marcy and Holt believed that the importance of the investigation went beyond the subject of multinationals to nothing less than the committee's reputation: "The Committee's capacity to accomplish these other things—ending the war, reasserting Senatorial prerogatives vis-a-vis the Executive Branch—will be impaired if it loses credibility."[20]

Perhaps with this warning in mind the committee decided that it should not treat the multinationals issue as just another subject on its agenda. The issue required more attention. Some senators worried also that a hurried look at ITT would be unfair to the corporate community. In their estimation, a broad inquiry into the multinationals would show that big businesses played a constructive role abroad and that ITT was not a typical company. At the end of May the Foreign Relations Committee thus established a subcommittee with an estimated budget of $400,000 to conduct a "long-range, in-depth study" of multinational corporations and their implications for U. S. foreign policy. The study was supposed to take at least two to three years. Several members of the Foreign Relations Committee suspected that, even with that much time, the assignment was impossible; multinational businesses comprised too huge and complex a subject. Some senators, especially Minority Leader Hugh Scott of Pennsylvania, had more immediate political concerns. Alarmed that the inquiry might harm Richard Nixon's reelection campaign, they forced an agreement stating that the subcommittee would not make an interim report until after January 1, 1973.[21]

On May 31, 1972, Fulbright appointed the subcommittee's members, all of them Senate veterans: Republicans Clifford Case of New Jersey, Jacob Javits of New York, and Charles Percy of Illinois; and Democrats Stuart Symington from Missouri, Hubert Humphrey from Minnesota, William Spong, Jr. of Virginia, and, as chair, Frank Church. When Spong lost his reelection bid that fall, Maine's Edmund Muskie replaced him. To protect the subcommittee from charges of being anti-corporation, Fulbright made sure that a majority of its members had business backgrounds. Symington had been president of the Emerson Electric Manufacturing Company of St. Louis; Humphrey's close friend was Dwayne Andreas, a millionaire in agri-business, hotels, and banking; Case had been a Wall Street lawyer; Javits's law firm had specialized in corporate reorganization; and Percy, the former boy wonder at Bell and Howell, had been the youngest chief executive of a major U. S. corporation.[22]

III

Church's designation as chair was no surprise. For one thing, he was already presiding over the Foreign Relations subcommittee that examined Latin American issues, so ITT's activities in Chile fell naturally under his scrutiny. Moreover, since at least 1970 he had advocated a Senate study of U. S. businesses south of the Rio Grande. In articles and speeches he had warned of a collision between economic nationalism in Latin America and "colonialist economics." By 1968, as he pointed out, private U. S. investments in Latin America and the Caribbean had reached almost $13 billion. Growing resistance to this "Yankee imperialism" presented business with two alternatives, in Church's opinion: accepting or fighting economic nationalism. Choosing to fight would encourage the U. S.'s " 'send-the-marines' reflex" which, in turn, would increase Latin American resentments.[23]

Anxious to head off another round of "gunboat diplomacy," Church wanted to investigate U. S. businesses abroad. On February 25, 1972, more than a month before Jack Anderson's disclosures of ITT's actions in Chile, he had made his wishes clear to Carl Marcy. According to

Marcy, Church was "all hot to go after. . . multinational corporations," and was "willing to chair hearings on this subject."[24]

Although Church got his wish to chair the new multinationals subcommittee, Fulbright was not enthusiastic about appointing him. Fulbright, along with several other senators and staffers on the Foreign Relations Committee, doubted Church's capacity to handle the assignment effectively. The subcommittee's top aides, chief counsel Jerome Levinson and associate counsel Jack Blum, were surprised to encounter so much skepticism about Church's leadership qualities. Some members of the Foreign Relations Committee staff warned them that Church was unpredictable and would not support them "when the chips are down." Fulbright, pacing in his office, lamented that he could not appoint one of the Senate "giants" as chair—for example, Alaska's Ernest Gruening, who had failed to win reelection in 1968, or Tennessee's Albert Gore, Sr., who had been defeated in 1970. As Blum recalled, Fulbright and Clifford Case "viewed Church as strong on rhetoric but likely to fold up in the clutch." When Blum insisted that he, as an investigator, had to know the committee was solidly behind him, Case offered reassurances. The New Jersey senator said, according to Blum, "We have carried Frank through the door from time to time and we wouldn't be afraid to do it again."[25]

These misgivings about Church reflected the ongoing suspicion that he compromised too much, too soon; but they also indicated an awareness of the enormous political pressures that confronted the subcommittee. "Everybody and his brother was on our case to stop the investigation one way or another," Blum remembered. Some skeptics thought the subcommittee had partisan designs. Senator Aiken, for example, guessed that it might "be used largely for witch-hunting purposes to discredit the President." Other critics contended that the subcommittee might injure U. S. corporations. A *Newsweek* cover story in late 1972 thus reported that "every international lawyer in Washington worth his attache case has been hired by one or another multinational company to prepare for the barrage."[26]

Corporate executives were quick to warn Church of the damage that his investigation might cause. In November 1972 several of them approached him at a conference. Suspicious and hostile, they admonished him that the multinationals inquiry would subvert U. S. interests abroad. "Not in twenty years," Church complained afterward, "had I heard so many businessmen echoing the simplistic doctrine

Charlie Wilson enshrined in one pungent sentence: 'What's good for General Motors is good for the United States.' "[27]

George Aiken's observation that the big companies were "considerably" agitated was even more evident on another occasion. In a move that Church interpreted as pure intimidation, around fifteen of the most powerful members of the American business community invited him to a private, black-tie dinner in a posh New York City apartment overlooking the East River. Because his old friend Carl Burke happened to be in New York on business, Church brought him along for moral support. Burke, who arrived somewhat late and was at first unsure of the nature of the dinner, asked the man next to him what work he did. The man replied that he "worked" for American Express. Somewhat later an embarrassed Burke realized the man was the chief executive officer of that company.[28]

As a large group of waiters served dinner, the executives expressed concern that Church was bent on destroying U. S. businesses abroad. Church tried to reassure his hosts that he had no such motive. The problem, he said, was that some corporations were misusing their power in foreign countries. According to Burke, the corporate leaders were initially "cool" toward the senator. Although Burke believed Church had eventually impressed his hosts during the "lively exchange" over several hours, Church told Jerry Levinson the next day that the conversation had gotten "pretty nasty." Church kept the lavish evening in perspective. When he and Burke left the dinner around 1:00 a.m. he breathed deeply the crisp fall air and joked how improbable it was that "a couple of little guys from Boise, Idaho," would end up at such a fancy private dinner in New York City and not even have to pay for it.[29]

Despite pressures from business and elsewhere, and despite the doubts of some of his colleagues, Church pursued the multinational investigations aggressively and persistently. Levinson and Blum, initially unsure about him, ended up applauding his tenacity and firmness. "He sure as hell didn't let me down," Levinson insisted. "The guy was terrific. I mean he was terrific."[30]

Misgivings about Church's toughness reflected less on the senator's resolve than on his personality. Church's accommodating disposition did not suit him for the role of "horse trader" or for one-on-one confrontations. "The normal rule of thumb in the Senate," Blum joked later, "is that the more you are concerned with humanity at large the worse you treat the people within thirty feet of you." Church did not fit that rule. Many individuals attested to his capacity for empathy and his sensitivity to other people's needs. These admirable character traits could be a liability in hard-nosed negotiations, however. A good bargainer, as Blum explained, puts on brass knuckles, scowls, bluffs, and makes the other side beg for concessions. Church's demeanor and temperament did not fit him for the tough guy role. He was, in Blum's words, "so acutely aware of the feelings of others that he fell over himself to accommodate those feelings. That's the worst guy on earth for negotiation."[31]

Church's pleasing nature could nevertheless be deceptive. It conveyed too easily the impression that he would give ground. In fact, his tendency to moralize made him quite ready for combat once he perceived that large principles were at stake. As his old friend Stan Burns recognized, morality was in him "as big as a horse." Church might easily have been a minister, an aide told him, because he was always thinking of a sermon. Indeed, his desire to set things right increasingly resembled "a reflex action."[32]

Initially, even Jerry Levinson found his boss's moralism "excessive" and understood why the senator sometimes annoyed people. According to the longtime congressional doorkeeper, "Fishbait" Miller, it was common wisdom on Capitol Hill that the senator took "his name too seriously. Church. Christ, he's more like a cathedral." In that regard an aide heard Church's colleagues mutter more than once, "Here comes Senator Cathedral."[33]

Over time, however, individuals such as Levinson recognized that Church's moralism was neither simplistic nor affected. Instead, it flowed from a firmly-held, well-considered set of values and assumptions about what kind of country the United States was supposed to be. Delaware senator Joe Biden summed up succinctly one of Church's bedrock political principles: "power out of the hands of the people is a dangerous, dangerous thing." The Emergency Powers Act certainly embodied this conviction. So did Church's wariness of big business.[34]

No businesses were larger, or from Church's view more economically threatening, than the sprawling multinational corporations which stretched into scores of countries. Multinational companies had been important for several centuries, as the history of Britain's East India Company proved; but they were rapidly becoming the dominant international economic force. By 1968 they accounted for around 23 percent of total world production; by the year 2000, according to some projections, that percentage would more than double. Of the ten largest companies in the world by the early 1970s, eight—including General Motors, Exxon, Ford Motors, IBM, and ITT—were based in the United States. The annual sales of General Motors alone exceeded the gross national product of all but around fifteen countries. Church believed these massive businesses were in fact "economic nation-states" that viewed the world as "their oyster." As evidence of their arrogance, he related an incident in which Henry Ford II had reportedly pointed his finger at British Prime Minister Edward Heath and warned, "Behave yourselves or we will go elsewhere."[35]

Frank Church "really had a visceral distrust of the big companies," recalled Jerry Levinson. In this regard he revealed his intellectual debt to the "wild jackass" side of Idaho politics, a side that had long resented eastern profiteers who milked the state's extractive economy. Even as a youngster he had disliked eastern-based companies that sought a favored position in the state. "It was arrogant of eastern corporate officers to be piping the tune for an Idaho legislature," he later reminded a high school classmate. "That was a matter for Idahoans alone."[36]

Church had entered the Senate without the backing of big business. Oil companies outside Idaho had supported Herman Welker during the 1956 election; and, inside the state, the Idaho Power Company had clashed with him over the public power issue in Hells Canyon. Church, in turn, distrusted most of the people who ran Idaho Power and large businesses like it. During his first Senate term he delivered a speech with a title that would have made William E. Borah proud, "The Scourge of Giantism in Business and Politics." In his ringing defense of small shopkeepers, Church had criticized the growth of "a remote corporate hierarchy" that diverted power from local communities and produced economic monopolies. "The bigs," he said, "have ways of rendering competition painless to each other." Nine years later, in 1971, he castigated the Nixon administration's proposed $250 million loan to the struggling Lockheed Corporation as "socialism for the rich and free enterprise for the poor." Where, he wondered, was the administration's concern for the 10,000 small or medium-sized businesses that had gone bankrupt the previous year? Jack Anderson's revelations in early 1972 about ITT confirmed his dislike of large corporations. His view resembled Anderson's: multinationals, as the journalist described them, were "the modern buccaneers, well tailored and turned out, whose quarry is the world," and whose primary motive was profits, not patriotism. One evening at a reception for some of the most powerful corporate executives in America, including the presidents of General Motors and General Electric, Church commented to an aide, "I just don't like these people."[37]

Ideologically and temperamentally, Church was thus predisposed to pursue the multinationals investigation aggressively, uncovering the extent to which government-business relationships threatened democratic processes and the constitutional bases of U. S. foreign policy. In his own eyes, he was no enemy of the big corporations. He saw himself, instead, as saving them from themselves, convincing them that corruption and concentrated power were ultimately not even good for business. But he knew that his allies in this mission would have to be people outside the Wall Street business establishment.[38]

Jerome Levinson, his choice for chief counsel, met that requirement. Levinson was less concerned than Church about the moral implications of the multinationals, and he often tried to convince his boss that the subcommittee's task "was not to remake corporate morality in America." But Levinson was a rigorous investigator who drew some of his ideas from the revisionist diplomatic historian, William Appleman Williams. Citing Williams, he wrote that "the ultimate question for this study is whether American foreign policy is necessarily the handmaiden of U. S. capital."[39]

Church and Levinson developed a close relationship. At first glance they were the "odd couple," as different from each other as Felix and Oscar in the Broadway play and television series. Levinson was a Jew from Brooklyn, balding, intense, driven; Church was a lapsed Catholic from Boise, with a thick head of hair and a relaxed manner. Relationships between them were exceptional, however, and they generally viewed the world in the same way. Levinson believed that he represented Church's "populist side," a side which he encountered many times when they drove to work together, discussing history, politics, economics, and the committee's agenda.[40]

For Church, the investigations offered a splendid opportunity to combine moral convictions with personal advantage. The inquiry could bring him substantial national exposure if he chaired it effectively. He thus broke precedent by insisting upon having a subcommittee staff quite apart from that of the Foreign Relations Committee. For one thing, he wanted to remove the subcommittee as much as possible from under Fulbright's wing. He also recognized that the full committee staff owed its primary loyalty to the Arkansas senator. There was already considerable rivalry and jealousy between his own office aides and Fulbright's people.[41]

IV

"It's a classic inquiry you're onto," *Washington Post* reporter Bernard Nossiter enthusiastically told a Church aide. "Could be as big as La Follette Civil Liberties in the 30s." Nossiter's analogy was appropriate. During the Great Depression, Robert La Follette, Jr.'s Senate Civil Liberties Committee had dramatically influenced public policy and opinion by exposing corporate abuses of labor's right to organize. Forty years later, the multinationals investigations had the same political potential.[42]

Since the mid-1960s, public concerns about corporate misconduct and power had risen markedly, allowing reformers to launch, in effect, a second New Deal of economic regulation. Between 1964 and 1977 Congress created no fewer than ten new agencies to protect the public from corporate wrongdoing, and passed numerous laws, ranging from the Fair Packaging and Labeling Act to the Truth in Lending and Child Protection acts. Activist Ralph Nader led the surging consumers' rights movement, and "Nader's Raiders," a dedicated group of public interest attorneys, battled with large businesses. An explosion of corporate mergers at the end of the Sixties dramatized the question, as one reporter phrased it, of "whether too much economic power is falling into too few hands." International Telephone and Telegraph, for example, not only operated telephone systems in over 120 countries by 1969; after a series of mergers it also controlled the Avis rent-a-car company, Levitt and Sons builders, Continental Baking, and Sheraton Hotels. Harold Geneen, ITT's outspoken president, candidly admitted to running "a colonial empire."[43]

In the early 1970s the Watergate investigations fueled anti-business sentiments by revealing blatant examples of corporate malfeasance. These revelations of corporate misdeeds surfaced against an economic backdrop of rising unemployment and inflation. During the first half of 1973 the inflation rate soared 9.2 percent, eliciting angry protests from shoppers.[44]

Multinational corporations thus constituted "a subject whose time has come," in Frank Church's words. "Global Companies: Too Big to Handle," *Newsweek* warned in a cover story, even before the Senate subcommittee commenced its public hearings in early 1973. A small flood of books also signaled the sudden interest in multinationals. Leading the way were *The American Challenge*, Jean-Jacques Servan-Schreiber's best-seller; *The Anderson Papers*, Jack Anderson's exposé of ITT; *Global Reach*, a scholarly analysis that one reviewer described as "hair raising"; *America After Nixon: The Age of the Multinationals*, which maintained that democracy had fallen victim to "several hundred superlarge multinational corporations, themselves out of control"; Ovid Demaris's carefully researched *Dirty Business*; and Anthony Sampson's readable *The Sovereign State of ITT*, which relied so heavily on the findings of the multinationals subcommittee that Church joked he deserved a share of the royalties.[45]

Church recognized from the outset that the subcommittee existed in a political fishbowl. Anti-business reformers would be quick to criticize it for signs of timidity. Corporate leaders, on the other hand, would be eager to blame it for endangering the U. S. economy. "If we are to compete overseas," admonished ITT's Harold Geneen, "we can't be hamstrung at home." Church thus had to be careful indeed if he hoped to avoid bringing discredit on the committee and himself. He unquestionably shared Bernard Nossiter's "go, go, go" fervor for the subcommittee's task; but he also respected Nossiter's advice to proceed "with loving care."[46]

Church was himself at first so uneasy about the subcommittee's future that he told Levinson the inquiry would probably not last more than a year. The subcommittee might hurt itself by seeming to be sensationalistic, by making mistakes, or by venturing too far into dangerous political waters. "We'll never be able to get through" the investigation, Church predicted. "There is just too much money, too many interests."[47]

The subcommittee's own dynamics presented an additional challenge. This was quickly evident after only a few months when Jacob Javits and Hubert Humphrey left the inquiry. The two senators had reportedly decided that the investigation was going to turn into a media carnival and then self-destruct.[48]

With the membership down to five, Church concentrated on the subcommittee's internal politics. He believed, correctly, that Muskie would be a reliable ally. Although Symington approached some business interests gingerly, he usually supported Church. Indeed, the Missouri senator once dazzled Jack Blum with a ferocious grilling of oil company executives. Charles Percy was considerably more problematic. More than anyone on the subcommittee, he identified with big business and fretted about the investigation's possible harmful effects. Additionally, Percy and Church disliked each other; as a subcommittee staffer observed, Percy "drove Church up the wall." To isolate Percy, and to steer the inquiry away from purely partisan lines, Church worked assiduously to keep the backing of Clifford Case. From one angle, the Church-Case alliance was a natural. It flowed in part from their efforts to end the war in Southeast Asia and from shared political instincts. Case's credentials were solidly liberal and, like Church, he had far more sympathy for labor than for big business. Also like Church, Case was very moralistic and was genuinely appalled when the subcommittee exposed corporate corruption. Although the Church-Case partnership was no surprise, it still required cultivating. The New Jersey senator could be cranky, eccentric, and difficult. He recognized his strategic position on the committee and made the most of it. Church, meanwhile, consciously relied on Case to force Percy into choosing between being outvoted four-to-one, joining the majority, or taking his battle to the larger Foreign Relations Committee. The Church-Case alliance thus formed the subcommittee's cornerstone, as the ITT hearings demonstrated.[49]

V

International Telephone and Telegraph posed a crucial test for the fledgling subcommittee. At the outset no one knew if the subcommittee would undertake work any more impressive than its nondescript office space in an old hotel, with a floor too weak for a safe and with a bath tub as a storage place for files. The subcommittee's reputation and integrity depended on how it handled Jack Anderson's much-publicized charges regarding the ITT/CIA underground war against Salvador Allende.[50]

A possible strategy emerged when Richard Nixon appointed former CIA director Richard Helms as ambassador to Iran. Helms's nomination made him more vulnerable to senatorial scrutiny than he had been as head of the CIA from 1966 to 1973. Still, during his February 5 and 7, 1973 confirmation hearings the Senate Foreign Relations Committee provided a friendly forum. Jerry Levinson and others on the multinationals staff urged Church to summon Helms before the subcommittee for a more rigorous grilling. Church initially demurred. To call Helms would put the subcommittee on a collision course with Fulbright, who looked respectfully upon the former director as one of the few officials who had been candid on the subject of Vietnam. Levinson pressed harder, insisting that the subcommittee desperately needed Helms's testimony if there was any hope of doing more than merely echoing Jack Anderson. At this point, the teamwork of Church and Clifford Case made the difference. The two senators jointly requested that Fulbright recall Helms under the auspices of the Senate Foreign Relations Committee. Unwilling to deny a bipartisan request from two senior members of the committee, Fulbright consented.[51]

By then, the CIA was much alarmed. On February 12, Levinson and Blum had submitted a series of questions to the agency regarding its role in the 1970 Chilean elections. Worse, Levinson had indicated that the subcommittee might well need additional information from Helms, whose recent Senate testimony contradicted ITT's documents.[52]

The CIA, anxious to head off Church's subcommittee, turned to Senator Henry Jackson for assistance. Jackson, a friend of Helms and a long-time supporter of the CIA, was also, according to a CIA memo, "discreet and can be counted on not to comment further on what he learns about CIA or ITT actions in Chile during 1970." The agency knew that it would have to brief the Washington Democrat on the CIA/ITT relationship in Chile but decided that it was "a risk worth taking, for the net gain from such action favors the CIA if the desired results are obtained." Specifically, the CIA wanted Jackson to help shift testimony regarding Chile to the Senate Armed Services subcommittee on CIA oversight, a body that met infrequently, seldom asked questions, and followed the "shut your eyes" advice of its chair, Mississippi's John Stennis. The CIA hoped that Stennis's subcommittee would listen sympathetically to the agency and perhaps get Church's panel to settle for a "controlled presentation" from the new director, James Schlesinger. Such a presentation would not preclude Schlesinger from invoking executive privilege before Church's subcommittee. The CIA's goal was "to avoid answering any questions that might compromise instructions which the Agency received from the President, Dr. Kissinger or the 40 Committee" which oversaw the CIA's covert activities.[53]

On February 23 Jack Maury, the CIA's legislative counsel, and Theodore Shackley, chief of the Western Hemisphere Division, met for about an hour with Jackson. They found him "extremely helpful." According to Shackley, Jackson feared "that the Church Subcommittee was planning to zero in on the whole question of the military industrial complex and its impact on American policies, both foreign and domestic."

Because Stennis was still recovering from a bullet wound that he had received during a robbery, Jackson offered to contact Arkansas senator John McClellan. Jackson was confident that McClellan would use the CIA oversight subcommittee to protect the agency from Church's investigation. Perhaps the CIA could then get by with a brief statement to Church's panel that Helms's Senate testimony had been accurate. Determined to guard the CIA against a Church-style inquiry, Jackson promised to do everything possible to help the agency. Immediately after Jackson talked with Maury and Shackley, Schlesinger asked him to contact McClellan.[54]

But McClellan and Jackson failed to deter Church. When they warned him that he was impinging on their committee's jurisdiction, Church offered a challenge of his own. Did they really wish to be responsible for a situation in which ITT could emerge unscathed and be able to tap millions of tax dollars to pay for its losses in Chile? McClellan backed off, indicating that no one had explained that aspect of the problem to him. "Jackson just shut up," according to Levinson, with whom Church discussed the conversation.[55]

On March 6, following the CIA's failure to guide the Chilean inquiry onto friendlier turf, Helms met behind closed doors with the Foreign Relations Committee. He quickly learned that this session would be different from his meetings with the committee several weeks earlier. In the past, the senators had typically questioned the witness; this time, per Church's instructions, Levinson started the interrogation. Moreover, it was soon apparent to Helms that Levinson was working from a lengthy script of detailed questions. As Church had predicted, Levinson and Blum were better prepared than the senators could have been. The staff people were able to start a line of inquiry which provided ideas for the senators' own questions.[56]

Church excelled in such situations. He was by all accounts a "quick study." Although he often had trouble finding his glasses, brief case, car keys, or the parking place in which he had left his car, he had an eye for substantive details and ideas. Even when he seemed distracted or uninterested, he typically absorbed huge amounts of information. He surprised people by appearing to be oblivious to what they were saying and then later repeating their words almost verbatim. During Senate hearings this ability served him especially well.[57]

As Levinson recalled the March 6 hearing, Helms soon resembled "a cornered rabbit," desperately trying to avoid contradicting himself when Church and Case boxed him in with questions about the CIA's relationship with ITT and the agency's role in subverting the Chilean government. Fulbright, realizing that his colleagues were not engaged in a fishing expedition with Helms, became more and more intrigued and was soon himself asking questions. Thereafter, in Levinson's estimation, Fulbright had more confidence in the subcommittee and was more protective of it.[58]

For Helms the experience was bitter. He resented the hostile attitude of Levinson and Blum. And he believed that Church had acted irresponsibly, turning the inquiry into a political investigation for personal gain. Helms later admitted that he had not told the whole story of the CIA's activities against the Allende government, but he had no regrets about his omissions. Indeed, he insisted that his patriotic duty had required the protection of an ongoing CIA operation, and that Church should have been more sympathetic to his predicament.[59]

Stuart Symington rallied to Helms's defense. As Church and Case bore in on the former CIA director, Symington interjected that it would be more appropriate to interrogate William Broe. Broe, the CIA's head of clandestine services for Latin America, had been the intermediary with ITT in 1970. The subcommittee subsequently summoned Broe, who became the first CIA agent to testify openly before a congressional body. In Levinson's words, "to save Helms, they had to give us Broe."[60]

The door on the ITT-CIA presence in Chile now opened more rapidly. Broe's testimony implicated Harold Geneen, ITT's chief executive officer, as well as Helms, in the plans to interfere with the Chilean election. The subcommittee interrogated other government and CIA officials, including John McCone. The white-haired, grandfatherly McCone, who had been a CIA director before moving to ITT's board of directors, portrayed ITT as a patriotic company that wanted to resist the advance of international communism. McCone seemed to regret the corporation's lack of success in getting the U. S. government to act more vigorously. His testimony made the situation more difficult for the last witness, the imperious Geneen, the highest paid corporate officer in the United States and the driving force behind ITT's record profits over the previous twelve years. Geneen tried to take the offensive by insisting that ITT had simply wanted to protect its shareholders and employees, most of whom were "U. S. taxpayers and citizens," and to prod the government "to do more to help the Chileans help themselves," rather than allow Chile to go Marxist. But, by then, Church and Case were relentless. Church branded the ITT-CIA relationship as nothing less than "incestuous."[61]

During the hearings in March and April 1973, the multinational subcommittee pushed beyond Jack Anderson's findings of a year earlier. Anderson had shown that CIA and ITT personnel had discussed ways in which the corporation might intervene in Chile's internal affairs, and he had also proven that ITT had offered the CIA millions of dollars to use in Chile. The multinationals subcommittee revealed that contacts between the CIA and ITT had occurred at the highest levels of both organizations. It also ascertained that, despite the corporation's claims, ITT had not intended to channel its proffered dollars into humanitarian projects in Chile: ITT president Harold Geneen had himself offered corporate money to block Allende's election. The subcommittee subsequently criticized ITT for conduct incompatible with the formulation of U. S. foreign policy and recommended legislation prohibiting U. S. citizens from providing government agencies with funds to interfere in foreign elections. The subcommittee also wondered by what authority the CIA had approached ITT about fomenting economic chaos in Chile. On this last issue, however, the senators hedged. They could neither prove nor disprove that the executive branch's 40 Committee knew anything about the ITT connection.[62]

Church himself was more outspoken. He intimated to the *Chicago Tribune* that the Nixon administration was probably behind the CIA's actions. The CIA, Church suspected, had responded to orders "from above."[63]

For Church, the ITT-CIA discussions about blocking Allende's presidency provided additional evidence that the U. S. had lost its moral compass. A huge American corporation had presumed to dictate the course of another country's politics and had attempted to enlist the CIA in its efforts. The CIA, in turn, had urged ITT to help create economic chaos in Chile in order to keep Allende from ruling. Church shrugged off arguments that the Allende government threatened the security of the United States. Chile, he joked, was "a dagger pointed at the heart of Antarctica." More important was the simple fact that Allende, whom the CIA and ITT had plotted to keep from power, had been freely and legally elected in a country with a long democratic tradition. What, Church wondered, if the situation were reversed and a foreign government attempted to intervene in the election of an American president? When John McCone stressed that Allende had won the election by a plurality and not a majority, Church reminded him that Richard Nixon in 1968 had also received only a plurality. The senator found it disturbingly ironic that, while American troops were dying in Vietnam ostensibly to protect free elections, ITT and the CIA were trying to keep from office a man who had won a popular election, openly and legally.[64]

Church hoped that ITT would at least be unable to collect on its losses in Chile. The company wanted the Overseas Private Investment Corporation (OPIC) to approve its $92.5 million insurance claim for property that the Chilean government had expropriated. Since 1969 OPIC, a federal agency, had insured U. S. businesses against foreign losses. Unless ITT had provoked the nationalization of its holdings, the company was eligible to collect on its lost investments.

Frank Church liked neither ITT's massive insurance claim nor OPIC. Earlier, he had unsuccessfully opposed the formation of OPIC on grounds that it would provide special subsidies to big U. S. corporations and encourage them to invest abroad rather than at home. If ITT now collected on its losses in Chile, OPIC's flaws would be even more apparent. Church was thus delighted to learn from Jerry Levinson that ITT might indeed have invalidated its insurance claim by ignoring a negotiated settlement with Chilean officials, "in favor of plotting with CIA and actively implementing 'economic chaos' strategy." "Good!" the senator wrote on his copy of Levinson's report. In early April 1973, Church told the press that OPIC should deny ITT's huge insurance claim on the basis of the subcommittee's hearings. He said that the hearings also proved the need to reexamine the OPIC program. Taxpayers, he argued, should not have to underwrite the risks of companies who preferred to invest abroad. And make no mistake, he emphasized, taxpayers would be the ones who bailed out ITT, because OPIC had insufficient funds to do so. Church claimed "a major victory" when OPIC, on April 9, denied the ITT claim.[65]

For a moment OPIC itself seemed politically vulnerable. Church and others on the multinationals subcommittee fought its June 1974 renewal on grounds that it was unsound actuarially, protected big business unfairly, and encouraged U. S. government intervention in the politics of host countries. On October 17, 1973 the subcommittee recommended phasing out by 1980 OPIC's role as the primary insurer of overseas investment. The Nixon administration, seeking a two-year OPIC extension, responded with what the *Wall Street Journal* described as "an all-ought fight." In a well-publicized letter, for example, Secretary of State Henry Kissinger told Church that terminating OPIC would be contrary to the national interest.[66]

Contrary to Jack Blum's sense that Church was temperamentally a weak combatant against the likes of Jacob Javits, OPIC's hard-knuckled legislative parent and chief protector, the Idaho senator weighed in heavily against the corporation. On December 11 he obtained a 9 to 7 Foreign Relations Committee vote endorsing his subcommittee's October recommendations. The bill which Church subsequently brought to the Senate floor stipulated specific phaseout deadlines for OPIC–"sudden death" deadlines, as the agency's defenders unhappily called them. To avoid abrupt termination, for example, OPIC had to get private insurance companies to assume responsibility for 25 percent of new policies against expropriation and inconvertibility of U. S. currency by the end of 1975 and 50 percent by 1978. In the Senate on February 16, 1974, Church went head-to-head with Javits. The formidable New York Republican wanted, among other things, to delete the "sudden death" deadlines. Squaring off tenaciously, Church argued that OPIC's policies jeopardized "some *three and one-half billion dollars* of the United States taxpayers' money." Labeling OPIC's programs as "socialism for the rich," he pointed out that "approximately *eighty percent* of the insurance issued by OPIC is to corporations in the Fortune Magazine list of the largest 500 corporations and the fifty largest banks." Church so wanted to stop subsidizing America's largest corporations abroad that he said he "would not weep any crocodile tears" if the Senate opted for Clifford Case's suggestions to abolish OPIC immediately. Sparring verbally with Javits, Church compared the New Yorker's defense of OPIC to the shopworn "articles of faith" that had marked U. S. foreign policy in the more innocent 1950s. "Are we going to stand here on this floor and repeat old axioms because they fit like old shoes?" Church wondered. By only two votes, 48-46, he lost his fight to save the sudden death provisions. He settled ultimately for more open-ended legislation extending OPIC for two years (the conference agreement raised it to three), legislation that clearly signaled congressional intent to limit the agency's role.[67]

Although Church was disappointed that the OPIC legislation was not tougher, he had astutely chaired the ITT hearings and gotten the multinationals subcommittee off to a blazing start. "Church himself," wrote British journalist Anthony Sampson, "dominated the show, shooting the key questions and providing his own running commentary; gazing sternly down at the witnesses, shaking his head, twiddling his glasses, occasionally flashing a wide but disconcerting smile." Pat Holt, a top aide of the Foreign Relations Committee, found the hearings "magnificent," the best staffed of any he had witnessed in twenty-five years on Capitol Hill.[68]

Church was convinced that the hearings had contributed significantly to public knowledge. They had exposed the ITT-CIA stance toward Chile for what it was—immoral, because it violated the American ideal of self-determination; impractical, because it was ultimately counterproductive and bad for business; and subversive, because it was contrary to democratic and constitutional processes. "So the tangled web we weave entraps us," he said sadly. "The imagination is set free to assume the United States is involved in every shady deal on God's earth." Even worse, he conceded, those suspicions might well be correct. "Who can blame others for thinking the worst of us," he asked, in light of America's recent record.[69]

On September 10, a few months after the ITT-CIA hearings, Church stared dejectedly at a note that an aide handed him. A military coup had just toppled Salvador Allende's government in Chile. Church gloomily scrawled on the back of the note, "The military will inherit the world!"[70]

VI

Allende's overthrow and assassination underlined the relevance of the Church subcommittee's work, but so did dramatic developments in the Middle East. On October 6, 1973, as the subcommittee conducted research on the major oil corporations, a massive Arab attack on Israel catapulted oil to the top of the national economic agenda. Within weeks, an "energy crunch" forcefully reminded Americans of their vulnerability to outside events.

The winter of 1972-73 had already provided a hint of things to come. Fuel oil shortages had hurt much of the country, temporarily closing schools in Denver and factories in Des Moines. As early as April 1973, according to a Louis Harris poll, a large majority of Americans suspected the existence of "a conspiracy among utility and fuel companies." By mid-year, popular news magazines like *Time* and *Newsweek* reported growing speculation that the petroleum industry giants were manipulating the supply of gasoline and oil to drive out independent marketers and raise profits.[71]

Against this backdrop of growing suspicion, the oil crisis of late 1973 erupted. The Nixon administration's mid-October decision to send war materiel to the beleaguered Israelis set off an economic explosion. The administration had initially been reluctant to help Israel. For one thing, new Secretary of State Henry Kissinger assumed that the Israelis would win a quick victory. Also, the White House was reluctant to antagonize the Arab oil-producing nations. But on October 9, as Egyptian and Syrian forces pounded Israel, Nixon and Kissinger reversed U. S. policy. Within a few days an immense airlift was underway. "Get them in the air, *now*," Nixon said of U. S. planes to Israel. ". . .Send everything that can fly."[72]

The Arabs responded to the gigantic airlift and a subsequent $2.2 million aid package to Israel by promptly cutting off oil shipments to the United States and several other nations. For the next five months, oil shortages staggered the U. S. economy and oil prices skyrocketed. During the previous twenty years the price of a barrel of oil had gone up just 50 percent, from $2 to $3; but on October 16 alone the price soared 70 percent, to $5.12. Automobile drivers, whose command "Fill 'er up" had long brought immediate results, now waited in lines for hours in hopes they could purchase at least a half-tank of gasoline. Panic buying and hoarding made the situation worse. In three months oil prices more than tripled. Diesel fuel shortages stranded some truckers. Several dozen New Hampshire towns were without police and fire protection for lack of gasoline. In Milwaukee, the public safety committee met by candlelight. "Our growing demands have bumped up against the limits of available supply," President Nixon informed the country in November.[73]

Many Americans were skeptical. The fast-breaking scandals in politics and business over the past months had heightened public distrust. According to a Gallup poll, half of the American public blamed the energy crisis less on the Arab-dominated Organization of Petroleum Exporting Countries (OPEC) than on sources closer to home. A quarter of the sample blamed Nixon; another quarter pointed at the U. S. oil companies. Embittered customers learned angrily that the 1973 fourth-quarter profits of the major American oil corporations had jumped 57 percent from what they had been a year earlier. First-quarter earnings for 1974 were even larger for some of the giant companies. Texaco's profits leaped by 70 percent over the previous year, Mobil's by 68 percent, Exxon's by 59 percent. "The industry's profits amid scarcity have reduced the public image of the oil company to a new low," *Time* reported.[74]

In December 1973, Frank Church publicly chastised the oil corporations for their eagerness "to profiteer upon the present adversity." It was time, he said, to examine the prevailing assumption of the nation's energy policy–"that what's good for the oil companies is good for the United States." Already, he noted, the *Washington Post* had reported that the Nixon administration was protecting the U. S. oil companies from antitrust prosecutions in exchange for their cooperation in ending the energy crisis. "There is no excuse here for secret covenants, secretly arrived at," Church objected. Indeed, he suspected that such agreements lay at the heart of the current crisis. "The cult of secrecy," democracy's great enemy, was again reaping a bitter harvest. Church indicated that the multinationals subcommittee would soon open a full public inquiry into the oil industry. "We Americans," he explained, "must uncover the trail that led the United States into dependency on the Arab sheikdoms for so much of its oil."[75]

Church's concern for the historical record helped to distinguish the subcommittee's inquiry from other investigations of the energy crisis on Capitol Hill. Robert Sherrill, a muckraking journalist who wrote often for *The Nation* magazine, ultimately concluded that the other investigations provided mainly television time for politicians. More valuable, he believed, was the work of the subcommittee on multinationals. By bringing before the public "mountainous piles of explicit details," it had exposed "much of the melancholy history of the federal government's subservience to the oil companies."[76]

The subcommittee's top staff people attributed this achievement directly to Church. Jack Blum lauded his patience and tolerance. Because Church had allowed the staff to dig deeply into the historical record, the public had gotten an unprecedented look "under the circus tent" of government's relationship with the oil industry. Blum could think of few senators who would have allowed their staffs to hold, for example, three days of long, laborious hearings on a subject as arcane as foreign tax credits, "a topic so deadly that when you get six lawyers around the table to talk about it, three argue and three fall asleep." Jerry Levinson agreed, recalling that his confidence in Church grew the more he worked with him.[77]

This "academic" side of the subcommittee nevertheless rivaled in importance the more publicized aspects of the multinational hearings. The information the subcommittee gathered was indispensable, according to David Ignatius, "for the arrogance of the multinationals in large part stems from the fact that they alone understand how their business is transacted—and who pays and who benefits." Ignatius, a former lobbyist for Ralph Nader, believed that Church and his colleagues were "building a case for a reorientation of American economic policy abroad as far-reaching as the critique of American military policy that has resulted from the Vietnam war."[78]

VII

A combination of diligence and luck facilitated the subcommittee's glimpse behind what Church called the oil companies' "curtain of secrecy." In early 1973, Levinson sent two staff members to the Justice Department to see what information they might find. Justice officials eagerly took them to a huge assortment of dusty files tucked away in a department annex. "Wonderful," Levinson later imagined the people at Justice saying. "We'll get these guys off contemporary issues. Get them into ancient history." Soon, however, the staffers were on the telephone, excitedly telling Levinson what they had found. Levinson hurried to the Justice Department and rummaged through the files in disbelief. The records dealt with subjects such as the so-called "golden handshake" by which the government had extended tax credits to the oil companies in the 1950s, and the Eisenhower administration's relationship with the Iranian oil consortium. Levinson quickly concluded that the documents were invaluable. He and the other staff members frantically carried carton after carton down the stairs and out into a driving rain, where they loaded them in taxi cabs destined for the subcommittee's offices. By the time the Justice Department realized what was happening, the papers were in the subcommittee's possession. While Justice tried unsuccessfully to get the documents back, the subcommittee staff pored through them, compiling a record of the U. S. government's growing dependency on the major oil companies, and the companies' increased reliance on Middle Eastern crude oil. By the spring of 1974, the subcommittee had made public scores of previously classified documents.[79]

The revealed history had several themes, one relating to the evolution of the companies and the other concerning U. S. policy toward them. The story of the oil cartels had little to do with the free market. Instead, since the 1920s, a powerful oligopoly had maintained its control over Middle Eastern oil production and prices. The oligopoly had protected itself through secret agreements and by absorbing emergent companies that moved into new fields, like Saudi Arabia's after World War II. According to a subcommittee background paper, the oil industry had long resembled "one gigantic company." Five of the seven corporations that dominated the petroleum industry by the 1950s were based in the United States; by 1974, the smallest of these U. S. firms, Standard Oil of California (Socal), had assets of over $8 billion.[80]

United States government policies had dramatically facilitated this hugely profitable entry of the American-based companies into the Middle Eastern oil fields. As Church emphasized, the government had provided financial and diplomatic support for the companies while leaving them in control of their own operations. The Cold War had magnified this pattern of operation. From the government's perspective, the American oil companies were indispensable agencies of U. S. foreign policy, crucial to keeping the oil-rich Persian Gulf nations from spinning into the Soviet orbit. Government support for the companies had taken several forms. In 1950, for example, the National Security Council had worked out a system of indirect subsidies. According to this arrangement, the companies paid taxes to the Persian Gulf sheikdoms, thereby making the oil-producing nations in the Middle East dependent on the U. S. rather than the Soviets; in turn, the U. S. government credited these foreign payments toward the companies' U. S. taxes. "For reasons of state," in Church's words, the U. S. Treasury "forfeited billions of dollars in tax revenues. . .to the treasuries of oil producing states." In 1953, the U. S. government more directly aided the companies by sponsoring the overthrow of Iran's Mossadegh government. The ousting of Mossadegh, who had nationalized the properties of the Anglo-Iranian Oil Corporation, cleared the way for U. S. oil companies to enter the Iranian fields through the newly formed Iranian Consortium. Because the companies were "saving" Iran from communism, the government protected the consortium members from antitrust laws, thereby establishing what *The Nation* magazine described as a " 'National Security' Cartel."[81]

The government had assumed that the United States and the American oil companies shared identical interests—a dangerous assumption, as Church's subcommittee discovered. Indeed, a subcommittee working paper drew a troubling historical analogy: blind confidence in the oil companies had lured the United States into a Middle Eastern nightmare just as surely as unquestioned Cold War premises had resulted in the Vietnam war. Parallels existed as well between the growth of the imperial presidency and the multinational oil corporations. "These corporations, like the U. S. presidency," the working paper asserted, "have been given extraordinary prerogatives, privileges and powers in return for very few obligations and responsibilities for which they are accountable." As an example of how the oil companies spurned accountability, Church recalled that their top attorney, John J. McCloy, told the State Department in the mid-Sixties that a tax audit of the petroleum industry's records would not be in the national interest.[82]

From Church's perspective, the oil companies were no more deserving of trust than was the imperial presidency. Misplaced confidence in the companies had been disastrous for virtually everyone except the OPEC countries. By the 1970s the corporations themselves were among the losers as OPEC, by shrewdly adopting the companies' monopolistic strategies, had gained ascendancy in the petroleum industry—at least over the control of crude oil production. Meanwhile, U. S. government policies, such as oil company tax credits, had hurt the nation's economy by encouraging the migration of U. S. capital and technology abroad.[83]

VIII

More disturbing was evidence that the oil companies had elevated their own interests above the national interest. To document the companies' substitution of profits for patriotism, the subcommittee again benefitted from a blend of luck and perseverance. This time the ever-vigilant Jack Anderson played an even more crucial role than he had during the ITT investigations.

In January 1974, Anderson brought serious charges against the American oil multinationals. His target, in newspaper columns as well as in closed testimony before the subcommittee, was the Arabian-American Oil Company (Aramco)—a partnership of Exxon, Mobil, Texaco, and Socal that enjoyed access to Saudi Arabia's fields. According to Anderson, Aramco had been apprehensive for some time about its oil supply, having long neglected its American fields in favor of the profitable concessions that it had worked out with the Saudis. By late 1972, however, the company feared that Saudi Arabia might nationalize its oil fields. At that point, Aramco had taken two steps. It decided to modernize its American fields and to pump the Saudi fields as rapidly as possible. Financing the modernization of the U. S. fields required a boosting of prices. To deflect public anger about these rising fuel costs from Armaco to Saudi Arabia, the company had encouraged the Saudis to raise their crude oil prices. While Aramco sought higher profits via increased prices, it pumped the Saudi fields furiously, ignoring the technological precautions necessary to preserve the wells. By 1973, Aramco's race to make money was leading to an economic calamity, as huge pressure drops in the wells jeopardized the company's oil supply in Saudi Arabia.[84]

Anderson's grave allegations offered the multinationals subcommittee an investigative challenge as well as an opportunity. The challenge, of course, was to obtain corroborative evidence that Aramco had colluded in boosting oil prices and had mismanaged the Saudi fields. To protect themselves against such charges, the companies ran up the American flag.

This patriotic strategy was evident when the aging John J. McCloy, attorney for many major oil companies, testified before the subcommittee. As Levinson recalled, "McCloy was supposed to be able to turn off an inquiry like this in the name of national security." Certainly the elderly New Yorker had impressive credentials. A Harvard Law School graduate, he had been among the handful of men who shaped America's Cold War foreign policy. Besides holding a number of high government positions and advising a series of presidents, he had also chaired the Chase Manhattan Bank. *New Yorker* columnist Richard Rovere had once called him the "cornerstone" of the American establishment. According to a Senate veteran, "McCloy was the one guy who could get the biggest company executives and the top government officials in the country together. . .and decide what gets done." Most importantly for the multinationals subcommittee, he had since 1961 represented some two dozen oil companies in their negotiations with the departments of State and Justice.[85]

On February 6, the seventy-eight-year-old McCloy appeared grandly before the subcommittee, waving confidently at the senators. His demeanor reminded one reporter of Winston Churchill. McCloy indicated almost nonchalantly that antitrust agreements between the government and the oil companies had seldom been put in writing; these were agreements among gentlemen, and had been passed from one attorney general to another. Several pointed questions from Church served as a warning that the subcommittee did not intend to praise such arrangements. Indeed, before the day ended, McCloy appeared to believe that the subcommittee was putting him and his ideas on trial. Fidgeting in his chair and visibly uncomfortable as the hearing wore on, he sent a message of his own: the United States was hardly helping itself by criticizing the petroleum producers. Outside the hearing room, he described as "almost masochistic" the American attack on its oil companies.[86]

Unable to impress the subcommittee by waving the banner of national security, the oil companies used other tactics. Under subpoena to turn over documents, Exxon, Mobil, and Texaco flooded the subcommittee with innocuous materials. Socal, in contrast, chose to produce virtually nothing. Socal's strategy, as Levinson subsequently said, was to "stonewall" the subcommittee in hopes that the investigators would back off. Determined to meet this challenge to the subcommittee's authority, Church got the other senators to agree that individual subpoenas should go to Socal's top executives. Facing interrogations behind closed doors, the Socal officials suddenly reversed themselves and offered to cooperate fully with the subcommittee. At the end of May, Levinson and Jack Blum flew to San Francisco to talk with the company's executives and collect documents.[87]

Jack Anderson made the Levinson-Blum trip more productive than Socal could ever have anticipated. Anderson's friendly relationship with Church and his staff, already helpful, now became pivotal. When Church asked if he could use Anderson's sources and files, the columnist agreed. "He was an honorable man," Anderson observed later of Church. "I never knew of a dishonorable thing he ever did." Anderson and Church occasionally discussed the investigations in "a little hideaway," and the journalist regularly communicated with Levinson and Blum. As long as Anderson could protect the identity of his informants, including several key officials at Socal, he was willing to do everything possible to aid the subcommittee. When Levinson and Blum went to San Francisco, he was helpful indeed. He contacted his inside sources at Socal to ascertain the exact location of specific documents the subcommittee needed. Armed with these invaluable details, Levinson and Blum descended on Socal's offices.[88]

It did not take the Socal people long to realize that Levinson and Blum had crucial inside information. When the officials tried to take the investigators to one location, Levinson and Blum would say no, they had something else in mind—for example, access to the lower left file drawer in the unmarked room on such-and-such a floor, where the silver-haired woman with the Irish name worked. Socal's executives were aghast and subsequently hired a battery of private detectives in an unsuccessful effort to find where the subcommittee staff had gotten such accurate details. When Levinson and Blum returned to Washington, D. C., with two file drawers of documents, a much relieved Frank Church could only shake his head and say, "I can't believe it." Until that moment Church had worried that the subcommittee would ultimately come up with little tangible documentation of Aramco's machinations. "He then would have had mud all over his face," in Levinson's words, and the companies would have controlled the public record.[89]

Levinson informed the subcommittee that the documents yielded "a unique insight into the workings of international oil." The evidence showed that the Aramco companies had curried favor with the Saudi government by lobbying to make U. S. policy more pro-Arab. To Levinson the meaning was clear: "Aramco and the companies are instruments of the Saudi Arabia Government and carrying out Saudi orders in terms of influencing U. S. foreign policy." More than innocent lobbying was involved. The companies had cooperated actively with the Saudis during the oil embargo from October 1973 until mid-March 1974. "Specifically," Levinson reported, "the companies provided information with respect to quantities of products supplied by them to the U. S. military in their refineries from crude shipped from Saudi Arabia." Knowledge of the military's reliance on Saudi crude allowed the Saudis to scale back their production accordingly. Grateful for such support, the Saudis promised to reward Aramco. The U. S. oil companies had in effect passed a loyalty test—to King Faisal, Saudi Arabia's seventy-year-old ruler.[90]

On August 7, Church told the press that the subcommittee had substantiated many of Jack Anderson's charges. Although Anderson's allegation that the companies had encouraged the Saudi price increases remained unproven, there was no doubt that Aramco had administered the Saudi oil embargo. For Aramco, in fact, the embargo could not have come at a better time. The oil companies had indeed been overproducing their fields, although the overproduction may not have been deliberate, as Anderson alleged. If for technical reasons only, Aramco's pumping of the fields had created severe drops in oil pressure that might soon have forced a curtailment of production. The embargo had thus been a godsend, allowing the companies a much-needed opportunity to cut back on production despite growing demand.[91]

Church discerned ominous meanings in the subcommittee's findings. "The companies," he said, "are hostages of the Saudis and forced to operate at their beck and call." Church believed, moreover, that Aramco's "objectives are not necessarily best for the American consumer." He rejected any devil theory in this regard. The companies were understandably pursuing their own interest. But, by seeking exclusive access to Saudi oil, they had made themselves prisoners of the Saudis. The basic lesson was simple enough, in Church's opinion: because the interests of the companies and the American people did not necessarily coincide, the U. S. government needed to reverse its permissive approach and supervise negotiations between Aramco and the Saudis.[92]

Church's comment that the oil companies "ride in tandem with Arab governments" infuriated representatives of the petroleum industry. So did his criticism of Aramco's high profits. In March 1974, for example, Church indicated that Aramco's earnings had increased by 350 percent since 1969. Moreover, in 1973 the corporation had paid only $609,000 in U. S. income taxes, or less than one-hundredth of one percent of its profits. Church indignantly compared that to the much higher percentage that American workers paid.[93]

Some of the industry's anger at the senator surfaced in the *Oil and Gas Journal*, where editor Gene Kinney objected to the unflattering portrait that Church and the press drew of the international oil companies. In Kinney's estimation, Socal vice-president J. Dennis Bonney—not Church—was the real hero of the hearings. The editor portrayed Bonney as a self-sacrificing man who spent days away from his family, negotiating with the Arab governments, refusing to "knuckle under to the demands for inordinate tax hikes," and enduring "untold tongue lashings from OPEC for taking the side of the consumer." Kinney claimed that the public needed to know what was really happening in the hearings. "The literate and urbane Bonney," for example, had forced Church into a "stammering retreat."[94]

Despite the efforts of Kinney and other defenders of the oil industry, Church and his subcommittee successfully conveyed to the public a message critical of the multinational companies. "Oil Firms Obeyed Faisal," the *Washington Post* reported on August 7, the day that Church released the subcommittee's findings about Aramco. "Big Oil Firms Tried to Shape U. S. Policy in Mideast at Arabs' Behest," echoed the *Wall Street Journal*.[95]

The oil companies were not alone in resenting Church. Vermont senator George Aiken questioned his leadership of the subcommittee. In Aiken's estimation, Church was playing politics with explosive issues, "going pretty far out" to win a fourth Senate term.[96]

IX

Church's role on the multinationals subcommittee probably helped the Idaho senator's 1974 campaign very little, if at all, however. True, the big oil companies had few friends among Idaho residents. A mid-1974 survey of the state's political climate revealed that a whopping 88 percent of Idahoans with an opinion on the subject blamed the energy crisis on "oil company desires for higher profits." Surprisingly, these people considered the Arab oil boycott and environmental laws as only minor contributors to the crisis. The same survey showed that 65 percent of Idaho voters strongly favored, while only 4 percent strongly opposed, political candidates who advocated strict controls on the oil companies. This information boded well for Church, except for an astonishing additional fact: a majority of voters was unaware that he had been presiding over hearings on the petroleum industry. As late as June 1974, 53 percent were unsure that Church was doing anything to "control the big oil companies."[97]

In some respects, Church's chairmanship of the multinationals subcommittee may have even been a political liability. Partly because of the subcommittee's demands, Church visited his home state less often in 1974 than usual. Campaign workers heard all too often, "Where is Church? We never see him." They worried that an alarming number of voters believed Church was spending too little time with his constituents.[98]

Moreover, the senator's emerging national reputation carried a price. His "star quality" made some citizens uncomfortable when they were around him. "You have to become good old Frank again," warned aide Mike Wetherell. Forced by a tight campaign schedule in 1974 to do more speaking than conversing, Church gave some people the impression that he was lecturing them "from Olympus." According to one northern Idaho resident, many folks had begun to wonder if the senator had lived in Washington, D. C., too long. Church, from this perspective, had become a suave, sophisticated Easterner—a damaging perception for a senator from a rural, western state.[99]

In this regard, Wetherell fretted that Church's support among small businesses was slipping. The aide surmised that small town entrepreneurs were less concerned about "big economic issues" than with "petty nuisances," such as growing piles of bureaucratic paperwork. From the point of view of the Main Street business owner, multinational corporations seemed less immediately threatening than the Occupational Safety and Health Act of 1970, which Church had supported.[100]

Church's 1974 Republican opponent, Nampa attorney Bob Smith, pitched his campaign accordingly. Taking aim at big government, he insisted that the federal bureaucracy's "war on the businessman" was ruining the economy. Smith blamed the oil shortages on government regulations of free enterprise – not on the oil companies. Describing himself as "the real Idahoan," he claimed that out-of-state interests were spending huge amounts to buy Church "another six years of adulation from eastern liberals."[101]

Smith also tried to capitalize on public bitterness and disenchantment. According to a Harris poll in late 1973, 55 percent of Americans felt "powerless" and "alienated." A staggering 94 percent intended to express their anger at government by voting "against a public official." This "throw the rascals out" sentiment was larger than it had been in years, giving added credibility to Bob Smith's assertion that it was time to "get rid of career politicians" like Church.[102]

Like other Americans, Idahoans were restless and discouraged about the nation's economy and politics. A survey of public opinion showed that, by mid-1974, 77 percent of Idaho voters believed the nation was moving in the wrong direction. Although they had overwhelmingly helped Richard Nixon defeat George McGovern less than two years earlier, their support for the president had evaporated. Only 10 percent believed he was telling the truth about the Watergate scandals, and the ratio of his "excellent to poor" ratings was a disastrous 1 to 8. The potential bad news for Church in such statistics was that Idahoans attributed the country's woes more to Congress than to the president. While 19 percent blamed Nixon, 37 percent held Congress responsible, and 37 percent blamed both governmental branches.[103]

In Idaho, the John Birch Society mounted a huge offensive against Church's reelection. Targeting the incumbent as one of the worst of the big government, pro-communist liberals, the society came after him with a vengeance. The Birchers' major weapon consisted of 100,000 copies of a reprinted article, dripping with innuendo and misinformation, that dubbed him "the Chameleon in the Senate." In a more populous state, 100,000 pamphlets might have counted for little, but Idaho's voting population numbered only around 300,000. Also, Idaho had already provided fertile ground for the Birchers. In 1972 no state had given a higher percentage of votes – almost 10 percent – to the American Independent party presidential candidate, John Schmitz, a Birch Society member who maintained that "Americanism is not trusting your leaders." Schmitz had run better than George McGovern in some Idaho counties.[104]

Alan Stang, the Birch Society's top publicist, wrote the well-circulated diatribe against Church as the Senate's chameleon. Stang accused Church of posing as a true American while in fact aiding the Rockefellers, "the actively pro-communist Council on Foreign Relations," "labor monopolists," the "professional revolutionary Cesar Chavez," socialists bent on cutting off America's oil supply, and communists. Oil millionaire Armand Hammer, like "other notorious radicals," was reputedly "bankrolling" Church's campaign. Stang was especially abusive of Church's chief administrative assistant, Verda Barnes, denouncing her as a dedicated communist whom Walter Reuther of the United Auto Workers had handpicked to work in the senator's office. Perhaps, Stang conjectured, "the Communists use her to control" Church. Stang found evidence of Church's communism in numerous places, including the senator's investigations of ITT in Chile. Despite the outrageous allegations, Stang's lengthy essay had an air of authority about it. Stang quoted Church at length, citing sources such as the *Congressional Record*. Casual readers had no way of knowing how badly Stang twisted the facts, dropped crucial parts of quotations, or left out vital bits of information. As Jack Anderson noted, Stang's kind of quoting would have had Abraham Lincoln "saying he would carry on his work 'with malice,' without adding the words 'toward none.' "[105]

Bob Smith lent credence to the Birch Society's attack on Church, seeming to condone their tactics and echoing some of their main charges. A former Methodist missionary and a ruggedly handsome ex-Marine with thick dark hair and long sideburns, Smith reflected a growing libertarian dimension of Idaho conservatism. He was a close ally of Steve Symms, whom the Birch Society had described as its "Number One Congressman." In 1972 Symms, a southwestern Idaho apple grower, had shocked state Republican Party professionals by winning a congressional seat, even though he had never run for political office before. Substituting ideological purity for political experience, Symms championed unimpeded free enterprise. In his 1972 campaign he endorsed Ohio's archconservative John Ashbrook–not Richard Nixon–for president. Bob Smith had managed Symms's campaign and then served as the new legislator's administrative assistant. Like Symms, he glorified untrammeled free enterprise and believed that governmental regulations threatened American freedoms. For starters, Smith wanted to slice the federal budget by two-thirds and bury regulatory legislation such as the Occupational Safety and Health Act.[106]

Although Smith apparently welcomed the backing of the John Birch Society, he was uneasy about Alan Stang's invective against Church. Stang's essay was so virulent that some state Republicans were urging him to disown it. But Smith could hardly repudiate it without alienating Symms, who in mid-1974 was the keynote speaker at the annual Birch Society convention. In retrospect, Smith conceded that he "was in a very difficult spot on that article." He chose not to denounce it. Indeed, he in effect sanctioned it by claiming that liberals were using the Birch Society as "a whipping boy." Moreover, his own literature was in some ways as questionable as Stang's essay. One campaign document, for example, accused Church of being "antagonistic toward countries that show pro-American tendencies while showing deep concern for the welfare of unfriendly nations."[107]

The bitter attacks caught Church off guard. Recent political polls in Idaho may have made him overly confident. Surveys of Idaho voters had portrayed him as virtually invincible. In September 1973, 66 percent of those polled had given him an excellent or good job rating; in mid-1974, the figure had dropped somewhat, but was still a reassuring 62 percent. The pollsters' "feeling thermometer" was also encouraging. On a scale in which 1 represented constituents' coldness toward him and 10 signified warm feelings, Church's median score was an impressive 7.1. This number contrasted dramatically with Nixon's dismal 3.3, or with Symms's ratings, which had dropped in eight months from 5.9 to 5.5. "Steve Symms is in decline," the mid-1974 survey concluded, an interpretation that did not augur well for Bob Smith. Buoyed by such information, Church chose to ignore the attacks on his character and Americanism. His constituents, he said, were "much too fair-minded" to believe silly charges that he was a communist.[108]

As the campaign entered its final weeks, however, Church sensed that he had miscalculated badly and might be in real political trouble.

In retrospect, he believed he should have replied immediately to his critics. "I didn't answer them, thinking that people wouldn't believe them. But that's wrong. People will believe the worst." At the least, as several campaign workers discovered, some Idahoans decided that the criticisms of Church must have been true because he was not denying them. By the time he realized that he had to confront his adversaries, his campaign coffers were almost empty. He had almost completely expended the money that the new election laws allowed. Unable to afford full newspaper or television coverage, he fought back frantically, targeting key areas in the state. "I almost trapped myself," he recalled.[109]

Scrambling to fend off Smith, Church stumbled badly over the issue of Cesar Chavez's lettuce boycott. Two years earlier, a petition in support of the boycott had circulated at the state Democratic convention in Sun Valley. The petition provided Republicans with an important issue. In the 1972 senatorial election, Jim McClure attacked his Democratic opponent, Bud Davis, for signing it. McClure's newspaper advertisements warned of a threatened potato boycott which would "bring all Idaho agriculture under the Chavez United Farm Workers thumb." No matter how emphatically Davis stated his opposition to a potato boycott, his signature on the Sun Valley petition allowed the victorious McClure to portray him as an enemy of Idaho's farmers.[110]

In 1974, rumors of a potato boycott still made many Idahoans nervous. They hardly needed Alan Stang's reminder that such a boycott could devastate the state's economy. But Stang's diatribe against Church sketched out a larger, even more chilling scenario. Cesar Chavez supposedly intended "to take control of crop after crop, and worker after worker, so that the Communists can control our food supply by threatening destructive strikes." Stang implicated Church in this plot by noting that, at Sun Valley in 1972, the senator had signed the petition supporting the lettuce boycott.[111]

For Church by mid-1974, the petition was a heavy political weight. Richard Napolitano made it heavier. Once an organizer of California's fields, Napolitano had broken with Chavez. In May, Napolitano told an Idaho audience that his old friend Chavez was a dangerous hypocrite whom Frank Church "blindly" endorsed. "It is people like Frank Church," Napolitano insisted, "who are responsible for the farmworker and grower getting hurt."[112]

Clumsily, Church tried to defuse the boycott issue. He claimed that he did not recall signing the pro-boycott petition at Sun Valley in

1972. Verda Barnes desperately tried to find the damaging petition, but no one seemed to know what had happened to it. Worried that the Smith forces somehow had it, Church explained that he might have signed it "inadvertently." Years later, Church stuck by his shaky story. "I told the truth," he insisted, "but the truth was so implausible" that few people could believe it.[113]

The senator's "lame answer," as journalist Bill Hall wrote, "was not his finest hour." Hall criticized more than Church's memory lapse. He took the occasion to castigate Church, not for signing the petition, but for aligning himself less with the poor farm workers than with "the skinflints who employ them." Hall had a point. Shortly after the 1972 state Democratic convention, in fact, Church had gone on record against the Chavez lettuce boycott. At the national party convention in Miami, his deciding vote had prevented the Idaho delegation from supporting the boycott. Hall initially decided that the only plausible explanation for Church's signature on the Sun Valley petition was that the senator had momentarily been swept up in the convention's liberal enthusiasm. After further investigation, however, Hall concluded that Church's account was true. Church had mistakenly put his name on the petition when he was in the process of signing autographs.[114]

Bob Smith scoffed at such explanations. "Each day seems to add another leaf to Senator Church's lettuce boycott coverup," he said. "It is difficult in this instance," agreed one newspaper editor, "to swallow a head of lettuce."[115]

On election day, however, the boycott issue failed to stop Church from winning a fourth term. With Bethine working the hustings furiously with him, he captured 55 percent of the vote. By his own admission, his campaign was nevertheless the "worst" he had run to that point.[116]

Church had dodged a political bullet. He was fortunate that 1974 turned out to be a hugely successful Democratic year. The Watergate scandals, Richard Nixon's resignation, and Gerald Ford's September 8 unconditional pardon of Nixon exacted a terrible toll on the Republicans. After the elections there were more Democratic officeholders in the United States than ever before. Democrats controlled most state legislatures, added four governorships to their already dominant numbers, increased their control over the Senate by four seats, and pushed their control of the House to 290-145 by gaining an impressive forty-nine positions. "The whole earth moved for the Democrats," quipped NBC television's director of elections. A substantial number of the new

Democratic representatives came from formerly strong Republican districts; Vermont elected its first Democratic senator. Democrats not only racked up stunning victories. In notable instances, they represented a new political breed–"Watergate babies," as one political analyst described them. They tended to be anti-establishment, committed to political reform, and independent of their party's hierarchy. A striking number had been grassroots activists in the Sixties' civil rights and antiwar movements. They shared as well a revulsion to Watergate. "We had a real sense of urgency," said California's George Miller. "We came [to Washington D. C.] to take the Bastille."[117]

Idaho Democrats also benefitted from the political reaction to Watergate, even though the state sent Republicans Steve Symms and George Hansen to the House of Representatives. In 1970, Cecil Andrus had barely won the governorship; in 1974, he received an astonishing 70 percent of the vote. Republicans still controlled the state legislature, but Democrats picked up eleven seats, including some from the traditional Republican bastion of Ada County. Not since 1940 had Ada County sent Democrats to the legislature.[118]

The Democratic trend unquestionably aided Church, but polls suggested that he had helped his own cause despite a wobbly campaign. "Quite frankly," concluded a large survey of political attitudes in Idaho, "in an age of cynicism it is extremely impressive to find a Senator who is so well respected among his constituents." Significant personal strengths had allowed him to win reelection by a fairly comfortable margin. He enjoyed a strong reputation for honesty, and voters gave him high marks for helping the elderly and protecting Idaho's interests, especially regarding water rights. Moreover, Church had been able to bridge political ideologies. He was considerably more liberal than most of his constituency, 51 percent of whom described themselves as conservatives and only 22 percent as liberals. Significantly, however, 42 percent of Idahoans classified Church as conservative, the same percentage as those who viewed him as liberal. Sixteen percent put him in the middle-of-the-road. When asked if Church was "too liberal," 58 percent said no, and only 26 percent answered yes. Clearly, Church was walking the state's ideological tightrope with considerable finesse. There were encouraging indications, too, that Idaho was becoming more "conservation-conscious," a trend that suited Church.[119]

Despite these favorable signs for Church, the 1974 election carried some ominous messages as well. Mike Wetherell conceded that his boss had made "a good showing for a liberal Democrat in conservative Idaho," but he felt the senator could have done even better. Wetherell noted, for example, that Governor Andrus's 70 percent of the vote was considerably more imposing than Church's showing. There was another troubling fact. Bob Smith had gained on the senator during the campaign's closing weeks. Polls indicated that Church's support had slipped more than it should have, particularly among farmers. Although Church had won a fourth term, Wetherell sensed that troubling currents were at work.[120]

Looking toward 1980, Church had much to ponder. Bob Smith had turned a potential Church landslide into a respectable race. What if the senator's next opponent were more experienced and better known? What if, next time, the attacks on Church were more sustained and even uglier? What if the political tide by 1980 favored Republicans, not Democrats?

These were questions that Church had six years to consider. More immediately, he prepared to return to the nation's capital. There, the multinationals subcommittee was geared up for more hearings. Additionally, Church would soon begin one of the most important assignments of his career—that of chairing the Senate investigations of the CIA and the Federal Bureau of Investigation.

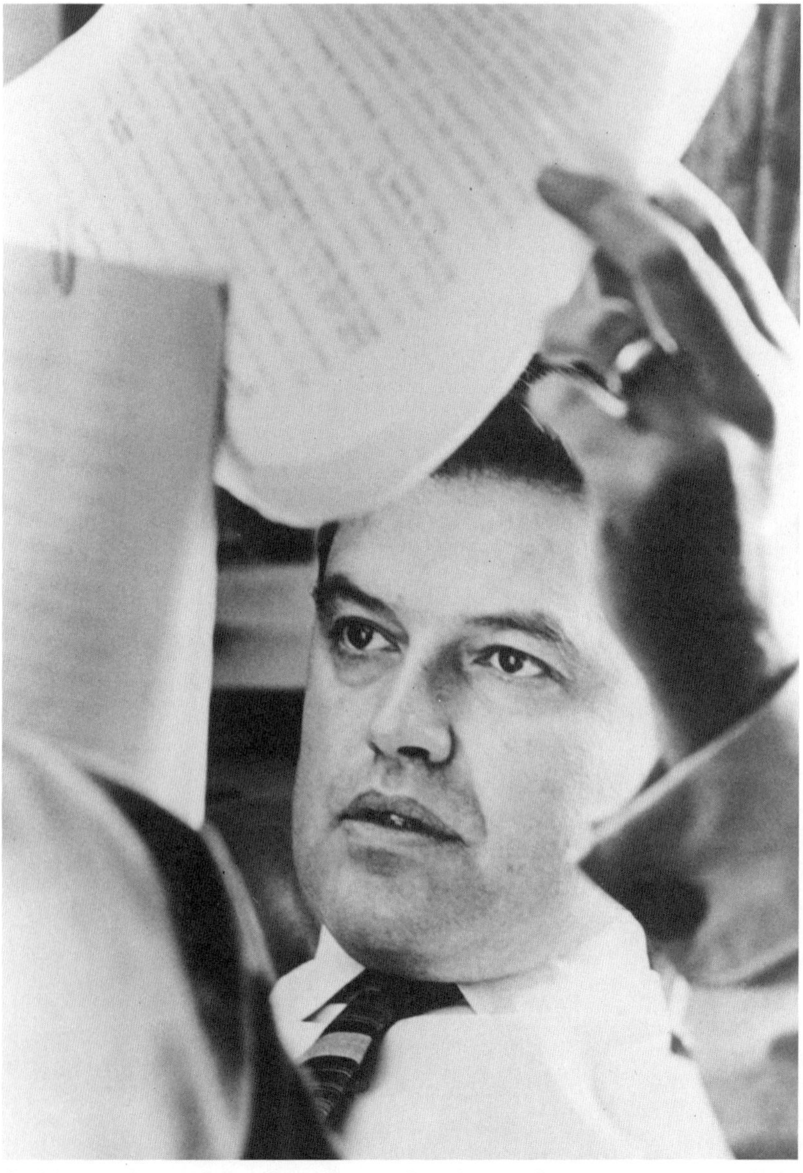

Chairing the Senate Select Committee on Intelligence, Church peruses some documents. *Courtesy Boise State University.*

Chapter Sixteen
Senator Sleuth: 1975-1976

FRANK CHURCH'S ANGER at the Vietnam war, at the ITT-CIA plots in Chile, and at governmental complicity in oil company profiteering had turned him into a kind of sleuth, determined to expose corporate and governmental meddling abroad and wrongdoing at home. Throughout 1975 and into 1976, as rumors circulated that he would soon be a presidential candidate, Church presided over two sensational probes, one focusing on the Federal Bureau of Investigation (FBI) and Central Intelligence Agency (CIA), and the other on high-level corporate bribery so explosive that its disclosure shook several foreign governments. He relished his investigative role, a role that challenged the system while working within it. According to Bill Miller, who knew him well, Church liked the prospects of "cleaning the Augean stables. That was a part of him that made him feel good: To right something. If it was wrong, get rid of it, clean it out."[1]

Old-fashioned idealism drove him as much as ambition or indignation at institutional lawlessness. Indeed, he imbued his sleuth's role with a sense that he was a modern-day political evangelist, infusing the old democratic faith with new energy, strengthening the moral dimension of public life. His intellectual debt had never been clearer to one of the fundamental premises of such early twentieth-century liberals as William Jennings Bryan, "Fighting Bob" La Follette, and Borah—namely, that the people shall rule. He sometimes invoked the progressive tradition of muckraking and its assumption that the spiritual health of a democratic culture depends on public access to information. Although events over the past decade had sorely tried his political convictions, he remained at heart a believer in the United States, its founding principles, its democratic form of government, its people, and its emphasis on a government of laws. "America," he still insisted, "does best when it follows its best instincts."[2]

I

Although 1975 proved to be "the year of the investigation" for Church, the collapse of the South Vietnamese government initially captured his attention. That government had grown shakier throughout 1974 as intensified attacks and desertion cost the South Vietnamese army a record 240,000 troops. In March 1975 the North Vietnamese launched a devastating offensive. Within days, hundreds of thousands of refugees and fleeing, looting South Vietnamese soldiers poured out of the highlands. On April 4, General Fred C. Weyand warned President Gerald Ford that South Vietnam was "on the brink of total military defeat." Weyand, who had just completed a whirlwind fact-finding mission at Ford's behest, confidentially recommended the reintroduction of B-52 bombing attacks against the communists. He also called for an additional $722 million for South Vietnam, an amount that would more than double the funds Congress had allotted for 1975. "What is at stake in Vietnam now," Weyand argued, "is America's credibility as an ally." Ford ignored the bombing request but asked Congress for the money.[3]

Church adamantly opposed any such boost in funding. A month earlier he had pressed Ford to phase out all aid to South Vietnam. The senator had hoped to strike a bargain: the administration could promise South Vietnam diminishing amounts of aid for three more years; in return, Congress would know exactly when the aid would stop. On March 4, Church and Kansas Republican James B. Pearson had discussed this possible agreement with Ford.[4]

Speculation about a "Viet-aid bargain" irked some long-time members of the antiwar movement who resented Church's willingness to compromise with the administration. Two of them, Jane Fonda and Tom Hayden, stopped by the senator's office to urge him to sponsor legislation that would extricate the U. S. from Vietnam immediately, not at some distant point. They were in a grim mood and anything but friendly. After they left, Church's own exasperation bubbled over. Considerably annoyed, he told an aide that they wanted to end the war tomorrow morning on their terms. He believed they lived in a political fantasy land, unable to recognize that the war was all but over and that confrontational politics would simply rekindle it as an issue.[5]

As irritated as he was with Fonda and Hayden, he was far angrier with the administration. In March, when Ford requested military aid for the Lon Nol regime in Cambodia, Church declared that "Indochina has become the opiate of the American presidency." Ford's subsequent request for $722 million in emergency military assistance for South Vietnam riled him even more. Pounding his fist on the mantle in his office, he wondered when the United States would learn from its past. Additional military aid to the South Vietnamese would end up as a gift to the communists. On April 18 he accused the administration of playing "the same old shell game" with the American public, and insisted that the Vietnam war, a creation of wrong-headed policies from the outset, was lost.[6]

A substantial majority of Church's colleagues on Capitol Hill now agreed with him. Congress in April approved only $300 million in aid, limiting it to "humanitarian" purposes and the evacuation of U. S. citizens who were in South Vietnam. Meanwhile, the Saigon government quickly fell apart.[7]

On April 29, fifty-five days after the North Vietnamese mounted their offensive, the South Vietnamese government surrendered unconditionally. The "nation" of South Vietnam ceased to exist. By then, Frank Church could only hope that Americans would not turn upon each other in a divisive search for someone to blame.[8]

By then, too, other matters were demanding his time. The newly formed Senate Select Committee on Intelligence was battling the Ford White House over access to executive documents. And, on the day that the Saigon government collapsed, the subcommittee on multinationals voted to investigate payoffs to foreign officials from the California-based Northrop corporation.

II

The subsequent investigations of Northrop and other companies for bribery and payoffs abroad breathed new life into the multinationals subcommittee, which had otherwise fallen on troubled times. In early 1975, Church expressed concern about "serious misunderstandings" regarding its "lifespan, role and jurisdiction," and he vigorously objected to a draft Foreign Relations Committee report that called for terminating the subcommittee in order to save $400,000 per year. The "misunderstandings" may have grown in part from struggles over turf. Hubert Humphrey, for example, fretted that Church's subcommittee was preempting the work of his own Subcommittee on Foreign Assistance and Economic Policy.[9]

Caught up in jurisdictional disputes, the subcommittee also provoked a fierce reaction in 1975 when it examined the influence of large commercial banks on foreign policy. Major bank presidents and several voting members of the Federal Reserve Board warned the subcommittee in executive session that queries about the soundness of the banking industry could jeopardize the entire financial system. David Rockefeller, powerful head of the Chase Manhattan Bank, flew down in his private jet to meet separately with Church and Clifford Case to argue the same point.[10]

Divisions plagued the subcommittee itself. The banking probe worsened the already bad chemistry between Charles Percy and Church. During a short, rancorous session on October 9, Percy indicated that he was "really fed up with coming to these meetings" and wanted to "drop the whole thing" about banking. The subcommittee, he claimed, had moved onto "perilous ground" and was "dealing with dynamite." 'We have better things to do with our time," he lectured Church. "I think you are beating a dead horse here. For some reason you don't want to give it up." Percy also balked at Church's efforts to obtain information regarding bank deposits from oil-exporting countries and loans to developing nations. "You are not going to get subpoenas out of this committee," he said threateningly. Stuart Symington sided with Percy on grounds that the banking industry did not need investigating.[11]

Church continued to press for subpoenas anyhow. The bankers and the administration fought back, arguing that Congress had no right to information about specific deposits. The ambassador from Kuwait said ominously that, if the banks revealed their accounts, his nation would remove its money. With the opposition "pulling out all the stops," in the words of a subcommittee staffer, Church nevertheless forced a compromise. The Federal Reserve agreed to collect the information from the banks, but to pass it along to the subcommittee only in aggregate form.[12]

Determined to keep the subcommittee from fracturing, and recognizing the strength of his opponents, Church accepted such compromises. Jack Blum, the subcommittee's associate counsel, wished the situation would have been different. "If there was ever an issue where we should have taken them apart, upside down and backwards, it was banking," he said later. He regretted that "we didn't hold their feet to the fire," but he understood the politics behind Church's decision not to press the issue.[13]

The subcommittee at least pointed to a massive problem involving oil money. Large U. S. banks, flooded with oil money deposits and anxious to recirculate those funds, eagerly offered loans to developing countries with perilously spiraling indebtedness. If those countries ever defaulted on their giant debts, the high price of oil money and politics would be all too clear. As journalists Jack Anderson and James Boyd subsequently warned, the debt hung "like the sword of Damocles over the West's financial structure." In 1975, however, this danger stirred little public interest in the United States. "Too much money was sloshing around out there," recalled Jerry Levinson, the subcommittee's chief counsel. "Too many banks were doing well." Church had nevertheless sounded an alarm about the debt and about how petro dollars could become, like oil itself, a kind of Middle Eastern weapon. The subcommittee, despite outside pressures and its own divisions, had raised the specter of impending financial disaster, focusing on bank policies that bore directly on the national interest.[14]

While the subcommittee ran up against the banks' brick walls, events helped to provide more promising targets – particularly the arms industry. Church had long been apprehensive about the sale of U. S. arms abroad. His 1967 essay, "From the U. S. A. to All the World with Love," had served a warning: in the name of fighting communism, the United States was "fueling regional arms races," thereby encouraging local conflicts that could all too easily explode into larger wars. In 1975 the Watergate scandals provided Church with an opportunity to investigate the arms trade.[15]

Watergate had exposed corruption within some of the nation's largest corporations as well as in the Nixon White House. Throughout 1973 and 1974, Americans heard much about "slush funds" and "off-the-books" money transactions involving businesses and the administration. Evidence of secret corporate payments to the president's men was so extensive that it overwhelmed the Securities and Exchange (SEC) enforcement division, the governmental watchdog of big business. Stanley Sporkin, the division's head, the son of a judge, and a dedicated investigator, recognized that his small staff could not possibly cover the rapidly surfacing expanse of corporate malfeasance. He tried to make the situation more manageable by offering companies a chance to admit their wrongdoing and in effect throw themselves on the mercy of the SEC, or to face governmental suits, outside audits, and undoubtedly harsher penalties. Exxon and Gulf Oil were among the major companies that subsequently submitted "voluntary disclosures" about payoffs. But Sporkin was not happy. Some companies were obviously not telling everything, and the State Department was pressuring the SEC to curtail its investigations rather than inflict further damage on U. S. interests abroad. Seeking help, Sporkin on a number of occasions approached Levinson. "Jerry," he would say, "I think there is something that you ought to know."[16]

It was important to know, for example, about the Northrop case. The Northrop Corporation had, during the 1960s, reaped huge profits from Pentagon-sponsored export sales, especially of its F-5 Tiger military plane. The Watergate investigations subsequently embarrassed the company. Northrop had contributed $150,000 (some of it laundered) to Nixon's reelection campaign; although company officials did not know it, the money went to a secret fund to defend the Watergate burglars. The corporation's activities were in fact worse than the public at first learned. Northrop's disclosures to the SEC also revealed overseas payoffs to gain sales. The corporation had literally set up a secret network, using inside contacts and bribes to sell military planes and electronic hardware, especially to Iran and Saudi Arabia. When the State Department successfully persuaded the SEC not to publicize this information, Stanley Sporkin looked to the multinationals subcommittee for assistance.[17]

Church informed the subcommittee that he favored nothing less than maximum disclosure of Northrop's wrongdoing and would oppose any inquiry that held back information. Percy objected initially, but switched his position after a 4-1 vote sustained Church. On June 9, Church opened the Northrop hearings by telling the packed room that company documents illustrated "in excruciating detail a sordid tale of bribery." Percy, to Church's surprise, also came out swinging, calling for a zealous investigation and full disclosures. As Church listened incredulously to the Illinois senator's opening statement, he muttered to Levinson that the scene was hard to comprehend: Percy, who had been dragged "kicking and screaming" into the inquiry, was now holding forth as its great champion.[18]

By the start of the Northrop hearings, the subcommittee and the executive branch were at loggerheads over the definition of acceptable corporate conduct abroad. A month earlier the subcommittee had elicited stunning testimony that Gulf Oil had bought favors, most notably in South Korea and Bolivia. "Can you believe this?" an astonished Church had whispered to Levinson as he listened to Gulf's top executive. Although Church emphasized that the subcommittee was studying the practical effects of corporate activities on U. S. foreign policy, he refused to ignore the ethical side of the issue. "Each country," he had written a few years earlier, "must live by the ideals it prizes most highly." Not surprisingly, then, he objected in 1975 when the Northrop executives defended their actions as a way of life, something they had to do. That way of life, he countered, was unacceptable: "It is no longer sufficient to simply sigh and say that this is the way business is done."[19]

Secretary of State Henry Kissinger took a starkly different view. The simple truth, he said, was that corporate payments such as Gulf Oil's were "not illegal by American law." The executive branch seemed generally to share Kissinger's opinion. *Newsweek* revealed that a Defense Department report advised American arms dealers to expect to pay bribes to local officials in the Middle East.[20]

Officials such as Kissinger drew upon traditional understandings: "Bribery overseas was foreign policy, not domestic crime." But Church and his allies seemed determined to change the rules. They wanted to apply some universal ethic to business practices at home and abroad.[21]

This struggle over the ethics of foreign policy and business intensified throughout 1975. In July, following the Gulf Oil and Northrop hearings, Exxon and Mobil Oil acknowledged that they had paid millions of dollars to several Italian political parties. The Church panel seemed suddenly to have uncorked a bottle. Revelations poured forth, in *Newsweek*'s words, "week by week, name by name, country by country, like some neatly plotted thriller of international intrigue." As more and more corporations admitted to spending millions on bribes and payoffs, some commentators spoke of "Watergate II." According to Jack Blum, a "can-you-top-this" mentality soon prevailed on the subcommittee.[22]

III

The Lockheed investigation, which the subcommittee opened in September, would have been difficult to top. Like Northrop, the Lockheed corporation had paid bribes to sell its military hardware abroad. But the shock value and repercussions of Lockheed's actions far exceeded those of Northrop.

The Lockheed scandal illustrated with particular force a dangerous trend in U. S. foreign policy. During the early 1970s, the Nixon Doctrine and the OPEC oil embargo had pushed to new levels America's sale of arms to Cold War allies. Deputy Secretary of Defense David

Packard had spelled out concisely the thinking behind the Nixon Doctrine: "The best hope of reducing our overseas involvements and expenditures lies in getting allied and friendly nations to do even more in their own defense." This strategy had guided the administration's Vietnamization program as well as its efforts in the Middle East, where the withdrawal of British forces had encouraged a power vacuum. By providing military hardware to anti-communist nations, the U. S. would supposedly be able to exert enormous influence without sending troops. Selling arms abroad thus became, more than ever, a central component of U. S. diplomacy. By the mid-1970s one American diplomat remarked cynically that "perhaps selling arms is the only influence we have left." Such sales became increasingly important also as a means by which to gain a favorable balance of trade. In 1971, for the first time since the late nineteenth century, a trade deficit jolted the United States. Two years later that deficit roared upward, propelled largely by the OPEC embargo and surging oil prices. To stanch the outward flow of money, the U. S. economy desperately needed exports, and few were more profitable than military weaponry.[23]

There were nevertheless real perils in exporting arms, as Frank Church pointed out. It was "pure folly," he told the Senate Finance Committee in 1975, "to make this country's financial and economic well-being dependent on building up an arms race in a politically volatile area such as the Persian Gulf." Corporate payoffs to foreign interests were counterproductive and shortsighted. Bribes might boost sales for a while, but the long-term results wreaked havoc abroad and at home. Abroad, they fostered "the conditions which bring to power political forces that are no friends of ours, whether a [Muammar al] Qaddafi in Libya or Communists in Italy." At home, they encouraged Watergate-style corruption.[24]

The Lockheed case confirmed Church's arguments. It evoked adverse reactions in foreign countries and endangered the stability of several pro-American governments. It showed, as the oil industry had done, that what immediately benefitted a U. S. multinational corporation might in fact be contrary to America's long-term interests. And it demonstrated how easily corruption, hidden behind a curtain of national security, could infect America's own government.[25]

Although the Lockheed scandal had been building for some time, the multinationals subcommittee first called the public's attention to it during the Northrop investigation. On June 10, Church shrewdly extracted information about Lockheed from Northrop's chief executive officer, Thomas V. Jones. Well aware that Northrop's incriminating documents contained scattered references to Lockheed, Church pressed the handsome, debonair Jones to concede that Northrop's pattern of bribes was not unique. Jones initially hedged his answers. He had no love for his company's bitter corporate rival, but he knew that the Lockheed trail could lead to more information about Northrop itself, especially regarding bribes to Prince Bernhard of the Netherlands. Church finally asked Jones directly if Northrop had patterned its activities "after the Lockheed arrangement"—an arrangement using dummy corporations, connections with foreign agents, and bribes. Despite Jones's guarded response, the "Lockheed scandal" quickly moved front and center, prompting Church's committee and the SEC to subpoena company documents.[26]

In what the *Wall Street Journal* described as "an end run," the subcommittee secured masses of documents from Lockheed's auditors before the company could intervene. Receipts from Japan that had long puzzled the auditors suddenly began to make sense. A reference to "one hundred peanuts," for example, was part of a code by which a peanut represented a million yen.[27]

On August 24, Lockheed's fifty-four-year-old vice president and treasurer, Robert N. Waters, killed himself. After referring in a suicide note to business problems, he held a hunting rifle to his temple and pulled the trigger. Waters was dead and the Lockheed corporation badly wounded.[28]

For some time the southern California-based aircraft company had been struggling. Throughout the 1960s it had been the nation's largest defense contractor and the world's biggest arms dealer, but late in the decade it had encountered hard times. A series of setbacks, including cancellations and reductions of U. S. government purchases, as well as the loss of important European sales, had created what Lockheed president A. Carl Kotchian described as "a disastrous situation." In 1971 the Nixon administration barely got Congress to bail out the faltering corporation with a loan guarantee of $250 million. The loan won House approval by only three votes and slipped through the Senate, despite Church's determined opposition, by a margin of one vote. Kotchian had already concluded that Lockheed's future rested in the Far East. "There is no way left," he said, "but to win in the biggest market, Japan." To secure a contract with All Nippon Airways, he agreed to pay millions of dollars to several Japanese government officials. Buying favors was not new to Lockheed. West Germany's Defense Minister, Franz Joseph Strauss, had once joked that Lockheed's "salesmen are everywhere. I can't open a drawer in my desk without a Lockheed man falls out of it." Strauss might well have referred to Lockheed's money falling out of desks. Over the years, the corporation had given huge amounts of cash to influential people in Indonesia (under the cover of a fund for widows and orphans) and in countries such as the Netherlands, the Philippines, Turkey, Saudi Arabia, and Italy. In mid-1975, Church's multinationals subcommittee closed in on Lockheed.[29]

To Church's dismay, however, William Proxmire's Senate Banking Committee almost stole the case in late August by opening its own "Lockheed Bribery" hearings. But the committee lacked the documentation that Church's staff had been gathering. Proxmire's inquiry thus elicited little more than some humorous exchanges with Lockheed's chairperson, Dan Haughton. Haughton at one point told Proxmire, for example, that the company's attorney preferred that he call the Lockheed's payment system a "kickback, but, you know, if you want to call it bribes, I guess it's all right."[30]

On September 12, amid a pile of documentation regarding Lockheed bribes in Asia and the Middle East, Church's subcommittee grilled Haughton. Church observed disdainfully that Lockheed's corruption abroad made "crookedness in politics look like a Sunday school picnic by comparison." Haughton again tried to distinguish a bribe from a kickback, but then claimed that he was "not an authority on these matters." Church shot back with a laugh, "If you are not one, I don't know who is." The senator then picked up on the company's admission that it competed abroad, not just against other airplane manufacturers, but, in Haughton's words, "for sales dollars that would be spent on something else." "Such as Kellogg Corn Flakes," Church retorted. "You see, this is where the whole practice becomes so venal." By bribing high government officials to purchase airplanes, "you force these governments in the direction of military sales purchases when other purchases might be far more beneficial to them and to their people." To sell its planes, Lockheed had paid over $106 million in bribes to Saudi Arabia alone. Most of that money had gone to Saudi entrepreneur Adnan M. Khashoggi, one of the world's biggest arms dealers, the owner of luxury homes and investments around the world, and a man whose friendship with and alleged contributions to Richard Nixon had intrigued the Watergate prosecutors.[31]

Church gets in step with Democratic presidential frontrunner Edmund Muskie in early 1972. *Courtesy Barry Kough.*

Two sides of the 1976 presidential campaign leadership: a modish Henry Kimelman and lawyerly Carl Burke. *Courtesy Boise State University.*

Church and supporters walk through Idaho City's snow-lined streets following the declaration of his presidential candidacy, March 18, 1976. *Courtesy Barry Kough*.

At New York City's Biltmore Hotel, Church awaits Jimmy Carter's call regarding the vice presidential spot on the Democratic ticket. Carter called a few minutes later with news that Walter Mondale was his choice. *Courtesy Barry Kough*.

After the frantic pace of Church's 1976 presidential campaign, staffer Peter Fenn, "Superman," and Forrest Church have some fun at a charity roast. *Courtesy Peter Fenn.*

Chief counsel Jerome Levinson was crucial to the effectiveness of the multinationals subcommittee. *Courtesy Jerome Levinson.*

Administrative assistant Mike Wetherell meets with Church in the late Seventies. In the 1990s, Wetherell became chair of Idaho's Democratic Party. *Courtesy Barry Kough*.

During the intelligence committee investigations, Church meets in his private office with the committee's chief of staff, William Miller. *Courtesy Barry Kough*.

Church talks with CIA director William Colby during the 1975 intelligence committee investigations. *Courtesy Barry Kough.*

Church and Charles Mathias, co-chairs of the Senate's Special Committee on National Emergencies, share a split gavel. *Courtesy Boise State University.*

Church and Paul Sarbanes meet with Jimmy Carter in the Rose Garden in April 1978, their expressions betraying the chilliness of the relationship between the senators and the president. *Courtesy Boise State University.*

Church as Senate Foreign Relations Committee chair, working with Republicans Jesse Helms and Jacob Javits. *Courtesy Boise State University.*

Beneath Ben Franklin's statue, Church in late 1979 discusses the Iranian situation with Senate Foreign Relations Committee chief of staff William B. Bader. *Courtesy George Tames and New York Times.*

Church and Senator Edward Kennedy during the 1980 hostage crisis in Iran. *Courtesy Boise State University.*

Church, cheeseburger in hand, campaigns in 1980 at the Corner Bar in Genesee, Idaho. *Courtesy Barry Kough*.

Bethine and Frank enjoy a relaxing moment on their Boise porch during the otherwise dispiriting 1980 campaign. *Courtesy Boise State University.*

Frank and Bethine Church in their typical dynamic duo role. *Courtesy Boise State University.*

Over the next few months documents about Lockheed's payoffs poured out of Church's subcommittee. "The press tables drowned in them," wrote a chronicler of the scandal. "Often the duplicated copies were left behind, unread and certainly not unravelled, to be shovelled into the janitors' waste-bins as the session adjourned."[32]

For the subcommittee itself, Lockheed provided a far more unifying target than the banks. The political implications of weapons sales were obvious. "Arms are not tennis shoes," as one journalist observed, regarding the lethal qualities of weapons. Moreover, the fight in 1971 over the governmental bailout of Lockheed had sorely tested the corporation's slim margin of support on Capitol Hill. On the multinationals subcommittee, Lockheed was unable to spark Charles Percy's usual corporate sympathies. The Illinois senator once enraged the company's interim chair, Robert Haack, by excusing himself from a meeting in order to escort movie star Elizabeth Taylor around the Senate. As Jerry Levinson recalled, Haack exploded: "I've got responsibility for 60,000 employees, and this guy is taking this actress around."[33]

Lockheed nevertheless drew upon a considerable reservoir of power. The company's attorney, William Rogers, had been Nixon's Secretary of State for almost five years. By applying what Jack Blum described as "tremendous pressure," Rogers at first got the subcommittee to focus in detail only on Lockheed's relationship with Saudi Arabia. Blum appealed anxiously to Church. "Look, this can't be," he remembered telling the senator. Investigative leads suggested that the scandal ran deeply into the North Atlantic Treaty Organization and Japan. Church backed Blum. "Go on, carry on," he instructed him. "Carry it to the end."[34]

Church's response may have reflected his anger at Henry Kissinger's intervention in the case in late 1975. At William Rogers's request, Kissinger on November 28 asked Attorney General Edward Levi to secure a "protective order" against the disclosure of the names of people who had received "covert payments from Lockheed." Kissinger maintained that disclosing the names could imperil America's foreign relations. Levi secured a federal court order forbidding the SEC from releasing names as it pressed its complaint against Lockheed. Church, reportedly irate at the efforts of Nixon administration holdovers to put a muzzle on the case, now plunged ahead with renewed zeal. He was undoubtedly also aware that bits and pieces of the Lockheed story were already breaking loose in a number of countries.[35]

In early 1976 the lid blew off the case. On February 4, Church's subcommittee reopened its Lockheed hearings to enormous publicity. Over the next few days the subcommittee released new Lockheed documents and questioned the company's president, Carl Kotchian. The white-haired, soft-spoken Kotchian, whose countenance at the hearings sometimes resembled that of an anguished and aging James Cagney, endured what he described as "a very painful two and a half hours" under glaring television lights. Although Kotchian preferred the term "gift" to that of "bribe," he admitted that the company's off-the-books operation had paid millions of dollars to people in countries such as Germany, Italy, Sweden, and Japan, and to "a high government official in the Netherlands." Kotchian withheld the name of the Dutch official, but a committee leak revealed that it was Prince Bernhard of the royal family.[36]

In late February *Newsweek* featured an eight-page special report, "Payoffs: The Growing Scandal." By then, the scandal's repercussions were world-wide. The Dutch launched an investigation of Prince Bernhard, their World War II hero and once-dashing symbol of royalty. According to the Church committee the prince had received $1 million from Lockheed in 1959, following the decision of the Dutch military to buy F-104 Starfighters. Bernhard had subsequently collected additional payments from the corporation (and also from Northrop). Italy likewise opened an investigation, after the Church hearings disclosed that Lockheed had paid Italian officials around $2 million to ensure the purchase of fourteen Hercules transport planes. The Lockheed revelations hit Japan with even greater force, shaking it, in the words of journalist Robert Shaplen, "more deeply than any comparable event since 1945, when the American Occupation began." Between 1969 and 1975, Japanese officials had received over $12 million in bribes from the company. Church's subcommittee determined that more than $1 million had gone to Lockheed's secret agent in Japan, Yoshio Kodama, a major power broker who had spent time in jail for his ultra right-wing activities. In March, the government indicted Kodama. That month a disillusioned young ultra-nationalist, convinced that Kodama had betrayed the right-wing cause, put on a red headband and killed himself by crashing his plane into Kodama's house. "Lockheedo," as the Japanese called the scandal, spread outward and, in July, public prosecutors arrested former Prime Minister Kakuei Tanaka. A Church aide quipped that the Senate "investigations would bring down more governments in a few hours than Lenin had in a lifetime."[37]

For a number of weeks the multinationals subcommittee was at the center of an international storm. The hearings attracted huge attention from the media, outside and inside the United States. Once, when American and Japanese reporters jostled over the limited number of seats, a writer from the *Wall Street Journal* shouted, to laughter, "Okay, Allies here; Axis here." Members of the press eagerly sought out Church and his staff. When Jack Blum answered the doorbell one evening, he confronted glaring television lights and a crowd of shouting Japanese reporters. The media's appetite for cops-and-robbers revelations seemed insatiable. Blum concluded that the subcommittee could sustain the high level of interest only via more and more lurid findings until, ultimately, it would have "to drag a still warm body to the witness table with a knife sticking in its back."[38]

Some critics believed that Church, in an effort to boost his presidential stock, encouraged the circus atmosphere. Pat Holt of the Foreign Relations Committee staff faulted the subcommittee for "just chasing more scandals" rather than digging deeper into the causes of problems. In his opinion, Church pursued the headlines. Holt talked with him about the need to look at less spectacular but still important issues, such as the export of agricultural products to the Soviet Union and Europe, but Church was not interested. "No, we're doing great," Holt remembered him saying.[39]

Not all observers sensed that Church was scrambling to get into the spotlight, however. A *Village Voice* reporter who attended the hearings thought he seemed "relatively oblivious to the impression he was making on the TV audience." In contrast to Charles Percy, who was ever attentive to the cameras and "was all slicked up to look like Robert Redford in 'The Candidate,' " Church slumped in his seat, often hid his face behind his hand, and "practically disappeared behind the big dais."[40]

Moreover, the investigation of corporate scandals was as significant as it was sensational. Church's subcommittee showed that officials in more than thirty countries, spread across four continents, had received payoffs from Lockheed and other corporations, including Gulf and Northrop. *Newsweek* referred dramatically to the hearings' "Great Global Fallout" and credited Church with having "been more responsible than any other individual for uncovering the flood of international scandals."[41]

Not surprisingly, Church was consistently under pressure to ease off the inquiry. The standard warning was that he would be responsible for the retaliations of other countries against U. S. businesses. A report in February that Lockheed had lost a $1.3 billion Japanese order for new planes, and that other U. S. aircraft manufacturers might lose the Japanese market, hardly helped his cause. Indeed, the report attracted the attention of the White House, which found the corporate scandals embarrassing as well as worrisome.[42]

The scandals were embarrassing partly because, in mid-1974, the Nixon/Ford administration had appointed as the U. S. ambassador to Japan one of Lockheed's senior vice presidents. James D. Hodgson had worked for the corporation for around twenty-five years before becoming Nixon's Secretary of Labor and, then, ambassador to Japan. The Ford administration now scurried to contain the growing scandal, while trying to avoid any implicit endorsement of Lockheed or other corporate corruption. On the one hand, the president expressed "deep concern" that the disclosures were upsetting American allies. On the other hand, as he looked to the November election, he wanted to dispel criticism that he was the captive of big business. On March 31 he thus established what he called "a Cabinet-level Task Force on Questionable Corporate Payments Abroad." He hoped that it would restore public faith in the honesty of major corporations and thus boost free enterprise. Ford also noted that the U. S. had asked the United Nation's Economic and Social Council (ECOSOC) to frame an international agreement regarding corrupt practices. Indeed, he portrayed the U. S. as the driving force behind ECOSOC's formation, in August, of a special group to deal with the matter.[43]

While the administration tried to put the best gloss possible on a bad situation, Church attacked "corporate lawlessness" as symptomatic of larger problems in U. S. politics and foreign policy. One of the problems, as the Watergate crisis had shown, was a chilling disrespect for law at the highest levels of American government. Church reminded several audiences of the wisdom of the great Supreme Court justice, Louis Brandeis, that government "'teaches the whole people by its example.'" In recent years, however, that example had been sorry indeed. "The executive branch's disregard for the law" had been so staggering that, ultimately, a president had resigned rather than risk impeachment.[44]

Another of America's problems that Church identified was the growing privatization of foreign policy, in defiance of the Constitution and democratic principles. When huge corporations interfered in the politics of other countries, as ITT had done in Chile, or when they used bribes to garner arms sales abroad, they in effect usurped the government's power to make U. S. foreign policy. Years earlier, only midway through his first term, Church had warned against turning the nation's military aid program over to private business. But that transferral of power had basically occurred. The multinationals subcommittee discovered, for instance, that the California-based Grumman company had sold F-14 fighters to Iran before the U. S. government approved such sales. Lockheed, in turn, had helped to subsidize the notorious Yoshio Kodama, whose shadowy right-wing politics had earned him the title of "the monster" to the Japanese left. Kodama's strident nationalism and militarism ran contrary to the kind of politics that the U.S. officially favored in Japan. "We had better make up our minds," Church announced in the multinational hearings, "whether we are going to have a United States or a corporate foreign policy."[45]

Governmental acceptance and even encouragement of corporate bribery abroad manifested yet again, as Church pointed out, the liabilities of Cold War thinking. Through oil purchases and arms sales, the U. S. hoped to counteract Soviet influence in areas such as the Persian Gulf. But, in Church's opinion, Saudi Arabia and Iran were not mere pawns in the struggle with communism. Those countries had used their oil to effect "a greater degree of destabilization in the West than the communists have ever been able to achieve," and were themselves turning into armed camps that threatened the peace.[46]

The "corporate immorality play," as Church described it, thus contained vastly unsettling implications. Jerry Levinson was surprised at how deeply the multinationals' behavior offended his boss. Commuting one morning to the Lockheed hearings with Levinson, the senator was emotionally as hot as the steaming cup of coffee in his hand. Levinson tried to make the point that the subcommittee's role was not to change corporate morals. Church remained unpersuaded. In several speeches he dismissed the argument that U. S. corporations needed to bribe foreign officials in order to conform to the old wisdom, "When in Rome, do as the Romans do." This rationalization had simply encouraged the bringing of bad habits to America. As evidence, Church noted the illegal corporate contributions to Nixon's 1972 campaign. When the senator pleaded that "we just have to put our house in order," *Newsweek* described him as "one of the most articulate and insistent proponents of the 'new morality' that has dominated American politics since Watergate."[47]

IV

Church's concern that America's house was not in order also reflected his growing skepticism about the nation's intelligence-gathering agencies. As a former intelligence officer, he recognized the need to collect information about one's foes and potential adversaries. For several decades, however, he had viewed the expanding power of the FBI under director J. Edgar Hoover as "scary." Driving past the bureau's headquarters with a friend one night in 1958, he remarked, "There's J. Edgar Hoover's lair—the man who made a police state out of America."[48]

He was also nervous about the CIA. Although he had apparently been uncritical of the agency during its formative decade, he concluded fairly early in his Senate career that its Cold War frame of reference blinded it to significant world trends. He laughingly told his staff that CIA director Allen Dulles and an aide had been unable to find the Congo on the map. And he joked about the possible medical consequences of being "briefed" by the CIA and then not debriefed. His humor nevertheless betrayed considerable apprehension about the CIA's bureaucratic hold on the government and the media. "You don't count unless you're part of the old in-crowd," he once commented when assessing the CIA's privileged position in policy-making circles. During the mid-Sixties he had supported Eugene McCarthy's unsuccessful call for an investigation of the agency. In 1971 he had told the Foreign Relations Committee's staff director that Congress needed to wrest back "the war-declaring function" from the CIA. To that end, he wanted to strip the agency of its ability to conduct covert military and para-military operations around the world. When he learned in 1973 about the CIA's dirty tricks in Chile, he was infuriated. It was impossible, he declared, "to insulate our constitutional and democratic processes at home from the kind of foreign policy we have conducted. . . ."[49]

On September 8, 1974 additional evidence of what one reporter dubbed "the 'Chileanization' of American politics" jolted Church. Information leaked from the House of Representatives suggesting that several people had lied to the multinationals subcommittee, among them former CIA director Richard Helms. According to the *Washington Post* and *New York Times*, the CIA had been deeply involved in the destabilization of Chile, despite the denials of Helms and others. The source of this startling news was testimony that the new CIA director, William Colby, gave on April 22 behind the closed doors of a House Armed Services subcommittee. Although members of the entire Armed Services Committee had access to Colby's testimony, only Massachusetts Democrat Michael Harrington took action. Shocked, he requested a thorough investigation of the U. S. role in Allende's overthrow. To his dismay he received no encouragement from either Senator Fulbright or Thomas Morgan, the chair of the House Foreign Affairs Committee, to whom he sent lengthy appeals. Fulbright doubted that there was sufficient Senate interest in such an investigation, or that such an inquiry would turn up new information. The public, and most members of Congress, thus remained unaware of Colby's testimony until stories about Harrington's letter to Morgan, describing the CIA's covert activities in Chile, appeared on the front pages of the *Post* and *Times*. Even then, congressional outrage was not directed at the CIA, but rather at the Harrington leak and its possible implications for "the national interest."[50]

Church, virtually alone among his Senate colleagues, was irate at the substance of Colby's reported testimony. Breaking off his reelection campaign in Idaho, he returned to Washington, D. C., telling reporter Seymour Hersh that he was "very much incensed" about the possible perjury before his subcommittee. "I'm not going to let this matter slide by," he threatened. He blamed "the Vietnam syndrome" for the growing willingness to lie to Congress and stated firmly, "It's a habit the Congress is going to have to break." Church announced that he would turn over to the Justice Department any "misleading" information that his subcommittee had received, and he instructed Jerry Levinson to gather the appropriate information.[51]

Over the next few weeks, however, Church fought an uphill battle. Fulbright and the Senate Foreign Relations Committee initially impeded his progress. Just a few hours before the committee was to discuss Levinson's confidential report, the *New York Times* and the *Washington Post* revealed the report's contents. Stormy committee debate followed, swirling around the source of the leak. Wyoming Democrat Gale McGee and Pennsylvania Republican Hugh Scott turned their fury on Levinson. Church rallied to his aide's defense and tried unsuccessfully to direct the committee's attention to the contents of the report. Although Levinson had been unable to say for sure that Helms or anyone else had lied to the subcommittee, he contended that their testimony was certainly "contumacious" and subject to contempt proceedings. The much-agitated committee set Levinson's report aside, however. Church had gotten no support from Fulbright, who was seething about the leak and more inclined than his Idaho colleague to downplay the CIA's intrusion into Chile's politics. "I don't approve of intervention in other people's elections," Fulbright told the press, "but it has been a long-continued practice."[52]

The deteriorating relationship between Church and Fulbright was evident shortly thereafter when they clashed during a Foreign Relations Committee interrogation of Henry Kissinger about Soviet detente. Church took the opportunity to ask Kissinger how he squared the spirit of detente with America's outrageous meddling in Chile. Fulbright objected strongly that Church's interrogation did not bear on the subject at hand. Church doggedly persisted. He criticized the U. S. subversion of the Allende government as a hypocritical act that undercut talk of detente. When Fulbright again interceded in Kissinger's behalf, Church left the room in disgust. One journalist believed that his angry departure had provided "the first sign of life that the committee has shown in many months."[53]

Church also rebuked the president. At a September 16 press conference, Ford had defended the CIA's covert activities in Chile on grounds that communist countries spent "vastly more money than we do for the same kind of purpose." Church was aghast. "He equates us with the Russians," the senator fumed. "I thought there was a difference, and the difference is what it's all about." What, Church wondered, distinguished Ford's justification for undermining Allende from the Soviets' excuse for invading Czechoslovakia in 1968? In Church's estimation, there was no defense for the CIA's sorry actions.[54]

Church was no happier with his Senate colleagues who were supposed to be overseeing the CIA. "The trouble is, the watchdog committee never really watched the dog," he said. Like him, a few senators wanted more supervision. Minnesota Democrat Walter Mondale urged the formation of a committee, resembling the Select Committee on Emergency Powers, to study the problem. By December, however, as reporter Judith Miller wrote, it appeared that Congress would probably "do what it has done in the past—nothing."[55]

That situation changed suddenly on December 22. Seymour Hersh, the investigative journalist whom *Time* called "Supersnoop," broke yet another story on the CIA. This time, Hersh revealed that the agency had illegally conducted intelligence operations against thousands of Americans, especially antiwar activists. His sources, as events proved, came from within the CIA itself. In 1973 new director James Schlesinger had ordered his subordinates to compile a report on agency activities that had perhaps violated the CIA's charter. Schlesinger's successor, William Colby, called the secret report the "Family Jewels" and later indicated that he had personally met with Hersh to confirm the reporter's information. Hersh's disclosures quickly mobilized the White House and the Congress. As Congress finally swung into action, the Ford administration worried about the start of a legislative "circus." To discourage such a circus and to evaluate Hersh's charges, Ford set up a commission with Vice President Nelson Rockefeller as chair—a step that columnist Tom Wicker likened to putting out a goat "to guard the cabbage patch."[56]

On January 14 and 20, Frank Church came out fighting at the Senate Democratic caucuses, where debate whirled around a possible inquiry into the CIA. At the first meeting, in what one observer described as a "very strong speech," he contended that the agency had "deceived" his subcommittee about Chile. On January 20 he endorsed the formation of a special Senate investigating committee. Mississippi senators John Stennis and James Eastland mounted a counterattack. "What's wrong with overthrowing the government of Chile?" Eastland demanded. "It was a commie government, wasn't it?" The overwhelming 45 to 7 vote in favor of a special investigating committee raised eyebrows. People leaving the meeting were heard discussing "the end of an era." Church could agree. He knew that the so-called Senate watchdog committees had historically ignored CIA actions. As Leverett Saltonstall, the dignified Massachusetts Republican, had once told him, "It's better for gentlemen not to know what's going on."[57]

By early 1975 the Senate was decidedly more interested in what was going on. On January 27, by a vote of 82 to 4, it established a Senate Select Committee on Intelligence Activities, to operate for nine months and charged with investigating the CIA, the FBI, and other intelligence-gathering agencies. Majority Leader Mike Mansfield promptly named Church and ten other senators to the ideologically balanced committee. The other Democrats included Mondale, Philip Hart of Michigan, Walter Huddleston of Kentucky, Robert Morgan of North Carolina, and Gary Hart of Colorado. The five Republicans were Charles Mathias, Jr. of Maryland, Howard Baker of Tennessee, John Tower of Texas, Richard Schweiker of Pennsylvania, and Arizona's Barry Goldwater.[58]

V

Eager to chair the committee, Church lobbied actively for the position and reportedly "almost knocked down Mansfield's door," as one acquaintance put it. Although Mansfield's first choice was reputedly Phil Hart, the Montana senator later insisted that he had considered no one other than Church, the "best man for the job." Hart, in any case, was suffering from cancer and was barely able to finish his term on the committee, let alone chair it.[59]

For Church, the committee offered an opportunity to combine principle with ambition. As a matter of principle, it allowed him to deal firsthand with issues about which he felt strongly, including U. S. interventionism and the growth of the national security state. "It's the culmination of what he has been talking about for years," an associate observed: "America doped on *hubris*, playing God in the world. It ties together his foreign policy and civil libertarian views." Philosophically, Church recognized the tensions within American history between nationalism and the constitutional guarantees regarding justice, personal freedom, and government under law. "Nationalism," he once said, "has always been the enemy of the republic." By feeding a rally-'round-the-flag mentality it jeopardized individual liberty and enhanced the powers of the state. To salvage America's basic freedoms, Church believed an investigation of the intelligence community could be nothing less than "redemptive."[60]

If the investigation could refurbish America's political ideals, it could also bring the senator much national exposure. Public hearings could turn him into what one magazine described as the "star of a long-running TV show with high ratings." The Ford administration hardly relished these prospects. The president's counsel, Roderick Hills, later indicated that the White House felt "considerable apprehension" about Church, who was "outspoken about the things he cared about," and able to gain headlines.[61]

The committee nevertheless got off to a slow start. Putting together a huge staff of around 150 consumed precious time. Moreover, the White House delayed in turning over documents. "We're not moving rapidly enough," Church said irritably on April 23. "The executive branch is setting the pace. We cannot make ourselves subject to their control."[62]

From the outset, the administration nervously eyed the committee as a possible threat to national security. Henry Kissinger, Vice President Rockefeller, and other top presidential advisers blamed Watergate for having exposed the intelligence community to unprecedented scrutiny. They warned Ford that the deteriorating situation allowed for " 'band-wagon' efforts" on Capitol Hill that endangered the nation's intelligence agencies. Public hearings especially worried the White House because they could easily spin out of control, leading the press and other congressional bodies to increasingly sensitive information. Convinced that it was protecting lives and the morale of the intelligence agencies, the administration decided early on to withhold certain information from the committee. When Ford talked in March with Church and Tower, he thus worked from the premise that "we are a great power and it is important that we be perceived as such—that our intelligence capability to a certain extent be cloaked in mystery and held in awe."[63]

White House advisers also saw the committee as a political hazard. They complained that its "massive efforts" put the White House on the defensive, giving the public the impression "that leadership rests in Congress rather than the White House." The administration looked for ways to circumscribe and even discredit the committee's activities. In that context, a Seymour Hersh article that greatly alarmed the White House nevertheless seemed useful as a potential political weapon. When the May 25 *New York Times* carried Hersh's essay claiming that U. S. submarines were staging spy missions inside Soviet waters, the administration was genuinely upset: Ford's advisers considered obtaining a warrant to search Hersh's apartment and seeking grand jury indictments of the *Times* and of Hersh. At the same time, the president's aides wondered if they might use Hersh's story "to bolster" their efforts to put limits on the Church committee.[64]

Partisanship inevitably ensnared the committee itself. Goldwater, for example, passed information concerning the committee's proposed agenda to the White House, and Tower informed a Republican leadership meeting in the cabinet room that he had blocked Church's move to go public with hearings on the National Security Agency (NSA). Tower wrote later that minority leader Hugh Scott had asked him to serve as the G. O. P.'s "damage control officer."[65]

Political intrigue suffused the committee's massive staff room, which resembled a cross between what staffers described as "a World War II bunker" and a "rat's maze," and was so crowded that private telephone conversations were virtually impossible. When Tower's personal staff person, Charles Kirbow, resorted to making calls from an outside pay phone, Church's people laughingly waved at him. Once, when

Church loyalists returned from a meeting and heard Kirbow warning the NSA office not to give material to the committee, they peered over the partition and greeted him. Goldwater's staff designee candidly told the committee's chief counsel, Fritz Schwarz, "Fritz, I'm not here to work for you. I'm here to spy on you."[66]

VI

Despite a shaky start, in the late spring the committee opened a sensational investigation of the political assassinations of foreign leaders. Here "was the hottest item in town since Watergate," recalled a committee staffer; "it demanded attention." Church hinted publicly that the committee was digging up some astounding information. After a closed hearing with William Colby on May 21 he indignantly told the press, "It is simply intolerable that any agency of the government of the United States may engage in murder." Without offering any details, he had piqued considerable curiosity. Although Church's critics were certain that he had staged his anger for public effect, the senator conveyed the same impression of shock and disgust when he listened to Colby behind closed doors describe cloak-and-dagger activities in which the CIA had engaged.[67]

The assassination topic became even more compelling after the Rockefeller Commission largely ducked it. Although the panel's 299-page report in early June criticized the CIA for "unlawful and improper invasions" of constitutional rights, it relegated specifics about assassinations to a secret, eighty-six-page supplement for the president. Church promptly criticized the report for revealing only "the tip of the iceberg"; the commission, he said, had done little more than murmur, "naughty, naughty, tich, tich." Ford defended Rockefeller's panel, noting that its charge had been to examine domestic intelligence abuses. He then indicated that he would turn over to Congress the documents on political assassinations that the commission had gathered—"a surprise," according to Loch Johnson, a Church committee investigator.[68]

Speculation swirled around why Ford was facilitating the congressional inquiry into assassinations. *Newsweek* conjectured that he wanted to avoid charges of a cover-up and was happy to let a Democratic Congress "investigate supposed murder plots, hatched mostly under Democratic presidents." White House aide Phil Buchen later guessed that Ford had indeed "decided to let the committee squirm." Conservative commentator Fulton Lewis III could not contain his glee. Church was supposed to "ride forward on his white horse" and save the U. S.; instead, he was going to end up embarrassing himself and the Democrats by exposing the misdeeds of the Kennedy and Johnson administrations. "Some of my colleagues are calling me 'Kamikaze Church,' " the senator admitted.[69]

A substantial number of committee staffers soon concluded that the assassination issue was leading the investigation into a swamp, consuming precious time and diverting the committee's attention from other forms of covert action and domestic spying. As one staff member put it: "The CIA said, 'Oh, please don't throw us in the assassination brier patch!' and that's exactly what we did—to their delight." To Seymour Bolton, however, that interpretation was silly. According to Bolton, the CIA's liaison with the committee, the assassination "plots did more to make the CIA look ridiculous than any other disclosures in its history."[70]

Church himself had no doubts about the matter. As he told columnist Mary McGrory right after the Rockefeller Commission had dodged the subject of assassinations, "I knew we had to face it. There was really no way out." Several months later, as the committee wound down, he remained convinced that its most important findings were those that documented "CIA murder plots and murder attempts" abroad.[71]

Throughout the summer and into the fall of 1975 the committee pursued the grim topic of assassinations. The White House, claiming it was understaffed, only grudgingly released information. The fact was, as William Colby said later, "They just didn't want to turn over documents." According to the committee's chief counsel, "The CIA and the White House always gave us only what they thought we already knew." Bit by bit, however, the staff followed leads and gathered specific pieces of evidence. "These specifics were our lifeblood," remembered Loch Johnson, "the key to new vaults, new files, new memoranda hidden somewhere within the bowels of the CIA." And steadily the staff fleshed out files with code names such as "Operation MONGOOSE." MONGOOSE was the name of a covert-action plan by which the Kennedy administration hoped to destabilize Cuba and bring down Fidel Castro's government. The committee discovered that the CIA had indeed plotted to murder Castro, as well as Patrice Lumumba, the premier of the Belgian Congo, who in 1960 seemed anxious to lead his newly independent nation into the Soviet orbit. The agency's failed attempts to assassinate Castro included several schemes that enlisted the aid of organized crime. Congolese rebels killed Lumumba in early 1961, before the CIA could itself act. In three other instances, the committee found that the CIA had not actually killed leaders, but had encouraged and armed dissidents to overthrow their governments. The three cases involved the Dominican Republic's long-time dictator, Rafael Trujillo, South Vietnam's Ngo Dinh Diem, and General René Schneider of Chile. Although the committee lacked conclusive proof, it found evidence that the CIA might also have been involved in plots to murder Indonesia's Achmed Sukarno and Haiti's Francois Duvalier.[72]

Some critics believed, unfairly, that the committee tried to whitewash the Kennedy and Johnson administrations. In fact, as Loch Johnson observed, the Kennedy "administration became the centerpiece of the investigation," and none other than John Tower said that Church had been "totally fair and honest" regarding Kennedy. Although the committee hedged on John Kennedy's own responsibility for the attempts on Castro's life, it nevertheless spelled out the incriminating details of Operation MONGOOSE; and it acknowledged, for example, the administration's complicity in Diem's overthrow. Church himself told the press that it "strains credulity" to conclude that Eisenhower, Kennedy, and Johnson had been ignorant of the plots to kill Castro. The assassination investigation helped to revise Church's own feelings about the Kennedy presidency. "The more I learned about what was going on," he said later, "the less impressed I became."[73]

Nonetheless, Church himself had invited some of the charges of a whitewash in a mid-July interview when he suggested that the CIA may have been behaving "like a rogue elephant rampaging out of control." The comment haunted him and the committee thereafter. Senator Schweiker and others charged Church with deflecting responsibility from the presidents who presided over the agency. Other critics, such as presidential counsel Rod Hills, were furious that Church had tarred the entire CIA because of the wrongs of a small group of individuals. Hills chastised the senator when they met in Church's hideaway office, telling him that his remark was gratuitous, a sorry response to the White House's efforts to work with the committee.[74]

Church's response to Hills revealed much about his mood and sense of mission. Although the senator regretted his statement somewhat, he defended himself. His indignation at the CIA's conduct had simply boiled over, he explained. But his admitted showmanship and flamboyance had been for a good purpose. He compared himself to an evangelist trying to strike a moral chord in the American audience. Indeed, as he saw it, his role on the committee demanded that he stir the public's conscience. Church, according to Bill Miller, assumed that a kind of national catharsis might follow the exposure and excoriation of abuses.[75]

He was working against the clock, however. By mid-summer the committee was running out of time, even with the six-month extension that the Senate granted it. The assassination issue was dominating the agenda and had precluded the holding of public hearings. To meet its schedule, the committee divided up responsibilities and moved quickly along several tracks, one dealing with the domestic abuses of the intelligence agencies, and the other reviewing systematically the intelligence community's activities over some thirty years.[76]

On September 16, nine months after its formation, the committee finally opened its long-awaited public hearings. "We need to begin hearings with something dramatic," Church had instructed a staff member several days before. His chosen topic involved hidden poisons in the CIA's arsenal. In closed sessions the committee had just learned that the agency possessed various lethal chemicals and their delivery systems. Particularly shocking was the agency's admission that it had stored enough of a deadly shellfish toxin to kill thousands of people, despite a presidential order in 1970 to destroy it. One staff member joked sadly that the committee's final report should bear the title, "Bugs, Drugs, and Thugs," but others believed that the investigation should pursue more important issues, such as U. S. intervention in Chile. They feared that the klieg lights were drawing Church like a moth to a flame.[77]

VII

"I want that gun there!" Church ordered his staff just before the first public hearing. He was referring to a large pistol that the CIA had developed to shoot a tiny poison dart. The gun provided a dramatic exhibit when the session opened in the Senate Caucus Room, the site of the Watergate hearings. Spectators and newspeople packed the room, with public television on hand for live coverage. For several hours the committee focused on the CIA's biochemical program, which could spread deadly diseases and devastate crops and livestock. Church electrified the crowd by holding up the dart pistol for everyone to see, and then passing it along to his colleagues. Predictably, photographs of Church displaying the dart gun appeared in many newspapers and magazines. The gun had indeed caught the public's attention, providing the kind of "splash" that the senator wanted, but also opening him to criticism for his theatrics. The issue was not the pistol itself, however, as the committee's chief counsel later explained. The issue was that the CIA had illegally stored poison gases and chemicals in defiance of a presidential order.[78]

Despite the startling opening session, the hearings quickly bogged down in a dull discussion of various chemicals. By the third day, seats in the huge room were half empty, and many reporters had turned to other stories. Dwindling public interest suggested that the committee had chosen its subject poorly. Morton Halperin, the director of the Project on National Security and Civil Liberties, disagreed, arguing that the committee had performed a real service. "The three days of hearings were the beginning of a public education into how the CIA functions," he wrote. He applauded the "amazing discipline" with which the committee pursued the subject of biological weapons. Church's panel, unlike that for the Watergate scandals, had not wandered from the issue.[79]

Racing the calendar, the committee tried to cover as much of its business as possible. Sometimes it appeared to lack a focus and an agenda. "This is like building your boat as you go out to sea," Gary Hart grumbled as he left one meeting. Disagreements over strategies and topics were common.[80]

Ultimately, however, the committee conducted over 800 interviews, met as a group 126 times, held 21 public and 250 executive hearings, and gathered over 110,000 pages of documentation. It probed the FBI's domestic counterintelligence programs (COINTELPRO), which had declared a virtual war against civil rights groups and Native American organizations such as the American Indian Movement. Church described COINTELPRO as "one of the sordid episodes in the history of American law enforcement." The committee also revealed that a special unit within the Internal Revenue Service had "politically harassed" thousands of political activists, and that for over thirty years major communications companies such as ITT and RCA had routinely provided the CIA with access to telegrams that Americans sent abroad. A twenty-year mail intercept program that the CIA had conducted apparently included the opening of a letter that Church had mailed in 1971 to his mother-in-law in Boise; a CIA official remembered seeing the letter, but concluded that it and others had recently been destroyed. The committee probed as well the efforts of the Nixon White House to cajole the FBI, CIA, NSA, and the Defense Intelligence Agency to mount a massive, and grossly illegal, domestic surveillance campaign.[81]

At one point, Church and the other committee members themselves marched into the FBI office, demanding to see the files that the bureau had gathered on them. Suddenly, the surveillance issue was no longer an abstraction. Goldwater reportedly brushed off the existence of his file by saying that he was ashamed of nothing in it. But Church was extremely upset that the FBI had kept newspaper clippings about him as well as random charges regarding his possible disloyalty. "He was about as mad as I had ever seen him," recalled Bill Miller.[82]

VIII

These were frantic months for Church. As the demands of the intelligence committee increased, he also presided over the subcommittee on multinationals, which was by then enmeshed in the investigation of Lockheed and other arms dealers. Meanwhile, his supporters pressed him to lay the groundwork for his presidential campaign. And he continued to chair the Special Committee on Aging, where Utah senator Frank Moss was heading up an important inquiry into fraud and abuse in the Medicaid program. On the aging committee, Church fought in 1975 to ensure that Social Security beneficiaries received the 8 percent cost-of-living increase, rather than the administration's proposed 5 percent; and he assumed a variety of other duties, including chairing hearings in Boston about the impact of the high cost of living on the elderly. That fall, the National Council of Senior Citizens described him as "the leading voice in Congress on behalf of aged and aging Americans." Listing twenty-two pieces of legislation that he had sponsored or cosponsored, the council said that his record in behalf of the aging was "unequaled by any other Member of Congress."[83]

Church, constantly on the move, granted interviews, greeted visitors from Idaho, appeared on numerous news shows, delivered speeches, and coordinated his committee work. Loch Johnson remembered frantically trying to brief him as they hurried "at a near jog" to the next committee meeting. The emotional and psychological stress sometimes visibly fatigued Church.[84]

Bethine Church had never known him to be so angry or tense. He paced the floor at home, trying to work out his feelings and struggling to contain his emotions. The previously hidden assaults on constitutional government and civil liberties affronted him. He began to do what was unusual for him: he personalized his rage, lashing out bitterly at specific individuals who had betrayed American ideals and endangered the Constitution. Socially, as well, this was an especially trying period for the Churches, more so in Bethine's opinion than the years of the Vietnam war. During the war, there had been an exchange of ideas, however heated, and a sense of camaraderie with colleagues. But the investigations of the multinational corporations and the intelligence agencies isolated the Churches.[85]

"We were subject to incredible pressures," Church himself recalled of those frenzied months. The CIA regularly swept his office to make sure it was secure, prompting his staff to joke that the only bugs the agents found were from Idaho potatoes (a comment the CIA team apparently did not find amusing). The intelligence hearings attracted the attention of a variety of cranks. Church's speechwriter Bill Hall had been a journalist for years, but he had "never seen anything to equal the parade of paranoiacs who passed through Frank Church's office." He remembered a call from a woman in Denver who insisted that the CIA and FBI had been wiretapping her phone for a long time. As she became more and more upset, Hall improvised; he spoke very loudly into the phone that whoever was tapping her conversations had to stop immediately, by order of Frank Church, the chair of the Senate's select committee. Seemingly reassured, the woman hung up.[86]

The Lockheed hearings even triggered a threat against the senator's life. A radical Japanese group known as Chrysanthemum and Water claimed it had dispatched a team to kill Church and several members of his staff. Shortly thereafter, a terrified Japanese reporter, who had hoped to interview Church one evening, suddenly found himself against the wall outside the senator's office, facing a Capitol security team with snarling attack dogs.[87]

To maintain his own equilibrium during a period of great stress, Church looked as usual to his family. In order to attend his son Chase's high school graduation, he left an intelligence committee meeting early, even though former CIA director Richard Helms was testifying. The senator's advisers sometimes grumbled about his spending too much time with his family, but Jack Blum believed in retrospect that Church was in fact preserving "something extraordinary": an emotionally happy family and a balanced view of himself. Blum judged Church as "one of the few totally sane" politicians that he had known.[88]

As often as possible Church drove with Bethine and Chase to their rented cabin in the Pennsylvania woods. The small log house dated back to before the Civil War, and was accessible only by fording a creek. Church fished in the creek, shot skeet with Chase, lounged around, and read. As a concession to the intelligence committee, he temporarily installed a phone at the cabin. In significant ways, however, he protected his private life from the Senate's growing demands; and that life in turn bolstered him during a period of enormous personal commitment.[89]

IX

Although Church kept his investigative work in perspective, he found it bracing and drew from it a sense that he was defending fundamental ideals. The intelligence committee was his in more than name only. Like the senator himself, the committee had several sides, and there were no better expressions of its contrasting dimensions than the two staff leaders whom he picked, Bill Miller and F. A. O. ("Fritz") Schwarz, Jr.[90]

Miller, like Church, was a consummate political realist, aware of votes, the need to compromise, and the importance of working within institutional boundaries. He was Church's logical choice as staff director. When he had been John Sherman Cooper's top aide, and later when he headed the National Emergency Committee's staff, Miller had earned Church's trust and respect. He had also become a target of conservatives, who criticized him for heading "a cabal" of Senate staffers intent on softening America's Cold War policies. Some conservatives viewed his appointment to the intelligence committee as "an absolute disaster." Miller had indeed questioned the nation's foreign policy for some time but, as one of his associates observed, he was in fact "the quintessential Washington insider." He believed passionately in the political process. As staffer Patrick Shea put it, he would "walk into the street assuming the light will change, as it always has." For the gentle, soft-spoken Miller, the challenge on the committee was in "dealing with a large group of aggressive litigators."[91]

Schwarz, the committee's chief counsel, was exactly that kind of tough litigator. The grandson of a wealthy New York City toy manufacturer, Schwarz had gone from Harvard Law School to one of the nation's largest and most prestigious legal firms. His typically disheveled appearance disguised a sharp adversarial temperament and a zest to ferret out the facts and build the evidence—to "identify the wrongdoing," in his words. "I wanted to press for exposure," he said of his role on the Church committee. Unlike Miller, Schwarz was a political outsider who knew none of the senators before joining the committee. Yet he, as much as Miller, represented an important side of Frank Church, a side that had emerged more fully during the years of Vietnam and Watergate. Schwarz, like Church, was much the moralist, the product of idealism and indignation, the skeptic of established, powerful interests.[92]

Church knew that Miller and Schwarz were a combustible combination. They nevertheless echoed in their contrasting ways his own thoughts. Hence Church, the moral watchdog, instructed his staff that the committee existed "to investigate wrongdoing." In retrospect, he was proud that he had "taken on very powerful interests in this country. I chose to take them on. I did take them on." But Church, the consensus politician, simultaneously sought harmony on the committee and in his negotiations with the executive branch. "You don't win by losing," he reminded Loch Johnson. The intelligence investigation was thus "dual-headed," manifesting Church's blend of the moral and the practical.[93]

Church thus combined his crusading zeal with a keen appreciation for the consensus politics that the committee demanded. With a 6 to 5 party split, the panel was by design bipartisan. Senate leaders such as Mike Mansfield recognized that the investigation would be controversial enough without a highly charged partisan agenda. Close votes along party lines would have devastated the committee and tainted its findings. It was essential that it be as unified as possible. Church was well aware that criticism of the intelligence community would be more convincing if it bore Goldwater's and Tower's names, though he ultimately proved unsuccessful in obtaining them.[94]

Although Church was not alone in cultivating the political consensus that generally ruled the committee, his role was crucial. His preference for letting his colleagues make up their own minds, and his reluctance to twist arms, frustrated some of the staff. "Why," Schwarz moaned, "is Church so unwilling to lobby other senators?" Church knew, however, that too much pressure on the likes of Tower and Goldwater would only widen the committee's political and ideological lines. The select committee could all too easily have duplicated the sad fate of the House Intelligence Committee, which conducted a parallel investigation. Under New York Democrat Otis Pike, the House panel self-destructed; eventually, the House overruled its own committee and voted 146 to 124 to allow the White House to censor the Pike report. The Church committee had its share of battles with the White House, but the results were ultimately more tempered. Initially, White House counsel Rod Hills feared the worst from Church's panel—perhaps "a year of pure hell." Hills was never happy with the existence of the Senate committee, but he contrasted Church's reasonable and professional conduct with that of Pike, who was "difficult, uncompromising, unable to deal with anything" and altogether "the most disreputable representative" that Hills had met.[95]

Some of Church's critics faulted him for being too agreeable, unwilling to fight when "the right-wingers get rough." Columnist Nicholas Von Hoffman labeled him a "noble-profiled marshmallow." Complaints surfaced time and again that he was bending backward to please the CIA, the White House, or Goldwater and Tower. Although Seymour Hersh believed that Church's multinationals committee had done a creditable job in digging up information on Chile, he decided by late 1975 that the intelligence panel was treating the CIA far too easily. A member of the House committee went so far as to call Church "an artful dodge."[96]

For Church, of course, the central question was how much leverage he had within the committee. Tower and Goldwater were both, in Miller's words, "King's Party men" who had long believed that foreign policy and defense were the president's prerogative. Although Tower told the White House that Church was "sometimes after his own publicity," the two men developed a surprisingly good working relationship. Still, Tower was well aware of Church's desire for a unanimous committee, and he used that knowledge to gain concessions. In Goldwater, Church faced not only a faithful defender of the intelligence community, but also a man whom he had publicly criticized a decade earlier for not living in the real world. The Arizona conservative was unhappy enough with Church anyhow. "I have never," he wrote later, "more severely questioned the conduct of a U. S. senator than I have Church's display of ambition during those televised hearings." Although Goldwater and Tower both refused to sign the final report, the committee, in April 1976, made public its multi-volume findings. *Newsweek* described the report as "probably the most comprehensive and thoughtfully critical study yet made of the shadowy world of U. S. intelligence." Its existence constituted a remarkable achievement, and Church deserved a great deal of credit for it.[97]

Church had been conciliatory but stood by his principles. When it appeared in early November 1975 that the committee might obey Ford's plea to keep the assassination findings secret, he threatened to resign. His stunned colleagues sat quietly for several minutes. Then, overwhelmingly, in one of the few votes the committee took, they sent the report to the Senate and recommended that it be made public. The report, which the Senate released in late November, "uncovered some maggoty horrors," in the words of columnist Mary McGrory—horrors that the *New York Times* categorized as the "inexcusable" products of "an amoral secret bureaucracy." Although Church tried to avoid confrontations with the White House, he made clear from the start his willingness, if necessary, to go to the courts to obtain documents. His threats apparently carried some weight. In the months after Watergate, according to the CIA's chief liaison to the committee, the president and his advisers were "terrified of subpoenas. They did not want to force a resolution of constitutional questions."[98]

Church publicly castigated the administration on many occasions. In November, for example, when Ford fired William Colby, Church was so angry that his voice literally shook during a press conference. "Concealment is the order of the day," he protested. "Hiding evil is the trademark of a totalitarian government." On TV a few days later, the senator told reporters that Colby's firing was part of a pattern "to disrupt this investigation." And he objected loudly when Ford named George Bush as Colby's replacement, an appointment nothing less than "astonishing." At the very time the CIA needed to become less politicized, Ford made a highly partisan appointment. "We need a CIA director who has the courage to say 'No, Mr. President,' " Church argued, "not one who is hoping the President will choose him as a running mate."[99]

Complaints that Church's committee should have pursued the intelligence agencies more relentlessly overlooked the huge backlash against it. "We seem to face increasing resistance on every front," Church observed in late 1975. Wherever he turned, he encountered warnings that he and his panel were destroying the defense community. Whether the attack came from Ford in a public letter to him, or from angry constituents, or from movie star Bing Crosby, or from former congresswoman and ambassador Clare Boothe Luce—who sat next to Church at a luncheon for Egypt's president Anwar Sadat—the message was the same: the committee was endangering America's national security. When Bush was sworn in as the CIA's new director, Ford visited the agency headquarters and told a cheering audience, "We cannot improve this agency by destroying it."[100]

The most potent weapon against the committee was the assassination of Richard Skeffington Welch, the CIA station chief in Greece. After masked terrorists killed Welch in Athens on Christmas day 1975, condemnation rained down on the Church panel. "The Welch murder was *the* event," Church recalled. "It was stage-managed." Thirty-one CIA officers had previously died in the line of duty, but not one of them received the attention that Welch did. Television's "Today Show" was on hand when his body returned to the U.S.; indeed, the plane bearing the dead man circled the field for almost an hour in order to guarantee live coverage. Ford and other top officials attended a large public funeral. Jim McClure, Church's Republican counterpart from Idaho, also made much of Welch's assassination. Defenders of the intelligence community "danced on the grave of Richard Welch in the most cynical way," Fritz Schwarz said bitterly. At least one White House aide admitted confidentially that the White House "exploited" Welch's death. Church, incensed, pointed out again and again that his panel had never published Welch's name nor that of any other agent. In fact, throughout the investigation Church insisted on not having any agent's name. But the damage to Church and his committee was substantial. Letters calling him a "murderer!" flooded his office. A vigilante group, Veterans Against Communist Sympathizers, threatened to kill him. By year's end, as the committee completed its public hearings and worked on its final report, public good will was quickly dissipating. Even before Welch's assassination, an opinion poll had revealed that only 38 percent of the public viewed the Church committee positively. Welch's death helped to turn growing public skepticism about the investigation into a powerful backlash.[101]

X

The backlash gained additional momentum because of rumors that Church was using the investigation to become president. Ford's advisers were certain that the senator was capitalizing on the inquiry at every step. On the select panel itself, one of Tower's top aides noted sarcastically that he was working "for the Church for President Committee." Even staffers who sympathized with Church suspected that he sometimes "milked" the investigation for publicity. By late fall a number of people on the committee were grumbling about his growing inattention and his apparent eagerness to wrap up the intelligence work. He was under fierce pressure from both sides—from people urging him to press on with the inquiry, and from aides eager for him to get into the presidential race. Looking back, one of Mondale's aides concluded that Church's interest in seeking the presidency in 1976 had hurt the investigation.[102]

Church indeed wanted to be president, but he did not sacrifice the committee to his ambition. In important respects, as he realized, chairing the intelligence panel could damage as well as help him politically. Southern Democrats reportedly warned him that a "witch hunt" against the CIA would ruin his presidential hopes. The intelligence community unquestionably enjoyed wide popularity and had been glamorized for years on TV shows such as "Mission Impossible." Televised hearings of the assassination issue might have helped to demystify the CIA and to publicize Church, but the Idaho senator opposed them and settled for a published report summarizing the panel's findings. Partly because so much of the committee's work occurred behind closed doors, the intelligence investigation lacked the intense drama of the Watergate hearings. When the committee met publicly, Church occasionally played to the cameras. Still, according to none other than William Colby, even when he brandished the poison dart gun, he was posturing no more than were the others on the panel, including Barry Goldwater.[103]

In reality, Church put his word ahead of his political ambition. He had promised Mike Mansfield that he would see the inquiry to its completion. He may have regretted that pledge, but he honored it. On the day he took command of the committee he told a delegation of liberals who wanted to open his presidential campaign that he would not mix the panel's business with election politics. The group left his office believing that his message was, "No, not now, but come back later." By mid-autumn, it was later and the press was touting him as a presidential "dark horse"; but he was still not a candidate and the investigation was continuing. Visibly anxious, he anguished as he urged Schwarz and Miller to wrap things up—but also to do good work. On December 13, although he had not yet announced his candidacy, he consented to the formation of the Church for President Committee. By then the hearings were over, even though the committee's final seven-volume report, cataloging intelligence abuses and recommending a permanent Senate oversight committee, would not be complete for several more months.[104]

On balance, the committee probably damaged Church's candidacy far more than his candidacy may have hurt the committee. Bill Miller was certain that Church had ultimately sacrificed his presidential hopes to meet his committee obligations. Because Church stayed with the investigation as long as he did, he entered the presidential race late. Even after he began campaigning, he spent much time working on the final intelligence report. "To charge that Church used the committee to run for president is unfair," insisted Fritz Schwarz. In some respects his role as chair of the committee may have even undercut his senatorial base in Idaho, where the investigation was hardly popular among the growing number of conservatives. Certainly the assignment detracted enormously from his other work and conveyed no direct benefits to his constituency.[105]

XI

By chairing the committee he also opened himself to the destructive charge that he had put his own country at risk. "Sen. Church aids Reds," blared a headline in a Missouri newspaper. The senator's staff acknowledged that he was receiving mail from across the country attacking him as unpatriotic. One CIA source contended that the intelligence committee had "left us naked before our enemies." Another CIA person declared bitterly, "You don't have a country, you have a church—no pun intended."[106]

Defenders of the national security state reviled Church. Conservative columnist James J. Kilpatrick looked upon him as a "hanging judge," and attacked the select committee's report as "a massive piece of folly." Patrick Buchanan, Nixon's former aide, complained that the committee had sought headlines, not the truth, in order to advance the "Big Lie" of America's left wing and aid "the ambitions of chairman Frank Church." According to Buchanan, a nation that treated its police and security officers so shabbily courted defeat. Another conservative commentator, Bill "the Iron Duke" Severin, weighed in against "ultra-liberals" such as Church, who placed the rights of bomb-throwing radicals ahead of their innocent victims. Newscaster Paul Harvey scored the committee for "sticking pins in the FBI" and ignoring the bureau's "mission to protect our established order against the wreckers." An editorial in *TV Guide* claimed that "a hundred KGB agents working overtime for the Kremlin" could not have damaged national security as much as had Church's committee.[107]

The White House was scarcely more temperate. In his State of the Union address, Ford referred to "the crippling of our foreign intelligence agencies" in a dangerous world. Vice President Rockefeller accused the Church committee of aiding America's enemies by exposing U. S. intelligence operations. And Henry Kissinger, who later described Church as "our scourge on Vietnam and constant critic of 'deceitful' methods," called on the country to stop undercutting its ability to conduct foreign policy. Years later, Kissinger continued to say that Church had "practically wrecked" the CIA.[108]

Although Church was certain that he was rescuing the U. S. from practices that subverted the country's ideals and were dangerously counterproductive, Kissinger and the others believed that he was naive, and held a "boy-scoutish" view of the world. "The world is not the sweet place that Frank Church liked to portray it," argued Richard Helms. After a quarter of a century battling Soviets and other groups "in the back alleys of the world," the former CIA director believed that he, far more than Church, recognized threats against the United States. Barry Goldwater placed himself with Helms in "the old school," a school that would protect the nation from "self-seekers and weak sisters" at home, and the deadly menace of international communism. The issue, Goldwater argued, was not what the intelligence community had done but what its intentions were: "If the intent is to keep us from national harm," then "dirty tricks" were necessary and patriotic.[109]

Another member of the old school was James Angleton, the CIA's fabled chief of counter-intelligence until late 1975. Angleton, like Church, had been born in Boise, but he otherwise had almost nothing in common with the senator, whom he saw as "a political celebrity within Washington's liberal left-wing Establishment." The Church committee, from Angleton's perspective, was part of a "diabolical plot" to expose the nation's jugular to the Soviets. The intelligence investigation attested frighteningly to the fact that the U. S. was losing its mortal struggle with the communists. "The country is going to hell," a distraught Angleton told Loch Johnson. "There is no interest in national security these days." The U. S. had fallen, but not to another nation, the legendary spycatcher asserted: "We have been occupied by Congress."[110]

Officials of multinational companies such as Lockheed were no less inclined to see themselves as clear-eyed patriots in an international jungle. Themselves Cold Warriors, they found it difficult to distinguish between their profits and patriotism. Lockheed's long-time president, Carl Kotchian, often ruminated on the communist threat. From the vantage point of Kotchian and his counterparts, the selling of arms and aircraft was part of the anti-communist crusade to save the West. Companies needed to protect their stockholders, boost the American economy, and save the world for market capitalism. From this perspective, payments to foreign leaders constituted good business and political savvy rather than bribes. There was little indication that the U. S. government disagreed. The CIA, for example, more than likely knew about Lockheed's payments to Kodama in Japan.[111]

Steadfast defenders of both the national security state and the multinational corporations were convinced that the real world of international politics and business did not allow for moralizing. From their vantage point, Frank Church's sermons on proper conduct and decent behavior seemed foolish and dangerous. As James Kilpatrick complained, Church and his ilk expected the United States to "go abroad in a dangerous world, accoutered like Little Lord Fauntleroy, to play patticake with gangs who fight with switchblade knives."[112]

Church disagreed that he was a fuzzy-minded innocent. He believed that he was far less naive than Henry Kissinger, who sought "a world restored to the ordered condominium of superpower hegemony." Kissinger and other so-called realists mistakenly ignored the relationship between morality and American interests. In Church's opinion, doing the right thing was as good for national security as it was for the soul. Indeed, immoral behavior created bad foreign policy and actually hurt the national interest. "Dirty tricks," whether at the hands of the CIA or multinationals, sullied the U. S. image abroad and encouraged anti-American sentiments and protests. Italian communists, claiming that they had "clean hands," had thus gained politically after the exposure of Lockheed's bribes to high officials. And the relationship of the oil multinationals with Libya's King Idris had encouraged the coup that put Colonel Muammar al-Qaddafi in power.[113]

International reaction to the bribery scandals seemed to confirm Church's opinion that high moral standards could provide the basis for a realistic foreign policy. Nations such as Japan not only survived momentary political crises following the revelations of payoffs; they also took steps to curtail corruption. In the Netherlands, the prime minister denounced Prince Bernhard for having "damaged the national interest," and parliament stripped the humiliated prince of virtually everything except his royal title. In Italy, the president eventually resigned under pressure and several officials were convicted for "aggravated corruption." In Japan, where videotapes of Church's multinational hearings were extremely popular, former prime minister Tanaka was convicted of accepting Lockheed's bribes and sentenced to four years in prison; sixteen other government and corporate officials were charged and ten convicted for their role in "Lockheedo." Such actions suggested that nations could agree upon a universal ethic. British journalist Anthony Sampson, who had followed the history of U. S. multinationals for some time, was surprised to discover little resentment of the U. S. in Japan, Holland, and elsewhere. "The Lockheed revelations," he wrote, "encouraged self-questioning and internal criticism, rather than anti-Americanism." Church himself received thanks from members of the reform wing of Tanaka's ruling Liberal Democratic Party. They applauded him and his subcommittee for exposing the bribery and the role of the shadowy Yoshio Kodama.[114]

These developments gratified Church. Again and again, he had heard that his investigations would destabilize America's allies and destroy crucial alliances. Events, however, had not justified such panic.[115]

Similarly, Church believed that the United States had strengthened itself by looking more closely at its darker side. Totalitarian governments hid their evils behind veils of secrecy; democracies depended upon well-informed electorates. "Our society," he said proudly, "has drawn its inspiration from the Biblical injunction, 'Ye shall know the truth and the truth shall make you free.' "[116]

XII

Together, the multinationals and intelligence investigations marked some of Church's finest hours. They fused in compelling ways his views on foreign policy and civil liberties. In both investigations, he dealt with issues that cut to the heart of American democracy, asking who, or what, ruled America.

His search for answers helped to produce one of the most important inquiries in American history regarding corporate power and influence. "Seldom has Congressional muckraking yielded such explosive material," observed *The Nation*, which described the multinationals subcommittee as "one of the most potent investigative bodies of the postwar period." There was quite simply "nothing like it," according to Judith Miller, who covered the multinationals subcommittee for the *Progressive* magazine. Years later, its "unparalleled" body of work still provided the basic raw materials for understanding the impact of the oil, banking, and weapons industry on foreign policy. The subcommittee's findings in many respects hardly reassured believers in American democracy. As political scientist Andrew Hacker wrote during the multinational investigations, "Our real centers of sovereignty are corporate bodies with inelegant names." Although Church wanted Congress to enact stiffer legislation than it ultimately did in 1976-77, he still found comfort that the subcommittee had confronted "the biggest, richest companies in the world" and demonstrated that they were secretly shaping American foreign policy.[117]

Such revelations raised another vital question for American democracy: who controls information and how much should the public know? Again, Church's findings were not reassuring. He observed that the executive branch's "imperial view" increasingly conflicted with the right of the people to find out what their government was doing. America's presidents seemed more and more to believe that, if public opinion precluded sending in the Marines, they could secretly send the CIA. The president too often resembled "a glorified Godfather." Ironically, in the name of democracy, the U. S. had accepted "the value system of the 'enemy' "–a system that depended upon subterfuge and disguised its attempts to overthrow democratically elected leaders.[118]

Church also questioned the definition of "national security" that often disguised the most sordid acts. The sad truth, he argued, was that U. S. policies often hinged far less on real issues of national security than on inflated views of America's role abroad, exaggerated Cold War fears, and the desire to shield powerful interest groups. The CIA's intervention in Chile thus had more to do with guarding "American business investments" than with subduing a foreign threat. Additionally, the U. S. had arrogated to itself the role of a world police officer. "Like Caesar peering into the colonies," Richard Nixon had watched the Chilean elections; and because the president had disliked the choice of the Chilean people, he had instructed the CIA to bring down their democratically chosen government. "When will this country stop being so uptight about the world?" Church asked an aide as they headed toward an intelligence committee meeting. "The foundations of the Republic will not crumble away if someone we don't like takes over Chad." Church compared the U. S. to a drug addict "hooked" on the Cold War and imperial pretensions; to feed its habit it backed some of the world's most brutal dictatorships and created a security system that was more and more "a mirror image of the evil it is designed to combat." It was time, the senator argued, to reject the idea that, "since the Soviets do it, we must do it, too." It was time to square American conduct with the nation's historic ideals – ideals which had once served as "a beacon of hope for the downtrodden and oppressed throughout the world."[119]

Just as Church preferred stricter legislation than Congress passed to deal with the multinational corporations, he wanted to limit notably the powers of the CIA. "All covert activity unrelated to the gathering of essential intelligence should be severed entirely from the CIA," he recommended unsuccessfully in the select committee's final report. He was well aware that the permanent oversight panel, which the committee recommended (and which the Senate established in 1976), would be vulnerable to shifting political winds. The requirement that the president had to justify in writing the need for each covert action was equally vulnerable. But Church accepted these institutional changes as compromises. "We did not want to end up on the cutting room floor," he explained. The committee had helped to provide the means to police the intelligence community more effectively. The political will to use those means was not, however, something that Church or anyone else could guarantee.[120]

Church continued to believe in his country's best instincts, even as he criticized its politics and foreign policy. "Ours," he insisted, "is not a wicked country and we cannot abide a wicked government." When columnist Mary McGrory contemplated Church's forthcoming presidential campaign, she thus believed that his agenda would involve nothing less than "the soul of the nation." She predicted, moreover, that if Americans were not tired of post-Watergate soul-searching, Church might even become president.[121]

Church announcing his presidential candidacy in Idaho City, March 18, 1976. *Courtesy Boise State University.*

Chapter Seventeen

The Late, Late Candidate: Seeking the Presidency, 1976

On March 18, 1976, along a crowded, snow-banked street in the small mountain town of Idaho City, Frank Church finally announced his presidential candidacy. As a late entry into the race, he had considerable ground to make up in the primaries. Although he subsequently won several stunning upsets over the heavily favored Jimmy Carter, Church correctly described himself as the campaign's "Don Quixote," tilting with ideas and ideals.[1]

Unlike conservative Democrats who sought to cut their party's ties to the "New Politics" of 1972, he continued to call for a dramatic rethinking of Cold War foreign policy. At the same time, he tried to recapture middle- and working-class Democrats who had fled their party because they opposed its recent emphasis on causes that seemingly ignored them. He focused mainly on honesty in government, America's role abroad, and jobs. Populistic overtones suffused his overarching message, a blend of new and old themes in which he urged Americans to take back their government, returning it to the rule of law and making it the servant of more than just "the ownership people of this country."[2]

On a personal level, Church's campaign demonstrated how far he had traveled since winning his first election twenty years earlier. He had come a long way from the Senate's backbench, and now had a national reputation. Columnist George Will aptly described him as "a rising star," and Church's presidential campaign provided additional evidence. Moreover, Church's ideas regarding government and foreign policy had evolved considerably over those two decades. He was still a liberal, but with a difference. Bit by bit, he had significantly detached his liberalism from its original Cold War moorings and its confidence in federal solutions. By now a committed anti-interventionist abroad, he also favored domestic policies that looked more to communities than to the federal bureaucracy for implementation. Yet, while his 1976 presidential candidacy attested to his political growth and emerging stature, it at the same time contained baggage from the past. Church's boy orator image still haunted him, as did reminders that he remained a political outsider.[3]

I

Church had thought seriously about seeking the presidency since at least 1974. On New Year's Day 1975 he again broached the subject. Sitting upstairs in a small pine-paneled study full of political memorabilia in his Boise home, he discussed his plans with Mike Wetherell. Church indicated that he wanted Wetherell to become his administrative assistant when Verda Barnes retired in the near future. But he wanted Wetherell to know he was thinking of running for president.[4]

Church's presidential plans were far from pipe dreams. Because the Watergate scandals had wounded the G. O. P. badly, the Democrats had reasonable expectations of regaining the White House in 1976. And because major Democrats such as Hubert Humphrey and Edward Kennedy declined to enter the primary elections, a less prominent individual had a real opportunity to capture the party's nomination. In September 1974 Jack Anderson reported that Church was already gaining support in Democratic backrooms, as party members looked for "a fresh face." A year later, columnist Joseph Kraft described Church as a potential "dark-horse compromise candidate." By then, as the senator watched a number of relatively anonymous Democrats declare their candidacies, he was seriously considering his own prospects. "If these people can run," he recalled thinking, "and the Kennedys and the Humphreys are not going to be involved, then why not. . . have a fling at" running himself.[5]

Throughout 1975 and into 1976, his chairmanship of the Select Committee on Intelligence greatly influenced his political calculations. He had difficulty knowing to what extent the assignment was either quicksand or a springboard for his presidential ambitions. It trapped him in several ways—delaying his announced candidacy, allowing his critics to say that he used the investigations for his own ambitions, and opening him to charges that he jeopardized national security. At the same time, the intelligence committee allowed him, a senator from a remote, lightly populated western state, to reach more visible political heights. Prior to the intelligence investigations, a Gallup poll indicated that only one of four Americans had heard of him; by the fall of 1975 pollsters discovered that two of three knew about him. Partly because Church had identified himself with some of the era's most important issues, one reporter went so far as to say that the senator's "name had become a household word."[6]

On July 30, 1975, as the intelligence committee waded into the swamp of political assassinations, and as the multinationals investigation probed the Lockheed scandals, eight Church staffers gathered at Verda Barnes's apartment to weigh the prospects of their boss's presidential candidacy. They knew that Church desperately needed to establish an election committee to lay the groundwork for a campaign. Yet he had pledged to keep out of the presidential race until he had concluded the intelligence investigation. His aides considered ways in which he might at least start positioning himself to enter the race. He could cultivate important contacts in, and perhaps even visit, key primary states. He could try to get on informal talk shows, with formats more relaxed and popular than press conferences. And he could perhaps set up a series of lunches with people, a kind of brain trust, whom he could "tap for information and ideas" about issues.[7]

During the last half of 1975, Church and his aides quietly followed some of the strategies that emerged from the July meeting. For example, Church's staff arranged for the Committee on Aging to hold hearings in Portland, an important city in the May 1976 Oregon primary. Upon his arrival at the Portland airport in late November, Church held a press conference. Following the two-and-a-half hours of hearings on issues concerning elderly citizens, he devoted the rest of his schedule to politics. He conducted two television interviews, dined with Portland's popular young mayor Neil Goldschmidt, met with the Multnomah County Central Labor Council, and called Oregon governor Robert Straub. The next morning Church had an early breakfast with a dozen potential supporters. Wetherell had come along on the trip, supposedly to help with the hearings. His real role, however, was to lay the foundation for an Oregon campaign. Indeed, Wetherell remained in Oregon an extra day to make political contacts which might be helpful in the primary.[8]

Such maneuvering was tricky, given Church's pledge not to campaign for the presidency until the intelligence inquiry ended. Shock waves thus traveled through Church's office when Rowland Evans, of the Evans and Robert Novak writing team, called about Tom Lantos.

Lantos was one of Church's "deep-cover organizers" in California. "Somehow Evans and Novak found out" about him, recalled Church's press secretary Bill Hall. The last thing Church wanted was for Evans and Novak, who disliked him anyhow, to raise additional questions about his proclaimed allegiance to the intelligence investigation. Although Church was in fact not yet investing much time in preparing for his candidacy, he was doing "more than we were letting on," as Hall conceded later. Hall remembered telling Evans that Lantos was "a Frank Church fanatic who was adamant that the senator run for President, which was true, and that I didn't know much more about it than that, which wasn't true." The response seemed to satisfy Evans. But several weeks later, Evans called again, wanting Lantos's phone number. Hall knew he would arouse the reporter's suspicions if he refused to give the information. While he talked with Evans, however, another Church staffer immediately phoned Lantos, telling him, in Hall's words, "to make himself scarce."[9]

Despite the close call with Evans, Church's staffers still thought the senator was not doing enough to prepare a successful campaign. When Jeff Shields reviewed his boss's fall schedule, he noted happily that it did not signal obvious presidential campaigning. But Shields then realized that it did not help Church's cause either. "Unfortunately," he informed the senator, "the present schedule does nothing to establish the personal contacts necessary for a fund raising and organizational base." Shields warned Church that other candidates were building strong organizations and that people who preferred the Idaho senator would "not wait forever" on him. In the strongest terms, Shields advised Church at least to sanction a fund-raising committee no later than November 1.[10]

November 1 came and went. On November 11 several Church supporters and aides met at a restaurant to discuss what was turning out to be his lack of a candidacy. The next night, eighteen of them gathered for dinner at Church's home. Out of these crucial meetings the rudiments of a campaign organization finally emerged. Carl Burke would chair it. Henry Kimelman would be in charge of finances. Kimelman, a wealthy resident of the Virgin Islands, had known Church since the early 1960s and had handled the finances of George McGovern's 1972 campaign.[11]

On December 9, Kimelman hosted a strategy meeting in his Georgetown home. Among the dozen present were Verda Barnes, Hall,

Shields, Wetherell, Jerry Levinson, and Frank Mankiewicz, a former Kennedy campaigner who had worked for McGovern in 1972. They discussed issues that might separate Church from the other candidates. They pondered which primaries the senator should enter. And they waited for Church to join them. Around 6 p. m. the senator arrived. Kimelman informed him that the fund-raising could start as soon as Church filed his campaign papers. Campaign headquarters would be in an old building near Capitol Hill which McGovern had used four years earlier. Kimelman reminded everyone that all of Church's travels had to include fund-raising efforts.[12]

On December 12, Verda Barnes and Church's close Senate colleague, Rhode Island's Claiborne Pell, filed papers establishing a Church "exploratory committee." Church could now legally organize and raise money for a campaign. Even before newspapers publicized the committee, he received encouraging news. The previous weekend, although he was not yet officially a candidate, he had placed third in an endorsement convention sponsored by the Massachusetts Reform Democratic Conference.[13]

But Church's campaign slowed to a virtual halt almost as soon as the exploratory committee formed. Over the Christmas holiday the senator announced that he would postpone announcing his candidacy until February 29 because the intelligence committee was taking longer than expected to finish its work. "The recommendations to be made by the committee are so important," he told reporters, "I have decided I cannot walk away from them." He had again placed his obligations to the committee above his presidential ambitions. The delay meant that he would not enter the Massachusetts primary, where he might have benefitted from strong liberal sentiments and his friendship with Ted Kennedy.[14]

Jeff Shields believed, however, that it was best for Church to avoid Massachusetts anyway. The senator's lapsed Catholicism and his opposition to gun control might hurt him, and a disappointing showing would be disastrous. Moreover, raising sufficient money in time for television ads would be difficult. Shields told Carl Burke that there were advantages to entering the campaign after the initial primaries. Other liberal candidates such as Birch Bayh, Fred Harris, and Morris Udall might by then have exhausted their resources or floundered. Shields also touched on a problem that was already surfacing: the lack of leadership in Church's camp. Burke was bogged down in a court trial in Idaho so no one in the East was making decisions. According to Shields, the campaign needed some central control immediately.[15]

Early 1976 was a frustrating time for Church's backers. They had a campaign staff, a campaign committee, and they were raising money. But they still had no candidate. Church himself recalled that the situation "looked pretty bleak." He believed that his chances of winning the Democratic nomination diminished the longer he waited to get into the race.[16]

But wait he did. Because each member of the intelligence panel needed time to review the committee's report, he would not be able to enter the presidential race until mid-March. He began to joke about his "late, late strategy."[17]

While Church continued to delay his announcement, Jimmy Carter established himself as the clear Democratic front runner. Months earlier the former Georgia governor had started his pursuit of the presidency as a virtual unknown. In early 1976, a Gallup poll showed that he was the choice of only 4 percent of Democrats. But he shrewdly capitalized on the anti-Washington mood. "I'm not a lawyer, I'm not a member of Congress, and I've never served in Washington," he said repeatedly. His outsider status supposedly proved his merit. Many Americans were losing faith in an expanding government which seemed unresponsive to their problems. They worried about inflation, budget deficits, the claims of special interest groups, and the competence and integrity of their leaders. "I'll never tell a lie," Carter promised voters. And he took advantage of fissures among the Democrats, who were divided between the McGovern wing, the hawkish Henry Jackson wing, which rejected the "New Politics," and Alabama governor George Wallace, who promised to rescue the party from the "ultra-liberal, exotic left-wing few" and return it to "average Americans."[18]

After beating a large field of challengers in the Iowa caucuses and the New Hampshire primary, Carter stumbled in Massachusetts, finishing fourth and well behind Jackson, the winner. But a week later he won the Florida primary and, shortly thereafter, emerged victorious in North Carolina, thereby effectively driving Wallace from the race. By then Carter had also forced out candidates such as Bayh and Harris. And by then, Mo Udall, the remaining liberal candidate, had personally contacted Church. Udall said he hoped "to head him off" and persuade the senator not to become a candidate. The prevailing assumption was that Church would compete for Udall's campaign dollars and votes.[19]

Church was already having second thoughts about entering the race. In February he summoned Kimelman, Burke, and the campaign treasurer William Landau to his Capitol hideaway office and confided to them that he might not run. According to Landau, "a big argument" ensued. Burke reminded Church not to forget all those citizens, many in Idaho, who had contributed to his cause because they expected him to be a candidate. Church finally concurred that he did not want to disappoint people who had counted on him. As Bethine said, "It's like outer space and the moon shot. There's a certain point at which there is no return."[20]

In February Jimmy Carter stopped by Church's office to discuss the senator's intentions. He wanted to know if Church planned to enter the primaries as part of the Washington establishment's stop Carter effort. Church replied that he had no desire to be a spoiler; he would be his own candidate.[21]

II

On the morning of March 18 in Boise, two buses pulled up in front of the old Clark mansion on Idaho Street. One bus contained Church's key staff members and supporters, the other some thirty members of the press. They would accompany Church on the winding forty-five mile drive to Idaho City, where he would declare his candidacy.

Church had decided not to make his announcement in Washington, D. C., despite the media exposure that he could receive there. He picked tiny Idaho City instead, although his advisers worried that the crowd and the press corps might be small. "I am a romantic," he said later. His grandparents had settled in that once booming mining community, which he described as the state's "true pioneer town." And his father had been born there. Church wanted to go back to his roots.[22]

In Idaho City residents ignored the storm clouds overhead and eagerly awaited the caravan. They had removed two feet of snow from the streets and decked out the boardwalks in red, white, and blue. Not since the gold rush days of the 1800s had the community seen such activity. By now fewer than two hundred people lived there, but another five thousand spectators were present, many in blue jeans, cowboy boots, and western hats. The crowd continued to wait while Church and a few of his closest friends and family gathered in the home of the town mayor, John Brogan. In the street the mood was festive, but inside the house people nervously checked their watches and glanced anxiously at each other. Suddenly, Church tossed his raincoat in the air and announced, "I've changed my mind. I can't go through with it." A hush fell over the room. Then Church erupted in laughter. Idaho governor Cecil Andrus placed his hand on Church's shoulder and said, "Listen, you do that and you'll need more than the secret service to protect you." The group then filed out the door and crossed the street to the historic, red-brick Boise County courthouse. Cheers and waving placards greeted the entourage.[23]

Just after 10 a. m., Church stepped up to the bank of microphones on the podium. His dark hair contained traces of gray, but his face still preserved his boyish good looks of twenty years earlier. As he began to speak, the sun broke through the clouds. Over the next half hour, applause and shouts of encouragement continually interrupted him. At the end of his speech, he responded to people who might think he was entering the race far too late. "I reply," he said, "that it's never too late—nor are the odds ever too great—to try. In that spirit the West was won, and in that spirit I now declare my candidacy for President of the United States."[24]

As Secret Service agents immediately began to protect him, he knew that his life would change a great deal during at least the immediate future. He would be under public scrutiny as never before. Reporters had already speculated on whether the removal years earlier of one of his testicles had left him impotent. Bethine responded that his sex life was normal in every way, with one exception which the nation's capital would have difficulty understanding: "He's monogamous." When Bill Hall apologized to Church for continually pestering him about other information for the press, Church replied, "No problem. I'm just grateful you've finally got your mind off my sex life." The senator then laughed uproariously. At one point on the campaign trail he came out of the restroom and noted the Secret Service agents guarding the door. "You know," he sighed, "if I get elected, I'll never go to the bathroom alone again."[25]

III

"Enter Frank Cathedral," *Newsweek* reported after Church declared his candidacy. The magazine wondered if his "Scout's-honor style and a tardy start" would hurt his cause. The *New York Times* guessed that, if nothing else, "in terms of the nation's self-education on the issues, the Church candidacy can only be a positive event."[26]

As Church made clear in his Idaho City announcement, and in numerous speeches and interviews over the next twelve weeks, his candidacy rested on three main themes: restoring integrity to government, removing foreign policy from the "compulsive interventionists," and rejuvenating the economy. His issues-oriented campaign rejected simple political labels. Seeking to build a broad-based coalition, he described himself as a conservative regarding "the preservation of constitutional government and individual liberties," an old-style progressive in his anti-trust sentiments, a Franklin D. Roosevelt liberal concerning government's obligation as an employer of last resort, and a common-sense politician who would keep the U. S. out of "senseless foreign wars." He called for a more active federal government that was also less bureaucratic and more responsive to local conditions. And he portrayed himself as both a political insider and an outsider. Although his twenty years in the Senate had educated him well about the intricacies of the federal government, he had never belonged to "the Establishment" nor was he "a go-along senator." Indeed, he emphasized, "I've been a critic of much of the policy in Washington."[27]

Governmental lawlessness received the brunt of his criticism. He understood why the polls showed an overwhelming public distrust of politicians and why, in the nation's bicentennial year, there was "no spirit of jubilation in the land." Public officials from the former president on down had engaged in illegal, immoral conduct that undermined government's legitimacy. Federal agencies had unlawfully opened people's mail, used tax investigations for political harassment, tried "to destroy a great American like Martin Luther King," investigated thousands of Americans who were simply exercising their First Amendment freedoms, bullied citizens, and abused power in many other ways. "Only when the government begins treating people with respect again will it regain the respect of the people again," Church predicted. For that reason he placed the restoration of obedience to the law at the top of the nation's agenda. He rebuked President Ford, not for being personally dishonest but for pardoning Richard Nixon and for downplaying the crimes of the CIA and other agencies. In recent years the federal government had set a horrid example that helped to spread cynicism, immorality, and disrespect for law across American society. Church told about a Pennsylvania farmer, a good Republican, who had asked him if the U. S. government had indeed arranged with the Mafia to kill a foreign leader. When the senator conceded that the story was true, the farmer replied sadly, "How, Senator, are we ever going to teach our children to grow up honest, if their government is in cahoots with the Mafia?"[28]

According to Church, the government's disrespect for law and morality had also produced a failed foreign policy. Covert actions, ranging from abduction to conspiracy to murder, had seriously impaired America's moral leadership. In place of the nation's once formidable moral force, policy makers had increasingly substituted physical coercion and interventionism. Church advocated a "discriminating foreign policy" that did not plunge compulsively into third world countries in an effort to dictate their futures. Striking at a long-standing Cold War premise, he argued that no nation could long establish satellite countries around the world. African and Asian countries wanted to escape foreign domination, not submit to it. Neither the U. S. nor the Soviets could maintain "the *status quo* in the regions where there is no *status*, and there is no *quo*." Church lashed out at Ronald Reagan, who was seeking the Republican presidential nomination. The former California governor had claimed that ongoing negotiations to end U. S. control of the Panama Canal would sacrifice America's vital interests in Latin America. Church believed that Reagan's "reprehensible" charges ignored complex realities and played politics with an issue that could lead to conflict in Central America. "I am tired of old men in politics who are so ready, and so willing, to send the young men to war," he said repeatedly.[29]

Church used discussions of foreign policy to probe another main theme: salvaging the U. S. economy. "Foreign policy isn't foreign at all," he liked to say. The main cause of America's economic ills, he argued time and again, was a foreign policy that encouraged big businesses to move jobs and investments abroad. Because of government tax and insurance programs, an estimated 150,000 jobs per year left the United States. Church's quarrel was not with corporations who invested in other countries, but with public policies that elevated foreign over domestic investments. Existing policy taxed profits earned abroad at a lower rate than profits earned within the U. S. If he were president, Church would try to change that policy as well as to repeal the tax-subsidized government insurance program (OPIC) that protected business investments in other countries. Church's message to the corporations would be simple: "You will get no advantages for going abroad." It was time, Church contended, for the big corporations to get "a good dose of free enterprise. I'm tired of socialism for the rich and free enterprise for the poor." He scoffed at arguments that corporate profits abroad returned to the United States: "the profits don't come home to the American working people who lose their jobs. They come home to the people with stock, the ownership people of this country."[30]

In Church's opinion, it was time for a president who would "face up to these companies" and recognize that the Constitution said nothing "about the obligation of the federal government to maximize the profits of General Motors abroad." He urged tougher anti-trust actions against the big oil companies and other monopolies. "I believe in competition," he emphasized. As president, he would "take on this OPEC cartel instead of cooperating with it." He would also institute a crash program to find alternative energy sources.[31]

Convinced that people were "hungry to hear issues talked about," Church stated his views on a host of controversial subjects. To protect economically strapped farmers, he recommended a guaranteed price on agricultural goods to cover the costs of production. He supported the Humphrey-Hawkins jobs bill, a "liberal touchstone," as journalist Elizabeth Drew described it. He opposed right-to-work laws. He approved of clearcutting in national forests if regulations existed to prevent abuses. He advocated an "urban conservation corps" to help provide employment, especially for young African Americans. He wanted savings and loan institutions to set aside part of their earnings for investments in devastated urban areas. He opposed building the B-1 bomber, which was expensive, unnecessary, and would put the U. S. in the position of creating "the twentieth-century version of the Spanish Armada." He backed a national health insurance plan, starting immediately with universal catastrophic insurance and with a model comprehensive program for the elderly. He endorsed the Equal Rights Amendment along with Title IX, which was aimed at halting gender discrimination in extracurricular school activities. He objected vigorously to a proposed national secrets act ("the most dangerous piece of legislation" before the Senate), which he said would pull an even heavier national security curtain over illegal activities. He favored a national, federally funded railroad and transportation system. He was against legalizing marijuana but would reduce penalties for its use and possession.[32]

The *Washington Post*'s Paul Edwards noted "the unrelenting specificity" of Church's responses to questions as well as his efforts to mix conservative and liberal thinking. The senator seemed determined, in

Edwards's words, "to turn the Democratic primaries into an ideas forum." Columnist Mary McGrory believed that he was approaching the country as if it were a "a larger Idaho, where an essentially conservative electorate has to be coaxed into voting for a liberal candidate." Eight years earlier, when he had won his third Senate term, that strategy had worked so well that motorists in Idaho had stuck both "Wallace" for president and "Church" for senator stickers on their automobiles.[33]

In 1976, Church attempted again to reach across the political spectrum. He recognized that many people resented big government and feared the social upheavals of recent years. According to one analysis, he was "a law and order liberal." Church himself spurned any "warmed-over New Deal." He carefully distinguished between his views and those of liberals who seemed to think that the federal government could solve all problems. On the campaign trail he criticized "runaway bureaucracy" and called for "better, not bigger, government" with decentralized federal programs. He wanted to "move the decision making power down to the lowest level of government, closest to the people" who knew the most about local needs and circumstances. Welfare and other programs, he believed, were too concentrated in Washington, D.C. Regulations that made sense in one context were foolish in another. Church disliked, for example, the effort to apply standards from the Organization of Safety and Health Administration (OSHA) to mom and pop stores or to small, family farms. The growth of the bureaucracy, he said, resembled that of an orchestra which had spilled beyond the pit to fill the entire theater—an orchestra far too large for anyone to conduct. Church thought that a decentralizing process would allow for more discriminating policies and for a reduction of the size of the federal government by at least 5 percent per year over a four-year period.[34]

Contrary to at least one headline, however, Church in no sense advised Democrats to abandon the New Deal heritage. For one thing, he emphasized that he did not advocate a reduction in the federal funding of social programs. "Unlike Mr. Reagan and other self-styled conservatives," he told one reporter, "I think it would be utterly ridiculous to think about meeting the housing, transportation and educational needs without federal money." He specifically invoked the New Deal when he talked about the federal government as "the employer of last resort in times of high unemployment" and as a stimulator of the economy. He, like Franklin Roosevelt, preferred that the government provide work—rather than welfare—for the able-bodied unemployed. Although he supported the so-called "sunset bill," which would stop federal programs after five years unless Congress renewed them, he did so on grounds that government agencies needed periodically "to justify their existence," not because he philosophically opposed government action. His objections were to needless red tape and to skewed policies that funded wealthy foreign allies and military dictators rather than Americans. "If this country can spend $100 million for a bomber plane or $2 billion for a submarine," he told an enthusiastic Los Angeles audience, "it can afford a decent and dignified retirement for its senior citizens." Church wanted the government to show more concern for Americans than for propping up other nations. Indeed, he argued, the much-cited domino theory applied less to the world at large than "to our own falling cities right here at home."[35]

Church regretted the liberal tendency to expand administrative machinery and to divide into dozens of factions. As one reporter sensed, deep down he had "a genuine contempt for the arrogance of the Eastern establishment and many of its causes." The "causists," or practitioners of "cocktail-party liberalism," as Church called them, were purists who allowed for no flexibility. "They support 1,000 causes, and if you are not 100 percent in their particular cause, you are not acceptable."[36]

As an example, he mentioned the abortion issue. He emphasized that, as president, he would enforce the Supreme Court's *Roe vs. Wade* decision. But he had trouble understanding why some who supported the right to choose an abortion would force Catholic hospitals to perform that procedure. In 1973, following the Supreme Court's ruling, he had successfully sponsored a "conscience clause" protecting hospitals, doctors, and nurses from performing abortions in violation of their religious beliefs. "I would never be the party to forcing others to abort their beliefs in order to help others to abort their babies," he explained during his presidential campaign. He found hypocritical the tendency of pro-choice advocates to dismiss the religious views of their opponents and then "to lecture others on liberalism."[37]

In contrast to liberals who tried "to keep step with one hundred different drummers," Church chose as his dominant message in 1976 the need for Americans to regain control of their government. It was time, he said, "to put the American people first for a change." And it was time to return to first principles, those that comprised the country's revolutionary heritage. Officials, including the president, needed to learn that they were servants of the people and under the law.[38]

When Church talked about "rekindling the spirit of 1776," he also had in mind restoring the nation's sense of community. He was certain that the outbreak of lawlessness, from the White House to corporate boardrooms, the CIA, and the streets, had devastated the country's civic values. "That sense of community—of the duty of each citizen to his fellow citizens—seems to be evaporating," Church observed. "A social cannibalism is emerging in its place. We are beginning to feed on each other." It was time for Americans to think of the common good, of the social bonds that connected them. Speaking, for example, of the need to respond to the problems of the elderly, he quoted from a poem: "Hear, O our Children! We are not a special interest group./ We are your parents and grandparents. We are your roots." Church urged Americans to recall that their power once rested on their ability to represent a "great, moral force." And he appealed not to their fears but to their faith in what had made America great. "I believe," he told one audience, "in the power of principle and the power of ideas." Although he described his presidential candidacy as "late, late," he hoped that his message was not.[39]

IV

To explain his "late, late strategy," Church drew upon his experience as a guest on NBC's "Tomorrow Show," which followed Johnny Carson's popular "Tonight Show." He had discovered that six million people stayed up to watch the "Tomorrow Show." After the program, he joked with Bethine that he would win over America's insomniacs and then expand his campaign. In political terms, the "insomniacs" were the late May and June primaries in Nebraska, Oregon, Rhode Island, Ohio, and California. "If I could win those against the conventional wisdom," Church told the Washington Press Club, "it would astonish the country and I will come into the convention not with a lot of votes but with a lot of momentum." That momentum, and the accompanying media attention, would place him in a splendid strategic position if no one had already locked up the nomination. If he subsequently received the nomination, people would praise his foresight and ingenuity. But, he laughed, if his scenario proved incorrect he would simply reply, "Well, as everybody told me, it was too late."[40]

The problem with Church's late strategy, however, was that he was unable to patent it. On March 12, California's recently elected governor entered the race. When the thirty-eight-year-old Jerry Brown made his surprise announcement during an interview with four reporters, Carl Burke happened to be in San Francisco visiting with Leo McCarthy, the speaker of the California Assembly. McCarthy had already promised to direct Church's California campaign, unless Brown decided to run. But McCarthy was confident that Brown would not be a candidate. Indeed, McCarthy had just reassured Burke on this point when one of the legislator's aides rushed in with news that Brown was in the race. McCarthy was "flabbergasted," Burke recalled. The legislator need not have felt badly that Brown had failed to notify him; the youthful governor had not even told his father, former California governor Pat Brown. "There wasn't room for two late candidates, and Brown pre-empted California," Church said later. "My plan was based on the assumption that he wouldn't run."[41]

Although Brown's sudden entry surprised him, Church was not yet willing to concede California. Within hours after he announced his own candidacy, he headed for a fund-raising reception in Hollywood. Several top entertainers, including Ed Asner, Dennis Weaver, Milton Berle, Steve Lawrence, and Edie Gorme, were present. The next day Church paid a courtesy call on Jerry Brown in Sacramento. The two men clearly did not like each other, and their banter had an edge to it. Church suggested that Brown was doing such a good job as governor that Californians might want him to remain in his job. Shifting uncomfortably, Brown responded that California voters had a voice in that regard. Church jabbed back, noting that "the Presidency is more than a glorified governorship." When Brown countered that his responsibilities in California in many ways resembled those of the presidency, Church smilingly replied, "I think we have already started the debate."[42]

The immediate fate of Church's presidential hopes rested not in California, however, but elsewhere—with finances, Jimmy Carter's growing momentum, the press, and the Nebraska primary. Church's campaign never had much money. At one point a Secret Service agent peered out the window of Church's small chartered plane, which was parked alongside Carter's Boeing 727, and said, "Senator, there is one thing that is certainly clear: you are the poor man's candidate."[43]

At an April 8 meeting in Church's Capitol office, campaign treasurer William Landau reported difficulties in raising funds. The campaign had a mere $200,000 in the bank and contributions were averaging only $34. Kimelman, Wetherell, and Peter Curtin joined Landau in urging

Church to seek endorsements from other senators. "I can't plead with my colleagues," Church protested. "When the water's at the second deck, it's every man for himself. Endorsements don't mean a thing in the countryside." As the meeting continued, frustrations surfaced. Church, eating a hamburger and drinking a Coke, became testier. At one point, when someone suggested that he needed to "reassert" himself again and again in the campaign, Church snapped irritably that the "problem with this campaign is not the candidate."[44]

As Church looked anxiously to the May 11 Nebraska primary, Carter won another election, barely edging Mo Udall in Wisconsin. Udall had initially believed that he might beat Carter in Nebraska. But the lanky Arizonan now concluded that he would only split votes with Church and lose another primary. Udall thus decided to stay out of Nebraska, giving Church a chance to upset Carter. Kimelman helped to work out the deal, explaining later that "it wasn't a stop Carter [effort] as much as it was help Udall or help Church."[45]

The Idaho senator still believed that he needed a "political miracle" to win. Indeed, in March when his son Forrest arrived in Nebraska to help set up the campaign, a local poll in the Omaha *World* showed Church in seventh place, with only 1 percent. Carter, who had set up a campaign organization in the state a year earlier, held the lead. Moreover, for some reason, the Republican Secretary of State had added the names of non-candidates Humphrey and Kennedy to the ballot. Church thus talked only of making a "good showing." Some of his staffers were so skeptical about his chances that they talked with Carl Burke about Church's withdrawing from Nebraska. "We had a hell of a battle," Burke recalled. "We never told Frank about that."[46]

A continuing problem for Church was the national media, which either ignored him or completely discounted his candidacy. A *Newsday* reporter dismissed him as "Chuckles Church," a man "with a smile in his heart and a cascade of fatuous cliches on his lips," who had no more chance of winning the Democratic nomination than "a knock-kneed girl at the Miss America contest." Steve Ahrens, of the *Idaho Statesman*, resented the attitude of the national press representatives who with several exceptions viewed their assignment to cover Church as "strictly second rate."[47]

Despite the obstacles, Church forged on in Nebraska. He summoned almost all of his eastern campaign headquarters staff to Nebraska, but was so crimped for funds that each worker received a paltry $10 per day allotment for board and room. Several aides slept on the floor in a cheap one-room apartment for several nights before discovering that prostitutes occupied the noisy apartments downstairs.[48]

Staging what one reporter called a "bread-basket blitz," Church took to the political stump. As always, Bethine campaigned with him. Indeed, over the next few weeks, he proudly introduced her to audiences, sometimes referring to her as his "secret weapon." One reporter who observed the Churches in Nebraska was amazed at the "almost uncanny communication" between them. Each seemed intuitively to know what the other was thinking and needed.[49]

The Churches and three busloads of volunteers moved slowly across Nebraska, following the Platte River. "Church is in search of 'folks' as he put it," *Time* quipped, noting that in one hour he had encountered only "a herd of antelope, some buffalo, and two horsemen who were moving too fast to be approached." Not until Church "reached the 'cowboy capital' of Oglalla (pop. 4,976)," according to *Time*'s account, did he find a hand to shake. Only a few reporters, such as CBS's Jed Duvall, sensed that the Idaho candidate was finding a receptive audience in Nebraska's tiny communities.[50]

After Henry Jackson lost the April 27 Pennsylvania primary to Carter and withdrew from the race, Church hoped to pick up some of Jackson's union supporters. With sleeves rolled up, he spoke to several hundred members of the building trades electrician's local, one of the most active locals in Omaha. The crowd, initially wary and unresponsive, began to warm up as Church responded candidly to their questions and discussed democracy and fairness. One man, an unemployed electrician, asked him how he would respond to the complaint that he lacked the guts to be president. Church stared straight at the worker and recounted his Senate record. He had stood up to the president of his own party during the Vietnam war. He had challenged the most powerful multinational corporations in the world. He had helped to expose the CIA's and FBI's flagrant abuses of authority. He had championed many unpopular causes. "If that's not enough guts for you," Church declared, "go vote for somebody else." Church's fiery words brought the crowd to its feet with a thundering ovation. The unemployed electrician moved that the local endorse Church for president. His motion carried with a loud voice vote.[51]

Church's confidence grew, even though polls in Nebraska showed him with only half the support that Carter enjoyed and trailing even

Hubert Humphrey. Looking out the bus window one day, the senator saw a jackrabbit dart into the road and run alongside the vehicle. As the bus pulled away from the hare, he laughed, "The tortoise is doing it again." By then, the turtle had become the symbol of his campaign, and he had even named his chartered airplane, "The Tortoise." He was starting genuinely to believe that he could upset Carter in Nebraska.[52]

In the primary's closing days, Church heard rumors that the front-runner might make a sudden appearance. Carter had not campaigned personally in Nebraska, focusing instead on more populous states such as Pennsylvania. He had even declined to address the annual Jefferson-Jackson dinner of Nebraska Democrats. Church agreed to be the featured speaker, but pondered what to do if the Georgia candidate showed up unexpectedly. A strategy meeting with several staffers convinced Church that humor would be his best weapon. By the time he took the podium in Omaha, he had a surprise ready for Carter.[53]

Church dazzled the eighteen hundred guests with one of the best talks that journalist Steve Ahrens had ever heard. Ahrens got goose bumps just watching him play the audience "like a symphony," holding his listeners spellbound. As Church finished his speech, a small commotion occurred at the back of the room. Carter had just arrived, following a last-minute flight from the Midwest. With his picture on the most recent covers of *Time* and *Newsweek*, he seemed primed for victory in Nebraska's upcoming primary. After Church received a lengthy standing ovation, Lieutenant Governor Gerald Whelan indicated with a trace of irritation that Carter was present and wished to say a few words. Surprised at the blatant attempt to steal the evening from Church, the audience applauded weakly. At the podium, Carter stirred little enthusiasm. His quiet southern drawl proved no match for Church's smooth, rich tones. After speaking for several minutes, Carter stepped back. "The crowd was a Church crowd by then," recalled Ahrens. The senator capitalized on the moment by unveiling his surprise. He handed Carter some Idaho "peanuts"–a bucket of potatoes.[54]

Carl Burke believed the incident marked a political shift toward Church. Two days later, Lieutenant Governor Whelan, still angry over Carter's effort to upstage Church, endorsed the Idaho senator. "I've dealt with a lot of rascals in the legislature," Whelan told reporters, but he ranked Carter as "the worst."[55]

On May 11, despite the polls and the media predictions, Church squeaked by Carter 39 to 38 percent, and won fifteen of Nebraska's delegates. What *Newsweek* described as "very nearly a mom-and-pop show" had produced a stunning upset. One analysis suggested that Church had captured "virtually all" of the liberal support that had previously favored Udall, Humphrey, and Kennedy. Elated with his victory, Church claimed that it "launches my campaign and gives it legitimacy."[56]

Carter shrugged off the Nebraska results by saying, "I can't win them all." To the Idaho senator's despair, CBS anchorman Walter Cronkite subscribed to Carter's interpretation and downplayed Church's accomplishment. On May 12, Cronkite asked Church if his victory did not really attest to the fact that he had spent more days and money in Nebraska than had Carter. Years later, the query still rankled Church, who could not imagine "a more loaded question." Church replied that Carter had appeared on the *Time* and *Newsweek* covers on the eve of the election, thereby gaining publicity worth millions of dollars. Moreover, Carter had been on the network news every night for weeks. Church wished that Cronkite would take those elements of the campaign into account.[57]

In fact, as several journalists pointed out, Carter now seemed more vulnerable. His severe loss a few days later to Brown in Maryland, and his razor-thin victories over Udall in Michigan and Connecticut suggested that he was stumbling. Suddenly the May 25 Oregon primary had real significance. "O follows N—it's on to Oregon," Church told his Nebraska supporters as he looked westward.[58]

V

Although Church's Nebraska "miracle" had gotten "a little band wagon in gear," as Bill Hall wrote later, the Oregon primary road was terribly steep. Two weeks before the primary, a local poll showed Carter leading Church by 32 to 8 percent. Even non-candidates Humphrey and Kennedy were ahead of Church. Church's position improved after his Nebraska victory, but he was still ten points behind Carter and five behind write-in candidate Brown. Carter, moreover, was determined to bounce back from his two recent losses. His son Jack later told Bill Hall, "We underestimated Frank Church in Nebraska, and it gave us fits the rest of the way." Carter's people were not about to overlook Church this time. Church was thus not exaggerating when he told Mike Wetherell, "We've got a lot of work to do."[59]

Again, Church received help from Mo Udall. Despite the advice of his campaign manager, John Gabusi, Udall stayed out of Oregon, giving Church a better chance against Carter. Church's candidacy had already infuriated Udall's people. After they had spent two years organizing a campaign, the Idaho senator had suddenly made his appearance. From Gabusi's perspective, Church had no chance to win the Democratic nomination and was engaged in nothing but a "dilettantish" ego trip, trying to increase his national reputation and angling for the vice presidency. The Udall camp justifiably resented Church's bid as surely as Church and his people did Brown's; in both cases, last-minute spoilers were ruining the best-laid plans. One of Gabusi's most "agonizing" assignments was having to call Udall's Oregon people, after they had been organizing for months, and tell them that their candidate would not campaign in the state after all. "It was not a pleasant time," Gabusi recalled bitterly.[60]

Carter, equally miffed, charged that his two opponents had struck a "secret deal" to divide up the primary states in order to beat him. Church flatly denied the accusation, even though his and Udall's staffs had in fact been consulting—or "conspiring," as Udall's brother later said—with each other. "I've had no discussions with Udall," Church said, insisting that he was following his initial strategy. The senator's statement was true, but misleading. Agreements with Udall aside, Church could not help but tweak Carter for complaining: "No one ever promised him a rose garden."[61]

In a small propeller-driven plane, Church took his campaign to Oregon's hinterlands. Mixing stump speeches with question-and-answer sessions, he said that he was placing "substance over style." Seemingly intent on proving columnist Elizabeth Drew's point that he was "not considered one of the more colorful campaigners around," he insisted on giving lengthy, individualized answers not tailored to fit different audiences. Observers found his style both stiffly cerebral and reminiscent of "a tough-minded preacher." The *Washington Post*'s David Broder, surprised at how "cool, controlled and highly effective" the senator was, found that Church's performance contrasted markedly with his reputation as "a plump, sometimes pompous, pillowfighter of a politician."[62]

Church's campaign was gathering momentum. Bill Hall sensed that "there was something in the air," something intangible that augured well despite polls that showed Carter still in the lead. Several hundred Church volunteers labored across the state. Larry LaRocco, who was coordinating the Oregon campaign, had established a huge phone bank that he believed was contacting "damn near everybody" in the state. Meanwhile, the candidate himself worked hard. In Portland he appeared one day at 6:30 a. m. with his sleeves rolled up to speak to a local union; he finished the day's campaigning, looking very tired, on a 10:30 p. m. radio call-in show. On other occasions, he mixed in what Elizabeth Drew called "trite stunts" for the media, wobbling along on a borrowed bicycle for a few blocks in an environmental parade, for example. And on the Thursday before the election, he posed at the Portland zoo with a giant tortoise. He even wore his official campaign necktie with pictures of turtles all over it. "We're going to start a stampede of tortoises throughout the land," he laughingly told the press.[63]

"Go to Church on Tuesday," urged the senator's campaign slogan—and many voters did, boosting him to an impressive 35 to 25 percent victory over Carter. A *New York Times*/CBS poll determined that he had drawn particularly well from the ranks of the elderly, blue-collar workers, and union members. His effort to build a cross-party coalition also paid dividends: former Humphrey, McGovern, and Wallace supporters backed him. Moreover on the same day, across the border, Idahoans had predictably awarded him with a whopping win over Carter. Church had now beaten Carter in three consecutive primaries.[64]

But Church's successes were still politically suspect. For one thing, Carter continued to pick up delegates, even in Oregon. "The calculus of the convention" was beginning to take hold, as Church later observed. "We were losing even as we were winning." Church desperately needed to prove that he had more than regional appeal.[65]

Despite the senator's recent triumphs, his late, late candidacy was running out of time. Church had counted on winning California, but Brown now blocked the way. The governor was turning into a formidable competitor. In Oregon, he had polled an amazing 23 percent of the vote, all write-ins. His simple message, "Don't write me off, write me in," had appealed especially to voters under thirty and to people with some college education and independent political leanings. In his delegate-rich home state, Brown looked unbeatable. "I mean, good Lord," Church said as he ticked off the obstacles that faced him in a state the size of Spain. With limited funds and time he faced "a popular governor who is running as a favorite son." He thus looked for help elsewhere, hoping that he had found it in the Rhode Island and Ohio primaries.[66]

VI

Church was optimistic about his chances in Rhode Island, small, compact, and easy to traverse. He had the active support of Senator Claiborne Pell and Representative Edward Beard. And he planned to spend the crucial last days before the June 1 primary campaigning in the state. Montana would hold its primary on the same date, but he assumed that his earlier stops there, and the state's proximity to Idaho, made it protected ground.[67]

In Rhode Island, however, virtually nothing worked as Church had planned. Carter, bent on invigorating his candidacy, campaigned hard. And Jerry Brown, whose name was not on the ballot, urged residents to pull the uncommitted lever to vote for him. Even voters who were sincerely in the uncommitted column would thus appear to be for Brown. Church's own campaign faltered badly. Its dwindling funds did not allow for extensive advertising. And Church fell ill with a sore throat and began to lose his voice. He began to sense that he would lose. At one point, he heard a television announcer say that he was "relatively unknown in Rhode Island" and running an "underdog campaign." The senator had assumed that he was in a stronger position than the description suggested. "I suddenly began to get the perspective on where I stood," he said later.[68]

On June 1, Church easily carried Montana but finished third in Rhode Island. Brown's "uncommitted" slate won 31 percent of the vote, Carter received 29 percent, and Church 27 percent. Only a dismal 10 percent of the state's voters turned out on a rainy day following the long Memorial Day weekend. Looking back, Church was certain that he could have won in Rhode Island. But he had not. Ohio—and controversy—loomed ahead.[69]

The controversy involved Mo Udall's camp, which insisted that Church had broken a promise to stay out of Ohio. Udall had finished second in a number of primaries and believed he might finally win in the Buckeye state, where he had been building a campaign organization for months. If Carter lost the June 8 primaries in Ohio and California, there might still be an open Democratic convention. For weeks, Udall's brother Stewart and Henry Kimelman had been informally dividing up the primary states to avoid Udall-Church confrontations. Church had stayed out of Michigan and South Dakota; Udall had avoided Nebraska and Oregon. According to Stewart Udall, the two political camps had "tacit understandings," rather than outright agreements on these primaries. The Udall brothers had no doubt what the understanding was regarding Ohio: Church would stay away.[70]

When Church opted to enter the Ohio primary, the Udalls and their staff believed that he had violated a trust. "Our people were extremely bitter," Morris Udall recalled. "I didn't like it either," he said of Church's decision. "I didn't understand what he was doing." But Church vehemently denied rumors that he had ever agreed to stay out of Ohio. "I have made no deals," he told the press. "If he [Udall] asks me to stay out I will tell him I will make my decision on my own assessments."[71]

Henry Kimelman pleaded with Church over the phone to stay out of Ohio. Mike Wetherell remembered taking the call in Church's hotel room. According to Wetherell, Kimelman asked Church not to go into Ohio because of the understanding with Udall. Wetherell wondered who had made such a deal. Kimelman replied that he had. Wetherell put his hand over the telephone and asked Church if there was such an arrangement. Church denied it and took the telephone to talk with Kimelman. "I have no intention of not campaigning in Ohio," Wetherell recalled Church saying. After he hung up the phone, Church indicated that his candidacy would be over if he did not enter Ohio.[72]

Despite Church's denials of knowledge about any understanding with Udall, Kimelman later was adamant: "Sure he knew about all the agreements. . . . I didn't make any agreements on my own."[73]

Any understandings with Udall aside, top members of Church's organization, including Kimelman, Landau, and Burke, believed that the senator should concentrate on California rather than Ohio. Burke noted that Church had received many commitments there and should not alienate his supporters. Moreover, Burke's personal discussions with Ohio political leaders had been anything but encouraging. One adviser, Peter Curtin, believed that the best strategy was to focus on New Jersey, the third of the June 8 primary states. But New Jersey depended so heavily on the expensive media markets of New York City that the Church campaign could not afford it. According to Burke, "a whale of a battle" developed in Church's camp over whether he should concentrate on Ohio, which Church favored, or California. Bill Hall recollected that "one faction would win one week and the other the next." Meanwhile, valuable time disappeared. "We were split on the issue," Burke observed, "and so we delayed the decision until it was too late."[74]

The indecision and confusion over the Ohio primary was symptomatic of deeper problems in Church's campaign. While the candidate staged some impressive battles, his organization was in turmoil. "Frank Church's national campaign headquarters was open warfare from morning 'til night," recalled Bill Hall. "Day after corrosive day, we vilified each other with sincere and heartfelt obscenities. We maneuvered and backstabbed and outflanked and threatened to tell Frank Church on each other—or, when truly provoked, threatened to tell Bethine Church." The problem was not "mere factionalism; this was a four-month firestorm of emotion."[75]

Someone identified the main competing factions as the "Idahoans" and the "Jews," because Church's volunteers tended to be either from Idaho or Jewish supporters like Kimelman and Landau. Bill Hall hated the labels because they were so destructive and he worried that the media would learn about them. The fact that the labels were also inaccurate was abundantly clear one day when Mort Schwartz, a Jewish volunteer from Miami, burst into Hall's office shouting, "Do you know what those Jews have done now?" Hall reminded him that the "Jew" he was complaining about was in fact "a Gentile from Blackfoot, Idaho." In turn, Hall heard the so-called "Jewish" faction lumping Schwartz among "those damned Idahoans" who should return to their own state.[76]

The factions more accurately broke down into the partisans of Burke and Kimelman. Burke had known the senator considerably longer and had managed his earlier campaigns. Kimelman had met Church in the early Sixties when the senator had been on a fact-finding mission to the Virgin Islands, where Kimelman was John Kennedy's Commissioner of Commerce. They had struck up a close friendship. Church had introduced George McGovern to Kimelman, who subsequently presided over McGovern's 1972 campaign finances.

Except for their devotion to Church, Kimelman and Burke were as different as Idaho and the Virgin Islands. The handsome Kimelman was deeply tanned from the Caribbean sun. One observer laughingly described his modish clothes as "late-Hippie" in style. Wearing sandals and shorts, and with his shirt unbuttoned halfway to his belt, exposing a gold necklace or two, he sometimes dispensed advice to the staff while sitting, "cross-legged, guru-style, on the floor." Burke, on the other hand, looked like the reserved Boise lawyer that he was. Balding and easy-going, he wore neatly tailored business suits. The contrasting appearances of the two men attested to their sharply different temperaments. Burke was mild-mannered; Kimelman could be equally engaging but also eccentric and difficult. As the pressure to fund Church's campaign intensified, Kimelman sometimes treated the people around him rudely and insensitively, as if they were, in Hall's words, "witless, obedient flunkies."[77]

Years later, Kimelman attributed his disagreements with Burke to their different personalities. Kimelman described himself as a "fast-moving guy," whereas Burke was more of a "country boy-type lawyer." Burke remembered that the divisions were deep and real and went to the heart of who was running the Church campaign. "One of us had to win," he said, noting that he had personally found Kimelman "particularly detrimental." But Burke also resented the fact that a few of the eastern campaign workers treated the Idahoans as "bumpkins." Church, aware of these conflicts, talked about them several times with Kimelman and Burke. In retrospect, the senator believed that Kimelman sometimes erroneously saw himself, not Burke, as running the campaign.[78]

While the national headquarters resembled a "two-headed monster," in Hall's words, the candidate and his field staff comprised another faction, the "road show," with Frank and Bethine in charge. Indeed, looking back, Church believed that he and Bethine commanded the campaign, "subject to vetoes of various kinds. . . . I found that running my own campaign was one of the hardest things I had to do because I had to keep bucking people in Washington who thought they knew better."[79]

Nowhere was that conflict more evident than over the decision to enter the Ohio primary. Years later, Church said that he really had no choice. "I made my decision to go into Ohio because there was no place else to go." He still thought there was a chance to stop Carter from controlling the first ballot at the convention.[80]

Church's Ohio effort sputtered from the beginning, however. Curiously, the day after the Rhode Island primary, he flew to California for a quick campaign swing. The trip not only wasted time, but further drained his health. After a brief press conference in Los Angeles, he was so sick that he stayed in bed at the hotel, except for making a twenty-minute appearance at a fund-raising dinner in his behalf. He canceled his next day's visit to northern California in order to nurse a 102-degree temperature and strep throat. On Friday, when he returned to Ohio, he still looked tired and ill.[81]

Because of a missed plane connection in Chicago, he was an hour late for a scheduled appearance with Carter in Toledo's heavily

Democratic Polish-American fourth ward. Carter arrived early enough to shake hands with virtually all of the two thousand people in the wooden bleachers at the local high school's football field. His standard speech received a warm reception. By the time Carter left, Church had still not arrived. Many reporters and about half of the audience gave up on the senator appearing. Although he was still sick, Church summoned up the energy that had marked his appearances in Nebraska and Oregon. His ringing speech included a scathing attack on Gerald Ford and Ronald Reagan for turning their Republican primary into a jingoistic debate over the Panama Canal.[82]

During the next three days before the primary, Church needed desperately to campaign hard. Neither his body nor events cooperated. On Saturday afternoon, he was so tired that he had to cancel an appearance at the "World's Greatest Garage Sale" in Berea, Ohio. That night, with large bags under his eyes, he forced himself to make a scheduled stop at a suburban shopping center near Cleveland. The inattentive audience and the noisy children only detracted from his speech. As Church moved wearily to the next stop, he learned that the newly completed Teton Dam in eastern Idaho had collapsed a few hours earlier. A fifteen-foot-high wall of water had surged through the upper Snake River Valley, killing several people, leaving hundreds homeless, and inflicting millions of dollars in damage. Church had no choice but to interrupt his campaign and visit the devastated area.[83]

Canceling his scheduled appearance on ABC's "Issues and Answers" program the next morning, Church headed immediately for Cleveland to catch a plane back to Idaho. But even that effort was ill-fated. An airport baggage truck somehow broke loose, disabling his chartered jet. As aides looked for a replacement plane, Church talked with reporter Elizabeth Drew about the fortunes of his late, late strategy. He indicated that in many respects his campaign had gone as he had hoped, allowing him to win four primaries, and almost a fifth in Rhode Island, and to legitimize his candidacy. But he had not anticipated a number of troubles. He believed that he could have won the California primary if Brown had not entered the race. Moreover, a "shoestring" budget had handicapped the senator from the start. "And now," he said, "I have to return to Idaho. But that's Kismet." He had no regrets. His campaign had gone fairly well, up to these last days. "And then it all came apart."[84]

While Church awaited his flight out of Cleveland he still hoped that his campaign would not lose too much valuable time. He assumed that he would at least have the national press corps flying with him back to Idaho. But the tiny Lear jet that he was finally able to charter had additional room for only a CBS pool reporter. In the meantime, while arrangements were still underway to charter the plane, he decided to tape his segment for "Issues and Answers." The taping at a local television station did not end until after 1 a. m. When the interview aired the next morning, one reporter commented that Church resembled someone who had just completed "a night on the town, a few rounds with Muhammad Ali, and perhaps an invasion of Normandy." By contrast, the other candidates on the program looked rested and refreshed.[85]

At 5 a. m. on Sunday, Church's plane at last departed Cleveland and headed for Pocatello, some two thousand miles away. In Idaho, Church and other state leaders flew over the flooded section. Perhaps the senator recalled the warning three years earlier from geologist Robert Curry about the site's geologic defects. At that time, Church had ignored Curry's nay-saying and strenuously supported the locals who wanted a dam to help water the area's crops. Now, he looked down on a muddy tragedy. The little town of Wilford had literally been washed away. In nearby Rexburg water had reached half-way up the first stories of buildings on Main Street. A mobile home park outside Sugar City had disappeared, as had tens of thousands of acres of topsoil. The scene was unnerving, but would have been far worse had the dam given way in the middle of the night, rather than the daytime. After touring the area, Church conferred with officials on ways to provide relief to the victims.[86]

He then headed back to Ohio and arrived ashen-faced at the Hollenden House hotel in Cleveland that evening. "Show me where my bed is," he commented tiredly as he stepped toward the elevator.[87]

The final day of the campaign hardly lifted his spirits. He went to a television studio to make a desperate appeal for support only to discover there was no time for his program. That night, he, Bethine, and about a dozen staffers gathered at a seafood restaurant in Cleveland for a private dinner. Everyone knew that Church would lose the primary the next day. Halfway through the dinner, he realized that he was eating turtle soup. Recalling that the tortoise had become the symbol of his campaign, he felt like a cannibal. "But," he laughed, "it's better to eat turtle than to eat crow."[88]

On Tuesday, Carter swept to an overwhelming victory in Ohio, with 52 percent of the vote. Udall received 21 percent and Church 14. Carter's big Ohio win compensated for his setbacks in California and New Jersey. Brown carried California easily, and his uncommitted slate in New Jersey also rolled over Carter. But Carter that day had picked up another 218 delegates and seemed virtually assured of receiving the Democratic nomination. In California, Church's 7 percent of the vote placed him a distant third, way behind Brown's 59 and Carter's 21. The Idaho senator had still not conceded, but on television that night he looked battered and dazed. Elizabeth Drew noted that the usually articulate Church seemed hesitant and even confused a few words. Someone asked him if he had considered the vice presidency. "Yes, I've thought about it," he said, and then contradicted himself: "It's presumptuous to think about the Vice-Presidency."[89]

VII

Church had nevertheless been thinking about the vice presidency for at least several weeks. Campaigning in Oregon, he asserted that he would accept the Democratic ticket's second spot: "You know how it is," he explained, "lightning strikes and they tell you you have to do it for the party." On the eve of the Ohio primary, in a conversation with his long-time friend Bryce Nelson, he left no doubts that he was interested in the vice presidency and was making himself available for the position. Publicly, he contended that the vice-presidential candidate should come from the ranks of someone who had won a primary, as he had done. And at one point, when his campaign was faltering, he stopped pacing in a motel room to ask Mike Wetherell, "What do you think is going to happen with the Vice Presidency? Do you think that I've got a shot at it?"[90]

Rumors circulated, especially in Mo Udall's camp, that Church had entered the Ohio primary mainly to position himself for the vice presidency. As a stalking horse for Carter, Church had helped the former governor by siphoning off Udall's votes. Church himself later admitted that he had probably taken more votes from Udall than from Carter. And journalist Elizabeth Drew learned that Carter's people had approached some Church staffers about coaxing the senator into Ohio.

Mo Udall himself reportedly believed initially that Church, to advance his vice-presidential cause, had cooperated with Carter. Stewart Udall, although miffed at the time, ultimately rejected that interpretation because he doubted "that Frank Church would play that crass a game." In his estimation, Church was "a class person."[91]

Church's Ohio decision remained cloaked in mystery. The senator insisted that political realities dictated his choice; his chances were better in Ohio than in California. If he was in fact angling for the vice presidency, he was politically naive. John Gabusi, Udall's campaign director, had come to know Carter's people over the past two years, and he was certain about one thing: they would not accept any of Carter's challengers as their candidate's running mate. Nor was Carter himself inclined to take kindly to his opponents. "I don't have to kiss his ass," he snapped in response to rumors that Ted Kennedy was perhaps part of a Stop Carter drive. Church, by entering the primaries, in effect eliminated himself from the vice presidency. He apparently did not think so himself, however, because he continued to talk about his prospects.[92]

Church's later contention that Carter would have won Ohio regardless of who opposed him did little to mollify Mo Udall, who viewed the senator's Ohio campaign as a "gratuitous, final kick." The misunderstanding with Udall clearly bothered Church because he contacted him to try to repair relations. The senator insisted that he had hoped only to derail Carter and secure an open convention. After all, despite months of trying, Udall had been unable to defeat Carter in any primary; yet Church had beaten the former governor several times. Udall was still puzzled about Church's motives. Why, he wondered, had the senator returned to Ohio after having left the state because of the Teton Dam tragedy? Udall confronted Church directly: had the senator, or any of his people, made a deal with Carter regarding the vice presidency? Church was emphatic. Neither he nor, to his knowledge, anyone on his staff had reached any understanding with Carter. Udall ultimately held no grudges against Church. "In retrospect," he said, "I can see his point of view."[93]

Events subsequently showed that Church had no deal with Carter. Following the Ohio primary he promoted himself as Carter's possible running mate. He wrote out in longhand a series of "talking points," and then heavily edited his draft remarks. Emphasizing his "distinguished record of proven achievement," he contended that none of the other senators on Carter's reported list of possible choices matched his preparation and legislative accomplishments. He noted that he had done well in the primaries, winning four of six where he had been "able to conduct an adequate campaign." He emphasized his strength in the West, "the only region in the country in which Governor Carter was unable to win a single primary." He stressed that he and Carter agreed on major issues. And he described himself as a political outsider, like Carter. He even anticipated that "the Washington 'club' " would push for another vice-presidential candidate, "as part of a subtle, persistent effort to take over Jimmy Carter." Church then used Congressman Carroll Hubbard as his intermediary with Carter. Hubbard, who like Carter was a southern Democrat and Southern Baptist, sent Church's "talking points" to the Democratic frontrunner, along with a letter endorsing the senator for the vice-presidential nomination.[94]

Other Church advocates contacted Carter's people. Henry Kimelman asked his old friend Morris Dees, Jr. to help Church's cause. Dees, an influential southern lawyer who had raised funds for Carter, put Kimelman in touch with Carter's top aide, Hamilton Jordan. Jordan in turn arranged a meeting between Church and Carter in the senator's hideaway Capitol office. After the meeting, Dees told Kimelman that Church had impressed Carter.[95]

For a while, Church's chances of becoming Carter's running mate seemed excellent. Carter himself wrote later that, "if an instant choice had been required at that time, it would have been Senator Frank Church of Idaho or perhaps Senator Henry Jackson of Washington." Mike Schneiders, Carter's personal aide, believed that Church was Carter's preference. Carter, he said, "thought Church was the most qualified, would add the most to the ticket, and also had the advantage of going through the primary system."[96]

Carter quickly began to have second thoughts, however, especially regarding his and Church's compatibility. As Carter expanded the list of choices, Church tried to strengthen his position. On June 14 the senator released his 79 delegates to vote for Carter.[97]

In late June, Carter's trusted friend and adviser, Charles Kirbo, visited Church to confirm that the senator was one of Carter's top choices. Church nevertheless feared that his conversation with Kirbo went badly. "I didn't respond the way he thought I should, I guess," the senator recalled. "So, he was certainly not in my camp. It was just one of those personality things." Church informed Kirbo that he planned to take his family fishing in the Caribbean for a few days and that Carter would be able to contact him there. Looking back, Church guessed that Kirbo may have thought that the timing of the trip was inappropriate if the senator really wanted to be vice president.[98]

More serious obstacles blocked Church's path, however. Several of his Senate colleagues advised Carter not to choose the Idaho senator. They reportedly criticized his handling of the CIA investigation and his reputation on Capitol Hill. Church later heard that two or three influential senators who had supported the Vietnam war did not want a "dove" a heartbeat from the presidency. Other individuals also weighed in against Church. Among the thirty or so politicians, journalists, academics, and notable citizens whom Carter consulted, support for the senator was muted. According to journalist Richard Reeves, Carter "kept hearing that Church was something of a windbag." Carter's rating sheet eventually indicated that Church had done well in the primaries but was "a lightweight." Increasingly, Carter looked to Minnesota senator Walter Mondale as his running mate.[99]

Church understandably interpreted as a bad sign the news that Carter would interview senators Edmund Muskie, John Glenn, and Mondale at his Plains, Georgia, home. At the convention in New York, Carter planned to interview Church, Henry Jackson, Illinois senator Adlai Stevenson III, and New Jersey representative Peter Rodino, who had chaired the Watergate investigation. As Church prepared to leave with his family for the Caribbean, ABC reporter Sam Donaldson called from Plains. "What's happened?" Donaldson asked. "Yesterday, you were everyone's top pick around here, but now it appears from what I hear that you have been dropped from consideration." The *Atlanta Constitution* also reported that Church was out of the running.[100]

Puzzled by his declining fortunes, Church embarked on his Caribbean trip. He and his staff established an elaborate system, utilizing the marine radio, by which his aides could reach him if Carter called. They even agreed on a code so that anyone listening would not know they were discussing Jimmy Carter. When Wetherell contacted Church to report on the latest developments concerning the vice presidency, he was horrified that Church started talking openly about the subject. The senator had forgotten about the code.[101]

Church had concerns other than the code on his mind. As he and Forrest stood on the boat's bridge watching darkness settle in, he commented suddenly, "You know, I have been terribly naive." He proceeded to inform his son that, just before leaving Washington, he had received a call from the CIA. The agency thought he should know about unconfirmed reports that in October the *Economist* magazine would contain an article showing that the KGB had infiltrated Church's intelligence committee. Church was not worried about the truth of the essay. But, he noted to Forrest, "can you imagine any rumor more certain to spook a presidential candidate than that his prospective vice president has overseen an operation which was infiltrated by the KGB?" Church predicted that the rumored story would disappear after the convention. "He was right," Forrest wrote later. "The man who was named as prospective author of the article did not even exist," and the *Economist* never published the article.[102]

On July 11, when Church arrived in New York for the Democratic convention, he sensed quickly that his interview the next day with Carter would be a mere formality. When the senator encountered Carter's key advisers, Hamilton Jordan and Jody Powell, at a reception, they were conspicuously aloof. He recalled that "they just really cold-shouldered me, walked right past me, hardly even said hello."[103]

The Monday morning interview in Carter's hotel room proved awkward. Church immediately felt ill at ease when he showed up in a suit and found Carter barefoot and in blue jeans. Carter proceeded to put on socks and tennis shoes. Mike Wetherell, camera in hand, stepped back to get a better picture of Church and Carter together. To his embarrassment, he stepped on the foot of Carter's wife, Rosalynn. Bethine was horrified and the senator glared at his aide. After a few minutes Carter and Church went into the next room to talk privately. Church sensed that Carter was simply going through the motions, and that he had already selected someone else as his running mate. Subsequently, back in his own hotel room, the senator told his staff that he would not be Carter's choice.[104]

VIII

On Tuesday evening, shortly before midnight, Church delivered a short speech before the convention. He followed a parade of speakers whom the delegates had virtually ignored. The enthusiastic response to his appearance was gratifying. *Washington Post* and Associated Press polls showed that a majority of the delegates favored him for vice president. His ten-minute address reiterated the major themes of his recent Senate and campaign speeches. He condemned governmental secrecy and deception, noting the examples of Nixon's bombing of Cambodia and the more recent covert actions in Angola. He chastised the Nixon and Ford administrations for showing "contempt for those traditional goals of self-determination and human liberty that were once the hallmark of American diplomacy." And he predicted that a new Democratic administration would be more attentive to human rights, more willing to accommodate a revolutionary world. The convention interrupted him some twenty-five times with applause and chants, "We want Church!" "Dyn-o-mite," said one delegate after the speech. Church looked upon his comments as a satisfying cap to his presidential bid. "It was the last hurrah of this particular chapter of my life."[105]

The next morning Carter called with news about his chosen running mate. Church hung up the phone and told his family and aides, "Well, it is not going to be us." Mondale would join the ticket.[106]

At the time, Church seemed disappointed, but in retrospect he believed Carter had made the right selection. The senator concluded that he would have found the vice presidency "much too confining" and that he would not have been happy. He suspected also that he would not have pleased Carter, who in November went on to win the presidential election against Gerald Ford.[107]

The more Church pondered his own fate, the more he wondered how he could ever have thought that he would end up on the Democratic ticket. "I've got enemies in high places," he told an interviewer shortly after the convention. "There are certain powerful board and conference rooms where I am friendless." In part, he was rationalizing his recent setbacks and covering his disappointment; more prosaic reasons accounted for why Carter had not chosen him as a running mate. But Church's suspicions were not altogether unfounded. The senator had given many powerful individuals and groups every reason to oppose him. In his post-convention interview he brandished their opposition as his badge of courage, proof that he was "a loner," as he called himself, who had "never been part of the Washington establishment."[108]

His renewed sense of being an outsider, and his basic fatalism, had been apparent even before the Democratic convention, when he vacationed briefly in the Caribbean with his family. Watching the stars very late with Forrest, Church had said quietly, "Kismet. Some things are simply meant to be or not to be. We cannot worry about them. The other things, they are the ones that matter." His relationship with his son mattered, for one thing. They had come a considerable distance since the late 1960s, when the Vietnam war and cultural issues had divided them. Now, they stood side by side, singing songs from *Camelot* and *Man of La Mancha*. There on the deck, on that warm summer night, the long campaign trail of recent months must have seemed very distant. Kismet. Some things are simply meant to be or not to be.[109]

Church and Fidel Castro during Church's August 1977 Cuba trip. *Courtesy Bethine Church*.

Chapter Eighteen
Change and Resistance: 1977-1978

FOR FRANK CHURCH, the Jimmy Carter presidency got off to a promising start in several respects. Carter's initial emphasis on a non-militaristic foreign policy and human rights pleased him. And, in 1978, he played a towering role in the administration's historic fight to ratify the long-overdue Panama Canal treaties.

Church was nevertheless often disheartened, and not just because of his strained relationship with the White House. He was disenchanted also because of the Cold War's continuing grip on the American political culture, a grip evident in the revitalized rightward movement. For a while during the Seventies, the trauma of the Vietnam war and the Watergate scandal had opened the national security state and long-standing Cold War premises to unparalleled scrutiny. Church had seized the moment to raise fundamental questions about U. S. foreign policy and to publicize some of the more glaring ways in which government and corporate policies had endangered the Constitution. But, by the late Seventies, his limited victories against secrecy, deception, and interventionism appeared increasingly tenuous. While the Panama Canal treaties signaled the emergence of the anti-colonial, non-interventionist foreign policy that he had long espoused, the bitter fight to ratify them provided depressing evidence of a resurgent jingoism, stridency, and mean-spiritedness. Moreover, the administration's decision in 1978 to sell fighter jets to the Saudis was an unpleasant reminder that U. S. policies, in this case regarding arms dealing, had not changed much.

I

Going into 1977, Church seemed somewhat jaded. He was at a turning point in his career. His bid the previous year for the presidency had failed. The investigations that had consumed so much of his time over the past four years had ended. Verda Barnes, who had been on his staff since he entered the Senate, and who had served as his administrative assistant for eleven years, had retired. Tom Dine, Bill Hall, and several others who had recently worked for him had moved on. Church still had talented, experienced people on his staff, but his office was nevertheless in transition. Although he believed that he would soon chair the Foreign Relations Committee, it was at the time drifting under the leadership of Alabama's John Sparkman, whose energy and intellectual powers were slipping rapidly. Indeed, Sparkman kept falling asleep during public hearings and the committee's chief of staff would have to nudge him awake. For several months in 1977 the Idaho senator "was kind of down," according to Church aide Peter Fenn. The previous year, during his presidential campaign, he had confided to his friend Bryce Nelson that the Senate was beginning to bore him and that he did not intend to stay there for the rest of his life. He wanted new challenges. In early 1977 Mike Wetherell observed that staffers found him rather "testy, difficult to approach with any new idea." They seemed to have to fight to get him to do something and found him less agreeable and more remote than he had been previously. "The presidential election is over," Wetherell reminded him. "It's time to stop reliving that election and focus on your next one, in 1980."[1]

Political changes complicated Church's search for direction. For the last eight years he had battled Republican administrations. With a Democrat again in the White House, his familiar role as a critic became more difficult, even though he often lacked confidence in Carter.

Indeed, the new administration had been in power only a few weeks before it jolted Church regarding the problem of secrecy and the CIA. When the *Washington Post* revealed that the CIA had secretly paid Jordan's King Hussein millions of dollars over two decades, Carter appeared more upset about the breach of secrecy than about the payments. Although the president stopped the payments, he also urged the formation of a joint congressional committee that would limit Congress's access to information about covert activities. Church must have wondered where Carter had been during the recent investigations of illegal CIA conduct. Clearly agitated, Church published an essay chastising the new administration for its "draconian response," which he hoped reflected inexperience rather than policy. "The dynamic of an open society, by definition, works in favor of disclosure," he lectured the White House. Public information was the best guard against wrongdoing. And Church had no doubts that the CIA payments were wrong: "If you don't believe it," he wrote, "ask yourself how you would feel if it were disclosed that the President of the United States had gotten secret payments from King Hussein."[2]

Church's uneasy association with the administration was partly philosophical but also mirrored the tensions between Carter and Congress. Throughout his presidency Jimmy Carter was, in the words of one scholar, "a stranger in a strange land." That was perhaps Carter's preferred role. In 1976 his main campaign theme had been that he was not part of the national political establishment; as president, he took pride in remaining an outsider. He was never at ease in dealing with Congress, even though his own party controlled it. He made his disenchantment with the legislative branch clear in his memoirs, where he entitled a chapter "My One-Week Honeymoon with Congress." As Maryland senator Paul Sarbanes said, "The kind of close partnership a lot of us hoped for just didn't really develop with the President."[3]

Church was among the many people on Capitol Hill who had trouble dealing with the administration. "I feel no closeness with those people at the White House," he said. Several times after returning from a White House meeting or event he observed disdainfully that Carter was not the greatest president he had met. When Carter delivered a national television speech on energy during his first weeks in office, Church and Arkansas senator Dale Bumpers slipped out of a side door at the White House rather than tell the press what they thought of the president's proposals. For one thing, Carter had not discussed his ideas with Congress. For another, he was not very persuasive. As the two senators made their hasty exit, Bumpers muttered to Church that Carter would be unable to sell a prostitute's services on a troop train.[4]

Further undercutting Church's relationship with the White House was the senator's sense that Carter's aides resented his brief entry into the 1976 Democratic primaries. Carter's staff "couldn't have been cooler," recalled Bethine Church. She was equally certain that Carter himself never liked her husband.[5]

Time and again the White House displayed either ineptitude or striking insensitivity to political protocol. During the tense debates over the Panama Canal treaties, for example, an Idaho resident telephoned Church's office to say that he and a state delegation received invitations to a presidential briefing aimed at building grassroots support. Peter Fenn, who took the call, was appalled to learn that Carter had extended invitations to various opinion leaders in Idaho without first consulting Church. Fenn immediately got on the phone to the White House, angrily trying to find out why. He learned that a twenty-three-year-old presidential aide, who was working on his B. A. degree in night school, had compiled his own list of people from Idaho and other northwestern states to invite to the briefing. The apologetic young man had been oblivious to political etiquette and had not considered checking with the offices of Church or of Washington senators Henry Jackson and Warren Magnuson. Years later, Fenn was still aghast at the bungling of "those bozoes" in the White House.[6]

Even when Carter tried to build bridges with Church, the results fell short. Presidential advisors suggested at one point, for example, that Carter should invite the Churches over for lunch. According to Bethine Church, the lunch, which included Rosalynn Carter, "couldn't have been nicer." Curiously enough, however, Jimmy Carter said little to the senator. Bethine speculated that perhaps he was tired. In any case, the luncheon was awkward and no real rapport developed between the two men. The president's friendly gesture had been inconsequential and even counterproductive. Bethine thought the occasion was typical of Carter's dealings with Church: "Something. . . never comes off right." Within Church's camp there was considerable puzzlement regarding the president's seeming reluctance to recognize the number of times that the senator, in the words of staffer Steve Emerson, "was out on the gang plank for Carter and not really getting the support he needed."[7]

II

Among the political risks that Church took on behalf of the administration was a trip to Cuba in 1977. That spring, when a Cuban delegation invited him to visit Havana, he initially decided not to go. Although he was as anxious as Carter to seek more normal relations with Cuba, he wanted to make sure that any trip to Havana justified the bad publicity that it would most certainly generate in Idaho. "I did not want to be a part of Castro's dog and pony show," he recalled. He had already declined to join several members of the Foreign Relations Committee who visited Cuba earlier. But when the Cubans in 1977 extended a second invitation to him and intimated that Fidel Castro had something important to discuss, Church consulted the White House. Carter convinced him that it would be useful to determine what was on Castro's mind.[8]

On August 8, Frank and Bethine Church flew to Havana on a plane that Carter provided, a signal to Castro that Church spoke for more than himself. Indeed, the U. S. Air Force plane that carried the Churches, along with several staff members and fourteen reporters, was the first to land in Cuba since 1960–"legally, that is," as Castro joked. Over the next three days Castro himself served as a kind of tour guide for the group. At one point, he drove (although not well, Bethine remembered) an open jeep through a driving rainstorm, showing the Churches the Cuban countryside and talking excitedly about a wide range of non-political issues. Extremely cordial and witty, he laughingly apologized for the downpour soaking his guests: "I will get you down here on a high level mission like this, you will catch cold, and they will say that I did it on purpose because I am such a terrible man."[9]

On the third day Church and Castro engaged in serious, lengthy talks. Well into the early morning hours, they had a freewheeling and open conversation. At the State Department's request Church emphasized three main issues: the release of American political prisoners; the right of American citizens living in Cuba to bring their Cuban families to the U. S.; and the right of several hundred "dual nationals," who were eligible for either American or Cuban citizenship, to move to the United States. Castro consented immediately to allow the families of the U. S. citizens to leave Cuba, and to do so with their savings and personal belongings. "Just give us a list," he said. He agreed also to review the cases of seven Americans whom the State Department classified as "political prisoners," and of sixteen more in jail for drug smuggling, hijacking, or other charges. Castro, in turn, asked nothing of the Carter administration, but clearly expected some kind of reciprocation on down the line. Church subsequently recommended to the Senate Foreign Relations Committee that the U. S. should respond to Castro's "good-faith" gestures by relaxing America's trade embargo, stamping out U. S.-based anti-terrorist activities against Cuba, and expanding cultural and other exchanges between the two countries.[10]

An off-the-cuff statement that Church made just before departing Cuba, however, threatened to overshadow the positive features of his visit. Castro, when bidding his guests farewell at the Havana airport, praised the senator effusively. Church, obviously embarrassed and fumbling for a reply, said that he had "found a friend" in Castro. Cleve Corlett, who was handling the press for Church, was dumbstruck: "Oh shit," he thought to himself. He knew the statement would haunt the senator. It did, providing additional ammunition for the growing right-wing campaign against Church. In the *National Review,* for example, William Buckley described the senator as Castro's "altarboy," a gullible liberal whom the Cuban dictator had reduced "to moral idiocy." According to Buckley, "Romeo never said to Juliet sweeter things than Frank Church had to say about Fidel Castro." Heading back to the United States, Church admitted to Corlett that he had not chosen his words well. "I had to say something," he explained lamely, but he sorely regretted his comment.[11]

For Church, who usually spoke carefully and precisely, the statement was particularly unfortunate because it misrepresented the nature of his visit. True, Castro's charm and "charismatic" presence had impressed him. And Church's understanding of Cuba's "bitter history" stirred his sympathies. The United States, he said, had for decades "regarded Cuba much like a colony," and by the late 1950s had controlled much of that nation's economy. Church believed that U. S. policies after the overthrow of the dictator Batista in 1959 had perhaps played a "compelling" part in driving Castro toward the Soviets. But Church had no illusions about Castro. In his report to the Foreign Relations Committee he described the Cuban as unquestionably "a grass-roots communist" who presided over "a regimented state" where freedom was "conspicuously absent." The government controlled public information and rounded up political prisoners. During his meetings with Castro, moreover, Church had been quite critical of Cuban policy, especially that of sending troops to Africa. The senator in fact angered Castro by comparing the Cuban's rationale for intervening militarily in Angola with that earlier of Dean Rusk and Henry Kissinger regarding the U. S. presence in Vietnam. When Castro objected on grounds that the Africans had asked for Cuban troops, Church reminded him that American policy makers had also said they were simply honoring requests. Castro, he warned, was repeating the same kind of mistake that Americans had made in Southeast Asia.[12]

Church believed that his visit to Cuba had been productive. He had gotten Castro to allow the Cuban families of almost a hundred U. S. citizens to relocate in America. Over the next few weeks Castro also freed several political prisoners. "Thanks to efforts by U. S. Senator Frank Church," a Georgia newspaper reported, a Baptist minister who had been in jail for ten years was finally rejoining his family in Cobb County. Church had also helped to reverse what he viewed as

America's ill-fated efforts to isolate Cuba and topple Castro—policies that he said had "failed monumentally." In an effort to improve communications between the two countries, Church had spent more time with Castro than had any U. S. official since the severing of relations in 1961.[13]

He knew that his trip would trigger hostile responses in Idaho. Indeed, shortly after his return, Idaho conservatives reprinted a photograph of him talking with Castro; a cartoon-like box in the photo contained the senator's comment about finding a friend. In south-central Idaho's sprawling farm country, a group circulated advertisements saying that Castro was part of a communist drug-smuggling scheme "to enslave youths of the Western Hemisphere." "Senator Church," the group asked, "What do you think of your 'friend' now?"[14]

III

A far more politically charged issue than Cuba, however, was the Panama Canal. Difficulties over the canal were rooted in the original 1903 treaty. Under questionable circumstances, the treaty had granted the U. S., in perpetuity, a ten-mile-wide strip across the middle of Panama. On that slim band of territory, the U. S. had constructed a massive canal. Panamanians increasingly resented this invasion of their sovereignty. In the late 1950s, and especially in 1964, their anger exploded in bloody anti-American riots. To salvage America's role in Central America and to maintain access to the canal, the Johnson, Nixon, and Ford administrations had sought a new treaty with Panama. By the fall of 1977, after more than a decade of volatile negotiations, two agreements were finally ready for a national vote in Panama and for Senate ratification in the U. S. The first called for a joint U. S.-Panamanian operation of the canal until the end of 1999, when Panama would assume full control; the second (known as the Neutrality Treaty) dealt with America's rights to defend the canal subsequently. Together, the agreements would restore Panamanian sovereignty over the Canal Zone.

Given the American public's general lack of knowledge about the canal by the mid-Seventies, there was perhaps little reason to anticipate major problems over ratification. According to a June 1975 poll, only a third of the respondents knew that the U. S. owned the canal. The emerging "New Right," however, subsequently invested the canal with huge symbolic meaning and turned the treaties into a bitterly contested issue. In the fall of 1977 the Republican National Committee voted to oppose the agreements.[15]

More than anyone, Ronald Reagan made "saving" the canal a rallying point. In his 1976 effort to wrest the Republican nomination from incumbent Gerald Ford, he discovered that the issue galvanized large numbers of Americans who wanted their country to "stand tall" again. Following the setbacks of the Vietnam war and the Arab oil boycotts, many citizens welcomed Reagan's stand against "the giveaway." "We bought it, we paid for it, it's ours and we're going to keep it," Reagan said repeatedly to wildly receptive audiences. He brushed off the Panamanian leader, General Omar Torrijos, as a "tinhorn dictator."[16]

In 1977 conservatives mounted a ferocious attack on the Panama Canal treaties. "THERE IS NO PANAMA CANAL, THERE IS AN AMERICAN CANAL AT PANAMA," the American Conservative Union (ACU) proclaimed in a slick, thirty-minute TV film that fall. By then, conservatives had fielded congressional "truth squads" to battle the treaties, and the Young Americans for Freedom were selling buttons, "Give'em Plains [Georgia, home of Jimmy Carter], Not Our Canal."[17]

Although Jimmy Carter had insisted during the 1976 campaign that he would not concede "practical control of the Panama Canal Zone" any time soon, as president he championed the new treaties. His sudden reversal was not surprising, given his evolving world view. Carter was no conceptualizer and inclined to analyze problems in an "item-by-item engineering" way, according to his speechwriter James Fallows. Nevertheless, Carter initially represented an intellectual shift among some U. S. policy makers and scholars away from traditional Cold War perceptions of a bipolar world, torn between Soviet-sponsored communism and U. S.-backed freedom. The emerging revisionism was more attentive to historical complexities, nationalism, local conditions, and Third World problems. Cold Warriors had focused mainly on military and ideological threats to the U. S.; Carter and his advisors, as well as Church, were more likely to see dangers abroad in terms of economic scarcity, inequities, ancient regional conflicts, and the spread of weaponry. The old containment policies, oriented mainly toward defending territory, had been largely resistant to change; the newer post-Vietnam perspective was concerned with accommodating change in ways that advanced human rights and moderated conflicts. To the incoming Carter administration, the Panama Canal issue pointed up the need for flexible, fair policies in a rapidly changing world. During the first half of Carter's presidency, the canal agreements embodied the administration's efforts not only to improve relationships with Latin

America, but also to deal with small, developing nations in open, non-militaristic ways. Church shared these goals.[18]

They were also formidable goals to achieve. The patriotic backlash that Frank Church had encountered during the intelligence committee hearings now threatened to prevent ratification of the canal agreements. Just as Church had hoped his investigations would help America turn a historical corner, Carter wanted the Panama treaties to inaugurate a series of foreign policy initiatives regarding human rights, arms limitations, and better relations with the Soviets and Chinese. But American public opinion, as Church discovered on the intelligence committee, was not turning a corner after all. Instead, the national mood was circling back, boomerang-like, seeking Cold War certainties and evidence of previous U. S. strength – before the defeats, humiliation, and turmoil of the recent past. Thus, whereas Carter hoped the treaties would give his presidency a rousing start, the battle over them developed into what he later called "an extended nightmare." And the canal issue plunged Frank Church into what William Jorden, the U. S. ambassador to Panama, described as "the longest, most detailed, and certainly most rancorous foreign policy fight in Congress in more than fifty years."[19]

IV

Despite the growing political risks, Church backed the treaties. As early as 1960 he had favored internationalizing the canal even though he knew such action was politically impossible. Although following the 1964 rioting in Panama he said he wanted the U. S. "to keep" the canal, by 1967 he openly advocated new treaties as the best defense against the threat of violence and subversion in Latin America. In March 1974 he refused to support Senator Strom Thurmond's resolution opposing any relinquishment of U. S. control over the Canal Zone. James McClure, Idaho's freshman senator, was among the resolution's thirty-five co-sponsors – more than enough to defeat the treaties, which required a two-thirds Senate vote. "Where's Frank," an Idaho member of the militantly right-wing Posse Comitatus asked ominously, as he surveyed the resolution's backers. Was the senator perhaps implicated in the "subversion" behind the treaties?[20]

Church recognized the canal's powerful symbolism. Many U. S. citizens looked fondly on the canal because it summoned up memories, he said, "of a time when we did pretty much as we pleased." To

Central Americans, however, it had become a painful reminder of Yankee dominance. Church empathized with them, especially after what he had learned during the multinational investigations. He understood why they resented U. S. intervention "every time the local government displeased. . .the big American companies, like United Fruit." He had also concluded that the canal, three quarters of a century old, no longer met the economic and military needs of the U. S. The time was thus ripe, he believed, for the U. S. to enhance its position in Central America by trying "to do justice by a small country."[21]

A May 1977 poll showed that most Americans disagreed with him: 78 percent wanted to maintain U. S. control of the canal. Later that year a survey revealed that 79 percent of Idahoans felt the same way. Church thus set out to put the treaties in a more favorable light.[22]

On September 26, 1977 the Foreign Relations Committee opened three-week hearings on the treaties that quickly revealed a problem: Panamanian and U. S. officials interpreted the agreements differently. Church was among several senators who informed the administration that the treaties had no chance of ratification unless they contained a clearer understanding of the United States' right to protect the canal. "He didn't threaten us," recalled Robert Beckel, a Carter aide who worked mainly with the Senate, but he summed up forcefully some political realities on the Hill. At one point, Carter queried him at length over the telephone and then, clearly annoyed, slammed the phone down. Turning to Sol Linowitz, a treaty negotiator who was visiting at the White House, Carter wondered why Church was being so difficult; the senator was supposed to be championing the treaties, not changing them. In retrospect, however, neither Beckel nor Linowitz faulted Church. They believed that he had correctly alerted the administration to obstacles that lay ahead.[23]

In October, Carter invited Torrijos to the White House to clarify the agreements. The resulting Carter-Torrijos Understanding of October 14 became an essential ingredient in the treaty fight. According to the understanding, the U. S. and Panama each had the right to defend the canal against any threat, and American ships could move to the front of the line during any emergency. On October 23, after Torrijos had read his and Carter's understanding over Panamanian television, two-thirds of Panama's voters accepted the treaties. But on Capitol Hill some senators were unsure whether the understanding—unsigned and separate from the treaties—had any legal weight.[24]

To ease his colleagues' minds, Church engaged in some skillful legislative maneuvering. His strategy was to formalize the Carter-Torrijos Understanding by adding it verbatim to the Neutrality Treaty's existing articles. The administration consented, but reluctantly: it did not want to endanger the treaties in Panama by seeming to change them. By a fourteen to one vote, the Foreign Relations Committee subsequently recommended Senate ratification of treaties which incorporated the Carter-Torrijos Understanding. Significantly, however, the committee itself did not offer the necessary amendments, a decision loaded with political meaning. Majority Leader Robert Byrd and Minority Leader Howard Baker wanted personally to offer floor amendments because they had pledged to support the treaties only if the security portions included "significant changes." The treaties' success depended on both men. Baker, who was risking his 1980 presidential hopes by supporting the agreements, had decided to work closely with Byrd. Indeed, Carter's congressional liaison, Frank Moore, reported that the Tennessee Republican was even willing to serve the White House "as a back channel of information" regarding the Senate. Baker and Byrd wanted to offer "Leadership Amendments" that would incorporate the Torrijos-Carter Understanding into the treaties. Their amendments were nevertheless, as Bob Beckel and others later emphasized, essentially Church's creations.[25]

Despite Church's early support for the treaties, the Idaho senator hardly relished the prospects of leading the floor fight to ratify them. That assignment awaited him, however, because of John Sparkman's poor health. "What do you think I should do?" Church asked aide Mike Wetherell. Wetherell urged him to let somebody else, perhaps Rhode Island's Claiborne Pell, take the point position in the Senate. The treaties, Wetherell argued, were "dynamite" that could destroy Church politically. Church needed no such warning. He told Sol Linowitz that he preferred to back the treaties as inconspicuously as possible.[26]

Preferences aside, Church realized that he had no choice but to be the treaties' floor manager. Sparkman backed the treaties and, as Foreign Relations Committee chair, was the logical floor leader; but the seventy-eight-year-old Alabaman was not up to the task. Church, next in line on the committee, cared too deeply about the agreements to dodge his responsibilities for them. Sol Linowitz sensed that the senator nevertheless struggled with himself over what role to play. As Linowitz recalled, it was almost as if Church hesitated, then gulped and said, " 'Yes, I will step up and take the leadership.' And then he gave it all he had."[27]

At Sparkman's request, Church and Maryland's freshman senator Paul Sarbanes led the floor fight. Sarbanes chaired the sub-committee on the Western Hemisphere, but Linowitz suspected that the Democrats turned to him also because he was new in the Senate and in no position to turn down the assignment. For Church, who had insisted that he needed help, Sarbanes became an indispensable ally; together, they made an effective team. Both men were intelligent and quick. And Sarbanes balanced Church's eloquence and experience with the determined resolve of a soldier in the trenches.[28]

V

On February 8, 1978 the treaty debates started with the capital on edge, still recovering from the worst blizzard of the winter. The mood in the Senate was tense. Not only was the ratification fight going to be close, but, for the first time, a Senate debate would receive gavel-to-gavel radio coverage over the Public Broadcasting System. That evening, Ronald Reagan kept up his own kind of pressure by delivering a nationally televised address warning that acceptance of the treaties might eventually cost Americans their "own freedom."[29]

For the next ten weeks Church and Sarbanes managed the floor debate—"one of the most demanding assignments in recent Senate history," according to Ambassador Jorden. Procedurally, the job was especially onerous because the Senate chose to operate as a Committee of the Whole, voting as a body on each proposed amendment. It had been fifty-five years since the Senate had last considered a treaty in such a manner. As if this institutional arrangement were not enough of a challenge for the floor managers, the White House guessed in early February that the treaties were nine votes short of ratification. Church and his allies clearly faced a huge task.[30]

The treaties' opponents complicated that task through interruptions, vitriolic talk, and "killer amendments" aimed at wrecking, not improving, the agreements. On the first day alone, Alabama's conservative Democrat James B. Allen raised fourteen parliamentary questions. Church at one point became so exasperated with the constant interjections of Paul Laxalt, the leader of the Senate's anti-treaty forces, that he insisted the Nevada Republican stop interrupting him: "I do have the floor." When Laxalt almost immediately interrupted him again, Church chastised him for always shifting the argument. How could Laxalt say, as he just had a few minutes earlier, that the treaties would benefit the communists and then turn around and say that the agreements would serve eastern bankers? "I believe it is both," Laxalt answered. Church found such logic baffling. "How can it be both?" he demanded. "The two interests conflict."[31]

Listening to the radio in Panama, Ambassador Jorden wished the debates would have matched the standard of Church's "smooth oratory." Instead, an "unremitting trickle of poison" fouled them with "chauvinism, self-righteousness, and contempt." At least twice General Torrijos had found the debates so insulting that he smashed radios on the floor.[32]

Church likewise detested the opposition's distortions and scare tactics. The treaties' opponents included some of the people whom he disliked most in the Senate – North Carolina's Jesse Helms, South Carolina's Strom Thurmond, Utah's Orrin Hatch – people who in his opinion traded on simplicities, fear, and prejudice. Thurmond, he once told an aide, was the only "truly evil" man in the Senate. But he also detested Hatch. During the treaty debates, Church whispered to a staffer, "One more day with him and I'll be ready for a padded cell."[33]

Equally difficult to tolerate was the rancorous anti-treaty campaign of archly conservative groups. *The Phyllis Schlafly Report* called the treaties "highly immoral" and warned against turning the Caribbean into a "Red Lake." "Save *Your* Panama Canal," urged the ACU's "Panama Canal Task Force" in full-page ads. The Conservative Caucus declared February 22, 1978 as "Keep Our Canal Day" – a day during which citizens were supposed to drive with their headlights on. The American Federation of Small Business sent out flyers opposing the "Giveaway of U. S. Canal to Marxist Dictator." The Houston-based "Committee of Tax-Weary and Concerned Citizens" ran full-page newspaper ads condemning the treaties as symbolic of America's "moral disintegration," and quoting Idaho Representative George Hansen. The *Spotlight*, a strident right-wing publication, featured a column by Orrin Hatch describing the treaties as "phony" and offered special "Friendship Tours" through the Panama Canal. Cards and letters with pennies attached, proclaiming an old U. S. battle cry, "Millions for Defense, but Not One Cent for Tribute!" poured into offices such as Church's.[34]

In Idaho, Church felt considerable additional pressure because the treaties' opponents included the rest of the state's congressional delegation: McClure, Symms, and Hansen. McClure and Symms were both board members of the ACU, which had launched an imposing campaign to keep the canal. Symms added his signature to a full-page ACU appeal in the *Idaho Statesman*: "Senator Church. . . before you vote to give away the Panama Canal, please consider all the facts." Hansen headed up a "Panama Canal Defense Campaign" and claimed that nothing less than America's "national survival" hinged on U. S. sovereignty over the canal. He also played a prominent role in the *Spotlight*'s tours of the canal.[35]

Meanwhile, local citizens across Idaho went after Church and the treaties with a vengeance. Bumper stickers carried an unsettling message: "Frank Church For a Stronger Russia." Various committees circulated save-the-canal petitions, attacking Church for his role as the treaties' floor manager and accusing him of pushing the agreements "down our throats." A rally in Pocatello turned out a crowd of three hundred, reportedly the largest conservative gathering in that community's history. Republican gubernatorial candidate and former state legislator C. L. "Butch" Otter initiated a petition demanding that the U. S. government "return" federally owned Idaho land to the state's residents if it gave away the canal.[36]

Church decided to ignore the spreading political firestorm back home as much as possible. His speechwriter, Cleve Corlett, advised against such a passive strategy and urged him to meet his critics head-on. But Church chose not to take the offensive lest he make the grassroots situation more combustible. He hoped that, over the next two years, the treaties would cease to generate such emotional heat. Quite deliberately, he sharply limited the number of canal-related press releases in Idaho and, unlike James McClure, never devoted an entire newsletter to the Panama issue. His press releases and newsletters emphasized instead his work for his Idaho constituents.[37]

On a rare occasion when he mentioned the canal issue in a newsletter, he showed himself with an otherwise unlikely ally, Hollywood's quintessential patriot, John Wayne. The "Duke" knew Panama well. His first wife of many years was a Panamanian and he had visited her country often. After talking with Torrijos in 1977, he expressed support for the new treaties. Over the next few months he and Ronald Reagan clashed publicly over the canal issue. At one point Wayne wrote an angry five-page letter disputing Reagan's "untruths" and saying, "I'll show you point by God damn point in the Treaty where you are misinforming people."

In mid-January 1978, Frank Church met Wayne. The senator and several other members of the Foreign Relations Committee were on a fact-finding visit to Panama when they encountered the movie star in a hotel dining room. While cameras clicked, Wayne shook hands and talked with them. As Ambassador Jorden observed, "a picture with John Wayne was pure gold in the political bank." Church drew subsequently upon that bank, reminding his constituents that "even John Wayne" backed the treaties. In his March 1978 newsletter he featured a photograph of himself and Bethine talking with the Duke, "a treaty supporter."[38]

As Church tried to finesse the politics of the treaty fight in Idaho, he labored at the center of the Senate debates. While the treaty's opponents attacked with myriad arguments and statistics, he and Sarbanes relied on a small team of researchers, the "Gang of Four," for details and information. Using as their base a tiny office in Vice President Walter Mondale's Senate suite, the researchers listened to the debates over the radio and frantically supplied the two floor managers with information to counter the ever-shifting arguments. Church sometimes believed he was "redigging the canal with a teaspoon." Not since the civil rights debates of the mid-Sixties had he spent so much time on the Senate floor. In the evenings he came home physically and emotionally drained.[39]

Doubts about Church's tenacity and toughness seemed to fade during the struggle. Arkansas Democrat Dale Bumpers would never forget how Church stood "in the well of the Senate day after day after day." George McGovern had the impression that Church "just lived on the Senate floor during that debate." Watching from the gallery, author David McCullough marveled at the Idaho senator's "simple staying power."[40]

McCullough, an award-winning historian, offered a special perspective on the treaty fights. His book *The Path Between the Seas* was, according to Church, "a bible for most senators" who studied the canal issue. When McCullough discussed the canal with the Foreign Relations Committee in 1977, he met Church for the first time. Subsequently, as a kind of one-man lobbyist for the treaties, he sought the senator's advice on several occasions. The more he watched the floor fight and came to know Church, the more he respected him. During a small dinner party at columnist Mary McGrory's house, he was amazed when Church started singing "The Road to Mandalay." The senator not only had a rich, powerful voice, but was using it in behalf of a song from the era of Rudyard Kipling, a song that, in McCullough's words, "is sort of a hymn to the romanticism of imperialism." The incongruities of that occasion lingered in McCullough's mind: Church, the resolute opponent of imperialism, singing with gusto a nineteenth-century colonial anthem. Church, well aware of the irony, clearly enjoyed the moment. The sheer joy, the playful sense of humor, the exuberance that Church exuded in private impressed McCullough greatly. Moreover, in McCullough's estimation, Church's eloquence provided the otherwise boring treaty debates with a few moments of "grandeur." McCullough admired not only Church's sense of history, but also his "righteous indignation." No other pro-treaty senator "had a greater sense that we [Americans] had really wronged the Panamanians."[41]

To the treaties' opponents, of course, Church's leadership role helped to make the agreements suspect. "Frank was known as a fellow who was sometimes in the bleeding heart category," Sol Linowitz recalled. His critics viewed him as "this big, bleeding-heart liberal who could hardly wait to give that canal away to this dictator." Admiral Thomas H. Moorer, who chaired the Joint Chiefs of Staff from 1970 to 1974, had long detested "Frank Church and his assault on everything"; testifying in 1977 against the canal agreements, Moorer rebuked him: "All I hear out of you is emotion." Senator Laxalt proudly contrasted himself to the likes of Church – people who wanted Americans to apologize for having built the canal and engaged in guilty "breast-beating." The comment prompted Church to reply that Laxalt apparently preferred to beat "a strawman," because the treaty supporters were seeking no such apology from the American people and in fact wanted to protect "the vital interest of the United States."[42]

VI

The anti-treaty obstacle that Church almost tripped over, however, was the creation not of zealous Republican conservatives but of Dennis DeConcini, a moderate freshman Democrat from Arizona. Although DeConcini had been in the Senate only a year, he became a main figure in the ratification fight. In December 1977 he told Carter's aides that he agreed with the treaties philosophically and wanted to vote for them. But with polls showing that 80 percent of his constituents opposed the agreements, he was hesitant to jeopardize his budding career. He thus proposed a reservation to the Neutrality Treaty whereby the U. S.

retained the right to do whatever "it deems necessary" to keep the canal operating. In his comments, he indicated that he was concerned about internal Panamanian threats, such as labor strikes, a statement to which irate Panamanians objected vehemently, charging that DeConcini's reservation would permit the U. S. to intervene at will in their country.[43]

DeConcini pressed blithely ahead. On March 15 he told Carter that, without the proposed reservation, he and at least two other senators would oppose the Neutrality Treaty. Fearing the loss of crucial votes, the president chose to ignore warnings from Ambassador Jorden and others that DeConcini's condition would doom the agreements in Panama. Rather than allowing senior senators a chance to deal with DeConcini, Carter abruptly accepted the condition as the price for Senate ratification. He hoped to win over the Panamanians later. On March 16 the Senate thus added the reservation to the Neutrality Treaty and then, with only one vote to spare, 68-32, ratified the agreement. By accepting DeConcini's wording, however, the Senate had indeed rendered the treaties unacceptable to the Panamanians. As the press focused on "the DeConcini fiasco," the administration recognized its mistake. White House aide Hamilton Jordan informed a small group at Vice President Walter Mondale's home that "the president told me today he should have seen the problem with the DeConcini thing and not accepted it. He said he'd been foolish not to see it."[44]

The bumbling management of the Neutrality Treaty fight during its final hours reflected far worse upon the Carter administration than upon Church and the other pro-treaty senators. Ambassador Jorden subsequently laid the blame squarely on the White House. Carter erred, whether out of a misreading of Panamanian sentiment, inadequate information from his aides, or a frantic pursuit of DeConcini's support. By doing so he had jeopardized the treaties and in effect given DeConcini more leverage than the Arizona senator might otherwise have enjoyed. Church, Sarbanes, and their allies had assumed that the administration's acceptance of DeConcini's reservation grew out of discussions with the Panamanians. As they turned now to the second treaty (which dealt with the transfer of the Canal Zone to Panama), they learned of the Panamanian outrage at DeConcini's "colonialist" reservation. Sarbanes was furious when he called Jorden to discuss the Panamanian reaction. According to Jorden, "he felt he and his fellow senators had been misled, and that the White House had mismanaged the whole affair." Church was equally unhappy. When Gabriel Lewis, the Panamanian ambassador to the U. S., complained that the DeConcini reservation violated the charters of the United Nations and the Organization of American States, Church agreed "100 percent." Somehow, to save the treaties, the senators now had to repair the damage that DeConcini had wreaked. That task, Alabama's anti-treaty senator James Allen claimed gleefully, "is just like trying to restore Humpty Dumpty. It cannot be done."[45]

With the Panamanians irate about the Neutrality Treaty, with the anti-treaty senators now attacking the second agreement, and with Ronald Reagan claiming that the battle to save the canal had "just begun," Church and Sarbanes were in an unenviable position. "The outlook on the second Treaty is far from certain," White House aides lamented to Carter. "Laxalt claims 33 solid votes against" it. For the moment, the crisis involving Arizona's junior senator seemed to have paralyzed the administration. Seeming to thrive on the publicity he was receiving, DeConcini told the press, "It's not my problem what Panama thinks." As the debates dragged on, Church, tired and discouraged, slumped on a couch in his hideaway office and said, "My version of hell is having to listen to DeConcini drone on about the Panama Canal for eternity."[46]

Behind the scenes Church and Sarbanes joined Byrd in trying to smother DeConcini's reservation, without turning the Arizona senator and his backers against the treaties. They "walked a tightrope," Ambassador Jorden wrote later, "and there was no safety net beneath them." By then, the Idaho senator may himself have been wondering if he could vote for agreements that did not make clear the U. S.'s firm commitment to stay out of Panama's internal matters.[47]

Waving off the White House, Church, Sarbanes, and Byrd seized the initiative. They followed up on a Panamanian suggestion that Ambassador Gabriel Lewis should meet with Church, whom Lewis, Torrijos, and other Panama leaders respected highly. On Sunday, April 16, at 11 a. m. the critical meeting occurred in Church's office. Church and Lewis gathered anxiously around a coffee table with Lewis's deputy, Ricardo Bilonick, and four other Americans: Sarbanes, Byrd, Deputy Secretary of State Warren Christopher, and William Rogers, who had become a key contact person for the Panamanians. Carefully, word by word, they worked on phrasing that might save the treaties. Church typed out the final version, which endorsed "the principle of non-intervention." According to the agreement, any U. S. action to assure the canal's accessibility and security "shall not have as its purpose nor be interpreted as a right of intervention in the internal affairs of the Republic of Panama or interference with its political independence or sovereign integrity."[48]

The Panamanians were satisfied. "We have gone to Church on Sunday," Gabriel Lewis joked, "and we shall have a treaty." Senate ratification was still problematic, however.[49]

At least Dennis DeConcini was now more conciliatory. Robert Byrd shrewdly got him to co-sponsor the new "leadership reservation"–the April 16 agreement that had taken shape in Church's office. When the Arizonan tried to make an additional adjustment in the wording, Byrd eyed him coldly and said, "It has to be like this, Dennis. I will not accept any changes." Alert to Senate politics, and perhaps believing that he had satisfied his constituents, the freshman senator chose not to defy the Majority Leader. Perhaps he also realized that, as Carter's congressional liaison people observed, he had "hurt himself badly with his colleagues." To some of them, his amendment smacked more of opportunism than principle. But Church patiently worked with him, helping to bring him into the pro-treaty camp. Even minutes before the final vote, he talked intently with the Arizona senator. DeConcini later praised the Idaho senator for treating him fairly and tolerantly, and for being so well prepared and persuasive. The treaties, he insisted, would not have passed without Church's leadership.[50]

In the early evening of April 18, after adopting the leadership reservation, 73-27, the Senate barely ratified the second treaty, 68-32. For Church, pride mingled with relief. "You were terrific!" Warren Christopher told him. Sol Linowitz described his leadership as "brilliant," Robert Byrd called it "*superb*," and Indiana senator Birch Bayh dubbed it "courageous." From Panama, William Jorden assured him that "none can claim a larger share" in the treaties' success. Years later, McGovern, Sarbanes, Bumpers, DeConcini, and others insisted that Church's political courage and tenacity during the ratification debates constituted one of his greatest moments. Even some of his long-time skeptics on the Foreign Relations Committee staff complimented him. Immediately after the April 18 vote, Church chose not to stick around for the victory celebration. Fighting off a terrible cold and fatigue, he told the press that he was heading home in search of his first good night's sleep in almost two months.[51]

At home, he stayed up long enough to watch Carter's press conference. The president, jubilant over his major foreign policy victory, thanked many people—but not Church or Sarbanes. Apparently forgetting the two floor managers, Carter instead thanked John Sparkman for leading the troops. Bethine Church recalled how "stunned" she and Frank were as they watched Carter that night on television. She was "livid." Her husband laughed wryly, indicating that Carter had stayed in character. When White House aides discovered how much Carter's lapse had annoyed pro-treaty senators, they urged the president to make amends. He subsequently wrote a note to Church, congratulating him for "a superb job" and inviting him and Sarbanes to the White House. "Too little, too late," Bethine told her husband.[52]

Church nevertheless felt good about his role in behalf of the treaties. Columnist Carl Rowen, looking to the future, believed that the Idahoan had "truly won the mantle of the Senate Foreign Relations Committee." Despite such praise, however, Church had a nagging sense that the canal issue might prove to be a larger political burden than the Vietnam War had been.[53]

VII

Events bore out his suspicions. "Now hear this," warned the vice commander of Idaho's American Legion, in a published letter to Church. According to the Legionnaire, Church had sold his constituents "down the river" and might as well "kiss. . . re-election in 1980 goodby [sic]." At a meeting of angry citizens in Post Falls, one person announced that it was "time to separate Church and state." Several hundred miles to the south, in Idaho Falls, petitions for Church's resignation were reportedly "coming in by the hundreds daily." In Rupert, a group of parents tried to rescind Church's invitation to speak at the local high school's upcoming commencement exercises.[54]

Church increasingly regretted his decision not to confront more forcefully the treaties' critics in Idaho. The canal issue had unleashed even greater furies than he had expected. Looking back, he thought that he might have educated his constituents more effectively.[55]

Such thinking was probably wishful. Later study suggested that Americans became more emotional about the Panama Canal the more they thought about it. Preconceptions about "our" canal seemed to defy logic or the facts. The "loss" of the canal stirred larger fears of national decline, social flux, and economic uncertainty. As much as any issue at the time, the treaties catalyzed broad-based anxieties about a host of threats to the American way of life.[56]

In that context, arguments that Church hoped would make the treaties more acceptable collided with a wall of public opinion. Church tried, for example, to show how unfair it was for the U. S. to claim permanently what was in effect "an American colony stretching across this little country" of Panama. At one point he asked Paul Laxalt to "suppose there was a strip of land 10 miles wide and 40 miles long in Nevada." Would Nevadans accept the "humiliation" of having that area "occupied by a foreign power, controlled by foreign military forces"? Church concluded that Americans could hardly expect Panamanians to accept an arrangement that U. S. citizens themselves would find intolerable. Contrary to Church's argument, however, a Harris poll found that few Americans believed it was wrong for the U. S. to own a canal that bisected another nation.[57]

A similar reaction awaited Church's warning that Panamanians would forcibly resist continued U. S. intrusion on their sovereignty. Church worried that the U. S., in order to protect the canal against sabotage and guerrilla warfare, might have to send tens of thousands of troops to Panama, thereby setting the stage for another Vietnam. He believed it was precautionary, not cowardly, to avoid such a conflict. Sixty-five percent of Americans disagreed with him, according to one poll. They believed instead that "we should not let the threat of mob action or sabotage from a little country like Panama force us to give up what is ours." Another poll indicated that Americans, above all, did not want to let a tiny nation intimidate them.[58]

Many Americans, as Church observed, were distressed "that somehow things are not as they used to be." Their feelings in that regard may have been even stronger than he assumed. As a whole, Americans might have applauded, as Church did, the retreat of empires and the growing "respect for the rights of others"; but a solid majority still saw no reason for the U. S. to "give up" its canal. More than property was at stake. Also in danger was an era full of nostalgic memories of national power and destiny. As that era grew more remote, many Americans clutched all the more tightly to its vestiges. In April 1978, toward the end of the treaty debates, 60 percent of the public still opposed "giving control of the Panama Canal to Panama."[59]

As he confronted what to him were often "preposterous" arguments that defied common sense, facts, and logic, Church sometimes wondered if he had plunged into "some chapter out of Alice in Wonderland." Opponents of the treaties seemed not to have given much thought to how they would protect the canal against violent upheaval in Panama. The threat of bloody conflict was no figment of Church's imagination. Ambassador Jorden discovered later that Omar Torrijos had placed special National Guard units in the field on the night of the final treaty vote to stop operation of the canal if the Senate rejected the agreements. Torrijos himself, upon learning that the Senate had approved the treaties, said publicly that the canal had come "within two votes of being destroyed." Jorden concluded that Torrijos was not exaggerating: ". . . After three months of insults and personal attacks, acting on impulse and out of bitterness, he could have done it, and probably would have." Jorden believed that sixty-eight senators had kept the canal open and perhaps prevented a war that could have claimed thousands of American lives. Flying to Washington, D. C., after the treaties' approval, he reflected gratefully upon the key individuals who had saved the agreements, among them "Church and Sarbanes, masters of the floor, protectors of the right."[60]

VIII

By late April Church was already worried about another controversial foreign policy issue: the sale of arms to Saudi Arabia. "Just when nobody needs it," wrote columnist James Reston, here was one more divisive problem. Congress squared off again, but this time, according to the *Baltimore Sun*, "over an issue it feels should never have been forced upon it and in this form."[61]

At the center of the Carter administration's decision to force the issue was a fundamental reality: the oil crisis of 1973-74 had catapulted Saudi Arabia to a position of staggering influence. The Saudis had reaped massive revenues and demonstrated with stunning effectiveness the industrial world's reliance on their oil. Good relations with them had never seemed more necessary to U. S. policy makers, but the political price tag was increasingly expensive. In early 1978 the Saudis asked to buy sixty F-15s, America's top fighter jets, as protection against internal revolt and outside invasion. According to the Saudi minister of petroleum, a refusal to sell would indicate that Americans were "not concerned with our security and you don't appreciate our friendship."

Carter approved the deal in order to maintain American access to moderately priced Saudi oil. He also hoped to enhance a peace settlement that he was trying to effect between Israel and Egypt, a settlement that the Saudis might wreck. The Israelis, however, feared that the proposed transaction only placed them in greater peril. They and their U. S. supporters found it psychologically unsettling as well as militarily threatening. Sale of the F-15s would mean, as a representative of the America Jewish Committee asserted, that the U. S. had rejected "its special relationship with Israel."[62]

To make the sale acceptable to Israel and Egypt, as well as to Congress, the Carter administration designed an arms package. Israel would receive fifteen F-15s, plus seventy-five F-16s; Egypt would get fifty F-5s. The F-16s were not quite as powerful or versatile as the F-15s, and the F-5s were even less sophisticated. Church opposed the sales. When he first heard of Carter's arms package, he thought immediately of America's earlier mistake in supplying weapons to India and Pakistan. That mistake had helped to produce a savage war. Providing the Israelis, Saudis, and Egyptians with weapons could produce equally tragic results. Church also disapproved of the administration's tactics. By tying $5 billion worth of aircraft sales to three countries into one legislative package, the administration limited the Senate's opportunity to consider the separate sales on their own merits. "It's an insult to the Foreign Relations Committee," Church said heatedly one evening at Connecticut senator Abraham Ribicoff's house. The White House was in effect handing the Senate a complex, multi-layered arms deal and saying, "Take it or leave it." Church objected as well to the timing of the proposed sales. Few plans seemed more likely to jeopardize the fragile peace process in the Middle East than one that injected additional sophisticated weaponry into it.[63]

Although Church personally rejected the arms package, his course of action regarding it resurrected the familiar charge that he was unreliable. In a surprise move, he presented the administration's case for the arms sales to the Foreign Relations Committee and then, in another apparent flip-flop, he voted with the opposition. In retrospect, he understood why people had trouble making sense of what he had done. "I've always had a weakness, if it is a weakness, for trying to get things accomplished legislatively," he explained later. His penchant for building coalitions had led him to work with the administration and had likewise probably encouraged the administration to turn to him.[64]

Carter desperately wanted the arms package to pass and, if possible, without a highly publicized, bruising congressional debate. He thus claimed that the deal, as a key to peace and stability in the Middle East, represented nothing less than "a vital test of our national purpose." The aircraft sales, he argued, would be gestures of friendship to the three countries, would bolster moderate governments, and would dissuade Saudi Arabia, "a firm friend of the United States," from turning elsewhere to protect itself from Soviet-armed neighbors. While Carter portrayed the arms deal as offering a "stark and fundamental" choice to the United States, he anxiously tried to defuse the issue on Capitol Hill. This strategy proved impossible, given intense feelings and vigorous lobbying between Israelis and Saudis over their contested "special relationships" with the U. S.[65]

In late April top administration officials looked to Church for help, asking him to present the case for the arms package to the Foreign Relations Committee. To get his support they spent considerable time with him and acceded to several of his demands: the U. S. would strip the F-15s of much of their offensive capability and would condition their sale by requiring the Saudis to station them as far from Israel as possible; the Saudis would not buy additional planes from France; and Carter would avoid future arms packages.[66]

Church agreed to seek a consensus on the committee – but without saying whether he would vote for the arms deal. Although he personally opposed the transaction, he, like the administration, worried that a bitter debate would seriously hurt the U. S. in the volatile Middle East. He explained later that he wanted "to avoid a showdown" or "a jungle-like situation in the Senate." To that end, he consented to present the administration's proposal on its own terms, but not as its advocate or as someone committed to voting for it. "I would see whether the committee would buy it," he recalled. He was even prepared to swing his own vote behind the deal, but only if the committee overwhelmingly approved it. His support at that point would simply make the committee verdict more decisive and might thereby head off a rancorous Senate debate. Looking back, he wished that he had told the administration to "go elsewhere" for help. Instead, he put himself in an awkward and perhaps untenable situation. Although he believed that he had disassociated himself from the administration's case when he presented it, several committee members found him so persuasive that he reportedly convinced them to vote for the arms package.[67]

Church nevertheless quickly determined that the arms package lacked the broad support necessary to avoid a harsh Senate debate. At that point, as he later explained, he "had no further interest in pressing for a compromise that was not going to produce the desired result"–namely "some show of unanimity." Because the Senate would be badly divided anyhow, he chose to stand by his own preferences. On May 11, just before the Foreign Relations Committee voted, he went to the Senate floor to inform Robert Byrd that the deal lacked support. The Majority Leader was puzzled. By his count, the committee was going to back the administration 9-7. Not so, Church told him. Flabbergasted, Byrd discovered that Church himself would oppose the arms package. Shortly thereafter, the Idaho senator's vote resulted in a committee split, 8-8.[68]

The administration nevertheless eked out a victory. Only a majority vote on the committee could have killed the arms package. The proposal thus went to the Senate, albeit without recommendation. On May 15, following ten hours of impassioned debate that Carter had wanted to avoid, the Senate approved the deal, 54-44. Never before had the Israeli lobby taken such a beating in Congress. Church not only voted against the sale, but tried to rally the opposition.[69]

Church's apparent flip-flop opened him to criticism. Several exasperated White House officials claimed that the senator had not kept his word. Carter rebuked his staff: "The next time you get a commitment, let's get some earnest money." *Time* especially criticized Church for seeming "to lose his nerve." The magazine even concluded that, except for his "stunning switch," the unpleasant floor debate might not have occurred.[70]

On the Foreign Relations Committee, Church surprised none other than his old friend George McGovern. Like Church, the South Dakota Democrat strongly objected to U. S. arms sales and to the timing of Carter's aircraft deal. Yet he concluded that the deal was already on the table, and was thus difficult for the Senate to reject. United States-Saudi relations would suffer unnecessarily. The Saudis would probably buy French aircraft whose placement and capacities lacked U. S.-imposed conditions. As a result, Israel would be no safer and the Saudis would believe the U. S. had rebuffed them. Following Church's May 9 presentation of the administration's case to the committee, McGovern concluded that the Idahoan now also favored the Mideast deal. Church's subsequent vote against the arms package astonished and disappointed him.[71]

To some observers, including McGovern and National Security Advisor Zbigniew Brzezinski, Church had caved in to pressure from the Israelis. The Idaho senator, like a large majority of his colleagues, had long been sympathetic to Israel. Some people believed that Tom Dine had cultivated his pro-Israel sentiments. After serving as the senator's chief foreign policy assistant for five years, he had become the director of the American-Israeli Public Affairs Committee (AIPAC), a powerful lobbying group. In fact, however, he may not have championed Israel all that much when he worked for Church. One Foreign Relations Committee staffer had not even realized that Dine was Jewish until he took charge of AIPAC. More influential in Church's thinking about Israel, according to some individuals, was the increasing importance of Jewish contributions to the senator's campaigns.[72]

Church's pro-Israeli sympathies went far beyond campaign politics, however. The senator emphasized that Israel had the only democratic government in the Middle East and was America's "only reliable ally" in that region. "I don't remember ever having held a different view," he said. "Israel is about as old an independent state as I am a senator. We have coexisted together." He admired the Israelis not just as valued allies but also for their history of survival against overwhelming odds. When he discussed privately the mass killing of Jews in places such as Babayar and Auschwitz, he verged on tears. Moreover, he liked the political liberalism of many American Jews. "Among the well-to-do business people of this country," he said with amused hyperbole, "it's only the Jews who tend to be liberals." The big-money conservatives tended to be "WASPs." For a variety of reasons, Church thus considered the Jews to be "a rather exemplary people."[73]

That was not his opinion of the Arabs. Cleve Corlett noted, for example, that "he had a rather visceral reaction to the Saudis," whom he saw as "fair-weather friends." The multinational investigations of the oil embargo had shown, for example, that King Faisal had even ordered the companies to withhold fuel from the U. S. Navy.[74]

In 1977-78, from what had been the multinationals subcommittee, Church received additional information detrimental to the U. S.-Saudi relationship. By then the multinationals subcommittee had disappeared into the more traditional Foreign Economic Policy Subcommittee, which had a smaller staff and a diminished investigative role. The staff, however, continued to turn up troubling data. In early 1977, OPEC raised oil prices by 10 percent; the Saudis went along with the price hike, claiming that bad weather had forced them to cut back on their oil production. When Jerry Levinson shrewdly placed a call to the U. S. Naval Station in Saudi Arabia and asked innocently, "How's the weather?," he made a telling discovery. The weather had been fine for months. Church, who received regular staff briefings, had to ponder what was happening. Perhaps the Saudis were less of a moderating force than U. S. policy makers made them out to be. Perhaps the administration, alert to the power of the Saudis' oil weapon, had downplayed Saudi complicity in the price hikes. Or, another possibility, perhaps the oil fields were not as healthy as they were supposed to be—which, if true, meant that the Saudis had less of an economic stranglehold on industrial countries than many people believed. When the vote on Carter's arms package occurred, Church's subcommittee staff was still pulling together its findings; but the senator could only wonder if the administration was accommodating the Saudis too much.[75]

Despite his firm views on the Middle East, Church had seemed to waffle during the arms package debate, thus raising the old questions about his dependability. A headline for a Rowland Evans/Robert Novak column dubbed him "the inconstant senator." And several people who dealt with him regarding the aircraft sale felt betrayed. National Security Advisor Zbigniew Brzezinski dismissed him as a man who "in the end failed to come through." According to Brzezinski, Church had "irritated Carter profoundly."[76]

He had, however, adhered more firmly to his convictions and wavered far less than his critics said. His insistence that he had not reversed his position, and had not violated any understanding with the White House, was no mere attempt to save face. He had considerable evidence on his side. Any number of times he had objected to the arms deal, publicly and privately. In late April, when Carter invited him and Sarbanes to the White House to thank them belatedly for managing the Panama treaties, the two senators seized the opportunity to express their opposition to the arms sales. But, as Sarbanes recalled, Carter in effect ignored their protests and limited the discussion to "some small talk." On May 9, Church had indeed told the Foreign Relations Committee that the White House had "made a bona fide effort to meet" Senate concerns, and he had urged his colleagues to consider fairly the administration's proposed arms sale. But beyond that he had done little more than note briefly several ways in which the administration had tried to accommodate critics of the arms sale, and he had prefaced his remarks by questioning the timing of the proposed transaction.[77]

Robert Beckel's account of the backstage maneuvering over the arms sale echoed Church's. Beckel, who worked as closely as any White House aide with Church on the aircraft deal, was certain that the senator had never indicated that he would vote for it. Church had agreed simply, in Beckel's words, "to find a consensus that would avoid a brutal fight between the Carter administration and the Israeli lobby." His efforts in that regard had been genuine. Beckel recalled that Church had told the administration "flat out" that he personally would oppose the deal. To Beckel's chagrin, some White House people subsequently told the press that Church "had stabbed us in the back." The charge was simply not true, Beckel claimed. Frank Moore, Carter's congressional liaison, and Douglas Bennet, who handled congressional relations for the State Department, were equally adamant that Church had not acted in bad faith.[78]

IX

Church's vote against the arms package was still bad news for the White House. It portended rocky times for Carter, according to columnists Rowland Evans and Robert Novak. They guessed that when John Sparkman retired in a few months and Church became chair of the Foreign Relations Committee, the Idaho senator would make the administration miserable. "With friends like Frank Church," one Democratic senator told them, "the President needs no enemies." The comment was misleading from one angle. After all, as Beckel pointed out, Church had been cooperative and helpful in presenting the administration's case to the committee. Still, the fact remained that he had ultimately gone his own way. And a few days after the arms package vote he published an article that faulted the administration for jeopardizing peace in the Middle East and for showing the Arab countries that their "oil weapon" could alter U. S. policy. The White House had better stay "on the good side of Frank Church," warned an unidentified Foreign Relations Committee aide. "For with the troubles the President is having on Capitol Hill, the White House needs Frank Church more than Frank Church needs the White House."[79]

In some respects, moreover, the distance between Church and the White House seemed to be growing. He kept emphasizing that, as chair of the Foreign Relations Committee, he would follow an independent course. In no sense would he serve as the White House's "agent."[80]

He also criticized the administration for falling back on Cold War kinds of rhetoric. In mid-1978, at a breakfast meeting with reporters, he observed that Carter's message seemed more and more to be that "the Russians are coming." The president apparently felt compelled to justify his policies, including the sale of the F-15s to the Saudis, by placing them in a Cold War context. Beware of globalizing disputes, Church warned the White House. The old habit of invoking the communist threat imposed huge ideological burdens on U. S. policy and was also politically dangerous. "If you keep throwing this red meat to the lions in the Senate," Church asked, "how do you expect to tame them?" How, for example, did Carter hope to gain support for normalizing relations with Cuba and China, and for reaching an arms limitation agreement with the Soviets?[81]

Church sensed accurately that the administration was shifting direction. Although in September 1978 Carter negotiated superbly the Camp David peace accords between Israel and Egypt, his administration was otherwise moving from its early reformist, non-military agenda. The president's "brief, fragile experiment in revisionism," in the words of journalist William Greider, had run up against an increasingly anxious and security-minded American public. Having exhausted exorbitant amounts of political capital fighting for the Panama treaties, the administration was now more susceptible to militaristic appeals.[82]

Right-wing pressures were building on Church as well. The New Right had narrowly lost the brawl over the Panama treaties, but it had not failed in its larger political war. "We've raised money," New Right organizer Richard Viguerie said excitedly, "and rallied our troops for the battles ahead." Church unquestionably preferred not to fight those battles, filled as they increasingly were with appeals to fears and prejudice. Once again, the civic-minded, democratic culture that he prized seemed all too vulnerable.[83]

Although he looked forward to becoming chair of the Foreign Relations Committee in 1979, he suspected that time was running out for him politically. Even before the Panama treaties fight, he commented pessimistically about his future. A four-term Democrat from Idaho, he said, constituted a kind of miracle that could not last.[84]

The Churches encounter a gun-toting Idaho constituent in a small Idaho town during the 1980 campaign. *Courtesy Barry Kough.*

Chapter Nineteen

"A Conspiracy of Circumstances": 1979-1980

"CONGRATULATIONS ON your chairmanship," read the telegram in early 1979 from "William E. Borah." "What took you so long?" The message amused Church, who had just taken charge of the Committee on Foreign Relations (CFR). "Borah keeps watch over me from his portrait on the wall," Church replied, noting how pleased he was to follow in the footsteps of his boyhood idol.[1]

Although Church had attained a long-sought goal, the last years of his fourth term proved bittersweet. As one of his top assistants observed later, "a conspiracy of circumstances" worked against him. Foremost among them was the growing power of the New Right across the country and especially in Idaho, where Church became the target of a vicious campaign to prevent his reelection. As he tempered political courage with caution, some disappointed liberals concluded that he had suffered a failure of nerve. Such criticism, while understandable in some respects, slighted his accomplishments: his perceptive, well-articulated critiques of America's changing place in the world, for example, as well as his legislative achievements in protecting wilderness areas. And such criticism also overlooked the fact that, by 1979, he was already fighting for political survival in the dirtiest campaign of his career.[2]

I

Initially, however, he attended more to the politics of the CFR than his reelection. Following J. William Fulbright's 1974 defeat, the CFR had lost visibility and influence, a trend that Church intended to reverse. Like Fulbright, who had guided the committee from 1959 to 1975, he wanted the CFR to strengthen Congress's foreign policy role. He talked, for example, of getting away from a "crisis management" approach by using televised hearings to address such long-range issues as the growing economic challenges from Germany and Japan, informing the public and providing the administration with ideas. He reiterated as well his opposition to the unfortunate belief "that anything that happens in the world is our business"– a belief that had fueled grievous examples of U. S. interventionism.[3]

Church's expectations regarding the CFR were clear, but observers differed sharply over what kind of leader he would be. Former Pennsylvania senator Joseph S. Clark, who had worked on the CFR with him and under Fulbright, predicted that Church would be "the greatest chairman of the committee of the past half-century." While Clark articulated liberal hopes, the *Richmond News Leader* expressed conservative fears that U. S. foreign policy would resemble "a china shop into which a bull by the name of Frank Church has plunged."[4]

Heading the CFR turned out to be far more frustrating than such commentators, or the senator himself, could have imagined. Soon he had reason to rue the timing of his chairmanship. Under Fulbright, the committee's reputation had been more liberal than that of the Senate as a whole. The 1978 elections, however, had cut sharply into the CFR's liberal base, especially with the defeats of Iowa Democrat Dick Clark and Clifford Case, Church's long-time Republican ally from New Jersey. One-third of the committee's fifteen members were new and included arch-conservative Republicans Jesse Helms of North Carolina and California's S. I. Hayakawa. Moreover, there were indications that Howard Baker and Charles Percy wanted to regain credibility they had lost among GOP conservatives when they voted for the Panama Canal treaties.[5]

In 1979 the Republican conservatives bolstered their position by establishing for the first time on the CFR a separate minority staff. For years the CFR had been remarkably bipartisan in structure and approach. In 1973 long-time chief of staff Carl Marcy emphasized that "the staff's loyalties belong to the Committee as an *institution*, and not to any individual or group within it." He once complimented a staffer for his work on a committee trip: "Neither your name nor your picture appeared anywhere." By the late 1970s, such assumptions about discreet, anonymous aides were outdated. With the implementation of separate majority and minority staffing, the CFR formally adopted a partisan format.[6]

The change was primarily the work of Jesse Helms. With a sharp tongue, a country-boy demeanor, and a true-believer mentality, Helms had done more than any other senator to shape the hard-core conservatism of the New Right. Church, according to one aide, looked upon him "as a total disaster." But the North Carolina senator was a growing political force who relished the title of "Senator No"—evidence, he said, of his opposition to liberalism. Moving to the CFR in 1979, he seized upon Senate reorganization rules by which a majority of the minority could demand a budget and office space. Over the objections of New York's Jacob Javits, the committee's ranking Republican, Helms prevailed. With a separate minority staff, he and his conservative allies now had more leverage and were eager to apply it, although Javits was able to mitigate Helms's influence somewhat by insisting that his own person, the very capable Peter Lakeland, head the staff. Nevertheless, during the CFR's mark-up of the strategic arms limitation treaty between the U. S. and the Soviet Union (SALT II) in the fall of 1979, one observer noted that the relationships between the majority and minority staffs were so adversarial that the situation resembled that of a courtroom.[7]

While the new staff structure undercut Church's authority, so did the CFR's nine subcommittees. Ironically, Church himself had added to their power and independence. As a very junior member of the committee he had pushed for separate subcommittee staffs despite Carl Marcy's warning that a fragmented committee would be difficult to manage. In 1972, Church's subcommittee on multinationals became the first CFR unit to have a separate staff. Church also turned his subcommittee into a powerful, highly publicized vehicle, and jealously guarded its prerogatives. Marcy and others believed he was setting a bad precedent and warned him that he might someday inherit a fractured CFR. When that time came, Church replied, he would deal with the problem.[8]

In 1979 that moment arrived. Under John Sparkman's sleepy leadership, the subcommittee chairs had built tiny fiefdoms. When Church tried to move major legislation from the subcommittees to the central committee, he encountered stiff resistance. "The time when committee chairmen ruled as dictators is over," one senior senator protested. Ohio Democrat John Glenn was especially miffed at what he perceived as heavy-handed efforts to centralize the committee. By 1980 he and Church, mainly because of clashing personalities, were barely on speaking terms.[9]

In order to take command of the CFR, Church desperately needed not only to curb the power of the subcommittees, but also to reorganize the staff, whose morale was sagging. "A good many" of the staffers, according to Church partisan Ira Nordlicht, shared neither his views nor his investigative bent. Nordlicht recommended that he create "a lean, fast-moving professional staff" more in tune with his sentiments. In this regard, Church encountered powerful legislative currents. A 1975 resolution allowing senators to hire personal legislative assistants for committee work had, within its first year, added almost three hundred staffers to the Senate. By 1979 senators' personal designees constituted a substantial layer of additional personnel at the CFR. When Church took control of the committee, the staff of seventy-eight people resembled an assortment of tiny constituencies, each protective of its own interests. His subsequent effort to impose discipline on the staff and alter its personnel created bad feelings and controversy.[10]

Hoping to assert more control, Church chose William B. Bader as staff director. Confident and experienced, Bader, a foreign policy intellectual, had a Ph.D. in Modern European History from Princeton and had worked briefly at the Central Intelligence Agency (CIA), writing national intelligence estimates with people such as William Bundy. As a staffer on the CFR from 1965 to 1969, he had brilliantly helped to expose the Johnson administration's deceptions during the 1964 Tonkin Gulf incident. In the mid-Seventies he had headed a task force on Church's Select Committee on Intelligence. His respect for the Idaho senator had improved substantially since the 1960s, when he had considered him rather egotistical. Indeed, by the late Seventies probably no one but Church could have attracted him back to Capitol Hill. Certainly he shared his boss's desire to resuscitate the CFR and, as a protégé of Carl Marcy, who had retired in the mid-Seventies, he hoped to restore some of the sense of anonymity, professionalism, and nonpartisanship that had marked the staff a decade earlier.[11]

Opinions about Bader were seldom equivocal. Several people at the CFR, including one of its senior senators, viewed him as a terrible choice. Critics nicknamed him "Darth Bader," after the Darth Vader villain in the popular *Star Wars* movies. Some individuals complained that his loyalties rested less with Church than with the foreign policy "establishment" at the Pentagon or the State Department. One senator even referred to the new staff director as "that creep from the Pentagon," even though Bader had spent only sixteen months there in a policy position.[12]

But Bader had notable defenders, including Maryland senator Paul Sarbanes, arms negotiator Ralph Earle, II, and journalist John Averill, who had watched Capitol Hill for years. Columnist Jack Anderson described him as "a scholarly but tough professional" who was helping Church strengthen the CFR. And CFR staffer Rick Inderfurth insisted that the "Darth Bader" nickname was far off the mark. Drawing a different analogy from the *Star Wars* movies, he laughed that Bader more closely resembled the wise and effective Obi-Wan-Kenobi character.[13]

Bader labored under less than optimum conditions. To reduce the CFR staff from seventy-eight, which according to Averill included "an awful lot of deadwood," to around fifty-two, and to hire people with expertise in particular foreign policy areas, was an unenviable task. Unfortunately for Bader, Church also wanted to streamline the CFR but shied away from the necessary personnel decisions. The senator had many considerable skills, but personnel management did not rank high among them. Most people found him kind, caring, and sensitive; he could generate fierce loyalties. Because he disliked confrontation, however, he was reluctant to "get tough" with staffers or colleagues. Twice, his administrative assistant Mike Wetherell fired individuals, only to have them plead successfully with Church to reinstate them. Aide Patrick Shea recalled urging the senator again and again to take someone to task: "He would say, 'Yes, I'll do it tomorrow.' Then, tomorrow would never come."[14]

Bader's difficult job of firing more than two dozen CFR staffers within several months thus became even harder. Sometimes the director believed that he had been "left hanging." In retrospect, Church wished that he would personally have asked for resignations from all the CFR staff and then rehired people he wanted. Instead, all of the employees initially stayed on, not knowing who would survive Bader's "Friday afternoon massacres." The situation encouraged suspicion, unhappiness, and political intrigue. "It just became a ship of fools, in terms of people fighting with one another," Pat Shea remembered. Moreover, partly because of the addition of ten GOP minority staffers, the staff was soon back up to seventy. "Instead of a lean, highly qualified staff, we now have a fat, mixed staff," one member complained.[15]

Evaluating Church's first few weeks as CFR chair, columnists Rowland Evans and Robert Novak described him as a "Senate rough rider" who had dismayed the administration and alienated his colleagues.

The administration had anticipated difficulties with him, but was reportedly surprised that he was so quick to question its policies. "We were hopeful" about Church as an ally, a presidential advisor told *Time* magazine, "but the hope is fading." Evans and Novak compared the senator's style to that of a "preacher," and said that he had angered particularly Helms and Glenn.[16]

"Strain and Rivalry Plague Senate Foreign Relations Committee," read a May 23, 1979 *New York Times* headline. White House officials contended that friction on the CFR impeded foreign policy legislation. A State Department aide wondered if anyone was in charge.[17]

Nine months later, collisions within the CFR still produced sparks. Nebraska's conservative Democrat Edward Zorinsky, a new member, objected that "the committee and its staff are rapidly becoming the laughing stock of Capitol Hill." The committee, he contended, lacked "credibility and clout."[18]

Columnist Jack Anderson disagreed, arguing that by 1980 Church had rebuilt the CFR into a "bulwark of strength." By then Bill Bader proudly viewed the staff as truly first rate. He believed, moreover, that the committee's internal divisions had made it more effective. Previously, its predominantly liberal membership had typically encountered opposition on the Senate floor. The committee's virtual unanimity on the Panama Canal treaties, for example, had contrasted jarringly with the mood of the full Senate, where almost a third dissented. The arrival of conservatives such as Helms, Hayakawa, and Zorinsky added to Church's woes, but increased the CFR's leverage outside its doors. Because the committee now more reflected the Senate as a whole, according to Bader, its internal debates mirrored those of the larger institution. Compromises that the CFR hammered out in its own ranks thus had a better chance of Senate passage. "It is far better to fight those battles out in the committee," Bader argued, than on the Senate floor. He was certain that, after a rocky beginning, the CFR staff was poised for greatness. Church was equally confident that the committee was making progress.[19]

II

Impeding the committee's advance, however, were trends within the Senate as a whole that bothered Church. Centrifugal tendencies marked not just the CFR, but also its parent body. Sixty-one of Church's colleagues had entered the Senate within the past decade, and *Time* described them as "aggressively independent." Church appreciated the fact that many of them, in reaction to the tragedies of Vietnam and Watergate, favored a stronger Congress over the imperial presidency. He also applauded their political independence, a trait that he associated with himself. But what Robert Byrd described as "a growing spirit of 'doing one's own thing' and of resisting the established way of doing things" exacted a price that made the Idaho senator uneasy.[20]

All through his career, Church had affectionately viewed the Senate as an institution with hallowed traditions of seniority, etiquette, and order. Granted, over the years he had himself challenged old-style politics. Although his organization had come to represent what one Idaho Democrat described as "the lifeblood of the party," he had largely avoided involvement in the party's business back home. In the 1960s he had challenged his party's president on Vietnam. And in 1972, he had championed the "new" versus "status quo" politics. He nevertheless had a deep fondness for tradition and was increasingly ambivalent about the Senate's shift from its hierarchical and deferential past.[21]

After more than two decades in the Senate, he spoke wistfully of his early years on the Hill. His younger colleagues were freer of their Senate elders and discipline than he had been, but he was uncertain if the change was "for the better or the worse." Institutional efficiency and loyalty had declined, encouraging legislative chaos. In notable ways Church, by now in his mid-fifties and the eighth-ranking senator, missed the old days.[22]

III

As the passage in early 1979 of the Taiwan Relations Act demonstrated, however, Church had not lost his enthusiasm for building legislative coalitions. In his debut as chair of the Foreign Relations Committee, he took to the trenches, helping to achieve a historic breakthrough in America's Asian relations. The act was a political victory, salvaging a normalized relationship with the People's Republic of China (PRC) and, at the same time, providing for continued U. S. relations with the Republic of China (ROC) on Taiwan. Given the inflammable political setting, the achievement was remarkable.

Polls in the late Seventies showed consistently that Americans favored diplomatic ties with the PRC by wide margins, but not at Taiwan's expense. Following the communist takeover of China in 1949, the U. S. had recognized only the exile ROC government and, in the 1954 Mutual Defense Treaty, guaranteed its security. In 1972, however, Richard Nixon and Henry Kissinger had taken steps toward a new U. S. Asian policy by establishing informal relationships with mainland China.[23]

Jimmy Carter hoped to formalize those ties but, to do so, he raced the clock. As his China specialist, Michel Oksenberg, warned, domestic situations within China and the U. S. rarely allowed for improved relations. "We may be nearing the end of such a period—if it has not already passed—and we must seize the opportunity," Oksenberg advised. Carter was determined not to let that opportunity slip away, but at the same time was well aware of the lingering power of the pro-Taiwan forces in Congress and did not wish to spark a disruptive political debate resembling that over the Panama Canal. He thus opted for secret negotiations with the PRC. The PRC, in turn, continued to demand that the U. S. end official relations with Taiwan and abrogate the 1954 security guarantee. On December 15, 1978, without previously consulting Congress, Carter announced an agreement to normalize relations with Beijing at the start of the new year. The agreement extended full diplomatic recognition to the PRC as China's only government, broke diplomatic relations with the ROC, and terminated, within one year, the 1954 treaty. The administration sent Congress an ambiguous, hastily-drafted bill by which the U. S. would conduct purely informal relationships with "the people on Taiwan."[24]

Carter had touched one of the most sensitive nerves in post-World War II American politics. "*BETRAYAL*," cried Dr. W. S. McBirnie, president of the Community Churches of America. Here was more evidence that the U. S. was giving ground to communism. "TODAY THE PANAMA CANAL, TOMORROW TAIWAN," read a sign on Capitol Hill during the canal debates, and the prophecy seemed to be coming true. Ronald Reagan rebuked the administration for having "abandoned Taiwan to the Red Chinese," providing yet another example of "Uncle Sam putting his tail between his legs and creeping away. . . ." He also cabled an apology to the Taiwan government.[25]

Frank Church had no quarrel with Carter's desire to normalize relations with the PRC. For years he had criticized America's "absurd" view of mainland China as a nonentity. He thus praised the administration for having finally brought "American policy into line with Asian realities."[26]

He realized, however, that Carter's treatment of the Taiwan issue had created a political flashpoint. Polls in 1978 showed that Americans, by a three-to-one margin, would not accept the "derecognition" of Taiwan as the price for better relations with the mainland. According to the American Conservative Union, sixty-four senators held the same position. Even rumors that the administration would terminate the mutual defense treaty with Taiwan had precipitated an anxious response. Six months before Carter announced the China agreement, the Senate, by a vote of 94 to 0, added a nonbinding amendment to the International Security Assistance Act of 1978, asking that Carter not alter the treaty's status without first consulting Congress. By subsequently ignoring Congress, the president surrounded himself with legislative dynamite. On December 12, 1978, Barry Goldwater and twenty-three other members of Congress brought a federal suit against the administration, contending that it had no constitutional authority to terminate a treaty without the Senate's consent.[27]

Despite Church's overall approval of Carter's China policy, the Idaho senator agreed that the president had mishandled the Taiwan issue. On February 5 he characterized the administration's recent agreement as "woefully inadequate to the task, ambiguous in language, and uncertain in tone." Although Church had left China in 1946 with little respect for Chiang Kai-shek's Nationalists (the creators of the ROC), as a senator he had always deemed Taiwan "a loyal ally and a major trading partner." Any understanding that threatened the security of the Taiwanese was unacceptable to him personally and was, he knew, politically doomed. Certainly in his own state, he found little maneuvering room on the issue and may have been reluctant to add yet another obstacle to his reelection chances. Idahoans, as aide Larry LaRocco informed him, believed "that an old friend [Taiwan] is now left out in the cold." Both houses of the Idaho legislature had already petitioned Congress and the president "to maintain diplomatic relations and the mutual defense treaty with the Republic of China."[28]

Well aware that he faced his first test as the CFR's chair, Church set out to rescue the China agreement, knowing that its success depended on a wide consensus within the United States. In February he thus held extensive hearings on U. S.-China relations and, as journalist Robert Kaiser observed, "ardently courted" the support of Jacob Javits in order to build a bipartisan coalition.[29]

Javits, like John Sherman Cooper, Clifford Case, and Charles Mathias, was the kind of liberal Republican with whom Church had allied so successfully over the years. In foreign policy, Javits had supported the Cooper-Church amendment and authored the War Powers Act. His praise for Church's "first-rate intellect" carried special weight because of his own brilliant reputation. But he also considered his Idaho colleague a "warm friend" and a truly "great senator." Church, in turn, respected Javits greatly.[30]

In February, as the administration watched nervously, Church and Javits labored over legislation that would protect both Taiwan and Carter's agreement with Beijing. "The Carter administration was quite upset," recalled Church aide Cleve Corlett. "There was a lot of handwringing and fear that the PRC would call the whole thing off," if the Senate altered the original agreement. *Time* reported that Church's interest in Taiwan's security had "startled" the administration, which had assumed that his chief objective would be to normalize relations with the PRC. Some White House officials angrily blamed him for another "flip-flop," like that over the Saudi arms sale.[31]

On February 22 the Foreign Relations Committee approved unanimously what the *Washington Post*'s Robert Kaiser labeled as "the Church compromise." The compromise sought to articulate America's concern for Taiwan without unraveling the new ties between the U. S. and the PRC. With painstakingly chosen words, the committee recommended legislation by which the United States would view anything "other than peaceful means" to unify Taiwan and the mainland as "a threat to the peace and security of the Western Pacific area." Furthermore, the U. S. would "maintain its capacity to resist" coercive actions that threatened "the security or social or economic system of the people on Taiwan."[32]

Grudgingly, the administration accepted the wording but still worried about the PRC's reaction. "We can live with" the compromise, said the assistant secretary of state for congressional relations Douglas Bennet, Jr. "But I'm not saying I'm happy with it."[33]

Despite such doubts, the compromise formed the basis of the Taiwan Relations Act, which saved the China agreement within the U. S. The act was, of course, a complex piece of legislation that ultimately included several Senate and House modifications. But, more than anyone, Church and Javits had given it life. Javits believed that their "spirit of cooperation" had set the tone for the broad consensus that developed. As Church noted proudly, the predicted acrimony on the Senate floor never developed: "We were able to obtain a united committee on the bill and, in the end, it was approved on the floor almost unamended." In late March, despite the New Right's efforts to inflame the Taiwan issue, the act won easy approval, 85-4 in the Senate and 339-50 in the House. Carter wavered before signing it, partly because some of his advisors wanted him to veto the bill lest the PRC conclude that he had negotiated in bad faith. On April 10 he signed it anyhow. Later that year Goldwater's legal challenge to the president's termination of the 1954 defense treaty failed.[34]

The administration's recognition of the PRC, combined with the Taiwan Relations Act, constituted what Harvard's John K. Fairbank called "a great diplomatic achievement." The recognized dean of America's China scholars believed the results were better than many China experts could have anticipated: "Since Peking now has latent sovereignty, we need not confront Chinese nationalism. Since Taiwan will be defensible, we have not 'abandoned' it."[35]

Although PRC officials objected to the Taiwan Relations Act, they went along with it. In mid-April, when Church and four other members of the Foreign Relations Committee visited China, Deputy Prime Minister Deng Xiaoping lectured them firmly that the act had almost derailed the normalization process. But Cleve Corlett, who was there with Church, noted that Deng's comments on Taiwan consumed only a very brief segment of the hour-long meeting. For the most part, Deng was friendly and seemed to agree with Church that the U. S. and China both shared a long-term interest in establishing good relations.[36]

In Taiwan, as well, initial fury over America's recognition of China gave way to a reluctant acceptance. When Carter first announced the China agreement, outraged demonstrators had taken to the streets, breaking windows of the car containing Deputy Secretary of State Warren Christopher. The turmoil diminished, however, once the Taiwan Relations Act placed the U. S. and Taiwan in what one scholar later described as "a unique relationship"–one that cut the old ties while paradoxically maintaining previous associations. Church received expressions of "deepest appreciation" from the ROC's premier and "profound gratitude" from Taiwan's Deputy Representative in the United States. Americans who subsequently visited the island learned that its residents looked upon Church as a kind of benefactor.[37]

Within the United States, the Taiwan Relations Act attested to Congress's assertiveness in the area of foreign relations—a development that Church unquestionably applauded. He undoubtedly agreed with Javits that Congress had shown it could strengthen U. S. foreign policy. At the least, Church had helped to buy time for America's changing Asia policy, thereby allowing the Chinese issue to work itself out as the older generation departed.[38]

IV

While Church had very capably passed his first major legislative challenge on the Foreign Relations Committee, he also discovered that his status as the CFR's chair provided him with the kind of podium he had long sought. His February 1 call for a "fundamental review" of U. S. policy toward Saudi Arabia undoubtedly captured attention in part because it was his first public address as head of the committee (even though it had in fact been scheduled months earlier and without his new position in mind). As a vigorous indictment of Carter's Middle Eastern policy, it also drew considerable criticism.[39]

Addressing the Anti-Defamation League of B'nai B'rith, Church scored the administration for undercutting the Camp David Accords between Egypt and Israel. The accords, in his opinion, comprised "one of the most remarkable achievements in modern diplomatic history." But, according to the senator, the administration's susceptibility to pressure—particularly from Saudi Arabia—had jeopardized peace in the Middle East. Because U. S. policymakers hoped that Saudi Arabia would moderate OPEC's prices, they indulged its role in the Pan-Arab effort to isolate Egypt for having negotiated with Israel. Church feared that American expectations regarding the Saudis and OPEC were as misplaced as had been those about the Shah of Iran. The Shah's recent overthrow confirmed that the U. S. had gambled on "a rotting regime." Church worried "that we are equally out of touch with Saudi Arabia and pinning our policy to false assumptions." He advised the administration to speak forthrightly to the Saudis rather than merely accommodate them.[40]

A number of political commentators described Church's speech as irresponsible, an offense to the Saudis, whose oil and influence on OPEC were indispensable. "Church should be more sensitive to fragile political situations," complained journalist Charles Bartlett.[41]

Church had opened himself to criticism in part because of his chosen forum. By chastising the Saudis before a pro-Israeli audience, he had seemed anything but impartial. A Saudi newspaper protested that his speech resembled "a document prepared by the Israeli Foreign Ministry," and guessed that he had delivered it in order to attract "fat campaign checks" from pro-Jewish contributors. Although his $500 honorarium was relatively small, it nevertheless suggested a conflict of interest. As columnist Nick Thimmesch pointed out, the chair of the CFR should refuse honorariums from groups with special connections to particular nations just as surely as the head of the Senate Banking Committee should reject payments from banking organizations. Bill Bader, the CFR staff director, wished sorely that Church had not given the speech.[42]

Church, certain that his remarks were completely justified, had no regrets about the lecture. The Saudis, he insisted, were blocking the road to peace in the Middle East and brandishing their oil weapon. He resented the deference with which U. S. policy makers treated them. Such treatment encouraged them to believe that they controlled the conditions for friendship with the U.S. "I thought it was time for somebody with some stature in American politics to speak plainly to the Saudis," he said. He had deliberately sharpened his comments. Shrugging off criticism that his speech lacked balance, he explained that "even-handedness is alright, unless the policy is not advancing the national interest." In his mind, the U. S. had yielded too much to Saudi pressure. Church "relished every minute of the speech," according to one staffer.[43]

V

Although he created a stir regarding U. S.-Saudi relations, his efforts to release a startling report on Saudi oil largely failed. For weeks in 1978, the staff of his Foreign Economic Policy subcommittee had been drafting the report which contained what one CIA oil and energy expert described as "the most shocking information" he had seen. Its stunning description of mismanagement and deception in the Saudi oil fields showed, for example, that the oil companies had justified high production rates by deliberately overestimating the amount of Saudi petroleum. The information bore directly on how much power the Saudis had in the high-stake politics of oil. Pressure to suppress the report was immense, not only from the Saudis and the oil companies but also from the Carter administration. Determined to protect America's energy supply, Carter and his advisors wanted to do nothing to alienate the Saudis, who had agreed to stabilize oil prices and increase production. Well aware of the building opposition and convinced that America would soon confront a massive energy crisis, Church urged his staff to complete the report before it was "too late."[44]

By early 1979, when the subcommittee voted on whether to release the information, it was already too late. The oil companies and the State Department had furiously lobbied the subcommittee not to damage U. S.-Saudi relations. And, per Senate rules, Church had relinquished his place on the subcommittee in order to chair the CFR. Although he lacked a vote, he attended the subcommittee discussions of the report. Defying telephone appeals from Secretary of State Cyrus Vance, he exhorted his colleagues to make the report public. By a count of three-to-two, however, the subcommittee disagreed with him, at least partly on grounds that the report was an anti-Saudi diatribe. The version that the public finally saw, on April 14, 1979, warned against American dependence on Saudi oil, but contained only 37 of the original 130 pages and omitted quotations, names, and dates of meetings. Although Bill Bader, who co-authored the final report, believed the streamlined rendition had replaced polemics with analysis, subcommittee staffer Steve Emerson later insisted that most of the revelations "never saw the light of day." Whatever the merits of the initial report, Church, by pressing so hard to release it, unquestionably rankled the administration and the Saudis. "Tell him to watch out," Saudi Commerce Minister Suleiman Solaim advised Morrison-Knudsen, a large Boise-based construction firm with extensive contracts in the Middle East.[45]

VI

Church's concern about America's vulnerability to the politics of oil reflected his growing conviction that the real issue was, as he told an aide, "no longer foreign policy but foreign *economic* policy." In the late 1970s he argued eloquently in a variety of forums that America's real adversary was not the Soviet Union but changing economic conditions. United States power and security, he maintained, were falling victim to a soaring trade deficit, recurrent inflation, dependence on foreign oil, declining industrial productivity, and rising foreign economic competition.[46]

With a growing sense of urgency, Church implored Americans to break from the familiar Cold War frames of reference. "We keep looking at the world in ideological terms," he lamented. As a result, Americans continued to pursue geopolitical supremacy over the Soviet Union, emphasizing defense spending and military strength. Church warned, however, that "a ship of state is not necessarily more seaworthy because she carries lots of cannon—indeed, without a sturdy hull, she is more likely to capsize and sink." America's economic hull, he argued, had in fact weakened over the years as military spending skewed research, development, and industry away from non-military areas. While Americans kept their eyes on the Soviet Union and produced masses of weapons, the Germans, Japanese, South Koreans, and Taiwanese churned out cars, steel, television sets, and a variety of consumer goods. Make no mistake, Church emphasized: America's greatest challenges came from its closest allies—especially "the rising new super powers of Germany and Japan." In several speeches he used a clever play on words to make his point about the need to consider America's plight in the context of global economic competition. "I have a Yen to make a Mark for the Dollar," he said.[47]

The Organization of Petroleum Exporting Countries had, of course, delivered the U. S. economy yet another blow, but Church asserted that U. S. foreign policy was again at fault. He reminded his audiences that, in the early days of the Cold War, U. S. policymakers had encouraged the formation of "a giant oil company cartel" in order to tie the Persian Gulf countries to the West. As the U.S. became increasingly dependent upon Middle Eastern oil, Republican and Democratic administrations alike had scrambled to accommodate OPEC with weapons, technology, and more money for oil. "We embraced Saudi Arabia with such fervor," Church declared, "that every time the Saudis sneeze, the United States catches cold." In Iran, the U. S. had indulged the Shah's "orgy of arms buying." Then, in early 1979, a revolutionary upheaval had driven the unpopular government from power, cutting off Iranian oil and precipitating another energy and inflationary crisis.[48]

Americans simply had to understand, Church contended, that global changes had unseated them from the king-of-the-mountain status they had enjoyed at the end of World War II. This did not mean that the U. S. was a second-rate power. It meant that Americans would have to adjust to a world in enormous ferment. And it meant that they would have to recognize that their security rested not on weaponry but on making their nation more competitive in the world marketplace. "For those who wish a tidy world," he said, "the times are not propitious." The huge number of new nations, the often desperate struggles in these new countries against poverty and oppression, the staggering diversity of the modern world, and the rising economic competition from Europe and Asia had ended " 'the American era' " and created turbulent and confusing times. Americans were going to have to live with enormous change. Church believed that the lessons of the Vietnam war had been instructive in that regard, stripping away the old "illusion of omnipotence." Now the U. S. was perhaps ready to put its own house in order. "The only thing we can't do—and this we must remember," Church emphasized—"is to put a lid on that changing world." The Cold War had already prompted the U. S. foolishly to protect the status quo. And, while the U. S. had funnelled much of its wealth into armaments, other nations such as Germany and Japan had increased their industrial capacity.[49]

Because his comments were often at least implicitly critical of the president's policies, Church exasperated the administration. At the State Department, for example, his "Yen for a Mark for a Dollar" speech received a decidedly cool reception. Karin Lissakers recalled that her colleagues at State were "furious" at what they believed to be a gratuitous assault on major American allies.[50]

Actually, Church's remarks about America's declining competitiveness in the world economy were as prophetic as they were perceptive. His warnings about the U. S.'s diminished productive capacity, the rising economic power of Germany and Japan, the dependency on OPEC oil, the baneful effects of producing and selling arms, and the measuring of national security in military—rather than economic terms—foreshadowed debates that, by the 1990s, were central to the nation's political discourse.[51]

VII

By the late Seventies, however, as storm clouds gathered over the troubled U. S. economy, a different kind of tempest threatened the senator's political future. In January 1979 a well-funded Anybody But Church (ABC) organization emerged in Idaho. With the election still almost two years away, the New Right opposition to him was already formidable. The prospects that Jesse Helms might go to Idaho to help the opposition also bothered him, according to one of his top staffers, who believed that Helms really held "a knife over Church's head."[52]

Church's apprehensions about the shifting political winds were evident shortly after he became chair of the CFR. After discussing floor strategy one afternoon with staffer Michael Glennon, he fell strangely silent, awaiting the Senate buzzer. Watching him, Glennon had an "eerie" feeling. "I remember looking at him," he recalled, "thinking that this was the unhappiest man I'd ever known." After finally attaining his childhood dream of chairing the CFR, Church appeared to sense that his success would be short-lived. "I felt incredibly sad for him," Glennon commented later. "The dream was slipping through his fingers, and there was nothing he could do about it."[53]

Events, as Bill Bader observed, seemed to be conspiring against the senator. "There wasn't anything out there in that forest but wolves," Bader said as he reflected back upon the obstacles that confronted his boss. Wherever Church looked, troubles awaited him, whether the source was the White House, the intelligence community, or the changing political mood. "History provided him with a lousy sense of timing," as Bader ruefully observed.[54]

The White House remained a problem for the senator. He was increasingly impatient with Carter's economic policies, which he criticized as "ill timed and poorly orchestrated." He objected, for example, to the president's use of budget cuts and credit restraints to curb inflation. In his opinion, the White House remedy victimized Americans by driving up interest rates and unemployment when the nation was already suffering from a recession. He compared Carter to "a driver, who, upon sighting a red light 100 yards away, places his foot down sharply on the accelerator only to have to jam on the brake at the stop line, unnecessarily jostling his passengers."[55]

Church's continued difficulties with the White House went beyond matters of policy to a relationship that Bader described as downright "adversarial," full of "living, breathing hostility." Several of Carter's advisors informed him that they were certain Church intended to challenge the president in 1980. Years later, thoughts of those "miserable, arrogant bastards from Georgia" still made Bader fume. He recalled how, in the spring of 1980, the administration failed to alert Church that Carter was going to name Senator Edmund Muskie as the new Secretary of State. When Bader discovered that the head of the Foreign Relations Committee was one of the few informed people in the city who had not yet heard about Carter's choice, he angrily called the White House and threatened to take the story to the press. Even then, Carter did not tell Church; the news came instead via Cyrus Vance, the outgoing secretary with whom the senator had a good relationship. In retrospect, Senator Richard Lugar cited the administration's relationship with Church as an example of how *not* to treat a committee chair. Undersecretary of State David Newsom agreed that Carter and National Security Advisor Zbigniew Brzezinski "were never very high on Frank Church." They considered him "much too soft on the Soviets" and generally "a liability" for the administration. Ralph Earle II, Carter's chief arms negotiator, likewise sensed that they viewed the senator as too independent and "big for his britches."[56]

If, as Earle believed, there was "no love lost" between Church and the White House, an even deeper antipathy existed between him and the intelligence community. Steve Emerson, who became an award-winning investigative journalist after leaving Church's staff, encountered many national security people who viewed the senator as a traitor. Church, in turn, fretted that the intelligence agencies were again retreating behind a veil of secrecy. He was outraged when, on February 9, 1979, the Justice Department dropped the long-standing perjury charges against Robert Berrellez. In 1973, the International Telephone and Telegraph official had faced six counts of lying to the multinationals subcommittee during the investigations of ITT/CIA activities in Chile. Church denounced as "spurious" the Justice Department's explanation that prosecuting Berrellez would expose highly sensitive information. The real reason for the department's action, he believed, was that the case "might have embarrassed major corporations, the CIA and the Nixon administration." He feared that the decision would encourage witnesses "to mislead Congress with impunity."[57]

Congress, and Church by implication, sustained political wounds on other fronts as well. In 1973 historian Arthur Schlesinger, Jr.'s *The Imperial Presidency* had articulated growing apprehensions about presidential power. But six years later, political scientists Thomas Franck and Edward Weisband published an important study, *Foreign Policy By Congress*, indicating that the resurgent legislative branch had yet to convince Americans that it could protect the national interest. Insofar as the public doubted Congress's abilities, Franck and Weisband predicted that "power will run off Capitol Hill." Opinion polls already boded ill for Congress. A 1977 Harris poll showed, for example, that voter confidence in the legislature had plunged from 66 percent in 1966 to a paltry 15 percent. In early 1979 columnist Carl T. Rowan summed up what appeared to be the growing sentiment. "We deplored the 'imperial presidency,' " he wrote, "and now the pendulum has swung to congressional irresponsibility." He pointed to Church as a prime example of congressional bungling. According to Rowan, the Soviets had recently made notable gains abroad because their leaders were "not burdened by 535 noisy lawmakers"– such as the Idaho senator–in hot pursuit of "political brownie points." Church's "absurd and destructive" criticism of Carter's handling of the Saudis especially galled the journalist. In Rowan's estimation, Church's conduct demonstrated that Congress had chosen "a hell of a way to conduct foreign policy."[58]

For Church, however, public skepticism about Congress paled alongside what one author called "thunder on the right." By the late Seventies the New Right was an expanding political force, drawing upon the finances of millionaires such as beer manufacturer Joseph Coors, the dedication of single-issue "family" lobbies such as Phyllis Schlafly's anti-ERA Eagle Forum, the shrewdness of direct-mail political organizers like Richard Viguerie, and the religious fundamentalism of the Reverend Jerry Falwell's Moral Majority, Inc. and Pat Robertson's Christian Broadcasting Network. Fear and resentment galvanized it. To its aggrieved members, the American way of life was under siege. Their long list of America's enemies included liberals, homosexuals, feminists, unions, big government, bureaucratic and media elites, "anti-life Baby Killers," and individuals who "surrendered" U. S. security and territory (the Panama Canal, for example) to the communists. These enemies together were part of what the head of Christian Voice, a fundamentalist political lobby, called *"a master plan to destroy everything that is good and moral here in America."*[59]

In 1979 the ABC movement was not alone in targeting Frank Church for defeat. The National Conservative Political Action Committee (NCPAC), a creation mainly of former Jesse Helms aide Charles Black, took direct aim at him and several other Democratic liberals, including George McGovern. Church was their primary prey because of his visibility as chair of the Foreign Relations Committee and his vulnerability in Idaho. Defeating him "would send a shiver down the spines of every liberal in the Senate," said Terry Dolan, the twenty-eight-year-old NCPAC director. In Dolan's estimation, "He's one of the most radical members of the U. S. Senate." By summer the NCPAC/ABC alliance was flooding Idaho with negative advertisements against him.[60]

A NCPAC flyer, "Frank Church's Record of Shame," claimed that he had gutted America's national defense by conducting "the anti-CIA witch hunt," voting to surrender the Panama Canal to "a marxist dictator," and generally building a "record of radicalism." Over a five-day period, NCPAC aired one radio spot 150 times. A television ad featured an empty missile silo and suggested that Church was responsible for disarming it. Actually, the silo was empty because it had housed an obsolescent missile system that had since been modernized.[61]

Joining NCPAC's onslaught against Church were other New Right groups, such as the National Right to Life Movement. Stop the Baby Killers, for example, placed him among people "who apparently think it's perfectly okay to slaughter unborn infants." The Citizens Committee for the Right to Keep and Bear Arms dismissed his opposition to gun control as insincere. Terry Dolan rejoiced at these attacks: "Frank Church is screaming like a stuck pig."[62]

With the election still some eighteen months away, Church was already, as *Newsweek* reported, "running scared." The backers of his likely Republican opponent, Congressman Steve Symms, were preparing a $250,000 anti-Church television blitz. Symms's organizer, Helen Chenoweth, criticized the senator as a liberal who responded to "the pressures of the Eastern Seaboard."[63]

The reference to the Eastern seaboard was telling. It summoned up images of Wall Street, fancy-pants aristocrats, and suave, sophisticated, swelled heads. "I think one of the worst insults you can use in Boise is the word 'expert,' " said one resident. "It's amazing how many people automatically think of experts as enemies." The problem for Church, in the opinion of one of Idaho's most successful Republican politicians, was that he confronted an unflattering fact: "Idaho people have a kind of passion for mediocrity, and tend to sort of resent anybody who rises visibly above the mouldering throng." Church thus worked at being "just folks." Once, when he was taping a television program, he borrowed a sheepskin jacket from a men's store—and promptly returned it after the filming. By the late Seventies, however, former governor Robert Smylie sensed that the senator's changing act was becoming more difficult. It was harder for Church not to appear, "in Idaho terms, to be pontifical and even a little pompous."[64]

Time seemed to be against Church, who in many ways had been a political anomaly. As his friend Jerry Levinson observed, much about "the politics of Idaho conflicted with his natural instincts" and frustrated him considerably. In Levinson's words the senator had always walked "on the knife's edge."[65]

By the end of the Seventies that edge was getting sharper. Resentment "is building up against you," staffer Mike Wetherell warned the senator as early as 1977. Church's Idaho field staff sensed that their boss's popularity had deteriorated seriously across the state. Constituents grumbled that the senator seemed remote, inaccessible. Some complained that they seldom saw him anymore. Wetherell noted that around thirty thousand people had moved to Idaho since Church's 1974 reelection campaign. "My bet is a lot of them are conservative."[66]

In 1979 pollster Peter Hart confirmed that Idahoans had indeed "moved far to the right" since Church first entered the Senate. They were also overwhelmingly negative about the direction in which the nation seemed to be headed, and "only a bare majority" were positive about Church's record. Seniority appeared to count for less than it once had; indeed, 59 percent indicated that his chairmanship of the CFR would not influence them to vote for him. "I don't think this body politic out here gives a damn about" his chairmanship, said former governor Smylie. "They're not even impressed." Perhaps most disconcertingly, 25 percent of Idahoans believed that Church thought more about foreign policy than about Idaho—a troubling statistic in light of his constituents' tendency to "view the world as a hostile place," in the words of one long-time resident.[67]

Staffer Mike Wetherell had already warned Church that chairing the CFR could be the senator's political Achilles' heel. Begging his boss to make more trips to Idaho, Wetherell reminded him that he needed to make his personal presence in the state as high a priority as, for example, questioning arms negotiator Paul Warnke. But, according to Wetherell, Church's staff sensed that the senator disliked "any proposal that entails a trip to the state."[68]

On the issues as well, Church was at variance with many of his constituents. A hefty 39 percent of Idaho voters disliked his support of the Panama Canal treaty and "other measures which weaken America's position in the world." Idahoans, who often seemed "xenophobic or militant" to the pollsters, favored more defense spending by a resounding 65 to 22 percent. Additionally, in a state where self-identified conservatives outnumbered liberals 52 to 17 percent, Church's reputation "as definitely liberal" magnified his difficulties. "In Idaho," as former CIA director William Colby joked, "being a flaming liberal is like wanting stuffing instead of potatoes." *Newsweek* placed Church on "the Democrats' most-endangered-species list."[69]

At first, the senator put up a brave front as he faced the rising political opposition. He laughed in early 1979 that the ABC movement would provide "a battle of the networks": ABC versus NBC, "Nobody But Church." And as the target of a March 29 charity "roast" in Washington, D. C., he leaped good-naturedly around the stage in a Superman sweatshirt and cape.[70]

Despite his cheerful demeanor, he could not understand the virulence of his opponents' attacks. He had long been accustomed to dealing with constituents more conservative than he but who at least tolerated his "apostasies." To his dismay, however, politics in recent years had become more abusive and vindictive. Efforts to portray him as a baby killer sickened him. He noted sadly that "not a single Republican politician" in Idaho had denounced the tactics of distortion and innuendo. More than ever, he missed his old colleague Len Jordan. During the 1967 recall campaign, Jordan had lashed out at efforts to portray him as a traitor. Church regretted that "there aren't men of that caliber and character any longer dominating the Republican scene." Aides attested to his deep distrust of James McClure, who had replaced Jordan, and who kept his distance from the senior senator. George Hansen continued to infuriate Church, most recently by serving as honorary chair of the group that classified him as a baby killer. And although Church reportedly did not dislike Steve Symms personally, he once compared him to a "puppy dog" oblivious to the consequences of his actions.[71]

VIII

Fighting back against his New Right opponents, Church vigorously defended Idaho's economic interests. In mid-1979 he introduced legislation to preserve passenger train service in the state. "Idaho Wins One," the *Statesman* celebrated in early August when the measure passed. "Church's effort cannot be under-estimated." After talking with Jimmy Carter, the senator also broke loose the funding for Boise's downtown development program.[72]

More importantly, in behalf of Idaho's beleaguered sugar beet industry, he doggedly took the administration to the mat in order to boost domestic sugar prices. As his "bargaining chip," he held the proposed International Sugar Agreement hostage in the CFR, refusing to allow the treaty to come to a vote until he received assurances from Carter that the administration would raise sugar support prices. Only after Carter agreed to protect the minimum domestic price of sugar, at a level that was almost a cent a pound above the existing amount, did he allow the treaty to come to a successful vote in the Senate. Critics argued that Church's move would increase inflation, hurt the Caribbean countries, and encourage the production of high-cost beet sugar (as opposed to cheaper sugar cane). Church answered that he was protecting an important American industry, but one staffer sensed his discomfort in trading off a larger international issue to protect the "home folks." When she pressed him on the matter, asking what the implications were for, say, the Jamaican economy, he grew defensive.[73]

While he championed Idaho's economy, he also guarded his right flank on social issues, as his position on gun control illustrated. Since entering office, he had voted against every federal gun control proposal that came to the Senate. But even this record did not satisfy New Right groups. The Citizens' Committee for the Right to Keep and Bear Arms, for example, claimed that he acted on politics rather than principle. The committee apparently accepted Terry Dolan's characterization of him as "a political prostitute" who tailored his rhetoric to fit the votes that he needed. Alan Gottlieb, a leading member of the committee, thus claimed that Church would support gun controls if he were not afraid that Idaho voters would tar and feather him for doing so. In the face of such criticism Church tried to prove the purity of his convictions. A few years earlier he had avoided a relationship with the National Rifle Association; by 1980 he was seeking contributions from it. His campaign manager told the association that "perhaps no person is more effective than Frank Church on this issue" of gun control. In 1979, in his foreword to *Restricting Handguns: The Liberal Skeptics Speak Out*, the senator went so far as to claim that human rights activists "are coming to understand that gun controls work against their interest." The truth of the matter, he said, was that "in the inner cities, where the police cannot offer adequate protection, the people will provide their own." This chilling scenario was a far cry from his objections, in 1967, to regulating "the right of the people of my state to keep and bear their sporting arms."[74]

In 1979 the gun control issue apparently influenced Church's astonishing vote against the confirmation of Abner Mikva as a federal judge. As a liberal congressman from Illinois, Mikva had joined Church in opposing the Vietnam war. He enjoyed so much respect on Capitol Hill that, when Carter appointed him to the District of Columbia Appeals Court, even Republicans such as House Minority Leader John Rhodes offered endorsements. But, after the gun lobby mounted fierce protests against Mikva because he supported gun controls, Church opposed his confirmation. The senator's feeble justification was that Mikva, despite his stated goal of making "unprejudiced decisions," refused to disqualify himself from hearing gun-control cases. Church's vote shocked a number of prominent liberals. Under a huge headline, "Church's Reelection Frenzy Went Too Far With Vote Against Mikva," columnist Mary McGrory rebuked the senator, quoting from one of his colleagues who said, "There must be a limit to what a man will do to come back here." Leon Shull, head of the Americans for Democratic Action, was certain that Church acted out of political expediency. "We really do have a right to expect something of our senators other than that," he said.[75]

While the gun control issue plagued Church, so did that of abortion. The Life Amendment Political Action Committee hoped to defeat him in 1980 on grounds that he favored "abortion on demand"–an accusation he called "an outlandish, bald-faced lie." He reminded his critics that he had authored "conscience" legislation protecting members of the medical community from having to violate their religious beliefs in order to perform abortions. His stand had opened him to attack from pro-choice advocates; they noted that the law created hardships for rural women, who had to search for the relatively few hospitals that allowed abortions. According to a leader of the Religious Coalition for Abortion Rights, the "conscience clause" limited freedom of choice on reproductive issues. Church countered that he was protecting religious freedom. It was unreasonable, he said, for a woman who did not want the state to coerce her into giving birth to expect the state to force others to perform an act that violated their conscience. Personally, he approved of abortion only in extreme circumstances, when the mother's health was in danger or when rape or incest caused the pregnancy. He also endorsed a constitutional amendment that would allow the states to regulate abortions. During his 1976 presidential bid he had "stood by" the *Roe* ruling because it was the law of the land; by 1980 his emphasis was elsewhere: "I am one of a handful in Congress who has actually done something to restrict the Supreme Court's decision." "Right to life" groups remained unconvinced and insisted that he favored abortion on demand.[76]

Battling the New Right's shameless misrepresentations of his record, Church sought in other ways to show that he was, in his words, "conservative on some of the important social issues." He supported legislation "to restore prayer to the public schools." He opposed plans to register women for the draft. He voted against the confirmation of the District of Columbia Court of Appeals judge Patricia Wald, a children's rights activist whom the Christian Voice lobby considered "a leading proponent of secular humanism." He co-sponsored legislation to designate a "National Family Week" in order "to recognize the importance of the family in American life." And he also countered conservative charges that he was weak on defense issues by noting that, since entering the Senate, he had voted for "every Defense Department and Appropriation Bill."[77]

IX

Wisecracks that he was a "born-again conservative" were nevertheless misleading in several respects. On moral issues he had always been downright "old-fashioned," as his son Forrest remarked. He had never aligned himself with the cultural and social kinds of liberalism that had spun out of the Sixties and that the GOP had attacked so successfully. His positions on issues such as abortion, school prayers, and pornography were not new. For years he had opposed restrictions on prayer or on reading from the Bible in public schools. He had also insisted that sex education for children was a matter for local school boards to determine. He favored the death penalty as "fitting punishment" for particularly terrible crimes. And, although he did not want to infringe upon "legitimate exercise of free press and free speech," he had joined Illinois conservative Everett Dirksen in sponsoring legislation to prevent the mailing of obscene and pornographic material. He emphasized that he had no sympathy for " 'smut peddlers' " and "their dirty business."[78]

While over the years he had compiled a generally conservative record on social issues, he remained liberal on economic, environmental, and social welfare questions. In contrast to the New Right's slash-and-burn approach to government, he held to the activist traditions of the New Deal and Great Society. Granted, he increasingly worried about the soaring national deficit and opposed instituting a host of new federal aid programs. But he nevertheless still looked to the federal government as the catalytic agent regarding matters for which there was a clear national commitment—for instance, in cleaning up air and water; helping communities build transportation systems, new sewer systems, and better schools; reducing unemployment; and providing mass transit and an improved infrastructure. He wanted to make domestic food programs (such as the Nutrition Program for the Elderly, the Food Stamp program, and school lunches) more accessible to poor and needy people. He backed the Women and Infant Children program, which provided pre- and post-natal care. And he advised Jimmy Carter not to raise taxes or interest rates to curb inflation. Such steps constituted "the traditional Republican approach to cooling off the economy," he wrote, and hurt working-class people. Moreover, as his views on foreign economic policy suggested, he thought in terms of industrial planning, especially regarding energy. In that regard, he wanted the government to promote the development of alternative energy sources—gasohol, for example—to help protect the environment and to end U. S. dependence on foreign oil.[79]

X

Church's renewed zeal for wilderness legislation illustrated dramatically his willingness to stand up to the New Right in behalf of a national commitment. Wilderness protection was still a "high risk" issue, former Secretary of the Interior Stewart Udall noted. In Idaho, a 1979 public opinion poll revealed that voters were "split right down the middle" between those wanting more emphasis on economic development and those favoring wilderness areas. The poll also showed that voters overwhelmingly recognized Church's bent toward wilderness preservation.[80]

Church's fight for the Endangered Wilderness Act helped to set the stage for his environmental battles with the New Right. On March 30, 1977 the senator introduced a bill to add specifically defined areas of National Forest land to the National Wilderness System that had been established thirteen years earlier. These endangered places would receive immediate protection while they were still relatively undisturbed. Moreover, the act would reduce local uncertainty about what the Forest Service might recommend regarding future wilderness spots. The result, Church hoped, would be "a comprehensive view of the system we intend ultimately to create." In all, he proposed eleven new wilderness areas, plus eight additional places that would receive interim protection to allow for further study. Church said that he hoped soon to amend his bill by adding Idaho's Gospel-Hump region to the wilderness areas. That amendment, however, hinged on what he could work out among the competing groups in Idaho.[81]

The contested Gospel-Hump region in north-central Idaho comprised five hundred thousand spectacularly rugged acres between Buffalo Hump Mountain on the east and Gospel Peak on the west. Environmentalists had filed a series of suits to stop timber cutting there, while residents fought back to protect their mills and jobs. With no resolution in sight, the situation had turned ugly, as groups squared off against each other.[82]

Church stepped into the explosive situation, defying conventional wisdom that conservationists and developers could never agree. Carefully, he set out to put together a coalition. On April 28, 1977 he convened a motley group of environmentalists, timber people, and members of the local Chamber of Commerce to decide among themselves how to handle the issue of Gospel-Hump. The site of the meeting was Grangeville, Idaho, where anti-wilderness feelings ran so high that he was hung in effigy.[83]

On the eve of the meeting, Church got together separately with the competing interest groups. In a hotel room in nearby Lewiston he helped push the furniture back so there would be room for maps on the floor. While he crawled on hands and knees around the maps and asked questions, he puffed on a huge cigar, filling the room with clouds of smoke that made some people woozy. The next day the Grangeville Elks Club crackled with tension as he presided over a lunch that brought the conflicting groups together into a small task force. After lunch they retreated to a back room to pore over more maps. Church set a tone of give-and-take, telling the participants he would get out of the way and let them hammer out details regarding what should be pristine wilderness and what should be set aside for multiple use. If they could reach an agreement, he promised to try to turn it into legislation.[84]

The Grangeville negotiations continued, off and on, for several months. Doug Scott of the Sierra Club, a participant, marveled at the results. "If anybody had said to me the Sierra Club would be sitting down at the Elks Club in Grangeville week after week with the Chamber of Commerce, I would have said that's ludicrous." Nevertheless, at 1 a. m. on July 13 the participants arrived at an agreement, designating some 220,000 acres as "wilderness." "This is a bright day," Church said when he learned of the settlement. "The agreement between conservationists and local representatives proves that it is possible to resolve volatile issues. . . in a rational manner." On August 5 he introduced his Gospel-Hump amendment to the Endangered American Wilderness bill.[85]

Over the next few weeks he guided the amendment and bill through the Senate. Always trying to be flexible and accommodating, he never tried "to put you in a box," Oregon's Mark Hatfield recalled appreciatively. According to Hatfield, he "could fight hard for his cause," break into a marvelous smile, and never gloat if he won. At one point he startled environmentalists by accepting Jim McClure's amendment to permit the conditional use of snowmobiles. Later, he explained that he had done so knowing that McClure's proposal would not survive the House-Senate conference. But his negotiating tactics allowed him, on October 20, to win unanimous Senate approval of his Gospel-Hump Amendment and an 89-3 vote for the Endangered Wilderness Act. Armed with the huge Senate vote, Church had greater bargaining power when he asked the House conferees to add the amendment to the House version of the act. Among the conferees was Steve Symms, who viewed the Wilderness Act of 1964 as "a bill of goods" and opposed "locking up" western lands such as Gospel-Hump. Symms believed that Church and his Grangeville task force were trying "to divide up Idaho." The House conferees nevertheless supported Church and attached his amendment to the wilderness bill. In the spring of 1978 Carter signed the Endangered Wilderness Act into law.[86]

Church had emerged victorious. "In as tough and difficult a state as Idaho, Gospel-Hump got resolved," said a coordinator of Citizens for America's Endangered Wilderness, the Sierra Club's Doug Scott. "There's history there; it did work." And it was vintage Church.[87]

The Gospel-Hump law had prepared the way not only for Church's next environmental round, but also for his building political clash with Symms. By 1979 the issue had shifted to the senator's proposed River of No Return legislation. And by then, his opponents were joining a movement known as the "Sagebrush Rebellion."

Church acted courageously in the late Seventies when he set out to make Idaho's majestic River of No Return region the largest area in the National Wilderness Preservation System. On the eve of what clearly was going to be a rough reelection battle, he chose to forge ahead, knowing that another wilderness fight would further polarize the electorate. "If ever there was a tough political decision, that was it," recalled Cleve Corlett.[88]

On January 18, 1979, Church introduced three Idaho wilderness bills in the Senate. Each concerned the future of the Idaho and Salmon River Breaks Primitive Areas. One of the proposals came from a preservationist group, the River of No Return Wilderness Council, which wanted to create 2.3 million acres of protected wilderness in central Idaho. The "citizens' bill," as its backers called it, had the support of national environmental organizations. The second, competing, proposal was the idea of the Idaho Forest Industry. It would limit the wilderness area to 1.3 million acres and keep 850,000 more for multiple use. The third bill represented the Department of the Interior's position, calling for 1.9 million acres of wilderness, but, according to environmentalist Michael Frome, leaving out "critical river drainages and wildlife habitat." The Wilderness Council and the administration also wished to add all 237 miles of the Salmon River's main stem to the National Wild and Scenic Rivers System.[89]

As always, Church sought a consensus, well aware that legislative success demanded trade-offs and compromise. He listened sympathetically to residents of logging communities while at the same time making the most of his positive relationships with environmentalists and Secretary of the Interior Cecil Andrus, Idaho's former governor. "We need your help on the inside," Church had implored Andrus during the push for the Endangered Wilderness Act, knowing that his long-time political ally would be reasonable and obliging. Certainly, Andrus's shared interest in environmental protection, as well as his willingness to work with Church, aided the senator as the Idaho wilderness struggle intensified. In this legislative battle, as with others, Church was no purist, demanding one solution. His approach to the environment was practical yet principled. Genuinely committed to protecting wilderness areas, he liked to quote the novelist and preservationist Edward Abbey: "Wilderness needs no defense—it needs more defenders." But defenders, as Church realized, also needed a strategy. And, as usual, the senator had a plan, this time regarding specifically the River of No Return. By introducing three competing bills he was buying time, not setting himself up as a stationary target for his opponents. All three proposals reflected a basic agreement that at least part of the central Idaho area should be preserved as wilderness. With that main idea before the public, he hoped to use open discussion and a series of hearings to forge an agreement. To protect local economies, he was quite literally willing to give ground. But always he thought in terms of "careful use" and "stewardship," trying to balance the future against the past. With his three contrasting bills before the public, he tried to negotiate a compromise.[90]

Doing so was not easy, however. The weak U. S. economy was taking a toll on Idaho, especially its timber industry. Inflation and rising interest rates curtailed housing construction, which in turn hurt the lumber market. In the central and northern sections of Idaho, growing numbers of workers faced layoffs. Several lumber mills expected at least temporary shutdowns. Idaho Women in Timber groups in many small towns warned Church that additional wilderness legislation could ruin their communities. "It frightens me," wrote one woman, "when I see first one mill close, then another, and some people say 'Well, it's not so bad. We have to make *some* sacrifices.' But Senator Church, where will it end?" From Elk City came an appeal from a ten-year-old boy, "Please do not take my home away." And when Church held a wilderness hearing in Salmon, Idaho, an angry cowboy rode his horse through the hall in protest.[91]

In this volatile situation, the "Sagebrush Rebellion" erupted. Taking their cue from Nevada, where the state legislature laid claim to federal lands, Idahoans took action. They formed the Sagebrush Rebellion, Inc.—"which," one of its founders joked, "is the first time in the history of man they ever incorporated a rebellion." Although the Sagebrush rebels were concerned mainly about lands under the jurisdiction of the Bureau of Land Management, the movement had broad implications for all of the thirty-four million acres of federal land that comprised two-thirds of Idaho. Convinced that the federal government was the source of most of their problems, the rebels wanted to shift control of the lands closer to home. As one person summed up their philosophy: "We've been here longer than the Forest Service, and those trees are ours, and those hills are ours and those deer are ours."[92]

The Sagebrush Rebellion placed additional strains on the coalition that Church was trying to build. Whereas the senator wanted a compromise, the rebels believed they had nothing to negotiate. "WHY SHOULD WE COMPROMISE?" asked the mayor of one logging town. Why should local people ruin their lives "so that some rich flatlander can come visit for a week and watch the natives run around"?[93]

Politically, the rebellion grew more ominous for Church insofar as Steve Symms identified with it. A vigorous defender of unbridled capitalism (which he called the world's "most humanitarian" system), Symms opposed obstacles to economic development. He jokingly saw "some advantages to having a hamburger stand on every peak." More immediately, he wanted to end the federal government's role as an "absentee landlord" and let Idaho deal with the lands inside its borders.[94]

Church nevertheless won the River of No Return fight. On November 20, 1979 the Senate voted 69-18 to set aside 2.2 million acres in central Idaho for wilderness (about 5 percent of the state), 915,000 adjacent acres for multiple-use purposes, and 125 miles of the Salmon River as part of the Wild and Scenic Rivers System. A compromise agreement kept open existing landing strips and several cobalt mining areas. "We were able to provide for *both* wood and wilderness," Church said. Although he and Jim McClure had cooperated on important aspects of the bill, McClure in the end opposed it. On June 1, 1980 the House approved it, 271-137, and shortly thereafter Carter signed it into law. Church had been anything but a silent bystander in obtaining the legislation. He had lobbied his Senate colleagues far more than usual, and he had telephoned House members, appealing for their votes. Symms and George Hansen tried to rally the House opposition. At one point, a vote on Symms's substitute motion for a much smaller wilderness area reverberated with election politics. Support for the motion took on the appearance of an implicit endorsement of Symms, who was by then actively seeking Church's Senate seat. Church could take heart in winning that symbolic House vote, and in securing the River of No Return legislation; but otherwise he was stumbling in his pursuit of a fifth term.[95]

XI

In late summer 1979 he tripped badly over an issue involving a Soviet "combat" brigade in Cuba. By the time the dust settled, he had opened himself to charges of sacrificing a major arms limitations agreement with the Soviets (SALT II) in order to prove his toughness to Idaho voters. He also inadvertently accelerated a conservative shift in U. S. foreign policy toward what one senator described as "a new sense of macho."[96]

The situation was full of irony because Church disliked the renewed emphasis on America's military might and he strongly supported the SALT II treaty, which the brigade issue ultimately helped to derail. On 10 May 1979, five weeks before Jimmy Carter and Leonid Brezhnev of the Soviet Union signed the SALT II agreement, Church delivered a spirited defense of its guiding principles. At issue, he said, was America's most basic national interest: "the survival of our people and our system." To that end, the nuclear arms race had brought insecurity, not security; the "addictive habit" of stockpiling weapons raised the odds that an accident or miscalculation might trigger an unthinkable nuclear war. "The great moral blindness of our time," Church told his audience, inured people to live with the threat of nuclear terror and to accept passively "the abstract mumbo jumbo of the nuclear priesthood" about kill ratios and survival rates. "As though Armageddon could be reduced to a computer printout," he scoffed. Now was the time, he insisted, to begin decreasing the number of nuclear weapons. Commenting on the upcoming Senate debates over SALT II, he urged people not to think they had to choose between arms control or national defense. "Arms control is part of our national security," he argued. He concluded what Bill Bader believed was one of his finest addresses with three words: "The debate begins."[97]

A few weeks later, as the CFR prepared to open its hearings on SALT II, the New Right started airing in Idaho its TV spots featuring the empty missile silo and suggesting that Church opposed a strong national defense. Although a pollster found that Idahoans favored SALT II by a 52 to 40 percent margin, he warned the senator to treat the SALT agreement "very carefully."[98]

That summer Church nevertheless sometimes seemed willing to abandon caution. "I've accomplished about all I can in a Senatorial career," he told *Newsweek*. "If SALT II is grounds for my defeat, so be it. Disarmament is essential to our survival." Starting on July 8, he presided day in and day out over the CFR's hearings. Bader sensed that Church believed SALT II would be "one of the hallmarks of his time as chairman." The hearings were serious, careful, and exceedingly professional. "I had never seen a chairman who was as tenacious in staying with the process," Bader recalled. "He gave it his all."[99]

At the same time, he gave some observers the impression that he was beginning to worry about his reelection. In little ways, he seemed determined to prove that he was no patsy when dealing with the Soviets. Ralph Earle, the U. S. arms negotiator whom Church had impressed favorably a year earlier, thought that he was now assuming a "tougher" stance.[100]

The senator was not alone, however, in showing a tougher side. By mid-1979 the administration was retreating from its earlier reformist, non-military policies. In June, the same month that Carter signed the SALT II agreement, he also yielded to National Security Advisor Zbigniew Brzezinski's pressure to approve the MX missile program—"the largest new nuclear-weapons program since Harry Truman ordered the development of the hydrogen bomb in 1950," according to historian Gaddis Smith. The MX was a mobile intercontinental missile with ten warheads, designed to give the U. S. a first-strike capacity to match what the Soviets reportedly enjoyed. Paul Warnke, America's chief arms negotiator, summed up Brzezinski's viewpoint: "The bigger, the uglier, the nastier the weapon—the better." In Warnke's opinion, the message that Brzezinksi hoped to send the Soviets was an emphatic "Shape up, buster." As the administration weaved along the arms control road, the New Right pummeled the SALT II treaty. "We'll fight it to the end," promised Conservative Caucus leader Howard Phillips. Insofar as Phillips and his allies could equate SALT II with a weakened U. S., the treaty's future was gloomy. That summer, as the renewed energy crisis created long lines at gasoline pumps, Americans were in an intractable mood, resentful of signs that the U. S. was a wounded giant.[101]

In that setting Frank Church, whom Vice President Walter Mondale described as "the most important man in America" regarding SALT II's fate, learned about a Soviet brigade in Cuba. He heard the news late in the afternoon on August 30, during a visit to Idaho. Bethine summoned him to the phone from the backyard, where he was repairing the fence. David Newsom at the State Department was on the line with startling information: the press would soon be reporting leaked intelligence reports that had just revealed Soviet combat troops in Cuba. Church was "stunned," according to Newsom. "Well," he sighed, "SALT is dead." He asked if the administration planned to make an announcement. "No," Newsom replied, "we just wanted to alert you to the existence of this information," before it appeared in the press. After the call, Church returned to the yard and hammered furiously on the fence.[102]

As his mind raced over the news he had just received, he must have felt a terrible sense of *deja vu*. During his 1962 reelection campaign, after he had reassured Idahoans that there was no Soviet military threat in Cuba, revelations of the missile crisis had almost swamped him politically. Now, in 1979, the Cuban issue was back. To prove that the senator was soft on communism, the New Right was already showing a news clip of his visit a year earlier with Castro. And recently, during the SALT II hearings, he had denied rumors of a Soviet military buildup on the island. He had done so on July 17, after Senator Richard Stone (D-Florida) told the CFR that an armed Soviet brigade was in Cuba. Stone reportedly hoped that his tough talk about Cuba would win back constituents whom he had infuriated by voting for the Panama Canal treaties. The administration denied that the Soviet presence had grown on the island and hurriedly drafted a press statement which Church and Javits issued. Now, some six weeks later, Church had just learned that the statement was wrong. Once again, as in 1962, he was vulnerable to charges of naiveté or deception regarding the Soviet threat in Cuba. Information about the brigade would not only "sink SALT," as he predicted, but perhaps him as well. The Panama Canal battle had recently forced him "to walk the plank," he said in retrospect. He believed it was sometimes "possible to walk the plank once and survive, but it's very unlikely that you'll survive if you have to walk it twice." On that late August afternoon in Boise, he knew that news of the brigade was again pushing him over the political edge.[103]

Suddenly, he stormed back into the house. Bethine thought he had hit his finger with the hammer, but he was fuming instead at the administration's handling of the brigade issue. "They just can't let this leak," he told her angrily, as he reached for the phone. He tried unsuccessfully to get hold of Carter, who was out of town. Finally, he contacted Secretary of State Vance, who confirmed Newsom's report. Church argued that someone in the U. S. government should announce the news, rather than rely on the press to do so. Indeed, he threatened to make a public statement himself if some top official in the administration did not. Vance left that decision to him. "My expectation was that Church would say nothing," he wrote later.[104]

At 8:30 that evening, to Vance's surprise and the administration's chagrin, Church held a dramatic press conference in his home to announce "a recent development" in Cuba: "the buildup of Soviet ground forces to brigade strength" of from 2,300 to 3,000 troops. He urged the president to demand "immediate withdrawal of all Russian combat troops from Cuba."[105]

For the next several days, the administration was "in shambles," in Ralph Earle's words. Earle himself was stunned that Church had "panicked" and acted so hastily. The senator's conduct confirmed the uneasy feeling at the State Department that one never knew quite what to expect from him during an election year. One dismayed official suspected that "if it [the brigade] had been kept quiet, we could have negotiated something. It's going to be a big deal, now." It was indeed, and the administration complicated the situation by issuing contradictory statements that, although the brigade was neither new nor a threat, the U. S. would, in Vance's words, "not be satisfied with the maintenance of the status quo."[106]

At first Church refused to link SALT II and the troops. But then, on September 5, he did so—a move that Jimmy Carter irately described in his diary as "absolutely irresponsible." The senator told reporters that there was "no likelihood whatever" of Senate ratification of the treaty until the Soviets withdrew their combat troops from Cuba. By a 13-2 vote, the CFR subsequently approved a Church-sponsored reservation: the treaty would not take effect until Carter assured Congress that Soviets in Cuba were not engaged in a combat role and did not threaten the Western Hemisphere. All of this maneuvering baffled the Soviets, who insisted that they were adhering to their 1962 agreement with Kennedy. They contended that opponents of SALT II had manufactured an excuse to defeat the treaty. "Church has painted himself into a corner," complained a State Department official, "unless he plans to torpedo SALT." The senator in his own defense contended that he was in fact trying to save the treaty, clearly outlining the actions necessary for the CFR's approval of the agreement.[107]

Although on November 9 the CFR endorsed the treaty, SALT II was floundering. Majority Leader Byrd hesitated to bring it to the floor because he doubted that he could get the required two-thirds vote for ratification. The CFR's 9-to-6 vote was itself a warning in that respect. On December 20 the Senate Armed Services Committee threw more dirt on SALT by concluding, 10 to 0, that the treaty did not serve the national interest. A week later, the Soviet invasion of Afghanistan virtually buried the agreement.[108]

Ironically, by then the Soviet combat brigade had turned out to be a silly non-issue. Additional intelligence information revealed that the soldiers in Cuba were in fact successors to units that had been on the island since the settlement of the 1962 missile crisis. They in no strict sense constituted a "combat" unit, or even a "brigade." Moreover, some three thousand Soviet troops, without immediate sea transport or airlift, scarcely threatened the United States.[109]

For several months, however, the much-ballyhooed "combat brigade" incident had resounded throughout U. S. foreign policy. It supplied

SALT II opponents with evidence of Soviet treachery. The alleged Soviet military buildup in Cuba fit well with anti-SALT films such as *Soviet Might, American Myth: The United States in Retreat*, which the American Conservative Union aired on some four hundred television stations. In the Carter administration, the hawkish Brzezinski accused the State Department of being too acquiescent toward the Soviets. The U. S., he told the president, needed "a tough line on Soviet adventurism."[110]

Actually, the brigade crisis may have encouraged such adventurism by making easier the Soviet decision to invade Afghanistan. The Soviets could infer that SALT II and improved relations with the U. S. were lost causes anyhow. The brigade incident, from the perspective of the U. S. S. R., made no sense except as proof that Americans did not want the SALT II treaty. When Ralph Earle, who had spent years negotiating the agreement, tried to explain that the brigade issue was the product of foolish mistakes, a Soviet official responded, "No government could be that stupid."[111]

After Carter decided in early 1980 to shelve the treaty, its supporters were quick to blame Idaho's senior senator. Many of them were convinced that he had acted recklessly, even demagogically, to save his political hide. Carter and Brzezinski both accused him of using the brigade issue to offset his liberal, dovish reputation as he pursued a fifth term. In the press, a disappointed Mary McGrory attributed his "huffing and puffing" to his desire to appease Idahoans furious about the Panama Canal treaties. "The Soviet brigade," she wrote, "offered him a chance to show that he can stand up to those Commie canal-rustlers." Columnist Mike Royko chided him for "hyperventilating" over three thousand Soviet soldiers. The *Christian Century* hoped that he would stop his "jingoistic posturing" in pursuit of votes. "Doonesbury" cartoonist Garry Trudeau portrayed a general congratulating him for aiding "Operation Manhood," thereby giving Americans "another chance to show that they're still number one!" Even Church's former speechwriter, Bill Hall was embarrassed. "It was not a proud moment to have the Senate Foreign Relations chairman from Idaho trying to outdo every right-wing wacko in the Senate," he said.[112]

Hall was surely correct about Church's concern over "how his words were playing at home." More than a dash of bravado marked some of the senator's statements. After his August 30 press conference he canceled a Labor Day appearance in Idaho by indicating that he was returning "to Washington for urgent consultations with the President." The

Soviets, he asserted, were "testing us in the Caribbean, right in our own front yard." He hoped "to persuade the President to take effective action in dealing with this challenge." On NBC's October 2 "Today Show," he asked: "If one brigade is acceptable in a combat role, then what about two? And if Cuba can be used as a base for ground combat forces, then what about naval forces?" On November 2 he threw down a challenge to the Soviets, saying that they had "to decide what matters most, the SALT II treaty, or a brigade of combat troops in Cuba."[113]

George McGovern cautioned him at the time not to blow the issue out of proportion. But he sensed that it was difficult for Church to back down, once the Idaho senator had taken his initial stand. McGovern guessed that "it was one of those cases where he made a mistake"—indeed, the "greatest mistake" of his career.[114]

In retrospect, Church apparently agreed. He subsequently told Bethine and Forrest that he wished he had not broken the brigade story. And in 1981, over lunch, he implicitly acknowledged his error to Ralph Earle. Earle recalled that he said sadly, "Well, Ralph, you look back on how you performed and it's not always perfect, is it?"[115]

Church nevertheless bridled at suggestions that he was the primary culprit behind the troop controversy and, by extension, the treaty's failure. There was, as he observed correctly, more than enough blame to share. The crisis produced no heroes. According to Carter's CIA director Stansfield Turner, the intelligence community committed "serious errors" in collecting and interpreting data about Cuba. The administration made matters worse, as a group of sixteen senior statesmen (including McGeorge Bundy and Henry Kissinger) candidly informed Carter. By mid-1979 the White House was in considerable disarray. In July, suffering from approval ratings that were below Nixon's worst figures, the president in two days had fired four Cabinet members and accepted the resignation of a fifth. Against that backdrop of confusion and growing public distrust, the brigade controversy badly divided Carter's advisors, some of whom worried primarily about SALT while others focused on improving the president's image. Official statements were occasionally inflammatory. Brzezinski, for example, warned "of possible retaliation" if the Soviets did not help to resolve the brigade issue. Meanwhile, anti-SALT senators seized upon the "combat" unit as evidence of Soviet duplicity. The nation's poor institutional memory permitted erroneous interpretations of "new" Soviet units in Cuba. Intelligence agencies thus overlooked continuities in the Soviets' Cuban presence. The media did not help. *Time* magazine showed what was supposed to be a Soviet-built intelligence station that was in fact a complex that ITT had built before Castro's takeover.[116]

When Church pointed out, quite rightly, that almost everyone involved in the crisis had made mistakes, he wisely did not exclude himself. He "created a mine field through which we've had to walk each day," one White House official commented bitterly as the controversy entered its fifth week. The senator had done what he himself had advised against—tying SALT to other issues. "He preached against linkage," said one Senate aide, "and at the first obstacle, he caved in." Although Church insisted he had simply stated a fact—namely that the brigade sorely damaged SALT II's chances for ratification—a senior Carter advisor probably guessed correctly that people must have thought: "If Frank Church says the Russians are coming, boy, things must really be in bad shape."[117]

If anyone should have been cautious about a leaked intelligence report, it was Church. But competing with his recent skepticism of the intelligence community was the memory of 1962, when information about Soviet missiles had been accurate. In retrospect, David Newsom wished that he would have informed Church about the Soviet brigade somewhat differently. At the time, however, the undersecretary was unaware that seventeen years earlier the senator had been "stung" when revelations about the missiles in Cuba had momentarily made him look like a liar or a fool. Newsom also emphasized that Church's August 30 announcement regarding the brigade accurately reflected information that the senator had just received. Moreover, Newsom conceded that Church may have been correct in wanting the public to learn about the brigade from an official source, rather than a newspaper leak. Perhaps, too, Church worried rightly that a leaked story would provide SALT II's opponents with more ammunition, allowing them to argue that the administration (and Church as well) had been engaged in a coverup. Still, the senator had acted precipitously. Looking back, he wished that he would at least have delayed overnight his decision to meet with the press. But no amount of second guessing could obscure the political content of his actions.[118]

Although Church was not without fault, his critics unfairly turned him into "the fall guy." The chances of ratifying the SALT II treaty were problematic all along. Some of Church's defenders argued that the agreement had no chance, even before the brigade crisis. In contrast, officials such as Ralph Earle were optimistic about the treaty, even after the Soviet invasion of Afghanistan. It was Carter who had dashed the optimists' hopes. In early 1980 he had given up on the agreement without first consulting Robert Byrd, Earle, Church, and others beyond his small White House circle. Still, in the effort to assign blame for the agreement's fate, many fingers pointed at Church. He became the scapegoat for errors only partly his. Bethine Church believed with some justification that the administration had "sandbagged" her husband, letting him bear the burden for "losing" SALT. At the least, Ralph Earle thought, Newsom should have urged him not to announce the brigade's existence.[119]

Ironically, the brigade incident only intensified the New Right's criticism of Church. Anyone But Church director Don Todd brushed off the senator's "saber rattling" as hypocritical and opportunistic—a desperate effort to salvage his battered political reputation in Idaho. If Church were really anxious about the Soviets, Todd declared, he would "lead the battle against the SALT II treaties." George Hansen accused Church of having covered up the brigade's existence for as long as possible to protect SALT. Steve Symms wondered why the senator, unlike Idaho's other congressional members, had so recently discovered the Soviet threat. "It is unfortunate," Symms said, "that he expresses his new-found concern about Soviet adventurism only when it will make headlines." Shortly after Church's August 30 press conference, his adversaries launched another blitz of TV advertisements against him.[120]

XII

Church's political road was getting steeper and steeper. Despite the senator's objections that NCPAC/ABC grossly distorted his record, the New Right continued to portray him as an enemy of Idaho and the United States. Terry Dolan of NCPAC happily predicted that "by 1980 there will be people voting against Church without remembering why." According to Dolan, the senator's challenger would "never have to say anything negative about Frank Church. We'll talk about all the negative stuff." Steve Symms certainly accommodated such a strategy. Into September of 1980, he protested not at all as the ultraconservative organizations staged a scurrilous campaign against the incumbent. His detached pose was misleading. With the election only weeks away, a television crew recorded Symms, who had apparently forgotten his wireless microphone, prompting someone at a political rally to raise a particularly damaging question about Church. The person subsequently asked if Church had weakened the CIA. Symms acted surprised at the question and turned to Jim McClure on the stage, saying that the senator would have more knowledge about the subject. McClure then attributed Richard Welch's death to Church. The former CIA agent in Greece had reportedly told McClure that Church was emboldening America's enemies and would cause the deaths of U. S. agents. Shortly thereafter, Welch had himself been assassinated. McClure's response to the question put Church in a terrible light, while still allowing Symms to play the role of the good guy above dirty politics.[121]

Affable and easy going, the forty-two-year-old Symms was a New Right favorite. A product of Caldwell, Idaho, where his family owned a large fruit ranch, he had graduated from the University of Idaho. The discipline of fraternity life and of football training camp, he said later, had been formative influences on him. After graduation, he served three years in the U. S. Marines. During the Cuban missile crisis his unit had been shipped to Guantanamo Bay, where it prepared to invade Cuba. When Kennedy reached an agreement with the Soviets, Symms angrily concluded that the president had deprived the U. S. of an opportunity to clean the communists off the island. After returning to Idaho he left the Presbyterian Church on grounds that it was becoming too liberal. He helped to publish *The Idaho Compass*, a pro-marketplace, anti-government newsletter. Among its goals was to have the University of Idaho offer a degree in capitalism to offset what Symms called the school's "bias" against the market economy. By 1971 he was so convinced that the U. S. was turning socialist that he considered moving his family to Australia's Great Barrier Reef. He entered politics instead. In 1972, to virtually everyone's surprise, he won election to the House of Representatives. Quickly establishing himself as a leading congressional conservative, he gained reelection by increasingly wide margins. And in 1980 his long-anticipated candidacy against Church was doing well indeed.[122]

While Symms focused on traditional pocketbook issues such as inflation and unemployment, NCPAC and ABC slammed Church with brutally negative ads. As the campaign progressed, the New Right attacks kept Church on the defensive. He had encountered political mudslinging before, but never this sustained or hateful. The ABC literature accused him of betraying the Republic of China on Taiwan; voting "to give away our Panama Canal"; voting in 1977 to boost his own salary (when, in fact, he had voted against the raise); and conducting a "witch hunt against the CIA and FBI" which destroyed America's intelligence agencies. Moral Majority literature repudiated Church for his "anti-tax-payer, anti-defense, anti-family votes." The National Pro-Life Political Action Committee pictured a sixteen-week-old fetus who was "*RUNNING FOR HIS LIFE* RIGHT NOW!," trying to get away from Church and several other "consistently. . . pro-abortion" senators. Right-to-Life supporters leafletted churches with a similar message. The ABC organization even started a telephone hotline over which callers could listen to minute-long diatribes against Church—a new one each day.[123]

New Right groups also brought to Idaho former intelligence officers and government officials who castigated Church for undermining U. S. security. In a radio advertisement, former CIA deputy director Daniel Graham said that agents blamed Church, more than anyone, for eroding America's intelligence capabilities abroad. Retired Army General John K. Singlaub and former U. S. ambassador to Chile Edward Korry blistered Church for harming the United States. Singlaub accused him of "emasculating" the CIA and helping the Soviets surpass the U. S. militarily while Korry charged him with suppressing evidence regarding Chile in order to protect the communists and the Kennedy and Johnson administrations. Church "put out a black and white morality fable presenting the U. S. as some kind of bully boy," Korry protested. "I have often stated publicly that if I could ever use my voice. . .to remove Frank Church from public office, I would put aside everything to travel to this state."[124]

The viciousness of these attacks gave rise to frightening expressions of grassroots rage. Several constituents angrily returned Church's campaign literature with threats and obscenities written on it. One man razored out Church's throat from a campaign photo and accused him of selling out Idaho "to the commies." "*Go to Hell*!! you God Damn Communist," wrote another person. Another man described him as " 'The sell-out Snake' who's as queer as a 3 dollar bill." People called his office "all the time," recalled Penny Gross, saying such things as "I hope he gets run over by a truck." Bethine Church found Idahoans so furious about her husband's alleged disloyalty that she sometimes feared for his life.[125]

The sheer ugliness of the attacks kept Church off balance. According to his campaign manager Carl Burke, he was "really hurt" and "felt like Idaho itself was changing and the people in it were changing." His staffers were divided on how to respond. Some favored a direct counter-attack; others reasoned that such tactics only dignified the outrageous charges. "On the one hand, you'd sit there saying, 'Nobody is going to believe this crap,' " recalled Cleve Corlett. "On the other hand, people do start to believe if you tell a lie often enough." Church had previously relied upon volunteers. The question now was whether they could match the New Right's sophisticated mailings and heavy advertising. For the first time, Church ended up hiring phone bank operators to advance his cause. Burke, watching the expenses roar upward, commented that the senator was spending more on helium for balloons than he had spent in the entire 1956 campaign.[126]

Burke sensed that the ABC assault "really got under [Church's] skin." The senator began to lose his sense of humor and even his confidence. He became more strident. On several occasions he lost his composure. Once, he placed some red, white, and blue bunting around his shoulders and said that he, too, could wrap himself in the flag. His staff was "horrified," and told him so. At Ricks College, he lost his temper during a series of barbed, even malicious, questions. A young woman held up *The Spike*, a novel about communist subversion. Among its characters was a senator who had weakened the CIA by investigating it. "Does this remind you of anyone you know," the woman asked nastily as she waved the book. Church snapped back at her for believing such "political fiction" and then, in frustration, told the next questioner to learn the facts before making charges: "You are in college now."[127]

As the long campaign dragged on, Church seemed so exhausted that aide Garry Wenske worried about his health. The senator himself may have had similar concerns. One afternoon he paced anxiously in his Boise living room while talking with Peter Fenn. Suddenly he sat down. After what seemed an interminable moment of silence, he asked suddenly, "Peter, who's going to take care of Bethine when I'm gone?" The startled aide asked what his boss was talking about. "Bethine's going to outlive me by a long time and I'm worried about it," Church replied. The conversation ended at that point, but Fenn wondered later what kinds of premonitions were going through the senator's mind.[128]

With the election only a few weeks away, the polls were sending out discouraging signals as well. By mid-September Church was trailing

Symms 42 to 49 percent. Pollster Peter Hart warned the senator's campaign staff that "Frank Church has come across as a man under siege," looking "worn down" and unsure of himself. The senator was also losing the battle of the media. Symms's anti-government message was a factor, but many voters appeared to be thinking less about the challenger than about ousting Church. Increasingly, according to Hart, they viewed him as "one of 'them' instead of one of 'us.' " Thirty percent continued to believe that his support for the Panama Canal treaties was by itself reason enough to vote against him. The abortion issue was apparently hurting him very badly among Catholics (12 percent of Idaho voters), where his support had plummeted from 66 to 46 percent in four months. In southeast Idaho, Church's plunging fortunes suggested how much he missed the redoubtable Verda Barnes, who died in mid-1980. For years she had tapped her eastern Idaho background and Latter-day Saints connections to round up the Mormon vote in that part of the state. Her death, as historian Ron Hatzenbuehler later conjectured, "may have left a hole in Church's campaign staff that no one could fill."[129]

Nor could Church look to the Carter administration for help. A year earlier, the president's fortunes had been bad enough, slumping in mid-1979 to a dismal public approval rating of only 30 percent. Since then, Carter had suffered additional setbacks. The energy crisis had driven inflation into double digits. Interest rates were rocketing upward. For Church, as well as for Carter, the economic news was devastating because Idaho, like many states, was reeling. "The oppressed middle class is about to vote Church out," Peter Hart discovered. Among the 54 percent of Idaho voters whose income ranged from $10,000 to $25,000, Church's support was sinking dramatically. The fact that only 23 percent of his constituents knew about his opposition to the big oil companies was no more reassuring.[130]

Crises abroad also battered the administration and, by extension, Church. In November 1979 Iranian students had seized the U. S. embassy in Teheran, taking fifty American hostages. Throughout 1980 "America Held Hostage" was a dominant news story, supplying further evidence of U. S. humiliation abroad. Former ambassador Edward Korry blamed part of that humiliation on Frank Church. The senator, he said, was "the one American most responsible" when the Iranian rebels invoked "Chile" to justify their resistance to U. S. "imperialism." In December the Soviet invasion of Afghanistan dealt the administration yet another blow.[131]

While Carter's growing unpopularity added to Church's political burdens in Idaho, the rising tide of Ronald Reagan washed across the state. The Republican presidential candidate articulated dramatically the growing public disillusionment with government and with America's image abroad. He denounced big government along with "gloom and doom" talk about America's limits and decline. And he championed a stronger America abroad. By the fall of 1980, Reagan had a two-to-one lead over Carter in Idaho and seemed on his way to carrying the state by as much as 70 percent. "But for the honor of it all," Church quipped, "I would just as soon be running in a different year."[132]

Caught in a dramatic transition in American politics, Church had to fend off not only the New Right's unprincipled attacks but also a widespread sense in Idaho that he had lost touch with his constituency. An incident in a small town in the Salmon River country suggested a shift in the way voters viewed him. A Church supporter was surprised to see a Symms bumper sticker on a friend's truck. The friend expressed gratitude for what Church had done in the past, but explained that "it's just time for a change. We just got to change what's going on in Washington."[133]

XIII

That desire for change, and the state's growing conservatism, clinched Church's defeat. In Idaho, Ronald Reagan received two and a half times the number of votes that Carter did. The election also strengthened considerably the hold of conservative Republicans on the state legislature. In the House they outnumbered Democrats 56 to 14; in the Senate their margin was 23 to 12. In this context, the surprise was that Church barely missed winning a fifth term. Despite the New Right's onslaught against him and the conservative juggernaut in Idaho, Church lost to Symms by only 4,262 ballots, less than 1 percent of the vote. Significantly, for the first time in Idaho history more people cast votes in the Senate race than in the presidential contest; Church and Symms received thirty thousand more votes than Reagan and Carter. Some people were certain that Jimmy Carter's early concession in the presidential race several hours before the western polls closed had cost Church his Senate seat. Church himself was "mad as hell" about Carter's hasty concession. But generally he took his defeat stoically. Patting the shoulders of his mother and mother-in-law, he said, "I guess your son has to go out and find another job."[134]

On the afternoon after the election, Church sat quietly at his kitchen table, drinking a glass of milk. Obviously tired, he accepted his defeat philosophically. He predicted that the Reagan/Symms confidence in unfettered free enterprise would produce more problems than solutions. And he doubted that the new administration would be able to boost defense spending, cut taxes, and balance the budget. But whatever the future held, one thing was certain: for the first time in twenty-four years, Frank Church would no longer be a U. S. senator.[135]

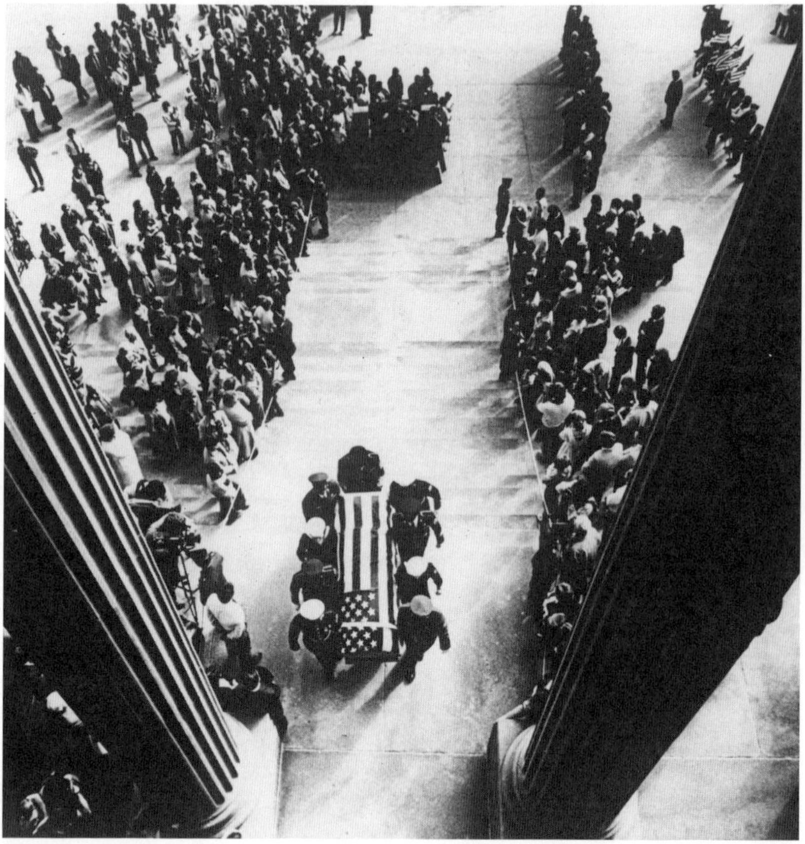

The final trip home. Bearers carry Church's body into the Idaho statehouse. *Courtesy Idaho Statesman.*

Epilogue

"MAYBE PEOPLE ARE like geraniums," Frank Church said two years after leaving office. "Maybe it's best that they are uprooted once in a while and replanted in different soil." For Church, the soil outside the Senate proved quite nourishing. Financially, he and Bethine prospered for the first time. The large law firm that he joined allowed him to pursue his interests in international issues. And, although the ascendancy of Ronald Reagan discouraged him greatly, he used his status as an ex-senator to critique the administration's policies in speeches, articles, and public letters. Church found, in Bethine's words, that " 'Yes, there is life after the Senate.' " It was, however, all too brief. In early 1984, he learned that he was terminally ill.[1]

I

Except for the last few months, Church's post-Senate career was extremely active. In early 1981 he joined the Washington office of Whitman and Ransom, a prestigious New York City law firm that was expanding its international practice. Church's friend William Landau helped him find the job. According to Landau, Church had been "a little at loose ends" as he wrapped up his Senate career, unsure about his future and uncomfortable about hunting for a position elsewhere. Landau even negotiated his salary because Church found the whole process embarrassing. After Church's first two years on the job, members of Whitman and Ransom were well pleased with their new partner. "Since he came to our firm," one of them said, "our international practice has become our most rapidly growing area."[2]

Church was equally satisfied. His partnership with Whitman and Ransom allowed him time to lecture, write, remain somewhat active in the public sector, and finally enjoy a considerable salary. His income had jumped substantially, he said, from the $60,000 that he had earned at the end of his Senate career to something "in the six figures." He joined organizations such as the Center for Democratic Policy, the Center for Responsive Politics (whose goal was campaign finance reform), and George McGovern's Americans for Common Sense, which sought in part to counter the radical right. He and Bethine traveled widely.[3]

His new affluence was welcome. Although money had never been particularly important to him, he worried about Bethine's economic status if anything serious happened to him. "He really had nothing," according to William Landau, who often helped him figure out his finances. Granted, he was far from impoverished, but evidence abounded that he had not used his twenty-four years in the Senate to enrich himself. The Churches had little except for the quite comfortable home in which they had lived for over two decades and the tiny Pennsylvania cabin they finally purchased in the 1970s. He drove an old car, and the house in Bethesda needed repairs. After he signed on with Whitman and Ransom he joked about flying first class instead of "in the tail of the plane." And he laughingly grabbed the check when he and Bethine took several friends to a fancy restaurant. "I can afford to pay now," he said.[4]

He appreciated the fact that his work with Whitman and Ransom did not require extensive lobbying on Capitol Hill. For one thing, he had never been comfortable pressuring people for support. For another, he had always been uneasy about the ethics of former officeholders who traded on their connections. Now that he was out of office, he preferred to avoid the Senate as much as possible. He recalled how depressing it was to watch former senators trying to relive their glory days. "I'd rather have a new and different life," he said.[5]

In important respects he did not even regret leaving the Senate. He speculated that a fifth term would have brought only frustration. The Republicans had captured the Senate in 1980, so he would have lost his position as chair of the Foreign Relations Committee. Moreover, he disliked the growing ugliness of American politics. In 1980, the New Right's campaign of innuendo and smear had helped not only to defeat him, but other well-known Democratic liberals such as McGovern, Iowa's John Culver, Indiana's Birch Bayh, and Wisconsin's Gaylord Nelson. Certainly Church would not miss dealing with the embittered, vengeful groups that had become increasingly active in Idaho. Looking to the future, he had no interest in trying to reclaim his Senate seat. "I can't say that I miss the Senate as much as I thought I might," he commented after being out of office for a year.[6]

He was gloomy about America's political future. The Democrats seemed adrift, content to wait in hopes that Reagan would soon lose favor. Church wished that they would more aggressively define their own programs and ideas, and articulate the principles for which they stood rather than simply seek shelter during the Republican storm.[7]

Wherever Church looked, he found additional evidence that the world was "strange and dangerous." The New Right was an ominous example. Church criticized its intolerance, its rejection of democratic pluralism, its strident efforts to impose one viewpoint on others, and its pursuit of single issues–which made it, he said, like a horse with blinders. On March 29, 1981, on the David Suskind television show, he faced off against representatives of the Reverend Jerry Falwell's Moral Majority. The state, he insisted, should not attempt to force one group's version of morality upon another. Nothing less than the principles of political and religious freedom were at stake. As Church said elsewhere, he was always wary "when political action programs are wrapped in religious garb." Persecution too often resulted.[8]

In part because of its ties to the Moral Majority, the Reagan administration made Church nervous. He worried also that the administration would set back civil rights, environmental laws, and social programs for the needy. To Church, everything seemed "topsy-turvy." Federal spending had jumped enormously, largely because of the vastly expanded military budget; but the public seemed to think that government expenses were diminishing. The deficit continued to soar; but people cheered Reagan's talk about balancing the budget. The 1981 tax cut aided mainly the very rich; but rank-and-file citizens seemed pleased with it.[9]

As much as the administration's domestic actions bothered Church, he found Reagan's foreign policy even more appalling. For almost two decades Church had battled the simplistic assumptions behind the Cold War. The Carter administration's increasing hawkishness had perturbed him, but Reagan and his advisors seemed even more determined to shore up the aging Cold War edifice. Church found Casper Weinberger "indeed frightening," because the new Secretary of Defense backed such huge increases in defense spending. Worse, he said, was the fact that Weinberger apparently mirrored the president's own wishes. The administration, obsessed with the Soviet threat, overlooked America's slumping position in the world economy. It single-mindedly attributed international ferment, from El Salvador to Namibia, to the Soviets. It backed brutal right-wing regimes simply because they were anti-communist. And it called for a massive rearmament program. Church believed that ideology, not reality, accounted for this chip-on-the-shoulder style of foreign policy whose guiding principle seemed to be "Poke the Russians." He feared for the results. The U. S. would become a scapegoat, as it recently had in Iran, by continuing to back anti-communist dictators in nations seething with unrest. At home, meanwhile, the immense arms buildup would shift resources from the civilian budget to the military, cutting social services and wrecking hopes of balancing the budget.[10]

Church was also alarmed at the resurgence of the CIA, now under the direction of Reagan's campaign manager William Casey. In 1981, for example, the Reagan administration proposed an Executive Order by which the agency would be able to conduct certain covert operations within the United States. The CIA could open mail without warrants, collect information on Americans who were not under investigation, and gain access to bank and medical records. On November 12, in testimony before a House Judiciary subcommittee, Church attacked the proposals as threats to the rule of law in a democracy. His earlier investigations of the intelligence community had revealed its tendency to see the law as an obstacle, "an impediment to national security." The administration's proposed Executive Order would encourage intelligence abuses. At one point Church's suspicions of the CIA boiled over. In other countries, he said, it operated "in utter disregard of the consequences of the law. . . .When you bring these people home, you invite trouble, serious trouble." The fact that Barry Goldwater, in January 1981, took charge of the Senate intelligence committee hardly reassured Church. "I think that the CIA is going to find a very cordial reception here," Goldwater said.[11]

In Church's opinion, the Reagan administration was headed down the bloody path that the U. S. had taken in the 1960s and early 1970s—a path that blurred distinctions between America's international conduct and that of the Soviet KGB. Church recalled how the CIA's covert actions in Cuba and Chile had sullied America's reputation abroad and made the U. S. seem as imperialistic as the Soviets. He denied the administration's claims that covert action was a realistic necessity. It was instead a euphemism "for unacknowledged proxy wars, for murder, coercion, blackmail, bribery, the spreading of lies and any other dirty trick that is deemed useful in serving U. S. interests abroad." Church was incensed at reports that the administration was secretly intervening in Nicaragua. "Such criminal activity on our part," he snapped, "should be stopped cold, once and for all!" He also urged the administration not to repeat past mistakes in Latin America by "hustling in the Marines to suppress each local uprising." Reagan's treatment of Central America infuriated him. "The stupidity of it!" he said when talking with columnist David Broder. "This country," he told Broder, "has become so conservative – so fearful – that we have come to see revolution anywhere in the world as a threat to the United States. It's nonsense."[12]

In the fall of 1983, unlike the majority of Americans, he criticized the administration's handling of Grenada. For several months the president had been virtually obsessed that the small Caribbean island was turning into a communist beachhead. On October 25 he ordered an invasion force of five thousand troops to Grenada to rescue U. S. medical students reportedly endangered by an outbreak of violence. After two days of fighting against a few hundred Cubans on the island, the U. S. restored order on its own terms. "We blew them away," the U. S. task force commander said triumphantly. Polls suggested that most Americans viewed the Grenada invasion as "a lovely little war," in one reporter's words. Church was skeptical that the president's main concern had been to save the students. "I think that in due course it will be revealed that our government's real objective was to displace the local government and put in its place a government of our own choosing," he said.[13]

Church was also angry with Jimmy Carter. In late 1982 the former president's newly published memoirs, *Keeping Faith*, enraged him. On one level, Carter had portrayed Church condescendingly as "a favorite of the Washington press"– a characterization that the *Washington Post*'s Robert Kaiser guessed would "surprise ex-Sen. Church." More seriously, Carter had also mixed up the facts regarding Church and the Soviet brigade incident, making the senator look shabby indeed. The day after Church looked at the book he was "livid," according to his secretary, so "visibly upset" that he could not do his work. Finally, he put everything else aside and furiously scribbled out a reply to Carter, which the *Washington Post* published. After setting forth his own version of what had happened during the brigade crisis, he offered some advice to the ex-president: "For those of us who were involved, it is time to sheathe the long knives."[14]

II

While Carter's jabs and Reagan's policies distressed Church, he was also having trouble physically. Shortly after leaving the Senate he complained of thirstiness, tingling feet, and terrible backaches. Tests revealed that he had diabetes. From that point on he was dependent on insulin, and Bethine learned how to administer the injections.[15]

By the spring of 1983 he was clearly not his old self. Some mornings he was late coming to work; sometimes he stayed away until after lunch. He was tired and losing weight. On a trip to France that summer he had difficulty keeping his food down. Back in the United States he took several pills at lunch one day. Penny Gross, his secretary, asked how long he was going to have to take them. "For the rest of my life," he said. He paused before adding, "However long that may be."[16]

Despite his fatigue and premonitions that he might have serious health problems, he continued to deliver speeches around the country. In what turned out to be his last appearance in Idaho, he spoke in October at Boise State University for Russian Awareness Week. Controversy erupted when Steve Symms charged that sponsors of the event had misused federal funds by spending them for a conference on the Soviet Union. A representative of the National Endowment for the Humanities claimed that Church's speech, a critique of U. S. foreign policy, was "very intelligent" but "didn't have a great deal to do with the humanities."[17]

On November 17, in New York City, a discouraged Frank Church gave a relentlessly bleak assessment of American politics and foreign policy. "The Imperial Presidency still rides tall in the saddle," he said. "Far from having curbed presidential wars, Congress isn't even told which country the United States will invade next!" Church believed that the War Powers Act counted for little, once the president waved the flag and banged the drum. He was equally pessimistic about the prospects of nuclear disarmament. "Good luck can't last forever," he predicted. "As long as the missiles remain poised on hair-trigger alert, mathematical odds make certain that one day there will be a nuclear holocaust." He felt no better about the capacity of the president to manipulate anti-communist sentiments. The invasion of Grenada was a case in point. "President Reagan has cowed the Democrats by nailing a little Marxist pelt on the White House wall," Church declared. " 'Happy 1984.' "[18]

Physically, he looked worse and worse. He had developed yellow jaundice and a bacterial infection. Another round of tests had still not ascertained the major reason for his illness. As Christmas approached, he was determined to spend the holiday in New York City with Forrest's family. In previous years, he and Bethine had flown to Boise to be with their mothers. This Christmas, however, because his mother had died the previous spring, they decided to visit their grandchildren. The day before they were to fly to New York, he had to cancel the trip. He was simply too sick to enjoy it. Forrest sensed that he knew he was dying.[19]

On January 12 he underwent surgery for a blocked bile duct in New York's Memorial Sloan-Kettering Cancer Center. The evening before the operation he received a call from Steve Symms. Idaho's new senator undoubtedly meant well, but his comments were badly timed. "I just want to tell you, Frank, that the last three years have been the greatest of my life," Symms said happily. "I really love the Senate." Bethine was irate at such insensitivity; Church simply smiled.[20]

During the operation, the doctors discovered that he had pancreatic cancer which had spread to his liver. The prognosis gave him no more than four months to live. He remained in good humor nonetheless. Once, as he maneuvered down the hospital hall, with Bethine helping him and pushing the intravenous stand, he asked a bystander what the speed limit was. On a foggy, frigid January 24, he endured a bumpy, painful flight back to Washington, D. C. He hated hospitals and wanted to return to his Bethesda home, where he intended to stay to the end, in his own bed and without life supports. Three times he submitted to chemotherapy, but did not tolerate it well. He hoped the treatments would nevertheless buy "a little springtime."[21]

His health failed rapidly. During February, despite breathing difficulties and a terribly weakened condition, he pushed himself to complete his last article, "We Must Learn to Live With Revolutions." "You can't imagine the amount of energy it takes to think," he said. In mid-March, a bacterial problem raised his temperature to 104. By the end of the month, however, he felt somewhat stronger. Still interested in current events, he expressed concern about Reagan's ability to reshape the U. S. Supreme Court. "For American jurisprudence," he said, "the idea is simply staggering."[22]

His main thoughts were understandably on life and death. He admitted feeling "outraged" at having to fight cancer yet another time. He had once told Forrest that he hoped to die via a massive heart attack, suddenly and quickly. "What he feared most, and secretly expected," Forrest wrote later, "was a recurrence of cancer." His suspicions proved correct, but he tried to remain philosophical about his fate. "It again proves to me," he said, "that life goes by too fast, and the only solace Bethine and I have is that we've deeply savored the time we've had since my first bout with cancer 35 years ago." Bethine, in turn, grieved that "he will leave me too soon." With Chase's constant help, she cared for her husband around the clock. And she prayed that he would make it until spring so he could watch the flowers bloom in their yard. In the meantime, he was locked in battle with what he called "the invader which is threatening me now."[23]

He had long been skeptical about an after-life, and gave no indication that he was changing his mind on the subject. According to Forrest, who in 1978 became the minister of New York City's All Souls Unitarian Church and talked with him many times about theological issues, "his belief was that this life was the life we had and it was miracle enough, challenge enough." The act of dying frightened him, because of the pain and the loss of control over his body. But, in Forrest's opinion, "he was not afraid of death." He was stoical about it, and "needed no belief in immortality to sustain him."[24]

For Church, even these terrible days brought their own rewards and satisfaction. Bethine and Chase were always with him, and Forrest flew down each week for brief visits. Church's brother Richard stopped by regularly. "Well, Frank," he would say, "I'm here for my daily lesson in foreign policy." Although Church increasingly had difficulty talking, his interest in foreign relations did not flag. He was also extremely pleased when Congress, on March 1, added his name to Idaho's River of No Return Wilderness. James McClure, despite having opposed the wilderness area, now kindly introduced legislation to rename it. And on March 11 the *Washington Post* published Church's essay on learning to live with revolutions.[25]

The flood of well-wishers and sympathy cards and letters for Church was overwhelming. Even before he left the hospital, attendants brought thick bundles of letters to him from around the country. Urging him to "fight on," one writer called him the "only person we have ever believed in." When Church was back home in Bethesda, friends and former colleagues streamed by. He insisted that people not keep quiet downstairs, even if he was resting in his room. "He wanted to be able to hear the household," his secretary remembered. "He wanted people to laugh. He wanted to hear them talking." Until his last few days, he looked forward to gathering around the dinner table and reminiscing. One evening he put an opera on the phonograph and then sang along with the record, enjoying himself immensely. Senator Ted Kennedy visited him a number of times, sometimes sitting quietly beside the bed and holding his hand. "I think it's coming soon," Church told him when they last saw each other. George McGovern, paying a final visit, thought his old friend was asleep. Somewhat awkwardly, McGovern leaned over the bed and hugged him. He then heard Church's weak whisper, "You are a dear man." Overwhelmed with emotion, McGovern simply held him.[26]

Church had avoided painkillers in order to keep his mind clear, but the night before he died Bethine requested morphine to comfort him. He lay in bed, emaciated, his hair almost white, with Bethine still trying to get liquids down him. By then he was virtually unable to speak. He managed to wink and smile sometimes in response to his visitors. "The last thing to go," Forrest recalled, "was his incandescent smile." Church had hoped to survive long enough for one more visit to his beloved Pennsylvania cabin, where he could see and listen to the creek. He never made the trip. On April 7, at 7:45 a. m., he died. He was fifty-nine.[27]

III

Twenty-four hours after Church died, former congressman Otis Pike picked up the morning newspaper and knew it was a bad day. Alongside the headlines of Church's death were stories that the Reagan administration had been mining Nicaraguan harbors and preparing contingency plans to send U. S. combat troops to Central America. Pike had been Church's House counterpart during the investigations of the intelligence community. More than ever, he now thought, the times needed Frank Church. Pike praised him as "a class act" who "taught us that all conduct that brings us dishonor must, in the long run, fail."[28]

On April 10, hundreds of mourners jammed National Cathedral for Church's memorial service. Church would have been astonished. With great reluctance, he had bowed to his family's urgings that there should be a service in the Washington, D. C. area; but he had wanted it in a small chapel so there would not be a lot of empty seats. As Ted Kennedy surveyed the packed audience in the huge cathedral, he remarked that he now knew why Church had smiled during their last meeting: "I believe he chuckled that morning because he knew the best orator of our time in the Senate would not be available for this service, so he was asking some of the rest of us to do the best we could."[29]

Toward the end of the service, the haunting melody, "Dream the Impossible Dream," elicited many tears. The song was from *Man of La Mancha*, a musical about the life of Don Quixote. Church had loved the play, and often sang its tunes as he drove along in his aging Ford Mustang. In the mid-Sixties, during a visit from his long-time Boise friends Stan and Marylu Burns, he had played the record after dinner, sometimes acting out the parts with great gusto. While Bethine had not chosen to include "Dream the Impossible Dream" in Church's memorial service, several staffers inserted it because they thought it told much about his own life. He apparently thought so, too. When he was dying he expressed regret to one old friend that "I can't continue to pick up the cudgels with you as we play Don Quixote in this mad world." Like Quixote, he had challenged those with power, whether in the form of multinational corporations, the intelligence community, or the Imperial Presidency. And like Quixote, he had often tilted at windmills in his pursuit of ideals.[30]

Following the memorial service in the National Cathedral, Church's body was flown to Boise for the funeral. "And home he comes today," wrote former staffer Bill Hall, "home to Idaho, home to the soil from which he sprang, home to the state he made so proud, home to the place where he found Bethine."[31]

Hall was not alone in paying tribute to Bethine. It was impossible to honor Frank Church without honoring her. He had believed, quite literally, that she had saved his life during his first battle with cancer. She had been his best friend and his constant companion; by all accounts, their love for each other ran deep. He had always needed her. Now, at the end, she was still with him, walking alongside his casket at the funeral.

The funeral services occurred April 12 at Boise's First Methodist Church. On that brilliant but sad spring afternoon, people such as Carl Burke and Stan Burns reminisced about their old friend. Forrest compared his father to "the day star, rising early to prominence, brilliant in the dusk and against the darkness," gone with the dawn. "God love him," said an unidentified elderly woman who was among the thousand people in attendance. Church was buried in Boise's Morris Hill cemetery, a short distance from his boyhood hero, William E. Borah.[32]

Endnotes

Endnote Abbreviations

BC–Papers in the personal possession of Bethine Church
CP–Frank Church Papers, Boise State University
CR–Congressional Record
GRF Library–Gerald R. Ford Presidential Library, Ann Arbor, Michigan
HJP–Senator Henry Jackson Papers, University of Washington, Seattle
JEC Library–Jimmy Carter Library, Atlanta, Georgia
JFK Library–John F. Kennedy Presidential Library, Boston, Massachusetts
LC–Library of Congress
LBJ Library–Lyndon Baines Johnson Presidential Library, Austin, Texas
LJP–Senator Len Jordan Papers, Boise State University
MSHS–Minnesota State Historical Society
NA–National Archives, Washington, D. C.
NPMP–Richard M. Nixon Presidential Materials Project, National Archives, Washington, D. C.
POF–Personal Office File
WHCF–White House Central File
WHSF–White House Staff File

Notes for Prologue

1. Frank Church, "We Must Learn to Live With Revolutions," *Washington Post*, 11 March 1984; interviews: Jerry Levinson, 2 Aug. 1984; Penny Gross, 11 Aug. 1984; Steven Emerson, 31 July 1984; also Frank Church to Wendy Morgan, 28 March 1984, CP, 12/3/20.
2. Detroit *Free Press*, 16 March 1975 (complex); *Lewiston Tribune*, 15 April 1984 (chances).
3. Re borrowed time, Bethine Church interview, 12 March 1985; also David Morrissey in Vancouver, Wa., *Columbian*, n.d., clipping in CP, 12/3/1.
4. Kennedy qtn., *CR*, 12 Dec. 1980, p. 33836.
5. Qtns., "Frank Church, R I P," *National Review* (4 May 1984): 21; McGrory in *Idaho Statesman*, 12 April 1984.
6. Church qtn. in *The Frank Church Papers: A Summary Guide* (Boise: Boise State University, 1988), p. 32.
7. Church qtn., *Philadelphia Inquirer*, 21 Sept. 1975; Hawley qtn., *Washington Post*, 8 April 1984; David Morrissey interview, 17 Nov. 1987, re audience.
8. Dieter in *Idaho Statesman*, 11 April 1984; Wayne Cornell in *Idaho Press-Tribune*, 11 April 1984, re potatoes.

9. Church, "We Must Learn to Live With Revolutions."
10. Qtn., F. Forrester Church, *Father and Son: A Personal Biography of Senator Church of Idaho* (New York: Harper & Row, 1985), p. 162.

Notes to Chapter One

1. Richard Church to Ashby, 28 Feb. 1987; interviews: Richard Church, 5 Aug. 1984; Stan Burns, 16 March 1988; Laura Church (by Sam Day), 23 June 1971, CP, Audio tape A71012.
2. Richard Church interview, 5 Aug. 1984; Richard Church to Ashby, 28 Feb. 1987.
3. F. Forrester Church, *Father and Son: A Personal Biography of Senator Frank Church of Idaho* (New York: Harper & Row, 1985), pp. 14-15; Richard Church interview, 5 Aug. 1984, re religion.
4. On the family tree, see especially Church, *Father and Son,* pp. 14-17, and *Idaho Statesman*, 7 March 1943, copy in CP, 5.2/2/13.
5. Interviews: Richard Church, 5 Aug. 1984, and Stan Burns, 29 Jan. 1984; Richard Church to Ashby, 28 Feb. 1987.
6. Harmon Holvorson interview, 5 Sept. 1984.
7. Interviews: Frank Church, 18 June 1979; Holvorson, 5 Sept. 1984; and Forrest Church, 25 July 1984; Richard Church to Ashby, 28 Feb. 1987.
8. Richard Church to Ashby, 28 Feb. 1987; Richard Church interviews, 5 Aug. 1984 and 28 May 1987.
9. Richard Church to Ashby, 28 Feb. 1987.
10. Richard Church interview, 5 Aug. 1984, and Church to Ashby, 28 Feb. 1987; Laura Church interview. Frank Church interview, 18 June 1979, re his father and Gonzaga University in Spokane, Washington.
11. Richard Church to Ashby, 28 Feb. 1987, re tantrums; Laura Church interview re July 4.
12. For example, see Burns interview, 24 April 1984.
13. Richard Church to Ashby, 28 Feb. 1987, and interviews, 5 Aug. 1984 and 18 May 1987.
14. Richard Church to Ashby, 28 Feb. 1987; interviews: Jim Baxter, 25 April 1984; Richard Church, 5 Aug. 1984; Stan Burns, 16 March 1988.
15. Interviews: Burns, 22 March 1979; Holvorson, 5 Sept. 1984.
16. Tommie Ward interview, 16 May 1987.
17. Quotation from Carl Burke, *South Idaho Press*, 13 April 1984; Frank Church to Bethine, 30 Nov. 1945, in Bethine Church's possession.
18. Interviews: Burke, 23 May 1979; Burns, 22 March 1979 and 16 March 1988.
19. Interviews: Frank Church, 18 June 1979; Burns, 16 March 1988.
20. Perry Swisher to Ashby, 31 Dec. 1987; Burns interview, 22 March 1979, and Tom Spofford, 30 April 1984.
21. Richard Church to Ashby, 28 Feb. 1987.
22. Richard Church to Ashby, 28 Feb. 1987; Frank Church to Bethine, 30 Nov. 1945 (in Bethine Church's possession), re Wardwell and the cave.
23. Burke to Church, 9 April 1958, CP, 10.3/1/5.
24. Quotation in F. Ross Peterson, *Idaho: A Bicentennial History* (New York: Norton, 1976), p. 5. See also Carlos A. Schwantes, *In Mountain Shadows: A History of Idaho* (Lincoln: University of Nebraska Press, 1991).
25. Quotation in Merle Wells, *Boise: An Illustrated History* (Woodland Hills, Cal.: Windsor Publications, 1982), p. 6; Richard Church to Ashby, 28 Feb. 1987.

26. Burns interview, 16 March 1988.
27. Richard Church to Ashby, 28 Feb. 1987, and interviews: Frank Church, 18 June 1979; Laura Church re the economic situation; Burns, 16 March 1988, re the bike.
28. Interviews: Burns, 22 March 1979, and Carl Burke, 23 May 1979; *Boise Capital News*, 27 April 1939.
29. Esther Huse interview, 23 April 1984. See, also, several poems and essays for Miss Semple's English class, CP, 10.1/1/5,7.
30. Interviews: Margaret Baxter, 1 May 1984, Holvorson, and Laura Church; Paul A. Carter to Church, 17 Oct. 1956, CP, 12/3/1.
31. *Boise Highlights*, 18 April 1941; Boyd B. Stutler, "There Burns a Light," *The American Legion Magazine* (June, 1941): 24-25, 41; quotation from Perry Swisher to Ashby, 31 Dec. 1987.
32. Stutler, "There Burns a Light"; Frank Church, "The American Way of Life," CP, 10.1/1/8.
33. Stutler, "There Burns a Light," p. 40.
34. Interviews: Church, 18 June 1979; Burke, 22 Nov. 1987; also Burns, 16 March 1988.
35. Sam Day interview with Jean Elizabeth Clark, CP, A71011, re voting.
36. Interviews: Burns, 24 April 1984 and 16 March 1988, and Jean Elizabeth Clark.
37. Frank Church, "Borah the Statesman," *Idaho Yesterdays*, 9 (Summer 1965): 2-3. On Borah see, for example, LeRoy Ashby, *The Spearless Leader: Senator Borah and the Progressive Movement in the 1920s* (Urbana, Ill.: University of Illinois Press, 1972).
38. Interviews: Frank Church, 18 June 1979; Richard Church, 5 Aug. 1984.
39. Interviews: Frank Church, 18 June 1979; Richard Church, 28 May 1987; Burns, 29 Jan. and 4 April 1984; quotation about converting himself in pamphlet, "Distinguished Young Americans," p. 17, CP, 10.1, Box 1.
40. Richard Church interview, 5 Aug. 1984; Burns interview, 24 April re the kidding.
41. Forrest Church interview, 25 July 1984.
42. Jim Baxter interview, 25 April 1984.
43. Church to "Dear Ron," 9 November 1979, CP, 12/3/1.
44. Burns interviews, 29 Jan. 1984, 16 March 1988.
45. Richard Church interview, 28 May 1987.
46. Church keynote address, 2 Sept. 1952, at the state Democratic convention, CP, 12/3/2.
47. *Boise Capital News*, 27 April 1939.
48. Burke interview, 23 May 1979.
49. Quotation in Lily Jay Silver's biographical sketch of Frank Church, February, 1963, containing Church's corrections, CP, 10.1, Box 1; Frank Church interview, 18 June 1979, re the mock hanging. See also Frank Church, "Boise High Schools Buy Stamps," *The Idaho Journal of Education*, Feb., 1942, pp. 133-34, copy in CP, 10.1/1/6.
50. *The Penguin* (29 May 1942) re the play, CP, 10.7, Box 1; Burke interview, 23 May 1979, re the magic act.
51. Interviews: Burns, 24 April 1984; Bethine Church, 3 Aug. 1984.
52. Interviews: Burns, 16 March 1988; Burke, 23 May 1979.
53. Interviews: Bethine Church, 25 Jan. 1989; Burns, 16 March 1988.
54. Unidentified clippings, CP, 10.1/1/6, re the debates; Church, *Father and Son*, pp. 22-24; Burke to Ashby, 5 Aug. 1986.
55. Tim Woodward column, Idaho *Daily Statesman*, 15 April 1984, re the barroom initials.

Notes to Chapter Two

1. Edwin Randall interview with Church, n. d., but shortly after his 1956 election to the Senate, CP, A-65001.
2. See "Military Service Record of Senator Frank Church," CP, 10.1/1/6.
3. Church to Mother, Dad, and Eva, 19 Jan. 1944, and to Dad, 8 March 1944, BC.
4. Church to Mother, Dad, and Eva, Easter, 1944, re officer; 13 May 1944, re enema and bivouacs; Church's handwritten addition to the Lily Jay Silver draft biographical sketch, CP, 10.1/1/8, re the last drill.
5. Church to Mother, Dad, and Eva, 7 Sept. 1943, BC.
6. Church to Mother and Dad, 21 Oct. 1944, BC, and to Carl Burke, 28 Jan. 1945, CP, 12/3/2.
7. Church to Mother and Dad, 27 April 1945, BC.
8. Church to Mother and Dad, 8 May, 19 June, 18 July 1945; to Dear Folks, 21 Sept. 1945, to Bethine, 22 Sept. 1945, BC; F. Forrester Church, *Father and Son: A Personal Biography of Senator Frank Church of Idaho* (New York: Harper & Row, 1985), pp. 27-28.
9. Church to Mother and Dad, 4 Oct. 1944, BC, re loathing military life; Richard Church interview, 5 Aug. 1984.
10. Church to Mother and Dad, 22 Oct. 1945, BC.
11. Church to Mother and Dad, 4 Oct. 1944, and to Bethine, 5 March 1945, BC.
12. Church to Kathy Fong, 12 Feb. 1969, CP, 2.2/24/3, re "Mainstreet"; to Folks, 22 Nov. 1945, re Shanghai; to Mother and Dad, 5 April 1945, and to Bethine, 6 April 1945, BC, re India.
13. Church to Bethine, 18 Oct. 1945, BC.
14. Church to Bethine, 6 April 1945, BC, re India; to Bethine, 18 June, 8 and 24 July 1945, and to Mother and Dad, 27 April and 19 June 1945, re China; to Bethine, 18 Oct. 1945, re Idaho.
15. Church to Mother and Dad, 27 April, 8 May, and 22 July, 1945, and to Bethine, 13 May 1945, BC.
16. Church to Mother, Dad, and Eva, 22 July 1945, re communists; to Bethine, 9 Dec. 1945, re Chiang, BC. Also, Church, *Father and Son*, pp. 30-31.
17. Church to Mother and Dad, 17 April 1945, BC, re "stoic hostility"; Randall interview of Church re revolutionaries.
18. Church to Bethine, 7 June 1945, and to Mother, Dad, and Eva, 2 Aug. 1945, BC.
19. Randall interview of Church.
20. Church to Bethine, 6 Sept. 1945, BC.
21. Church to Bethine, 21 Aug. 1945, BC.
22. Church to Mother, Dad, and Eva, 14 Nov. and 7 Dec. 1943, BC.
23. Church to Mother, Dad, and Eva, 9 Dec. 1943, BC; Church to Carl Burke, 28 Jan. 1945, CP, 12/3/2, re "Liberal conviction."
24. Church to Bethine, 21 Aug. 1945, BC.
25. *Ibid.*
26. *Ibid.*
27. *Ibid.*
28. Church to Bethine, 6 Sept. 1945, BC.
29. *Ibid.*, and to Mother and Dad, 1 Oct. 1945, BC.
30. Church to Bethine, 6 Sept. 1945, BC.
31. Church to Mother and Dad, 1 Oct. 1945, BC.
32. Church to Bethine, 6 Sept. 1945, BC.
33. Church to Mother and Dad, 9 Sept. 1945, BC.

34. Church to Dear Folks, 21 Sept. 1945, and to Bethine, 22 Sept. 1945, BC.
35. Church to Mother, Dad, and Eva, 20 Aug. 1945, re promotion; to Dear Folks, 21 Sept. 1945, and to Bethine, 22 Sept. 1945, re "big way," BC.
36. Church to Bethine, 30 Sept. 1945, BC.
37. Church to Mother and Dad, 11 Feb. 1945, BC.
38. Church to Mother and Dad, 23 Dec. 1945, re intelligence; 28 March and 17 April 1946 re college, BC.
39. Church to Mother, Dad, and Eva, 13 Aug. 1943, re morale, and to Bethine, 12 April 1944, re ring, BC.
40. Bethine Church interview, 25 Jan. 1989.
41. Church to Carl Burke, 28 Jan. 1945, CP, 12/3/2; Bethine Church interview, 28 Oct. 1984.
42. Church to Mother and Dad, 8 May 1945; to Bethine, 6 April, 26 May, 7 and 18 June, 21 Aug. 1945, BC.
43. Bethine to Church, 28 June and 27 Oct. 1945, BC.
44. Church to Bethine, 18 Nov. 1945, BC.
45. Church to Bethine, 9 Jan. 1945, re strangers, and 30 Nov. 1945, BC, on Wardwell. On Boise, see Merle Wells, *Boise: An Illustrated History* (Woodland Hills, Cal.: Windsor Publications, 1982), p. 107.
46. Interviews: Stan Burns, 24 April 1984 and 16 March 1988; Bethine Church, 18 June 1979.
47. Frank and Bethine Church interview, 18 June 1979.
48. Interviews: Burns, 24 April 1984 and 16 March 1988; Frank and Bethine Church, 18 June 1979; Bethine Church, 13 June 1979 and 3 Aug. 1984.
49. Church to Bethine, 9 Nov. 1946 and, re fraternities, 27 Feb. 1947, BC.
50. Church to Bethine, 26 Oct. and 2 Nov. 1946, BC.
51. Church to Bethine, 26 Jan. 1947.
52. Church to Bethine, 26 Jan. 1947, and notes for Church's speech, BC.
53. Church to Bethine, 27 Feb. 1947, BC.
54. Church to Bethine, 23 March and 30 May 1947, BC; unidentified clippings, CP, 10.1/1/6.
55. Church to Bethine, 14 Oct. 1946, BC, re study; unidentified clippings, CP, 10.1/1/6.
56. Interviews: Bethine Church, 25 Jan. 1989, and Richard Church, 5 Aug. 1984.
57. Bethine Church interview, 25 Jan. 1989; on his controlled emotions, many interviews, for example, Myrna Sasser, 20 March 1988.
58. Bethine Church interview, 25 Jan. 1989, re not liking the Northeast; Church to Carl Burke, 23 March and 15 April 1948, CP, 12/3/2, about Harvard's setting; Church, *Father and Son* (New York: Harper & Row, 1985), p. 6, re the car.
59. Interviews: Richard Church, 5 Aug. 1984, and Frank Church, 18 June 1979.
60. Frank Church, "I Was Told I Had Only Six Months to Live," *Good Housekeeping* (January 1976): 26.
61. Church, "I Was Told," p. 26; Church, *Father and Son*, pp. 6-8.
62. Church, "I Was Told," p. 26.
63. *Ibid.*, pp. 26, 28.
64. Church, *Father and Son*, p. 8.
65. Church, "I Was Told," pp. 28, 30.
66. *Ibid.*, p. 30.
67. Bethine Church interview, 25 Jan. 1989, on the bar exam.
68. *Ibid.*

69. See, for example, Geofrey T. Mills, "Harry S. Truman and Price Controls: Two Episodes of Inflation Control, 1945-1952," in William F. Levantrosser, ed., *Harry S. Truman: The Man from Independence* (New York: Greenwood Press, 1986), pp. 265-79. Quotation in Robert J. Donovan, *Tumultuous Years: The Presidency of Harry S Truman, 1949-1953* (New York: Norton, 1982), p. 368.
70. Bethine Church interview, 25 Jan. 1989; also Richard Church interview, 5 Aug. 1984, re his father's OPA experience.
71. Quotations from undated notes for two Church speeches, probably early in 1951, CP, 10.1/1/16.
72. Class notes for "Public Speaking," CP, 10.1/1/16.
73. Burke interview, 30 May 1986.
74. Typescript of Church's radio address, Halloween, 1952, CP, 12/3/2, re ghostly voice; Burke and Church response to Jack Hawley, *Idaho Daily Statesman*, 1 Nov. 1952.
75. Carl Burke interview, 22 Nov. 1987.
76. See Church and Burke joint reply to Jack Hawley, *Idaho Daily Statesman*, 1 Nov. 1952; campaign cards, sketch of flyer, and typescript for Church's Halloween radio address, CP, 12/3/2; Burke interview, 22 Nov. 1987, re the finances; Bethine Church interview, 25 Jan. 1989, on their intentions.
77. *Idaho Daily Statesman*, 5 Nov. 1952. All four Republicans garnered more than 23,000 votes each; Church received 12,931 and Burke, 12,428. Two other Democrats received almost 5,500 votes each.
78. Typescript of Church's 2 Sept. 1952 keynote address, CP, 12/3/2.
79. *Ibid.*
80. Steven M. Gillon, *Politics and Vision: The ADA and American Liberalism, 1947-1985* (New York: Oxford University Press, 1987), pp. 3-130, on the ADA's early years; Tyler qtn., p. 116.
81. Church interview, 10 Jan. 1979.
82. Typescript of Church's 1954 TV comments, CP, 10.2/6/15; *Idaho Daily Statesman*, 4 Feb. 1954 and 13 Feb. 1955, on the balloons.
83. Church to A. L. Alford, 21 Dec. 1954; copies of Leland Stowe, "They Hit the Communists Where It Hurts Most," *Reader's Digest* (Feb. 1954) and advertisement in CP, 10.2/6/15.
84. Church interview, 10 Jan. 1979. On the CIA and Radio Free Europe, see John Prados, *President's Secret Wars: CIA and Pentagon Covert Operations from World War II through Iranscam* (New York: William Morrow, 1986), pp. 34-35, 312-13, and John Ranlegh, *The Agency: The Rise and Decline of the CIA* (New York: Simon and Schuster, rev. ed., 1987), pp. 216, 307-09.
85. Church quoted in 21 Jan. 1955 news release, CP, 10.2/6/15.
86. Church interview, 10 Jan. 1979.
87. Church quotation in Loch K. Johnson, "Operational Codes and the Prediction of Leadership Behavior: Senator Frank Church at Midcareer," in *A Psychological Examination of Political Leaders*, ed. Margaret G. Hermann and Thomas W. Milburn (New York: Free Press, 1977), p. 107.
88. Interviews: Dale Nelson, 1 March 1988, and Sam Day, 4 Oct. 1987.
89. Dwight Jensen interview, 7 Nov. 1987; *Idaho Daily Statesman*, 4 April 1954.
90. Jensen interview, 7 Nov. 1987; *Idaho Daily Statesman*, 4 April 1954.
91. Nelson interview; Church to G. C. Pennell, 20 March 1956, CP, 12/3/2.
92. Bethine Church interview, 10 June 1986.

Notes to Chapter Three

1. Quotation in *Boise Journal*, 21 Sept. 1956; Verda Barnes interview, 8 June 1979, re hair.
2. Richard B. Church to Ashby, 18 Aug. 1988.
3. Bethine Church to "Frosty," n. d., CP, 12/3/3.
4. The estimates of miles traveled and hands shaken are in outline notes to a Church speech on the 1956 campaign, undated, but in 1957, CP, 12/3/3.
5. Interviews: Frank and Bethine Church, 18 June 1979; Frank Church, 10 Jan. 1979; and Bethine Church, 10 June 1986.
6. Alan Minskoff, "The Church Campaign: Carl Burke, Campaign Manager" (typescript, 1976), copy in authors' files.
7. Bethine Church interview, 10 June 1986.
8. F. Ross Peterson, *Prophet Without Honor: Glen H. Taylor and the Fight for American Liberalism* (Lexington: University of Kentucky Press, 1974), pp. 1-33.
9. *Ibid.*, pp. 34-179.
10. Church to R. B. Church, 28 March 1956, CP 12/3/3.
11. Peterson, *Prophet Without Honor*, p. 173n, re Taylor's success in a crowded election field; Glen H. Taylor, *The Way It Was With Me* (Secaucus, N. J.: Lyle Stuart, 1979), pp. 378-79, 387, 410.
12. Frank Church interview, 10 Jan. 1979.
13. Church to Allen Wheeler, 29 March 1956, CP, 12/3/3.
14. Church to Joel Jacobson, 24 April 1956, CP, 12/3/3. The other candidates were Frank Benson, an attorney and assistant state attorney general before turning to public school teaching in Caldwell, and Theron Ward, a Jerome County probate judge.
15. Bill Johnston to Ashby, 28 June 1986; Church interview, 10 Jan. 1979.
16. Church to Joel Jacobson, 24 April 1956, CP, 12/3/3; Carl Burke interview, 24 May 1986; Bill Johnston to Ashby, June 28, 1986. Benson and Ward withdrew.
17. Flyer in CP, 12/3/3.
18. Bryce Nelson, Banquet Speech for Idaho Press Club, 20 April 1985; Bethine Church interview, 10 June 1986.
19. Bethine Church interview, 10 June 1986; re the Utah incident, unidentified newspaper clipping and Church to John Evans, 20 June 1956, CP, 12/3/3.
20. Church to Claude Kent, to John Evans, 20 June 1956, re the dog; to Joel Jacobson, 24 April 1956 qtn., CP, 12/3/3; Bethine Church interview, 10 June 1986.
21. Douglas T. Miller and Marion Nowak, *The Fifties: The Way We Really Were* (Garden City, N. Y.: Doubleday and Co., 1977), p. 344; U. S. Dept. of Commerce, Bureau of Census, *Statistical Abstract of the United States, 1957* (Washington D. C., 1957), pp. 520, 832; *The Idaho Almanac* (Boise, 1963), pp. 570-71.
22. Bureau of Census, *Statistical Abstract, 1957*, p. 955; Edwin Diamond and Stephen Bates, *The Spot: The Rise of Political Advertising on Television* (Cambridge, Mass.: MIT Press, 1984), pp. 35-92.
23. "Budget for Citizens for Church," n. d.; Wade B. Fleetwood to KLIX-TV, 27 Sept. 1956, CP, 12/3/3.
24. Interviews: Carl Burke, 24 May 1986; Stan Burns, 16 March 1988; Bethine Church, 10 June 1986.
25. Film, "Idaho's Decade of Stunted Growth," CP, 56003.
26. Stan Burns interview, 16 March 1988, re the filming.
27. Films, "Build Your Idaho" and "Farming," CP, 56002, 56009.
28. Film, "Foreign Policy," CP, 56017; also film, "Why I am a Democrat," 56014.

29. Films on "Small Business," CP, 56007-08.
30. Church to John Glasby, 21 July 1956 (first two qtns.) and to Jim Charrier, 14 Dec. 1956 (last qtn.), CP, 12/3/3; Bethine Church and Carl Burke interviews, 10 June 1986 and 24 May 1986.
31. Carl Burke and Bethine Church, for example, cannot remember the other candidates using TV much, if at all.
32. *Lewiston Tribune*, 5 Aug. 1956. According to Forrest Church, his father spent under $14,000 in the primary, $6000 of which came from the sale of the house. See F. Forrester Church, *Father and Son: A Personal Biography of Senator Frank Church of Idaho* (New York: Harper & Row, 1985), p. 35.
33. Burke interview, 24 May 1986.
34. Figures compiled from *The 33rd Biennial Report of the Secretary of State of Idaho, 1955-56* (Boise, 1956), foldout page.
35. Church to George E. Byard, Jr., 31 Aug. 1956, and Church press release, 29 Aug. 1956; statement of Albert Gore, chairman of the Senate Subcommittee on Elections, n.d., all in CP, 12/3/3.
36. Unidentified clipping; qtns. in Taylor to Kay Pell, n. d., but sent to Church by Pell, 12 Oct. 1956, CP, 12/3/3.
37. Taylor, *The Way It Was With Me*, pp. 398-413; qtns. 401-02, 404, 400, 391.
38. Carl Burke to G. E. Agree, 17 Oct. 1956; George H. R. Taylor to Burke, 24 Oct. 1956, and to Church, 10 Sept. 1956 (qtns.), CP, 12/3/3; *New York Times*, 23 Oct. 1956.
39. Ad, "Glen Taylor Write-In? It's Up to You!," in many newspapers, but see *Statesman*, 17 Oct. 1956; Church to Harry W. Christy, 8 Oct. 1956 (twist), and to J. Ward Arney (rough), 1 Sept. 1956, CP, 12/3/3.
40. Burke to Church, 15 Oct. 1956, CP, 12/3/3.
41. *Idaho State Journal*, 4 Oct. and 9 Oct. (phony) 1956; George Agree to Burke, 24 Oct. 1956, re NCEC contributions of $5000; Burke "To Whom It May Concern," 2 Nov. 1956, re the spending figure, all in CP, 12/3/3.
42. *Idaho Daily Statesman*, 1 Jan. 1957; Doris Fleeson in the *Washington Star*, 5 Sept. 1956; *New York Times*, 2 Nov. 1956; Herbert Howe (Idaho chairman of the Natural Resources Division, National Democratic Party), to George H. R. Taylor, 11 and 19 Sept. 1956, Democratic National Committee Papers, JFK Library, Box 71.
43. George Reedy memo to Lyndon Johnson, 15 Oct. 1956, Johnson Papers, LBJ Library, Congressional File, Box 41. The encouraging letter from Johnson to Church, 23 Oct. 1956—written by Reedy per Johnson's instructions and saying "your chances. . .are excellent"—thus belied the actual feelings in Johnson's office. Indeed, as the Oct. 15 memo made clear, Reedy did not relish Johnson's dilemma if Church sought an endorsement (which Church did not). *New York Times*, 2 Nov. 1956.
44. Quoted in Joe Miller, "The Battle of Idaho: Welker vs. Church," *The Reporter*, 15 (1 Nov. 1956): 17; and in Thomas C. Reeves, *The Life and Times of Joe McCarthy* (New York: Stein & Day, 1982), p. 658 (champions).
45. Ad in *The Idaho Legionnaire*, 26 (Oct., 1956): 3; Blackfoot speech in United Press clipping, n.d., CP, 12/3/3.
46. Report of the NCEC, 17 Feb. (first qtn.) and 11 Oct. (second qtn.) 1956, copies in CP, 12/3/3; *New York Times*, 2 Nov. 1956; Bethine Church interview, 10 June 1986, re the NCEC's contact with Church. See Harry M. Scoble, *Ideology and Electoral Action: A Comparative Study of the National Committee for an Effective Congress* (San Francisco: Chandler, 1967), p. 106, re the $13,000.

47. Welker quoted in Miller, "The Battle of Idaho," p. 17; *Idaho Daily Statesman*, 10 April 1956 (running, honest); Church to Ferris Clark, 1 Oct. 1956, CP, 12/3/3.
48. See ad, "From one extreme you have heard," *Idaho Daily Statesman*, 4 Nov. 1956; Church to Ray Hill, 10 June 1982, CP, 12/3/3; Frank Church interview, 10 Jan. 1979. Also, Bethine Church interview, 10 June 1986.
49. See unidentified clippings of ads, CP, 12/3/3. The Pocatello *Intermountain* of 9 Aug. 1956 featured Swisher's editorial, which later appeared in advertisements with headlines such as "Republican Leader Blasts WELKER" and "Thinking Republicans are Voting for Church."
50. Copy of "The Deplorable Record of Herman Welker!" which contains these journalistic criticisms as well as partial reproductions of Pearson's column from the Rock Springs (Wyo.) *Daily Rocket*, 23 June 1954, Alexander's column from the Los Angeles *Times*, 26 Sept. 1956, and the New York *Daily News*, 17 Dec. 1955, CP, 12/3/3. See too the staff report, "Herman Welker, Six Years in Washington," *ibid*. On the burning of the pamphlets, Church, *Father and Son*, p. 37, and interviews, Frank Church, 10 Jan. 1979, and Bethine Church, 10 June 1986.
51. See, for example, unidentified clipping re food stamp speech; Carl Burke to Patrick Murphy Malin, 11 Oct. 1956; Church to P. Malcolm Hammond, 12 Oct. 1956, CP, 12/3/3.
52. Church to Women's Joint Legislative Committee for Equal Rights, 11 Oct. 1956; to A. G. Cornell, 25 June 1956; and to John H. Webb of Idaho Farm Bureau Federation, 21 Sept. 1956, CP, 12/3/3.
53. Church to various labor organizations, 1 Aug. 1956; Joel R. Jacobson to Al Barkan, 29 Feb. 1956; Church to "Dear Sir," n. d. (last qtns.), CP, 12/3/3.
54. Church to Thomas B. Wood, 21 July 1956, and 15 Sept. 1956 press release (re Eastland), CP, 12/3/3.
55. Statement for *Salt Lake Tribune*, October 19, 1956, CP, 12/3/3.
56. Church press release, 15 July 1956, argued strongly for a federal dam; compare with document, "The Senate Campaign in Idaho," and Church to John Glasby, 11 Sept. 1956; Church to Bill Johnston, 11 July 1956, and Burke to Jack Randall, 17 Oct. 1956, CP, 12/3/3. John Corlett briefly described the legal and legislative battles over the dam; see the *Idaho Statesman*, 1 Jan. 1957.
57. Press release, 30 Oct. 1956; Burke to P. J. Bennion, 26 Oct. 1956, and to Roger Swanstrom, 15 Oct. 1956, CP, 12/3/3.
58. Carl Burke to Ashby, 5 Aug. 1986; *Idaho State Journal*, 31 Oct. 1956. A complete list of contributors of $100 or more to Welker's campaign is in Democratic National Committee Papers, JFK Library, Box 23.
59. *Idaho Daily Statesman*, 30 Oct. (cookie, oil, philosophy) and 1 Nov. 1956 (faceless, eggheads, fringe); Burke to Ashby, 5 Aug. 1986 (bombshell). See also *Statesman*, 3 Nov. 1956; Twin Falls *Times-News*, 30, 31 Oct., 2 Nov. 1956; *Idaho State Journal*, 4 Nov. 1956.
60. Bethine Church interview, 10 June 1986.
61. *Ibid.*; *Idaho Daily Statesman*, 29 Oct. 1956.
62. *Boise Journal*, 9 Nov. 1956, on the betting odds; on Gooding County, see Corlett in *Idaho Daily Statesman*, 26 Oct. 1956. See also Boyd A. Martin, "The 1956 Election in Idaho," *Western Political Quarterly*, 10 (March 1957): 122, 124.
63. *New York Times*, 7 Nov. 1956; Les Fishman, "Church of Idaho," *The Nation*, 183 (17 Nov. 1956): 423; Corlett in *Idaho Daily Statesman*, 8 Nov. 1956.
64. Quoted in Miller, "The Battle of Idaho," p. 16.
65. *New York Times*, 18 Oct. 1956.

66. On the "Democratic advance in the West," see Frank H. Jonas, "Western Politics and the 1956 Elections," *Western Political Quarterly*, 10 (March 1957): 80-95.
67. Undated Kennedy staff report on "the media side of campaigning," pp. 2, 13, 15, Theodore Sorenson Papers, JFK Library, Box 2; Church quotation on his youth in Bethine Church interview, 10 June 1986; Fleeson in *Washington Star*, 5 Sept. 1956; Church quotation in *Labor* [Wash., D.C.], 13 Oct. 1956, p. 2.
68. *New York Times*, 17 Nov. 1956.
69. Carl Burke to Ashby, 5 Aug. 1986.
70. Qtn., Burke to Louis A. Mankus, 25 March 1958, CP, 12/3/3.

Notes to Chapter Four

1. Qtn. in Carl Burke to Wade Fleetwood, 15 Oct. 1957, CP, 12/3/4; *Oregon Journal*, 8 Dec. 1956, re "baby."
2. "Real soul" in Church's speech on race relations, n. d., but late 1957 or early 1958, and delivered to a Virginia audience, CP, 10.6/1/24. Cited hereafter as Church, "Race Relations."
3. On the list that John Kennedy's administration put together concerning which people and groups influenced which senators, Carver was the only staff person mentioned. He and Montana's Senator Mike Mansfield were identified as key influences on Church. Undated document, "Senators," Lawrence O'Brien Papers, JFK Library, Box 32. On Carver, John Gerassi, *The Boys of Boise* (New York: Macmillan, 1966), pp. 51-52, *Washington Daily News*, 4 Feb. 1961, and Carver interview, 30 June 1987; also interviews with Ward and Phyllis Hower, 11 April 1987, Tommie Ward, 16 May 1987, and Myrna Sasser, 20 March 1988.
4. Interviews: Carver, 30 June 1987 and Bethine Church, 26 June 1993. Verda Barnes resumé (1956) and Paul M. Butler to Church, 3 Dec. 1956, CP, 9.7/1/2.
5. Salt Lake *Tribune*, 6 Jan. 1957; Bethine Church to "Dear Everybody," 29 Jan. 1957, CP, 12/3/4.
6. See, for example, profile of Church in *Washington Post*, 3 Jan. 1957; limericks in notes for Church's Martinsburg, W. Va., speech, 6 April 1959, Church Papers, 10.6/3/13; F. Forrester Church, *Father and Son: A Personal Biography of Senator Frank Church of Idaho* (New York: Harper & Row, 1985), pp. 47-48.
7. Bethine Church to "Dear Everybody," 29 Jan. 1957, CP, 12/3/4; Johnson quotation in Salt Lake *Tribune*, 6 Jan. 1957.
8. Bethine Church to "Dear Everybody," 19 Jan. 1957, CP, 12/3/4.
9. See, for example, Harvard Sitkoff, "The Preconditions of Racial Change," in William Chafe and Harvard Sitkoff, eds., *A History of Our Time*, 2d ed. (New York: Oxford University Press, 1987), pp. 151-60.
10. Richard L. Neuberger, "Democrats' Dilemma: Civil Rights," *New York Times Magazine* (7 July 1957): 7.
11. Steven F. Lawson, *Black Ballots: Voting Rights in the South, 1944-1969* (New York: Columbia University Press, 1976), p. 162, for the voting statistics.
12. Reedy qtn. in memo to Johnson, 25 Dec. 1956, Office Files of George Reedy, LBJ Library, Box 418. Reedy to Ashby, 13 Jan. 1987, emphasizes the importance of the Rocky Mountain region and of Church.
13. Transcript, Frank Church Oral History Interview, 1 May 1969, by Paige E. Mulhollan, pp. 1-2, LBJ Library.
14. McGrory in *Washington Evening Star*, 1 Jan. 1957; Church Oral History (Mulhollan), p. 6.; Church interview, 10 Jan. 1979.

15. Church quoted by Mary McGrory, *Washington Evening Star*, 11 Jan. 1957. Useful re the fight over Rule XXII is Paul H. Douglas, *In the Fullness of Time: The Memoirs of Paul H. Douglas* (New York: Harcourt Brace Jovanovich, 1971, 1972), pp. 214-20, 277-85.
16. Church Oral History (Mulhollan), pp. 6-7; also, Church interview, 10 Jan. 1979.
17. Church interview, 10 Jan. 1979.
18. Church, "Race Relations"; typescript of Church speech, 22 Jan. 1958, before Tenth District Democratic Club of Virginia, and Church to Arne Robert Johnson, 24 Jan. 1958, CP, 12/3/4.
19. Douglas, *In the Fullness of Time*, p. 255, mentions the caucuses; also, Douglas memo to Church, 19 June 1957, CP, 12/3/4; Church Oral History (Mulhollan) p. 7.
20. Frank Church interview, 10 Jan. 1979.
21. Quoted by McGrory, *Washington Evening Star*, 11 Jan. 1957.
22. Church, Oral History (Mulhollan), p. 8; interviews: Frank Church, 10 Jan. 1979, Hower, 11 April 1957, Bethine Church, 8 Feb. 1989.
23. "January 4, 1957, on the Senate Filibuster Rule," NAACP Papers, LC, Box "Civil Rights, Rule 22 Legislation, 1956-61." Also, Walter Reuther to Church, 11 Jan. 1957, CP, 12/3/4. Howard E. Shuman, "Senate Rules and the Civil Rights Bill: A Case Study," *American Political Science Review*, 51 (Dec., 1957): esp. 961, 974, emphasizes the importance of the Anderson vote.
24. Eastland quoted in Lawson, *Black Ballots*, p. 157; Shuman, "Senate Rules and the Civil Rights Bill," pp. 963-68, and Douglas, *In the Fullness of Time*, pp. 286-87, re the tactical maneuvering; *Washington Post*, 21 June 1957.
25. Douglas, *In the Fullness of Time*, pp. 286-87.
26. *CR*, 19 June 1957, pp. 9653-54.
27. *Ibid.*, pp. 9654-55.
28. *Ibid.*, pp. 9655-56.
29. *Ibid.*, pp. 9657-66.
30. John Carver interview, 30 June 1987; *CR*, pp. 9657-9666; qtns.: Morse, p. 9657; Douglas, Johnson, and Goldwater, p. 9666.
31. Clippings of Smith's and Nover's comments, and transcript of Morgan's 25 June 1957 broadcast in CP, 10.1/1/30.
32. Church Oral History (Mulhollan), p. 5; Church to Clinton Anderson, 22 June 1957, and to Lyndon Johnson, 22 June 1957, CP, 1.1/68/9; Carver interview, 30 June 1987, re Church's respect for Anderson.
33. Douglas, *In the Fullness of Time*, p. 287.
34. Rowland Evans and Robert Novak, *Lyndon B. Johnson: The Exercise of Power* (New York: New American Library, 1966), pp. 125-38, effectively summarizes the elements of the "deal," but see also C. Vann Woodward, "The Great Civil Rights Debate," *Commentary*, 24 (October 1957): esp. p. 289. Drew Pearson, *Washington Post*, 20 June 1957, re Eastland; John Carver interview, 27 Oct. 1979; Watkins quoted in *Washington Post*, 22 June 1957.
35. Gaylord Nelson interview, 21 May 1987, re Church and Senate etiquette.
36. Church's news releases, 30 Sept. and 23 Nov. 1957 re speeches in Wooster, Ohio, and Caldwell, Idaho; Church to Darrell B. Carter, 31 July 1957, CP, 12/3/4. On the intellectual climate, see for example John Higham, "The Cult of the American 'Consensus,' " *Commentary*, 27 (1959): 93-100; Peter Novick, *That Noble Dream* (Cambridge: Cambridge University Press, 1988), pp. 337-38.
37. Transcript, Clinton P. Anderson Oral History Interview, 20 May 1969, by T. H. Baker, p. 6, LBJ Library; Evans and Novak, *Lyndon B. Johnson*, pp. 131-32; Roy Wilkins telegram to Church and other senators, 19 July 1957, NAACP Papers, LC, Box "Legislative Congressman 1957, July 11-31."

38. Church to Darrell Dorman, 22 July 1957, and "Washington Report from Frank Church," Aug. 1957 (qtn.), CP, 12/3/4; King quoted in Reinhold Niebuhr, "The Civil Rights Bill," *The New Leader*, 40 (16 Sept. 1957): 9.
39. Transcript of Clarence Mitchell speech, 21 July 1957, NAACP Papers, LC, Box "Civil Rights Legislation Press Releases, 1956-57"; transcript of Edward P. Morgan broadcast, 30 April 1957, *ibid.*; Arnold Aronson memo to Cooperating Organizations, 17 April 1957, *ibid.*, Box "Civil Rights Legislation, General, 1956-April, 1957."
40. Church to Library of Congress, 1 May 1957, and reply 8 May 1957, CP, 12/3/4; Dean Acheson statement, 6 Aug. 1957, in Office Files of George Reedy, LBJ Library, Box 418; Benjamin V. Cohen to Lyndon Johnson, 13 Aug. 1957, Johnson Senate Papers, Box 290, LBJ Library.
41. Qtn. in Roy Wilkins to C. B. Powell, 22 Aug. 1957, NAACP Papers, LC, "Civil Rights Legis. Publicity—n/papers 1957."
42. John Carver interview, 27 Oct. 1979, re Church's liking O'Mahoney; O'Mahoney to Tracy S. McCraken, 30 July 1957 (qtn.), Joseph P. O'Mahoney Papers, American Heritage Center, University of Wyoming, Box 228; Douglas quoted in Shuman, "Senate Rules and Civil Rights," p. 972. Useful in following that "moving target" are Shuman, pp. 972-73; Douglass Cater, "How the Senate Passed the Civil-Rights Bill," *The Reporter*, 17 (5 Sept. 1957): esp. 11-12; and *Washington Evening Star* (4 Aug. 1957). Church to Dave Koonce, 6 Aug. 1957, CP, 12/3/4, described the *Star*'s summary as "a major accomplishment."
43. Carl A. Auerbach, "Jury Trials and Civil Rights," *The New Leader*, 40 (29 April 1957): 16 (qtn.)-18; Auerbach to Hubert Humphrey, 16 April 1957, Hubert H. Humphrey Papers, MSHS, Senatorial Files, 1949-64, 23.K.3.5B.
44. In the Senate, Church drew heavily upon Auerbach's argument; *CR*, 24 July 1957, p. 12544. Church qtn. in Church Oral History (Mulhollan), p. 9. See also John Carver to Mrs. Leonard Loring, 3 Aug. 1957, CP, 12/3/4.
45. See esp. Evans and Novak, *Lyndon B. Johnson*, p. 134.
46. Church Oral History (Mulhollan), p. 8; Walter Reuther to Church, 6 July 1957, and "Statement by the AFL-CIO Executive Committee," 30 July 1957, CP, 12/3/4. Also, Cater, "How the Civil Rights Bill Passed the Senate," pp. 11-12.
47. Andrew Biemiller to Church, 30 July 1957, with attached statement of AFL-CIO Executive Committee; copy of James B. Carey letter to Senators Johnson, Kefauver, and O'Mahoney, 27 July 1957; John L. Lewis telegram, 30 July 1957, and letter, 31 July 1957, to Church; G. E. Leighty telegram to Church, 1 Aug. 1957, CP, 12/3/4.
48. Humphrey in Cater, "How the Senate Passed the Civil-Rights Bill," p. 12; memo, with attachment, from Reedy to Lyndon Johnson, 29 July 1957, Office Files of George Reedy, LBJ Library. Box 418.
49. Interviews: Bethine Church, 8 Feb. 1989; Frank Church, 12 June 1979; Frank Church interview by Sheldon Stern, 5 Nov. 1981, p. 3, Oral History Program, JFK Library.
50. John Carver interview, 27 Oct. 1979.
51. Copy of letter from William E. Mahan to Church, 10 June 1957, and of Church's reply, 18 July 1957; Church to Johnson, 19 July 1957; Johnson to Church, 23 and 25 July 1957, LBJ Congressional File, LBJ Library, Box 41.
52. Interviews: Bethine Church, 8 Feb. 1989, re Galahad; Church Oral History (Mulhollan), pp. 8, 11; John Carver, 30 June 1987.
53. Church to William Foster, 6 Aug. 1957, CP, 12/3/4; interviews: Church Oral History (Mulhollan), pp. 10-11; Carver, 27 Oct. 1979 and 30 June 1987; Church, 21 June 1979.

54. Church Oral Histories (Mulhollan), p. 11, (Stern), p. 4.
55. Church interview, 12 June 1979.
56. *CR*, 31 July 1957, pp. 13153-54.
57. *CR*, 1 Aug. 1957, pp. 13324-26.
58. *Ibid.*, pp. 13325-26.
59. *Ibid.*, 1 Aug. 1957, p. 13356; on Hennings and Payne, Lawson, *Black Ballots*, p. 193.
60. George Reedy to Ashby, 13 Jan. 1987; on JFK, Roy Wilkins to "Dear John," 23 July 1957, NAACP Papers, LC, Box "Civil Rights Legislation, 1957, July"; on the importance of Church's addendum, Wilkins to C. B. Powell, 22 Aug. 1957, *ibid.*, Box "Civil Rights Legislation Publicity–n/papers 1957"; JFK on the amendment in copy of Kennedy letter to Samuel H. Beer, 3 Aug. 1957, in Theodore Sorenson Papers JFK Library, Box 9; Bethine Church interview, 8 Feb. 1989, re "your man."
61. *CR*, 1 Aug. 1957: vote, p. 13900; Douglas qtns., p. 13841; Morse's, pp. 13889-90. The NAACP echoed Douglas's point about hung juries. See NAACP press release, 1 Aug. 1957, NAACP Papers, LC, Box "Civil Rights Legis Press Releases, 1956-57."
62. Lawson, *Black Ballots*, pp. 197-99.
63. Interviews: Carver, 30 June 1987; Bethine Church, 8 Feb. 1989; Phyl and Ward Hower, 11 April 1987; Ward Hower to Ashby, 25 Jan. 1987.
64. Bethine Church to Dear Family, 29 July 1957, CP, 12/3/4; NAACP News Release, 21 July 1957, NAACP Papers, LC, Box "Civil Rts Legislation Press Releases, 1956-57."
65. C. W. Salter to Church, 23, 27, 1957; Bernard Kroechel to Church, 2 Aug. 1957; Frank Hough to Church, 8 Aug. 1957; F. D. Davant to Church, 19 July 1957, with staff memo attached; also Joseph Dale to Church, 23 July 1957, CP, 12/3/4. Dozens of telegrams to Joseph O'Mahoney also made it clear that white Southerners interpreted the jury trial amendment as a way to weaken civil rights legislation. See O'Mahoney Papers, Box 228.
66. Letters to Church from L. R. Zerbe, 4 Aug. 1957; Allan Metz, 6 Aug. 1957; Bradner W. Gilmore, 2 Aug. 1957, CP, 12/3/4.
67. State YDFL Newsletter, June-July 1957, Democratic-Farmer-Labor State Central Committee Records, MSHS, 48.I.2.9B; also minutes of YDFL dinner committee, 24 July 1957, 27.B.3.8F.
68. On the threatened protest, see *Christian Science Monitor,* 4 Sept. 1957; *Minneapolis Tribune*, 26 Sept. 1957, for the women's letter, but also Aug. 18, and Sept. 8, 12, 15, 22, 23; Attorney L. Howard Bennett to Hubert Humphrey, 7 Aug. 1957, Humphrey Papers, MSHS, Legislative: Civil Rights, 23.K.3.5B.
69. "Statement of Senator Frank Church," Sept. 1957, and Church to Paul Thatcher, 21 Aug. 1957, CP 12/3/4; Bethine Church interview, 8 Feb. 1989. The YDFL ultimately rescheduled the dinner for October 19; former Arkansas governor Sid McMath, who had sharply criticized Orval Faubus's handling of the Little Rock school crisis, was the speaker. *Minneapolis Tribune*, 3 Oct. 1957.
70. Humphrey to Samuel Scheiner, 4 Sept. 1957, Humphrey Papers, MSHS, Legislative: Civil Rights, 23.K.3.5B; interviews: Bethine Church, 8 Feb. 1989, and Ward Hower, 11 April 1987.
71. Church to Roy Wilkins, 17 Sept. 1957, NAACP Papers, LC, Box "Staff-Roy Wilkins Civil Rts, 1956-57."
72. Church to Arthur J. White, 12 Aug. 1957, CP, 12/3/4; on the addendum's contributions, see Church speech, Tenth District Women's Democratic Club, 7 Oct. 1957, ibid.; Kennedy to Julius Bernstein, 13 Sept. 1957, and to Samuel Beer, 3 Aug. 1957, Sorenson Papers, JFK Library, Box 9. Kennedy and Clinton Anderson were

both disgruntled about the criticisms they received from civil rights groups. "They blamed me for not doing a better job," recalled Anderson. "We did everything we could do. It was quite evident that our original position was hopeless, and one thing more would have broken the camel's back." Transcript, Clinton Anderson Oral History Interview, 20 May 1969, by T. H. Baker, p. 6, LBJ Library. Also, JFK to Roy Wilkins, 18 July 1957, Sorenson Papers, JFK Library, Box 9.

73. Wayne Morse to Roy Wilkins, 18 Sept. 1957, NAACP Papers, LC, Box "Staff-Roy Wilkins Civil Rts, 1956-57"; Church speeches, Tenth District Women's Democratic Club of Northern Virginia, 7 Oct. 1957, CP, 12/3/4, and "Race Relations."
74. Church speeches, Tenth District Women's Democratic Club of Northern Virginia, 7 Oct. 1957, CP, 12/3/4, and "Race Relations."
75. Roy Wilkins to John Sengstacke, 30 Aug. 1957; to C. B. Powell, 20 Aug. and 5 Sept. 1957; to Eustace Gay, 4 Sept. 1957; to E. Washington Rhodes, 4 Sept. 1957; to William O. Walker, 19 Aug. 1957, NAACP Papers, LC, Box "Civil Rights Legislation, Publicity—n/papers 1957."
76. Church qtn. in "Washington Report from Frank Church," August 1957, CP, 12/3/4; on Church voting "wrong," Henry Lee Moon to Clarence Mitchell, 24 Sept. 1957, with attachment, NAACP Papers, LC, Box "Civil Rights Legislation, Clarence Mitchell, 1956-59." On compromise, copy of Richard R. Huber to Archibald MacLeish, 3 Aug. 1957; George Agree to Church, 5 Aug. 1957, noted Huber's $6 contribution, CP, 12/3/4.
77. Church Oral History (Mulhollan), pp. 12-13; Johnson to Church, 8 Aug. 1957, LBJ Congressional File, LBJ Library, Box 41; AP wirephoto in, for example, Great Falls (Mont.) *Tribune*, 3 Aug. 1957, clipping in O'Mahoney Papers, Box 228, and UP photo in *Christian Science Monitor*, 3 Aug. 1957; Reedy to Ashby, 13 Jan. 1987.
78. On the Argentina trip, Johnson to Church, 10 Aug. 1957, LBJ Congressional File, LBJ Library, Box 41; Evans and Novak, *Lyndon B. Johnson*, p. 103; Church Oral History (Mulhollan), p. 13; Drew Pearson card subject file, Drew Pearson Papers, LBJ Library.
79. Church qtn. in Ross K. Baker, *Friend and Foe in the U. S. Senate* (New York: Free Press, 1980), p. 157; Hower interview, 11 April 1987.
80. *Washington Daily News*, 26 Aug. 1957; *Baltimore News-Post*, 7 Aug. 1957; Baltimore *Sun*, 9 Aug. 1957; AP photos: unidentified clipping, CP, 1.1/68/10, and (re civil rights) *Christian Science Monitor*, 3 Aug. 1957; UP photo in Great Falls (Mont.) *Tribune*.
81. Bethine Church to "Dear Family," 29 July 1957, CP, 12/3/4; George Smathers to Church, 19 Aug. 1957, 8.1/1/2; "Washington Newsletter from George Smathers," #196 (n. d., but Aug. 1957), George Smathers Papers (University of Florida), Box 13; Paul Douglas, "The Bright Young Men of Politics," *Esquire*, 50 (Sept. 1958): 36; *Baltimore News-Post*, 7 Aug. 1957. The award from the U. S. Junior Chamber of Commerce claimed that, "without the Church [jury] amendment, it is doubtful the recent Civil Rights Bill would have been enacted." CP, 10.1/1/30.
82. Frank Church news release, 12 Sept. 1957, CP, 12/3/4.

Notes to Chapter Five

1. John A. Carver, Jr. interview, 30 June 1987.
2. Bethine Church interview, 12 March 1985; Forrest Church interview, 27 Aug. 1979. One of the senator's closest colleagues confirmed Bethine's suspicions, but not for attribution.

3. F. Forrester Church, *Father and Son: A Personal Biography of Senator Frank Church* (New York: Harper & Row, 1985), pp. 40-41; Forrest Church interview, 27 Aug. 1979.
4. See, for example, Church to his brother, 10 Oct. 1957, CP, 10.3/1/1, re Chase; Bethine to "Darling," 11 Aug. 1961, 10.3/1/5, re the boys; Bethine to "Darling," 18 Aug. 1960, 10.3/1/3, and Church to Bethine, 22 Aug. 1961, 10.3/1/5, for examples of letters.
5. Interviews: Stan Burns, 22 March 1979; Penny Gross, 11 Aug. 1984; Moscow, Idaho, *Daily News/Idahonian*, 9-10 March 1985; Jules Witcover, *Marathon: The Pursuit of the Presidency, 1972-1976* (New York: Signet Books, 1978), p. 349; transcript of Cincinnati interview, 27 May 1976, CP, 8.2/14/6, re slippers; *Lewiston Tribune*, 12 April 1984, re extra senator.
6. Interviews: Mike Wetherell, 14 May 1979, and Ward Hower, 11 April 1988; McGovern qtn., *Idaho Statesman*, 20 July 1980; *Minneapolis Tribune*, 29 Sept. 1957, re "Kissable." Also, Myra MacPherson, *The Power Lovers: An Intimate Look at Politics and Marriage* (New York: Putnam's, 1975), pp. 424-32, and many interviews.
7. Interviews: Carver, 23 July 1989, Gross; former aide, speaking anonymously, re campaigning; Burke to Wade Fleetwood, 15 Oct. 1957, Carl Burke Papers (Boise State University), Box 1; Bryce Nelson interviews, 26 June 1986, re the Democratic party and the film, and 7 April 1993.
8. Joe Biden in *Idaho Statesman*, 20 July 1980; interviews: Bryce Nelson, 1 Feb. 1987; Peter Fenn, 16 May 1987; Ward and Phyllis Hower, 11 April 1987; Carver, 27 Oct. 1979 and 23 July 1989; David Morrissey, 17 Nov. 1987; Karin Lissakers, 1 July 1992; Alice Dieter, 22 Dec. 1987.
9. Forrest Church interview, 27 Aug. 1979.
10. Carver interview, 27 Oct. 1979.
11. Bill Hall interview, 7 Aug. 1986.
12. Drew Pearson note card file on Church and statehood, May 9, 1958, Drew Pearson Papers, LBJ Library, and Daniel Inouye to Ashby, 23 July 1986, re Church's early interest in statehood; also, Church news releases, 15 April 1957, and Church to the President, 12 April 1957, CP, 12/3/5; Church to Johnson, 28 Jan., 5 June, and 16 Dec. 1958, Lyndon B. Johnson Senate Papers, LBJ, Box 365.
13. Church to Johnson, 28 Jan. 1958, and news release, 26 April 1957 (qtn.), CP, 10.6/1/4.
14. George Sundborg interview, 19 Sept. 1988; Church in *CR*, 5 May 1958, p. 7986.
15. *CR*, 5 May 1958, pp. 7983-96.
16. Paul Douglas to Church, 8 May 1958, CP, 12/3/5; *CR*, 5 May 1958, pp. 7984, 7995. See also clippings in CP, 12/3/5.
17. Sundborg to Ashby, 17 Aug. 1988.
18. *CR*, 24 Aug. 1959, p. 16738; "Washington Report from Frank Church," 16 March 1959, CP, 7.7/1.
19. Sundborg to Ashby, 17 Aug. 1988; Ernest Gruening to Church, 29 April 1958, CP, 12/3/5; Ernest Gruening, *Many Battles: The Autobiography of Ernest Gruening* (New York: Liveright, 1973), p. 405. Sundborg served for ten years as Gruening's administrative assistant.
20. Porter Ward memo to Church on "Idaho Newspaper Coverage During 1959," undated, CP, 12/3/6.
21. Hower interview, 11 April 1987; Carver interview, 30 June 1987.

22. See, for example, *Washington Daily News*, 16, 26 July 1958; Washington *Evening Star*, 29 July 1958; "A Fretful Form 57," *Newsweek* (28 July 1958): 44; "Washington Report from Frank Church," 26 Aug. 1958, CP, 7.7/1.
23. *Time* (29 June 1959): 8; Dwight D. Eisenhower, *Waging Peace: 1956-61* (Garden City, N. Y.: Doubleday, 1965), p. 392.
24. Richard A. Baker, "A Slap at the 'Hidden-Hand Presidency': The Senate and the Lewis Strauss Affair," *Congress and the Presidency*, 14 (Spring 1987): 3-5.
25. *Ibid.*, pp. 5-6.
26. On the liberal bloc, Carver interview, 30 June 1987; transcript, Joseph Clark Oral History Interview, 16 Dec. 1965, by Ronald S. Grele, p. 27, JFK Library, and transcript, Joseph Clark Oral History Interview, 1 Oct. 1978, by Ronald S. Grele, p. 9, Former Members of Congress, Inc., LC; Clark to Lyndon Johnson, 26 March 1959, Papers of Lyndon Baines Johnson as Senator, LBJ Library, Box 365.
27. Baker, "A Slap at the 'Hidden-Hand Presidency,' " pp. 5-9.
28. Church to "Dear Pop," 13 June 1959, CP, 10.3/1/2.
29. Goldwater quoted in Baker, "A Slap at the 'Hidden-Hand Presidency,' " p. 13.
30. Meany quoted in Arthur M. Schlesinger, Jr., *Robert Kennedy and His Times* (New York: Houghton Mifflin, 1978), p. 143; on McNamara, Chicago *Sun-Times*, 1 Apr. 1958.
31. Interviews: Church, 10 Jan. and 12 June 1979; Carver, 30 June 1987; Dick Clark, 30 July 1984 (re voting); Ross K. Baker, *Friend and Foe in the U. S. Senate* (New York: Free Press, 1980); p. 157.
32. Church to Bethine, 18 Jan. 1947, BC; Randy Stapilus, *Paradox Politics: People and Power in Idaho* (Boise: Ridenbaugh Press, 1988), p. 227, re Idaho union membership.
33. San Francisco *People's World*, 25 Oct. 1958, on Idaho; Saginaw, Michigan, *Labor News*, 31 Oct. 1958, and *Wall Street Journal*, 16 Oct. 1958, on right-to-work blitz and deMille's quotation; clippings in Robert F. Kennedy Pre-Presidential Papers, JFK Library, Senate Select Committee Newsclippings, Microfilm Roll 2.
34. Church to Archie Kennedy, 25 Aug. 1959, and to Harold Holmes, 3 March 1959, re labor abuses; Howard Roe to Church, 10 Sept. 1959, and Church reply, 14 Sept. 1959, re defense of labor; Church to Paul Maness, 15 July 1958, re management, CP, 12/3/5; handwritten notes for Church speech re appreciating Idaho, *ibid.*, 10.6/2/14.
35. Transcript of an oral history interview, John A. Carver, Jr., 8/19/68, by John F. Stewart, p. 11, JFK Library; New York *Daily News*, 16 Sept. 1958, Church qtn.
36. Church interview, 12 June 1979; Frank Church to Robert Kennedy, 11 Sept. 1959, and Kennedy to Church, 14 Nov. 1959, Robert Kennedy Papers, Pre-Administration Political Files, Correspondence, JFK Library, Box 6; Robert F. Kennedy, *The Enemy Within* (New York: Harper & Brothers, 1960), pp. 224-25, 301.
37. Interviews: Frank Moss, 11 May 1987; Quentin Burdick, 18 May 1987; also, Patrick Shea, 15 Oct. 1988, a staffer for both Moss and Church.
38. Church to Opal Silva, 10 Feb. 1964, CP, 12/3/5; transcript, John A. Carver, Jr., Oral History Interview, 25 Nov. 1969, by William W. Moss, p. 97, JFK Library (hereafter, Carver Oral History).
39. Susan M. Stacy, "Frank Church and the Termination Policy," unpublished paper, 2 Dec. 1989, pp. 3-12, CP, 12/1/7; Church to Joseph Thorpe, Jr., 19 Sept. 1958 (unsent), 1.1/71/13; *CR*, 22 Sept. 1961, p. 20873-74, re programs.
40. Carver Oral History, p. 97; interviews: Sam Day, 4 Oct. 1987, and Hal Gross, 11 Aug. 1984; Perry Swisher to Ashby, 31 Dec. 1987. Also, Frank Moss interview,

11 May 1987; transcript, Stewart Udall Oral History Interview, 16 Feb. and 2 June 1970, by W. W. Moss, pp. 40, 129, JFK Library. Church similarly relented on a case involving the Kalispel tribe in the Northwest. In 1964 he, along with Washington senator Henry Jackson, shocked the tribe by trying to hold an Indian Claims Commission settlement hostage to the Kalispels' acceptance of some kind of termination. After tribal representatives met personally with Church, however, he (unlike Jackson) had a change of heart and reversed himself. Robert C. Carriker, "The Kalispel Tribe and the Indian Claims Commission Experience," *Western Historical Quarterly*, 9 (Jan. 1978): esp. pp. 26-29.

41. Church to Patricia K. Ourada, 29 Dec. 1980, CP, 12/3/5. In 1971 he backed with "full support" a joint resolution repudiating termination. The policy, he said, had "failed so miserably" that it was time to end it. Two years later, at the urging of LaDonna Harris, a Native American, he co-sponsored legislation to reverse the termination of the Menominee tribe. Stacy, "Frank Church and the Termination Policy," pp. 19-20.
42. Moss interview, 11 May 1987; also Carver Oral History, p. 97.
43. Carl Marcy interview, 2 Nov. 1983, by Donald A. Ritchie, *The U. S. Senate Historical Office Oral History Collection: Interviews with Senate Staff* (Wilmington, Del: Scholarly Resources, 1987), p. 260.
44. Robert A. Divine, *Blowing on the Wind: The Nuclear Test Ban Debate, 1954-1960* (New York: Oxford University Press, 1958), pp. 237-47.
45. *CR*, 2 March 1959, pp. 3127-34, which included Church's letter to Herter; "Senator Church of Idaho," *The Atlantic*, 204 (Aug. 1959): 8; Divine, *Blowing on the Wind*, pp. 248, 250.
46. *San Francisco Chronicle*, 25 April 1959; *Christian Science Monitor* editorial, 14 April 1959; Ernest K. Lindley, "Atom-Free Air," *Newsweek* (16 March 1959): 33.
47. Divine, *Blowing on the Wind*, pp. 247-48, 253-55.
48. Divine, *Blowing on the Wind*, pp. 248, 262-69; Frank Church, "We Must Stop Poisoning the Air," *The Reporter*, 20 (16 Apr. 1959): 18-19; "Washington Report from Frank Church," 16 Mar. 1959, CP, 12/3/5.
49. Church qtn., 4 Feb. 1958 news release, CP, 12/3/5; "Senator Church of Idaho," p. 8; Mansfield, Church's 8 Jan. 1960 letter, and the State Department proposal in *CR*, 11 Feb. 1960, pp. 2412-13, 2420-21.
50. *CR*, 28 May 1959, pp. 9318-21; Church news release, 12 June 1959, CP, 12/3/5.
51. *Salt Lake Tribune*, 27 July 1959.
52. *CR*, 28 April 1960, pp. 8896-99.
53. John Lewis Gaddis, *Strategies of Containment: A Critical Appraisal of Postwar American National Security Policy* (New York: Oxford University Press, 1982), pp. 192-93, and Divine, *Blowing on the Wind*, pp. 259, 314 re the administration.
54. Text of 27 May 1958 speech at Arizona State University, CP, 12/3/5.
55. Church's keynote address to biennial convention of Young Democratic Clubs of America, Reno, Nevada, 7 Nov. 1957, CP, 12/3/5; typed notes of Church's speech before Woman's National Democratic Club, 25 Feb. 1960, *ibid.*, 10.6/6/10; Church to Albert T. Church, Jr., 26 Aug. 1959, re brush fires, 12/3/5; re his doubts about who was winning, Church's handwritten notes for speech, "The Communist Challenge," n. d., but probably early 1960, 10.6/6/10; on Castro, Church news release, 19 Aug. 1960, 7.4/1/8.
56. Church speech, "The Communist Challenge."
57. Church to J. E. McGoran, 12 May 1959, and Church speech, "The Role of College Education in a Free Society," Easton, Penn., 8 May 1958, CP, 12/3/5.

58. Qtn. in Church to Ralph G. Simpson, 30 June 1959, CP, 12/3/5.
59. Church to Dick Bearg, 14 Aug. 1959, CP, 12/3/5, re rigidity; *CR*, 2 March 1959, pp. 3130-31.
60. Church speeches, Grand Rapids, Mich., 9 Feb. 1957, CP, 10.6/3/13, re total war; "The Role of College Education in a Free Society," and 1958 Arizona State address; also, "Public Education at the Crossroads," 9 March 1958, in San Francisco, for another reference to anti-intellectualism, CP, 12/3/5.
61. Carl Marcy to Morella, 24 March 1972, Carl Marcy Papers, Box 1972-73, in Senate Foreign Relations Papers, NA; Louis Harris and Associates, Inc., typed report on "The Issues of Concern in Idaho," Democratic National Committee Papers, JFK Library, Box 212; James B. Donart to Frank Church, 9 Sept. 1960, copy in JFK Pre-Presidential Papers, JFK Library, Box 978; Burke to Church, 29 March 1961, CP, 12/3/5.
62. Ward Hower interview, 11 April 1987; Church memo to Carver, n. d., but concerning an 11 Dec. 1959 letter from Mackay, Idaho, CP, 7.5/4/2; interviews: Tommie Ward, 16 May 1987; Myrna Sasser, 20 March 1988; Rick Raphael, 21 Jan. 1988; man in audience at Frank Church conference, Boise State University, 30 Sept. 1988.
63. Tommie Ward interview, 16 May 1987.
64. Interviews: Ward and Phyllis Hower; Tommie Ward, 16 May 1987; Sam Day, 4 Oct. 1987; *Idaho Statesman*, 25 May 1960, re speech.
65. Moss interview, 11 May 1987.
66. Carver memo to Church, n. d., but April, 1959, and Church to Gardner Jackson, 29 April 1959; Pat McNamara to Church, 8 June 1959, with attached memo from Hower and Carver, CP, 12/3/5.
67. James B. Donart to Church, 9 Sept. 1960, copy in JFK Pre-Presidential Papers, JFK Library, Box 978, re dangers of criticizing Ike; Donart and Louis Harris poll on "The Issues of Concern in Idaho," Democratic National Committee Papers, JFK Library, Box 212, re economic concerns.
68. "Washington Report from Frank Church," Aug., 1957; reprint of Church's 24 Aug. 1959 speech from *CR*, CP, 12/3/5.
69. For example, see Church to Prescott Bush, 11 Jan. 1960, re the lead pigs; "Washington Report from Frank Church," 26 Jan. 1959, re Pocatello; newsletter #86-2-3 (n. d., but fall, 1960) re timber; reprint from *CR* of Church's 19 June 1958 remarks on excise tax rates, CP, 12/3/5.
70. Ward Hower interview, 11 April 1987.
71. Carver Oral History, 19 Aug. 1969, pp. 14-15, and Carver interview, 27 Oct. 1979; Harry Wall to Paul M. Butler, 7 Oct. 1959, copy in CP, 6/2/6; *Lewiston Tribune*, 23 Jan. 1960.
72. Washington *Evening Star*, 20 Jan. 1960. Harry Wall made many of these same points when he recommended Church to Paul Butler, 7 Oct. 1959; copy in CP, 6/2/6.
73. John Kennedy to Church, 8 Oct. 1959, CP, 12/3/5; Carver interview, 27 Oct. 1979.
74. Robert A. Wallace to John and Robert Kennedy, 14 March 1960, JFK Pre-Presidential Papers, JFK Library, Box 1038; Carver Oral History, 19 Aug. 1968, p. 16; interviews: Frank Church, 10 Jan. 1979; Bethine Church, 8 Feb. 1989, re LBJ's assumption.
75. Church to Bryce Nelson, 6 June 1960, CP, 10.3/1/3.
76. Script, "Keynote Address of Senator Frank Church. . .to Biennial Convention of Young Democratic Clubs," Reno, Nev., 7 Nov. 1957, CP, 12/3/5; Church to R. B. Church, 6 June 1960, CP, 10.3/1/3.

Notes to Chapter Six

1. *Los Angeles Times*, 7 July 1960; Bethine Church interview, 8 Feb. 1989.
2. Interviews: Tommie Ward, 16 May 1987; Eugene McCarthy, 22 March 1990; Verda Barnes, 8 June 1979; Ward and Phyllis Hower, 11 April 1987.
3. Church to Bryce Nelson, 6 June 1960, CP, 10.3/1/3.
4. *Los Angeles Times*, 10 July (Reston) and 11 July 1960 (Lubell).
5. *Los Angeles Times*, 7, 10, and 11 July 1960; Richard Church interview, 5 Aug. 1984, re Church's nervousness.
6. Interviews: John Corlett, 15 March 1988; Frank Church, 10 Jan. 1979.
7. Bethine Church interview, 14 March 1985; F. Forrester Church, *Father and Son: A Personal Biography of Senator Frank Church of Idaho* (New York: Harper & Row, 1985), pp. 48-49.
8. Text of keynote speech, CP, 12/3/6.
9. *Ibid.*
10. *Los Angeles Times*, 12 July 1960.
11. Interviews: Sam Day, 4 Oct. 1987; McCarthy, 22 March 1990; Corlett, 15 March 1988; Ward, 16 May 1987; Ward and Phyllis Hower, 11 April 1987; Myrna Sasser, 20 March 1988; Barnes, 8 June 1979; transcript, John Carver Oral History interview, 19 August 1968, by John F. Stewart, p. 17, JFK Library; Broder qtn. in Loch K. Johnson, *A Season of Inquiry: The Senate Intelligence Investigation* (Lexington: University Press of Kentucky, 1985), p. 249. The dozens of letters that Church received were critical by about three-to-one. Most of the criticism took umbrage at his criticism of the Eisenhower administration. A number of writers attacked his 'communist' leanings. CP, 6.0/3/1-3, 11.
12. Qtn., *New York Times*, 8 April 1984; Patrick Shea interview, 15 Oct. 1988.
13. Interviews: Church, 10 Jan. 1979, and John Corlett, 15 March 1988; Church to Bryce Nelson, 10 Aug. 1960, CP, 10.3/1/3. Church recounted his encounter with JFK to Nelson, but John Corlett was present when it occurred.
14. Bethine Church interview, 8 Feb. 1989; transcript, Frank Church Oral History Interview, 1 May 1969, by Paige E. Mulhollan, pp. 13-14, LBJ Library.
15. *Idaho Statesman*, 13 July 1960.
16. *Idaho Statesman*, 14 July 1960; interviews: Robert McLaughlin, 12 Sept. 1979, and John Corlett, 10 Dec. 1978.
17. *Idaho Statesman*, 14-15 July 1960; John Corlett interview, 15 March 1988, re Church's plea.
18. Church to Robert Kennedy, 24 Oct. 1960, Robert Kennedy Pre-Administration Political Files, Correspondence, JFK Library, Box 6, re campaigning.
19. *Idaho Statesman*, 10 Nov. 1960; John A. Carver, Jr. to Lloyd J. Walker, 17 Nov. 1960, CP, 9.7/1/13, re the statistics.
20. Lloyd J. Walker to Frank Church, 15 Nov. 1960, CP, 9.7/1/13.
21. *CR*, 29 June 1961, p. 11759.
22. Frank Moss, typed diary of 1960 Africa trip, p. 3, in Former Members of Congress Oral History Project, LC, Box 8, Frank Moss, folder 2; Church's handwritten notes of trip--hereafter, African notes--CP, 10.6/1/1.
23. African notes; Moss diary, pp. 6-29; Bethine Church interview, 23 June 1993.
24. African notes; Moss diary, pp. 29-52.
25. African notes, 15 Nov. entry, for qtn. (Church's emphasis); Moss diary, pp. 29-68.
26. Moss diary, p. 69; African notes, 'Conclusions.'

27. Transcript, Frank Church Oral History Interview, 5 Nov. 1981, by Sheldon Stern, p. 7, JFK Library, re JFK's request; Thomas J. Noer, "New Frontiers and Old Priorities in Africa," in Thomas G. Paterson, ed., *Kennedy's Quest for Victory: American Foreign Policy, 1961-1963* (New York, Oxford University Press, 1989), pp. 253-83; Richard D. Mahoney, *JFK: Ordeal in Africa* (New York: Oxford University Press, 1983), esp. pp. 244-48.
28. African notes, "Conclusion"; handwritten notes for Idaho Falls Kiwanis-Rotary speech, 1 March 1961; text of Church's extemporaneous remarks, Naval Academy Foreign Affairs Conference, 27 April 1961, CP, 10.6/1/1; *CR*, 29 June 1961, p. 11761.
29. Notes of Church's Idaho Falls speech, 1 March 1961; African notes; re Forrest, notes for unidentified speech (c. 1961), CP, 10.6/1/1.
30. Church's African notes; Idaho Falls speech, 1 March 1961; *CR*, 29 June 1961, pp. 11759-63.
31. *San Francisco Examiner*, 28 Dec. 1960.
32. *CR*, 29 June 1961, pp. 11759-62.
33. Jonathan Kwitny, *Endless Enemies: The Making of an Unfriendly World* (New York: Congdon & Weed, 1984), pp. 50-51, 56-58.
34. Quotation in Robert A. Pastor, *Condemned to Repetition: The United States and Nicaragua* (Princeton, N. J.: Princeton University Press, 1987), p. 76.
35. Church to Sidney Hyman, 15 June 1961, and typed outline, "Myths that Plague American Foreign Policy," CP, 10.6/1/1. Church's emphasis.
36. Church to Lester Markel, 22 July 1961, and handwritten notes for U. P. I. interview, n. d., but around 1960, CP, 12/3/6; Newsreel, "Personal Profiles II" (1958), video #58007; Church biography, July 1960, 10.1/1/5.
37. Handwritten notes for U. P. I. interview, n. d., but around 1960, CP, 12/3/6; text of speech, "The Scourge of Giantism in Business and Politics," 12 Feb. 1962, 12/3/15.
38. See, for example, Church to Reid Gardner, 22 June 1961; to Nelda Lien, 5 Feb. 1962; to DeForrest Smith, 5 June 1962, CP, 12/3/6.
39. Tommie Ward interview, 16 May 1987.
40. Arthur Schlesinger, Jr. to Ashby, 17 Feb. 1987; interviews: Ward Hower, 11 April 1987, re "Old Jack," and Bryce Nelson, 7 April 1993.
41. Khrushchev qtn., David Burner, *John F. Kennedy and a New Generation* (Boston: Little, Brown, 1988), p. 73; Michael R. Beschloss, *The Crisis Years: Kennedy and Khrushchev, 1960-1963* (New York: HarperCollins, 1991), pp. 171-78, 223, 232-88, for a detailed discussion of the crisis.
42. Bryce Nelson interview, 1 Feb. 1987; Church to Lester Markel, 22 July 1961, CP, 12/3/6.
43. *CR*, 16 Aug. 1961, pp. 16002-10, 16007 (qtn.).
44. Church to Bethine, 22 Aug. 1961, CP, 10.3/1/5.
45. Memo to Ted Kennedy, et al., re 13 Oct. 1961 testimonial banquet for Church, p. 2, which stressed his need to be independent, CP, 10.6/1/43; Church to A.M. Horrall, 31 Aug. 1961, 2.2/3/14, re Berlin.
46. Memo, Ken O'Donnell to Larry O'Brien, 26 May 1961, John F. Kennedy Papers, Presidential Name File: "Church," JFK Library, for example of Church's candor; Church qtn. in Church's JFK Oral History, JFK Library, p. 19; Theodore White, *The Making of the President, 1960* (New York: Atheneum, 1961), p. 458; re Church's awe of the presidency, interviews: Bryce Nelson, 1 Feb. 1987; Ward and Phyllis Hower, 11 April 1987; and Forrest Church, 25 July 1984.
47. Church's handwritten comments on Kennedy's "First Hundred Days," 5 May 1961, CP, 10.6/3/19.

48. Church qtn. in text of speech (n. d., but early 1962), CP, 10.1/1/6; photo and re potatoes in newsletters 87-2-1 and 87-2-2 (n. d., but 1962), 12/3/6; Church and Ralph R. Harding to "Dear Friend" (n. d., but 1961) with enclosure, "Reasons for Reinstating the Wheat-Mixture Exemption. . . ," 10.6/2/14; Louis Harris & Associates, Inc., "A Survey of the Race for U. S. Senate in the State of Idaho" (July, 1962), 12/3/6 (hereafter, Harris survey).
49. Interviews: Orval Hansen, 2 Aug. 1984, and Chase Church, 7 Aug. 1984, re Church's views of nature; John Carver, 27 Oct. 1979.
50. Carver interview, 27 Oct. 1979; transcript, Stewart L. Udall Oral History interview, 2 June 1970, by W. W. Moss, p. 117, JFK Library.
51. Carl Pease to Church, 7 March 1961, and P. W. Jungert to Church, 21 Feb. 1961, CP, 1.1/151/20; cartoon enclosed with C. J. Hopkins to Church, 29 March 1961, 1.1/152/2.
52. Church to Herman Dobroth, 9 March 1961, as example of reply, CP, 1.1/152/20; Jack Tacke interview, 9 Aug. 1984.
53. Richard A. Baker, *Conservation Politics: The Senate Career of Clinton P. Anderson* (Albuquerque: University of New Mexico Press, 1985), pp. 135-36, 139; *CR*, 28 March 1961, pp. 4975-76; Church news release, 14 July 1961, CP, 1.1/151/18.
54. Clinton P. Anderson to Church, 14 July 1961, CP, 10.3/1/4.
55. Clinton P. Anderson, *Outsider in the Senate* (New York: World Publishing Co., 1970), p. 233.
56. *CR*, 5 Sept. 1961, pp. 18045-47.
57. *CR*, 5 Sept. 1961, p. 18046; 6 Sept. 1961, p. 18365.
58. *CR*, 5 Sept. 1961, pp. 18046; Church to "Dear Friend," 26 Sept. 1961, with excerpts from Senate debate, CP, 1.1/151/18.
59. On Anderson's role, *CR*, 6 Sept. 1961, p. 18398, and Church to Anderson, 12 Sept. 1961, CP, 1.1/152/11; Anderson, *Outsider in the Senate*, p. 233; copy of Olaus J. Murie to Albert Van S. Pulling, 1.1/152/5; Carl W. Buchheister to Church, 13 Sept. 1961, and Thomas Kimball to Church, 8 Sept. 1961, 1.1/152/5.
60. Baker, *Conservation Politics*, p. 143, re Church's belief; Anderson, *Outsider in the Senate*, p. 233; Drew Pearson and Jack Anderson, *The Case Against Congress* (New York: Simon & Schuster, 1968), p. 425.
61. Qtn., Frank Church, "Whither Wilderness?" *American Forests* (July 1977): 12.
62. Script, Industries of the Coeur d'Alenes Information Service, 28 Sept. 1961, CP, 1.1/152/3; number of critical letters, 1/1/152/1-5; Church, "Whither Wilderness," p. 11, re crowds.
63. E. C. Rettig of Potlatch Forests, Inc., to "Dear Fellow Employees," 23 Feb. 1961, CP, 1.1/152/6; script, Industries of the Coeur d'Alenes Information Service, 28 Sept. 1961, 1.1/152/3; *Idaho Daily Statesman*, 10 Aug. 1961, re Derr. David Underhill, "Out of the Labyrinth and Into the Wilderness," reprinted from *The "I"* (May 1962), esp. pp. 23-24, astutely discussed how the "mock battle" over wilderness jeopardized Church's political base; 1.1/152/10.
64. Church to William F. Johnston, 30 Sept. 1961, and C. Knutson to Church, 10 Sept. 1961, with *Idaho Statesman* editorial, n. d., but early Sept. 1961, CP, 1.1/152/5.
65. Burke to Church, 3 May 1962; also Burke to George E. Agree, 3 March 1962, and Joseph S. Miller, 5 Feb. 1962, on Hawley, CP, 12/3/6.
66. Text of Hawley's speech, CP, 5.2/1/2; Hawley flier, 12/3/6.
67. Burke to Church, 13 Feb., 27 March, 3 May 1962, CP, 12/3/6.
68. Burke to Fred A. Picard, n. d., but early Feb., 1962; to William S. Hawkins, 3 March 1962; to Stanley Mortimer, Jr., 20 March 1962, CP, 12/3/6.

69. Church to Lyndon Johnson, 8 Oct. 1962, re folly of the gambling plan, CP, 12/3/6; Harris survey, pp. 3, 5, 24-27.
70. Harris survey, pp. 20-22; anonymous comments of former Church staffer to Ashby.
71. Burke interviews, 22 Nov. 1987 and 23 May 1979; also, Church to Lyndon Johnson, 8 Oct. 1962, CP, 12/3/6.
72. Harris survey, pp. 3, 7-8, 14-16, 20-22, 31.
73. CP, 5.2/1-3, audio tapes, A62002-04; and video tapes 62001-2, 62037, 62039-40, 62043-44.
74. Woman quoted in Baltimore *Sun*, 17 Feb. 1980; Carver interview, 27 Oct. 1979.
75. Thomas G. Paterson and William J. Brophy, "October Missiles and November Elections: The Cuban Missile Crisis and American Politics, 1962," *The Journal of American History*, 73 (June 1986): 93-98.
76. Gale McGee interview, 6 March 1988; Church press release, 1 Oct. 1962, CP, 12/3/6; Barnes interview, 8 June 1979, and Church, *Father and Son*, p. 57, re newsletter.
77. Barnes interview, 8 June 1979; Church, *Father and Son*, p. 57.
78. Bethine Church interview, 8 Feb. 1980.
79. Interviews: Ward Hower, 11 April 1987; Bethine Church, 8 Feb. 1989; Church, *Father and Son*, p. 57.
80. Hower interview, 11 April 1987; Church, *Father and Son*, p. 57.
81. Interviews: Hower, 11 April 1987; Bethine Church, 8 Feb. 1989.
82. Interviews: Bethine Church, 8 Feb. 1989, and Frank Church, 13 Feb. 1979.
83. Interviews: Bethine Church, 8 Feb. 1989; Frank Church, 13 Feb. 1979; Barnes, 8 June 1979, re Hawley and his campaign; Spokane, Wash., *Spokesman-Review*, 11 Nov. 1962, re counties.
84. See William O. Lewis, "The 1962 Election in Idaho," *Western Political Quarterly*, 16 (June 1963): 432-38.
85. Corlett in *Idaho Statesman*, 1 Jan. 1963; voter quoted in Randy Stapilus, *Paradox Politics: People and Power in Idaho* (Boise: Ridenbaugh Press, 1988, p. 92.
86. Stapilus, *Paradox Politics*, p. 204, re memo; Dale Nelson interview, 1 March 1988.

Notes for Chapter Seven

1. Handwritten notes for speech, n. d., but in 1961, CP, 10.6/3/6. See, for example, "Frank Church of Idaho," *Atlantic* (August 1959): 8, re Church's liberalism.
2. Qtn. re JFK, transcript, Frank Church Oral History interview, 5 Nov. 1981, by Sheldon Stern, p. 17, JFK Library; Church to George Sloneker, 22 March 1963, CP, 2.2/46/13, re danger, and to Lillian Pickrel, 1 May 1964, 2.2/47/1, re Cuba.
3. Church to Paul Shrum, 28 March 1962, CP, 2.2/25/10.
4. Church handwritten notes of Southeast Asia trip, CP, 10.6/8/7—hereafter, Church Notes; Frank Moss, Southeast Asia diary, Former Member of Congress Oral History Project, LC, Box 8, Moss Folder 2—hereafter, Moss Diary—pp. 1-37 (qtn., p. 36); U. S., Cong., Senate, *Study Mission to Southeast Asia, November-December 1962*, 88th Cong., 1st sess., 1963, p. 11. Gale McGee interview, 6 March 1988, re hunting.
5. *Study Mission*, p. 7.
6. Statistics in Neil Sheehan, *A Bright Shining Lie: John Paul Vann and America in Vietnam* (New York: Random House, 1988), p. 183; Nhu qtn., David Halberstam, *The Making of a Quagmire: America and Vietnam During the Kennedy Era* (rev. ed., New York: Knopf, 1988), p. 23.

7. Church interview, 13 Feb. 1979; Church Notes. See, also, Moss Diary, pp. 35, 37-39.
8. Interviews: Church, 13 Feb. 1979, and Frank Moss, 11 May 1987.
9. Church Notes; Church interview, 13 Feb. 1979; Moss interview, 11 May 1987; *Study Mission*, pp. 1, 7; L. K. Johnson, "Preliminary Analysis of Church Dissent," July, 1970, CP, 10.6/8/2, re the Dec. 20 quotation. Johnson, a Church aide, compiled this chronology from files in the senator's office.
10. See, for example, "Christian Brotherhood" and "Closer up" newsletters, CP, 7.5/4/3; Cinema Educational Guild pamphlets, 1.1/152/12 and 7.5/4/3; Church to Charles Hendricks, 25 May 1961, 7.5/4/3, re the film.
11. See, for example, Church to Ronald E. Eggert, 6 April 1961; to Charles J. Hendricks, 25 May 1961, CP, 7.5/4/3; and to Hillis Griffin, 31 Aug. 1961, 7.5/4/2.
12. See, for example, any number of letters in CP, 7.5/4/2-3.
13. Phyllis and Ward Hower interview, 11 April 1987.
14. Bethine to Church, 18 Aug. 1960, CP, 10.3/1/3; Church to Bethine, 14 Aug. 1960, 10.3/1/5; Church to Robert W. Barlett II, 11 Oct. 1963, 12/3/7; Rick Raphael interview, 21 Jan. 1988.
15. Frank Church, "What is a 'Liberal'? A 'Liberal' Senator Answers," *U. S. News and World Report* (6 May 1963): 117.
16. *Ibid.*, pp. 117-18.
17. *Ibid.*, pp. 118-19.
18. *Ibid.*, p. 119.
19. Script for Salmon, Idaho, speech, "Report from Washington" (n. d., but spring, 1961), CP, 10.6/1/43.
20. See, for example, Church to Loyd E. Johnson, 18 Feb. 1964, and to Ginger Jones, 14 Aug. 1964; draft letter from Lloyd Walker to Paul Cross, n. d., but responding to a 2 May 1963 editorial (Church himself edited the letter for Walker), CP, 12/3/7.
21. Church, "Stemming the Goldwater Flood: A Western Responsibility," 19 Sept. 1963 keynote address for Western States Democratic Conference, Salt Lake City, Utah, reprinted in *CR*, 23 Sept. 1963, pp. 17777, 17781; Church, "The Private World of Barry Goldwater," *Frontier* (Nov. 1963): 5-7.
22. Church, "Stemming the Goldwater Flood," pp. 17781-82, and "The Private World of Barry Goldwater," pp. 5, 7.
23. Church to Alton S. Windsor, Jr., 13 April 1964, CP, 12/3/7, re the ACA rating.
24. Qtn., Charles and Barbara Whalen, *The Longest Debate: A Legislative History of the 1964 Civil Rights Act* (softbound ed., New York: New American Library, 1986), p. 17.
25. Statistic in Whalen, *The Longest Debate*, pp. 24-25; interviews: Bryce Nelson, 1 Feb. 1987; Myrna Sasser, 20 March 1988; Fariborz Fatemi, 15 May 1987.
26. See, for example, Halberstam, *The Making of a Quagmire*, pp. 101-20.
27. William C. Gibbons, *The U. S. Government and the Vietnam War: Executive and Legislative Roles and Relationships*, Part II, 1961-1964 (Princeton, N. J.: Princeton University Press, 1986), pp. 148-62.
28. Handwritten notes of 5 Sept. 1963 meeting in James Thomson Papers, JFK Library, Box 6; qtn., Drew Pearson clipping, n. d., but Sept. 1963, CP, 2.2/26/19; Roger Hilsman, *To Move a Nation: The Politics of Foreign Policy in the Kennedy Administration* (New York: Doubleday, 1967), p. 505.
29. Gibbons, *The U.S. Government and the Vietnam War*, pp. 160, 166-67; Roger Hilsman interview, 6 Feb. 1984; Hilsman cable to U. S. embassy in Saigon, 5 Sept. 1963, JFK Papers, POF Country File, JFK Library, Box 128a; "JWN" [Joseph Neuber] to "RH" [Roger Hilsman], n. d., but probably 6 Sept. 1963, Thomson Papers, JFK Library, Box 23.

30. Interviews: Hilsman, 6 Feb. 1984, and Bryce Nelson (by Gibbons and McAdams), 12 Dec. 1978, copy in Gibbons's possession; "Draft Resolution, Proposed by Senator Church," 5 Sept. 1963, Thomson Papers, Box 23; "Statement from Mr. Bundy's Office" (n. d., but Sept. 1963), and Carl Marcy to Church, 7 Sept. 1963, CP, 2.2/26/19.
31. Hilsman interview, 6 Feb. 1984.
32. Typed notes of Church-Hilsman meeting, 10 Sept. 1963, Thomson Papers, JFK Library, Box 23.
33. Minutes of State Department meeting, 10 Sept. 1963–Subject Vietnam, Kennedy Papers, NSF Meetings and Memos, JFK Library, Box 316-17; McGeorge Bundy interview, 23 July 1984.
34. Memo of Conference with the President, 11 Sept. 1963–Subject: Vietnam, Kennedy Papers, NSF Meetings and Memos, JFK Library, Box 316-17.
35. *CR*, 11 Sept. 1963, pp. 16783-87; statistic and qtn. from Humphrey's aide in Herbert S. Parmet, *JFK: The Presidency of John F. Kennedy* (New York: Penguin Books, 1983), pp. 315-16; see, for example, H. E. Iverson, 1 and 22 Sept. 1963, CP, 12/3/7.
36. Alsop in *Washington Post*, 22 Sept. 1963.
37. Memo, Ginny to RH [Hilsman], 12 Sept. 1963, Thomson Papers, JFK Library, Box 23; script of Church's speech, with corrections added, Roger Hilsman Papers, JFK Library, Box 4; speech and resolution in *CR*, 12 Sept. 1963, p. 16824.
38. Hilsman interview, 6 Feb. 1984, (qtn.); see, for example, Roger Hilsman to Secretaries of State and Defense, 16 Sept. 1963, including "Pressure Plan–Phase 1" of "Action Plan for South Vietnam," Kennedy Papers, NSF Meetings and Memos, JFK Library, Box 316-17; copy of Frederick G. Dutton to J. W. Fulbright, 14 Oct. 1963, CP, 2.2/27/3.
39. R. W. Komer to the President, 19 Aug. 1963, Kennedy Papers, NSF-Subjects, JFK Library, Box 296-98.
40. *CR*, 17 June 1963, pp. 10976-85; Mike Manatos to Larry O'Brien, 9 Oct. 1962, Mike Manatos Papers, JFK Library, Box 1.
41. Craig Raupe to Claude Desautels, 7 Oct. 1963, Kennedy Papers, NSF-Subjects, JFK Library, Box 296-98.
42. Church, "The Liberal Revolt Against Foreign Aid," 24 Oct. 1963, CP, 8.3/4/26.
43. Arthur Schlesinger, Jr., *A Thousand Days: John F. Kennedy in the White House* (1965; softbound ed., New York: Fawcett, 1967), p. 551; Church to Eric Sevareid, 12 Nov. 1963, and to Richard Humphrey, 19 Nov. 1963, CP, 12/3/7.
44. Church's comments on, and copy of, Halberstam's 15 Sept. 1963 *New York Times* article, and clipping of Meagher in Los Angeles *Times*, 8 Sept. 1963, CP, 2.2/26/20; newscaster Roger Mudd re "no reform, no aid," CBS News transcript, 8 Sept. 1963, p. 1, 12/3/7.
45. Church to Eli Oboler, 28 March 1963, CP, 2.2/26/18.
46. Ben [Bryce Nelson] to Senator, n. d., but October, 1963, CP, 2.2/26/20.
47. JFK on "our offspring" in George C. Herring, *America's Longest War: The United States and Vietnam, 1950-1975* (2d ed., New York: Knopf, 1986), p. 43.
48. *CR*, 5 Nov. 1963, p. 21056; Church to McGovern, 19 Nov. 1963, CP, 2.2/3/17.
49. Church interview, 13 Feb. 1979; Parmet, *JFK*, pp. 328, 333, 336.
50. Church interview, 13 Feb. 1979; Church's JFK Oral History, pp. 8-9.
51. *CR*, 11 Dec. 1963, p. 24135; Hilsman, *To Move a Nation*, pp. 352-53; Hilsman interview, 6 Feb. 1984.
52. *CR*, 11 Dec. 1963, p. 24135.
53. Church to Dear Fellow-American, 2 Dec. 1963, with clippings of Ralph McGill, Doris Fleeson, and Lippmann articles, CP, 12/3/7.

54. Church to "Dear Bob," 16 Dec. 1963, Robert F. Kennedy Papers, Attorney General's Correspondence, JFK Library, Box 2.
55. Whalen and Whalen, *The Longest Debate*, pp. 70, 89-91, 157-58.
56. For Church's reassurances, see, for example, Church to Ira Hoffman, 20 Dec. 1963, CP, 12/3/7.
57. Resolution by Hailey, Idaho, Chamber of Commerce, n. d. but Dec., 1963, and Church to Ira Hoffman, 20 Dec. 1963; *Lincoln County Journal*, 9 Jan. 1964; re Birchers, Church to Clark Eaton, 9 Dec. 1963, CP, 12/3/7. Re the Committee for Fundamental American Freedoms, see also Church to Carl Burke, 18 Dec. 1963, and the Group Research, Inc., publication, 9 Dec. 1963, CP, 12/3/7.
58. Church to Jack Stevens, 12 March 1964; to Guy Whitaker, 12 May 1964; and to Lee Ester, 3 April 1964, re morality, CP, 12/3/7. See also 1.1/29.
59. Church to Gerald Fosbenner, 5 Dec. 1964, and to Carl McIntyre, 23 March 1964, CP, 12/3/7.
60. *Lewiston Tribune*, 12 Jan. 1964; Lois Chaffee to Church, 25 Dec. 1963; Naomi Stebbins to Church, 23 Dec. 1963; Robert Fanning to Church, 30 Dec. 1963; Mr. and Mrs. Sidney Chaffee to Church, 28 Dec. 1963; Church to Lois Chaffee, 14 Oct. 1964; Church to Mr. and Mrs. Art Nolen, 7 Feb. 1964, CP, 12/3/7.
61. Whalen and Whalen, *The Longest Debate*, pp. 141-42, 145, 164-65.
62. See, for example, Bipartisan Civil Rights Newsletters in Papers of Leadership Conference of Civil Rights, Library of Congress, Box G 9, which regularly listed Church's assigned watch; Jerry Brady interview, 7 Nov. 1987.
63. *CR*, 30 April 1964, pp. 9640-41; Bipartisan Civil Rights Newsletter #76, 19 June 1964, Leadership Conference on Civil Rights Papers, LC, Box G 9, for the statistic.
64. Brady interview, 7 Nov. 1987; Church to Perry Swisher, 27 April 1964, and Church news release, 3 June 1964, CP, 12/3/7.
65. Whalen and Whalen, *The Longest Debate*, pp. 202-03, 218-19, 232; on the law's accomplishments, Steven F. Lawson, *Black Ballots: Voting Rights in the South, 1944-1969* (New York: Columbia University Press, 1976), pp. 301-02.
66. *CR*, 19 June 1964, p. 14514.
67. Church to John M. Bailey, and to James Farmer, 28 July 1964, CP, 12/3/7; Goldwater qtn., Whalen and Whalen, *The Longest Debate*, p. 216.
68. Cleveland Sellers with Robert Terrell, *The River of No Return* (New York: William Morrow, 1973), p. 106.
69. White quoted in Lawson, *Black Ballots*, p. 302; Dennis in Allen J. Matusow, *The Unraveling of America: A History of Liberalism in the 1960s* (New York: Harper and Row, 1984), p. 349.
70. Westmoreland in Herring, *America's Longest War*, p. 112.
71. Goldwater in Thomas Powers, *Vietnam: The War at Home* (1973; reprint, Boston: Twayne, 1984), p. 3; Johnson in Gibbons, *The U. S. Government and the Vietnam War*, p. 223.
72. *Washington Star*, 15 March 1964.
73. *The Intermountain Observer*, 17 April 1971; *CR*, 23 June 1964, pp. 14790, 14792.
74. *CR*, 6 Aug. 1964, p. 1429. Idaho state senator Carl Moore was in the Senate gallery when Church spoke. His brief description is in an *Intermountain Observer* clipping, 3 Sept. 1964, CP, 10.6/8/11.
75. Herring, *America's Longest War*, pp. 119-122; Gibbons, *The U. S. Government and the Vietnam War*, pp. 284-303. See also Anthony Austin, *The President's War* (Philadelphia: J. B. Lippincott, 1971).
76. Church news release, 6 Aug. 1964, 2.2/27/3; *CR*, 6 Aug. 1964, pp. 18415, 18421.

77. Church interview, 13 Feb. 1979; Tom Dine interview, 14 June 1979, re scarlet letter; Church to Sherrie Porter, 30 Nov. 1971, CP, 12/3/7, and to Eric Seitz, 15 Jan. 1973, 2.2/25/17.
78. Interviews: Church, 13 Feb. 1979; Nelson (by Gibbons & McAdams), 12 Dec. 1978.
79. Fulbright in Gibbons, *The U. S. Government and the Vietnam War*, p. 313; Gaylord Nelson interview, 21 May 1987.
80. Church's speech, "Battle Call for the Republic," delivered in Salt Lake City, 26 June 1964, CP, 12/3/7, in Milwaukee, 1 Aug. 1964, reprinted in *CR*, 12 Aug. 1964, pp. 19173-74.
81. *CR*, 12 Aug. 1964, p. 19173; also, Church to Mrs. Knifong and others, 1 Oct. 1964, CP, 2.2/27/3.
82. Church to Daniel Inouye, 10 Sept. 1964, and, re the challenge to Harding, typescript of Edward P. Morgan's 10 Dec. 1964 ABC broadcast, CP, 12/3/7; on Hansen and the Birchers, Randy Stapilus, *Paradox Politics: People and Power in Idaho* (Boise: Ridenbaugh Press, 1988), p. 115.
83. Re the Idaho elections, Stapilus, *Paradox Politics*, pp. 118-19; Peter D. Hart, "A Survey of Voter Attitudes in the State of Idaho, July 1979," pp. iii-iv, CP, 5.7/1.
84. Church to Jim Gray, 3 June 1964, CP, 2.2/27/2.

Notes for Chapter Eight

1. Bethine Church to Church, 18 Aug. 1960, CP, 10.3/1/3.
2. Transcript, Frank Church Oral History interview, 1 May 1969, by Paige E. Mulhollan, pp. 17-18, LBJ Library.
3. Transcript, Church's dictated memo (n. d., but probably mid-April 1965) re the Vietnam debate and his encounters with Johnson, p. 2, CP, 10.6/8/7 (hereafter, Church, "Narrative")—the tape itself is in CP, A64001; interviews: Bethine and Frank Church, 13 Feb. 1979, and Bethine Church, 24 July 1979.
4. Draft "memorandum on Vietnam," 8 Dec. 1964, with attachments, Carl Marcy to Fulbright, 8 Dec., and Ben [Bryce Nelson] to Church, n. d., but Dec. 1964, CP, 2.2/27.
5. Bethine Church interview, 24 July 1979.
6. Frank Church "Interview," *Ramparts* (Jan.-Feb. 1965): 17-22.
7. Frank Church interview, 13 Feb. 1979; Hubert Humphrey to Church, 6 Jan. 1965, CP, 2.2/27/5; Tristram Coffin, *Senator Fulbright: Portrait of a Public Philosopher* (New York: Dutton, 1966), p. 226.
8. *The New York Times*, 27 and 28 Dec. 1964; Church, "Narrative," pp. 3-4.
9. Memo, Ben [Bryce Nelson] to Church, n. d., but late 1964, CP, 2.2/27/3; Church telephone memo to Bryce Nelson, 30 Dec. 1964, 2.2/27/3; Church to Hans Morgenthau, 28 Dec. 1964, 2.2/27/5.
10. Frank Church interview, 13 Feb. 1979; Peter Fenn interview, 16 May 1987, re Church's pragmatic concerns.
11. George C. Herring, *America's Longest War: The United States and Vietnam, 1950-1975* (2nd ed., New York: Knopf, 1986), pp. 127-29.
12. Frank Church, "We Are In Too Deep in Asia and Africa," *The New York Times Magazine*, 14 Feb. 1965: 30-31, 84, 86; Walter Lippmann to Church, 15 Feb. 1965, CP, 2.2/27/6; F. Forrester Church, *Father and Son: A Personal Biography of Senator Frank Church of Idaho* (New York: Harper & Row, 1985), p. 60, re Bethine Church's opposition.
13. *CR*, 17 Feb. 1965, pp. 2869-72.

14. *Ibid.*, p. 2872.
15. LBJ quoted in U. S. Congress, Senate, Committee on Foreign Relations, *The U. S. Government and the Vietnam War: Executive and Legislative Roles and Relationships*. 100th Cong., 2d sess., 1988, part 3, p. 107. Hereafter, *Government and Vietnam War*, III.
16. Church, "Narrative," pp. 6-7; George McGovern, *Grassroots: The Autobiography of George McGovern* (New York: Random House, 1977), p. 106.
17. Church, "Narrative," pp. 7-8; on Humphrey's 15 Feb. 1965 memo to LBJ, see *Government and Vietnam War*, III, pp. 92-95.
18. *CR*, 18 Feb. 1965, pp. 3146-51; qtns. p. 3146.
19. Church, "Narrative," pp. 5-6.
20. *Ibid.*, pp. 5-6, 9-11; Church, *Father and Son*, p. 61.
21. Bethine Church interview, 12 March 1985; Church, "Narrative," p. 11.
22. Church, "Narrative," pp. 11-13; transcript, "Interview with Frank Church," 5 July 1983, by William C. Gibbons, p. 3—hereafter, Church interview (Gibbons), in Gibbons's possession; Church Oral History (Mulhollan), p. 22; Bethine Church interview, 12 March 1985.
23. Interviews: Ralph Yarborough, 19 March 1987, Bethine Church, 12 March 1985; Church (Gibbons), p. 3; and Church "Narrative," pp. 13-14.
24. Church, "Narrative," pp. 14-15; Bethine Church interviews, 22 June 1979 and 12 March 1985.
25. Church, "Narrative," pp. 15-18; Church interview (Gibbons), p. 4.
26. News release, 1 March 1965, CP, 2.2/27/12; clippings re Detroit speech, 2.2/28/5; news release for 2 March 1965, re Stanford, 2.2/3/20.
27. Church to the President, 19 Feb. 1965, CP, 12/3/8; Newsletter 89-1-1, 10.6/8/14.
28. Interviews: Bethine Church, 22 June 1979; Jerry Brady, 7 Nov. 1987; Tommie Ward, 16 May 1987; Verda Barnes, 8 June 1979.
29. Church interview (Gibbons), p. 10; Paul Kalbfleish to Church, 5 March 1965, and Grant Jones to Church, 8 March 1965, 2.2/27/10; *Lewiston Tribune*, 13 May 1965, re McMurray.
30. Interviews: Forrest Church, 27 Aug. 1979, and Bethine Church, 24 July 1979; Church, *Father and Son*, p. 60.
31. John Warner to Church (n. d., but early 1965), with translated 29 Dec. 1964 radio transcript, CP, 2.2/17/3.
32. Transcript, Bryce Nelson interview, 12 Dec. 1978, by William Gibbons and Patricia McAdams, pp. 3-4, in authors' possession; Nelson interview, 22 March 1993.
33. LBJ quoted in Doris Kearns, *Lyndon Johnson and the American Dream* (1976; softbound ed., New York: Signet, 1977), p. 263. Re saving the Great Society, see also Larry Berman, *Planning a Tragedy: The Americanization of the War in Vietnam* (New York: Norton, 1982), esp. pp. 122, 127, 145-50, and Brian VanDeMark, *Into the Quagmire: Lyndon Johnson and the Escalation of the Vietnam War* (New York: Oxford University Press, 1991), esp. pp. 54-55, 96-97, 178-81, 211-14.
34. Richard N. Goodwin, *Remembering America: A Voice from the Sixties* (Boston: Little, Brown, 1988), pp. 386, 361 (re McNamara), 366; McGovern *Grassroots*, pp. 104-05 (LBJ qtn.).
35. Memo for the President, 5 March 1965, Name File, White House Central File, Box 220, LBJ Library; *Washington Post*, 22 Jan. 1984.
36. Herring, *America's Longest War*, pp. 130-31. See, also, Nancy Zaroulis and Gerald Sullivan, *Who Spoke Up? American Protest Against the War in Vietnam, 1963-1975* (New York: Holt, Rinehart & Winston, 1984), p. 36, who note that U. S. Marines first landed in Vietnam in 1845 to rescue a Catholic bishop.

37. Frank Church, "We Should Negotiate a Settlement in Vietnam," *Saturday Evening Post*, 238 (24 April 1965): 10, 14.
38. *Government and Vietnam War*, III, p. 144, re the poll; re the continuing discontent see, for example, Mike Mansfield to Johnson, 24 March 1965, LBJ Papers, Ex ND 19/Co 312, Box 215, LBJ Library.
39. Douglass Cater memo to the President, 7 April 1965, Johnson Papers, White House Central File, Ex Sp 3-70, Box 168, LBJ Library; Church, "Narrative," p. 19; Church interview (Gibbons), pp. 4-5; Church Oral History (Mulhollan), p. 23; McGovern interview, 15 June 1979.
40. Church, "Narrative," pp. 19-20; Church interview (Gibbons), p. 5.
41. McGovern interview, 15 June 1979; Church, "Narrative," pp. 20-21.
42. Church, "Narrative," pp. 20-21; McGovern interview, 15 June 1979.
43. Press notice, 8 April 1965, CP, 2.2/27/12.
44. Interviews: Frank and Bethine Church, 13 Feb. 1979; McGovern, 15 June 1979.
45. Frank and Bethine Church interview, 13 Feb. 1979; Church Oral History (Mulhollan), pp. 24-25, re the problems of the middle ground.
46. Wm. Bundy quoted in Robert J. Donovan, *Nemesis: Truman and Johnson in the Coils of War in Asia* (New York: St. Martin's, 1984), p. 68; McG. Bundy and LBJ quoted in *Government and Vietnam War*, III, p. 222. Re the demonstration, Todd Gitlin, *The Sixties: Years of Hope, Days of Rage* (New York: Bantam, 1987), pp. 183-85.
47. Jack Valenti memo to LBJ, 23 April 1965, LBJ Papers, Ex ND 19/CO 312, Box 215; *Government and Vietnam War*, III, pp. 224-25, re the FBI; Goodwin, *Remembering America*, pp. 368-416 (qtn. on p. 392).
48. UPI dispatch from Walter T. Phair, 5 May 1965, CP, 2.2/28/7; Church to Dwight Jensen, 14 May 1965, 12/3/8.
49. *Government and the Vietnam War*, III, pp. 239-42.
50. Church interview (Gibbons), pp. 12-13; Coffin, *Senator Fulbright*, p. 225, re the poll and pp. 240-41 re Russell; *Government and Vietnam War*, III, p. 238; George Herring, "The Executive, Congress, and the Vietnam War, 1965-1975," manuscript in authors' possession, esp. pp. 1-7 (Russell qtn., p. 2; McGovern, p. 7).
51. *Government and Vietnam War*, III, pp. 242-49.
52. Peter Fenn interview, 16 May 1987.
53. *CR*, 24 June 1965, pp. 14628-35; 12 July 1965, pp. 16434-35.
54. Goodwin, *Remembering America*, pp. 400-416; Jack Valenti's doubts about Goodwin's descriptions in *The New York Times Magazine* (21 Aug. 1988): 8; McGovern, *Grassroots*, p. 104.
55. Church to Bill Moyers, 23 June 1965, LBJ Papers, White House Central File, Sp/FG 130, LBJ Library.
56. Church interviews: 5 July 1983 (Gibbons), p. 7; 13 Feb. 1979.
57. *Ibid.*; Bethine Church interview, 12 March 1985; Donovan, *Nemesis*, pp. 103-04.
58. Church interviews, 13 Feb. 1979, and 5 July 1983 (Gibbons), pp. 7-8; Donovan, *Nemesis*, p. 104.
59. Church to Byron Johnson, 27 July 1965, CP, 2.2/28/10.
60. *Ibid.*
61. Cater memo to the President, 24 July 1965, LBJ Papers, White House Central File, Ex FG 431/F, LBJ Library; Bundy quoted in *Government and Vietnam War*, III, p. 351.
62. Church to Eli Oboler, 28 July 1965, CP, 2.2/28/10; Reedy memo to LBJ, 26 June 1965, LBJ Papers, Confidential File, Name File, LBJ Library.

63. Transcript, 18 July 1965 "Issues and Answers" program, CP, 2.2/28/10.
64. Church to Eli Oboler, 28 July 1965, CP, 2.2/28/10.
65. See, for example, Herring, *America's Longest War*, pp. 139-42; Wheeling qtn., p. 142.
66. Mansfield quoted in *Government and the Vietnam War*, III, p. 430.
67. Church Oral History (Mulhollan), pp. 19-20.

Notes for Chapter Nine

1. Church to Eli Oboler, 28 July 1965, CP, 2.2/28/10.
2. SNCC organizer quoted in Allen J. Matusow, *The Unraveling of America: A History of Liberalism in the 1960s* (New York: Harper & Row, 1984), p. 350; King in Stephen B. Oates, *Let the Trumpet Sound: The Life of Martin Luther King, Jr.* (1982; New York: Plume, 1983), pp. 375-76.
3. Nancy Zaroulis and Gerald Sullivan, *Who Spoke Up? American Protest Against the War in Vietnam, 1963-1975* (New York: Holt, Rinehart, Winston, 1984), pp. 64-66.
4. Todd Gitlin, *The Sixties: Years of Hope, Days of Rage* (New York: Bantam, 1987), p. 187, re the Dominican Republic; Gitlin to Ashby, 24 Jan. 1988, re Church.
5. On Dodd and Stennis, James Miller, *"Democracy Is In the Streets": From Port Huron to the Siege of Chicago* (New York: Simon & Schuster, 1987), p. 249.
6. Harry McPherson interview, 6 Aug. 1984.
7. Frank Church, "How Many Dominican Republics and Vietnams Can We Take On?" *The New York Times Magazine* (28 Nov. 1965): 44-45, 177-78; Frank Church, " '. . .the Basic Flaw in Our Asian Policy,' " *Washington Post*, 20 Feb. 1966; Church interview, 12 June 1979.
8. Church, "How Many Dominican Republics," and " '. . .the Basic Flaw.' "
9. *Ibid.*
10. *Ibid.*
11. *Ibid.* Compare to Hans Morgenthau, " 'Are We Deluding Ourselves in Vietnam,' " *New York Times Magazine* (18 April 1965): 25, 85-87; and "War with China?" *The New Republic* (3 April 1965): 11-14.
12. Melvin Small, *Johnson, Nixon, and the Doves* (New Brunswick, N. J.: Rutgers University Press, 1988), p. 80; Zaroulis and Sullivan, *Who Spoke Up?*, pp. 75-76; George Herring, "The Executive, Congress, and the Vietnam War, 1965-1975," pp. 8-9, mss. in authors' possession.
13. Fulbright quoted in Small, *Johnson, Nixon, and the Doves*, p. 75; Church to Ross Woodward, 4 Feb. 1966, CP, 12/3/9.
14. Joe Califano memo to the President, 19 Feb. 1966, LBJ Papers, National Security-Defense, ND19/CO 312, Box 219, LBJ Library, re confusion; Marvin [Watson] memo to the President, 21 Feb. 1966, FG431/F, re Connally; "Jake" to the President, 26 May 1966, National Security-Defense, Box 220, re White; Mike Manatos to the President, 17 Feb. 1966, Nat'l Sec.-Defense, ND19/CO 312, Box 219, re Lausche.
15. Transcript, Gale McGee Oral History interview, 10 Feb. 1969, by Joe B. Frantz, pp. 40-43, 47, LBJ Library; McGee interview, 6 March 1988.
16. Church to Ross Woodward, 4 Feb. 1966, CP, 12/3/9; Bundy quoted in Small, *Johnson, Nixon, and the Doves*, p. 78, and LBJ qtns. (Feb. 4), p. 81, (Oct. 21), p. 86; Zaroulis and Sullivan, *Who Spoke Up?*, pp. 76-77; LBJ on "Nervous Nellies" in Matusow, *The Unraveling of America*, p. 382.

17. Church interview, 13 Feb. 1979; transcript, Frank Church Oral History interview, 1 May 1969, by Paige E. Mulhollan, pp. 26-27, LBJ Library; Small, *Johnson, Nixon, and the Doves*, p. 138, re Cronkite.
18. Church interview, 13 Feb. 1979.
19. Frank Church, "Memorandum for the Files," 21 July 1966, CP, 10.6/8/7.
20. Michael Foley, *The New Senate: Liberal Influence on a Conservative Institution, 1959-1972* (New Haven, Conn.: Yale University Press, 1980), p. 277, re voting record.
21. Transcript, Church interview by William C. Gibbons, 5 July 1983, p. 6, in Gibbons's possession; Church interview (Mulhollan), p. 30.
22. John Macy memo, n. d., but April or early May, 1966, LBJ Papers, John Macy Files, Box 855; Mike Manatos memo to the President, 11 Oct. 1967, White House Central File, Name File, Box 220. Both in LBJ Library.
23. Mike Manatos memo to the President, 29 Aug. 1967, LBJ Papers, White House Central File, Name File, Box 220, LBJ Library.
24. Harry C. McPherson, Jr., memo to Bill Moyers, 8 Aug. 1966, White House Aides Files, McPherson, Vietnam, 1966, Box 28, LBJ Library; McPherson interview, 6 Aug. 1984.
25. *Washington Post*, 6 March 1966.
26. Church's draft comments, "In Reply to a Smear," n. d., but mid-March, 1966, CP, 2.2/30/11; also Church to Lyle Olson, 23 March 1966, *ibid*.
27. Church to Lyle Olson, 23 March 1966, which included the McCaffrey quotation; clipping from *London Observer*, 5 Dec. 1965, CP, 2.2/29/5.
28. Church interview, 13 Feb. 1979, on Morse.
29. Church speech, 5 Aug. 1965, Washington, D. C. Sheraton-Park hotel, CP, 10.6/8/1; Frank Moss interview, 11 May 1987.
30. Wayne Morse to Church, 6 Jan. 1966, CP, 2.2/29/8; J. William Fulbright to Church, 1 March 1966, 2.2/30/12; Clark Clifford to Church, 15 Feb. 1966, 2.2/30/12; Small, *Johnson, Nixon, and the Doves*, p. 141, for Rusk's quotation.
31. *Boston Globe*, 17 July 1966, and Church memo to Cleve Corlett, n. d., but July 1966, CP, 10.6/2/20.
32. Rick Raphael interview, 21 Jan. 1988; *Boston Globe*, 17 July 1966.
33. *Boston Globe*, 17 July 1966.
34. "A Plea for Sanity," CP, 10.6/8/7.
35. George McGovern interview, 23 Dec. 1987; Arthur Goldberg to Church, 10 Aug. 1966, CP, 12/3/9; *Idaho State Journal*, 26 July 1966.
36. William C. Gibbons interview, 13 May 1987.
37. Harry C. McPherson, Jr., memo to Bill Moyers, 8 Aug. 1966, LBJ White House Aide Files, McPherson, Vietnam, 1966, Box 28, LBJ Library.
38. Mike Manatos memo to Jim Jones, 2 June 1966, LBJ Papers, Mike Manatos Files, Box 10, LBJ Library; LBJ quoted in Herring manuscript, "The Executive, Congress, and The Vietnam War, 1965-1975," p. 8.
39. Walter Arnold Zelman, "Senate Dissent and the Vietnam War, 1964-1968" (Ph.D. diss., University of California-Los Angeles, 1971), pp. 308-09.
40. CIA translation of 27 April 1967 Moscow broadcast, CP, 2.2/30/17; re the "Plea for Realism," 2.2/29/6.
41. Transcript of Church press conference, 17 May 1967, CP, 2.2/30/17; Church to John Sherman Cooper, 2 May 1967, 10.6/8/12.
42. On McCarthy, Gruening, and the Church aide, see Zelman, "Senate Dissent and the Vietnam War," p. 309; *Time*, 89 (26 May 1967): 13. For the administration's contention that the senators acted independently, UPI story, 17 May 1967, CP, 2.2/29/6.

43. Mike Manatos memo to the President, 10 May 1967, LBJ Papers, White House Central File, Name File, Box 220, LBJ Library.
44. Transcript of Church's 17 May 1967 press conference, CP, 2.2/30/17. For an example of rumors that Church was caving in, see Bill Hall to Church, 26 Nov. 1965, 2.2/29/4.
45. Hans Morgenthau to Church, 7 Jan. 1967, re a Department of Defense movie, "Why Vietnam?," and Church reply, 17 Jan. 1967, CP, 2.2/30/16.
46. See, for example, Mrs. Cecil Lowe to Church, 12 Jan. 1966, and Church reply, 20 Jan. 1966, and Church to Stephen R. Haynes, 8 Dec. 1967, CP, 12/3/9.
47. Benjamin Spock to Church, 2 May 1967, and Church reply, 11 May 1967, CP, 12/3/9.
48. Church to Eileen Lund, 20 June 1967, re Hell, 2.2/30/18.
49. Quotation re white radical in William H. Chafe, *The Unfinished Century: America Since World War II* (New York: Oxford University Press, 1986), p. 326; Matusow, *The Unraveling of America*, pp. 357-58, re Fanon, and p. 363, re Cavanaugh; *New York Review of Books* (24 August 1967): 1.
50. George C. Herring, *America's Longest War: The United States and Vietnam, 1950-1975* (2d ed., New York: Knopf, 1986), pp. 145-51; Depuy qtn., p. 151.
51. Brown quoted in Matusow, *The Unraveling of America*, p. 366; Todd Gitlin, *The Sixties*, p. 217, re Reagan, and 247 re liberals.
52. F. Forrester Church, *Father and Son: A Personal Biography of Senator Frank Church of Idaho* (New York: Harper & Row, 1985) pp. 67, 75-76.
53. McGovern interview, 23 Dec. 1987; also on the caucuses, Gale McGee Oral History interview (Frantz), p. 47, and 6 March 1988 interview.
54. McGovern interview, 23 Dec. 1987; transcript, McGovern Oral History interview, 16 July 1970, by Larry J. Hackman, p. 12, Robert F. Kennedy Oral History Project, JFK Library. On Church's voting record in 1966, printout of Alan Clem, who for a number of years computed Senate votes at the University of South Dakota; copy in authors' possession.
55. McGovern interviews: (Hackman), pp. 8-9, and 23 Dec. 1987.
56. *San Francisco Chronicle*, 25 July 1966.
57. *CR*, 12 Jan. 1965, p. 562 ("fever"); *Washington Post*, 29 Nov. 1964.
58. Frank Church, "Conspiracy USA," *Look* (26 Jan. 1965): 21-23. See, for example, Hans J. Morgenthau, "Goldwater–The Romantic Regression," *Commentary* (Sept. 1964): 65-68, bearing Church's initials, CP, 10.6/2/25. Sevareid in, for example, *The Idaho Observer*, 17 Sept. 1964. On the Christmas present, Bill Hall's column in *Idaho State Journal*, 13 Jan. 1965.
59. Church, "Conspiracy, USA"; *CR*, 12 Jan. 1965, pp. 562-69.
60. Morse, *CR*, 12 Jan. 1965, p. 569; Mike Monroney to Church, 18 Jan. 1965; sheet from Radio TV Reports, Inc., re Downs; Stuart Chase to Church, 25 Jan. 1965; Mrs. James Helis to Church, March, 1965, with clippings, CP, 12/3/9.
61. Church to Dean Miller, 6 April 1965, CP, 12/3/9; interviews: Jerry Brady, 7 Nov. 1987 and Rick Raphael, 21 Jan. 1988.
62. James Waite to Church, 14 Feb. 1965; unidentified de Toledano clipping (early 1965); Daniel Lyons, S. J., "Accepting Defeat in Vietnam," brochure published by The Manion Forum (Feb. 1965): 12-13–all in CP, 12/3/9; "Manion Forum," 24 Jan. 1965, 2.2/27/6.
63. Randy Stapilus, *Paradox Politics: People and Power in Idaho* (Boise: Ridenbaugh Press, 1988), pp. 53-54, 64, 137, 140.
64. *Ibid.*, pp. 130-31.
65. On Tom Boise, *ibid.*, pp. 85-87, and obituary clippings in CP, 10.6/1/9.

66. Burke in Stapilus, *Paradox Politics*, p. 132; Sam Day interview, 4 Oct. 1987.
67. Stapilus, *Paradox Politics*, pp. 132-34; Rick Raphael interview, 21 Jan. 1988, re Barnes.
68. Interviews: Byron Johnson, 14 March 1988; George Klein, 3 Aug. 1979; Mike Wetherell, 25 April 1984.
69. William Barry Furlong, "A Dove Versus a Dogcatcher," *The New York Times Magazine* (25 June 1967): 49-50; Group Research Report, 31 May 1967, p. 34, CP, 12/3/9; Gene Mileck interview, 7 April 1979.
70. Furlong, "A Dove Versus a Dogcatcher," p. 49; Ronald Rankin interview, 7 April 1979; *Kansas City Star*, 24 July 1967.
71. Rankin interview, 7 April 1979.
72. *Ibid.*
73. Pamphlet, "Why Recall Frank Church?," CP, 12/3/9.
74. Group Research Report, 31 May 1967, CP, 12/3/9; *New York Times*, 25 May 1967; *Kansas City Star*, 24 July 1967.
75. Church interview (Gibbons), pp. 10-11; *San Francisco Chronicle*, 8 May 1967, for Pearson's column.
76. Group Research Report, 31 May 1967, p. 34, CP, 12/3/9; "The Fighting Dove," *Newsweek*, 69 (5 June 1967): 28-29; "In Trouble: Senator Church of Idaho," *The New York Times Magazine* (25 June 1967): cover; Seattle *Post-Intelligencer*, 28 July 1967; transcript of Edward P. Morgan's 15 June 1967 broadcast, CP, 12/3/9.
77. "The Fighting Dove," pp. 28-29; Furlong, "A Dove Versus a Dogcatcher," pp. 51-52.
78. Church to Mrs. Wally Bruner, 14 June 1967, CP, 12/3/9.
79. Raphael interview, 21 Jan. 1988.
80. *Ibid.*; script of 21 July 1967 video, CP, 2.2/30/19.
81. Neal Parsell to Ashby, 1 May 1988, and interviews: John Carver, 23 July 1989; Jerry Brady, 7 Nov. 1987; Bryce Nelson, 1 Feb. 1987; Michael Wright, 10 Aug. 1984.
82. Interviews: Myrna Sasser, 20 March 1988; Mike Wetherell, 14 May 1979; Patrick Shea, 15 Oct. 1988. "There are some issues so close to the emotions and pocketbooks of Congressman's constituents," wrote Carl Marcy, who presided over the Senate Foreign Relations Committee's staff for years, "that he does not in fact have a free personal vote. This is as it should be—after all, he is in Congress to *represent*." In Idaho, gun control constituted such an issue. Draft of Carl Marcy's comments, 2 Feb. 1962, Carl Marcy Papers in the Senate Foreign Relations Committee Papers, NA, Box 1962-1964.
83. Brady interview, 7 Nov. 1987.
84. Church quoted in Furlong, "A Dove Versus a Dogcatcher," pp. 50-51; Stapilus, *Paradox Politics*, p. 19, re resident; Alice Dieter interview, 22 Dec. 1987; graffiti in Lumberjack Restaurant, Troy, Idaho, early 1970s.
85. Quotations in Furlong, "A Dove Versus a Dogcatcher," pp. 50-51, 54; editorials in *Lewiston Tribune*, 25 May 1967, and *The Coeur d'Alene Press*, 2 June 1967.
86. Quotations in Blaine Schulz, "The Dove Who Flies with His Own Wings," *Northwest: The Sunday Oregonian Magazine* (3 Sept. 1967): 4; *Christian Science Monitor*, 4 Aug. 1967; Raphael interview, 21 Jan. 1988.
87. "BJ" memo re Jack Waugh information, 30 June 1967, on the billboards, CP, 12/3/9; Seattle *Post-Intelligencer*, 28 July 1967, re the signatures; William Buckley, "Recall Senator Church?" *National Review*, 19 (13 June 1967): 628; *Salt Lake Tribune*, 27 July 1967, and *Kansas City Times*, 6 July 1967, on Patrick.
88. Interviews: Rankin, 7 April 1979, and Mileck, 7 April 1979; Seattle *Post-Intelligencer*, 28 July 1967. Also, *Salt Lake Tribune*, 27 July 1967, and Boise *Statesman*, 26 July 1967.

89. Quotation in Church interview (Gibbons), p. 11.
90. Church to Paul Hovey, 18 Sept. 1967, CP, 2.2/31/1; Frank Church, "From the U. S. A. to All the World with Love," *Esquire*, 68 (July 1967): 83-85, 123-24.
91. *CR*, 4 Dec. 1967, pp. 34880-82, for the McCaffrey interview, which McGovern placed in the *CR*.
92. Schulz, "'The Dove Who Flies with His Own Wings," pp. 4-5.
93. *Ibid.*, p. 5; David Riesman to Church, CP, 2.2/30/12.

Notes for Chapter Ten

1. Church to C. W. Mulhall, 11 Jan. 1968 (reckoning), CP, 2.2/4/3; *CR*, 21 Feb. 1968, pp. 3811 (summer); Richard Rovere, "The Sixties: 'This Slum of a Decade,' " *The New York Times Magazine*, (14 Dec. 1969): 25 ff.
2. See Irwin Unger and Debi Unger, *Turning Point: 1968* (New York: Charles Scribner's Sons, 1988), p. 1, for the statistic and qtn.
3. Blaine Schulz, "The Dove Who Flies with His Own Wings," *Northwest Magazine*, (3 Sept. 1967): 6.
4. *Ibid.*
5. Church, "President and Congress in Foreign Policy: The Threat to Constitutional Government," CP, 10.6/2/19.
6. *Ibid.*
7. "Draft Speech for the Senate," 3 Oct. 1967, from W. W. Rostow to the President, LBJ Papers, NSF Country File, Box 102, LBJ Library.
8. George C. Herring, *America's Longest War: The United States and Vietnam, 1950-1975* (2d ed., New York: Knopf, 1986), pp. 181-83–Johnson qtn. to aides, p. 181; LN memo to Rostow, 4 Oct. 1967, LBJ Papers, National Security File, Box 103, LBJ Library, re the FBI checks; LBJ and Humphrey public statements in Robert J. Donovan, *Nemesis: Truman and Johnson in the Coils of War in Asia* (New York: St. Martin's, 1984), p. 122.
9. Paul K. Conkin, *Big Daddy from the Pedernales: Lyndon Baines Johnson* (Boston: Twayne, 1986), p. 212. On the fate of the Great Society, see, for example, Robert Lekachman, "Death of a Slogan: The Great Society 1967," *Commentary* (January 1967): 56-61.
10. Transcript, Frank Church Oral History interview, 1 May 1969, by Paige E. Mulhollan, pp. 31-32, LBJ Library; transcript, Church interview, 5 July 1983, by William Gibbons, pp. 8-9, in Gibbons's possession; Church interview, 10 Jan. 1979.
11. Church interview, 1 May 1969 (Mulhollan), p. 32; Conkin, *Big Daddy from the Pedernales*, p. 212.
12. Church's "Washington Report," Oct. 1967, CP, 10.6/4/15.
13. Statistics in Nancy Zaroulis and Gerald Sullivan, *Who Spoke Up? American Protest Against the War in Vietnam 1963-1975* (New York: Holt, Rinehart, Winston, 1984), p. 147; Church to Ernest H. Wells, 15 May 1967, CP, 12/3/10.
14. Church to Jane Fields, 25 March 1968, CP, 12/3/10.
15. Cronkite quoted in Charles Kaiser, *1968 in America* (New York: Weidenfeld and Nicolson, 1988), p. 63.
16. Church's "Washington Report," Feb. 1968, CP, 12/3/10.
17. Church to Eugene Chase, 14 March 1968, CP, 12/3/10, re State of the Union.
18. Interviews: Cleve Corlett, 22 May 1987; Fariborz Fatemi, 15 May 1987; Rick Raphael, 21 Jan. 1988; Myrna Sasser, 20 March 1988; Mike Wetherell, 15 July 1987; Patrick Shea, 15 Oct. 1988; David Underhill, 10 Aug. 1989; Church quoted in William H. Honan, "The Art of Oratory in the Senate of the United States," *Esquire*, 71 (May 1969): 164.

19. Honan, "The Art of Oratory in the Senate," p. 164.
20. Patrick Shea interview, 15 Oct. 1988.
21. Honan, "The Art of Oratory in the Senate," pp. 164-65.
22. *Ibid.*, p. 164.
23. *CR*, 21 Feb. 1968, pp. 3808-09.
24. *Ibid.*, pp. 3809-10.
25. *Ibid.*, pp. 3808-11.
26. Honan, "The Art of Oratory in the Senate," p. 164; Gruening, *CR*, 21 Feb, 1968, p. 3812.
27. Church news releases, 18 March and 31 July 1968, CP, 2.2/4/3.
28. Clipping, n. d., but early 1968, CP, 2.2/31/8; *CR*, 21 Feb. 1968, p. 3810, Church qtns.
29. Church to Eugene Chase, 14 March 1968, CP, 12/3/10.
30. George McGovern, *Grassroots: The Autobiography of George McGovern* (New York: Random House, 1977), pp. 110-11; Church interview, 13 Feb. 1979; McCarthy quoted in Zaroulis and Sullivan, *Who Spoke Up?*, p. 126.
31. Interviews: McGovern, 23 Dec. 1987; Church, 13 Feb. 1979. Also, Mike Wetherell, 25 April 1984.
32. Church, 31 March 1968 phone statement and 3 April 1968 press release, CP, 12/3/10.
33. On the peace talks, Herring, *America's Longest War*, pp. 209-10; on McCarthy, Zaroulis and Sullivan, *Who Spoke Up?*, pp. 157-58.
34. Kennedy quoted in Jack Newfield, *Robert Kennedy: A Memoir* (New York: Dutton, 1969), p. 224; Church interview, 13 Feb. 1979; re Church's unhappiness with Humphrey's candidacy, George McGovern interview, 23 Dec. 1987.
35. Church to Theodore Sorenson, 14 May 1968, Robert Kennedy Papers, 1968 Presidential Campaign, Box 5, JFK Library; William Dee to Church, 16 April 1968; Church reply, 2 May 1968, CP, 12/3/10.
36. Udall quoted in Kaiser, *1968 in America*, p. 114; Rick Raphael interview, 21 Jan. 1988; Church, "As I See It," in his "Washington Report," April 1968, CP, 10.6/4/15.
37. Church to Edward Kennedy, 8 March 1961, CP, 12/3/10.
38. Church, "Thoughts on the Train," in his "Washington Report," June 1968, CP, 10.6/4/15; Church's keynote speech, Idaho Democratic State Assembly, 14 June 1968, 12/3/10.
39. Church's keynote speech, Idaho Democratic State Assembly, 14 June 1968, CP, 12/3/10.
40. *Ibid.*
41. Byron Johnson interview, 14 March 1988.
42. Church interviews, 13 Feb. and 12 June 1979; Martin Peretz to Church, 5 Aug. 1968, CP, 12/3/10.
43. Church interviews, 13 Feb. and 12 June 1979.
44. *Ibid.*
45. Eugene McCarthy interview, 22 March 1990.
46. Brown quoted in Stanley Karnow, *Vietnam: A History* (New York: Viking, 1983), p. 580; on the peace plank and Humphrey, Kaiser, *1968 in America*, pp. 239-40.
47. Church interview, 13 Feb. 1979; Church to Michael McCrery, 17 Sept. 1968, CP, 2.2/31/9, re Humphrey; Church to Eugene McCarthy, 30 Aug. 1968, handwritten copy of telegram, 12/3/10.

48. Unidentified clipping re annual income, CP, 1.1/151/6; Church to C. R. Ricks, 30 March 1966, 1.1/151/6, re Harlem; pamphlet, "Hitler Youth Program for Nampa," and Church to Mrs. Theo Folkerts, 19 Nov. 1964, 1.1/151/6; re beating corps to death, Tommie Ward memo to Church and Verda Barnes, 13 May 1968, 12/3/10.
49. Interviews: Ward Hower, 11 April 1987; Patrick Shea, 15 Oct. 1988. Also, Cleve Corlett, 22 May 1987.
50. David Underhill interview, 10 Aug. 1989.
51. Benjamin DeMott, "The Age of Overkill," in DeMott, *Supergrow: Essays and Reports on Imagination in America* (New York: Dell, 1970), pp. 72-81.
52. Todd Gitlin, *The Sixties: Years of Hope, Days of Rage* (New York: Bantam, 1987), p. 287; other quotations in DeMott, "The Age of Overkill," pp. 73-75.
53. Irving Howe, "The New 'Confrontation Politics' Is a Dangerous Game," *The New York Times Magazine* (20 October 1968), esp. pp. 27-28, 134, 137, 140.
54. Church to B. M. Orchard, 28 Feb. 1968, CP, 2.2/4/3.
55. Church's 1 Oct. 1968 newsletter on lawlessness, CP, 12/3/10; re Wallace, Nixon, and law and order, see Liva Baker, *Miranda: Crime, Law and Politics* (New York: Atheneum, 1983), esp. pp. 39-42, 211, 243-49, and Garry Wills, *Nixon Agonistes* (softbound ed., New York: Signet, 1971), pp. 43-46, 58-60, 285-88.
56. Church to Donald Judd, 28 Dec. 1964; to Mrs. Frank Johnson, 25 Feb. 1966; to Francis and Ivel Griffin, 15 March 1967, CP, 12/3/10; and to D. E. Colvell, 13 March 1967, 3.4.1/1/1.
57. Church to Ernest Moore, Jr., 9 Oct. 1967, CP, 2.2/31/3; Church's 1 Oct. 1968 newsletter, 12/3/10.
58. John F. Kraft, Inc., "A Report of Attitudes of Idaho Voters," Oct. 1968, CP, 5.7/1, pp. 4-5, 8.
59. *Los Angeles Times*, 6 Oct. 1968; *Washington Evening Star*, 18 Oct. 1968; Michael McCrery, "Gunning for Senator Church," *The Nation*, 207 (16 Sept. 1968): 233; Church to Stephen Paine, 24 July 1968, CP, 12/3/10.
60. *Washington Evening Star*, 18 Oct. 1968; postcard from "Joe" to Church, n. d., but 1968, CP, 12/3/10; Mike Wetherell interview, 17 July 1987. Church's doubts about Hansen's honesty proved correct. In 1975, after Hansen pleaded guilty to misdemeanor charges regarding campaign financing, a federal judge sentenced him to two months in prison; in 1984 a jury convicted him of four felonies involving financial disclosure reports, for which in 1986 he served six months in prison. The next year he returned to jail for six months following a parole violation. See Randy Stapilus, *Paradox Politics: People and Power in Idaho* (Boise: Ridenbaugh Press, 1988), pp. 177, 183-85.
61. *Los Angeles Times*, 6 Oct. 1968, re statistics and the King service; McCrery, "Gunning for Senator Church," p. 233, re Hansen; Wetherell interview, 25 April 1984.
62. Robert Pierpoint interview, 12 July 1993. The committee secured a federal district court ruling desegregating the club, which a family operated as a kind of restaurant/resort.
63. McCrery, "Gunning for Senator Church," p. 234; Paul Wieck, "How to Survive in the Rockies," *The New Republic*, 159 (2 Nov. 1968): 16; "Season on Doves," *Newsweek* (7 Oct. 1968): 44.
64. Neal Parsell to Ashby, 1 May 1988; ad in, for example, Meridian *Valley News-Times*, 31 Oct. 1968; *Los Angeles Times*, 6 Oct. 1968; CP, videos 68001 and 68008.
65. CP, video 68001; brochure, "Church of Idaho," 12/3/10.
66. Pamphlet, "Frank Church of Idaho," CP, 10.1/1/13; pamphlet, "Church of Idaho," 12/3/10; video, 68001.

67. On Glasby and Walker's observations, Crickett Keough memo to KDG and TCS, 1 May 1968, Robert Kennedy Papers, 1968 Presidential Campaign, Box 5, JFK Library; Neal Parsell to Ashby, 1 May 1988; Carl Burke to FC, 22 April 1965, CP, 12/3/10.
68. See, for example, *Idaho Farm Roundup*, 20 Jan. 1968 and May, 1968, CP, 12/3/10; video 68001; Church to Robert Coiner, 30 Oct. 1967, 12/3/10; video 68015.
69. Tommie Ward memo to Verda Barnes and Church, 13 May 1968, CP, 12/3/10, re Walker; video 68001.
70. Pamphlet, "Church of Idaho"; video 68011.
71. *Washington Evening Star*, 18 Oct. 1968; "Can They Buy Idaho's Senate Seat?" CP, 12/3/10; Wieck, "How to Survive in the Rockies," p. 16.
72. Barbara Tuchman and Henry Steele Commager to "Dear Friend," Fall 1968, and NCEC pamphlet; Archibald MacLeish to "Dear Friend," Summer and Oct. 1968, CP, 12/3/10.
73. Archibald MacLeish to Church, 16 June 1968, and Church reply, 19 June; George Agree memo to Church and McGovern, 8 Nov. 1968, CP, 12/3/10.
74. "Can They Buy Idaho's Senate Seat?"
75. Interviews: Forrest Church, 25 July 1984; Pat Shea, 15 Oct. 1988.
76. Interviews: Pat Shea, 15 Oct. 1988, and Forrest Church, 25 July 1984; Forrest Church, *Father and Son: A Personal Biography of Senator Frank Church of Idaho* (New York: Harper & Row, 1985), p. 75.
77. Church, *Father and Son*, p. 76; Ward Hower interview, 11 April 1987.
78. Church, *Father and Son*, p. 76; interviews: Forrest Church, 25 July 1984; Bethine Church, 22 June 1979; Mike Wetherell, 23 Nov. 1987; David Underhill, 10 Aug. 1989; Peter Fenn, 16 May 1987.
79. Church, *Father and Son*, pp. 69-70.
80. "Church of Idaho" pamphlet; video 68022, CP.
81. Church, *Father and Son*, p. 78.
82. Church, *Father and Son*, pp. 75; interviews: Forrest Church, 25 July 1984; Martin Peterson, 2 April 1985; Myrna Sasser, 20 March 1988.
83. Peter Fenn interview, 8 Aug. 1984.
84. *Ibid.*
85. Rick Raphael interview, 21 Jan. 1988.
86. Church to Marriner Eccles, 14 Sept. 1968, CP, 12/3/10; Kraft, "A Report of Attitudes of Idaho Voters," pp. 2-3, 18-19. Unfortunately, the report does not define terms such as "upper class" or "cities."
87. Hansen quoted in *Idaho Statesman*, 15 June 1968; interviews: Rich Raphael, 21 Jan. 1988; Carl Burke, 22 Nov. 1987.
88. *Idaho Statesman*, clipping (n. d.), CP, 12/3/10, and 13 Oct. 1968.
89. Cleve Corlett interview, 22 May 1987.
90. Interviews: Jerry Brady, 7 Nov. 1987, and Byron Johnson, 14 March 1988; Burke to Church, 15 Dec. 1967, re his schedule, and Frank Moss to Church, 14 Nov. 1968, CP, 12/3/10.
91. Joke in Church, *Father and Son*, p. 74; Wieck, "How to Survive in the Rockies," p. 15.
92. Gene Mileck interview, 7 April 1979.
93. Martin Peterson interview, 2 April 1985.
94. Abstract of Votes, State of Idaho, 5 Nov. 1968, CP, 12/3/10; Cleve Corlett interview, 22 May 1987. Also Parsell to Ashby, 1 May 1988.
95. Church interviews, 12 June 1979 (Nixon) and 13 Feb. 1979 (war); Shannon qtn., Unger and Unger, *Turning Point: 1968*, p. 532.

Notes for Chapter Eleven

1. Frank Church interview, 13 Feb. 1979; notebook of anecdotes, p. "Vietnam," CP, 12/3/11.
2. Richard Nixon, *RN: The Memoirs of Richard Nixon* (New York: Grosset & Dunlap, 1978), p. 414.
3. Stephen A. Ambrose, *Nixon: The Triumph of a Politician, 1962-1972* (New York: Simon & Schuster, 1989), p. 252.
4. Sidey in Garry Wills, *The Kennedy Imprisonment* (Boston: Little, Brown, 1981, 1982), p. 181. See also Arthur M. Schlesinger, Jr., *The Imperial Presidency* (New York: Houghton Mifflin, 1973), esp. pp. 208-09.
5. The Carl Marcy Papers in the Senate Foreign Relations Committee Papers, NA, trace the committee's growing concerns. See, for example, unused draft of J. William Fulbright to Lyndon Johnson, May, 1965, Box 1965; Norvill Jones to Marcy, 12 Sept. 1966, Box 1966. Church quoted in Loch Johnson, "Operational Codes and the Prediction of Leadership Behavior: Senator Frank Church at Midcareer," in Margaret G. Hermann and Thomas W. Milburn, eds., *A Psychological Examination of Political Leaders* (New York: Free Press, 1977), p. 95.
6. Schlesinger, *Imperial Presidency*, pp. 218-19; chef quoted in J. Anthony Lukas, *Nightmare: The Underside of the Nixon Years* (New York: Viking, 1976; reprint ed., New York: Penguin Books, 1988), p. 343; Patrick Buchanan memo to the President, 17 Sept. 1971, NPMP, WHSF-Buchanan, Box 4; Raymond Price memo to the President, 13 Nov. 1970, *ibid.*, POF, Box 8.
7. Henry Kissinger, *White House Years* (Boston: Little, Brown, 1979), p. 11. See Seymour Hersh, *The Price of Power: Kissinger in the Nixon White House* (New York: Simon & Schuster, 1983), pp. 25-45.
8. On the siege-like complex of the administration, see Lukas, *Nightmare*, esp. pp. 9-40, and Jonathan Schell, *The Time of Illusion* (New York: Knopf, 1976; paper ed., New York: Vintage Books, 1976), esp. pp. 77-134. Nixon qtn. in Stanley Karnow, *Vietnam: A History* (New York: Viking Press, 1983; reprint ed., New York: Penguin Books, 1984), p. 577; aide's in Lukas, *Nightmare*, p. 11.
9. Nixon article quoted in Karnow, *Vietnam*, p. 579; Hersh, *The Price of Power*, pp. 46-65, re the "madman theory" and Cambodia.
10. Frank Church, "Impoundment of Appropriated Funds: The Decline of Congressional Control Over Executive Discretion," *Stanford Law Review* (June 1970): 1240; Lamar Alexander memo to Bryce Harlow, 17 May 1969, NPMP, WHCF, ExFG 30 to 31, Box 1, re foreign aid. Also Ambrose, *Nixon*, p. 292, for Nixon's unwillingness to consult Congress on an issue such as welfare.
11. Bryce Harlow memos to President, March 3 and 10, 1969, NPMP, WHCF ExFG 30 to 31, Box 1; Nixon, *RN*, p. 416. On the legislative significance of the fight, see Alton Frye, *A Responsible Congress: The Politics of National Security* (New York: McGraw Hill, 1975), pp. 15-46.
12. William Miller interview, 27 July 1984; Church to Harrison, Gilbert Harrison Papers, Box 1, LC. See also, Frye, *A Responsible Congress*, p. 22.
13. Nixon, *RN*, pp. 416, 418, on Alsop and Harlow; Bill Miller to John Sherman Cooper, 10 April 1969, William Miller Papers (in Miller's possession), on "fight to win."
14. Church interview, 13 Feb. 1979; Church to Gilbert Harrison, 9 July 1969, Harrison Papers, Box 1, LC.
15. Church to Harrison, *ibid.*
16. Frank Church, "Revolution and World Order," *Engage*, 1 (15 April 1969): 22-27; copy in CP, 2.2/31/13.

17. *Ibid.*, p. 27.
18. *Ibid.*, pp. 24-25.
19. *CR*, 11 July 1969, pp. 19241-42.
20. William C. Berman, *William Fulbright and the Vietnam War: The Dissent of a Political Realist* (Kent, Ohio: Kent State University Press, 1989), pp. 84-85, 101, 108.
21. On the resolution, see Robert J. Bresler, "The War-Making Machinery," *The Nation* (17 Aug. 1970): 105-09; Church qtn, p. 106.
22. Berman, *William Fulbright*, p. 113; Church to Danny O'Halloran, 18 March 1970, CP, 2.2/26/7.
23. William Miller interview, 27 July 1984, re the developing anti-war coalition; Berman, *William Fulbright*, p. 107, on the bombing (Berman cites his interview with Church regarding this); *Washington Evening Star*, 21 May 1969, re Church; Nixon quoted in Ambrose, *Nixon*, p. 277.
24. Frye, *A Responsible Congress*, re Miller and the staff caucuses; also Miller interview, 27 July 1984.
25. Miller interviews, 15 June 1979 and 27 July 1984, re the meeting and developing containment strategy.
26. Hersh, *Price of Power*, p. 119.
27. *New York Times*, 9 May 1969; on Laos, 8 Oct. 1969.
28. Church to Danny O'Halloran, 18 March 1970, CP, 2.2/26/7, re Laos; Symington quoted in John Prados, *President's Secret Wars: CIA and Pentagon Covert Operations from World War II Through Iranscam* (New York: Morrow, 1986), p. 285.
29. William S. White column, *Washington Post*, 16 Aug. 1969, re Church walking out; press release, 14 Aug. 1969, CP, 10.6/2/20, for his response.
30. Agnew quoted in Berman, *William Fulbright*, p 114.
31. Quotation in Church to Jesse Oppenheimer, 14 April 1969, CP, 2.2/31/13.
32. Charles Goodell interview, 30 July 1984.
33. Jack Anderson in *Washington Post*, 6 Oct. 1969, re Nixon.
34. Transcript, "Issues and Answers," 12 Oct. 1969, pp. 4, 11-12, CP, 10.6/2/20.
35. *CR*, 8 Oct. 1969, pp. 29106-07.
36. *Ibid.*, pp. 29106-09.
37. Nancy Zaroulis and Gerald Sullivan, *Who Spoke Up? American Protest Against the War in Vietnam 1963-1975* (New York: Holt, Rinehart, Winston, 1984), pp. 247, 264-66; letter from Church and others to Vietnam Moratorium Committee, 9 Oct. 1969, CP, 2.2/31/17; Church press release, 6 Oct. 1969, 2.2/31/16; *New York Times*, 7 Oct. 1969.
38. Transcript, "Issues and Answers" televised news program, pp. 7, 9, CP, 10.6/2/20.
39. Zaroulis and Sullivan, *Who Spoke Up?*, pp. 267-70; Melvin Small, *Johnson, Nixon, and the Doves* (New Brunswick, N. J.: Rutgers University Press, 1988), pp. 182-84; Charles DeBenedetti with Charles Chatfield, *An American Ordeal: The Antiwar Movement of the Vietnam Era* (Syracuse: Syracuse University Press, 1990), pp. 255-58.
40. Martin Peterson interview, 2 April 1985.
41. Circular announcing the staff vigil in CP, 2.2/31/17; Myrna Sasser interview, 20 March 1988.
42. Zaroulis and Sullivan, *Who Spoke Up?*, pp. 276-77, 286-89; "Bipartisan statement by United States Senators," 12 Nov. 1969, CP, 2.2/31/16.

43. U.S. Cong., Senate, *Hearings before the Committee on Foreign Relations*, 91st Cong., 1st sess., 18-19 November 1969, p. 27.
44. Nixon quoted in Curt Smith, *Long Time Gone: The Years of Turmoil Remembered* (South Bend, Ind.: Icarus Press, 1982), pp. 216-17; Agnew in Zaroulis and Sullivan, *Who Spoke Up?*, p. 277.
45. Nixon, *RN*, p. 409; Schell, *Time of Illusion*, pp. 62-65; Hersh, *Price of Power*, p. 131, re the poll.
46. *Hearings before the Committee on Foreign Relations*, 18-19 Nov. 1969, pp. 28-30; Frank Church, "The Only Alternative," *The Washington Monthly*, 1 (Dec. 1969): 46-58; Church article in *The Idaho Statesman*, 14 Dec. 1969.
47. Robert Schulman, *John Sherman Cooper: The Global Kentuckian* (Lexington: The University Press of Kentucky, 1976), esp. pp. 3-81.
48. *Ibid.*, pp. 5, 18.
49. *Ibid.*, pp. 5 (re Ingersoll), 7; Richard Harwood profile of Cooper in *The Louisville Times*, 27 Sept. 1957.
50. Cooper to Church, 2 May 1967, CP, 10.6/8/12.
51. John Sherman Cooper to Church, 30 Sept. and 9 Oct. 1969, CP, 2.2/31/17; *Hearings before the Committee on Foreign Relations*, 18-19 Nov. 1969, p. 104; William Miller interview, 15 June 1979, re Mansfield.
52. *New York Times*, 16-17 Dec. 1969; *Washington Post*, 16 and 18 Dec. 1969; Tom Dine interview, 14 June 1979.
53. *New York Times* and *Washington Post*, 17 Dec. 1969.
54. Dine's resumé, CP, 9.7/1/11; Dine to Alan White, 20 Jan. 1970, Dine Papers (Dine's possession); Tom Dine interview, 6 Feb. 1988.
55. Interviews: Tom Dine, 6 Feb. 1988; Lynda Clark, 30 Sept. 1988.
56. Schulman, *John Sherman Cooper*, p. 96.
57. Interviews: Miller, 27 July 1984, and Dine, 14 June 1979; Mary McGrory clipping, 4 Jan. 1970, CP, 2.2/32/2; Church to Edward Herman, 2 Feb. 1970, 2.2/32/4. Hersh, *Price of Power*, pp. 168-69, re Laos. Re the fading protests, Zaroulis and Sullivan, *Who Spoke Up?*, pp. 298-300.
58. Church news release, 29 Jan. 1970, and clipping, *The Cleveland Press*, 19 Feb. 1970, CP, 2.2/26/7; Dine to Allen White, 20 Jan. 1970, Dine Papers.
59. Hersh, *Price of Power*, pp. 175-83; Karnow, *Vietnam*, pp. 604-06; Walter Isaacson, *Kissinger: A Biography* (New York: Simon & Schuster, 1992), pp. 256-57, 793; William Shawcross, *Sideshow: Kissinger, Nixon and the Destruction of Cambodia* (New York: Simon & Schuster, 1979), pp. 112-33; Church interview, 13 Feb. 1979.
60. Interviews: Frank Church, 13 Feb. 1979; William Miller, 15 June 1979, 27 July 1984, 23 Dec. 1987 (qtn.).
61. "Senators," n. d., Lawrence O'Brien Papers, Box 32, JFK Library, re the Kennedy years; interviews: Frank Moss, 11 May 1987; Patrick Shea, 15 Oct. 1988; Bill Hall, 7 Aug. 1986; Church to Jeffrey Safford, 19 Sept. 1977, CP, 2.2/5/5.
62. Interviews: William Miller, 27 July 1984, on the importance of Mansfield and Aiken, and Cleve Corlett, 7 Aug. 1984, re Mansfield; Anderson in JA to DP, 23 Dec. 1956, Drew Pearson Papers, Box G 265, LBJ Library.
63. Church statement, 30 April 1970, CP, 2.2/32/7.
64. Nixon, *RN*, pp. 449-50; George C. Herring, *America's Second Longest War* (2d ed., New York: Knopf, 1986), p. 235; Hersh, *Price of Power*, pp. 187-88; Small, *Nixon and the Doves*, p. 200.

Notes for Chapter Twelve

1. Tom Dine interview, 6 June 1988 re Church; *Washington Post*, 1 May 1970, for text of Nixon's speech.
2. Tom Dine interviews, 14 June 1979 and 6 Feb. 1988.
3. *CR*, 1 May 1970, pp. 13829-30.
4. *Ibid.*, pp. 13831-33.
5. *Ibid.*, pp. 13834-36.
6. Richard Nixon, *RN: The Memoirs of Richard Nixon* (New York: Grosset & Dunlap, 1978), pp. 453-54; Walter Isaacson, *Kissinger: A Biography* (New York: Simon & Schuster, 1992), p. 269; Pentagon official quoted in Seymour Hersh, *The Price of Power: Kissinger in the Nixon White House* (New York: Summit Books, 1983), pp. 192-93; re staff talk, William Safire, *Before the Fall* (New York: Doubleday, 1975), p. 190.
7. Nancy Zaroulis and Gerald Sullivan, *Who Spoke Up? American Protest Against the War in Vietnam 1963-1975* (New York: Holt, Rinehart, Winston, 1984), pp. 318-19; *New York Times*, 2 May 1970.
8. See, for example, Zaroulis and Sullivan, *Who Spoke Up?*, pp. 319-35 (Kissinger qtn., p. 329); Melvin Small, *Johnson, Nixon, and the Doves* (New Brunswick, N. J.: Rutgers University Press, 1988), pp. 201-03.
9. F. Forrester Church, *Father and Son: A Personal Biography of Senator Frank Church of Idaho* (New York: Harper & Row, 1985), p. 76; Church telegram to college and student body presidents, 7 May 1970, and Church to Joseph Tydings, 6 May 1970, CP, 2.2/32/8.
10. *New York Times*, 2 May 1970, clipping in CP, 2.2/32/8.
11. Typescript, Frank Church, "America: Reclaim Your Birthright, Renew Your Ancient Faith," typescript of commencement address, 8 June 1970, Northwest Nazarene College, CP, 12/3/12.
12. *Ibid.*
13. *Ibid.*; compare to George McGovern, *Grassroots: The Autobiography of George McGovern* (New York: Random House, 1977), pp. 169-70.
14. Church, "America, Reclaim Your Birthright."
15. Sam Day, "Notes on the Revolution," *Intermountain Observer*, 16 May 1970, pp. 10-11; Agnew quote in *Washington Post*, 9 May 1970.
16. See any number of clippings, constituent letters, and the cards, "An Appeal to the Silent Majority," in CP, 2.2/36. Hundreds of the cards are also in 2.2/34-35.
17. *Washington Post*, 8 May 1970. See also American Law Division of Congressional Legislative Service to John P. Saylor, 20 Oct. 1970, for "a legislative history of the Cooper-Church Amendment," CP, 2.2/39/1, pp. 1-4.
18. Bob Haldeman's notes, 12 May 1970, NPMP, WHSF-Haldeman, Box 41.
19. Tom Charles Huston to Bryce Harlow, John Erlichman, H. R. Haldeman, William Timmons, Henry Kissinger, 23 May 1970, NPMP, WHCF-Subject Files, [Ex] FE4-1, Box 6. See also William E. Timmons to H. R. Haldeman, 15 May 1970, *ibid.*
20. Haldeman's handwritten notes, 2 May and 16-18 May 1970, NPMP, WHSF-Haldeman, Box 41.
21. H. R. Haldeman memo to Charles Colson, 12 May 1970; Colson memo to Haldeman, 13 May 1970, and typescript of Colson's conference call to "Commanders," n. d., NPMP, WHSF-Colson, Box 43; J. Milton Patrick to Dear Legionnaire, n. d., but mailed out 15 May 1970, and Ray Gallagher to Dear Madame President, n. d., WHSF-Colson, Box 42. Also UPI story, 13 May 1970, *ibid.*

22. H. R. Haldeman handwritten notes, 16 May 1970, NPMP, WHSF-Haldeman, Box 41.
23. *Washington Post*, 5, 9 May 1970.
24. "Talking Paper" memo re "PR," 20 May 1970, NPMP, WHSF-Haldeman, Box 152; Haldeman's handwritten notes, 19-20 May 1970, Haldeman, Box 41; Stephen E. Ambrose, *Nixon: The Triumph of a Politician, 1962-1972* (New York: Simon & Schuster, 1989), p. 360, re the press conference.
25. Bryce Harlow memo to Bob Haldeman, 25 May 1970, NPMP, WHCF-Subject Files [Ex] FE4-1; Carl Marcy to Fulbright, 18 May 1970, Carl Marcy Papers in Senate Foreign Relations Committee Papers, Box 1970, NA.
26. McGovern, *Grassroots*, pp. 164, 166; Charles Goodell interview, 30 July 1984.
27. Goodell interview, 30 July 1984; compare to McGovern, *Grassroots*, p. 166.
28. George McGovern, Harold Hughes, Frank Church to "Dear Senator," 11 May 1970, CP, 2.2/39/9; script, "The Amendment to End the War" TV broadcast, 12 May 1970, 12/3/12; also, Goodell interview, 30 July 1984, and McGovern, *Grassroots*, p. 166.
29. McGovern, *Grassroots*, p. 166; photo in "Special Report on the War from the Office of Senator Frank Church," p. 2, CP, 2.2/39/2; Church to E. N. Torbert and Stewart Mott, 28 May 1970, CP, 2.2/32/9.
30. Interviews: Mark Hatfield, 6 Aug. 1984; Erwin Knoll, 3 Nov. 1987; Tom Dine, 14 June 1979; Cleve Corlett, 7 Aug. 1984; Church, *Father and Son*, p. 77.
31. Anonymous detractor quoted in Carol Payne and Margaret Carpenter, "Frank Church," in *Ralph Nader Congress Project* (New York: Grossman, 1972), n. p.; interviews: Carl Marcy, 18 May 1987, and in *The U.S. Senate Historical Office Oral History Collection: Interviews with Senate Staff* (Wilmington, Del.: Scholarly Resources, 1987), 12 Oct. 1983, with Donald Ritchie, p. 179; Charles Goodell, 30 July 1984; also, John Averill, 8 June 1979.
32. George Ashworth interview, 14 June 1979.
33. Interviews: Tom Dine, 6 Feb. 1988; John W. Finney, 9 Sept. 1987.
34. Finney interview, 9 Sept. 1987.
35. Interviews: William Miller, 27 July 1984; Cleve Corlett, 7 Aug. 1984; Tom Dine, 14 June 1979.
36. Interviews: George Tames, 14 Sept. 1993; Cleve Corlett, 7 Aug. 1984; Tom Dine, 6 Feb. 1988; William Miller, 27 July 1984; Ross Baker to Ashby, 30 June 1986.
37. Interviews: Sam Day, 4 Oct. 1987; anonymous re "unseemly"; Pat Holt, 12 May 1987; Dwight Jensen, 7 Nov. 1987.
38. John Carver interview, 23 July 1989; typescript, Bryce Nelson's banquet speech for Idaho Press Club, 20 April 1985, pp. 15-16, in authors' possession.
39. Nelson speech, 20 April 1985, p. 15. Church's efforts to turn public opinion against the war "required getting headlines," according to CBS reporter Robert Pierpoint, who believed that criticism of Church as a publicity hound was unfair. George Tames of the *New York Times* agreed. Interviews: Pierpoint, 12 July 1993; Tames, 14 Sept. 1993.
40. Interviews: Mike Wetherell, 25 April 1984, 15 July 1987, and a staffer speaking anonymously.
41. See many examples in CP, 2.2/32 and 36.
42. Interviews: Mary McGrory, 8 Aug. 1984; Tom Dine, 14 June 1979; Garry Wenske, 22 March 1987; William Miller, 15 June 1979, 27 July 1984, 23 Dec. 1987; Gaylord Nelson, 21 May 1987. Also Mike Wetherell, 14 May 1979, and Richard L. McCall, 21 Sept. 1993.

43. Interviews: Frank Church, 13 Feb. 1979; Charles Goodell, 30 July 1984; J. William Fulbright, 11 June 1979; Mark Hatfield, 6 August 1984; William Miller, 15 June 1979, 27 July 1984.
44. Interviews: George McGovern, 23 Dec. 1987; Carl Marcy, 11 June 1979.
45. Payne and Carpenter, "Frank Church," n. p.; interviews: Charles Goodell, 30 July 1984, Mark Hatfield, 6 Aug. 1984.
46. Payne and Carpenter, "Frank Church," n. p.; Church interview, 13 Feb. 1979.
47. Interviews: McGrory, 8 Aug. 1984, Fulbright, 11 June 1979, Hatfield, 6 Aug. 1984.
48. Patrick Buchanan memo to the President, 17 June 1970, NPMP, WHSF-Haldeman, Box 139.
49. Payne and Carpenter, "Frank Church," n. p.; interviews: McGovern, 23 Dec. 1987, and William Miller, 29 Dec. 1987.
50. Interviews: Tom Dine, 14 June 1979; 6 Feb. 1988; William Miller, 27 July 1984. Re the phone: Myrna Sasser interview, 20 March 1988; Ross K. Baker to Ashby, 30 June 1986; and Church, *Father and Son*, p. 117.
51. Church to Harry Gilcrest, 1 March 1971, CP, 2.2/38/8; Mike Wetherell interview, 25 April 1984; Ambrose, *Nixon*, pp. 397-98, 433.
52. Mike Wetherell interview, 25 April 1984.
53. *CR*, 22 June 1970, p. 20744; William Miller interview, 27 July 1984.
54. Ross Baker to Ashby, 30 June 1986; interviews: George Lardner, 20 April 1979, and Jerry Brady, 22 March 1987.
55. "Dear Senator. . ." *The New Republic*, 6 June 1970: 6 (Loch Johnson, a Church aide, co-authored the essay); Church to Raj Singh, 29 June 1970, CP, 2.2/32/10. For speculation on Oregon Republican Robert Packwood's vote, see L. J. Evans, Jr. to Gene Bradley, 29 July 1970, NPMP, WHSF-Colson, Box 21.
56. Dine interview, 14 June 1979; "G" memo to Larry Higby, 25 May 1970, NPMP, WHSF-Haldeman, Box 41, re screwing it up; Haldeman notes, 12 June 1970, re dallying Senate; 16 May 1970, re Cooper, *ibid.*; and 25 May 1970, Box 19, re Cotton.
57. Tom Dine re "test votes," n. d., with clipping, "Senate Tests Set On Cambodia," *Washington Post*, 29 May 1970, CP, 2.2/32/9.
58. Church, *Father and Son*, pp. 77-78; interviews: Peter Fenn, 8 Aug. 1984, and Penny Gross, 11 Aug. 1984.
59. Church, *Father and Son*, pp. 78-81; Fenn interview, 8 Aug. 1984.
60. On Dole, Gail Sheehy, *Character: America's Search for Leadership* (1988; revised ed., New York: Bantam Books, 1990), esp. pp. 115-20, 123-25; Stanley G. Hilton, *Bob Dole: American Political Phoenix* (Chicago: Contemporary Books, 1988), pp. 78, 84-85; Dine interview, 6 Feb. 1988.
61. Frank Church news release, 3 June 1970, CP, 2.2/39/10.
62. Dole quoted in *Washington Post*, 29 May 1970; Nixon to Hugh Scott, 4 June 1970, NPMP, WHSF-Haldeman, Box 139; William E. Timmons to Chuck Colson, 5 June 1970, WHSF-Colson, Box 42, re the Legion; William Timmons to the President, 8 June 1970, WHSF–Haldeman, Box 139, re the vote.
63. Interviews: Patrick Shea, 15 Oct. 1988, re Church's dislike of Byrd; Church, 13 Feb. 1979; Church news release, 7 June 1970, CP, 2.2/39/10; "The Senate: Unloving Acts," *Time*, 1 June 1970: 10.
64. Church news release, CP, 2.2/32/11; Bryce Harlow to the President, 22 June 1970, NPMP, WHCF-Subject Files, Box 6, [Ex] FE4-1.
65. "A Legislative History," pp. 1-12; Marcy to JWF, 24 June 1970, Carl Marcy Papers, Box 1970, NA; William Timmons to the President, 18 June 1970, NPMP, WHSF-Haldeman, Box 139. See also Briefing Book Memo #2, Patrick Buchanan to President, 1 July 1970, WHSF-Buchanan, Box 14.

66. Patrick J. Buchanan to the President, 29 June 1970, NPMP, WHSF-Buchanan, Box 14; "News Analysis and Digest. . ." by PJB, 1 July 1970, *ibid.*, and briefing statement, 1 July 1970, *ibid*; "Winding Up the Cambodian Hard Sell," *Time* (13 July 1970): 7-8, re news conference; Nixon, *RN*, pp. 467-68.
67. Church interview, 13 Feb. 1979; Church to Ralph Hyslop, 1 July 1970, CP, 2.2/32/12, and to Jan Smith et al., 30 June 1970, 2.2/32/10; John Sherman Cooper to Church, 12 July 1970, re his and Aiken's views, 12/3/12.
68. Dine to Ashby, 12 Feb. 1988.
69. Stone, 13 July 1970 article, in I. F. Stone, *Polemics and Prophecies 1967-1970* (New York: Random House, 1970), pp. 138-41.
70. Charles Colson to H. R. Haldeman, 12 Aug. 1970, NPMP, WHSF-Colson, Box 123; Colson to Don Johnson, 27 July 1970, and "The Tell It To Hanoi Committee" "Fact Sheet," n. d., *ibid*, Box 121.
71. Carl Marcy to Lewis W. Douglas, 12 May 1970, Marcy Papers, Box 1970; Mark Hatfield to Church, CP, 2.2/32/15.
72. Frank Church, "The Doves Have Won and Don't Know It," reprinted in Church news release, 6 Sept. 1970, CP, 10.6/2/20.
73. Frank Church speech, "The Doves Are Winning—Don't Despair," Colorado State University, 26 Sept. 1970, CP, 10.6/8/8.
74. Carl Marcy document, 22 July 1970, Marcy Papers, Box 1970, NA.
75. Clipping, "Senators See Coup Threat in Article," Sacramento *Bee*, 26 July 1970, *ibid.*
76. H. R. Haldeman notes, 2, 12, 14, 17 Sept., 7 Nov. 1970, NPMP, WHSF-Haldeman, Box 42; Charles W. Colson to Jim Keogh, 22 Sept. 1970, WHSF-Colson, Box 44; Church, "The Doves are Winning—Don't Despair."
77. "Activities of McGovern-Hatfield Campaign," NPMP, WHSF-Colson, Box 21, pp. 1-3, 8-21.
78. Haldeman to Magruder, 11 Sept. 1970, NPMP, WHSF-Haldeman, Box 64; Charles Colson to Haldeman, 9 Sept. 1970, NPMP, President's Office Files, Box 7; re hitting back at Church: Jeb Magruder to Staff Secretary, 30 Sept. 1970, NPMP, WHSF-Haldeman, Box 64; also, L. Higby to Magruder, 8 Sept. 1970, WHSF-Subject Files, 1969-74, Box 15.
79. William E. Timmons to the President, 5 Aug. 1970, NPMP, POF, Box 7; Alsop in *Washington Post*, 2 Oct. 1970.
80. "Significant Events Relating to the Cooper-Church Amendment," 6 Jan. 1971, Carl Marcy Papers, Box 1971, NA; Church news release, 20 Jan. 1971, CP, 2.2/26/1; William C. Berman, *William Fulbright and the Vietnam War* (Kent, Ohio: Kent State University Press, 1988), p. 137; Mrs. Robert Cazden to Church, 12 Feb. 1971, and Church reply, 17 March 1971, CP, 2.2/38/8; draft constituent letter from John Sherman Cooper to William Miller, 11 March 1971, William Miller Papers (Miller's possession).
81. *Washington Post*, 1 Jan. 1971; Church to Cooper, 11 Dec. 1970, CP, 2.2/39/10.
82. Church interview in *Detroit Free Press*, 16 Aug. 1970.
83. Church to John Sherman Cooper, 4 and 22 Feb. 1971, CP, 2.2/39/11.
84. Church to Cooper, 1 March 1971, CP, 2.2/39/11; also Church to Cooper, 22 Feb. 1971, 2.2/39/11.
85. Church to Cooper, 1 March 1971, with draft of resolution; re the legislative limb, Church to Cooper, 4 Feb. 1971, CP, 2.2/39/11.
86. Church news release, 7 July 1971, CP, 2.2/39/11; see also drafts of resolution, 31 March and 26 April 1971, *ibid.*
87. Draft of William Miller analysis to John Sherman Cooper, 14 Oct. 1970, Miller Papers.

88. Church news release, 7 July 1971, CP, 2.2/39/11.
89. William Miller interview, 15 June 1979; Henry Kissinger, *White House Years* (Boston: Little, Brown, 1979), p. 513.
90. William Timmons memo to President, 23 Sept. 1971, NPMP, WHSF-Haldeman, Box 85. See also Chalmers Roberts's column, *Washington Post*, 14 March 1971.
91. Charles DeBenedetti and Charles Chatfield, *An American Ordeal: The Antiwar Movement of the Vietnam Era* (Syracuse: Syracuse University Press, 1990), pp. 318-19, on the amendment; William Miller to John Sherman Cooper, 24 Nov. 1971, Miller Papers.
92. Church news release, 17 Nov. 1971, CP, 2.2/39/11.
93. William Miller to John Sherman Cooper, 24 Nov. and 1 Dec. 1971, Miller Papers; Church to Cooper, with proposed text for modified amendment, 4 Nov. 1971, CP, 2.2/39/11.
94. DeBenedetti and Chatfield, *An American Ordeal*, pp. 319-20, re Cooper and McReynolds.

Notes for Chapter Thirteen

1. Church speech, "Foreign Policy and the Generation Gap," 3 Dec. 1970, reprinted in *CR*, 7 Dec. 1970, pp. 40045-46.
2. Jerry Levinson interview, 11 May 1987.
3. Church, "Foreign Policy and the Generation Gap," pp. 40045-47.
4. Stewart Udall interview, 11 June 1979; on Aspinall, Eleanora W. Schoenebaum, *Profiles of an Era: The Nixon/Ford Years* (New York: Harcourt Brace, 1979), pp. 31-32.
5. Stewart Udall interview, 11 June 1979.
6. *Ibid.*
7. Bill Hall interview, 8 April 1979; Church to Bob Johnson, 2 Dec. 1965, CP, 12/3/13.
8. See, for example, Frank Church, "The New Conservation," *Parks and Recreation* (Sept. 1969): 36-40, 80-83, and reprint of his 20 Feb. 1970 speech, "The Atom: Its Dangerous Aftermath," CP, 10.6/4/4.
9. Church, "Give Earth a Chance," typescript of 22 April 1970 speech, CP, 10.6/1/28. On the first Earth Day, see, for example, "The Earth Has Its Day," *Newsweek* (16 April 1990): 4.
10. George Lardner interview, 20 April 1979.
11. Mike Wetherell interview, 15 July 1987.
12. Church, "Give Earth a Chance."
13. Church, "Give Earth a Chance," re "willfulness."
14. *Washington Post*, 12 Jan. 1969; Baltimore *Sun*, 16 Jan. 1969; Church in *CR*, 22 Jan. 1969, pp. 1527-28 (doubt), and to John Eyre, 4 Feb. 1969, CP, 10.6/3/4 (shoulder); Thomas E. Dustin to Church, 3 Feb. 1969, *ibid.*
15. Carol Payne and Margaret Carpenter, "Frank Church," in *Ralph Nader Congress Project, Citizens Look at Congress* (New York: Grossman, 1972), n. p.
16. *Ibid.*
17. On Jordan, Randy Stapilus, *Paradox Politics: People and Power in Idaho* (Boise: Ridenbaugh Press, 1988), pp. 104-06, 136-37, 164. See also Howard Berger, "Leonard Beck Jordan," in Robert C. Sims and Hope A. Benedict, eds., *Idaho's Governors: Historical Essays on Their Administrations* (Boise, Ida.: Boise State University, 1992), pp. 156-65.

18. Interviews: John Carver, 27 Oct. 1979; Frank Church, 10 Jan. 1979; Myrna Sasser, 20 March 1988; Mike Wetherell, 25 April 1984; Cleve Corlett, 22 May 1987; Orval Hansen, 2 Aug. 1984. See also Ross K. Baker, *Friend and Foe in the U. S. Senate* (New York: Free Press, 1980), p. 14.
19. Stapilus, *Paradox Politics*, p. 35; Mike Wetherell to Bill Ashworth, 5 Oct. 1976, CP, 1.1/153/2; Church interview, 10 Jan. 1979. On Jordan and the issues, see "Battle of the Snake River–Who Will Share Its Riches," *U. S. News and World Report* (11 Nov. 1968): 104-05; Jordan to Mrs. Mardel K. Gale, 9 April 1969, LJP, Box 25, Folder 2, and Jordan, 16 Feb. 1970 statement, LJP, Box 32, Folder 4.
20. See, for example, *Lewiston Tribune*, 27 June 1971. Qtn., Hells Canyon Preservation Council, Inc., *Newsletter* 10 (2 Feb. 1970), LJP, Box 32, Folder 5.
21. Mike Wetherell to Bill Ashworth, 5 Oct. 1976, CP, 1.1/153/2, re the "delicate balance."
22. Carroll Wells to Len Jordan, 15 June 1971, LJP, Box 37, Folder 12, re hippies; Stapilus, *Paradox Politics*, pp. 37-38 (Samuelson qtn.); Mike Wetherell to Bill Ashworth, 5 Oct. 1976, CP, 1.1/153/2; Payne and Carpenter, "Frank Church." See also Jordan to Carol Freeman, 29 Dec. 1970, LJP, Box 32, Folder 12, and Jordan to Jon Larsen, 14 Dec. 1971, LJP, Box 37, Folder 12. On McClure and environmentalists, see Sven Erik Holmes, "James A. McClure," *Ralph Nader Congress Project*, n. p., and on Samuelson's administration, see Katherine G. Aiken, "Don Samuelson," in Sims and Benedict, *Idaho's Governors*, pp. 176-81. Another view received little attention–that of Native Americans, particularly the Lemhi, who had treaty claims to over five million acres in the Sawtooths. "It seems to us that everyone has had something to say about the land except the Indian people who still hold aboriginal title," complained LaNada Means of the Bannock-Shoshone Legal Research Project. In personal conversations with Church and Jordan, she received no satisfaction: "Neither office. . .showed any favorable response." LaNada Means to Cecil Andrus, 7 April 1971, copy in LJP, Box 37, Folder 10.
23. Payne and Carpenter, "Frank Church," n. p.
24. Stapilus, *Paradox Politics*, pp. 39-41.
25. Jordan to Don Evans, 20 July 1971, LJP, Box 37, Folder 18, and also Jordan to Walter Lenz, 4 Oct. 1971, LJP, Box 37, Folder 21; *Idaho Statesman*, 27 June 1971.
26. Qtns., Len Jordan to Don Evans, 20 July 1971, LJP, Box 37, Folder 18, and editorial "How Not to Pass a Bill," *Oregon Journal*, 29 June 1971. See also the Hells Canyon Preservation Council *News*, 4 (Aug. 1971), in LJP, Box 37, Folder 2; Church, Jordan, and Mark Hatfield to Dear Colleague, 23 June 1971, LJP, Box 37, Folder 18; *Lewiston Tribune*, 25 and 27 June 1971; *Oregon Journal*, 25 June 1971. Although Packwood had been in the Senate only two years, he had already developed a reputation for brashness by introducing legislation to end the Senate's seniority system and joining freshman Howard Baker's unsuccessful effort to defeat veteran Hugh Scott for minority leader.
27. *Lewiston Tribune*, 27 June 1971, re the coalition; Bill Ashworth to Bill Hall, 3 Feb. 1976, and Mike Wetherell to Ashworth, 5 Oct. 1976, CP, 1.1/153/2, re the Packwood bill; also, Wetherell interview, 23 Nov. 1987. Idaho's Republican Congressman Orval Hansen believed the White Clouds settlement constituted "a real bipartisan achievement." Hansen interview, 2 Aug. 1984.
28. *Lewiston Tribune* and *The Oregonian*, 26 June 1971, re Church's interceding with Jackson. Reporter Chris Carlson had a particularly good analysis of the Packwood-Church collision, *Lewiston Tribune*, 24 July 1971. On the Packwood hearings, see also *Oregon Journal*, 19 and 25 June 1971.

29. Payne and Carpenter, "Frank Church," re mining industry; Member of Congress Questionnaire, Ralph Nader Congressional Research Project, CP, 10.6/4/14; pamphlet, "Frank Church of Idaho, a Biographical Sketch" (July 1973), 10.1/1/16, re the award.
30. Gary Eisler, "Forest Practices Debated in Washington," *Not Man Apart* (June 1971): pp. 1-2; copy in CP, 7.7/2/3.
31. Mike Wetherell interview, 25 April 1979; William and Pat Oriol interview, 19 May 1987, re the committee and Barnes.
32. William and Pat Oriol interview, 19 May 1987.
33. VB [Barnes] memo attached to Frank Moss to Church, 3 Aug. 1970, CP, 12/3/13; interviews: William Oriol, 19 May 1987, and Cleve Corlett, 22 May 1987.
34. Church news release, 5 Feb. 1971, CP, 12/3/13; *New York Times*, 30 Jan. 1971.
35. *Washington Post*, 30 July 1971, and Church to Colman McCarthy, 3 Aug., 1971, CP, 12/3/13.
36. Church newsletter, 26 April 1971, CP, 12/3/13; also, "Memorandum: Special Committee on Aging," 28 April 1971, *ibid*.
37. Special Committee on Aging Memo, 5 July 1972, CP, 12/3/13, on the law; Cleve Corlett interview, 22 May 1987.
38. Church to Phillip Sanchez, 11 Feb. 1972, re legal services; Church to Ralph Graves, 7 Feb. 1972, re fraud; clippings from 13 Aug. 1972 *London Sunday Times* and 8 Aug. 1972 *Idaho Statesman* re "Death with Dignity"; 13 Sept. 1972 newsletter re World Assembly—all in CP, 12/3/13; *CR*, 27 Jan. 1972, p. 1504, re home repairs. See, also, compilation of Church's speeches and news releases in early 1971 by Martha Dula, for use in her class at the Harvard Business College, c. 1972, CP, 12/3/13. In 1982 the World Assembly on Aging finally convened with 124 participating nations in Vienna, Italy; William Oriol interview, 19 May 1987.
39. Pat and William Oriol interview, 19 May 1987.
40. *Senior Advocate* (July/August, 1973): cover, 7, in CP, 10.1/1/39; National Council of Senior Citizens press release, 14 June 1974, in CP, 12/3/13.
41. *CR*, 7 Feb. 1972, p. 2785.
42. Richard Nixon, *RN: The Memoirs of Richard Nixon* (New York: Grosset & Dunlap, 1978), p. 509; re Kissinger, Stephen E. Ambrose, *Nixon: The Triumph of a Politician, 1962-1972* (New York: Simon and Schuster, 1989), p. 447; Church news release, 16 June 1971, CP, 2.2/25/13; Church to Mr. and Mrs. William H. West, 20 July 1971, 2.2/38/9, re the Court's decision.
43. Joseph Biden interview (1974), CP, A74060. Senator Ralph Yarborough (D-Texas), 19 March 1987 interview, also noted Church's Jeffersonian views, as did Forrest Church, 25 July 1984, and Judith Miller, 10 Aug. 1992.
44. On Church's more radical side: Bryce Nelson, "Church: A Man Who Took Great Risks for America," *Los Angeles Times*, 16 April 1984; Nelson, 20 April 1985 banquet speech for Idaho Press Club (copy in authors' possession); and interviews: Bryce Nelson, 1 Feb. 1987; Sam Day, 4 Oct. 1987; Patrick Shea, 15 Oct. 1988; Jerry Brady, 7 Nov. 1987; Jerry Levinson, 11 May 1987; Mike Wetherell, 15 July 1987; Byron Johnson, 14 March 1988, Karin Lissakers, 1 July 1992. Church quoted in "The Word from Washington," *The Progressive*, 35 (Nov. 1971): 12.
45. Bryce Nelson, 20 April 1985 address to Idaho Press Club; interviews: Garry Wenske, 22 March 1987; Richard Church, 5 Aug. 1984; Levinson, 11 May 1987; Frederick A. O. Schwarz, Jr., 13 Aug. 1984. Another Church aide commented anonymously in 1987 about the "two Churches."
46. Bill Hall interview, 7 Aug. 1986; also, Levinson interview, 11 May 1987, re Church believing *Post* disliked him.

47. Church quoted in Myra MacPherson, *The Power Lovers: An Intimate Look at Politics and Marriage* (New York: G. P. Putnam's, 1975), p. 429; re his roots, interviews: Forrest Church, 25 July 1984; Jerry Brady, 27 June 1979 and 7 Nov. 1987; Bill Hall, 7 Aug. 1987. Re his basic shyness, Brady and Tommie Ward interview, 16 May 1987.
48. David Underhill interview, 10 Aug. 1989.
49. Martin Peterson interview, 2 April 1985; Ross Baker to Ashby, 30 June 1986. Also Peter Fenn interview, 16 May 1987.
50. Hall, "DC and Me," unpublished mss. in Hall's possession, pp. 20-23.
51. Interviews: Patrick Shea, 15 Oct. 1988; Jerry Brady, 7 Nov. 1987; Mike Wetherell, 15 July 1987; Garry Wenske, 22 March 1987; Johanna Munson, 5 Feb. 1988; Penny Gross, 11 August 1984; Lynda Clark, 30 Sept. 1988.
52. Unidentified clipping, Jack Beatty, "Frank Church 1924-1984," 12/3/13, re Church's reference to the "priesthood"; Ross K. Baker to Ashby, 30 June 1986; interviews: Tom Dine, 14 June 1979, and Bill Hall, 7 Aug. 1986; Church to Sam Day, 23 July 1970, CP, 2.2/32/13; Church to Members of the Arco, Idaho, English Class, 8 Oct. 1970, 2.2/32/16.
53. Robert Schulzinger, *The Wise Men of Foreign Affairs: The History of the Council on Foreign Relations* (New York: Columbia University Press, 1984), pp. x (qtns.) -xi, 1-164. Arthur H. Dean to Church, 31 Oct. 1963, CP, 10.6/2/1, re the invitation to join.
54. Church to Bayless Manning, 22 April 1971, CP, 10.6/2/31.
55. See for example, William O'Neill, *Coming Apart: An Informal History of America in the 1960s* (Chicago: Quadrangle, 1971), p. 355, re the American Medical Association; Jon Wiener, "Radical Historians and the Crisis in American History, 1959-1980," *Journal of American History* (Sept. 1989): 422, and J. Anthony Lukas, "Historians' Conference: The Radical Need for Jobs," *The New York Times Magazine*, 12 March 1972: 38-40, re the American Historical Association.
56. Schulzinger, *The Wise Men of Foreign Affairs*, pp. 209-14; see the letters from various Council members to John Templeton Swing and Cyrus Vance in CP, 10.6/2/4.
57. Church to Cyrus R. Vance, 10 Jan. 1972, CP, 10.6/2/3; to Council on Foreign Relations, 21 Feb. 1973, 10.6/2/5; to John Martinson, 7 May 1976, CP, 2.2/5/1.
58. Louis Harris and Associates, "A Survey of the Race for U. S. Senate in the State of Idaho," July 1962, CP, 12/3/6, p. 22; Church to Charles Hummel, 28 July 1961, CP, 2.2/3/13.
59. Forrest Church interview, 25 July 1984; Carl Marcy to Pat Holt and Don Henderson, 6 June 1968, Carl Marcy Papers, in the Senate Foreign Relations Committee Papers, Box 1968-69, NA.
60. *New York Times*, 26 and 30 Oct. 1971.
61. *CR*, 29 Oct. 1971, pp. 38252-58.
62. *Ibid.*, p. 38258.
63. Frank Church, "A Farewell to Foreign Aid," *Washington Post*, 7 Nov. 1971; Frank Church and Charles Percy, "Should We End Our Foreign Aid Program?" *The American Legion Magazine* (Jan. 1971): 36-37; Frank Church, "Why I Voted No," *New Republic* (13 Nov. 1971): 14-17.
64. Church to Carl Burke, 1 Nov. 1971, CP, 12/3/13; Richard Nixon to Hugh Scott, 27 July 1972, NPMP, WHCF, EX FO 3-2.
65. Seymour M. Hersh, *The Price of Power: Kissinger in the Nixon White House* (New York: Summit Books, 1983), pp. 444-45, 457.

66. Hersh, *The Price of Power,* pp. 445-64; Ambrose, *Nixon*, pp. 481-86. Also, Roger Morris, *Uncertain Greatness: Henry Kissinger and American Foreign Policy* (New York: Harper & Row, 1977), pp. 206-07, 213-29, contains a brief, eloquent overview.
67. *CR*, 6 Dec. 1971, pp. 44849-51; Chester Bowles to Church, 12 Oct. 1971, CP, 2.2/24/14; Church to Mary Dimond, 9 Dec. 1971, 2.2/24/4; Church's hand-corrected report, "The Road to Jessore: India's Refugee-and-Security Crisis," to the Foreign Relations Committee, Dec. 1971, 10.6/3/11.
68. G. S. Dhillon to Church, 31 Dec. 1971, CP, 2.2/24/14; *CR*, 6 Dec. 1971, pp. 44850-51.
69. Kissinger quoted in Hersh, *Price of Power,* p. 454; A. K. Dutta Chowdhury to Church, 14 Jan. 1972, CP, 2.2/24/14.
70. Birch Bayh interview, 14 May 1987.
71. *CR*, 2 Dec. 1971, p. 44040.
72. Church, "Impoundment of Appropriated Funds: The Decline of Congressional Control Over Executive Discretion," *Stanford Law Review,* 22 (June 1970): 1240-53; reprint from *CR*, 24 Sept. 1971, p. 33273, CP, 10.6/4/14.
73. Payne and Carpenter, "Frank Church."
74. Printouts of computerized record of Church's roll call voting, 1969-74, 1976, compiled by Professor Alan L. Clem, University of South Dakota, in authors' possession.

Notes for Chapter Fourteen

1. Theodore H. White, *America in Search of Itself: The Making of the President 1956-1980* (New York: Harper & Row, 1982), pp. 35-71, on "the Old Country"; on the "new politics" see, for example, Herbert S. Parmet, *The Democrats: The Years After FDR* (New York: Oxford University Press, 1976), pp. 253-54; Steven M. Gillon, *The Democrats' Dilemma: Walter F. Mondale and the Liberal Legacy* (New York: Columbia University Press, 1992), p. 103, and E. J. Dionne, Jr., *Why Americans Hate Politics* (New York: Simon and Schuster, 1991), pp. 46-49. Dionne, esp. pp. 116-21, discusses the collapse of the political center and the anger at status quo politics.
2. Frank Church, "Memorandum of Conversation with Edmund S. Muskie," 13 Dec. 1971, CP, 10.4/4/13.
3. On "life-style" liberalism, see Christopher Lasch, "Beyond Left and Right," *Dissent* (Fall 1991): 587-88; Dionne, *Why Americans Hate Politics*, p. 79.
4. Church speech, "Foreign Policy and the Generation Gap," 3 Dec. 1970, St. Louis, reprinted in *CR*, 7 Dec. 1970, p. 40045.
5. Barbara Ehrenreich, *Fear of Falling: The Inner Life of the Middle Class* (New York: Pantheon Books, 1989), pp. 97-143.
6. Wallace qtns., in Frederick Siegel, *Troubled Journey: From Pearl Harbor to Ronald Reagan* (New York: Hill and Wang, 1984), p. 200, re morons; and Ehrenreich, *Fear of Falling*, pp. 127-28.
7. Church to L. E. Lefler, 26 June 1972, CP, 12/3/14; see also, transcript of Church's taped diary, 19 July-7 Aug. 1972, CP, 10.6/1/15 (hereafter, Church diary, 19 July-7 Aug.), p. 17.
8. Church to L. E. Lefler, 26 June 1972, CP, 12/3/14, re populists; *CR*, 7 Dec. 1970, p. 40046 (China); Church memo of 8 June 1972 meeting with McGovern, CP, 10.6/1/15, re welfare.

9. Church, "Memo of Conversation with Muskie." Re Nixon's economic planning policies, see Otis L. Graham, Jr., *Toward a Planned Economy: From Roosevelt to Nixon* (New York: Oxford University Press, 1976), esp. pp. 198-203, 213-63. See also Tom Wicker, *One of Us: Richard Nixon and the American Dream* (New York: Random House, 1991), esp. pp. 529-41.
10. Church, "Memo of Conversation with Muskie."
11. *Ibid.*; McGovern to Church, 21 Dec. 1971, CP, 10.6/3/25.
12. George McGovern, *Grassroots: The Autobiography of George McGovern* (New York: Random House, 1977), p. 155; Church diary, 19 July-7 Aug., pp. 10, 13-15, re Humphrey and the old politics; Michael J. Glennon to Ashby, 28 Aug. 1986, for quotation.
13. Church, "Memo of Conversation with Muskie." Church voted with Muskie 89 percent of the time in 1970 and 84 percent in 1971, and with Jackson 82 percent in 1970 and 73 percent in 1971. Although he voted with Humphrey 84 percent of the time in 1971, he clearly could not put aside the negative impression he had formed of him over some fifteen years. Printouts of computerized record of Church's roll call voting, 1970-71, compiled by Professor Alan L. Clem, University of South Dakota, in authors' possession.
14. Church, "Memo of Conversation with Muskie"; Church to Muskie, 23 Dec. 1971, CP, 10.6/4/13.
15. Mike Wetherell interview, 25 April 1984.
16. *Intermountain Observer*, 26 Feb. 1972. See also Church news release, 23 Feb. 1972, CP, 10.6/4/13.
17. J. Anthony Lukas, *Nightmare: The Underside of the Nixon Years* (New York: Viking, 1976; reprinted, New York: Penguin Books, 1988), pp. 150-65.
18. Wetherell interview, 25 April 1984.
19. McGovern, *Grassroots*, pp. 135-51; Parmet, *The Democrats*, pp. 293-96. Also, Dionne, *Why Americans Hate Politics*, pp. 48, 119-20.
20. Re Nader, Church to Sharon Lichtenberg, 1 July 1970, CP, 2.2/32/12; re financial disclosure, "Idaho's Frank Church, A Biographical Sketch," May, 1974, 10.6/1/18; re Electoral College, Church news release, 14 Sept. 1970, 10.6/2/11; re the draft, for example, Church to Roy Nelson, 4 Sept. 1970, 12/3/14; Leadership Conference on Civil Rights, "A Civil Rights Voting Record for the 91st Congress," Oct. 1970, and "A Civil Rights Voting Record for the 92nd Congress, 1971-72," Oct. 1972, 12/3/14.
21. Emma E. Newton to Church, 10 Oct. 1957; Andrew Biemiller to Church, 15 Feb. 1957; Church to Newton, 19 Nov. 1957, and to Helen Holverson, 16 April 1958, CP, 12/3/14; Church's presidential campaign ad, *Los Angeles Times*, 9 March 1976, noted his long-time support for the Equal Rights Amendment.
22. Many staff interviews, but esp. Penny Gross, 11 Aug. 1984.
23. Karin Lissakers interview, 1 July 1992 (in 1977, Church appointed Lissakers as staff director of the Subcommittee on Foreign Economic Policy of the Senate Relations Committee); Forrest Church interview, 25 July 1984; Bill Hall, "DC and Me," unpublished mss. in Hall's possession, pp. 157-58.
24. Verda Barnes to Claire Wetherell, 23 Dec. 1965, CP, 12/3/14, re the Churches' recommendation.
25. Charles DeBenedetti, with Charles Chatfield, *An American Ordeal: The Antiwar Movement of the Vietnam Era* (Syracuse: Syracuse University Press, 1990), pp. 316-23, 335.

26. Nixon quoted in *ibid.*, p. 323, and Seymour Hersh, *The Price of Power: Kissinger in the Nixon White House* (New York: Summit Books, 1983), pp. 485-86; Fulbright in William C. Berman, *William Fulbright and the Vietnam War* (Kent, Oh.: Kent State University Press, 1988), p. 151.
27. *CR*, 23 March, 1971, pp. 7413-14 (people and slaughter); Church to Kenneth Hacking, 16 May 1972, CP, 2.2/38/13.
28. DeBenedetti and Chatfield, *An American Ordeal*, pp. 327-28.
29. Interviews: John Sherman Cooper, 4 Aug. 1984; William Miller, 27 July 1984, re Cooper's comment to Case.
30. Text of Roger Mudd comment on CBS Evening News, 12 Dec. 1970, Carl Marcy Papers in Senate Foreign Relations Committee Papers, Box 1970, NA, re the hair shirt; Eleanor W. Schoenebaum, *Profiles of an Era: The Nixon/Ford Years* (New York: Harcourt, Brace, Jovanovich, 1979), pp. 117-18; Clifford Case interview, 28 June 1979, on Church.
31. Tom Dine interview, 14 June 1979.
32. Richard Nixon, *RN: The Memoirs of Richard Nixon* (New York: Grosset & Dunlap, 1978), pp. 606-07.
33. *CR*, 5 May 1972, pp. 16103-06. See also Frank Church, "Bombs and Mines Won't Break the North's Will," *Los Angeles Times*, 11 May 1972.
34. George Aiken, *Senate Diary: January 1972-January 1975* (Brattleboro, Ver.: Stephen Greene, 1976), pp. 47-48, 53-54, 69; *New York Times*, 28 April and 16 May 1972; Tom Dine to "Charlie and Dan," 5 May 1972, Tom Dine Papers (Dine's personal possession).
35. *Washington Post*, 17 May 1972; *CR*, 5 May 1972, p. 16104, for the Civil War analogy.
36. Church to "Fellow Democrat," 25 May 1972, CP, 10.6/3/28; Church, "George McGovern for President," address at Idaho Democratic Assembly, 16 June 1972, CP, 10.6/3/27—hereafter, Sun Valley address.
37. Carl Burke interview, 22 Nov. 1987.
38. See, for example, Church memos to McGovern, 10 Aug. 1972, CP, 10.6/3/28, and (qtn.) 16 Aug. 1972, 10.6/1/15, re his concerns about ignoring key voting elements; Dionne, *Why Americans Hate Politics*, pp. 49-51, re the cultural shift within the Democratic Party.
39. Frank Church interview, 13 Feb. 1979.
40. Interviews: Carl Burke, 22 Nov. 1987, and Frank Church, 13 Feb. 1979; Church memo of 8 June 1972 meeting, 10.6/1/15, re the assurance from McGovern.
41. *Salt Lake Tribune*, 12 July 1972, re Church and the delegation; on the Chisholm petition, Church, "Memorandum for the File on the Convention in Miami (July 10-13)—The Episode of the Vice Presidency," n. d., but immediately after the convention, CP, 10.6/1/15—hereafter, Miami memo; on the lettuce boycott, Church, 13 Feb. 1979, and Mike Wetherell, 25 April 1984, interviews.
42. Church, Sun Valley address.
43. *Ibid.*
44. *Ibid.*
45. *Christian Science Monitor*, 8 May 1972, re cabinet; Church, memorandum of 8 June 1972 meeting, CP, 10.6/1/15, as example of advice.
46. Church, Miami memo.
47. McGovern, *Grassroots*, pp. 196-97; McGovern interview, 23 Dec. 1987.
48. Church, Miami memo.
49. Church diary, 19 July-7 Aug. 1972, pp. 1-2.

50. DeBenedetti and Chatfield, *An American Ordeal*, p. 333.
51. Aiken, *Senate Diary*, p. 75.
52. Gary Hart, *Right from the Start: A Chronicle of the McGovern Campaign* (New York: Quadrangle, 1973), p. 215, re the floor leaders; Paul F. Boller, Jr., *Presidential Campaigns* (New York: Oxford University Press, 1984), pp. 334-35, re McLaine, O'Hara, and the proceedings.
53. Church diary, 19 July-7 Aug., p. 4; Nixon quoted in Stephen E. Ambrose, *Nixon: The Triumph of a Politician, 1962-1972* (New York: Simon & Schuster, 1989), p. 590.
54. Church diary, 19 July-7 Aug., pp. 4-5; Scott quoted in *New York Times*, 25 July 1972.
55. Church diary, 19 July-7 Aug., p. 5; *Washington Post* and *New York Times*, 25 July 1972.
56. Church diary, 19 July-7 Aug., pp. 5-6. See also *Washington Post* and *New York Times*, 25 July 1972.
57. Church diary, 19 July-7 Aug., pp. 4, 6; *New York Times*, 25 July 1972; Scott quoted in *Washington Post*, 26 July 1972; Ed Harper to John Erlichman, 26 July 1972, NPMP, WHCF, EX FO 3-2, re warning Republicans.
58. Church diary, 19 July-7 Aug., p. 8; also, McGovern, *Grassroots*, pp. 199-208.
59. Church diary, 19 July-7 Aug., p. 9.
60. *Ibid.*, pp. 9-11.
61. *Ibid.*, pp. 11-12.
62. *Ibid.*, pp. 13-14.
63. *Ibid.*, pp. 16, 18. In retrospect, Church believed that he would have accepted the vice presidential spot on the ticket if it had been proffered a few weeks earlier at the Democratic convention. Church interview, 13 Feb. 1979.
64. Church diary, 19 July-7 Aug., p. 17.
65. *Ibid.*; Church memo of 8 June 1972 meeting with McGovern, CP, 10.6/1/15.
66. Memo of 8 June 1972 meeting with McGovern, CP, 10.6/1/15, re advice. On McGovern and the working class, see Steven M. Gillon, *The Democrats' Dilemma: Walter F. Mondale and the Liberal Legacy* (New York: Columbia University Press, 1992), p. 137.
67. Church diary, 19 July-7 Aug., p. 18; joke in Boller, *Presidential Campaigns*, p. 340.
68. Church diary, 19 July-7 Aug., pp. 19-20.
69. *Ibid.*, p. 20, re Church's disinterest; Boller, *Presidential Campaigns*, pp. 335, 340.
70. Church diary, 19 July-7 Aug., pp. 21-24.
71. *Ibid.*, pp. 24-27.
72. *Ibid.*, pp. 27-29.
73. *Ibid.*, pp. 27-28.
74. Mike Wetherell interview, 25 April 1984, re the quagmire analogy; Church memo to George McGovern, 16 Aug. 1972, CP, 10.6/1/15.
75. Godfrey Hodgson, *America In Our Time: From World War II to Nixon* (1976; paper ed., New York: Vintage Books, 1978), pp. 385-95.
76. Church to McGovern, 16 Aug. 1972, CP, 10.6/1/15.
77. Transcript of Church taped diary, 22-28 Aug. 1972, CP, 10.6/1/15, pp. 8-10.
78. *Ibid.*, pp. 11-13.
79. *Ibid.*, pp. 16-17; "Informal Remarks by Senator Frank Church at a Dinner Given for Him by Foreign Minister Abba Eban, King David Hotel, Jerusalem, August 23, 1972," CP, 10.6/1/15.

80. See, for example, Church's earlier comments on ideology in "Revolution and World Order," *Engage* 1 (15 April 1969): 22-27.
81. Christopher Lasch, "What Shall A Moral Man Do?," *The Nation* (28 Nov. 1966): 581-86.
82. Church memo to McGovern, 29 Aug. 1972, CP, 10.6/1/15.
83. Bryce Nelson interview, 7 April 1993, re sentiments and "Exodus"; U.S. Cong., Senate, *Prospects for Peace in the Middle East: The View from Israel—Report by Senator Frank Church to the Committee on Foreign Relations on a Study Mission to Israel, August 22-27, 1972*, Sept. 1972, p. 10, re Meir.
84. Tom Dine interview, 6 Feb. 1988; Church quotations in *Study Mission to Israel*, pp. v, 11; re the fear of bombs, Penny Gross interview, 11 Aug. 1984.
85. Church to McGovern, 9 Oct. 1972, and, re the elderly, to Dear Friend, 27 Oct. 1972, CP, 10.6/3/28; Church speech, "George McGovern for President," CP, 10.6/3/27.
86. Boller, *Presidential Campaigns*, pp. 338-39, 341.
87. McGovern interview, 15 June 1979.
88. Hodgson, *America in Our Time*, pp. 421-28; Boller, *Presidential Campaigns*, p. 338.
89. Wechsler in *New York Post*, 4 Jan. 1973; CDM ad in *Washington Post*, 7 Dec. 1972, and fliers in Henry Jackson Papers (University of Washington), #3560-6, 35/8; "Power Struggle," *New Republic* (16 Dec. 1972): 8; labor leader in William H. Chafe, *The Unfinished Journey: America Since World War II* (2d ed., New York: Oxford University Press, 1991), p. 418; see also, Parmet, *The Democrats*, pp. 304-05, re the old politics backlash.
90. Church to Editor, *Washington Post*, 12 Feb. 1973.
91. Nixon, *RN*, pp. 733-34; George C. Herring, *America's Longest War: The United States and Vietnam, 1950-1975* (2d ed., New York: Knopf, 1986), pp. 253-54; Aiken, *Senate Diary*, p. 137.
92. Aiken quoted in DeBenedetti and Chatfield, *An American Ordeal*, p. 345; Colson in Herring, *America's Longest War*, p. 254.
93. Verda Barnes note to Church, 16 Jan. 1973, CP, 2.2/29/3; DeBenedetti and Chatfield, *An American Ordeal*, pp. 346-47.
94. Seattle *Post-Intelligencer*, 26 Jan. 1973; Church-Case news release, 26 Jan. 1973, CP, 2.2/25/16.
95. Goldwater in Seattle *Post-Intelligencer*, 26 Jan. 1973; Tower in *CR*, 6 Feb. 1973, pp. 3515-16; Griffin, *CR*, 26 Jan. 1973, p. 2257.
96. *CR*, 26 Jan. 1973, pp. 2256-57.
97. Tad Szulc, *The Illusion of Peace* (New York: Viking, 1978), pp. 637-40. See also Nguyen Tien Hung and Jerrold L. Schecter, *The Palace File* (New York: Harper & Row, 1986), esp. pp. 1-171, which documents a series of promises, mostly via letters, from Nixon to Nguyen Van Thieu that, to protect South Vietnam after the Paris Peace Accords, the U. S. would respond with "full force," supplying "swift and severe retaliatory action" (qtns.), pp. 1-2.
98. Church, Wilmington, Dela., speech, 6 June 1973, reprinted in *CR*, 8 June 1973, pp. 18827-30; qtn., p. 18828.
99. Lukas, *Nightmare*, pp. 276-339. Nixon's comment to press secretary in Nixon, *RN*, p. 848.
100. Berman, *William Fulbright and the Vietnam War*, p. 174.

101. *Chicago Tribune*, 9 April 1973; Mr. Miller to Senator Mathias, 9 May 1973, CP, 2.2/16/2, re the committee meeting; *CR*, 14 May 1973, pp. 15436-37. For an interesting discussion of Fulbright's refusal to co-sponsor the Case-Church amendment, see Berman, *William Fulbright and the Vietnam War*, pp. 174-75.
102. Nixon, *RN*, pp. 887-88. Re the secret agreement, *ibid.*, p. 737; Herring, *America's Longest War*, pp. 255, 259; Hersh, *The Price of Power*, p. 637; Hung and Schecter, *The Palace File*, pp. 1-171.
103. Nixon, *RN*, p. 888-89; Henry Kissinger, *Years of Upheaval* (Boston: Little, Brown, 1982), pp. 124, 358-59. See also Berman, *William Fulbright and the Vietnam War*, pp. 176-78.
104. Church speech to World Affairs Council, Wilmington, Delaware, 6 June 1973, reprinted in *CR*, 8 June 1973, p. 18827.
105. *Washington Post*, 29-30 June 1973; Berman, *William Fulbright and the Vietnam War*, pp. 177-78; Frank Church interview, 13 Feb. 1979.
106. Dine memo for the record, 28 June 1973, Dine Papers; Dine interview, 13 Feb. 1979. Also, interviews: Cleve Corlett, 26 June 1979, and Church, 13 Feb. 1979.
107. *CR*, 29 June 1973, pp. 22307-08 (Mansfield), 22308 (Hatfield), 22309 (Kennedy).
108. *Ibid.*, p. 22310.
109. *Ibid.*, pp. 22310-11.
110. Dionne, *Why Americans Hate Politics*, pp. 121-24, on the McGovern constituency; Thomas Franck and Edward Weisband, *Foreign Policy by Congress* (New York: Oxford University Press, 1979), p. 13, re "Bastille Day"; Berman, *William Fulbright and the Vietnam War*, p. 178; Jacob Javits with Rafael Steinberg, *Javits: The Autobiography of a Public Man* (Boston: Houghton Mifflin, 1981), pp. 409-13, and Church interview, 13 Feb. 1979, re the War Powers Resolution.

Notes for Chapter Fifteen

1. Jerry Brady interview, 7 Nov. 1987, re lightning rod; Michael Glennon to Ashby, 28 Aug. 1986, re "State of Siege." Also interviews with Peter Fenn, 16 May 1987, and Rick Inderfurth, 14 Sept. 1993; and Bryce Nelson, "Church: A Man Who Took Great Risks for America," *Los Angeles Times*, 16 April 1984.
2. Miller to Senator Mathias, 23 April 1974, William Miller Papers, in Miller's possession, re "loophole"; also, Miller interview, 15 June 1979.
3. Frank Church, "Ending Emergency Government," *American Bar Association Journal* (Feb. 1977): 197.
4. *Ibid.*; interviews: Tom Dine, 6 Feb. 1988; Charles Mathias, 1 Aug. 1984.
5. Church, "Ending Emergency Government," p. 197; Mathias interview, 1 Aug. 1984.
6. Interviews: Bethine Church, 12 March 1985, and Miller, 24 Dec. 1988; Church, "Ending Emergency Government," p. 197.
7. Church, "Ending Emergency Government," p. 198; re the "loaded gun," Church's 20 Sept. 1976, Fresno, Cal., speech, CP, 10.6/1/17. Also, Church and Mathias to Howard W. Cannon, 11 Jan. 1974, CP, 12/3/15, and Dom Bonafede, "Emergency Powers Under Scrutiny," *National Journal Reports* (6 July 1974): 1021.
8. *Washington Post*, 7 Oct. 1973; Dine interview, 6 Feb. 1988; Church speech, "Watergate and Foreign Policy," 19 Nov. 1973, at the University of Delaware, Newark, reprinted in *CR*, 26 Nov. 1973, p. 37951.

9. William Miller memo to Senator Mathias, 3 Oct. 1974, Miller Papers; U. S. Cong., Senate, *The National Emergencies Act (Public Law 94-112), Source Book: Legislative History, Texts, and Other Documents*, 94th Cong., 2d Sess., 1976 (hereafter, *Legislative History*), pp. 25-28. Harold C. Relyea, "Reconsidering the National Emergencies Act: Its Evolution, Implementation, and Deficiencies," in R. Gordon Hoxie, ed., *The Presidency and National Security Policy* (New York: Center for the Study of the Presidency, 1984), pp. 274-323, is a thoughtful, thorough essay, which is extensively documented.
10. Stanley I. Kutler, *The Wars of Watergate* (New York: Knopf, 1990), pp. 518-46; Fish qtn., p. 525; Peter Fenn interview, 8 Aug. 1984, re the champagne.
11. Church speech, "Watergate and Foreign Policy," reprinted in *CR*, 26 Nov. 1973, pp. 37949-51.
12. *CR*, 22 Aug. 1974, pp. 29975-79; Memo, 21 Aug. 1974, from William E. Timmons re the meeting with Church and Mathias; Timmons memo to Ford, 22 Aug. 1974; Vince Rakestraw to the Attorney General, 15 Aug. 1974, William E. Timmons Files, Box 3, GRF Library.
13. On White House concerns, see Ron Nessen memo for the President, 18 Feb. 1976, with attachment, and Ford's approval, Gerald R. Ford Papers, Presidential Handwriting File, Box 8, GRF Library; Ford qtn. in Arthur Schlesinger, Jr., *The Cycles of American History* (New York: Houghton Mifflin, 1986), p. 284; Mathias interview, 1 Aug. 1984.
14. *New York Times*, 15 Sept. 1976; *Legislative History*, pp. 281-83, 338, 343; Mathias interview, 1 Aug. 1984. For White House objections, see Naomi R. Sweeney memo for the President, 8 Sept. 1976, Arthur F. Quern Files, Box 23, GRF Library. Relyea, "Reconsidering the National Emergencies Act," pp. 308-23, discusses some of the act's deficiencies, including its failure to provide "specific standards by which Congress may judge the propriety of an emergency declaration." He notes that the Special Committee's often-overlooked 28 May 1976 final report contained recommendations that Congress left out, regarding, for example, the improvement of presidential accountability. Had the Special Committee "remained in operation a little longer," according to Relyea, "it might have prompted a better statute. . ." (qtns. pp. 308-09).
15. *Washington Post*, 15 Sept. 1976; Mathias interview, 1 Aug. 1984.
16. Tom Dine interview, 14 June 1979; Church to Louise Sweeney, 17 Sept. 1976, CP 12/3/15; Church, "Ending Emergency Government," p. 199; Mathias interview, 1 Aug. 1984. The memoirs of Nixon, Ford, and Henry Kissinger contain no mention of the legislation.
17. Church speech, "Watergate and Foreign Policy," p. 37950.
18. Jack Anderson with George Clifford, *The Anderson Papers* (New York: Random House, 1973), pp. 13-62, 112; Anthony Sampson, *The Sovereign State of ITT* (New York: Stein and Day, 1973), pp. 259-60.
19. Staff Memorandum, "Origins of the Subcommittee on Multinational Corporations," 21 March 1975, CP, 10.6/4; George D. Aiken, *Senate Diary, January 1972-January 1975* (Brattleboro, Ver.: The Stephen Greene Press, 1976), pp. 37-39. Given Church's active role in early 1972, Roger Morris's admirable treatment of the Nixon administration's fiasco in Chile, *Uncertain Greatness: Henry Kissinger and American Foreign Policy* (New York: Harper & Row, 1977), pp. 230-44, seems unfair to Church. Morris implies, pp. 243-44, that Church's interest in Chile did not surface until 1975, during the investigations of the CIA.
20. Carl Marcy and Pat Holt to Fulbright, Church, and Case, May 2, 1972, CP, 10.6/4/10.

21. Staff memo, "Origins of the Subcommittee on Multinational Corporations"; on expectations of the pro-business senators, Jerry Levinson interviews, 2 Aug. 1984 and 23 May 1987; on politics, interviews with Tom Dine, 14 June 1979, and Pat Holt, 12 May 1987.
22. For business backgrounds, see Eleanora W. Schoenebaum, *Profiles of an Era, the Nixon/Ford Years* (New York: Harcourt, Brace, 1979), pp. 117, 327, 491, 630, and Carl Solberg, *Hubert Humphrey, A Biography* (New York: Norton, 1984). esp. pp. 166, 231-32.
23. Staff memo, "Origins of the Subcommittee on Multinational Corporations"; Frank Church, "Gunboat Diplomacy and Colonialist Economics," *Trans-Action*, 7 (June 1970): 25-32; *CR*, 25 Nov. 1970, pp. 38851-54.
24. Carl Marcy to Pat Holt, 25 Feb. 1972, Carl Marcy Papers in the Senate Foreign Relations Committee Papers, Box 1972, NA.
25. Interviews: Levinson, 2 Aug. 1984 and 11 May 1987; Blum, 10 Aug. 1984.
26. Blum interview, 10 Aug. 1984; Aiken, *Senate Diary*, p. 149; *Newsweek* (20 Nov. 1972): 97.
27. Church speech, "Inquiry on the Multinational Corporations and Its Relationship to United States Foreign Policy," New York City, 5 Dec. 1972, CP, 10.6/4/11.
28. Aiken, *Senate Diary*, p. 39; Carl Burke interviews, 12 Dec. 1985 and 22 Nov. 1987.
29. Interviews: Burke, 18 Dec. 1985, and 22 Nov. 1987; Levinson, 2 Aug. 1984.
30. Interviews: Blum, 10 Aug. 1984; Levinson, 11 May 1987.
31. Blum interview, 10 Aug. 1984; also *Los Angeles Times*, 13 Sept. 1975, re Church's not being "a tough-skinned, hard-nosed negotiator." Many interviews confirmed Church's gentle and caring disposition.
32. Interviews: Stan Burns, 24 April 1984, Patrick Shea, 15 Oct. 1988, re minister; William Oriol, 19 May 1987, re moral reflex. Once Church seized upon an issue he could be relentless, as Karin Lissakers noted (1 July 1992 interview).
33. Levinson interview, 2 Aug. 1984; William "Fishbait" Miller, *Fishbait: The Memoirs of the Congressional Doorkeeper* (Englewood Cliffs, N. J.: Prentice-Hall, 1977), p. 323; Church aide speaking anonymously.
34. Interviews: Levinson, 2 Aug. 1984, and Joseph Biden, 1974, CP, A74060.
35. Frank Church, "The Multinational Corporation—A Trial Balance," U. S. Senate, *Hearings Before the Subcommittee on Multinational Corporations*, March 20, 21, 22, 17, 18, 29, and April 2, 1973, Part 2, pp. 517-18, re percentages and "oyster"; Church speech to Council on Foreign Relations, Chicago, 16 Jan. 1973, reprinted in *CR*, 18 Jan. 1973, pp. 1513-15 (Ford qtn., p. 1514); "Global Companies: Too Big to Handle," *Newsweek* (20 Nov. 1972): 97, re the top ten. Also, Church speech, "Multinational Corporations, the Energy Debate and U. S. Foreign Policy: An Overview," Ames, Iowa, 3 Dec. 1973, CP, 10.6/4/11; hereafter, "An Overview."
36. Levinson interview, 2 Aug. 1984; Church to Milton J. Berrey, 27 Aug. 1975, CP, 2.2/4/17. Re Church's suspicions of big business, also interviews of Joe Sisco, 7 Aug. 1984, and Norvill Jones, 10 Sept. 1987.
37. Church speech, "The Scourge of Giantism in Business and Politics," 12 Feb. 1962, Washington, D. C., CP, 12/3/15; Church newsletter, June 1971, p. 1, re Lockheed, CP, 10.6/4/15; Anderson, *Anderson Tapes*, p. 109; Patrick Shea interview, 15 Oct. 1988, re the reception. Also, re Church's distaste for big corporations, interviews: David Underhill, 10 Aug. 1989, Bryce Nelson, 1 Feb. 1987, Steven Emerson, 20 May 1987; Joe Sisco, 7 Aug. 1984.
38. Marcy to Pat [Holt], 25 Feb. 1972, Marcy Papers, Box 1971, NA, re Church looking outside Wall Street; Bethine Church interview, 22 June 1979, for example, re helping business.

39. Levinson interview, 2 Aug. 1984, about remaking corporate morality; Levinson memo to Church, 12 Sept. 1972, CP, 10.6/4, re the questions.
40. Levinson interviews, 2 Aug. 1984 and 11 May 1987.
41. Interviews: Levinson, 23 May 1987; re separate staff, Levinson, 2 Aug. 1984, and Lissakers, 1 July 1992; Tom Dine, 14 June 1979, re rivalry; a Foreign Relations committee staffer spoke anonymously re the bad feelings among his colleagues toward Church.
42. Bernard Nossiter to Wes [Barthelmes], 4 April 1972, CP, 10.6/4/10. On the La Follette committee, see Jerold S. Auerbach, *Labor and Liberty: The La Follette Committee and the New Deal* (Indianapolis: Bobbs-Merrill, 1966) and Patrick J. Maney, *"Young Bob" La Follette: A Biography of Robert M. La Follette, Jr.* (Columbia: University of Missouri Press, 1978), pp. 170-88, 210-25.
43. David Vogel, *Fluctuating Fortunes: The Political Power of Business in America* (New York: Basic Books, 1989), pp. 37-112 re the consumer offensive; Robert Dietsch, "The Merger Boom: Who Owns What?," *New Republic* (22 Feb. 1969): 14 (qtn.)-16; Geneen quoted in Thomas S. Burns, *Tales of ITT; An Insider's Report* (Boston: Houghton Mifflin, 1974), pp. 17-18.
44. Peter N. Carroll, *It Seemed Like Nothing Happened: The Tragedy and Promise of America in the 1970s* (New York: Holt, Rinehart & Winston, 1982), pp. 129-31, re inflation.
45. Church, "Inquiry on the Multinational Corporations"; "Global Companies: Too Big to Handle," *Newsweek* (20 Nov. 1972); Jean-Jacques Servan-Schreiber, *The American Challenge* (New York: Atheneum, 1968); Richard J. Barnet and Ronald E. Muller, *Global Reach: The Power of the Multinational Corporations* (New York: Simon and Schuster, 1974)–"hair raising" on back cover; Robert Scheer, *America After Nixon: The Age of the Multinationals* (New York: McGraw-Hill, 1974), qtn. p. xii; Ovid Demaris, *Dirty Business: The Corporate-Political Money-Power Game* (New York: Harper's Magazine Press, 1974); Anthony Sampson, *The Sovereign State of ITT* (New York: Stein and Day, 1973). Bethine Church interview, 22 June 1979, re joke. By 1973 three other Senate and House subcommittees were also probing the multinationals, but Church's subcommittee emerged as the most potent and substantive. See John J. Reardon, *America and the Multinational Corporation: The History of a Troubled Partnership* (Westport, Conn.: Praeger, 1992), pp. 109-40. Reardon also describes the growing criticism of the multinationals in Congress and elsewhere.
46. Geneen quoted in Burns, *Tales of ITT*, p. 18; Nossiter to Wes Barthelmes, 4 April 1972, CP, 10.6/4/10.
47. Levinson interviews, 11 and 23 May 1987; 2 Aug. 1984, qtn.
48. Levinson interview, 23 May 1987.
49. Interviews: Blum, 10 Aug. 1984; Levinson, 11 May 1987; Lissakers, 1 July 1992; Pat Holt, 12 May 1987; Levinson memo to Fulbright and Church, 19 Jan. 1973, re Percy's reservations, CP, 10.6/4.
50. Levinson interview, 2 Aug. 1984, re the office.
51. Thomas Powers, *The Man Who Kept the Secrets: Richard Helms and the CIA* (paperback ed., New York: Pocket Books, 1981), pp. 281-84; Levinson interviews, 2 Aug. 1984, 11 and 23 May 1987, re the strategy.
52. Memo from Theodore G. Shackley for the Director of Central Intelligence, 21 Feb. 1973, re "Proposed CIA Response to Request for Information. . . From the . . . Subcommittee on Multinational Corporations," #3560-6, 51/2, HJP.

53. *Ibid.* Re Jackson's friendship with Helms see, for example, Jackson to Helms, 29 June 1973, #3560-5, 51/2, HJP. Loch Johnson, *A Season of Inquiry: The Senate Intelligence Investigation* (Lexington, Ken.: University Press of Kentucky, 1985), p. 7, re oversight and Stennis.
54. Theodore G. Shackley "memorandum for the record," 24 Feb. 1973, re "Discussions with Senator Jackson Concerning the Senate Foreign Relations Subcommittee Hearings On Multinational Corporations," #3560-6, 51/2, HJP. Jackson later tried to downplay the substance and importance of his meeting with the CIA. See "Remarks by Senator Henry M. Jackson," n. d., but early 1976, *ibid.*
55. Levinson interview, 23 May 1987.
56. Levinson interview, 2 Aug. 1984.
57. Bill Hall, "D. C. and Me," unpublished mss. in Hall's possession; Levinson interview, 2 Aug. 1984.
58. Levinson interview, 2 Aug. 1984.
59. Richard Helms interview, 2 Aug. 1984. Several years later, Helms faced felony perjury charges, partly because of his 6 March 1973 denials of the CIA's activities.
60. Levinson interviews, 2 Aug. 1984 and 23 May 1987; Seymour Hersh, *The Price of Power: Kissinger in the Nixon White House* (New York: Summit Books, 1983), p. 268n.
61. Sampson, *The Sovereign State of ITT*, pp. 267-73; Levinson interview, 23 May 1987; U. S. Cong., Senate, *Hearings Before the Subcommittee on Multinational Corporations---on the International Telephone and Telegraph Company and Chile, 1970-71*, 93rd Cong., 1973, pt. 1 (hereafter, *ITT Hearings*), pp. 93-125 re McCone's March 21 testimony, pp. 243-61 re Broe's on March 27, and pp. 457-515 (qtns., pp. 458, 484-85) re Geneen's on April 2; Church qtn. in *Chicago Tribune*, 9 April 1973.
62. Sampson, *The Sovereign State of ITT*, pp. 267-73; Hersh, *The Price of Power*, pp. 267-68; Levinson interview, 23 May 1987; Frank Church news statement, 22 June 1973, CP, 10.6/4. Several years later, the Senate Intelligence Committee discovered that Geneen had in fact sent at least $350,000 to Chile for political purposes. Hersh, *The Price of Power*, p. 268. Re the subcommittee's efforts to determine the Nixon administration's role in the ITT matter, see, for example, Brandon W. Sweitzer memo for Ambassador Peter G. Peterson, 19 March 1973, WFSC Files, John Dean Papers, Box 41, NPMP.
63. *Chicago Tribune*, 9 April 1973. As Hersh, *The Price of Power*, and Powers, *The Man Who Kept the Secrets*, pp. 281-304, show, Church was correct.
64. *Chicago Tribune*, 9 April 1973; *ITT Hearings*, pp. 112-13, 120-22; William Oriol interview, 19 May 1987, re dagger.
65. *The Idaho Statesman*, 5 April 1973; Jerome Levinson, "Working Paper #1 – ITT," 29 Sept. 1972, with Church's comment, CP, 10.6/4; Church to Richard Platt, 25 April 1973, 12/3/15, re victory; Sampson, *The Sovereign State of ITT*, pp. 267, 273.
66. "Overseas Private Investment Corp. Under Attack," *Congressional Quarterly Weekly Report* (3 Nov. 1973): 2921; *Wall Street Journal* and *New York Times*, 18 Oct. 1973; Henry Kissinger to Church, 3 Oct. 1973, CP, 12/3/15.
67. Blum interview, 10 Aug. 1984; "Committee Recommends Phaseout of OPIC Insurance," *Congressional Quarterly Weekly Report* (2 March 1974): 565; "Senate Bill Would Limit U. S. Role in Foreign Investment," *ibid.* (17 Aug. 1974): 2245; *National Journal Reports* (9 March 1974): 377-78; *Washington Post*, 12 and 18 Dec. 1973; *New York Times*, 18 Dec. 1974; *CR*, 26 Feb. 1974, pp. 4242-61. To facilitate the transition to the private sector, Church's bill allowed OPIC temporarily

and partially to reinsure private insurers against catastrophic global losses. The bill, after conference, proposed to give OPIC a purely reinsurer's role by 1981.

68. Sampson, *The Sovereign State of ITT*, pp. 268-69; Pat Holt interview, 12 May 1987.
69. Qtn. in Church news release, "In the Aftermath of the Chilean Affair," 13 Dec. 1974, CP, 2.2/46/3; re self-determination, Church to Milton J. Berrey, 27 Aug. 1975, 2.2/4/17.
70. Note, n. d., but attached to notes from 10 Sept. 1973 Kissinger confirmation hearings, in CP, 10.6/3/21.
71. Vogel, *Fluctuating Fortunes*, pp. 122-25.
72. Henry Kissinger, *Years of Upheaval* (Boston: Little, Brown, 1982), pp. 459-96; Richard Nixon, *RN: The Memoirs of Richard Nixon* (New York: Grosset & Dunlap, 1978), pp. 920-28. On the war's background and early days, see Daniel Yergin, *The Prize: The Epic Quest for Oil, Money, and Power* (New York: Simon & Schuster, 1991), pp. 588-605.
73. Steven Emerson, *The American House of Saud* (New York: Franklin Watts, 1985), pp. 38-39; Carroll, *It Seemed Like Nothing Happened*, pp. 117-19; Vogel, *Fluctuating Fortunes*, p. 124; local examples, "Cold Comfort for a Long, Hard Winter," *Time* (10 Dec. 1973): 33. On "the oil weapon" in the war, see Yergin, *The Prize*, pp. 605-12.
74. Carroll, *It Seemed Like Nothing Happened*, pp. 118-19; Vogel, *Fluctuating Fortunes*, pp. 125-26 (qtn.). See also Yergin, *The Prize*, pp. 610-11, 656-59. Although "the companies' profits were huge in absolute terms," Yergin cautions, p. 659, that "their rates of return were, except for 1974, somewhat below the average rate for all American industry."
75. Church, "An Overview."
76. Robert Sherrill, *The Oil Follies of 1970-1980* (New York: Anchor Press, 1980), pp. 211, 217-18. "Between 1973 and 1975," writes David Vogel, "fifteen of the thirty-nine permanent committees of the U. S. Congress conducted investigations into the energy crisis." *Fluctuating Fortunes*, p. 127.
77. Interviews: Blum, 10 Aug. 1984; Levinson, 2 Aug. 1984, 11 May 1987.
78. David Ignatius, "The Multinationals," *The New Republic* (14 Sept. 1974): 15, 19.
79. Church qtn., U. S. Cong., Senate, *Hearings Before the Subcommittee on Multinational Corporations. . .on Multinational Petroleum Companies and Foreign Policy*, 93rd Cong., 2d sess., 1974 (hereafter, *Hearings on Oil*), pt. 4, 30 Jan. 1974, p. 1 (veil); Levinson interview, 11 May 1987; Stephen Nordlinger, "Our Blundering Oil Diplomacy," *The Nation* (27 April 1974): 524.
80. Levinson memo to Church, 12 Sept. 1973, with attached "Background Paper—International Petroleum Industry," pp. 1-10, 13 (qtn.)—hereafter "Background Paper," CP, 12/3/15; *Hearings on Oil*, pt. 4, 30 Jan. 1974, p. 2.
81. *Hearings on Oil*, pt. 4, 30 Jan. 1974, pp. 2-5; Church speech, "Tax Subsidies and Multinational Corporations," before the International Fiscal Association, 23 Jan. 1975—hereafter, "Tax Subsidies"—(qtn.), and Church statement, 12 Jan. 1975, upon release of the subcommittee report on "Multinational Oil Corporations and U.S. Foreign Policy," CP, 10.6/4/11; Nordlinger, "Our Blundering Oil Diplomacy," p. 523. Also see Reardon, *America and the Multinational Corporation*, pp. 124-28, and Yergin, *The Prize*, pp. 446-47 (re foreign tax credits) and pp. 470-78 (re Iran).
82. "Background Paper," p. 2; and, re McCloy, Church, "Tax Subsidies."
83. Church, "Tax Subsidies."
84. *Hearings on Oil*, pt. 7, 28 Jan. 1974, pp. 1-12.

85. Levinson interview, 23 May 1987; Rovere and senator quoted in *San Francisco Chronicle*, 7 Feb. 1974. Walter Isaacson and Evan Thomas, *The Wise Men: Six Friends and the World They Made* (New York: Simon & Schuster, 1986), discuss McCloy and his impact on U. S. policy, but see also Jacob Heilbrunn, "The Real McCloy," *New Republic* (11 May 1992): 40-45, and Kai Bird, *The Chairman: John J. McCloy, the Making of the American Establishment* (New York: Simon & Schuster, 1992).
86. *San Francisco Chronicle*, 7 Feb. 1974; *Hearings on Oil*, pt. 5, pp. 247-87; qtn. in Schoenebaum, *Profiles of an Era*, p. 397. Also Church to McCloy, 11 April 1974, CP, 12/3/15, and McCloy's 24 Jan. 1974 closed testimony, *Hearings on Oil*, pt. 5, esp. pp. 65-68.
87. Levinson's 20 June 1974 testimony, *Hearings on Oil*, pp. 401-02; Levinson interviews, 2 Aug. 1984 and 23 May 1987.
88. Interviews: Jack Anderson, 6 Aug. 1984; Levinson, 23 May 1987.
89. Levinson interviews, 2 Aug. 1984 and 23 May 1987; *Hearings on Oil*, Levinson's 20 June 1974 testimony, p. 402.
90. *Hearings on Oil*, pp. 402-03; also, Emerson, *The American House of Saud*, chap. 2. Yergin, *The Prize*, pp. 620-25, discusses the enormous pressure on the companies from, on one side, the Arab government, and, on another side, the oil-consuming nations. ARAMCO officials saw no acceptable alternative except to implement the embargo. From their perspective, it was "better to cooperate and move as much oil onto the market as possible than to be nationalized and thrown out."
91. Church press statement, 7 Aug. 1974, CP, 12/3/15.
92. Church press statement, 7 Aug. 1974; *Hearings*, pt. 4, 28 Jan. 1974 executive session, p. 12; Church to Hugh Scott, 25 Sept. 1974, CP, 12/3/15.
93. Church qtn. and response in Gene T. Kinney, "What you don't read in the newspapers," *Oil and Gas Journal* (8 April 1975): 1; *Washington Post*, 28 March 1974, re taxes.
94. Kinney, "What you don't read in the newspapers."
95. *Washington Post* and *Wall Street Journal*, 7 Aug. 1974.
96. Aiken, *Senate Diary*, 21 Sept. 1974, p. 324.
97. Peter D. Hart Research Associates, "A Survey of the Political Climate in Idaho," July, 1974, pp. II-13, III-6-9, CP, 5.7/1. Hereafter, Hart Survey, 1974. Church had assuredly tried to keep Idaho's voters informed about his work on the multinationals subcommittee. See the letter, "The story behind big oil," which he mailed to constituents during the spring of 1974. Church to Dear Fellow Idahoan, n. d., but late April or May, 1974, CP, 9.7/1/10.
98. Memos on the 1974 campaign to FC from Mike Wetherell, 14 Nov. 1974, and Clareene Wharry, 15 Dec. 1974, CP, 12/3/15. Hereafter, Wetherell and Wharry memos.
99. Wetherell and Wharry memos.
100. Wetherell memo.
101. *Idaho State Journal*, 6 March 1974, re regulations; pamphlet, "Bob Smith for United States Senate," p. 1, CP, 12/3/15.
102. Smith quoted in *Kellogg Evening-News*, 8 April 1974; Democratic Senatorial Campaign Committee Campaign Bulletin #3, 20 Dec. 1973 (an analysis of the Harris poll by Michigan State political scientist Ada Finifter), CP, 12/3/15; also Mike Wetherell to Verda and FC, 21 Feb. 1974, 9.7/1/6.

103. Hart Survey, 1974, pp. I-2-3, 5, 11.
104. Loch Johnson, "Frank Church and the Birchers," *The Nation* (19 Oct. 1974): 358-59; Schmitz quoted in Curt Gentry, *The Last Days of the Late, Great State of California* (paperback ed., New York: Ballantine Books, 1968), p. 232. Also, Peter D. Hart Research Associates, "A Survey of Voter Attitudes in the State of Idaho," July 1979, CP, 5.7/1, p. iv, re Schmitz in 1972.
105. Alan Stang, "Frank Church, The Chameleon in the Senate," *American Opinion* (March 1974): 17-32; Anderson in *Washington Post*, 30 Aug. 1974. See "The *American Opinion* Attack on Senator Frank Church, A Fact Sheet," CP, 12/3/15, which the Church staff put together to show how Stang had twisted the record. Hereafter, "Fact Sheet."
106. Randy Stapilus, *Paradox Politics: People and Power in Idaho* (Boise: Ridenbaugh Press, 1988), pp. 187-93; Johnson, "Frank Church and the Birchers," p. 360; for Smith's thinking in 1974, see, for example, Twin-Falls *Times-News*, 29 July 1974, *Lewiston Tribune*, 11 April 1974; *Idaho State Journal*, 6 March 1974.
107. Stapilus, *Paradox Politics*, p. 193, re the Stang article; Johnson, "Frank Church and the Birchers," p. 360, re "whipping boy"; pamphlet, "Bob Smith for United States Senate," qtn. on p. 4.
108. Peter D. Hart Research Associates, "A Survey of Political Climate in Idaho," October, 1973, CP, 5.7/1, esp. pp. II-3-4, 7-13 (hereafter, Hart Survey, 1973); and Hart Survey, 1974, pp. II-4-11; Church quoted in Johnson, "Frank Church and the Birchers," p. 359.
109. Frank Church interview, 13 Feb. 1979; Hugh Horsley, "Notes on Senator Frank Church's 1974 Campaign," 25 Nov. 1974, and Dorothy Clobby to Carl Burke, 25 Nov. 1974, CP, 12/3/15. Also, Wetherell and Wharry memos, and Peter Fenn interview, 8 Aug. 1984.
110. Stapilus, *Paradox Politics*, p. 167.
111. Stang, "Frank Church," p. 24.
112. Clipping from *Caldwell News*, 2 May 1974, CP, 12/3/15.
113. Church interview, 13 Feb. 1979. Mike Wetherell interview, 25 April 1984, re Barnes.
114. Hall's *Lewiston Tribune* comments were quoted at length in the Burley *South Idaho Press*, 10 July 1974, in an editorial which the Smith campaign circulated, CP, 12/3/15; on the Miami vote, "Fact Sheet," p. 9. Also, Stapilus, *Paradox Politics*, p. 167, and Mike Wetherell interview, 25 April 1984.
115. Burley *South Idaho Press*, 10 July 1974. The Smith forces used the *Press* editorial as a campaign ad; copy in CP, 12/3/15.
116. Frank Church interview, 13 Feb. 1979; Hugh Horsley "Notes on the 1974 Campaign," 25 Nov. 1974, CP, 12/3/15, re Bethine Church.
117. Michael Barone, *Our Country: The Shaping of America from Roosevelt to Reagan* (New York: Free Press, 1990), pp. 533-34; William Schneider, "JFK's Children: The Class of '74," *The Atlantic Monthly*, 263 (March 1989) esp. pp. 35-38, re "Watergate babies" and Miller qtn; *Washington Post*, 7 Nov. 1974; Steven M. Gillon, *The Democrats' Dilemma: Walter F. Mondale and the Liberal Legacy* (New York: Columbia University Press, 1992), p. 154, re, for example, net gain.
118. Spokane *Spokesman-Review*, 7 Nov. 1974; Paul J. Buser, "Idaho Democrats Gain in Senate," unidentified clipping, CP, 12/3/15.
119. Hart Survey, 1974, II-3, 14 (qtn.), 17, III-16-19; Hart Survey, 1973, pp. II-1-2, 14 re ideologies.
120. Wetherell memo.

Notes for Chapter Sixteen

1. William Miller interview, 27 July 1984.
2. Church qtn. in his speech, "Multinational Corporations and East Asia: The Foreign Policy Implications of the Lockheed Affair," delivered 15 Oct. 1976 at the Harvard East Asia Conference, CP, 10.6/4/11—hereafter, "The Lockheed Affair." Church, mentioning Bryan and the muckrakers, himself drew comparisons between the 1970s and the Progressive Era, when abuses had generated a massive reform movement. Church speech, "The Last Quarter of the Twentieth Century: A Senator's Perspective," 26 Oct. 1976, CP, 12/3/16. See also Church speech, "A New Fashioned Patriotism" (1974), CP, 10.6/2/26.
3. George C. Herring, *America's Longest War: The United States and Vietnam* (2d ed., New York: Knopf, 1986), pp. 263-66; Fred C. Weyand to the President, 4 April 1975, with attached report, WHCF Subject File, CO 165-2, 3/1/75-5/30/75, Box 59, GRF Library.
4. Henry Kissinger memo to Ford re March 4 "Meeting with Senators Church and Pearson," n. d., WHCF FO 3-2, Box 15, GRF Library; "Viet-aid bargain," in *Christian Science Monitor,* 3 March 1975.
5. Bill Hall interview, 7 Aug. 1986, and Hall telephone conversation with Ashby, 14 July 1989.
6. Church news releases, 18 March and 18 April 1975, CP, 2.2/26/4; Hall interview, 7 Aug. 1986, and Hall phone conversation with Ashby, 14 July 1989. Ford included Church among the "incredibly short-sighted senators" who wanted the U. S. to "cut and run." Gerald R. Ford, *A Time to Heal: The Autobiography of Gerald R. Ford* (New York: Harper & Row, 1979), p. 255.
7. Herring, *America's Longest War,* pp. 266-67.
8. Church news release, 18 April 1975, CP, 2.2/26/4, re Americans not turning on each other.
9. Qtn. in Church to John Sparkman, 27 Feb. 1975, CP, 12/3/16; on the turf conflicts, see Humphrey to Church, 13 March 1975; Church to Sparkman, 21 March 1975, and unidentified memo sent to Church by Jerry Levinson, 18 March 1975, CP, 10.6/4/10.
10. Interviews: Jack Blum, 10 Aug. 1984; Jerome Levinson, 2 Aug. 1984 and 11 May 1987; Karin Lissakers, 1 July 1992.
11. U. S. Cong., Senate, 94th Cong., 1st Sess., *Hearings Before the Subcommittee on Multinational Corporations* (hereafter, *Hearings*), part 15, pp. 64-65, 68-72. Interviews: Blum, 10 Aug. 1984, Lissakers, 1 July 1992, and Hall, 8 April 1979, re bad feelings between Percy and Church.
12. Lissakers interview, 1 July 1992.
13. Blum interview, 10 Aug. 1984.
14. Jack Anderson and James Boyd, *Fiasco* (New York: New York Times Books, 1983), p. xii; interviews: Lissakers, 1 July 1992, Levinson, 2 Aug. 1984. See also, U. S. Cong., Senate, 94th Cong., *Hearings. . .on Multinational Corporations in the Dollar Devaluation Crisis and the Impact of Direct Investment Abroad on the U. S. Economy,* pt. 13, esp. pp. 1-61.
15. Frank Church, "From the U. S. A. to All the World with Love," *Esquire,* 68 (July 1967): 83-85, 123-24; qtn. p. 84. By the 1980s and 1990s, the Iraq/Iran and Persian Gulf wars made Church's warnings prophetic. In 1991, according to *The New Yorker,* the U. S. "sold more arms to the Third World than all other nations combined." By then, one study calculated that within a few years the U. S. would control at least 70 percent of the world arms market. "The Economics of Peace," *The New Yorker* (19 April 1992): 4.

16. David Boulton, *The Grease Machine* (New York: Harper & Row, 1978), pp. 255-57 [published in England as *The Lockheed Papers* (London: Jonathan Cape, 1978)]; Anthony Sampson, *The Arms Bazaar, from Lebanon to Lockheed* (New York: Viking, 1977), pp. 271-73; Levinson interview, 2 Aug. 1984.
17. Boulton, *The Grease Machine*, pp. 162-71, 255-58; Sampson, *The Arms Bazaar*, pp. 141-52; J. Anthony Lukas, *Nightmare: The Underside of the Nixon Years* (New York: Viking, 1976), p. 127.
18. *Hearings*, pt. 12, pp. 118-20 (Percy) and p. 107 (Church); Levinson interview, 2 Aug. 1984.
19. Levinson interview, 2 Aug. 1984; Frank Church, "Gunboat Diplomacy and Colonialist Economics," *Trans-Action* (June 1970): 32; *Hearings*, pt. 12, pp. 2, 108.
20. Kissinger in *New York Times*, 17 May 1975; "Spreading Stain," *Newsweek* (19 May 1975): 82.
21. John T. Noonan, Jr., *Bribes* (New York: Macmillan, 1984), pp. 660-63; qtn. p. 661.
22. *Hearings*, pt. 12, 16 July 1975, pp. 239-67 (Exxon); 17 July 1975, pp. 315-40 (Mobil); " 'All the Right People,' " *Newsweek* (16 June 1975): 65; "Spreading Stain," p. 80, re "Watergate II"; Blum interview, 10 Aug. 1984.
23. Sampson, *The Arms Bazaar*, pp. 241-43.
24. Text of Church's comments before the Senate Committee on Finance, 6 Oct. 1975, CP, 10.6/4/11. In the 1980s the Reagan/Bush administrations, in their dealings with Iraq's Saddam Hussein, might have benefitted from Church's advice.
25. See, for example, excerpts of Church's speech, "Americans and the Law," *CR*, 23 Oct. 1975, pp. 33850-51, and Church, "The Lockheed Affair."
26. Re Jones' testimony, Boulton, *Grease Machine*, pp. 262-64, and *Hearings*, pt. 12, pp. 149-91; *Hearings*, pt. 12, pp. 159-60, 165-67, re "the Lockheed arrangement."
27. *Wall Street Journal*, 29 Jan. 1976; Boulton, *The Grease Machine*, pp. 252, re peanuts.
28. Boulton, *The Grease Machine*, pp. 19, 265.
29. For detailed treatments of the Lockheed scandal, see Boulton, *The Grease Machine*—Strauss qtn., p. 63; Sampson, *The Arms Bazaar*, pp. 90-140, 207-40; Robert Shaplen, "The Lockheed Incident—I," *The New Yorker* (23 Jan. 1978): 48-74, Kotchian qtns., p. 62.
30. Boulton, *The Grease Machine*, pp. 264-66.
31. *Hearings*, pt. 12 (12 Sept. 1975), pp. 341, 367, 374; on Khashoggi, Sampson, *The Arms Bazaar*, esp. pp. 190-95.
32. Boulton, *The Grease Machine*, p. 266.
33. Judith Miller, "The Northrop Connection," *The Progressive* (August 1975): 36 (re shoes); Sampson, *The Arms Bazaar*, p. 275, re Percy; Levinson interview, 11 May 1987, re Haack.
34. Blum interview, 10 Aug. 1984.
35. Noonan, *Bribes*, pp. 660-61, and Boulton, *The Grease Machine*, pp. 267-69.
36. *Wall Street Journal*, 29 Jan. 1976; *Hearings*, pt. 14 (6 Feb. 1976), pp. 343-91; Noonan, *Bribes*, pp. 662-63—Kotchian qtn. p. 662; Kotchian's photo in *Newsweek* (23 Feb. 1976): 10.
37. *Newsweek* (23 Feb. 1976): 6-13, aide qtn., p. 11; Russell Mokhiber, *Corporate Crime and Violence* (San Francisco: Sierra Club Books, 1988), pp. 261-65, and Noonan, *Bribes*, pp. 663-70, contain brief summaries; Shaplen, "The Lockheed Incident—I," and "The Lockheed Incident—II," *New Yorker* (30 Jan. 1978): 74-91, is very informative re Japan; Boulton's *The Grease Machine* and Sampson's *The Arms Bazaar* provide detailed information.

38. Blum interview, 10 Aug. 1984; "Payoffs: The Growing Scandal," *Newsweek* (23 Feb. 1976): 29, re Blum at home. Also, Judith Miller interview, 10 Aug. 1992, re crowded press area.
39. Pat Holt interview, 12 May 1987.
40. Mary Perot Nichols, "Frank Church: The Hottest Liberal Dark Horse," *The Village Voice* (2 June 1975): 7.
41. "The Great Global Fallout," *Newsweek* (23 Feb. 1976): 11; " 'We Must Put Our House in Order,' " *ibid.*, p. 13, re Church.
42. Blum interview, 10 Aug. 1984, re the pressure; clipping from *Washington Star*, 11 Feb. 1976, re endangered U. S. firms, PF Comm Records, Press Office Files, Box G16, GRF Library.
43. Re Hodgson, Noonan, *Bribes*, pp. 662-63, and Eleanora W. Schoenebaum, *Profiles of an Era: The Nixon/Ford Years* (New York: Harcourt, Brace, Jovanovich, 1979), pp. 299-302; re Ford's response, *Wall Street Journal*, 11 Feb. 1976, and White House Issues Briefing Book, 18 Oct. 1976, Richard Cheney Files, Box 8, GRF Library, which sums up some of the administration's actions. Sixteen years later, as part of its deregulatory agenda, the Bush administration succeeded in closing down ECOSOC's special group, the UN Center on Transnational Corporations. The group had prepared a corporate code of conduct to recommend at the UN Conference on Environment and Development (the "Earth Summit"), scheduled for Rio in June, 1992. See Gerard Piel, "Globalopolies," *The Nation* (18 May 1992): 652-53.
44. Church, "Americans and the Law,"; see also, Church, "The Lockheed Affair," and typescript of Church speech, "U.S. Foreign Policy and the Future of the Multinational Corporation," 17 Feb. 1977, the Edwin R. Hodge Memorial Lecture in Toledo, CP, 10.6/4/11 (hereafter, Church, Hodge lecture).
45. Church, "Americans and the Law" and "The Lockheed Affair"; Church to Suzan Cantrell, 24 April 1959, CP, 12/3/16; Sampson, *The Arms Bazaar*, p. 224, re Kodama and the left; *Hearings*, pt. 14, p. 1, re Kodama and the qtn. Church anticipated here some of the central dangers that, in the 1980s, gave rise to the Iran-Contra scandal.
46. Frank Church, "The Lockheed Affair"; typescript of Church's 6 Oct. 1975 testimony to the Senate Finance Committee, CP, 10.6/4/11; "Oil and Confrontation," *Washington Post*, 13 July 1975 (qtn.).
47. Church, "The Lockheed Affair," re the play; Church, Hodge lecture; Levinson interview, 1 Aug. 1984; Church, "Americans and the Law," re Rome; " 'We Must Put Our House in Order,' " p. 13.
48. Qtns. re "scary," Stan Burns interview, 16 March 1988, and re "lair," Bryce Nelson, "Church: A Man Who Took Great Risks for America," *Los Angeles Times*, 16 April 1984.
49. David Underhill interview, 10 Aug. 1989, re the Congo, debriefing, and in-crowd; Eugene McCarthy to Richard Russell, 27 Feb. 1967, Carl Marcy Papers, Senate Foreign Relations Committee Papers, Box 1967, NA, and Marcy to "Don," 20 May, 1971, *ibid.*, Box 1971; Tom Dine to Don Henderson, 8 July 1971, Dine Papers (in Dine's possession); Church to David Underhill, 22 Feb. 1967, CP, 3.2.2/4/1; qtn. re processes in Judith Miller, "Criminal Negligence: Congress, Chile, and the CIA," *The Progressive* (Nov. 1974): 15.
50. Miller, "Criminal Negligence," pp. 15-17.
51. *New York Times*, 12 Sept. 1974 (qtns.); Miller, "Criminal Negligence," p. 17.
52. Miller, "Criminal Negligence," pp. 17-18; Fulbright qtd. in *Chicago Tribune*, 18 Sept. 1974.

53. Miller, "Criminal Negligence," and Nick Thimmesch column, *Baltimore Sun*, 24 Sept. 1974 (qtn.).
54. *New York Times*, 17 Sept. 1974; *Chicago Tribune*, 18 Sept. 1974; *Commonweal*, 18 Oct. 1974 (Church qtn.).
55. Church qtn. in *Chicago Tribune*, 22 Sept. 1974; Miller, "Criminal Negligence," p. 19. From 1947 to 1974 only two out of some 150 proposals to improve congressional oversight of the CIA even reached the floor of Congress. Thomas G. Paterson, "Oversight or Afterview?: Congress, the CIA, and Covert Actions Since 1947," in Michael Barnhart, ed., *Congress and United States Foreign Policy: Controlling the Use of Force in the Nuclear Age* (Albany: State University of New York Press, 1987), p. 160.
56. "Supersnoop," *Time* (6 Jan. 1975): 65; William E. Colby, *Honorable Men: My Life in the CIA* (New York: Simon & Schuster, 1979), pp. 340, 348-49; memo from Henry Kissinger and Max Friedersdorf, n. d., re 8 Jan. 1975 meeting with Mike Mansfield, Congressional Relations Office, Max Friedersdorf Files, Box 7, GRF Library; Wicker in "Ford Appoints CIA Panel," *U. S. News and World Report* (20 Jan. 1975): 22. Richard Cheney's handwritten notes, 27 Dec. 1974, White House Operations, Richard Cheney Files, 1974-77, Box 5, GRF Library, re concern with heading off congressional action. Loch Johnson, *A Season of Inquiry: The Senate Intelligence Investigation* (Lexington, Ken.: The University Press of Kentucky, 1985), pp. 9-11, discusses the impact of Hersh's disclosures.
57. *New York Times*, 15, 21 Jan. 1975; Eastland qtn. in "A Peek in the CIA's Closet," *Newsweek* (27 Jan. 1975): 30; Church interview, 24 June 1979, re Saltonstall.
58. *New York Times*, 28 Jan. 1975. The 1974 evaluations of the conservative National Security Index gave 0 percent ratings to Mondale, Hart, and Church, and 100 percent ratings to Tower, Goldwater, and Baker. Conversely, the liberal Americans for Democratic Action gave low marks especially to Tower and Goldwater, and 100 percent ratings to Mondale and Hart. Church's ADA score was 83 percent.; Frank Smist, Jr., *Congress Oversees the United States Intelligence Community, 1947-1989* (Knoxville, University of Tennessee Press, 1990), pp. 31-32, re the ratings.
59. Transcript of Senate Historical Office Oral History Interview of George Tames (by Donald Ritchie), 13 Jan. to 16 May 1988, pp. 179-81 (authors' possession), re Church's lobbying; qtn. in George Lardner, Jr., "Frank Church Joins the Pack," *The Nation* (17 April 1976): 468; Mike Mansfield to Rod Gramer, 24 May 1979. Johnson, *Season*, pp. 14-15, and others emphasize that Hart was Mansfield's preferred choice.
60. Associate's qtn. in James Barron and Marjorie Arons, "The Flexible Liberalism of Frank Church," *The Boston Phoenix*, 18 Nov. 1975; Church interview, 24 June 1979; "redemptive," in text of Church speech, "Neither a Vendetta Nor a Whitewash," 27 Feb. 1975, CP, 7.7/2/5. See also *Washington Star News*, 29 Jan. 1975.
61. *Washington Star*, 10 Sept. 1975; magazine qtn. in *New Times* (22 Aug. 1975); Roderick Hills interview, 10 Aug. 1984.
62. Johnson, *Season*, pp. 38-39 (qtn.).
63. Memo for the President from the Vice President, Henry Kissinger, and others, 18 Sept. 1975, WHCF, ND6, Box 5, GRF Library; interviews of Hills, 10 Aug. 1984, and of Phil Buchen, 30 July 1984, re withholding information; Patrick O'Donnell memo re presidential meeting with Church and Tower, 5 March 1975, Cong. Rel. Office, Max Friedersdorf Files, Box 7, GRF Library. See also Johnson, *Season*, p. 47; Smist, *Congress Oversees*, pp. 58-59.

64. Roderick Hills memo to Phil Buchen and others, 19 July 1975, Counsellors to the President, John Marsh Files, Box 81, GRF Library; re Hersh, Cheney's handwritten notes, 28 May 1975, White House Operations, Richard Cheney Files, Box 6, GRF Library.
65. Re Goldwater, Patrick O'Donnell to Hills, 31 July 1975, with attachment, William Miller to Church, 9 July 1975, Cong. Rel. Office, William T. Kendall Files, Box 3, GRF Library; Bob Wolthuis notes of GOP Leadership Meeting, 24 Sept. 1975, Robert K. Wolthuis Files, Box 2, *ibid.*; John Tower, *Consequences: A Personal and Political Memoir* (Boston: Little, Brown, 1991), p. 132; William Miller interview, 27 July 1984.
66. Smist, *Congress Oversees*, p. 48.
67. Johnson, *Season*, p. 42, re Watergate, and p. 46, re Church.
68. Church qtns., Mary McGrory column, *Washington Star*, 15 June 1975, and "The Cloak Comes Off," *Newsweek* (23 June 1975): 16-18; Johnson, *Season*, p. 54.
69. "The Cloak Comes Off," pp. 16-18; Phil Buchen interview, 30 July 1984; script of Fulton Lewis III commentary, 23 June 1975, CP, 2.6/1/2; *Washington Star*, 18 June 1975.
70. Johnson, *Season*, pp. 54-55 (qtns.), 272; William Miller interviews, 27 July 1984, 24 Dec. 1987. William Miller to John Sherman Cooper, 6 Oct. 1975, Miller Papers (in Miller's possession), described the assassination issue as "a red herring" and a "tar baby."
71. Church qtns. in McGrory column, *Washington Star*, 15 June 1975, and the *Charleston [W.Va.] Gazette* (interview), 13 Nov. 1975; also *New York Times*, 15 June 1975.
72. Johnson, *Season*, pp. 46-49.
73. Tower qtn. in unidentified UPI clipping, 17 Dec. 1975, CP, 12/3/16; Johnson, *Season*, pp. 61-62, and F. A. O. Schwarz, Jr. interview, 13 Aug. 1984; see, for example, "The C. I. A.'s Hit List," *Newsweek* (1 Dec. 1975): 28-32, re the prominence of JFK in the committee's assassination report; *Baltimore Sun*, 6 Oct. 1975, re "credulity"; Frank Church interview, by Sheldon Stern, 5 Nov. 1981, p. 18, Oral History Program, JFK Library.
74. *Baltimore Sun*, 16 July 1975; Johnson, *Season*, p. 57, re comment and Schweiker's response; Hills interview, 10 Aug. 1984; also Miller interview, 24 Dec. 1987.
75. Interviews: Hills, 10 Aug. 1984, and William Miller, 24 Dec. 1987; see also typescript of 17 Aug. 1975 "Meet the Press" program, CP, 12/3/16, in which Church explained that he meant simply that "there has been a good deal of looseness in the control of the CIA over all of these past administrations."
76. William Miller to Church, 22 July 1975, copy in Cong. Rel. Office, William T. Kendall Files, Box 3, GRF Library.
77. Johnson, *Season*, pp. 72-73.
78. *Ibid.*, pp. 73-76; Schwarz interview, 13 Aug. 1984; Phil Buchen interview, 30 July 1984, for an example of the criticism. *Time* (5 January 1976): 30, included Church holding up the gun among its "Images" from 1975. See also *New York Times Index*, 1975, II, p. 2583.
79. Morton H. Halperin, "CIA: Denying What's Not in Writing," *The New Republic* (4 Oct. 1975): 11-12.
80. Qtn. in Johnson, *Season*, p. 79.
81. Statistics in Smist, *Congress Oversees*, p. 79; Church qtn. in Ward Churchill and Jim Vander Wall, *Agents of Repression: The FBI's Secret War Against the Black Panther Party and the American Indian Movement* (Boston: South End Press, 1988), p. 62; *Washington Post*, 18 Oct. 1975, re Church's letter.

82. William Miller interview, 27 July 1984.
83. See, for example, Church newsletter, 28 March 1975, and typed proceedings of Boston hearings, 19 Dec. 1975, CP 12/3/16; U. S. Cong., Senate, 94th Cong., 2d Sess., *Fraud and Abuse Among Practitioners Participating in the Medicaid Program: A Staff Report Prepared for the Subcommittee on Long-Term Care of the Special Committee on Aging*, 1976; the National Council's article was reprinted in *CR*, 29 Oct. 1975, pp. 34227-28. See also Johnson, *Season*, pp. 166-67, re Church's schedule.
84. Johnson, *Season*, pp. 114, 151; Jay Shelledy, "Idaho's Lonely Frank Church," *Lewiston Tribune*, 12 Oct. 1975, described a typical day's work.
85. Bethine Church interviews, 22 June 1979 and 3 Aug. 1984.
86. Shelledy, "Idaho's Lonely Frank Church," re the bug joke; Bill Hall, "DC and Me," unpublished mss. in Hall's possession, pp. 122-23; interviews of Myrna Sasser, 20 March 1988, and Blum, 10 Aug. 1984, re CIA security sweeps.
87. Blum interview, 10 Aug. 1984.
88. *Washington Star,* 15 June 1975, re graduation; Blum interview, 10 Aug. 1984.
89. Interviews: Blum, 10 Aug. 1984; Penny Gross, 11 Aug. 1984; William Miller, 15 June 1979 and 27 July 1984; William Landau, 14 Aug. 1984.
90. Smist, *Congress Oversees*, pp. 36-37, effectively makes the point that "Miller and Schwarz reflected the two sides of Frank Church."
91. Evans and Novak column, *Washington Post*, 9 Feb. 1975, re conservative concerns; Smist, *Congress Oversees*, p. 36-37, re insider; Patrick A. Shea interview, 15 Oct. 1988; Miller to John Sherman Cooper, 6 Oct. 1975, Miller Papers.
92. Re Schwarz, Johnson, *Season*, esp. pp. 26, 74, 173; Smist, *Congress Overseas*, esp. pp. 36-37, 46 (qtn.).
93. Johnson, *Season*, p. 72 (qtn. re staff), p. 121 (qtn. re losing); Church interview, 4 April 1983; Smist, *Congress Overseas*, p. 37 ("dual-headed").
94. Miller interview, 24 Dec. 1987; re Goldwater, Bill Hall, "DC and Me," pp. 78-79.
95. Schwarz qtn., Johnson, *Season*, p. 192; Hills interview, 10 Aug. 1984; Johnson, *Season*, pp. 71, 182, 217 re the Pike committee's fate. Smist, *Congress Oversees*, pp. 41-45, described the Church committee as "a case study in consensual politics." Re Church's consensus style, interviews of Miller, 24 Dec. 1987, and Schwarz, 13 Aug. 1984; Smist, *Congress Oversees*, pp. 35-36, 42; Johnson, *Season*, pp. 56, 69, 159, 192, 218, 273.
96. See, for example, *New York Times*, 15 June 1975, and Jack Anderson in *Washington Post*, 27 May 1975; re Von Hoffman, Nichols, "Frank Church: The Hottest Liberal Dark Horse," p. 6; re Hersh, transcript of 2 Feb. 1975 "Face the Nation" program, p. 7, CP, 2.6/1/1, and Tom Dine to "the Files," 24 Oct. 1975, Mike Wetherell Papers (Wetherell's possession); re "dodge," Smist, *Congress Oversees*, p. 54. Smist, pp. 134-213, insightfully examines the House panel.
97. Re Church-Tower relationship, Miller to John Sherman Cooper, 6 Oct 1975, Miller Papers; Church interview, 24 June 1979; Robert Wolthuis notes of "GOP Leadership Meeting," 24 Sept. 1975, Cong. Rel. Office, Robert K. Wolthuis Files, Box 2, GRF Library; re Goldwater—Frank Church, "The Private World of Barry Goldwater," *Frontier* (Nov. 1963): 5-7; Barry Goldwater, with Jack Casserly, *Goldwater* (New York: Doubleday, 1988), p. 284 (qtn.)- 86; "Inquest on Intelligence," *Newsweek* (10 May 1976): 40.
98. Johnson, *Season*, pp. 109 (re threatened resignation), 222; William Miller, "Memo of Conversation" between Church, Ford, Kissinger, and others, 5 March 1975, Miller Papers, re courts; Smist, *Congress Oversees*, p. 61 (liaison's qtn.); McGrory

in *Washington Star,* 1 Dec. 1975; *New York Times*, 22 Nov. 1975. Intelligence committee staffer Rick Inderfurth praised Church's principled leadership; the senator had not caved in to the opposition but had instead "hung in there again and again." Inderfurth interview, 14 Sept. 1993.

99. *Washington Star,* 3 Nov. 1975; transcript of "Face the Nation" broadcast, 9 Nov. 1975, pp. 1-2, CP, 12/3/16; re Bush, *CR*, 11 Nov. 1975, pp. 35786-88, and Church to Mercer C. Hufford, 9 Dec. 1975, CP, 3.2.2/4/2.
100. *Charleston [W.Va.] Gazette*, 13 Nov. 1975 (Church qtn.); Ford to Church, in *New York Times*, 5 Nov. 1975; Bing Crosby to Church, 20 Nov. 1975, CP, 2.6/1/2; *Washington Star,* 29 Oct. 1975, re Luce; "Second Thoughts," *Newsweek* (9 Feb. 1976): 24 (Ford qtn.).
101. Re Welch and the backlash, Johnson, *Season*, pp. 161-62, 185, 215, and Smist, *Congress Oversees*, p. 64 (Church and White House aide's qtns.); Schwarz interview, 13 Aug. 1984; Bill Hall in *Lewiston Tribune*, 19 Oct. 1980, re the letters; *Washington Star,* 30 Dec. 1975, re the threat. Also, column, "Sharing the Blame," *Atlanta Journal*, 29 Dec. 1975.
102. Buchen interview, 30 July 1984, re the White House; "Capitol Chatter," *Rolling Stone* (15 Jan. 1976); Smist, *Congress Oversees*, pp. 38-40; Johnson *Season*, pp. 114-16, 150-51, 156-58, 176. For a stinging assessment like that of Mondale's aide, see Patrick Owens, "Nothing Works, No One Cares," *Newsday*, 2 May 1976.
103. Johnson, *Season*, pp. 16-17; *U. S. News and World Report* (8 Sept. 1975): 5, re southern Democrats; Nichols, "The Hottest Liberal Dark Horse," p. 7 ("Mission Impossible"); Smist, *Congress Oversees*, p. 39, and *Washington Star,* 27 June 1975, re opposition to televised hearings; William Colby interview, 18 May 1987. At the time, John Tower denied that Church used the committee to further his ambitions; unidentified UPI clipping, 17 Dec. 1975, CP, 12/3/16.
104. Church interview, 24 June 1979; *Washington Post*, 2 Feb. 1975; Lloyd Sherer, "Sen. Frank Church–Dark Horse Candidate for the Presidency," *Parade*, 21 Sept. 1975; Nichols, "The Hottest Liberal Darkhorse"; Smist, *Congress Oversees*, p. 39.
105. Smist, *Congress Oversees*, pp. 33, 39-40 (Schwarz qtn., p. 39); Miller interviews, 27 July 1984 and 23 Dec. 1987; Johnson, *Season*, pp. 215, 218.
106. Jefferson City, Mo., *Post-Tribune*, 20 Aug. 1975; the *Sunday Telegraph* (London), 15 Feb. 1976, re the mail; CIA people in transcript of Jack Anderson story, 9 Nov. 1975, CP, 12/3/16.
107. Church to Burns W. Roper, 21 Feb. 1975, CP, 10.6/1/22, qtd. Kilpatrick re judge; Kilpatrick, Buchanan, Severin, and Harvey clippings, n. d., but in 1976, CP, 2.6/1/4; "When the CIA is Gone," *Human Events* (23 Aug. 1975); *TV Guide* qtd. in Johnson, *Season*, p. 168.
108. Ford qtn., Johnson, *Season*, p. 168; Rockefeller in *New York Times*, 5 May 1976; Henry Kissinger, *Years of Upheaval* (Boston: Little, Brown, 1982), p. 495 ('scourge" qtn.), *Lewiston Tribune*, 22 Oct. 1988 ("wrecked"), and in McGrory column, *Washington Star,* 1 Dec 1975. Ford, *A Time to Heal*, p. 265, later wrote that "the Church probe was sensational and irresponsible."
109. Anonymous comments of Kissinger aide; Richard Helms interview, 2 Aug. 1984; Goldwater, *Goldwater,* pp. 286-87, 290-91, 294, 297.
110. James Angleton and Charles J. V. Murphy, "On the Separation of Church and State," unidentified clipping, June, 1975, CP, 12/3/16 (liberal); Johnson, *Season*, pp. 87, 189, and Tom Mangold, *Cold Warrior, James Jesus Angleton: The CIA's Master Spy Hunter* (New York: Simon and Schuster, 1991), pp. 349-50.

111. Sampson, *The Arms Bazaar,* pp. 123-24, 223, re Lockheed, Kotchian and Cold War; re CIA and Lockheed, *ibid.*, p. 223, and Shaplen, "The Lockheed Incident–II," pp. 76, 78.
112. Clipping of Kilpatrick column, n. d., but in 1976, CP, 2.6/1/4.
113. Church speech, "The Last Quarter of the Twentieth Century: A Senator's Perspective," 26 Oct. 1975, CP, 12/3/16; Church, Hodge Lecture; also, Bill Hall interview, 8 April 1979.
114. Noonan, *Bribes*, pp. 663-70; Mokhiber, *Corporate Crime and Violence*, pp. 264-65; Sampson, *Arms Bazaar,* p. 280; Tokuma Utsunomiya (member of Japanese House of Representatives) to Church, 12 Feb. 1976, with attached statement, CP, 12/3/16.
115. Church, Hodge Lecture.
116. Typescript of Church's statement in response to Ford's 31 Oct 1975 letter urging the suppression of the committee's assassination report, CP, 10.6/1/21. See also Church to Bing Crosby, 9 Jan. 1975, CP, 2.6/1/2.
117. "Frank Church," *The Nation* (21 April 1984): 469; Judith Miller interview, 10 Aug. 1992; Barron and Arons, "The Flexible Liberalism of Frank Church," p. 19; Andrew Hacker, "What Rules America?" *New York Review of Books* (1 May 1975): 12; Church interview, 24 June 1979, re his disappointment with legislation, and, re the subcommittee's accomplishments, see, for example, transcripts of Church's Dennison University speech, 22 Feb. 1977, CP, 10.6/4/11, and "The Lockheed Affair." The new legislation required public disclosure of corporate payments to foreign agents regarding arms sales, and made corporate bribery a felony. Church, "The Lockheed Affair"; Noonan, *Bribes*, p. 677.
118. Church made these points in many places, but see *Christian Science Monitor,* 21 March 1975, re "Godfather," and Church, "Covert Action: Swampland of American Foreign Policy," *Bulletin of the Atomic Scientists* (Feb. 1976): 7-11, re the enemy.
119. Church interview, *Charleston [W.Va.] Gazette*, 13 Nov. 1975, re investments; transcript of NBC's 21 Jan. 1976 "Tomorrow Show," CP, 12/3/16, re Caesar; Johnson, *Season*, p. 114, re Chad; Church, "The Last Quarter of the Twentieth Century," re drug habit and mirror image; Church, *ibid.*, and "Covert Action: Swampland of American Foreign Policy," pp. 7-11, re Soviets and ideals.
120. Re covert activities, U. S. Cong., Senate, 94th Cong., 2d Sess., *Foreign and Military Intelligence, Book I, Final Report of the Select Committee to Study Governmental Operations with Respect to Intelligence Activities*, 1976, pp. 563-65 (Church's comments); *CR*, 28 Sept. 1976, p. 32944 (qtn. re cutting room); *Washington Post*, 13 Nov. 1981, and Smist, *Congress Oversees*, p. 81, re political winds. A notable change that the investigations prompted grew out of the Church committee's discovery that the CIA was using federal agencies such as the Forest Service, in the words of the Seattle *Post-Intelligencer,* 25 Oct. 1993, "as cover for aircraft ownerships and staging areas in the United States for foreign operations." According to the newspaper, "the CIA agreed to divest itself of most of its American 'proprietaries,' companies the agency owned as fronts."
121. *New York Times*, 15 June 1975; *Washington Star,* 1 Dec. 1975.

Notes for Chapter Seventeen

1. *New York Times*, 19 March 1976, re Quixote.
2. Church speech, 4 June 1976 in Toledo, Ohio, CP, 8.2/14/6, re "ownership." On the struggle within the Democratic party, see, for example, Herbert Parmet, *The Democrats: The Years After FDR* (New York: Oxford University Press, 1976),

pp. 304-14, and Steven M. Gillon, *The Democrats' Dilemma: Walter M. Mondale and the Liberal Legacy* (New York: Columbia University Press, 1992), esp. pp. 99-185.

3. Will qtn., *Washington Post*, 10 May 1975.
4. Mike Wetherell interview, 14 May 1979.
5. Joseph Kraft, "The Cast," *New York Times Magazine* (17 Nov. 1974): 118; Jack Anderson column, released for publication 9 Sept. 1974, CP, 12/3/17; Frank Church interview, 14 June 1979.
6. *Washington Star*, 15 June 1975, re Gallup, and 10 Sept. 1975, re two of three; *Philadelphia Inquirer*, 15 June 1975, re issues, and 21 Sept. 1975, re word. For Church's own early reservations about the committee's political benefits, see Loch Johnson, *A Season of Inquiry: The Senate Intelligence Investigation* (Lexington: University Press of Kentucky, 1985), p. 17.
7. Memo from Mike Wetherell to Church, n. d., but summer 1975, Wetherell Papers, in Wetherell's possession.
8. Portland, Oregon, schedule, 24 Nov. 1975, Wetherell Papers.
9. Bill Hall, "D. C. and Me," unpublished mss. in Hall's possession, pp. 257-58.
10. Jeff Shields to Church, 16 Sept. 1975, CP, 12/3/17.
11. Carl Burke interview, 6 Jan. 1979; guest list, CP, 12/3/17.
12. Mike Wetherell's handwritten notes of the 9 Dec. 1975 meeting, Wetherell Papers.
13. *Idaho Statesman*, 12 Dec. 1975.
14. *Idaho Statesman*, 31 Dec. 1975.
15. Copy of Jeff Shields to Burke, 29 Dec. 1975, Wetherell Papers.
16. Frank Church interview, 14 June 1979.
17. *Idaho Statesman*, 13 Feb. 1976.
18. E. J. Dionne, Jr., *Why Americans Hate Politics* (New York: Simon and Schuster, 1991), p. 127, re poll and the divided liberals; Carter qtns. in Michael Barone, *Our Country: The Shaping of America from Roosevelt to Reagan* (New York: Free Press, 1990), p. 545; re Wallace, Jules Witcover, *Marathon: The Pursuit of the Presidency, 1972-1976* (1977; softbound ed., New York: Signet, 1978), p. 182. See also Richard J. Barnet, *The Rocket's Red Glare: War, Politics, and the American Presidency* (New York: Simon & Schuster, 1990), pp. 357-58.
19. Barone, *Our Country*, pp. 547-48; Elizabeth Drew, *American Journal: The Events of 1976* (New York: Random House, 1976, 1977), p. 75, re Udall; also Henry Kimelman interview, 25 Jan. 1992.
20. Interviews: Kimelman, 25 Jan. 1992; Carl Burke, 6 Jan. 1979; William Landau, 14 Aug. 1984; Bethine Church, 14 June 1979.
21. Frank Church interview, 14 June 1979.
22. *Ibid*.
23. *Idaho Statesman*, 19 March 1976, and other clippings in Church Scrapbooks, CP, 7.10.
24. *Ibid*.
25. Hall, "D.C. and Me," pp. 167-71; also, Mary Nichols, "Frank Church Faces the Ultimate Issue," *Village Voice*, 20 Oct. 1975; Mike Wetherell interview, 23 Nov. 1987.
26. "Enter Frank Cathedral," *Newsweek* (29 March 1976): 20; *New York Times*, 21 March 1976.
27. Qtns. re political labels from 29 May 1976 radio interview, Winsockett, R. I., CP, 8.2/14/7; re insider/outsider, Pendleton, Ore., press conference, 23 May 1976, and 27 May 1976 radio show in Cincinnati, 8.2/14/6.

28. This discussion of Church's campaign themes draws upon transcripts of numerous Church speeches and press conferences, CP, 8.2/14, and clippings, many unidentified, in Church Scrapbooks. Qtns. re jubilation, unidentified clipping in Scrapbooks; re King and respect, transcript of Church's CBS speech, 19 April 1976, CP, 12/3/17; re story of farmer, 21 May 1976 Portland, Ore., speech, 10.6/1/17.
29. See esp. Church's testimony before the Democratic Platform Committee, 19 May 1976, CP, 10.6/1/17. "Of those candidates with influence in the Democratic party," wrote one political observer, "Church probably represents the greatest departure from the main lines of current American foreign policy." Paul Lewis, "The Political Campaign at Home Takes Aim at Policies Abroad," *National Journal* (20 March 1976): 368.
30. See especially Church's testimony before the Democratic Platform Committee, 19 May 1976, CP, 10.6/1/17, and Church's speeches, 26 May 1976 at UCLA, 8.2/14/5; 27 May 1976 to the AFL-CIO in Cincinnati and 4 June 1976 in Toledo, 8.2/14/6.
31. Church's speeches, 26 May 1976 in UCLA, CP, 8.2/14/5, re standing up; 4 June 1976 in Toledo, 8.2/14/6, re GM; 24 May 1976 in Portland, 8.2/14/3, re competition; 29 May 1976 in Providence, R. I., re OPEC.
32. Qtns. re issues, unidentified clipping, 16 May 1975, CP, Scrapbooks; re corps and Armada, Providence, R. I., speech, 29 May 1976, 8.2/14/7; re Senate Bill One and secrets, 26 May 1976 UCLA speech. Drew, *American Journal*, p. 138.
33. *Washington Post*, 18 May 1976, re Edwards, and 18 April 1976, re stickers; McGrory in *Washington Star*, 14 March 1976.
34. Re New Deal, "Enter Frank Cathedral," p. 20; re government, for example, 19 May 1976 Winsockett, R. I., interview, CP, 8.2/14/71; re orchestra, Portland, Ore., press conference, 24 May 1976, 8.2/14/3.
35. *Idaho State Journal* headline, 3 Dec 1975; qtn. re money in article by Don Pieper, *Lincoln [Neb.] Journal* clipping, n. d., CP, Scrapbooks; James Barron and Marjorie Arons, "The Flexible Liberalism of Frank Church," *Boston Phoenix* (18 Nov. 1975): 13, re employer; *Los Angeles Times*, 28 April 1976, re submarine; 1 June 1976 Dayton, Ohio, press conference, CP, 8.2/14/6, re dominoes.
36. *Washington Post*, 26 April 1976 (qtns. re causes); George Lardner, Jr., "Frank Church Joins the Pack," *The Nation* (17 April 1976): 467 ("cocktail party"); also, *Lewiston Tribune*, 3 Dec. 1975.
37. Qtns. re abortion in *Lewiston Tribune* clipping, "Coming of Age in Nebraska," n. d., Church Scrapbooks, and lecturing in *Washington Post*, 18 April 1976.
38. Qtn. re drummers, *Lewiston Tribune,* 3 Dec. 1975; re people first, 29 May 1976 Providence, R. I., radio show, CP, 8.2/14/17.
39. Qtns. re 1776 and ideas, Portland speech, 21 May 1976, CP, 10.6/1/17; re epidemic, community, and cannibalism, *Idaho Statesman*, 9 Sept. 1975; re poem, 18 May 1976 Sacramento speech, CP, 8.2/14/5; re late, 27 May 1976 Cincinnati speech, 8.2/14/6.
40. Church speech to Washington Press Club, 26 March 1976, CP, 8.1/9/5.
41. Carl Burke interview, 6 Jan. 1979; Witcover, *Marathon*, pp. 347-52; Church qtn., p. 348.
42. *San Francisco Chronicle*, 20 March 1976.
43. Frank Church interview, 14 June 1979.
44. Mike Wetherell's handwritten notes of 8 April 1976 meeting, Wetherell Papers.

45. Interviews: Morris Udall, 8 June 1979, and Kimelman, 25 Jan. 1992; also, Witcover, *Marathon*, p. 348.
46. F. Forrester Church, *Father and Son: A Personal Biography of Senator Frank Church of Idaho* (New York: Harper & Row, 1985) p. 112; Carl Burke interview, 6 Jan. 1979; Frank Church qtns., unidentified clipping, 19 April 1976, Church Scrapbooks.
47. Patrick Owens, "Nothing Works, No One Cares," *Newsday*, 2 May 1976; Steve Ahrens interview, 26 April 1979; also unidentified clipping "Church's Unfair National Press," 16 May 1976, Church Scrapbooks; *Idaho Statesman*, 13 May 1976. *New York Times* photographer George Tames surprised his colleagues by choosing to follow Church's campaign, rather than Carter's, for a while. Tames had long admired Church, but the *Times* viewed the senator as a minor candidate, and other journalists were generally not eager to spend time with a campaign that they suspected would not capture headlines. Tames interview, 14 Sept. 1993.
48. Hall, "D. C. and Me," pp. 216-17.
49. *Lewiston Tribune*, 22 April 1976; re weapon, for example, 27 May 1976 Cincinnati speech, CP, 8.2/14/6; Ahrens interview, 26 April 1979.
50. *Lewiston Tribune*, 22 April 1976; "Senator Sunday School's Slow Start," *Time* (3 May 1976): 15-16; Ahrens interview, 26 April 1979, re the press.
51. Witcover, *Marathon*, pp. 327-28, 336, re Jackson; Wetherell interview, 25 April 1984, and John Greenfield to Church, 20 July 1983, CP, 12/3/17.
52. *New York Times*, 23 May 1976, and Ahrens interview, 26 April 1979, re turtle as campaign's symbol; *Idaho Statesman*, 7 May 1976, and *Lewiston Tribune*, 9 May 1976, re polls; *Lewiston Tribune* clipping, n. d., Church Scrapbooks, re the plane; "Senator Sunday School's Late Start," p. 15, re the rabbit.
53. Wetherell interview, 25 April 1984.
54. Interviews: Wetherell, 15 April 1984, and Ahrens, 26 April 1979; *Idaho Statesman*, 13 May 1976.
55. Burke interview, 6 Jan. 1979; *Idaho Statesman*, 10 May 1976 re endorsement; Whelan qtn., unidentified clipping, CP, 12/3/17.
56. Church qtn., Witcover, *Marathon*, p. 350; "Miracle Worker," *Newsweek* (24 May 1976): 21; *Washington Post*, 13 May 1976.
57. Carter qtn. in Witcover, *Marathon*, p. 350; Frank Church interview, 14 June 1979, and Hall, "D. C. and Me," p. 287, re Cronkite.
58. Church qtn., *Idaho State Journal*, 12 May 1976. Re the primaries, Witcover, pp. 350, 357-60; Drew, *American Journal*, pp. 175-78; also *New York Times* editorial, 13 May 1976.
59. Hall, "D. C. and Me," pp. 218, 287-88; Witcover, *Marathon*, p. 361, re polls; Wetherell interview, 25 April 1984.
60. John Gabusi interview, 7 June 1979.
61. Witcover, *Marathon*, p. 348, re Carter; interviews: Morris Udall, 8 June 1979, and Stewart Udall, 11 June 1979; Church qtn., *Idaho Statesman*, 24 May 1976.
62. Johnson, *A Season of Inquiry*, p. 249; *New York Times*, 23 May 1976; Drew, *American Journal*, p. 175; *Washington Post*, 18 May 1976, re cerebral, and 30 May 1976, re Broder; Portland *Oregonian*, 30 April 1976, re preacher.
63. Bill Hall, "D. C. and Me," pp. 378-84; *Idaho Statesman*, 22 May 1976; *Lewiston Tribune*, 21 May 1976; Drew, *American Journal*, p. 211.
64. Church's 27 May 1976 radio interview in Cincinnati, 27 May 1976, CP, 8.2/14/6, re slogan; *New York Times*, 26 May 1976; Witcover, *Marathon*, p. 363.

65. Qtn., Frank Church interview, 14 June 1979; Joseph Kraft in *Washington Post*, 27 May 1976.
66. Witcover, *Marathon*, p. 362, re Brown's campaign, and *New York Times*, 26 May 1976, re Brown's constituency; Church qtns., 1 June 1976 Toledo interview, CP, 8.2/14/6.
67. Church, *Father and Son*, pp. 117-18.
68. Drew, *American Journal*, p. 215; Frank Church interview, 14 June 1979. Also, David Underhill interview, 10 Aug. 1989.
69. Witcover, *Marathon*, pp. 363-64; Frank Church interview, 14 June 1979.
70. Interviews: Stewart Udall, 11 June 1979, Morris Udall, 8 June 1979, Gabusi, 7 June 1979.
71. Morris Udall interview, 8 June 1979; *Idaho Statesman*, 28 May 1976.
72. Wetherell interviews, 23 Nov. 1987 and 25 April 1984.
73. Kimelman interview, 25 Jan. 1992.
74. Interviews: Burke, 6 Jan. 1979, and Hall, 8 April 1979; Church's 1 June 1976 Dayton interview, CP, 8.2/14/6, re New Jersey.
75. Hall, "D. C. and Me," p. 318.
76. Hall, "D. C. and Me," pp. 306-07; also David Underhill interview, 10 Aug. 1989.
77. Hall, "D. C. and Me," pp. 321-22; interviews: Underhill and Peter Fenn, 8 Aug. 1984.
78. Interviews: Kimelman, 25 Jan. 1992; Burke, 6 Jan. 1979; Frank Church, 14 June 1979.
79. Hall, "D. C. and Me," p. 254; Frank Church interview, 14 June 1979.
80. Frank Church interview, 14 June 1979.
81. *Idaho Statesman*, 4 and 6 June 1976.
82. Martin Schram, *Running for President: A Journal of the Carter Campaign* (New York: Stein and Day, 1977), pp. 193-95.
83. Drew, *American Journal*, pp. 228-30.
84. *Ibid.*, pp. 230-32.
85. Church, *Father and Son*, p. 119; Schram, *Running for President*, p. 195.
86. Marc Reisner, *Cadillac Desert: The American West and Its Disappearing Water* (New York: Viking, 1986), pp. 398-425, re the Teton Dam and flood, and Church's support for the dam.
87. Schram, *Running for President*, p. 196.
88. Witcover, *Marathon*, p. 365; Hall, "D. C. and Me," p. 399; *Idaho Statesman*, 1 Jan. 1977.
89. Witcover, *Marathon*, p. 372; Drew, *American Journal*, p. 253; percentages in Richard Reeves, *Convention* (New York: Harcourt Brace Jovanovich, 1977), p. 237.
90. *Idaho Statesman*, 21 April 1976, re lightning; *Lewiston Tribune*, 7 June 1976, re primary winners; Bryce Nelson, 7 April 1993, and Wetherell interviews, 25 April 1984.
91. *New York Times*, 8 June 1976; Drew, *American Journal*, p. 228; Frank Church, 14 June 1979, and Stewart Udall, 11 June 1979, interviews. For an interpretation of a Church-Carter "deal," see Kandy Stroud, *How Jimmy Won: The Victory Campaign From Plains to the White House* (New York: Morrow, 1977), pp. 305-06.
92. Gabusi interview, 7 June 1979; Witcover, *Marathon*, p. 363, re Church and Carter's qtn.
93. Frank Church, 14 June 1979, and Morris Udall, 8 June 1979, interviews.
94. "Talking Points" for Senator Frank Church, n. d., typed and Church's handwritten copies, and copy of Carroll Hubbard to Jimmy Carter, 29 June 1976, CP, 10.6/1/18.

95. Kimelman interview, 25 Jan. 1992.
96. Jimmy Carter, *Keeping Faith: Memoirs of a President* (New York: Bantam Books, 1982), p. 36; Schneiders qtn., Witcover, *Marathon*, p. 386. See also Stroud, *How Jimmy Won*, p. 306.
97. Witcover, *Marathon*, p. 386; *Idaho Statesman*, 15 June 1976. Church's delegate count was: South Carolina, 1; Canal Zone, 3; Colorado, 2; Nebraska, 15; Utah, 5; Idaho, 14; Oregon, 14; Montana, 11; Nevada, 1; Rhode Island, 6; California, 7. See Reeves, *Convention*, pp. 223-37.
98. Frank Church interview, 14 June 1979.
99. Drew, *American Journal*, p. 287; Frank Church interview, 14 June 1979; Reeves, *Convention*, pp. 98-99.
100. Witcover, *Marathon*, pp. 386-88; Church, *Father and Son*, p. 120, re Donaldson; *Idaho Statesman*, 9-10 July 1976.
101. Penny Gross interview, 1 Aug. 1984.
102. Church, *Father and Son*, p. 122.
103. Frank Church interview, 14 June 1979.
104. Interviews: Wetherell, 25 April 1984; Frank Church, 14 June 1979.
105. Text of Church's speech, CP, 10.6/1/17; *Idaho Statesman*, 13-14 July 1976; Church qtn., *Lewiston Tribune*, 16 July 1976.
106. Wetherell interview, 25 April 1984.
107. Frank Church interview, 14 June 1979.
108. *Boston Globe*, 1 Aug. 1976; also Church, *Father and Son*, pp. 121-22.
109. Church, *Father and Son*, p. 123.

Notes for Chapter Eighteen

1. Interviews: Cleve Corlett, 7 Aug. 1984, Peter Fenn, 8 Aug. 1984, and Bryce Nelson, 7 April 1993; on Sparkman, Carl Marcy interview by Donald Ritchie, 2 Nov. 1983, *The U. S. Senate Historical Office Oral History Collection: Interviews with Senate Staff* (Wilmington, Del.: Scholarly Resources, 1987), p. 260; Mike Wetherell, handwritten "Memo to F. C.," n. d., but 1977, Mike Wetherell Papers, in Wetherell's possession.
2. Frank Church, "Which Secrets Should Be Kept Secret?" *Washington Post*, 14 March 1977.
3. Irwin B. Arieff, "Carter and Congress: Strangers to the End," in Congressional Quarterly, *Almanac*, 96th Cong., 2nd Sess. (Washington, D. C., 1980): 3-9 (qtn., p. 3); Charles O. Jones, *The Trusteeship Presidency: Jimmy Carter and the United States Congress* (Baton Rouge, La.: Louisiana State University Press, 1988), esp. pp. 1, 200, 206, 216-17; Jimmy Carter, *Keeping Faith: Memoirs of a President* (New York: Bantam Books, 1982), pp. 65-90; Paul Sarbanes interview, 15 May 1987. Also George McGovern interview, 23 Dec. 1987; Burton I. Kaufman, *The Presidency of James Earl Carter, Jr.* (Lawrence: The University Press of Kansas, 1993), pp. 30-31; William F. Mullen, "Perceptions of Carter's Legislative Successes and Failures: Views from the Hill and the Liaison Staff," *Presidential Studies Quarterly*, 12 (Fall 1982): 522-23.
4. Interviews: Frank Church, 13 Feb. 1979 (qtn.); Mike Wetherell, 25 April 1984; Fenn, 8 Aug. 1984, 16 May 1987; re Bumpers, anonymous comments of a Church staffer.
5. Bethine Church interview, 12 March 1985; also, Cleve Corlett interview, 26 June 1979, and *New York Times*, 12 Sept. 1979.

6. Fenn interviews, 8 Aug. 1984 and 16 May 1987.
7. Memo to Carter from Frank Moore and Dr. Brzezinski, 2 Feb. 1979, WHCF, Name File-Church, JEC Library; interviews: Bethine Church, 22 June 1979, and Steve Emerson 20 May 1987; also Myrna Sasser, 20 March 1988, and Fenn, 16 May 1987, interviews.
8. Interviews: Frank Church, 24 June 1979; Corlett, 26 June 1979. On Carter and Cuba, see Gaddis Smith, *Morality, Reason and Power: American Diplomacy in the Carter Years* (New York: Hill & Wang, 1986), pp. 115-17.
9. Interviews: Frank Church, 24 June 1979, Bethine Church, 22 June 1979, and Norvill Jones, 9 Aug. 1984; *Washington Post* and *Washington Star,* 9 Aug. 1977; U. S. Cong. Senate, 95th Cong., 1st Sess., *Report to the Senate Committee on Foreign Relations. . .by Senator Frank Church on a Trip to Cuba, August 8-11, 1977,* p. 1 (Castro qtn. re plane)—hereafter, *Report*; also, Bethine Church's 9-page transcript re the trip, n. d., CP, 12/3/18.
10. *Report*, pp. 6-7, 10; *Boston Globe*, 14 Aug. 1977; Frank Church interview, 24 June 1979.
11. Cleve Corlett interviews, 7 Aug. 1984, and 22 May 1987; William F. Buckley, Jr., "Scoop Campaigns for Neville Chamberlain," *National Review* (14 Nov. 1980): 1416.
12. *Report*, pp. 1-2, 4-5, 9; Corlett interview, 7 Aug. 1984.
13. *Boston Globe*, 14 Aug. 1977; *The Marietta* [Ga.] *Daily Journal*, 22 Aug. 1977; *Report*, pp. 6-8; interviews: Frank Church, 24 June 1979, and Cleve Corlett, 7 Aug. 1984.
14. Photo and ad, paid for by Magic Valley Sink or Swim Committee, CP, 2.2/49/3.
15. George D. Moffett, III, *The Limits of Victory: The Ratification of the Panama Canal Treaties* (Ithaca, N. Y.: Cornell University Press, 1985), p. 120, re the poll; "Opening the Great Canal Debate," *Time* (20 Feb. 1978): 19, re the GOP.
16. Lou Cannon, *Reagan* (New York: G. P. Putnam's Sons, 1982), pp. 210-19, 230; also, William J. Jorden, *Panama Odyssey* (Austin: University of Texas Press, 1984), pp. 315-25. Ronald Reagan to Sol Linowitz, 25 May 1977, and Linowitz to Cyrus Vance, 2 May 1977, WHCF, FO-15/FO31, JEC Library, are revealing on Reagan's opposition. Contrary to Reagan's claims, the U. S. never purchased the canal area. Walter LaFeber, *The Panama Canal: The Crisis in Historical Perspective* (New York: Oxford University Press, 1989 updated version), p. 35, notes, "The $10 million paid to Panama in 1903 was for treaty rights, not the purchase of territory as in the Louisiana acquisition of 1803 or the Alaska Purchase of 1861." See also pp. xi, 148-49, 216-19.
17. Alan Crawford, *Thunder on the Right: The "New Right" and the Politics of Resentment* (paperback ed., New York: Pantheon, 1980), p. 107; *Washington Post*, 28 Oct. 1977, re the film; *Miami Herald*, 11 Sept. 1977, on the squads; *Dayton Daily News*, 28 Aug. 1977. David Skidmore, "Foreign Policy Interest Groups and Presidential Power: Jimmy Carter and the Battle over Ratification of the Panama Canal Treaties," *Presidential Studies Quarterly*, 23 (Summer 1993): 479-83, 491 and Michael Hogan, *The Panama Canal in American Politics: Domestic Advocacy and the Evolution of Policy* (Carbondale, Ill.: Southern Illinois University Press, 1986), point up the size and effective grassroots techniques of the anti-treaty forces' campaign.
18. Jerel A. Rosati, "Jimmy Carter, a Man Before His Time? The Emergence and Collapse of the First Post-Cold War Presidency," *Presidential Studies Quarterly*, 23 (Summer 1993): 461-69; Moffett, *Limits of Victory*, pp. 50-69, and Jorden,

Panama Odyssey, pp. 341-456, are excellent re Carter's policy; also, Smith, *Morality, Reason and Power*, pp. 6-7, 27-30; Kaufman, *Presidency of Carter*, pp. 38-39. Walter LaFeber, "From Confusion to Cold War: The Memoirs of the Carter Administration," *Diplomatic History*, 8 (Winter 1984): 1-3, implicitly cautions, however, against finding much coherence in Carter's policies; Fallows qtn., p. 2.

19. Carter, *Keeping Faith*, p. 180; Jorden, *Panama Odyssey*, p. 495.
20. Church to Bryce Nelson, 10 Aug. 1960, CP, 12/3/18; Church to Lou Babb, 12 March 1964, 2.2/47/17; Church to many constituents, 23 Aug. 1967, 2.2/48/14; Sandpoint, Ida., *Daily Bee*, 5 April 1974; Jorden, *Panama Odyssey*, pp. 244-45, re the Thurmond resolution.
21. Qtn. re time in Moffett, *Limits of Victory*, p. 11; Frank Church interview, 13 Aug. 1979.
22. Moffett, *Limits of Victory*, p. 209, re U. S. poll; *CR*, 2 March 1978, p. 5344, re Idaho.
23. *Chicago Tribune*, 12 Oct. 1977; interviews: Robert Beckel, 12 June 1979, and Sol Linowitz, 3 Aug. 1984. On the treaty interpretations, Jorden, *Panama Odyssey*, pp. 468-77.
24. Jorden, *Panama Odyssey*, pp. 477-80; Church to Len Jordan, 1 Nov. 1977, CP, 2.2/48/14.
25. Jorden, *Panama Odyssey*, pp. 481, 504-09; Moffett, *Limits of Victory*, p. 91; Frank Moore memo, 13 Jan. 1978, re meeting with Howard Baker, WHCF, FO-18/FO 3-1, JEC Library; Beckel interview, 12 June 1979; Church to Cecil Calhoun, 2 Dec. 1977, CP, 2.2/49/7, and to Grant Hunter, 15 March 1978, 12/3/18; also Cleve Corlett interview, 26 June 1979, and Paul Sarbanes interview, 15 May 1987; *CR*, 10 Feb. 1978, p. 3213, re Church and the "Leadership Amendments." The actual wording of the Carter-Torrijos Understanding was the work of Linowitz and Romulo Escobar Bethancourt.
26. Interviews: Wetherell, 25 April 1984, and Sol Linowitz, 3 Aug. 1984; also Bethine Church, 3 Aug. 1984, and Dale Bumpers, 21 May 1987.
27. Linowitz interview, 3 Aug. 1984; Iowa senator Dick Clark later emphasized that Church had to take the lead, given his Senate position and principles. Clark interview, 30 July 1984.
28. John Sparkman to Church, 31 Jan. 1978, CP, 2.2/48/15; interviews: Linowitz, 3 Aug. 1984; Corlett, 7 Aug. 1984; and David McCullough, 7 Aug. 1984.
29. Jorden, *Panama Odyssey*, pp. 511-12; *New York Times*, 9 Feb. 1978, re Reagan.
30. Jorden, *Panama Odyssey*, pp. 512, 620 (qtn.); Frank Moore, et al., memo to Carter, 7 Feb. 1978, WHCF, FO-18/FO 3-1, and Moore to Carter, 1 Feb. 1978, WHCF, FO-15/FO 3-1, JEC Library.
31. "Opening the Great Canal Debate," p. 19, re Allen; *CR*, 10 Feb. 1978, p. 3211; also, Jorden, *Panama Odyssey*, pp. 511-26, 564-65.
32. Jorden, *Panama Odyssey*, pp. 511-26; Jordon qtns., pp. 520, 549.
33. Interviews: Garry Wenske, 22 March 1987; Wetherell, 15 July 1987 (evil); Patrick Shea, 15 Oct. 1988; Tom Dine, 6 Feb. 1988; Rick Raphael, 21 Jan. 1988; Michael Glennon to Ashby, 28 Aug. 1986 (cell).
34. *Phyllis Schlafly Report* (Nov. 1977), CP, 2.2/49/15; ACU ad, 12/3/18; Members Report, the Conservative Caucus (February 1978) and American Federation of Business Flyer (March 1978), 2.2/49/8; *Washington Post*, 18 April 1978, re Houston committee; *The Spotlight*, 20 Feb. 1978, 12/3/18; re the pennies, for example, 2.2/49/15.

35. See, for example, "Jim McClure Reports" re Panama, n. d., CP, 12/3/18; ACU ad in *Idaho Statesman*, 19 March 1978; George Hansen to "Dear Friend," n. d., but late 1977, Hamilton Jordan Papers, Box 50, JEC Library; *Spotlight* ad, 20 Feb. 1978, CP, 12/3/18.
36. Don Criddle to Church, 24 Feb. 1978, re the bumper sticker, CP, 2.2/49/1; clipping of Lester Clark letter to ed., *Post-Register*, n. d., 12/3/18; committees' ads in CP, 12/3/18; re the rally and petition, unidentified clippings, CP, 2.2/49/2.
37. Interviews: Corlett, 7 Aug. 1984; Fenn, 8 Aug. 1984.
38. Jorden, *Panama Odyssey*, pp. 487-90, 502-03; Church to Don Criddle, 14 March 1978, for example, CP, 2.2/49/1, and Church's March, 1978, "Washington Report," 12/3/18. See also copies of John Wayne to Editors, *Chicago Tribune*, 27 Jan. 1978, and Wayne's 13 Feb. 1978 statement, CP, 2.2/49/2. In his 1980 campaign Church again used photographs of himself with Wayne; "Frank Church on the Issues," 2.2/49/11.
39. Douglas J. Bennet, Jr. interview, 14 June 1979, and Jorden, *Panama Odyssey*, pp. 503-04, re the research team; Church to Louise Kerr, 10 April 1978, 12/3/18 (Church qtn.); Bethine Church interview, 3 Aug. 1984.
40. Interviews: Dale Bumpers, 21 May 1987, and George McGovern, 23 Dec. 1987; David McCullough, "Panama Diary," *Miami Herald*, 23 April 1978.
41. Church interview, 13 Aug. 1979, re book; McCullough, "Panama Diary"; McCullough interviews, 6 Feb. 1984 and 7 Aug. 1984.
42. Linowitz interview, 3 Aug. 1984; Moorer in Larry Engelmann, *Tears Before the Rain: An Oral History of the Fall of South Vietnam* (New York: Oxford University Press, 1990), pp. 153, 158; *CR*, 10 Feb. 1978, pp. 3210, 3212.
43. Bob Thomson and Bob Beckel to Frank Moore, 12 Dec. 1977, Hamilton Jordan Papers, Box 50, JEC Library; Jorden, *Panama Odyssey*, pp. 520, 537; Moffett, *Limits of Victory*, pp. 96-98. DeConcini's reservation, or "condition," as opposed to an amendment requiring formal approval of both signatory nations, was not legally binding but spelled out the U. S. understanding of the treaty. See LaFeber, *Panama Canal*, p. 178.
44. Jorden, *Panama Odyssey*, pp. 539-54, 560-62 (press and Jordon qtns, p. 560); Moffett, *Limits of Victory*, pp. 99-100, 104-05; Cyrus Vance, *Hard Choices: Critical Years in America's Foreign Policy* (New York: Simon & Schuster, 1983), p. 154; also Dennis DeConcini interview, 4 Aug. 1979.
45. Jorden, *Panama Odyssey*, pp. 551, 555-56, 561, 567, 572, 582 (Allen); also, Moffett, *Limits of Victory*, pp. 103-04, 106. For a contrary interpretation that Carter conducted a "virtuoso performance," see Skidmore, "Foreign Policy Interest Groups and Presidential Power," pp. 478, 486-90, 492-93.
46. Jorden, *Panama Odyssey*, pp. 559 (Reagan), 562, 566, 587 (DeConcini); Moffett, *Limits of Victory*, p. 102; Frank Moore, et al, to Carter, 20 March 1978, Hamilton Jordan Papers, Box 50, JEC Library; Karin Lissakers interview, 1 July 1992 (Church qtn.).
47. Jorden, *Panama Odyssey*, pp. 595 (qtn.), 598.
48. Agreement that Church typed, with brief, handwritten comments that he later added to it, explaining the nature of the meeting and who attended, CP, 2.2/49/2. Church mistakenly noted that the meeting occurred on 16 Oct. 1978. Also, Jorden, *Panama Odyssey*, pp. 591, 599-604. On Torrijos's respect for Church see, for example, copy of Omar Torrijos to Robert Byrd, 22 April 1978, CP, 12/3/18.
49. Bethine Church interview, 3 Aug. 1984, re qtn.

50. Bennet interview, 14 June 1979; Jorden, *Panama Odyssey*, pp. 613-16 – Byrd qtn., p. 613; Frank Moore, et al, to Carter, 20 March, 1978, Hamilton Jordan Papers, Box 50, JEC Library; Bennet, 14 June 1979, Beckel, 12 June 1979, and Deconcini, 4 Aug. 1979 interviews re Church's role; "How the Treaty Was Saved," *Time* (1 May 1978): 12, re talk.
51. Letters to Church from Warren Christopher and Dennis DeConcini, 19 April 1978; from Sol Linowitz, 18 April 1978; from Birch Bayh, n. d., CP, 2.2/49/2; and from William J. Jorden, 20 April 1978, 12/3/18; interviews: Linowitz, 3 Aug. 1984; McGovern, 23 Dec. 1987; Sarbanes, 21 June 1979; Bumpers, 21 May 1987; DeConcini, 4 Aug. 1979; Norvill Jones, 9 Aug. 1984 and 10 Sept. 1987; Pat Holt, 12 May 1987; Jerry Christianson, 22 May 1987; John Averill, 8 June 1979. *Idaho Statesman*, 19 April 1978. Unfortunately, events over the next decade and after suggested, as Walter LaFeber has shown, that "the 1978 treaties were less a break, a turn for the better, than they were a footnote to a ruthlessly continuing narrative." LaFeber, *Panama Canal*, pp. 188-215 (qtn., p. 213).
52. Bethine Church interview, 3 Aug. 1984; Congressional Scheduling Proposal, 20 April 1978, Church Name File, JEC Library; Jimmy Carter to Church, April 1978 CP, 12/3/18.
53. Chicago *Sun-Times*, 19 April 1978; Church interview, 13 Aug. 1979.
54. Don Chessman to Church, in *Lewiston Tribune*, 17 April 1978; Cameron Fuller to Church, n. d., but April 1978, CP, 12/3/18, re Post Falls; *Idaho Statesman*, 19 April 1978; unidentified clipping, c. 20 April 1978, CP, 2.2/49/3.
55. Interviews: Corlett, 7 Aug. 1984; Fenn, 8 Aug. 1984.
56. Moffett, *Limits of Victory*, pp. 108-37; Skidmore, "Foreign Policy Interest Groups and Presidential Power," pp. 480-83.
57. *CR*, 10 Feb. 1978, pp. 3210-11; Moffett, *Limits of Victory*, p. 133, re poll.
58. *CR*, 10 Feb. 1978, p. 3213; Moffett, *Limits of Victory*, pp. 132-33, re polls.
59. *CR*, 10 Feb. 1978, p. 3215, Church qtns.; Moffett, *Illusion of Victory*, pp. 133-34, 205, 212 (poll).
60. *CR*, 10 Feb. 1978, p. 3211-12, Church qtns.; Jorden, *Panama Odyssey*, pp. 623-26, re Torrijos, and p. 658, re Church.
61. *New York Times*, 27 Jan. 1978; *Baltimore Sun*, 15 May 1978.
62. Smith, *Morality, Reason and Power*, pp. 169-70; Seth P. Tillman, *The United States in the Middle East: Interests and Obstacles* (Bloomington: Indiana University Press, 1982), pp. 50-52, 98-100 (qtns.).
63. Church interview, 13 Aug. 1979; also, Church and Clifford Case to Dear Colleague, 15 May 1978, CP, 10.6/4/4; Neil MacNeil, "How a Deal Was Made – and Unmade," *Time* (29 May 1978): 14, re "insult."
64. Church interview, 13 Aug. 1979.
65. Jimmy Carter to Church, 12 May 1978, WHCF, Church Name File, JEC Library; Tillman, *The United States in the Middle East*, pp. 98-99, 103.
66. *Washington Post*, 17 May 1978; MacNeil, "How a Deal Was Made – and Unmade," pp. 14-15; Church interview, 13 June 1979.
67. *New York Times*, 24 May 1978; Church interview, 13 Aug. 1979; Church to Scott Rutherford, 31 May 1978, CP, 2.2/54/2; *Washington Post*, 17 May 1978, re influence.
68. *Washington Post*, 11 and 17 May 1978; MacNeil, "How a Deal Was Made – and Unmade," p. 15.
69. *New York Times*, 24 May 1978; Church and Clifford Case to Dear Colleague, 15 May 1978, CP, 10.6/4/4. According to the final deal, the Saudis received sixty

F-15s, the Israelis thirty-five F-15s and seventy-five F-16s, and the Egyptians fifty F-5Es. See "F-15 Fight: Who Won What?" *Time* (29 May 1978): 12-13. To block arms sales, both houses of Congress had to act. Following the Senate's favorable verdict, the House did not bother to vote. Smith, *Morality, Reason and Power,* pp. 171-72.

70. "The Fight Over Fighters," *Time* (22 May 1978): 17-18 (Carter qtn.); MacNeil, "How a Deal Was Made—and Unmade," pp. 15-16.
71. *New York Times*, 24 May 1978. McGovern and the arms package, U. S. Cong., Senate, *Action by the Congress on Certain Proposed Sales of Aircraft to Egypt, Israel, and Saudi Arabia*, Committee on Foreign Relations Report No. 95-806, 11 May 1978, pp. 5-6, CP, 10.4/4/4, and "Summary of May 11, 1978, meeting, U. S. Committee on Foreign Relations," CP, 10.6/4/5; re Church, McGovern interviews, 15 June 1979 and 23 Dec. 1987.
72. MacNeil, "How a Deal Was Made—And Unmade," p. 15; Zbigniew Brzezinski, *Power and Principle: Memoirs of the National Security Adviser, 1977-1981* (New York: Farrar, Straus, Giroux, 1983), p. 248; interviews: McGovern, 15 June 1979 and 23 Dec. 1987; Norvill Jones, 10 Sept. 1987; David Underhill, 10 Aug. 1989; and Bryce Nelson, 7 April 1993. Paul Findley, *They Dare to Speak Out: People and Institutions Confront Israel's Lobby* (Westport, Conn.: Lawrence Hill & Co., 1985), esp. pp. 27-32, discusses Dine.
73. Interviews: Church, 13 Aug. 1979; Jerry Levinson, 11 May 1987 (re Auschwitz); also Steve Emerson, 31 July 1984, and Bryce Nelson, 7 April 1993.
74. Interviews: Corlett, 22 May 1987; Church, 13 Aug. 1979; also, William Landau, 14 Aug. 1984.
75. Steven Emerson, *The American House of Saud: The Secret Petrodollar Connection* (New York: Franklin Watts, 1985), pp. 126, 133-38; Emerson interview, 31 July 1984; also, *New York Times*, 25 Dec. 1977.
76. *Washington Post*, 15 May 1978; Brzezinski, *Power and Principle*, p. 248.
77. Sarbanes interview, 15 May 1987; stenographic transcript of Hearings before the Senate Foreign Relations Committee, Executive Session, re the Middle East Arms Sales Proposals, 9 May 1978, CP, 12/3/18. Also Church to Cyrus R. Vance, 21 April 1978, and "Summary of May 3, 1978, SCFR Hearing," CP, 10.4.4/4; interviews: Corlett, 22 May 1987, and Fenn, 8 Aug. 1984.
78. Interviews: Beckel, 12 June 1979, and Bennet, 14 June 1979; re Moore, "Scrambling the Jets," *Newsweek* (22 May 1978): 18.
79. *Washington Post*, 17 May 1978; Frank Church, "Arms, Peace and the Mideast: The Logic of the Arms Sale," Baltimore *Sun*, 21 May 1978; aide qtd., *New York Times*, 19 April 1978. See also, "Church and State," *Time* (26 Feb. 1979): 17.
80. *New York Times*, 19 April 1978.
81. *Washington Star,* 8 June 1978.
82. Smith, *Morality, Reason and Power,* esp. pp. 8-9, 242; LaFeber, "From Confusion to Cold War," pp. 3-4, 6, 11-12; Rosati, "Jimmy Carter, a Man Before His Time?," pp. 461-69; Greider qtn., Moffett, *Limits of Victory,* p. 208.
83. Re Viguerie, "Canal Showdown," *Newsweek* (24 April 1978): 27.
84. Wetherell interview, 25 April 1984.

Notes for Chapter Nineteen

1. "William E. Borah" telegram to Frank Church, 22 Jan. 1979, with Church's handwritten comments, CP, 12/3/19.
2. Qtn., William Bader interview, 18 May 1987.

3. *New York Times*, 19 April 1978; transcript of 6 Dec. 1978 interview with UPI's Jim Anderson and Nick Daniloff, CP, 7.4/7/8; *Washington Post*, 31 Dec. 1979; *Idaho Statesman*, 12 Nov. 1978 (qtn. re interventionism).
4. *Philadelphia Inquirer*, 21 Sept. 1975, re Clark; *Richmond News Leader*, 20 Feb. 1979.
5. Interviews: Myrna Sasser, 20 March 1988, and Penny Gross, 11 Aug. 1984, for example, re frustrations of being chair; Ira Nordlicht to Church, 3 Nov. 1978, CP, 10.6/2/21—hereafter, Nordlicht memo—re Baker and Percy.
6. Carl Marcy to Fulbright, 1 Feb. 1973, Marcy Papers in Senate Foreign Relations Committee Papers, NA, Box 1972-73. Also, Bader interviews, 18 May 1987, 19 May 1993.
7. *New York Times*, 23 May 1979; interviews: Peter Fenn, 16 May 1987 (qtn.), Bader, 18 May 1987 and 8 June 1993, Hans Binnendijk, 4 Sept. 1987, Jerry Christianson, 22 May 1987, Rick Inderfurth, 9 Sept. 1993, Richard L. McCall, 21 Sept. 1993; re the mark-up, Ralph Earle, II interview, 20 March 1990. On Helms, see Ernest B. Furgurson, *Hard Right: The Rise of Jesse Helms* (New York: Norton, 1986), esp. pp. 13-18, 103-31.
8. Interviews: Carl Marcy, 11 June 1979, and Pat Holt, 12 May 1987; Donald Ritchie interview of Holt, 12 Dec. 1980, *The U. S. Senate Historical Office Oral History Collection: Interviews with Senate Staff* (Wilmington, Del.: Scholarly Resources, 1987), pp. 265-66. Also, "Church and State," *Time* (26 Feb. 1979): 17.
9. *New York Times*, 23 May 1979 (qtns.); Michael Glennon to Ashby, 28 Aug. 1986, and interviews: Patrick Shea, 15 Oct. 1988; Hans Binnendijk, 4 Sept. 1987; Norvill Jones, 10 Sept. 1987; William Bader, 18 May 1987.
10. Norvill Jones to Church, 7 Nov. 1978, CP, 2.2/3/5 re morale; Nordlicht memo; Bader interviews, 19 May and 8 June 1993. On Senate Resolution 60, see Harrison W. Fox, Jr. and Susan Webb Hammond, *Congressional Staffs: The Invisible Force in American Lawmaking* (New York: Free Press, 1977), pp. 13, 25, and Barbara Sinclair, *The Transformation of the U. S. Senate* (Baltimore: Johns Hopkins University Press, 1989), pp. 78-79.
11. On Bader's background and role in uncovering the Tonkin Gulf deceptions, Anthony Austin, *The President's War* (Philadelphia: J. B. Lippincott, 1971), esp. pp. 159-64, 168-80, 205-07; re his views of Church and the CFR, Bader interviews, 14 June 1979, 18 May 1987, 6 Feb. 1984, 9 June 1993. On Bader as a foreign policy intellectual, McCall interview, 21 Sept. 1993.
12. Opinions about Bader culled from several interviews, some anonymous, but including observations of Karin Lissakers, 1 July 1992, Steve Emerson, 20 May 1987, and Gross, 11 Aug. 1984; and Michael Glennon to Ashby, 28 Aug. 1987.
13. Transcript of Jack Anderson column, 4 March 1980, CP, 12/3/18; interviews: Earle, 20 March 1990, Paul Sarbanes, 15 May 1987, John Averill, 8 June 1979, and Inderfurth, 14 Sept. 1993. Richard McCall, who served on the CFR staff throughout the Seventies, believed that Bader was fair-minded and provided intellectual leadership without trying to "micro-manage" the staff. McCall interview, 21 Sept. 1993.
14. Interviews, several anonymous, but also Averill, 8 June 1979, Bader, 18 May 1987, Patrick Shea, 15 Oct. 1988, Steve Emerson, 20 May 1987; Mike Wetherell, 14 May 1979, and 15 July 1987; Ben Yamagata, 20 May 1987; Gross, 11 Aug. 1984.
15. Interviews: Shea, 15 Oct. 1988; Bader, 18 May 1987; George McGovern, 15 June 1979; *Idaho Statesman*, 25 Feb. 1980, re "massacres" and "mixed staff." Also, Glennon to Ashby, 28 Aug. 1987, re morale problems.

16. *Washington Post*, 9 Feb. 1979; "Church and State," *Time* (26 Feb. 1979): 17-18.
17. *New York Times*, 23 May 1979.
18. *Idaho Statesman*, 25 Feb. 1980.
19. Transcript of Anderson column, 4 March 1980, CP, 12/3/18; also Averill interview, 8 June 1979. Bader interviews, 14 June 1979, 29 July 1987, 8 June 1993; Church in *Idaho Statesman*, 25 Feb. 1980; re the more representative CFR, see also Robert Kaiser's assessment in *Washington Post*, 31 Dec. 1978. Also, McCall interview, 21 Sept. 1993.
20. Qtns. in "A Bold and Balky Congress," *Time* (23 Jan. 1978): 8-9.
21. Re "lifeblood," qtn. of Mel Morgan in Randy Stapilus, *Paradox Politics: People and Power in Idaho* (Boise: Ridenbaugh Press, 1988), pp. 234-35.
22. Ross K. Baker, *Friend and Foe in the U. S. Senate* (New York: Free Press, 1980), p. 158 (qtn.)-60; also Frank Church interview, 4 April 1983.
23. Leonard A. Kusnitz, *Public Opinion and Foreign Policy: America's China Policy, 1949-1979* (Westport, Conn.: Greenwood, 1984), p. 141, re polls.
24. Harry Harding, *A Fragile Relationship: The United States and China since 1972* (Washington, D. C.: The Brookings Institution, 1992), pp. 66-106, synthesizes the Carter administration's handling of the China issue, as does Gaddis Smith, *Morality, Reason and Power: American Diplomacy in the Carter Years* (New York: Hill & Wang, 1986), pp. 86-89; Michel Oksenberg to Zbigniew Brzezinski, 11 July 1977, WHSF, CO-15/CO34, JEC Library; Jimmy Carter, *Keeping Faith: Memoirs of a President* (New York: Bantam Books, 1982), pp. 187-88, 197. Harvey Feldman, "A New Kind of Relationship: Ten Years of the Taiwan Relations Act," in Ramon H. Myers, ed., *A Unique Relationship: The United States and the Republic of China Under the Taiwan Relations Act* (Stanford, Cal.: Hoover Institution Press, 1989), pp. 27-28, 46, re the bill.
25. "Dr. McBirnie's Newsletter," January, 1979, CP, 2.2/24/8; re the sign, Peter N. Carroll, *It Seemed Like Nothing Happened: The Tragedy and Promise of America in the 1970s* (New York: Holt, Rinehart & Winston, 1982), pp. 226-27; re Reagan, Smith, *Morality, Reason and Power*, p. 90, and Lou Cannon, *President Reagan: The Role of a Lifetime* (New York: Simon & Schuster, 1991), p. 343.
26. Church to Jennifer Wood, 9 June 1970, CP, 12/3/18, re "absurd"; Church press release, 15 Dec. 1978, 7.4/7/8, re Carter.
27. Kusnitz, *Public Opinion and Foreign Policy*, pp. 143-44, re polls and ACU; Edwin K. Snyder, A. James Gregor, and Maria Hsia Chang, *The Taiwan Relations Act and the Defense of the Republic of China* (Berkeley: Institute of International Studies, University of California, 1980), p. 14, and Robert G. Sutter, *The China Quandary: Domestic Determinants of U. S. China Policy, 1972-1982* (Boulder, Col.: Westview, 1983), pp. 76, 91, re the amendment; Richard M. Pious, "The Taiwan Relations Act: The Constitutional and Legal Context," in Louis W. Koenig, James C. Hsiung, and King-yuh Chang, eds., *Congress, The Presidency, and the Taiwan Relations Act* (New York: Praeger, 1985), pp. 150-51, re the suit.
28. Church press release, 5 Feb. 1979, CP, 7.4/7/10; re Taiwan, Church to Orrin Taysom, 23 Jan. 1979, 2.2/24/8, and to Monty J. Pearce, 15 Nov. 1978, 12/3/18; Larry LaRocco to Ira [Nordlicht], 21 Dec. 1978, CP, 2.2/24/7; Pat Harper to Church, 14 March 1978, with attached petition from the legislature, 2.2/24/6.
29. Cleve Corlett interview, 22 May 1987; U. S. Cong., Senate, Committee on Foreign Relations, *Taiwan*, Hearings, 5, 6, 7, 8, 21 and 22 Feb. 1979 (Washington D. C.: U. S. Govt. Printing Office, 1979); *Washington Post*, 22 Feb. 1979.
30. Interviews: Bader, 18 May 1987, Binnendijk, 4 Sept. 1987, and Norvill Jones, 10 Sept. 1987, re the alliance with Javits; qtns., Jacob Javits interview, 7 Feb. 1984.

31. Cleve Corlett to Ashby, 29 Jan. 1988; "Church and State," p. 18; Evans and Novak in *Washington Post*, 9 Feb. 1979.
32. *Washington Post*, 22 and 23 Feb. 1979. According to Michael Glennon, Lee Marks, the State Department's deputy legal advisor, hammered out most of the wording, but Bader credits Peter Lakeland. Glennon to Ashby, 28 Aug. 1986; Bader interview, 8 June 1993. See also John Felton, "New Status for Taiwan Voted by Senate Foreign Relations Committee," *Congressional Quarterly Weekly Report* (24 Feb. 1979): 346-47.
33. Bennet qtn. in *Washington Post*, 22 Feb. 1979.
34. Bader interview, 29 July 1987; Glennon to Ashby, 28 Aug. 1986; Jacob Javits, "Congress and Foreign Relations: The Taiwan Relations Act," *Foreign Affairs*, 60 (Fall 1981): 57; *New York Times*, 23 May 1979 (Church qtn.); Feldman, "A New Kind of Relationship," pp. 30-31, re Carter's advisors; Pious, "The Taiwan Relations Act," pp. 150-55, re the court case. On November 30, after a district court judge had ruled in favor of the plaintiffs, the U. S. Court of Appeals for the District of Columbia concluded that Carter could unilaterally abrogate the treaty. On December 13, the U.S. Supreme Court dismissed the case.
35. John K. Fairbank to Church, 14 Feb. 1979, CP, 2.2/24/9, responding to the emerging CFR drafts of the bill.
36. *New York Times*, 20 April 1979; Corlett interview, 7 Aug. 1984. William Ringle, a Gannett news reporter who was present, shared Corlett's impression of the meeting. Ringle interview, 8 June 1979.
37. Feldman, "A New Kind of Relationship," pp. 31-33; Ramon H. Myers, "A Unique Relationship," in Myers, ed., *A Unique Relationship*, p. 13; Premier Y. S. Sun to Church and S. K. Hu to Church, 2 April 1979, CP, 12/3/19; Corlett to Ashby, 29 Jan. 1988, re visitors.
38. Javits, "The Taiwan Relations Act," esp. pp. 54, 62; McGovern interview, 23 Dec. 1987. See also Cecil V. Crabb, Jr., "An Assertive Congress and the TRA: Policy Influences and Implications," in Koenig, Hsiung, and Chang, eds., *Congress, The Presidency, and The Taiwan Relations Act*, esp. pp. 96-102.
39. Church to Velma Morrison, 8 March 1979, CP, 2.2/54/5, and Emerson interview, 31 July 1984, re scheduling.
40. Church speech, "Return to Camp David," 1 Feb. 1979, CP, 7.4/7/8.
41. See, for example, columns of Nick Thimmesch, *The Arizona Republic*, 8 Feb. 1979; Charles Bartlett, *Seattle Times*, 7 Feb. 1979; Evans and Novak, *Washington Post*, 9 Feb. 1979; Carl T. Rowan, Spokane *Spokesman-Review*, 19 Feb. 1979; Ringle interview, 8 June 1979; Averill interview, 8 June 1979; "Church and State," p. 18.
42. Saudi paper quoted in *Los Angeles Times*, 5 Feb. 1979; Thimmesch in *The Arizona Republic*, 8 Feb. 1979; Bader interview, 29 July 1987.
43. Interviews: Frank Church, 13 Aug. 1979; Corlett, 7 Aug. 1984.
44. Steve Emerson, *The American House of Saud* (New York: Franklin Watts, 1985), pp. 127-28, 130, 135-43; also Lissakers interview, 1 July 1992.
45. Emerson, *The American House of Saud*, pp. 128, 144-47 (Vance, p. 145); "Saudi Oil Production Drop Seen," *Congressional Quarterly Weekly Report* (21 April 1979): 753; interviews: Emerson, 31 July 1984, and Bader, 8 June 1993; *Washington Post*, 12 Feb. 1979, re Sulaim. Voting to release the report were Paul Sarbanes and George McGovern; opposing the release were Delaware Democrat Joseph Biden and Javits, both from states in which the oil companies had enormous clout, and Indiana Republican Richard Lugar.

46. Comments of Loch Johnson at 12th Annual International Exchange Conference, Lewis-Clark State College, 7 Oct. 1992, re qtn.; *Lewiston Tribune*, 24 Sept. 1978.
47. *Lewiston Tribune*, 24 Sept. 1978; "The Yen To Make A Mark With the Dollar," 12 Dec. 1978 speech, CP, 7.7/2/5, and "The United States and the Developed Countries: The Rich vs. the Rich," 6 March 1979 speech, CP, 10.6/2/23.
48. Church, "Yen to Make a Mark"; *Lewiston Tribune*, 10 Jan. 1979; text of 1979 commencement address for various Idaho high schools, CP, 12/3/18; Church's 24 Feb. 1979 Jefferson-Jackson Day speech, 10.6/6/25; Church speech, "Between Two Decades: The Advance of Reason and the Unfinished Business of American Foreign Policy," 30 April 1979, 10.6/2/23.
49. "Yen to Make a Mark"; Jefferson-Jackson Day speech; "Between Two Decades"; Church speeches, "Terrorism: No Easy Answers," 2 March 1979, CP, 10.6/2/23, and "A Legislator's Perspective for the Turbulent Eighties," 23 June 1980, 12/3/19; Frank Church, "The Search for a Viable Foreign Economic Policy," *Northwestern Journal of International Law and Business*, I (1979): esp. p. 54.
50. "Church and State," p. 17; Lissakers interview, 1 July 1992.
51. During the 1992 presidential campaign, for example, America's eroded economic position was a major topic.
52. Interview, not for attribution, re Helms.
53. Glennon to Ashby, 28 Aug. 1987.
54. Bader interviews, 18 May 1987, 8 June 1993; also Inderfurth interview, 14 Sept. 1993.
55. Church, "A Legislator's Perspective for the Turbulent Eighties."
56. Interviews: Bader, 18 May 1987 and 8 June 1993; David Newsom, 10 Aug. 1984; Earle, 20 March 1990; Richard G. Lugar, *Letters to the President* (New York: Simon & Schuster, 1988), p. 60.
57. Bader, 18 May 1987, Emerson, 20 May 1987, Robert Pierpoint, 12 July 1993 (also re CIA), and Earle, 20 March 1990, interviews. Interior Secretary Cecil Andrus, on the other hand, thought Carter and Church got along well. Presidential aides Bob Beckel and Douglas Bennet believed that relations between the two men were somewhat problematic but, overall, positive. Interviews: Cecil Andrus, 8 June 1979; Beckel, 12 June 1979; Bennet, 14 June 1979. Re Berrellez, *New York Times* and *Washington Post*, 9 Feb. 1979.
58. Arthur Schlesinger, Jr., *The Imperial Presidency* (New York: Houghton Mifflin, 1973); Thomas M. Franck and Edward Weisband, *Foreign Policy By Congress* (New York: Oxford University Press, 1979), p. 9 (qtn.); polls in "A Bold and Balky Congress," *Time* (23 Jan. 1978): 8-9; Rowan in Spokane *Spokesman Review*, 19 Feb. 1979.
59. Alan Crawford, *Thunder on the Right: The "New Right" and the Politics of Resentment* (New York: Pantheon, 1980), esp. pp. 1-164; qtn., p. 145.
60. Crawford, *Thunder on the Right*, pp. 16-17, re NCPAC; Terry Dolan interview, 2 June 1980 (qtns.); *Idaho Statesman*, 26 Feb. 1979; "The New Right Takes Aim," *Time* (20 Aug. 1979): 20-21.
61. Flyer, "Frank Church's Record of Shame," CP, 2.2/5/19; "The New Right Takes Aim," p. 21.
62. *New York Times*, 27 Nov. 1978, re Right to Life; "The New Right Takes Aim," pp. 20-21.
63. "Running Scared," *Newsweek* (11 June 1979): 49.
64. John Gerassi, *The Boys of Boise* (New York: Macmillan, 1966), p. 65, re experts; anonymous qtn. re Idaho; *New York Times*, 27 Dec. 1979, re jacket; Robert Smylie interview, 27 Sept. 1979.

65. Jerry Levinson interviews, 2 Aug. 1984 and 11 May 1987; also Judith Miller interview, 10 Aug. 1992.
66. Mike Wetherell's handwritten "Memo to F. C.," n. d., but mid-1977, Mike Wetherell Papers, in Wetherell's possession. Wetherell wrote the memo by hand so that no other staffers could see it.
67. Peter D. Hart Research Associates, "A Survey of Voter Attitudes in the State of Idaho, July 1979," CP, 5.7/1—hereafter, Hart Survey—esp. pp. iii, 2, 9, 35, 54; Robert Smylie interview, 27 Sept. 1979; Byron Johnson interview, 14 March 1988, re "hostile."
68. Wetherell "Memo to F. C."
69. Hart Survey, pp. 40-42, 51, 68-72; Colby in *Washington Post*, 29 March 1979; "Running Scared," p. 49.
70. Jefferson-Jackson Day address, 24 Feb. 1979, CP, 10.6/6/25, re networks; *Washington Post*, 29 March 1979, re the spoof.
71. Church re changing political scene in *Philadelphia Inquirer*, 22 Jan. 1982; Church statement to Jim Boyd, 21 June 1979, CP, 7.4/7/12, and Church interview, 13 Aug. 1979, re Jordan and the GOP; re McClure, interviews with Myrna Sasser, 20 March 1988, Mike Wetherell, 23 Nov. 1987, Peter Fenn, 16 May 1987, Tommie Ward, 16 May 1987 (McClure, in turn, blamed Church's staff for some of the communications problems between the two senators—James McClure interview, 6 June 1980); re Hansen, "The New Right Takes Aim," p. 22; re Symms, Wetherell interview, 15 July 1987.
72. Church news release, 19 June 1979, CP, 7.4/7/12; *Idaho Statesman*, 5 Aug. 1979; Wetherell interview, 15 July 1987.
73. Church news releases, 5 March 1979, CP, 7.4/7/10; 1 and 30 Nov. 1979, 7.4/8/1; Lissakers interview, 1 July 1992. For criticism of Church, see *Forbes*, 18 Sept. 1978, p. 61; *Wall Street Journal*, 6 Oct. 1978; *New York Times*, 26 Feb. 1979.
74. Gottlieb in Mark K. Benenson, "Frank Church and the Politics of Guns," *Christian Science Monitor*, 9 April 1980; Dolan interview, 2 June 1980; Church news release, 29 Jan. 1980; *Blackfoot News*, 18 Oct. 1975, 7.10/4, re NRA; news release, 5 Sept. 1957; Carl Burke to National Rifle Association of America, 1 May 1980; Church to William W. Cowan, 12 March 1979, with foreword to Don Kates, ed., *Restricting Handguns*; script for Church film, 7 July 1967—all in 12/3/19. For a defense of Church's position, see Benenson, "Frank Church and the Politics of Guns."
75. *Washington Star*, 16 Oct. 1979; interviews: Leon Shull, 5 June 1980, and, also, Dick Clark, 30 July 1984.
76. Church's handwritten comments re "lie," CP, 12/3/19; copy of Church's guest opinion for the *Idaho Statesman*, 31 Jan. 1979, 7.4/7/8; Church newsletter (March 1979), 7.7/2/2; *Lewiston Tribune*, 21 June 1975. For a pro-choice critique of Church's position, see Sue Tenenbaum, "Liberals and Abortion: Talking Dirty in Congress," unidentified source, CP, 12/3/19.
77. "Interview with Frank Church," *Mountain Express*, 7 Aug. 1980, p. 18 (qtn. re conservative), CP, 10.1/1/43; Church to C. Y. Groseclose, 8 May 1979, 3.2.12/12/7, re prayer; Church newsletter, 30 Jan. 1980, 7.4./8/2, re draft; *CR*, 24 July 1979, p. 20324, and Christian Voice, "Congressional 'Report Card,' " for the 96th Congress, 1979, 12/3/19, re Wald (who was confirmed 77-21, with Church joining Helms, Strom Thurmond, and other conservatives in opposition); 27 March 1980 newsletter, 7.4/7/10, re week; Church to Mrs. Lee Garfield, 6 Aug. 1979, 2.2/5/19, re defense; news release, 3 Oct. 1980, 7.4/8/6.

78. *Lewiston Tribune*, 10 Jan. 1979, re "born-again"; Forrest Church interview, 25 July 1984. See, for example, Church to Willard Lacy, 7 May 1962, re Bible; to Thomas Hodgson, 29 June 1965, re prayer; to Ivan Rekow, 29 April 1966, re sex education and " 'smut,' " and 16 May 1969 news release re mails—all in CP, 12/3/19; James Barron and Marjorie Arons, "The Flexible Liberalism of Frank Church," *The Boston Phoenix* (18 Nov. 1975): 18, re death penalty.
79. See, for example, Frank Church interview, *Idaho Cities* (August 1978): 15-16; Church to The President, 4 April 1980, CP, 7.7/2/4. Re gasohol, for example, Church news release, 9 Nov. 1979, 7.4/8/1; re food programs and WIC, Church to Sister M. Geneva, 18 June 1980, 1.1/151/5. He also opposed efforts to reduce the Social Security cost-of-living increases; *CR*, 20 March 1980, p. 6097.
80. Stewart Udall interview, 11 June 1979; Hart Survey, pp. 77-78.
81. Church to Colleagues, 11 Feb. 1977; Church news release, 30 March 1977; Church and Morris Udall to Jimmy Carter, 25 March 1977, all in CP, 1.1/154/12.
82. Cleve Corlett interview, 26 June 1979, re the local situation. Charlie Creason, "The Gospel-Hump Controversy," Dec. 1977, unpublished University of Idaho Law School seminar paper, CP, 1.1/157/2, provides a useful overview.
83. Church newsletter, 6 April 1977, CP, 7.4/6/9; Diane Ronayne, "Frank Forrester Church," unidentified clipping, 10.1/1/16, and interviews, Corlett, 26 June 1979, and Fred Hutchinson, 6 Aug. 1984, re effigy.
84. Hutchinson interview, 6 Aug. 1984.
85. Scott qtn. in *Lewiston Tribune* clipping, n. d., CP, 12/3/19; Church news release, 13 July 1977, and copy of the Compromise Agreement, CP, 1.1/157/2; Morton Brigham to John Evans, 2 May 1977, 1.1/157/1; *CR*, 5 Aug. 1977, pp. 27546-49.
86. Church to Ernest Day, 8 Dec. 1977, and George Brumley, 17 Nov. 1977, CP, 1.1/153/12; Mark Hatfield interview, 6 Aug. 1984; Symms 4 August 1977 statement in Grangeville, copy in CP, 1.1/157/2.
87. Scott qtn. in *Lewiston Tribune* clipping, n. d., CP, 12/3/19; interviews: Hutchinson, 6 Aug. 1984, and Corlett, 26 June 1979.
88. Corlett interview, 7 Aug. 1984.
89. *CR*, 18 Jan. 1979, pp. 541-46; Michael Frome, "Idaho's Nature is Under Siege," *Los Angeles Times*, 29 April 1979.
90. Church's hand-corrected draft of a letter to "Dear Cece," n. d., but 1977, CP, 1.1/154/12, and Andrus interview, 8 June 1979, re the good relationship between the two men; Hutchinson interview, 6 Aug. 1984, re Church's philosophy and strategy; Ronayne, "Frank Forrester Church," re Abbey. See also reprint of Frank Church speech, early 1977, "Wilderness: The Challenge of Stewardship," CP, 1.1/153/6 (published as "Whither Wilderness?" *American Forests* (July 1977): 11-12, 38-41), and "An Interview on Wilderness with Senator Frank Church," *Western Wildlands* (Fall 1977): 2-5.
91. *Lewiston Tribune*, 9 Dec. 1979, re industry; Susan Frei to Church, 2 Oct. 1979, CP, 1.1/154/16; Jeff Seal to Church, 8 May 1979, 1.1/154/14; *Idaho Statesman*, 15 April 1984, re the cowboy.
92. Stapilus, *Paradox Politics*, pp. 44-49. For Church's dislike of the rebellion, see his speech, "Maintaining Idaho's Quality of Life," probably delivered 14 Oct. 1980 in Parma, Idaho, CP, 7.4/8/6.
93. Stapilus, *Paradox Politics*, p. 46 (qtn.).
94. Symms interview, 3 June 1980.
95. Church newsletter, January 1980, CP, 1.1/154/19; Church to Jerry Jayne, 17 Dec. 1979, 1.1/154/14; "Senate Votes to Create Huge New Wilderness Area in Central

Part of Idaho," *Congressional Quarterly Weekly Report* (1 Dec. 1979): 2709; *Idaho Statesman*, 2 July 1980; interviews: Symms, 3 June 1980; McClure, 6 June 1980; Hutchinson, 6 Aug 1984.

96. Lisa Myers, "A Sense of Macho Could be Changing U. S. Foreign Policy," unidentified clipping, probably 11 Nov. 1979, CP, 12/3/19.
97. Church, "SALT and the Senate: Principles of Decision," 10 May 1979 speech before the International Research and Exchanges Board, CP, 10.6/2/23; Bader interview, 29 July 1987. For "Highlights of SALT II Agreement," see *Congressional Quarterly Almanac* (1979): 413.
98. "The New Right Takes Aim," p. 21; Hart Survey, pp. 70-73.
99. Church qtn in "Running Scared," p. 49; Bader interviews, 18 May and 29 July 1987.
100. Earle interview, 20 March 1990.
101. Smith, *Morality, Reason and Power*, pp. 69-84; Warnke qtn., p. 83; Phillips qtn, "The New Right Takes Aim," p. 20.
102. Mondale in *Idaho Statesman*, 28 Oct. 1979; interviews: Bethine Church, 12 March 1985, and David Newsom, 10 Aug. 1984; Frank Church, "Carter on the Sinking of SALT: That's Not the Way I Remember It," *Washington Post*, 19 Nov. 1982. For important treatments of the brigade issue, see David D. Newsom, *The Soviet Brigade in Cuba* (Bloomington: Indiana University Press, 1987); Raymond L. Garthoff, *Detente and Confrontation: American-Soviet Relations from Nixon to Reagan* (Washington, D. C.: Brookings Institution, 1985), chap. 24; Gloria Duffy, "Crisis Mangling and the Cuban Brigade," *International Security* (Summer 1983): 67-87; Duffy, "Crisis Prevention in Cuba," in Alexander L. George, ed., *Managing U. S.-Soviet Rivalry* (Boulder, Col.: Westview Press, 1983): 285-318; William B. Bader, "The Making of a 'Non-Crisis': The Soviet Brigade," n. d., mss. in authors' possession.
103. Interviews; Newsom, 10 Aug. 1984; Cleve Corlett, 7 Aug. 1984; Peter Fenn, 16 May 1987; Newsom, *Soviet Brigade*, pp. 12-17, 20; Cyrus Vance, *Hard Choices: Critical Years in America's Foreign Policy* (New York: Simon & Schuster, 1983), p. 361; Bader, "Making of a Non-Crisis," pp. 6 ("plank" qtn.), 13.
104. Interviews: Bethine Church, 12 March 1985; Church, "Carter on the Sinking of SALT"; Vance, *Hard Choices*, p. 361.
105. *Idaho Statesman*, 31 Aug. 1979.
106. Earle interview, 20 March 1990; official qtd. in *Idaho Statesman*, 9 Sept. 1979; Burton I. Kaufman, *The Presidency of James Earl Carter, Jr.* (Lawrence: University Press of Kansas, 1993), pp. 155-56, re the administration's inconsistency.
107. *Idaho Statesman*, 6 Sept. 1979; Carter, *Keeping Faith*, p. 263; Garthoff, *Detente and Confrontation*, pp. 839-40, 844-45, 848, and Duffy, "Crisis Mangling," pp. 79-82, re Soviets; John Judis, "Church Move Threatens SALT," *In These Times* (19-25 Sept. 1979): 3 (State Dept. qtn.); Church, "Carter on the Sinking of Salt."
108. "World Events End Chances for SALT Approval," *Congressional Quarterly Almanac* (1979): esp. 427-28.
109. Newsom, *Soviet Brigade*, pp. 49-50.
110. "Dr. Strangelove Returns to Television," *Congressional Quarterly Almanac* (1979): 426; Smith, *Morality, Reason & Power*, p. 215, re Brzezinski.
111. Newsom, *Soviet Brigade*, pp. 51-52; Duffy, "Crisis Mangling," pp. 83-84; Earle interview, 20 March 1990.
112. Duffy, "Crisis Mangling," p. 68; Carter, *Keeping Faith*, pp. 262-63; Zbigniew Brzezinski, *Power and Principle: Memoirs of the National Security Advisor, 1977-1981* (New York: Farrar, Straus, Giroux, 1983), p. 347; McGrory in *Washington*

Post, 16 Oct. 1979; Royko clipping, 13 Sept. 1979, CP, 2.2/47/5; "Doonesbury" clipping, 12/3/19; "Reacting to the Right," *Christian Century* (3 Oct. 1979): 940; *Lewiston Tribune*, 23 Sept. 1979. Also, *New York Times*, 12 Sept. 1979. In retrospect, some reporters concluded resentfully that Church deliberately misled them for political purposes. "We were suckered," said James McCartney of the Knight-Ridder Newspapers. Leo Rennert of the McClatchy Newspapers agreed, noting that Church knew better than to make his Boise announcement: "He was chairman of the Foreign Relations Committee, privy to the CIA pipeline." Stephen Bates, ed., *The Media and the Congress* (Columbus, Ohio: Publishing Horizons, Inc., 1987), pp. 71-73.

113. Church news releases, 3 Sept. 1979, CP, 7.4/7/14, and 2 Nov. 1979, 7.4/8/1; transcript of 2 Oct. 1979 "Today Show," 7.4/7/15.
114. George McGovern interview, 23 Dec. 1987.
115. Interviews: Bethine Church, 12 March 1985, and Earle, 20 March 1990; F. Forrester Church, *Father and Son: A Personal Biography of Senator Frank Church of Idaho* (New York: Harper & Row, 1985), p. 141.
116. Harriman interview with Philip Geyelin, *Washington Post*, 15 Nov. 1981, blaming Church; Church to Harriman, 16 Nov. 1981, CP, 10.7/1/18; Church, "Carter on the Sinking of Salt"; Stansfield Turner, Foreword to Newsom, *Soviet Brigade*, pp. vii-xiii; Newsom, *Soviet Brigade*, esp. pp. 3-6, 20, 40, 44-46, 54-59; Garthoff, *Detente and Confrontation*, pp. 741 (re ratings), 829-32, 839 (re *Time*); Bader, "Making of a Non-Crisis," pp. 4, 6, 17-21, 27, 29, 32. On the White House disarray and the sixteen statesman, Kaufman, *The Presidency of James Earl Carter*, pp. 139-47, 156.
117. Church, "Carter on the Sinking of SALT"; *Idaho Statesman*, 3 Oct. 1979 (qtns. re minefield and linkage); Bader, "Making of a Non-Crisis," p. 3 (qtn. re Russians coming).
118. Newsom interview, 10 Aug. 1984, and Newsom, *Soviet Brigade*, pp. 55, 58; Duffy, "Crisis Mangling," pp. 77-78, 85-86; Bader, "Making of a Non-Crisis," p. 26.
119. Interviews: Peter Fenn, 16 May 1987; Bethine Church, 12 March 1985; Corlett, 7 Aug. 1984 and 22 May 1987; Penny Gross, 11 Aug. 1984; Garry Wenske, 7 Aug. 1984; Earle, 20 March 1990. David Newsom believed Church's defenders were "probably right" in saying that SALT II would not have passed without the brigade incident; Newsom interview, 10 Aug. 1984.
120. *Idaho Statesman*, 1 Sept. 1979 (qtns.); ABC Project news release, 25 April 1980, CP, 12/3/19.
121. *Idaho Statesman*, 1 Sept. 1979, re Church's complaints; Dolan in "The New Right Takes Aim," p. 21; transcript, ABC "World News Tonight," 13 Oct. 1980, CP, 12/3/19. Also, "Endangered Liberals," *Newsweek* (30 June 1980): 20-21.
122. Symms interview, 3 June 1980; Rod Gramer, "Steve Symms," *Idaho Statesman* election section, 20 July 1980, pp. 9-12.
123. Rod Gramer, "Idaho," *New Republic* (22 Oct. 1980): 17; Haynes Johnson, *Sleepwalking Through History: America in the Reagan Years* (New York: Norton, 1991), pp. 206-07; "Frank Church, A Moment Report," *MOMENT Magazine*, undated reprint, and draft of Church letter to constituents, n. d., both of which summed up some of the charges against Church; "Running" ad; Church to Patrick Leahy, 1 March 1981, re leafletting—all in CP, 12/3/19; Gramer, "Idaho," p. 17, re hotline.
124. Tape of Daniel Graham ad, authors' possession; Post Falls *Post-Register*, 21-22 Aug. 1980, re Singlaub and Korry; Loch Johnson, *A Season of Inquiry: The Senate Intelligence Investigation* (Lexington: University Press of Kentucky, 1985), p. 277.

125. Examples in CP, 12/3/19; interviews: Gross, 11 Aug. 1984, and Bethine Church, 3 Aug. 1984.
126. Stapilus, *Paradox Politics*, p. 218 (Burke qtn.); Corlett interview, 7 Aug. 1984; Fenn interview, 16 May 1987 (re balloons). Symms, Church, and the organizations supporting them divided up fairly evenly the $3.6 million in campaign expenditures. "This means that approximately $8.50 was spent for each of the 440,000 votes cast," according to Neil D. McFeeley and Robert H. Blank, "Idaho: A Conservative Republican Landslide," *The Social Science Journal*, 18 (Oct. 1981): 45.
127. Interviews: Carl Burke, 22 Nov. 1987, and Gross, 11 Aug. 1984; Stapilus, *Paradox Politics*, p. 213; authors' transcript of 16 Oct. 1980 Ricks College meeting.
128. Interviews: Carl Burke, 22 Nov. 1987; Gross, 11 Aug. 1984; Garry Wenske, 7 Aug. 1984; Fenn, 8 Aug. 1984, 16 May 1987.
129. Peter D. Hart, "A Survey of Voter Attitudes in the State of Idaho, September 1980," CP, 5.7/1—hereafter, Hart September Survey—esp. pp. 2-3, 6-8, 12, 14, 19-20, T-5; Ronald L. Hatzenbuehler, "Church and the Church: Frank Church, the Mormons, and Idaho Politics, 1956-1980" (1980), mss. in CP, 12/1/9.
130. Garthoff, *Detente and Confrontation*, p. 741, re Carter approval rating; Gramer, "Idaho," p. 16, re economy; Hart September Survey, pp. 11 (qtn.), 28.
131. Post Falls *Post-Register*, 21 Aug. 1984, re Korry. Worried that fast-breaking events in the Middle East jeopardized U. S. security, Church conceded that military strikes might be necessary to protect the nation's vital interests in the Saudi oil fields. He warned, however, that such action must be collective and include other economically and politically threatened countries. (*New York Times*, 2 Dec. 1979; Church to Jimmy Carter, 7 Feb. 1980, CP, 2.2/54/7.) Although he agreed with Carter that the Soviets should suffer at least some form of economic punishment for invading Afghanistan, he objected to the wheat embargo against the U. S. S. R. as unfair to American farmers: "If it serves the *national* interest to invoke the 'food weapon' against the Soviet Union, then the *nation*, as a whole, should bear the burden." To avoid heaping a disproportionate burden upon American farmers, Church urged the government to purchase the embargoed wheat for a gasohol program. "Here again," he complained, "the administration declines to take the lead." (Frank Church, "Let Justice Be Done," 16 Jan. 1980 speech, CP, 10.6/6/26.) Regarding Iran, he endorsed Carter's strategy of caution, diplomacy, and economic sanctions (not buying Iranian oil, for example) rather than military action. But, in April 1980, as Carter spoke increasingly of a military response, Church and Jacob Javits surprised the administration with a written reminder that the War Powers Act required presidential consultation with Congress. After the failed airborne rescue effort of the hostages on April 24, Church said that Carter, by not consulting in advance with Congress, had violated the act. (*New York Times*, 13 Nov. 1979; 25, 26 April 1980.)
132. Hart September Survey, p. 10; Gramer, "Idaho," p. 16 (Church qtn.).
133. Hart September Survey, pp. 2-3; Fenn interview, 16 May 1987.
134. McFeeley and Blank, "Idaho: A Conservative Republican Landslide," pp. 41-50; William Landau interview, 14 Aug. 1984, re Church's reaction; also Bader interview, 8 June 1993. Ronald L. Hatzenbuehler and Bert W. Marley, "Why Church Lost: A Preliminary Analysis of the Church-Symms Election of 1980," *Pacific Historical Review*, 56 (Feb. 1987): 99-112, emphasize the voting turnout and take issue with interpretations that Church owed his defeat to conservatism, Reagan's coattails, and Carter's early announcement. They trace the shift in votes

away from Church in the southeastern Idaho counties and argue that issues such as the Panama Canal had taken on huge symbolic value at the local level.

135. *Idaho Statesman*, 9 Nov. 1980.

Notes for Epilogue

1. Qtn., F. Forrester Church, *Father and Son: A Personal Biography of Senator Frank Church of Idaho* (New York: Harper & Row, 1985), p. 152, re geraniums; Bethine Church to Jim Ater, 21 March 1981, CP, 10.7/1/11.
2. William Landau interview, 14 Aug. 1984; Irwin B. Arieff, "Former Legislators Find Private Practice Rewarding," *Legal Times* (17 Jan. 1983): pp. 12-13.
3. Penny Gross interview, 11 Aug. 1984; Bethine Church to Jim Ater, 21 March 1981, CP, 10.7/1/11; and Frank Church to Ray Rigby, 16 Feb. 1981, 12/3/20, re his practice; Church to Ruth Flower, 9 Sept. 1981; Church to James Pearson, 4 May 1983 (re Center for Responsive Politics); and McGovern to Church, 3 Feb. 1982 (re Common Sense)–all in 12/3/20; Church to Drury Brown, 23 April 1982, 10.7/1/12; *Idaho Statesman*, 15 April 1984, re income.
4. Landau interview, 14 Aug. 1984.
5. Qtn., Arieff, "Former Legislators," p. 12; Church, *Father and Son*, pp. 162-63; Landau interview, 14 Aug. 1984.
6. Church to Drury Brown, 23 April 1982, CP, 10.7/1/12, and to Mark Adams, 7 Sept. 1982, 10.7/1/11; *Philadelphia Inquirer*, 22 Jan. 1982 (qtn.).
7. Church to Mark Ancel, 1 March 1982, CP, 10.7/1/11.
8. Church to Drury Brown, 23 April 1982, CP, 10.7/1/12, re "dangerous world"; Church to Alfred Gross, 11 June 1981, 12/3/20; Sonja Gilligan to Church, 30 March 1981, and Church reply, 9 April 1981, 10.7/1/17; Church to Sen. Patrick Leahy, 1 March 1981, 12/3/19; Church to Rabbi Alexander Schindler, 23 Jan. 1981, 12/3/20. See also Church statement re Jerry Falwell, n. d., 12/3/20.
9. See, for example, the two letters, n. d., that the Democratic Party sent out over Church's signature, and Church to Clareene [Wharry], 13 Aug. 1981 (qtn.), CP, 12/3/20.
10. Church to Eugene Jurs, 31 Aug. 1982, 12/3/20, re Weinberger and Reagan; Church to Sen. Robert Byrd, 22 July 1981, CP, 10.7/1/12; *Idaho Statesman*, 3 Sept. 1981; Frank Church, "America's New Foreign Policy," *New York Times Magazine* (23 Aug. 1981): 30-31, 65-66.
11. UPI release, 29 Oct. 1983, CP, 12/3/20; *New York Times*, 6 Oct. 1981, and UPI story by Ira Allen, 26 Nov. 1981, in CP, 12/3/20, re the proposals; Church's statement to the 12 Nov. 1981 Subcommittee on Civil and Constitutional Rights, CP, 10.7/1/6; *Washington Post*, 13 Nov. 1981; Goldwater qtn. in Rhodri Jeffreys-Jones, *The CIA and American Democracy* (New Haven, Conn.: Yale University Press, 1989), p. 232. Church's concerns about the CIA were not misplaced. Several years later the Iran/Contra scandal broke, revealing attempts by William Casey's CIA to mislead Congress, conduct secret wars, and raise funds for "off-the-shelf" covert operations that contravened the law. Also, the *New York Times* disclosed in 1993 that "The Central Intelligence Agency created an intelligence service in Haiti in the mid-1980s to fight the cocaine trade, but the unit evolved into an instrument of political terror whose officers at times engaged in drug trafficking." Spokane *Spokesman-Review,* 14 Nov. 1993.

12. Frank Church, "Do We Still Plot Murders? Who Will Believe We Don't?," *Los Angeles Times*, 14 June 1983; Frank Church speech, "Covert Intervention: Contradiction with Democratic Principles," 27 May 1982, CP, 12/3/20; Church, "America's New Foreign Policy," p. 31, re Marines; *Washington Post*, 22 Jan. 1984, re Broder.
13. Lou Cannon, *President Reagan: The Role of a Lifetime* (New York: Simon & Schuster, 1991), pp. 445-49, and UPI release, 29 Oct. 1983, CP, 12/3/20, for Church qtn.
14. Gross interview, 11 Aug. 1984; Jimmy Carter, *Keeping Faith: Memoirs of a President* (New York: Bantam Books, 1982), pp. 262-63; Robert Kaiser, "Wasn't Carter the President Who Said He'd Never Lie to Us?," *Washington Post*, 7 Nov. 1982, which is a scathing review of the book; Church, "Carter on the Sinking of SALT: That's Not the Way I Remember It," *Washington Post*, 19 Nov. 1982.
15. Gross interview, 11 Aug. 1984.
16. Interviews: Garry Wenske, 7 Aug. 1984; Stan Burns, 16 March 1988; Gross, 11 Aug. 1984.
17. *Idaho Statesman*, 15 April 1984, re the speech and reaction.
18. Church speech, "Domestic Constraints on American Foreign Policy," 17 Nov. 1983, CP, 12/3/20.
19. Gross interview, 11 Aug. 1984; *Idaho Statesman*, 11 Jan. 1984; Church, *Father and Son*, p. 154.
20. Church, *Father and Son*, p. 156.
21. Gross interview, 11 Aug. 1984; Church, *Father and Son*, pp. 156, 162, 169; *Idaho Statesman*, 22 Jan. 1984; Church to Paul Marx, 7 Feb. 1984, CP, 12/3/20 (qtn.).
22. Interviews: Gross; Steve Emerson, 31 July 1984; John Hechinger, 8 Aug. 1984 (qtn. re thinking); Church to Ward and Phyl Hower, 19 March 1984; to Wendy Morgan, 28 March 1984, CP, 12/3/20.
23. Church, *Father and Son*, p. 169; Church to Wendy Morgan, 28 March 1984; Bethine to Loey, 14 March 1984; and to Joane, 14 March, 1984, and Church to John Silkin, 17 Feb. 1984, CP, 12/3/20.
24. Forrest Church interview, 25 July 1984; also, Church, *Father and Son*, p. 172.
25. Richard Church interview, 5 Aug. 1984; *CR*, 1 March 1984, pp. 4049-50, re wilderness.
26. *Idaho Statesman*, 22 Jan. and 8 April 1984; Church, *Father and Son*, pp. 169, 171-72; interviews: Landau, 14 Aug. 1984, Gross, 11 Aug. 1984, and Marilyn Bickle, 17 March 1988.
27. Interviews: Gross, 11 Aug. 1984, Emerson, 31 July 1984, and Bethine Church, 23 June 1993; *Father and Son*, pp. 172, 174; *Idaho Statesman*, 8 April 1984; Church to Scott Read, 14 March 1984, and to Pete and Marge Gertonson, 20 March 1984, CP, 12/3/20.
28. Pike column in Twin Falls *Times-News*, 12 April 1984.
29. Church, *Father and Son*, pp. 163, 172 (Kennedy qtn.).
30. Church to John Silkin, 17 Feb. 1984, CP, 12/3/20; interviews: Stan Burns, 16 March 1988; Bickle, 17 March 1988; Gross, 11 Aug. 1984.
31. *Lewiston Tribune*, 12 April 1984.
32. Church, *Father and Son*, p. 179; *Idaho Statesman*, 13 April 1984 (woman's qtn.).

Bibliographical Note

Essay

Primary Sources:

Manuscript collections were crucial to this study, and are listed individually on the pages following. The huge collection of Frank Church Papers (Boise State University) is incredibly rich. It includes a wide range of materials, including personal correspondence, staff memos, notes that he wrote when he was touring Africa in 1960 and Southeast Asia in 1962, constituent mail, government documents, and drafts of speeches. Church had a strong sense of history. He kept all kinds of documents, and on several occasions he added diary-like comments to his files. Prime examples of his eagerness to document the historical record are evident in 1965 in a lengthy transcript regarding his recent troubles with Lyndon Johnson, and in several efforts in 1972 to keep a diary. A massive number of radio and video materials also constitute the Church collection. The Church Papers are well-indexed and very accessible.

Bethine Church has a small, quite useful collection of papers at Boise State University. She also has in her private possession dozens of exceptional letters that Frank Church wrote to her and his family from roughly 1942 to 1946. This study benefitted enormously from her willingness to share those letters with the authors.

The Carl Burke Papers (Boise State University) are particularly good regarding Church's campaigns, but contain a few other items as well. Frank Moss's lengthy, typed diaries of his trips with Church to Africa and Southeast Asia (Former Members of Congress Oral History Project, Library of Congress) are quite thorough. William G. Miller's Papers (privately held) are insightful regarding the Foreign Relations Committee during the late Sixties and early Seventies. Also illuminating re the Foreign Relations Committee are the papers of Carl

Marcy (National Archives). The John F. Kennedy Library (Boston) and the Lyndon Baines Johnson Library (Austin, Texas) contain large amounts of invaluable material on subjects such as Southeast Asia and civil rights. Although the Richard Nixon Presidential Project (National Archives, Washington, D. C.) has been under a kind of legal siege for years, it yielded some extremely good materials regarding, for example, Southeast Asia and the Nixon administration's relationships with Congress. The Gerald R. Ford Library (Ann Arbor, Michigan) contains a few items on the multinationals and intelligence investigations. The Hubert Humphrey Papers (Minnesota Historical Society) are quite good generally, but seem less so regarding Humphrey's vice presidential years. On civil rights, the papers of the National Association for the Advancement of Colored People and the Leadership Conference on Civil Rights (Library of Congress) are crucial. The Len Jordan Papers (Boise State University) reflect the good relations between Jordan and Church and have useful items on the Snake River moratorium and Sawtooth/White Clouds issues.

Several collections were disappointing. Because the Jimmy Carter Papers (Jimmy Carter Library, Atlanta) were still being processed, the records of the administration's congressional liaison office, and much of the 1976 campaign, were not yet available. The Robert F. Kennedy Papers (JFK Library) contain virtually nothing that illuminates the key issues of the day; they consist mainly of letters to Kennedy from constituents. The microfilm collection of newspaper articles in the Robert Kennedy Papers is more useful regarding, for example, the McClellan Committee. The Eugene McCarthy Papers (Minnesota Historical Society) and George Smathers Papers (University of Florida) are surprisingly thin in substance. So too are the Warren Magnuson Papers (University of Washington) because, for now, all political correspondence is closed. The Henry Jackson Papers have been culled of presumably important documents, although they unexpectedly contained several illuminating CIA memos regarding Church's investigations of the CIA, ITT, and Chile.

The CIA file on Church, which *Idaho Statesman* reporter Charles Etlinger obtained through the Freedom of Information Act and shared with the authors, is useful primarily as an excellent clipping file on Church during the ITT and intelligence investigations. The thinner FBI file is less important, but includes information about investigations of several threats on Church's life.

Vital Senate documents for this study included *Executive Sessions of the Senate Foreign Relations Committee*, 88th Cong., 2d Sess, 1964 (1988), and 89th Cong., lst Sess., 1965 (1990); *Hearings Before the Committee on Multinational Corporations* (1973-76), 13 vols.; and *Final Report of the Select Committee to Study Governmental Operations with Respect to Intelligence Activities* (1976), 6 vols.

Among newspapers, the *New York Times* and *Washington Post* are essential, partly because of their extensive indexes. The *Idaho Statesman* is basic on Idaho politics and benefitted, for many years, from the astute political writings of John Corlett, but also see the *Lewiston Tribune*.

Published memoirs are too often disappointing about their subjects and the times. Exceptions include Glen H. Taylor, *The Way It Was With Me* (Secaucus, N. J.: Lyle Stuart, 1979), as colorful and idiosyncratic as the man himself; Richard Nixon, *RN: The Memoirs of Richard Nixon* (New York: Grosset & Dunlap, 1978); George McGovern, *Grassroots: The Autobiography of George McGovern* (New York: Random House, 1977), and Paul H. Douglas, *In the Fullness of Time: The Memoirs of Paul H. Douglas* (New York: Harcourt Brace Jovanovich, 1971, 1972). Gary Hart, *The Good Fight: The Education of an American Reformer* (New York: Random House, 1993), is one of the more thoughtful Senate autobiographies. A lengthy unpublished manuscript, Bill Hall's "DC and Me," n.d., is a humorous, informative account by Church's press secretary in the mid-1970s.

Secondary Sources

On Frank Church, F. Forrester Church, *Father and Son: A Personal Biography of Senator Frank Church of Idaho* (New York: Harper & Row, 1985), is a sensitive, readable sketch, as well as a thoughtful meditation on life and death. Loch K. Johnson, a political scientist and former Church staffer, provides a useful analysis of Church, "Operational Codes and the Prediction of Leadership Behavior; Senator Frank Church at Midcareer," in Margaret G. Hermann and Thomas W. Milburn, eds., *A Psychological Examination of Political Leaders* (New York: Free Press, 1977), pp. 80-119. Carol Payne and Margaret Carpenter, "Frank Church, Democratic Senator from Idaho," in *Ralph Nader Congress Project* (New York: Grossman, 1972), n. p., is informative, especially regarding contemporary assessments of Church. For additional assessments of important aspects of Church's career, see Russell M. Tremayne, "Delusions and Reality: The Evolution of Frank Church's Ideas on U. S.-Latin American Policy, 1956-1980" (Ph.D. dissertation, University of Washington, 1990); Ronald L. Hatzenbuehler, "Church and the Church: Frank Church, the Mormons, and Idaho Politics, 1956-1980" (6 Oct. 1990), mss. in Church Papers; Hatzenbuehler and Bert W. Marley, "Why Church Lost: A Preliminary Analysis of the Church-Symms Election of 1980," *Pacific Historical Review*, 56 (Feb. 1987): 99-112; Gustaf Brock, " 'The Doves Have Won': Senator Frank Church and the Vietnam War" (M. A. thesis, University of Nebraska, 1989), and Susan M. Stacy, "Frank Church and the Termination Policy" (2 Dec. 1989), mss. in Church Papers.

An excellent overview of post-World War II American history is William Chafe, *The Unfinished Journey: America Since World War II* (2d ed., New York: Oxford University Press, 1991). Godfrey Hodgson, *America in Our Time: From World War II to Nixon* (New York: Random House, 1976), is first-rate. Michael Barone, *Our Country: The Shaping of America from Roosevelt to Reagan* (New York: Free Press, 1990), is packed with information on recent politics. Frederick F. Siegel, *Troubled Journey: From Pearl Harbor to Ronald Reagan* (New York: Hill & Wang, 1984) is a briefer, insightful analysis. Other leading studies of recent political trends in the U. S. include especially E. J. Dionne, *Why Americans Hate Politics* (New York: Simon & Schuster, 1991); Thomas Byrne Edsall with Mary D. Edsall, *Chain Reaction: The Impact of Race, Rights, and Taxes on American Politics* (New York: Norton, 1990, 1991); William E. Leuchtenburg, *In the Shadow of FDR: From Harry Truman to Ronald Reagan* (Ithaca, N. Y.: Cornell University Press, 1983), and Alonzo L. Hamby, *Liberalism and Its Challengers: From F.D.R. to Bush* (2nd ed., New York: Oxford University Press, 1992). Thomas G. Paterson, *Meeting the Communist Threat: Truman to Reagan* (New York: Oxford University Press, 1988) contains readable, insightful essays regarding foreign policy. Randy Stapilus, *Paradox Politics: People and Power in Idaho* (Boise: Ridenbaugh Press, 1988), a rich journalistic account, is superb on recent Idaho politics. More general views of Idaho history are in F. Ross Peterson, *Idaho: A Bicentennial History* (New York: Norton, 1976), and Carlos Schwantes, *In Mountain Shadows: A History of Idaho* (Lincoln: University of Nebraska Press, 1991). On Boise, see Merle Wells, *Boise: An Illustrated History* (Woodland Hills, Cal.: Windsor Publications, 1982). See, too, the fine sketches in Robert C. Sims and Hope A. Benedict, eds.,

Idaho's Governors: Historical Essays on Their Administrations (Boise, Ida.: Boise State University, 1992), especially those by Howard Berger on Len Jordan, Hope Benedict on Robert Smylie, Katherine G. Aiken on Don Samuelson, Stephen Shaw on Cecil Andrus, and Keith C. Petersen on John Evans.

Particularly good on issues with which Church wrestled during his first terms are Robert A. Divine, *Blowing on the Wind: The Nuclear Test Ban Debate, 1954-1960* (New York: Oxford University Press, 1968); Steven F. Lawson, *Black Ballots: Voting Rights in the South, 1944-1969* (New York: Columbia University Press, 1976); Steven F. Lawson, *Running for Freedom: Civil Rights and Black Politics in America Since 1941* (New York: McGraw-Hill, 1991), which includes an excellent bibliographical essay; Charles and Barbara Whalen, *The Longest Debate: A Legislative History of the 1964 Civil Rights Act* (paperback ed., New York: New American Library, 1986), a fascinating dissection of the making of a major law; and Michael R. Beschloss, *The Crisis Years: Kennedy and Khrushchev, 1960-1963* (New York: HarperCollins, 1991), the most thorough recent treatment of Kennedy's foreign policy, especially concerning the Berlin and Cuban missile crises. Rowland Evans and Robert Novak, *Lyndon B. Johnson: The Exercise of Power* (New York: New American Library, 1966), has considerable information on a number of subjects, including the fight over the 1957 Civil Rights Act.

A huge and rapidly expanding literature exists on Vietnam. Substantial histories include Stanley Karnow, *Vietnam: A History* (New York: Viking Press, 1983), and David Halbertstam's classic *The Best and the Brightest* (New York: Random House, 1972). Briefer but still insightful are George Herring, *America's Longest War: The United States and Vietnam, 1950-1975* (New York: Knopf, 1986); James S. Olson and Randy Roberts, *Where the Domino Fell: America and Vietnam, 1945-1990* (New York: St. Martin's Press, 1991), and David W. Levy, *The Debate over Vietnam* (Baltimore: Johns Hopkins University Press, 1991), all of which have fine bibliographies. Marilyn B. Young, *The Vietnam Wars, 1945-1990* (New York: HarperCollins, 1991), is a particularly commendable recent study. Larry Berman, *Planning a Tragedy: The Americanization of the War in Vietnam* (New York: Norton, 1982) and *Lyndon Johnson's War* (New York: Norton, 1989), and Brian VanDeMark, *Into the Quagmire: Lyndon Johnson and the Escalation of the Vietnam War* (New York: Oxford University Press, 1991), show how Lyndon Johnson wrestled with the war. Neil Sheehan's prize-winning *A Bright Shining Lie: John*

Paul Vann and America in Vietnam (New York: Random House, 1988), is a searing portrait. See also Doris Kearns, *Lyndon Johnson and the American Dream* (New York: Harper & Row, 1976).

An indispensable work in progress on the Senate and Vietnam is that of William C. Gibbons, *The U. S. Government and the Vietnam War* (Washington, D. C.: Congressional Research Service, Library of Congress) Part I: 1945-1960 (1984), Part II: 1961-1964 (1986), and Part III: January-July 1965 (1989). Princeton University Press has reprinted each volume. Prepared for the Senate Foreign Relations Committee, heavily documented, and based on formidable research, including many interviews, this multi-volume study is invaluable on its subject. William C. Berman, *William Fulbright and the Vietnam War* (Kent, Ohio: Kent State University Press, 1988), and Walter Zelman, "Senate Dissent and the Vietnam War, 1964-1968" (Ph.D. diss., University of California, Los Angeles, 1971) are quite useful regarding the Senate, as are Arthur M. Schlesinger's prize-winning *Robert Kennedy and His Times* (Boston: Houghton Mifflin, 1978), Gilbert C. Fite, *Richard B. Russell, Jr., Senator from Georgia* (Chapel Hill: University of North Carolina Press, 1991), and Richard A. Baker, *Conservation Politics: The Senate Career of Clinton P. Anderson* (Albuquerque: University of New Mexico Press, 1985). Gustaf J. Brock, " 'Congress Must Draw the Line': Frank Church and the Cooper-Church Amendment of 1970," *Idaho Yesterdays*, 35 (Summer 1991): 27-36, is a good sketch.

On the antiwar movement, see Nancy Zaroulis and Gerald Sullivan, *Who Spoke Up? American Protest against the War in Vietnam, 1963-1975* (New York: Holt, Rinehart & Winston, 1984), and Charles DeBenedetti with Charles Chatfield, *An American Ordeal: The Antiwar Movement of the Vietnam Era* (Syracuse: Syracuse University Press, 1990). Both are full, readable discussions. Melvin Small, *Johnson, Nixon, and the Doves* (New Brunswick, N. J.: Rutgers University Press, 1988) examines the impact of the antiwar movement on the Johnson and Nixon administrations.

Basic for understanding the domestic aspects of the 1960s are Allen J. Matusow, *The Unraveling of America: A History of Liberalism in the 1960s* (New York: Harper & Row, 1984), and Garry Wills, *Nixon Agonistes: The Crisis of the Self-Made Man* (New York: Houghton Mifflin, 1970). Todd Gitlin, *The Sixties: Years of Hope, Days of Rage* (New York: Bantam, 1987), and James Miller's *"Democracy is in the Streets" From Port Huron to the Siege of Chicago* (New York: Simon &

Schuster, 1987) are superior histories of the "movement" side of the era. Both works explore with insight and sensitivity the nuances and texture of a complex subject. On the political and social divisions that marked the end of the Sixties, see also Irwin Unger and Debi Unger, *Turning Point: 1968* (New York: Charles Scribner's Sons, 1988), and Charles Kaiser, *1968 in America* (New York: Weidenfeld & Nicolson, 1988).

Stephen E. Ambrose, *Nixon: The Triumph of a Politician, 1962-1972* (New York: Simon and Schuster, 1989), is admirable on Nixon's first term. Essential regarding Nixon's foreign policy are Roger Morris, *Uncertain Greatness: Henry Kissinger and American Foreign Policy* (New York: Harper & Row, 1977); Seymour M. Hersh, *The Price of Power: Kissinger in the Nixon White House* (New York: Summit Books, 1983); Walter Isaacson, *Kissinger: A Biography* (New York: Simon & Schuster, 1992); and William Shawcross, *Sideshow: Kissinger, Nixon and the Destruction of Cambodia* (New York: Simon & Schuster, 1979). Other basic treatments of the Nixon years include Jonathan Schell, *The Time of Illusion* (New York: Knopf, 1976); J. Anthony Lukas, *Nightmare: The Underside of the Nixon Years* (New York: Viking, 1976); and Stanley I. Kutler, *The Wars of Watergate: The Last Crisis of Richard Nixon* (New York: Knopf, 1990).

On the multinationals issue, John J. Reardon, *America and the Multinational Corporation: The History of a Troubled Partnership* (Westport, Conn.: Praeger, 1992), is an extremely helpful scholarly overview that makes clear the importance of Church's subcommittee. Other starting points are Anthony Sampson, *The Sovereign State: The Secret History of ITT* (New York: Stein & Day, 1973) and *The Arms Bazaar: From Lebanon to Lockheed* (New York: Viking Press, 1977); David Boulton, *The Grease Machine* (New York: Harper & Row, 1978); and Robert Sherrill, *The Oil Follies of 1970-1980* (New York: Doubleday, 1983)—but, unfortunately, they include few notes. Ovid Demaris, *Dirty Business: The Corporate-Political Money-Power Game* (New York: Harper's Magazine Press, 1974), contains more documentation. Steve Emerson's readable *The American House of Saud: The Secret Petrodollar Connection* (New York: Franklin Watts, 1985), combines the talents of award-winning investigative journalism with Emerson's inside views as a Church staffer. John T. Noonan, *Bribes* (New York: Macmillan, 1984), is a sweeping historical study with a thoughtful chapter, "The Ambassadors of America," on the multinationals' scandals of the 1970s. On the oil industry, see Daniel Yergin's justifiably acclaimed *The Prize: The*

Epic Quest for Money, Oil and Power (New York: Simon & Schuster, 1991). Jonathan Kwitny, *Endless Enemies: The Making of an Unfriendly World* (New York: Congdon & Weed, 1984), is a powerful indictment of U. S. business and covert actions abroad.

Regarding the intelligence committee, Loch Johnson, *A Season of Inquiry: The Senate Intelligence Investigation* (Lexington: The University Press of Kentucky, 1985), provides a political scientist's insights as well as an insider's perspective. Johnson's book is fair-minded and informative. Frank J. Smist, Jr., *Congress Oversees the United States Intelligence Community, 1947-1989* (Knoxville: University of Tennessee Press, 1990), uses interviews to excellent advantage in a fine, lengthy chapter on the Church committee. See also Smist's "Seeking a Piece of the Action: Congress and Its Intelligence Investigation of 1975-1976," in Bernard J. Firestone and Alexej Ugrinsky, eds., *Gerald R. Ford and the Politics of Post-Watergate America*, Vol. II (Westport, Conn.: Greenwood Press, 1993), pp. 463-89, plus the responses of discussants William Colby, Michael Raoul-Duval, James A. Wilderotter, Lucien N. Nedzi, and Bob Woodward, pp. 490-501. Gary Hart, *The Good Fight: The Education of an American Reformer* (New York: Random House, 1993), contains a brief, chilling chapter on the intelligence investigation. Paterson's *Meeting the Communist Threat* includes an overview of "The Clandestine Response: The CIA, Covert Actions, and Congressional Oversight."

For important background information on the CIA, see especially John Ranelegh, *The Agency: The Rise and Decline of the CIA* (New York: Simon & Schuster, 1986, 1987), which is thorough and balanced, and Thomas Powers's illuminating and thoughtful *The Man Who Kept the Secrets: Richard Helms and the CIA* (New York: Knopf, 1979). Also helpful are John Prados, *Presidents' Secret Wars: CIA and Pentagon Covert Operations from World War II through Iranscam* (New York: William Morrow, 1986), and Rhodri Jeffreys-Jones, *The CIA and American Democracy* (New Haven, Conn.: Yale University Press, 1989).

Notable examinations of Congress and foreign policy are Cecil V. Crabb, Jr., and Pat M. Holt, *Invitation to Struggle: Congress, the President and Foreign Policy*, 2d ed. (Washington, D. C.: Congressional Quarterly Press, 1984); Thomas W. Franck and Edward Weisband, *Foreign Policy by Congress* (New York: Oxford University Press, 1979); and John Rourke, *Congress and the Presidency in U.S. Foreign Policymaking* (Boulder, Col.: Westview Press, 1983).

Literature on the Senate is substantial, but see George E. Reedy, *The U. S. Senate: Paralysis or a Search for Consensus?* (New York: Crown, 1986); Michael Foley, *The New Senate: Liberal Influence on a Conservative Institution, 1959-1972* (New Haven, Conn.: Yale University Press, 1980); Barbara Sinclair, *The Transformation of the U. S. Senate* (Baltimore: Johns Hopkins University Press, 1989); Ross K. Baker, *Friend and Foe in the U. S. Senate* (New York: Free Press, 1980), a shrewd assessment by a former Church staffer; and Bernard Asbell, *The Senate Nobody Knows* (Baltimore: Johns Hopkins University Press, 1978), a fine case study that focuses on Maine senator Edmund Muskie and the changing legislative climate in the mid-Seventies regarding the Clean Air Act. Eric Redman, *The Dance of Legislation* (New York: Simon & Schuster, 1973), is a classic examination of the legislative process (specifically surrounding passage of the National Health Service Corps Act of 1970) during the year of the Cambodian invasion. J. McIver Weatherford, *Tribes on the Hill* (New York: Rawson, Wade, 1981), is a fascinating anthropological analysis of the Senate, including a provocative sketch of Church as a senator who had "the trappings of a Big Man" but nevertheless lacked power. The best guide to the history and literature of the National Emergencies Act is Harold C. Relyea, "Reconsidering the National Emergencies Act: Its Evolution, Implementation, and Deficiencies," in R. Gordon Hoxie, ed., *The Presidency and National Security Policy* (New York: Center for the Study of the Presidency, 1984). *Congressional Quarterly Weekly Report* and *National Journal Reports* are indispensable guides to the activities on Capitol Hill.

A good overview of the Seventies is Peter N. Carroll, *It Seemed Like Nothing Happened: The Tragedy and Promise of America in the 1970s* (New York: Holt, Rinehart & Winston, 1982). Steven M. Gillon, *The Democrats' Dilemma: Walter F. Mondale and the Liberal Legacy* (New York: Columbia University Press, 1992), is helpful on many issues, including Democratic politics in the 1970s and the Carter years. On the Carter administration, Haynes Johnson's critical early study, *In the Absence of Power* (New York: Viking Press, 1980), is readable and perceptive. A more recent scholarly synthesis that also judges Carter a mediocre president is Burton I. Kaufman's excellent *The Presidency of James Earl Carter, Jr.* (Lawrence: University Press of Kansas, 1993), which includes a fine bibliographical essay. Gaddis Smith, *Morality, Reason and Power: American Diplomacy in the Carter Years* (New York: Hill & Wang, 1986), astutely probes Carter's foreign policy, but see also Walter LaFeber's illuminating essay, "From Confusion to Cold War: The Memoirs of the Carter Administration," *Diplomatic History,* 8 (Winter 1984): 1-12, and Jerel A. Rosati's thoughtful article, "Jimmy Carter, a Man Before His Time? The Emergence and Collapse of the First Post-Cold War Presidency," *Presidential Studies Quarterly,* 23 (Summer 1993): 459-76. Gary W. Reichard, "Early Returns: Assessing Jimmy Carter," *Presidential Studies Quarterly,* 20 (Summer 1990): 603-20, and Edward R. Kantowicz, "Reminiscences of a Fated Presidency," *Presidential Studies Quarterly,* 16 (Fall 1986): 651-65, offer additional guides to themes and recent interpretations of the Carter years.

Studies that contain insights into Carter's relationships with Congress are Charles O. Jones, *The Trusteeship Presidency: Jimmy Carter and the United States Congress* (Baton Rouge, La.: Louisiana State University Press, 1988); Erwin C. Hargrove's less critical *Jimmy Carter as President: Leadership and the Politics of the Public Good* (Baton Rouge, La.: Louisiana State University Press, 1988); and Garland A. Haas, *Jimmy Carter and the Politics of Frustration* (Jefferson, N. C.: McFarland & Co., 1992).

William J. Jorden's splendid *Panama Odyssey* (Austin: University of Texas Press, 1984), provides the perspectives of America's ambassador to Panama. Significant treatments of their subjects are George D. Moffett III, *The Limits of Victory: The Ratification of the Panama Canal Treaties* (Ithaca, NY: Cornell University Press, 1985); Michael Hogan, *The Panama Canal in American Politics: Domestic Advocacy and the Evolution of Policy* (Carbondale, Ill.: Southern Illinois University Press, 1986); Walter LaFeber, *The Panama Canal: The Crisis in Historical Perspective* (updated ed., New York: Oxford University Press, 1989); Robert A. Strong, "Jimmy Carter and the Panama Canal Treaties," *Presidential Studies Quarterly,* 21 (Spring 1991): 269-86, a good summary; David Skidmore, "Foreign Policy Interest Groups and Presidential Power: Jimmy Carter and the Battle over Ratification of the Panama Canal Treaties," *Presidential Studies Quarterly,* 23 (Summer 1993): 477-97, a sympathetic treatment of Carter's performance; David D. Newsom, *The Soviet Brigade in Cuba: A Study in Political Diplomacy* (Bloomington: Indiana University Press, 1987); and Harry Harding, *A Fragile Relationship: The United States and China since 1972* (Washington, D. C.: Brookings Institution, 1992). Raymond L. Garthoff, *Detente and Confrontation: American-Soviet Relations from Nixon to Reagan*

(Washington, D. C.: Brookings Institution, 1985), is a major study with a fine chapter on the Soviet brigade issue. Also insightful on the brigade are Gloria Duffy, "Crisis Mangling and the Cuban Brigade," *International Security* (Summer 1983): 67-87, and "Crisis Prevention in Cuba," in Alexander L. George, ed., *Managing U. S. Soviet Rivalry* (Boulder, Col.: Westview Press, 1983), pp. 285-318. William B. Bader's unpublished essay, "The Making of a 'Non-Crisis': The Soviet Brigade," n. d., in Bader's possession, benefits from interviews and his perspectives at the time as director of the Senate Foreign Relations Committee staff.

Manuscript Collections

Anderson, Clinton (Library of Congress).
Church, Bethine (Boise State University).
Church, Bethine (Private).
Church, Frank (Boise State University).
Burke, Carl (Boise State University).
Carter, Jimmy (Jimmy Carter Library, Atlanta).
Democratic-Farmer-Labor State Central Committee Records (Minnesota Historical Society, St. Paul).
Democratic National Committee (JFK Library, Boston).
Dine, Tom (Private).
Ford, Gerald R. (Ford Presidential Library, Ann Arbor, Michigan), including files of Philip W. Buchen, James M. Cannon, Richard Cheney, James E. Connor, Arthur Fletcher, Max L. Friedersdorf, William T. Kendall, Roderick Hills, John O. Marsh, Stephen G. McConahey, Rogers C. B. Morton, Ron Nessen, Arthur F. Quern, Michael Raoul-Duval, William Timmons, Robert Wolthuis
Harrison, Gilbert (Library of Congress).
Humphrey, Hubert (Minnesota Historical Society, St. Paul).
Jackson, Henry (University of Washington).
Johnson, Lyndon B. (LBJ Library, Austin, Texas), including papers of Mike Manatos, Bill Moyers, and George Reedy.
Jordan, Hamilton (Jimmy Carter Library, Atlanta).
Jordan, Len (Boise State University).
Kennedy, John F. (JFK Library, Boston), including papers of Samuel Beer, Congressional Liaison Office (Lawrence F. O'Brien, Claude Desautels, Mike Manatos), Roger Hilsman, Frank Mankiewicz, Theodore Sorenson, and James C. Thomson, Jr.
Kennedy, Robert F. (JFK Library, Boston).
Leadership Conference on Civil Rights (Library of Congress).
McCarthy, Eugene (Minnesota Historical Society, St. Paul).
Magnuson, Warren (University of Washington).
Marcy, Carl (National Archives, Washington, D. C.).
Miller, William G. (Private).
Nixon, Richard M. (Nixon Presidential Materials Project, National Archives), including files of Dwight Chapin, H. R. Haldeman, John Dean, III, Charles Colson, Patrick Buchanan, John Ehrlichman.

National Association for the Advancement of Colored People (Library of Congress).
O'Mahoney, Joseph (University of Wyoming, Laramie).
Pearson, Drew (LBJ Library, Austin, Texas).
Smathers, George (University of Florida, Gainesville, Florida).
U. S. Senate Foreign Relations Committee (National Archives, Washington, D. C.).
Wetherell, Mike (Private).

Oral History Interviews

Anderson, Clinton (LBJ Library).
Bayley, Edwin R. (JFK Library).
Bell, David (JFK Library).
Bowles, Chester (JFK Library).
Carver, John A., Jr. (JFK Library).
Church, Frank, Congressional Research Service interview by William C. Gibbons (copy in Gibbons's possession).
Church, Frank (JFK Library).
Church, Frank (LBJ Library).
Clark, Joseph (JFK Library).
Clark, Joseph (Former Members of Congress Oral History, Library of Congress).
Dutton, Frederick (LBJ Library).
Gruening, Ernest (LBJ Library).
Humphrey, Hubert H. (LBJ Library).
McGee, Gale (LBJ Library).
McGovern, George (JFK Library).
McGovern, George (LBJ Library).
Moss, Frank E. (LBJ Library).
Nelson, Bryce, Congressional Research Service interview by William Gibbons and Patricia McAdams (copy in Gibbons's possession).
Pell, Claiborne (LBJ Library).
Proxmire, William (LBJ Library).
Sparkman, John (LBJ Library).
Udall, Stewart (JFK Library).
U.S. Senate Historical Office Oral History Collection: Interviews with Senate Staff (Wilmington, Del.: Scholarly Resources, 1987), especially the interviews with Pat Holt and Carl Marcy.

Unpublished Manuscripts, Miscellaneous

Bader, William B., "The Making of a 'Non-Crisis': The Soviet Brigade," unpublished mss., n. d., (authors' possession).
Central Intelligence Agency file on Frank Church (in possession of Charles Etlinger, *Idaho Statesman*, Boise).
Clem, Alan, printouts of Professor Clem's correlations of Frank Church's voting record, 1966-77 (in Clem's possession, University of South Dakota).
Federal Bureau of Investigation File on Frank Church (in possession of Charles Etlinger, *Idaho Statesman*, Boise).
Hall, Bill, "D.C. and Me," unpublished mss., n. d. (authors' possession).
Herring, George C., "The Executive, Congress, and the Vietnam War, 1965-1975," unpublished mss., n. d. (authors' possession).
Moss, Frank E., Diaries of Senate trips to Africa (1960) and Southeast Asia (1962), in Former Members of Congress Oral History Project (Library of Congress).

Nelson, Bryce, Banquet Speech for Idaho Press Club, 20 April 1985 (authors' possession).
Shea, Patrick A., "Politics, the Intelligence Community and Religion," speech at the Western Region-Catholic Press Association, 28 Oct. 1988 (authors' possession).

Correspondence

Ross K. Baker to Ashby, 30 July 1986.
Carl Burke to Ashby, 5 Aug. 1986.
R. M. Chastain to Ashby, 25 Feb. 1987.
Richard Church to Ashby, 28 Feb. 1987 and 18 Aug. 1988.
Cleve Corlett to Ashby, 29 Jan. 1988.
Tom Dine to Ashby, 12 Feb. 1988.
J. William Fulbright to Ashby, 1 July 1986.
Michael J. Glennon to Ashby, 28 Aug. 1986.
Morella R. Hansen to Ashby, 16 Oct. and 12 Nov. 1987.
Daniel K. Inouye to Ashby, 23 July 1986.
Edward M. Kennedy to Ashby, 11 July 1986.
Mike Mansfield to Gramer, 25 May 1979.
Claiborne Pell to Ashby, 15 July 1986.
Neal Parsell to Ashby, 1 May 1988.
Rick Raphael to Ashby, 22 Jan. 1988.
George Reedy to Ashby, 13, 26 Jan. 1987.
Arthur Schlesinger, Jr., to Ashby, 17 Feb. 1987.
Patrick A. Shea to Ashby, 2 Nov. 1988.
George Sundborg to Ashby, 17 Aug. 1988.
Perry Swisher to Ashby, 31 Dec. 1987.
David Underhill to Ashby, 5 Sept. 1989.
Garry Wenske to Ashby, 27 June 1986.

Interviews

Ahrens, Steve. 26 April 1979.
Anderson, Jack. 6 Aug. 1984.
Andrus, Cecil. 8 June 1979.
Ashworth, George. 14 June 1979.
Averill, John. 8 June 1979.
Bader, William B. 14 June 1979; 6 Feb. 1984 (phone); 18 May 1987; 29 July 1987 (phone); 19 May 1993 (phone); 8 June 1993 (phone).
Barnes, Verda. 8 June 1979.
Baxter, Marge. 1 May 1984.
Baxter, Jim. 25 April 1984.
Bayh, Birch. 5 June 1980; 14 May 1987.
Beckel, Bob. 12 June 1979.
Bennet, Douglas J., Jr. 14 June 1979.
Bickle, Marilyn. 17 March 1988.
Biden, Joseph. 5 June 1980.
Binnendijk, Hans. 4 Sept. 1987 (phone).
Blum, Jack. 10 Aug. 1984.
Brady, Jerry. 27 June 1979; 7 Nov. 1987 (phone).
Buchen, Philip W. 30 July 1984.
Bumpers, Dale. 21 May 1987.

Bundy, McGeorge. 23 July 1984.
Burdick, Quentin. 18 May 1987.
Burke, Carl. 6 Jan 1979; 27 Feb. 1979; 23 May 1979; 14 May 1980; 8 Aug. 1980; 12, 18 Dec. 1985; 24 May 1986; 22 Nov. 1987.
Burns, Stan. 22 March 1979; 29 Jan. 1984; 24 April 1984; 16 March 1988.
Carver, John A., Jr. 27 Oct. 1979; 30 June 1987 (phone); 23 July 1989.
Case, Clifford. 18 June 1979.
Chenoweth, Helen. 11 May 1979.
Christianson, Jerry. 22 May 1987.
Church, Bethine. 13, 22 June 1979; 24 July 1979; 9 June 1980; 3 Aug. 1984; 28 Oct. 1984; 12 May 1985; 10 June 1986; 25 Jan. 1989; 23 June 1993.
Church, Chase. 10 Aug. 1984.
Church, F. Forrester. 27 Aug. 1979; 25 July 1984.
Church, Frank. 10 Jan. 1979; 13 Feb. 1979; 12, 14, 18, 24 June 1979; 13 Aug. 1979; 30 Oct. 1980; 4 April 1983; 24 Oct. 1983.
Church, Richard. 5 Aug. 1984; 28 May 1987 (phone).
Clark, Dick. 30 July 1984.
Clark, Lynda. 30 Sept. 1988.
Colby, William. 20 June 1979; 19 May 1987.
Cooper, John Sherman. 4 Aug. 1984.
Corlett, Cleve. 26 June 1979; 7 Aug. 1984; 22 May 1987.
Corlett, John. 10 Dec. 1978; 2 Feb. 1979; 14 May 1979; 25 July 1979; 15 March 1988.
Cranston, Alan. 1 Aug. 1984.
Culver, John. 15 May 1987.
Day, Ernie. 8 Feb. 1984 (phone).
Day, Sam. 4 Oct. 1987 (phone).
D'Easeum, Dick. 30 April 1984.
DeConcini, Dennis. 4 Aug. 1979.
Destler, I. M. 12 June 1979.
Dieter, Alice. 22 Dec. 1987 (phone).
Dine, Tom. 14 June 1979; 6 Feb. 1988 (phone).
Dolan, Terry. 2 June 1980.
Earle, Ralph II. 20 March 1990.
Emerson, Steven. 31 July 1984; 20 May 1987.
Fatemi, Fariborz. 15 May 1987.
Fenn, Peter. 8 Aug. 1984; 16 May 1987.
Finney, John. 9 Sept. 1987 (phone).
Fulbright, J. William. 11 June 1979.
Gabusi, John. 7 June 1979.
Garn, Jake. 5 June 1980.
Gibbons, William C. 13 May 1987.
Goodell, Charles. 30 July 1984.
Gross, Hal. 11 Aug. 1984.
Gross, Penny. 11 Aug. 1984.
Hall, Bill. 8 April 1979; 7 Aug. 1986; 14 July 1989 (phone).
Halverson, Harmon. 5 Sept. 1984.
Hamilton, Barbara. 23 April 1984.
Hansen, Orval. 2 Aug. 1984.
Hart, Gary. 5 June 1980.
Hatfield, Mark. 6 Aug. 1984.

Hechinger, John. 8 Aug. 1984.
Helms, Richard. 2 Aug. 1984.
Hills, Roderick M. 10 Aug. 1984.
Hilsman, Roger. 6 Feb. 1984.
Holt, Pat. 12 May 1987.
Hower, Phyllis. 11 April 1987.
Hower, Ward. 11 April 1987.
Huse, Esther. 23 April 1984.
Hutchinson, Fred. 6 Aug. 1984.
Inderfurth, Rick. 9 Sept. 1993 (phone).
Javits, Jacob. 7 Feb. 1984 (phone).
Jensen, Dwight. 7 Nov. 1987.
Johnson, Byron. 14 March 1988.
Jones, Norvill. 9 Aug. 1984; 10 Sept. 1987 (phone).
Kimelman, Henry. 24 Jan. 1992 (phone).
Klein, George. 9 June 1979.
Knoll, Erwin. 3 Nov. 1987 (phone).
Landau, William. 14 Aug. 1984.
Lardner, George. 20 April 1979.
Levinson, Jerry. 2 Aug. 1984; 11 and 23 May 1987.
Linowitz, Sol. 3 Aug. 1984.
Lissakers, Karin. 1 July 1992 (phone).
Lowenstein, James G. 30 July 1980; 2 Nov. 1987 (phone).
McCall, Richard L. 21 Sept. 1993 (phone).
McCarthy, Eugene. 22 March 1990.
McClure, James. 6 June 1980.
McCullough, David. 6 Feb. 1984 (phone); 7 Aug. 1984.
McGee, Gale. 6 March 1988.
McGovern, George. 15 June 1979; 23 Dec. 1987 (phone).
McGrory, Mary. 8 Aug. 1984.
McLaughlin, Robert. 12 Sept. 1979.
McNichol, Ray. 1 June 1979.
McPherson, Harry. 6 Aug. 1984.
Mathias, Charles. 1 Aug. 1984.
Marcy, Carl. 11 June 1979; 18 May 1987.
Mileck, Gene. 7 April 1979.
Miller, Judith. 10 Aug. 1992 (phone).
Miller, William G. 15 June 1979; 27 July 1984; 23, 24, 28, 29 Dec. 1987 (phone).
Morrissey, David M. 17 Nov. 1987 (phone).
Moss, Frank E. 11 May 1987.
Munson, Joanna. 5 Feb. 1988 (phone).
Muskie, Edmund. 19 May 1987.
Nelson, Bryce. 1 Feb. 1987; 28 July 1987; 22 March 1993 (phone); 7 April 1993 (phone).
Nelson, Dale. 1 March 1988 (phone).
Nelson, Gaylord. 3 Aug. 1984; 21 May 1987.
Newsom, David. 10 Aug. 1984.
Oppenheimer, Arthur. 14 May 1979.
Oriol, Pat. 19 May 1987.
Oriol, William. 19 May 1987.
Pell, Claiborne. 19 May 1987.

Peterson, Martin. 2 April 1985.
Pierpoint, Robert. 12 July 1993 (phone).
Raphael, Rick. 21 Jan. 1988 (phone).
Reberger, Phil. 5 Aug. 1980.
Ringle, William. 8 June 1979 (phone).
Sarbanes, Paul. 21 June 1979; 15 May 1987.
Sasser, Myrna. 19 March 1988.
Schwarz, Frederick A. O., Jr. 13 Aug. 1984.
Shea, Patrick A. 15 Oct. 1988 (phone).
Schlesinger, Arthur, Jr. 4 June 1979.
Shull, Leon. 5 June 1980.
Sisco, Joseph. 7 Aug. 1984.
Smylie, Robert. 27 Sept. 1979.
Spofford, Tom. 30 April 1984.
Sundborg, George. 19 Sept. 1988 (phone).
Symms, Steve. 3 June 1980.
Tacke, Jack. 9 Aug. 1984.
Tames, George. 14 Sept. 1993 (phone).
Todd, Don. 17, 31 July 1980.
Udall, Morris. 8 June 1979.
Udall, Stewart. 11 June 1979.
Underhill, David. 10 Aug. 1989.
Ward, Tommie. 6 Aug. 1984; 16 May 1987.
Watkins, Don. 4 April 1979.
Wenske, Garry. 7 Aug. 1984; 22 March 1987.
Wetherell, Mike. 14 May 1979; 25 April 1984; 15 July 1987; 23 Nov. 1987.
Wicker, Tom. 1 April 1979.
Wright, Michael. 10 Aug. 1984.
Yamagata, Ben. 20 May 1987.
Yarborough, Ralph. 19 March 1987.

Acknowledgements

THIS BOOK BEGAN to take shape in the fall of 1978 during an interview that Gramer conducted for the *Idaho Statesman* with Senator Frank Church. Although Church had by then been in the Senate for some twenty-two years, his life and career had received little in-depth attention. Gramer decided to write a biography and turned to his friend and fellow journalist, Marc Johnson, for assistance. In 1980, a year after they had commenced research and interviews on the project, the *Idaho Statesman* assigned Gramer to cover the Senate campaign between Church and Idaho Representative Steve Symms. Following Church's defeat, Gramer and Johnson stopped work on the biography. In 1983 Gramer resumed the project, this time alone.

A year later Ashby commenced his own biography of the senator. When Gramer and Ashby continued to cross paths, they decided in 1988 to join forces, assuming that a collaborative effort would help to produce a better and more complete book. In a sense their decision mirrored an important theme in Church's life: the senator's faith in cooperative ventures, evident in his alliances with such people as John Sherman Cooper, Clifford Case, and Charles Mathias. Gramer and Ashby assumed that each could bring special strengths to the project—Gramer as a journalist who had covered Idaho politics for years as well as the latter stages of Church's career, and Ashby as a historian with a particular interest in twentieth-century American society and politics.

The authors owe a huge debt of gratitude to many individuals, but will have to settle for recognizing only a few. The exceptionally pleasant and cordial people at Boise State University who have worked closely with the Frank Church Papers, especially project director Ralph W. Hansen, head of special collections Alan Virta, and Leslie Pass and Mary Carter, deserve special thanks. Numerous other archivists shared their time and expertise at the presidential libraries of John Kennedy, Lyndon Johnson, Gerald Ford, and Jimmy Carter, the Richard Nixon

Presidential Materials Project, the Federal Archives, the Library of Congress, the Minnesota State Historical Society, the University of Washington, and the University of Wyoming. At Washington State University Lou Vyhnanck was particularly helpful.

Carl Burke, William Miller, Tom Dine, and Mike Wetherell kindly opened their private papers to the authors. Bill Hall made available the manuscript of his witty, informative memoir, "DC and Me," which is particularly illuminating regarding Church's 1976 presidential campaign. Other Church staffers, Cleve Corlett and Bryce Nelson, provided the authors with materials and considerable time. Journalist Charles Etlinger shared the FBI and CIA files regarding Frank Church that he had acquired through the Freedom of Information Act, and Professor Alan Clem of the University of South Dakota provided printouts of his correlations of Church's voting record, 1966-77.

Although this biography is in no sense "official" or "authorized," the authors owe much to Bethine Church. She has been open and honest, giving considerable time for interviews, sharing the many letters that Frank Church wrote to her and his family in the 1940s, and providing access to her private collection of photographs. Forrest and Chase Church were extremely helpful and, like their mother, made no effort to influence interpretations or cover up information.

Individuals who read all or parts of the manuscript include historians Robert H. Zieger of the University of Florida and Professor Emeritus Sam Merrill, University of Maryland; economist John Donnelly of Washington State University, and Sara Donnelly; former Church aides Bill Miller, Bryce Nelson, and William Bader; and two reviewers for the Washington State University Press, Robert Sims of Boise State University and Ron Hatzenbuehler of Idaho State University. The book has benefitted substantially from their useful suggestions and critiques.

The authors are also indebted to nearly 150 individuals who granted interviews, sometimes on several occasions. These individuals were invariably sensitive about lapsed memories and the difficulties of recollecting events. "That is the best that I can either remember or imagine it," David Underhill laughed as he struggled to recall a particular incident. Some individuals refused to grant interviews, however, and the authors regret not being able to draw upon their perspectives and knowledge.

Several exceedingly generous people shared their hospitality with the authors. Former Idaho Congressman Ralph Harding opened his home to the Gramers during their 1984 research trip to Washington, D. C.; Sam and Marion Merrill, as they have done so many times, provided the Ashbys with good company as well as a place to stay during research journeys to the same area. When the Gramers were researching in New York City, Mike Merrill made his apartment available. The importance of the Senate Historical Office to researchers continues to be abundantly evident, thanks to the dedication and talents of Dick Baker and Don Ritchie.

At Washington State University, Ashby received sabbatical leaves during the spring of 1987 and the 1992-93 academic year. He also received much encouragement and help from department chairs David Stratton and Richard Hume, and from John Pierce, dean of arts and humanities. Stan Schmid, vice president for university affairs, took a special interest in the project. Many people typed transcripts of taped interviews and helped gather library materials. For such services, the authors owe thanks to Mary Watrous, Daggy Weiler, Heather and Charli Hochsprung, Kelly Triplett, Lisa Hawkins, Paula Marley, John Rindell, and Deng Peng. Janice Morgan checked and printed the final draft of the manuscript. Diane Triplett, Janice Wright, and Pat Hawkins were also very helpful.

Ashby is grateful as well to the National Endowment for the Humanities for a Summer Stipend and a Travel-to-Collections Grant, and to the American Philosophical Society for a grant. The Margaret Pettyjohn Endowment to the Washington State University History department was a crucial source of funding. To these agencies and endowments, and to the review panels upon which they depend, the authors are indeed indebted.

The people at Washington State University Press have been ideal to work with and the authors greatly appreciate their enthusiasm and commitment. Keith Petersen, a fine historian in his own right, has been a careful, resourceful, and understanding editor. Others at the Press who made this book possible include director Tom Sanders, assistant director Mary Read, and Glen Lindeman, Dave Hoyt, John Sutherland, Arline Lyons, Beth DeWeese, Jean Taylor, Dwayne Downing, and Wes Patterson. Thanks also to indexer Caroline Hooper, and to photojournalist Barry Kough.

Mary Ashby and Julie Gramer have been involved with the project all along, helping with the research and interviews, reading chapters, offering suggestions and encouragement, and doing so much more as well. Our debt to them is unlimited.

About the Authors

LeRoy Ashby is professor of history at Washington State University. Among his publications are *The Spearless Leader: William E. Borah and the Progressive Movement in the 1920's*, *William Jennings Bryan: Champion of Democracy*, and *Saving the Waifs: Reformers and Dependent Children, 1890-1917.* He has won numerous teaching honors, including WSU's Distinguished Faculty Award, and has twice been named the State of Washington's outstanding professor.

Rod Gramer is a native of Idaho. He is director of news and public affairs for KTVB, the NBC affiliate in Boise. He moderates KTVB's "Viewpoint," the longest-running public affairs program in Idaho. For nearly fourteen years Gramer worked for the *Idaho Statesman,* where he served as political editor and editor of the editorial page. He has also written articles for the *Lewiston Morning Tribune,* the *San Diego Union, USA Today, The Progressive,* and *The New Republic.* Gramer has won numerous awards for his reporting.

Index